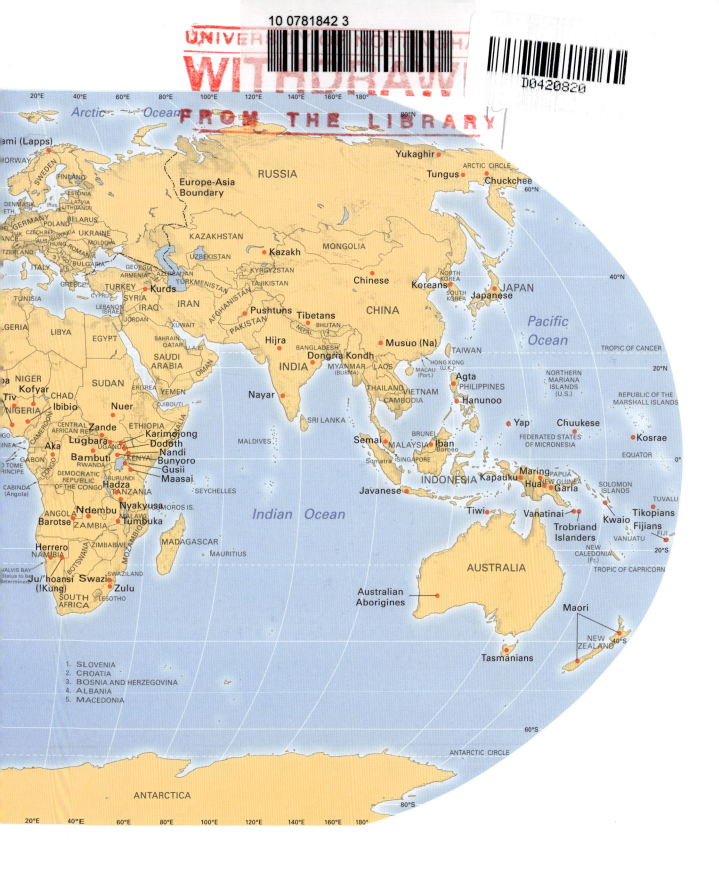

1. SLOVENIA
2. CROATIA
3. BOSNIA AND HERZEGOVINA
4. ALBANIA
5. MACEDONIA

EDITION
11

HUMANITY

AN INTRODUCTION TO CULTURAL ANTHROPOLOGY

JAMES PEOPLES

OHIO WESLEYAN UNIVERSITY

GARRICK BAILEY

UNIVERSITY OF TULSA

CENGAGE
Learning®

Australia • Brazil • Mexico • Singapore • United Kingdom • United States

Humanity: An Introduction to Cultural Anthropology, **Eleventh Edition**
James Peoples and Garrick Bailey

Product Director: Marta Lee-Perriard

Product Manager: Elizabeth Beiting-Lipps

Content Developer: Chrystie Hopkins, Lumina Datamatics

Product Assistant: Timothy Kappler

Senior Content Project Manager: Cheri Palmer

Art Director: Michael Cook

Manufacturing Planner: Judy Inouye

Production Service: Jill Traut, MPS Limited

Photo Researcher: Lumina Datamatics

Text Researcher: Lumina Datamatics

Text Designer: Diane Beasley

Cover Designer: Michael Cook

Cover Image: Martin Puddy/Getty

Compositor: MPS Limited

For product information and technology assistance, contact us at
Cengage Learning Customer & Sales Support, 1-800-354-9706

For permission to use material from this text or product, submit all requests online at **www.cengage.com/permissions**
Further permissions questions can be e-mailed to
permissionrequest@cengage.com

Library of Congress Control Number: 2016947234

10 07818423

Student Edition:
ISBN: 978-1-337-10969-7

Loose-leaf Edition:
ISBN: 978-1-337-11679-4

Cengage Learning
20 Channel Center Street
Boston, MA 02210
USA

Cengage Learning is a leading provider of customized learning solutions with employees residing in nearly 40 different countries and sales in more than 125 countries around the world. Find your local representative at **www.cengage.com**.

Cengage Learning products are represented in Canada by Nelson Education, Ltd.

To learn more about Cengage Learning Solutions, visit **www.cengage.com**.

Purchase any of our products at your local college store or at our preferred online store **www.cengagebrain.com**.

Printed in the United States of America
Print Number: 01   Print Year: 2017

BRIEF CONTENTS

CONTENTS

PART II   Theories and Methods of Cultural Anthropology

PART III   The Diversity of Culture

PART IV Anthropology in the Global Community

Preface

Perhaps it is presumptuous to title any textbook *Humanity*. The authors chose this title back in 1985, when we began working on the first edition. We thought *Humanity* captures the distinctive feature of anthropology—that it studies all the world's peoples, including those who lived in the prehistoric past, the historic past, and the present day, as well as peoples who live in every world region.

As a scholarly discipline, anthropology is very broad in its scope and interests. Several generations of anthropologists have discovered a vast amount of information about the human species. Paleoanthropologists are currently uncovering fossils and unwinding genetic relationships that show how and when the human species originated and evolved into modern *Homo sapiens*. Archaeologists are still digging into information about how prehistoric peoples lived their lives.

Another subfield, cultural anthropology, is the main subject of this book. Research done by cultural anthropologists (fieldwork) often involves years of study while living among some human community. Cultural anthropology describes and explains or interprets the fascinating cultural variability of the world's peoples. In this text, we try to convey to students the life-enriching and the educational value of discovering this variability. In the process, we hope students and other readers will experience a change in their attitudes about other cultures, about their own lives and nations, and about humanity in general.

We also hope the book leads readers to think about their own identities as individuals, as members of a particular society with its traditions and ways of thinking and acting, and as participants in an increasingly worldwide human community. To achieve this last goal, we discuss anthropological insights into some current problems, such as ethnic conflicts, national and global inequalities, hunger, religious intolerance, and the survival of indigenous cultures and languages. As we describe the diversity in humanity's cultures, we suggest the implications of such diversity for contemporary people and societies.

Finally, we want students and other newcomers to anthropology to grasp the full significance of the oldest anthropological lesson of all: that their own values, beliefs, and actions are a product of their upbringing in a particular human group rather than universal among all peoples. If understood properly and applied seriously, this principle leads individuals to question unconscious assumptions and to view themselves as well as other peoples through the complicated lens of cultural relativism.

Globalization has become an increasingly important theme throughout the last several editions. Each of the 17 chapters includes a feature on globalization, choosing a topic that is relevant for the chapter's content. Features in various chapters deal with issues such as how globalization affects cultural diversity, language survival, global warming, family and marriage practices, inequality among nations, religious diversity in the United States, production and sale of art, and cultural and religious fundamentalism. Some discussions are primarily case studies, whereas others present anthropological insights into the process or the results of globalization. Most chapters contain material that is relevant for modern North America, such as climate change, recent changes in family life and marriage practices, gender inequality, and religious accommodation.

New to the Eleventh Edition

To those instructors who are previous users of *Humanity*, the following summarizes the major changes in the eleventh edition.

Chapter 1 still introduces the four subdisciplines and discusses the importance of anthropological perspectives, methods, and factual knowledge about cultural diversity. We have included new information on human evolution. While retaining coverage of applied anthropology, we've updated the section on careers. We emphasize recent changes in anthropological interests and in research in modern societies and globalization.

To illustrate the complexity of the relativistic perspective, we add a new example of a Jarawa custom while retaining the example of female genital mutilation.

The topical structure and themes of Chapter 2 (culture) are intact. We continue to integrate terms like *cultural identity, subcultures, roles,* and *social learning* into an extended discussion of culture, with the goal of demonstrating that the concept of culture is more complicated than most people realize. New material appears in the section titled "The Origins of Culture."

Chapter 3 (language) retains coverage of the distinctive characteristics of language, structural linguistics, English's incorporation of Native American words, sociolinguistics, and the relationship between culture and language. Recent material appears about the use of language to acquire and enhance power, using examples from political speech in the American 2016 presidential campaign. The section titled "Language, Perceptions, and Worldview" now has a new and provocative argument about how verb forms might affect savings rates in countries with similar socioeconomic conditions. We again emphasize relationships among culture, language, thought, and behavior over the technical aspects of linguistics.

Chapter 4 (cultural diversity and globalization) provides the historical and cultural context for later chapters that discuss diversity among the world's peoples. We have updated sections, added a new Concept Review, and expanded the coverage of the globalization of academic training.

Chapter 5 (theory) continues its focus on two main areas: (1) historical contacts between the West and Others that gave rise to anthropology, and (2) distinctions between contemporary approaches, which we categorize (broadly) as scientific and humanistic. Where appropriate, we apply this distinction to material in other chapters by stating the interpretations or explanations each broad approach would offer.

Chapter 6 (methods) distinguishes between the methods and goals of the main ways anthropologists learn about humanity: fieldwork and comparisons. Generally ethnographic fieldwork is the primary method used to describe a given people, in time and space, whereas comparative methods are an essential part of efforts to explain or generalize.

In Chapter 7 (culture and environment) we updated some factual material, including dates for the beginnings and spread of agriculture and information about the 2015 Paris Accords on climate change. We have rewritten sections to clarify their meaning and wider implications. Like Chapters 2, 4, and 5, this chapter provides information referred to extensively later in the book.

In Chapter 8 (exchange) we include a new introductory vignette on the origin of credit cards to enhance student interest in the general topic. In covering reciprocity, redistribution, and market exchange forms, we provide examples of each in the United States, using a new example of the Affordable Care Act to illustrate political arguments over redistribution. We move on to describe capitalist economies, distinguishing between neoliberal/laissez-faire and social welfare capitalism and their strengths and weaknesses. We have also added new material on global markets in the Global Challenges and Opportunities feature.

In Chapter 9 (marriage and family), this edition includes the standard textbook topical structure: family forms, incest taboos, problems of defining marriage, marriage forms and their implications, marital transactions, postmarital residence patterns, and household forms. We have deleted the discussion of the avunculocal residence pattern to make room for an extensive revision of the section "Same-Sex Marriage and the Culture Wars," which includes recent court decisions and reactions to them. We argue that anthropology's relativistic and comparative perspective offer significant contributions to these topics.

Chapter 10 (kinship) also is standard, covering forms of descent and kinship, influences on these forms, and kinship terminologies, with examples of each topic. We give terminological systems as examples of cultural constructions introduced in Chapter 2. The chapter concludes by discussing the implications of cultural diversity for recent and future changes in marriage, family, and kinship forms and relationships.

The topics for Chapter 11 (gender) are unchanged from the last two editions. We have added new information about how recognition of the complexity of gender identity affects language, going beyond the obvious LGBTQIA to include new child naming practices. The ethnographic examples remain, but we have condensed some to reduce the length. Again, we suggest the relevance of anthropological evidence about diversity and anthropological theorizing to modern life.

In Chapter 12 (political life), portions of the Global Challenges and Opportunities feature have been expanded to include shell companies and tax haven countries; our discussion includes an examination of how these situations have allowed companies to increase their global economic power.

Chapter 13 (inequality and stratification) begins with a new vignette about the contrasting ideas of Bernie Sanders and Donald Trump about economic inequality. After describing contrasts between egalitarian, ranked, and stratified (including caste) societies, the chapter moves into stratification in the United States. We update numerical data on the distribution of income and wealth in the United States, including numbers that bring home the extent to which economic inequalities have increased since 1980. The distinction between religious and secular ideologies is applied to ideas and beliefs in the United States and the West. After discussing the strengths and weaknesses of the functionalist and conflict theories, we attempt to apply them to modern industrial society. We updated numerical data in the Global Challenges and Opportunities feature on China.

In Chapter 14 (religion), in the "Sociological Approaches" section, we added Richard Sosis's idea that costly rituals function to demonstrate commitment to group values and norms, noting its consistency with the evolutionary psychology general theory (discussed in Chapter 5) For each theoretical approach we note that religion creates as many cognitive, psychological, social problems as it allegedly alleviates. There is an entirely new section titled "Will Religion Disappear?" The section "Varieties of Religious Organization" now discusses the complexities of attempting to classify the great variety of humanity's religions into only a few forms or categories.

The introductory discussion of art has been rewritten in Chapter 15 (art), otherwise the chapter is basically the same with the exception of the Global Challenges and Opportunities feature. This new box addresses the question of how increased integration into the global economy and less expensive machine-made goods are changing the artistic visual traditions associated with handmade items.

Additions to Chapter 16 (ethnicity) include new and updated information on ethnic conflicts in the modern world.

Chapter 17 (world problems and the practice of anthropology) continues to discuss anthropological insights on health and health care, population growth, and world hunger. We have also updated the seemingly unending struggles of people like the San, Dongria Kondh, and Kayapo to protect their lands.

Special Features

The boxed features called A Closer Look are eliminated in this edition, in the interest of space and continuity. Each chapter still contains a feature on globalization, titled **Global Challenges and Opportunities**, a label that reflects the focus of most of their content. A photo accompanies each feature.

Several pedagogical aids are intended to help students understand and retain the material they have just read. Each chapter begins with a set of five to eight **Learning Objectives** that focus on the key concepts, ideas, and themes of the chapter. The learning objectives are tied to the end-of-chapter **Summary**. We hope this helps students come away with a solid understanding of the main points of each chapter.

We continue to include at least one **Concept Review** in the chapters to condense ideas and make sharp distinctions in just a few words. A **Glossary** again is included at the end of the book. **Key Terms** in bold are defined immediately at the bottom of the page where students first encounter them in the chapter.

Anthropology is a highly visual discipline, and *Humanity* holds to the highest standards in providing photographs, figures, and maps to illustrate the text. Maps on the inside front cover show the location of peoples and cultures mentioned in the book.

There are two **indexes**, one a traditional subject index and the other a list of peoples and cultures mentioned in the book.

Resources

Student Resources

CourseMate. The CourseMate for Peoples and Bailey's *Humanity*, eleventh edition, brings course concepts to life with interactive learning, study, and exam preparation tools that support the printed textbook. Access an integrated MindTap e-book, glossary, quizzes, videos, and more in the CourseMate for *Humanity*, eleventh edition. Go to CengageBrain.com to register or purchase access.

Instructor Resources

Online Instructor's Manual with Test Bank. This online supplement offers learning objectives, chapter outlines and summaries, key terms, suggested supplementary lectures, discussion questions, and more. The instructor's manual also includes updated references to relevant news articles, films, and videos for each chapter. The test bank provides approximately 40 multiple-choice, 15 true/false, and 5 essay questions per chapter.

Cengage Learning Testing Powered by Cognero. A flexible, online system, Cognero allows you to author, edit, and manage test bank content from multiple Cengage Learning solutions. Cognero also offers you the ability to create multiple tests in an instant and deliver them from your LMS, your classroom, or wherever you want!

Online PowerPoint Slides. These vibrant, Microsoft PowerPoint lecture slides for each chapter will assist you with your lecture by providing concept coverage using images, figures, and tables directly from the textbook.

CourseReader: Anthropology. *CourseReader: Anthropology* is a fully customizable online reader that provides access to hundreds of readings and audio and video selections from multiple disciplines. This easy-to-use solution allows you to select exactly the content you need for your courses and is loaded with convenient pedagogical features like highlighting, printing, note taking, and audio downloads. You have the freedom to assign individualized content at an affordable price. The *CourseReader: Anthropology* is the perfect complement to any class.

The Wadsworth Anthropology Video Library Volumes I–IV. Enhance your lectures with new video clips from the BBC Motion Gallery and CBS News. Addressing topics from the four fields, these videos are divided into short segments, perfect for introducing key concepts with footage sourced from some of the most remarkable collections in the world.

AIDS in Africa DVD. Expand your students' global perspective of HIV/AIDS with this award-winning documentary series focused on controlling HIV/AIDS in southern Africa. Films focus on caregivers in the faith community; how young people share messages of hope through song and dance; the relationship of HIV/AIDS to gender, poverty, stigma, education, and justice; and the story of two HIV-positive women helping others.

Classic Readings in Cultural Anthropology, **Fourth Edition.** Practical and insightful, *Classic Readings in Cultural Anthropology,* fourth edition, is a concise and accessible reader that presents a core selection of historical and contemporary works that have been instrumental in shaping anthropological thought and research over the past decades. Carefully edited by Dr. Gary Ferraro, the fourth edition includes classic readings from the disciplines of cultural anthropology and linguistics. Readings are organized around eight topics that closely mirror most introductory textbooks and are selected from scholarly works on the basis of their enduring themes and contributions to the discipline. These selections allow students to further explore anthropological perspectives on such key topics as culture, language and communication, ecology and economics, marriage and family, gender, politics and social control, supernatural beliefs, and issues of culture change. The book also addresses pressing topics such as globalization, ethnic violence, environmental issues, and more. *Classic Readings in Cultural Anthropology,*

fourth, delivers an excellent introduction to the field of anthropology and the contributions it makes to understanding the world around us.

Human–Environment Interactions: New Directions in Human Ecology. This module by Kathy Galvin begins with a brief discussion of the history and core concepts of the field of human ecology and the study of how humans interact with the natural environment. It then looks in-depth at how the environment influences cultural practices (environmental determinism), as well as how aspects of culture, in turn, affect the environment. Human behavioral ecology is presented within the context of natural selection and how ecological factors influence the development of cultural and behavioral traits, and how people subsist in different environments. The module concludes with a discussion of resilience and global change as a result of human–environment interactions. This module, in chapter-like print format, can be packaged for free with the text.

Medical Anthropology in Applied Perspective Module. This freestanding module is actually a complete text chapter, featuring the same quality of pedagogy and written content in Cengage's cultural anthropology texts. See your sales representative for information on bundling the module with this text.

Acknowledgments

Since the first edition was published in 1988, *Humanity* (the book, not the species) has benefited enormously from reviewers. Some reviewers are long-term users of the text, whereas others have not adopted it for their classes. Of course, we have never been able to incorporate all their suggestions for improvement, or the book would be twice as long as it is. But, over the last 25 years, we have added, subtracted, updated, rethought, and reorganized most of the book based on reviewers' comments. We thank all of them.

For the eleventh edition, both authors thank the reviewers listed here (their identities were unknown to us until publication):

Frank Araujo, American River College
Leslie Berry, De Anza College
Heidi Bludau, Monmouth University
Deborah Boehm, University of Nevada, Reno
Sheilah Clarke Ekong, Univesity of Missouri, St. Louis
Michael Dietz, College of DuPage
Anna Dixon, University of South Florida, St. Petersburg
Phyllisa Eisentraut, Santa Barbara City College

Becky Floyd, Cypress College
Henri Gooren, Oakland University
Jean Hatcherson, Western Connecticut State University
Rachel Hoerman, University of Hawaii Manoa
Bennett Judkins, Southern Adventist University
Ruurdje Laarhoven, Hawaii Pacific University
Paul Langenwalter, Biola University
Vienna Lewin, North Central University
Aurolyn Luykx, University of Texas at El Paso
Paul McDowell, Santa Barbara City College
Krista Moreland, Bakersfield College
Kevin Pittle, Biola University
Maureen Salsitz, California State University, Fullerton; Cypress College; Orange Coast College
Suzanne Spencer-Wood, Oakland University
Erin Stiles, University of Nevada, Reno
Cindi Sturtzsreetharan, California State University, Sacramento
Scott Vandehey, Linfield College
Mary Vermillion, Saint Louis University
Stephen Wiley, Normandale Community College
Andrew Workinger, University of Tennessee, Chattanooga
Stephen Zolvinski, Indian University Northwest

Although we were unable to make all the changes these scholars suggested, many of their comments are incorporated into the text. Their comments that the book needs to be more *explicit* about the relevance of anthropology in today's world were especially influential.

Both authors have benefited from the suggestions of colleagues and friends. Jim again thanks Thomas Love (Linfield College) for help with the text on energy in Chapter 7 and to Stacia Bensyl (Missouri Western State University) for assistance with Chapter 11. Garrick thanks James Faris for his assistance on Nuba body painting, and Robert Canfield for helping to clarify some points on the Pushtun and Afghanistan.

ABOUT THE AUTHORS

JAMES (JIM) PEOPLES is currently Professor and Chairperson of Sociology/Anthropology and Director of East Asian Studies at Ohio Wesleyan University in Delaware, Ohio. Peoples has taught at the University of California– Davis and the University of Tulsa in Oklahoma, among other colleges and universities. He received a BA from the University of California–Santa Cruz and a PhD from the University of California–Davis. His main research interests are human ecology, cultures of the Pacific Islands, and cultures of East Asia. His first book, *Island in Trust* (1985), describes his fieldwork on the island of Kosrae in the Federated States of Micronesia. His latest project is a coauthored book describing the prehistory, history, and contemporary culture of Kosrae Island in Micronesia, to which he most recently returned in July and August 2013. Since joining the faculty of Ohio Wesleyan University in 1988, he has taught courses on East Asia, the Pacific, human ecology, cultural anthropology, the anthropology of religion, world hunger, the prehistory of North America, and Native Americans of the southwestern United States. Since 2010, Peoples has been Secretary of the Japan Studies Association. When not teaching, writing, or attending meetings, he enjoys fly fishing, traveling, and gardening.

GARRICK BAILEY received his BA in history from the University of Oklahoma and his MA and PhD in anthropology from the University of Oregon. His research interests include ethnohistory, world systems theory, and ethnicity and conflict, with a primary focus on the native peoples of North America. His publications include *Navajo: The Reservation Years* (with Roberta Bailey); *Changes in Osage Social Organization 1673–1906; The Osage and the Invisible World;* and *Traditions of the Osage* and *Art of the Osage* (with Dan Swan, John Nunley, and Sean Standingbear). He also was editor of *Indians in Contemporary Society,* Volume 2 of the *Handbook of North American Indians,* Smithsonian Institution. Bailey has been a Senior Fellow in Anthropology at the Smithsonian Institution in Washington and a Weatherhead Resident Scholar at the School of American Research in Santa Fe. Actively engaged in contemporary Native American issues, he has served as a member of the Indian Health Advisory Committee, Department of Health, Education, and Welfare; of the Glen Canyon Environmental Review Committee, National Research Council; and of the Native American Graves Protection and Repatriation Act (NAGPRA) Review Committee, Department of the Interior. Bailey has taught anthropology at the University of Tulsa since 1968.

1 The Study of Humanity

Michael Doolittle/The Image Works

Cultural anthropology is the discipline that studies human cultural diversity, usually by visiting people where they live and interacting with them firsthand.

Subfields of Anthropology
Biological/Physical Anthropology
Archaeology
Cultural Anthropology
Anthropological Linguistics

Applications of Anthropology
Applied Anthropology
Careers in Anthropology

Cultural Anthropology Today

Anthropological Perspectives on Cultures
Holistic Perspective
Comparative Perspective
Relativistic Perspective

Some Lessons of Anthropology

After reading this chapter, you should be able to:

1. **LIST** the four major subfields of anthropology and describe their primary interests.

2. **DISCUSS** how anthropology differs from other disciplines that also study humans.

3. **EXPLAIN** some of the practical uses of anthropology in solving human problems.

4. **DISCUSS** how cultural anthropology has changed in the last four decades.

5. **UNDERSTAND** the meaning and importance of the holistic, comparative, and relativistic perspectives.

6. **DESCRIBE** the wider lessons one can learn from studying anthropology.

What makes humans different from other animals? What is human nature, or is there even such a thing? How and why do the peoples of the world differ, both biologically and culturally? Have affluent people in industrialized, urbanized nations sacrificed something important in their quest for what many consider the good life? What are the implications of living in a world whose diverse peoples have recently become connected by global corporations and international communications? These are just a few questions investigated by **anthropology**, the academic discipline that studies all of humanity.

Almost everything about human beings interests anthropologists. We want to know when, where, and how humanity originated and how we evolved into what we are today. Anthropologists try to explain the many differences among the world's cultures, such as why people in one culture believe they get sick because the souls of witches devour their livers, whereas people in another think that illness can result from tarantulas flinging tiny magical darts into their bodies. We want to know why most Argentinians and Australians like beef, which devout Hindus and Buddhists refuse to eat. We are curious about why some New Guinea peoples ritually engorge themselves with pork—the same animal flesh that some religions originating in the Middle East hold to be unclean and

prohibit eating. In brief, anthropologists of one kind or another are likely to investigate almost everything about human beings: our biological evolution, cuisines, values, art styles, behaviors, languages, religions, and so forth.

Anthropologists, then, study many different dimensions of humanity. The broad scope of anthropology is perhaps the one feature that most distinguishes it from other fields that also study humans, such as psychology and history. Anthropologists are interested in *all* human beings, whether living or dead, Asian or African or European. No people are too isolated to escape the anthropologist's notice. We also are interested in many different *aspects* of humans, including their genetic makeup, family lives, political systems, relations with nature, and beliefs about the dead. No dimension of humankind, from skin color to dance traditions, falls outside the interests of anthropology.

Subfields of Anthropology

Obviously, no single anthropologist can master all these subjects. Therefore, most anthropologists specialize in one of four principal subfields: biological (or physical) anthropology, archaeology, cultural anthropology, and anthropological linguistics. (The Concept Review summarizes the primary interests of each subfield.) A fifth area, applied anthropology, uses anthropological methods and insights to help solve real-world problems. Because cultural anthropology is the primary subject of this book, here we briefly summarize the other subfields and describe some of their major findings.

anthropology Academic discipline that studies humanity from a broad biological and cultural perspective.

Physical/Biological	Comparisons of human anatomy and behavior with other primate species; physical (genetic) variation among human populations; biological evolution of *Homo sapiens*
Archaeology	Excavation of material remains in prehistoric sites to reconstruct early human ways of life; study of remains in historic sites to learn more about literate peoples
Cultural	Differences and similarities in contemporary and historically recent cultures; causes and consequences of sociocultural change; impacts of globalization and contacts on the world's peoples
Anthropological Linguistics	Relationships between language and culture; role of language and speaking in social life of various peoples; how language might shape perceptions and thoughts

Biological/Physical Anthropology

Biological (also called **physical**) **anthropology** is closely related to the biological sciences in its goals and methods. It focuses on subjects such as the anatomy and

Steve Bloom Images/Alamy

One of the most surprising discoveries about the great apes is that they commonly use and even make tools. These two Ugandan chimpanzees are inserting a twig into a termite mound to access insects for food.

behavior of monkeys and apes, the physical (including genetic) variations between different human populations, and the biological evolution of the human species.

Within biological anthropology, researchers in **primatology** study the evolution, anatomy, adaptation, and social behavior of primates, the taxonomic order to which humans belong. Research on group-living monkeys and apes has added significantly to the understanding of many aspects of human behavior, including tool use, sexuality, parenting, cooperation, male–female differences, and aggression. Field studies of African chimpanzees and gorillas, the two apes genetically most similar to humans, have been especially fruitful sources of hypotheses and knowledge.

In the 1960s, famous British primatologist Jane Goodall was the first to observe toolmaking among African chimpanzees. Chimps intentionally modified sticks to probe holes in termite mounds. When termite soldiers locked their jaws onto the intruding objects, the chimps withdrew the probes and devoured the tasty insects. Goodall observed adult chimps teaching their young how to probe for termites, showing that humanity's closest animal relatives are capable of learning complex behaviors. Some chimpanzee groups wave tree branches in aggressive displays against other groups. Some wad up leaves to use as sponges to soak up drinking water. Working in West Africa, other researchers have observed some chimp groups using

biological (physical) anthropology Major subfield of anthropology that studies the biological dimensions of humans and other primates.

primatology Part of biological anthropology that studies primates, including monkeys and apes.

heavy round stones as hammers to crack open hard-shelled nuts. The chimps select stones of the proper shape and weight, control the force of their blows so that the nut does not shatter, and often leave the tools under nut trees for future use.

Other apes also use tools. Using sticks, African gorillas in the wild gauge the depth of water and even lay down tree trunks to cross deep pools. Researchers have seen one young female gorilla use stones to smash open a palm nut to get at the oil inside.

These and other observations of chimpanzees and gorillas dramatically altered our understanding of human–animal differences. Prior to such studies, making tools was widely considered to be one of the things humans could do that other animals could not. Now that we know that toolmaking is not unique to humanity, we look at other reasons for human uniqueness.

Biological anthropologists also investigate **human variation**, studying how and why human populations vary physically due to genetically inherited differences. All humanity belongs to a single species, which taxonomists call *Homo sapiens.* One of the most important findings of anthropology is that the physical/genetic similarities among the world's peoples far outweigh the differences. Nonetheless, peoples whose ancestral homelands lie in Africa, Asia, Europe, Australia, the Pacific Islands, and the Americas were once more isolated than they are today. During this time, they evolved differences in overall body and facial form, height, skin color, blood chemistry, and other genetically determined features. Specialists in human variation measure and try to explain the differences and similarities among the world's peoples in such physical characteristics. (We return to "racial" variation in Chapter 2.)

Often, genetic differences are related to the environment in which a people or their ancestors lived. Consider skin color. When exposed to sunlight, human skin manufactures vitamin D, a necessary nutrient. The melanin existing in human skin produces the color our eyes perceive as dark. High levels of melanin protect darker skin against sun damage, so melanin usually is beneficial in tropical environments, where sunlight is most intense. However, as humans migrated into more temperate regions tens of thousands of years ago, too much melanin

became harmful. In high latitudes, melanin reduces the penetration of sunlight in the skin, reducing its ability to make vitamin D. Thus, dark pigmentation is harmful in high latitudes like Europe and Siberia, and over many centuries skin grew lighter ("whiter") in such regions.

Human populations living in high altitudes also have evolved physiological adaptations. Andean peoples of South America have relatively large lungs and high levels of hemoglobin. The blood of Tibetans circulates more rapidly than most other people, allowing their muscles and organs to function more efficiently at elevations over 14,000 feet. Such populations evolved physiological adaptations to supply oxygen to their tissues.

Another aim of physical anthropology is understanding when and how the human species evolved from prehuman, apelike ancestors. **Paleoanthropology** investigates human biological evolution. Over decades of searching for fossils and carrying out meticulous laboratory studies, paleoanthropologists have reconstructed the evolution of human anatomy: limbs, feet, hands, skull, and other physical features.

In the late 1970s, paleoanthropologists began to use new methods to investigate human evolution. Scientists in the field of molecular genetics can now sequence DNA—the genetic material by which hereditary traits are transmitted between generations. By comparing DNA sequences, geneticists can estimate how closely different species are related. Studies comparing the genetic sequences of African apes with humans show that humans share 97.7 percent of their DNA with gorillas and 98.7 percent with chimpanzees and bonobos. DNA from modern humans and DNA sampled from bones of the extinct human species *Neandertal* are about 99.5 percent the same. Similarities in the DNA of two or more species are evidence that they share a common evolutionary ancestor. Also, the more similar the DNA between two or more species, the less time has elapsed since their divergence from a common ancestor. Thus, anthropologists study DNA sequences to estimate how long ago species separated.

Recent scientific work shows that the DNA of many modern humans resulted from our ancestors' interbreeding with now-extinct human species. Most people who are not African or African-derived have a small percentage of DNA from Neandertals. (Why not Africans too? Because Neandertal humans never lived in Africa.) Even more surprising is a 2016 finding that another extinct human species, called *Denisovan*, also interbred with the human branch now represented by you and me. Some Melanesian people of the southwestern Pacific have higher percentages of Denisovan DNA than people in other world regions. It is interesting (and food for thought) that the evolutionary line

human variation Physical differences among human populations; an interest of physical anthropologists.

paleoanthropology Specialization within biological anthropology that investigates the biological evolution of the human species.

Paleoanthropologists use evidence from laboratory research on DNA as well as fossil discoveries. Here paleoanthropologist Richard Leakey collaborates with a Kenyan in piecing together the skull of a human ancestor.

that led to modern humans bore offspring with two other human lines that went extinct.

Decades ago, Neandertals were depicted as thickly muscled humans who walked upright but had only the rudiments of technology and culture. Today's paleoanthropologists have a different view and recent research suggests they made significant accomplishments. Most recently, in 2016 archaeologists published evidence that Neandertals living over 170,000 years ago constructed structures deep inside a cave in France. They broke off hundreds of stalagmites and arranged them into six roughly circular structures. The structures were over 1,000 feet from the cave's entrance, so the builders must have used fire to provide light for their constructions.

Back in 2003, researchers unearthed bones of an extinct human relative that was so short—around 4 feet tall—that they nicknamed it "the Hobbit." This species so far has been found only on Flores, a tiny island in Indonesia. In 2016, scientists announced the discovery of a jawbone and six teeth of another small human relative on the same island. These remains are about 700,000 years old, which makes them far too ancient to be a member of our own species. "Hobbits" might

have descended from an earlier human ancestor and became smaller after migrating to Flores, due to the island's limited resources. Such dwarfism is well known among other species.

Through discovering and analyzing fossils, comparisons of DNA sequences, and other methods, the outlines of human evolution are becoming clear. Most scholars agree that the evolutionary line leading to modern humans split from the lines leading to modern African apes (chimpanzees and gorillas) by 6 million years ago, but the date of this separation is likely to change with additional research.

Most biological anthropologists work in universities or museums as teachers, researchers, writers, and curators. But many also apply their knowledge of human anatomy to practical matters. For instance, specialists in **forensic anthropology** work for or consult with law enforcement agencies, where they help

forensic anthropology Specialization within physical anthropology that analyzes and identifies human remains.

Robert Brenner/PhotoEdit

Prehistoric archaeologists investigate humanity's ancient past by carefully excavating and analyzing material remains.

identify human skeletal remains. Among their contributions are determining the age, sex, height, and other physical characteristics of crime or accident victims. Forensic anthropologists gather evidence from bones about old injuries or diseases, which are then compared with medical histories to identify victims. Forensic anthropologists have also excavated and analyzed mass graves containing the remains of victims of assassination, hoping to identify them and determine the cause of their death.

Archaeology

Archaeology investigates the human past through excavating and analyzing material remains. Modern

> **archaeology** Investigation of past cultures through the excavation of material remains.
>
> **prehistoric archaeology** Field that uses excavations and analysis of material remains to investigate cultures that existed before the development of writing.

archaeology is divided into two major kinds of studies: prehistoric and historic.

Prehistoric archaeology is the study of prehistoric peoples—that is, those who had no writing to keep records of their activities, customs, and beliefs. Much information about the lives of prehistoric peoples can be recovered from the tools, pottery, ornaments, bones, plant pollen, charcoal, and other materials they left behind in the ground. Through careful excavation and laboratory analysis of such remains, prehistoric archaeologists reconstruct the way people lived in ancient times and trace how human cultures have changed over many centuries and millennia.

Contrary to impressions given by many television documentaries and popular films, the main goal of archaeological excavations is not to recover valuable treasures and other artifacts but to understand how people lived long ago. Modern archaeologists seek to reconstruct as fully as possible how prehistoric peoples made their tools, lived in their environments, organized their societies, and practiced their religions. Over decades of meticulous field excavations and laboratory work, archaeologists have learned that agriculture first developed around 10,000 years ago, when some peoples of the Middle East began planting wheat and barley. For the first time, humans transformed certain edible wild plants into *crops*. A few thousand years later, peoples of China, Southeast Asia, and West Africa also domesticated plants like rice and millet. On the other side of the world, in what we now call the Americas, ancient peoples of southern Mexico, western South America, and the Amazon Basin domesticated plants like corn, squash, beans, tomatoes, potatoes, and manioc. Surprisingly, present evidence shows that these six regions where agriculture developed were independent—meaning that the people of one region domesticated plants on their own, rather than learning the idea of agriculture from other peoples. Similarly, civilization (living in cities) developed in several different regions independently, beginning about 5,000 years ago (see Chapter 7).

To investigate the past of societies in which some people could read and write, historians analyze written materials such as diaries, letters, land records, newspapers, and tax collection documents. **Historic archaeology** supplements historical documents by excavating houses, stores, plantations, factories, and other structures and remains. Historic archaeologists seek to uncover information lacking in old documents about how people lived at a particular time and place.

In May 2013, the *New York Times, USA Today,* CNN, and other media reported a startling find by historic archaeologists. In 1607, 104 settlers from England arrived in Jamestown, Virginia, to establish a settlement and make profit for the private company that financed the colony. Only a third of the settlers were alive after nine months, despite trade with the local Native Americans, the Powhatan. More colonists arrived in the next couple of years. However, in the winter of 1609, the English Jamestown settlers were starving: A drought the previous year had led to low agricultural yields, the fleet of nine ships from England that was supposed to supply the colony had been lost in a hurricane, and relationships with the Powhatan had turned hostile. A letter written in 1625 by the leader of the colony refers to the settlers digging up human corpses to consume their flesh during the Starving Time.

Archaeological excavations in the summer of 2012 led by William Kelso found hard evidence that cannibalism in fact had occurred at Jamestown. The archaeological team unearthed the remains of a girl about 14 years old. After her death, someone had struck the girl's head with several blows, splitting her skull, to remove the brain. Other cuts on her facial bones showed that facial tissues had been removed. Excavations in and around Jamestown continue.

Today, many archaeologists work not in universities but in museums, public agencies, and for-profit corporations. Museums offer jobs as curators and researchers. State highway departments employ archaeologists to conduct surveys of proposed new routes in order to locate and excavate archaeological sites that will be destroyed. The U.S. Forest Service and National Park Service hire archaeologists to find sites on public lands to help make decisions about the preservation of cultural materials. Those who work in *cultural resource management* (CRM) locate sites of prehistoric and historic significance, evaluate their importance, and make recommendations about total or partial preservation.

Since the passage of the National Historic Preservation Act in 1966, private corporations and government agencies that construct factories, apartments, parking lots, shopping malls, and other structures must file a report outlining how the construction will affect historical remains and which steps will be taken to preserve them. Because of this law, the business of *contract archaeology* has boomed in the United States. Contract archaeology companies bid competitively for the privilege of locating, excavating, and reporting on sites affected or destroyed by construction.

Cultural Anthropology

Cultural anthropology (also called **sociocultural anthropology** and **social anthropology**) studies contemporary and historically recent human societies and cultures. As its name suggests, the main focus of this subfield is culture—the customs and beliefs of some human group. (The concept of culture is discussed at length in Chapter 2.)

As we will see in future chapters, cultural anthropologists study an enormous number of specific subjects, far too many to list. Here are a few of the main interests of this subfield:

- Studying firsthand and reporting about the ways of living of particular human groups, including both indigenous peoples and peoples who live in modernized, industrialized nations

historic archaeology Field that investigates the past of literate peoples through excavation of sites and analysis of artifacts and other material remains.

cultural anthropology (social anthropology, sociocultural anthropology) Subfield that studies the way of life of contemporary and historically recent human societies and cultures.

- Comparing diverse cultures to seek general principles that might explain human ways of living or that might cause cultural differences
- Understanding how various dimensions of human life—economics, family life, religion, art, communication, and so forth—relate to one another in particular cultures and in cultures generally
- Analyzing the causes and consequences of cultural change, including the causes and consequences of what is commonly called globalization
- Enhancing public knowledge and appreciation of cultural differences and multicultural diversity
- Using anthropological methods and insights to aid understanding of life in today's industrialized, capitalistic nations, including the anthropologist's own nation

The last three objectives are especially important in the twenty-first century, in which individuals with diverse cultural backgrounds regularly come into contact with one another in the rapidly changing global system. Later chapters discuss some of the work cultural anthropologists have done on globalization and in modern nation-states.

To collect information about particular cultures, researchers conduct **fieldwork**. Most fieldworkers leave their own homes and universities, moving into the communities they study and living in close, daily contact with the people. If practical, they communicate in the local language. Daily interaction with the members of a community provides fieldworkers with firsthand experiences that yield insights and information that could not be gained in any other way. Most fieldwork requires at least a year of residence in the field site, and two or more years are common. Fieldworkers usually report the findings of their research in books or scholarly journals, where they are available to other scholars, students, and to the general public. A written account of how a single human population lives is called an **ethnography**, which means "writing about a

people." (We have more to say about the processes and problems of fieldwork in Chapter 6.)

Anthropological Linguistics

Defined as the study of human language, *linguistics* exists as a separate discipline from anthropology. The ability to communicate complex messages with great efficiency may be the most important capability of humans that makes us different from primates and other animals. Once we realize how complicated the knowledge of a language is, we realize that the communicative abilities of humans are truly unique. Certainly our ability to speak is a key factor in the success of humanity.

Cultural anthropologists are interested in language mainly because of how the language and culture of a people affect each other. The subfield of **anthropological linguistics** is concerned with the complex relationships between language and other aspects of human behavior and thought. For example, anthropological linguists are interested in how language is used in various social contexts: What style of speech must one use with people of high status? How do people of various social categories (like LGBT and ethnicities), classes (ultrarich, working), and political persuasions (supporters of Donald Trump and Bernie Sanders) use language to promote their political ideas and agendas? Does the particular language we learned while growing up have any important effects on how we view the world or how we think and feel? (Chapter 3 provides more information about language and social life.)

As our brief summary of the four subdisciplines confirms, anthropology is a vast and diverse field. Even by itself, cultural anthropology—the main subject of this text—is enormously broad: Modern fieldworkers live among and study human communities in all parts of the world, from the mountains of Tibet to the deserts of the American Southwest, from the streets of Chicago to the plains of East Africa.

Today's anthropology is quite different than 30 or 40 years ago. Still, the discipline does have a distinctive focus. More so than other fields, anthropology's focus is *human diversity*. Humankind is diverse in a multitude of ways, but two are most important to anthropologists. First, although all modern humans are members of the same species, the world's people differ somewhat in their genetic heritage, making humans diverse *biologically*. Second, the customs and beliefs of one society or ethnic group differ from those of other societies or ethnic groups, reflecting the fact that humans

fieldwork Ethnographic research that involves observing and interviewing members of a community in order to document and describe their way of life.

ethnography Written description of the way of life of some human population.

anthropological linguistics Subfield that focuses on the interrelationships between language and other aspects of a people's culture.

are diverse *culturally*. Prehistoric archaeologists investigate diversity in the distant past, between the world's major regions (e.g., how did the prehistoric peoples of Europe differ from those of East Asia 5,000 years ago?). Cultural anthropologists investigate and try to understand cultural diversity today and in the recent past.

Applications of Anthropology

Not too long ago, most professional anthropologists spent their careers in some form of educational institution, either in colleges and universities or in museums. However, since around 1990, more and more anthropologists have jobs in other kinds of institutions. The American Anthropological Association (AAA, often called "Triple A") is the professional association of anthropologists. In its 2006 *Annual Report*, the AAA reported that more than half of anthropologists work outside academic settings—in government agencies, international organizations, nonprofit groups, or private companies. Hundreds of others make their living as consultants to such organizations and institutions.

Applied Anthropology

Applied anthropology uses anthropological methods, theories, concepts, and insights to help public institutions or private enterprises deal with practical, real-world problems. Individuals in all subfields may do applied work—that is, work that contributes directly to problem solving in an organization. A few examples illustrate some of the work of applied anthropologists.

Development anthropology is one area in which anthropologists apply their expertise to the solution of practical human problems, usually in developing countries. Working both as full-time employees and as consultants, development anthropologists provide information about communities that helps agencies adapt projects to local conditions and needs. Examples of agencies and institutions that employ development anthropologists include the U.S. Agency for International Development, the Rockefeller and Ford Foundations, the World Bank, and the United Nations Development Programme. One important role of the anthropologist in such institutions is to provide policymakers with knowledge of local-level ecological and cultural conditions to help projects avoid unanticipated problems and minimize negative impacts.

Educational anthropology offers jobs in public agencies and private institutions. Some roles of educational anthropologists include advising in bilingual education, conducting detailed observations of classroom interactions, training personnel in multicultural issues, and adapting teaching styles to local customs and needs. Many modern nations, including those of Europe and the Americas, are becoming more culturally diverse due to immigration. As a response to this trend, an increasingly important role for educational anthropologists is to help educators understand the learning styles and behavior of children from various ethnic and national backgrounds. Persons trained in both linguistic and cultural anthropology are especially likely to work in educational anthropology.

Private companies sometimes employ cultural anthropologists full-time or as consultants, creating a professional opportunity often called *corporate anthropology*. As international trade agreements remove tariffs, quotas, and other barriers to international trade, people of different cultural heritages increasingly conduct business and buy and sell one another's products. The dramatic growth of overseas business activities encourages companies to hire professionals who can advise executives and sales staff on what to expect and how to speak and act when they conduct business in other countries. Because of their training as acute observers and listeners, anthropologists also work in the private sector in many other capacities: They watch how employees interact with one another, analyze how workers understand the capabilities of office machines, study how the attitudes and styles of managers affect worker performance, and perform a variety of other information-gathering and analysis tasks.

Medical anthropology is a rapidly growing field, partly because physicians, hospitals, and other health care providers want to understand how cultural and social forces affect their ability to deliver services. Medical anthropologists usually are trained both in biological and cultural anthropology. They investigate the complex interactions among human health, nutrition, social context, and cultural beliefs and practices.

applied anthropology Subfield applying anthropological perspectives, theory, empirical knowledge of cultures, and methods to help assess and solve real-world problems; practitioners are often employed by a governmental agency or private organization.

medical anthropology Specialization that researches the connections between cultural beliefs and habits and the spread and treatment of diseases and illnesses.

Medical anthropologists with extensive training in human biology and physiology study disease transmission patterns and how particular groups adapt to the presence of diseases like malaria and sleeping sickness. Because the transmission of viruses and bacteria is strongly influenced by people's diets, sanitation, sexual habits, and other behaviors, many medical anthropologists work as a team with epidemiologists to identify cultural practices that affect the spread of disease. Different cultures have different ideas about the causes and symptoms of disease, how best to treat illnesses, the abilities of traditional healers and doctors, and the importance of community involvement in the healing process. By studying how a human community perceives such things, medical anthropologists help hospitals and other agencies deliver health care services more effectively.

Careers in Anthropology

People who earn doctoral degrees in anthropology have a variety of career options, as the preceding discussion shows. What opportunities exist for those with an undergraduate degree in anthropology?

A place to start is the American Anthropological Association (AAA), which as mentioned above is the professional association of anthropologists. The AAA website provides information on jobs and careers that are suitable for those with an undergraduate degree in anthropology. Explore the www.americananthro .org site to find many resources for building a career in anthropology and to see the actual jobs obtained by those with a major in anthropology. An Internet search using the phrase "jobs in anthropology" returns many links, and a concise overview of the topic can be found at http://www.onedayonejob.com/majors /anthropology/.

More broadly, how can undergraduate training in anthropology help you build a career? Generally, in addition to learning to write, analyze, and think critically, students who study cultural anthropology are prepared to examine human life from many alternative perspectives, to study interactions between individuals and groups objectively and insightfully, to adjust to various social situations, to fit into diverse communities by respecting their ways of life, and to be sensitive to the multitude of differences between the world's peoples. Knowledge of the many ways of being human helps thoughtful graduates to have the capacity to consider alternatives that people with other kinds of formal education miss. Of course, along the way most students master other skills, such

as statistical analysis or foreign languages, which demonstrate ability and establish credentials for a variety of career paths.

Cultural Anthropology Today

Because this book deals mainly with the findings and conclusions of cultural anthropology, from now on when we use the word *anthropology*, we refer to cultural anthropology unless otherwise stated.

Many people imagine that cultural anthropologists go to far-off places to study "native" peoples. Except for some common but mistaken stereotypes about "natives," this image was reasonably accurate until the 1970s and 1980s. Until then, cultural anthropology differed from sociology and other disciplines that studied living peoples mainly by the kinds of cultures studied. Anthropologists focused on small-scale, non-Western, preindustrial, subsistence-oriented cultures, whereas sociologists tended to study large Euro-American, industrial, money-and-market countries. Not too long ago, many cultural anthropologists sought untouched tribal cultures to study because living among the "primitives" usually enhanced one's reputation.

All this has changed. As the Internet accelerates global communications, anthropologists publish books with titles like *Dreaming of a Mail-Order Husband: Russian-American Internet Romance* (Johnson, 2007). An anthropologist has done fieldwork among modern Americans who belong to Vineyard churches, an evangelical denomination, showing how they experience God's presence and hear his voice in their everyday lives (Luhrmann, 2012). Changing gender roles and working conditions lead to articles like "Man Enough to Let My Wife Support Me: How Changing Models of Career and Gender Are Reshaping the Experience of Unemployment" (Lane, 2009). In brief, cultural anthropology has widened its investigations well beyond the old idea of "natives." Today, we recognize we are all Natives.

Robin Nagle's engaging 2013 ethnography *Picking Up* is a study of New York City sanitation workers ("garbage collectors" to most of us). Nagle demonstrates the unsuspected job hazards and little-known skills of the men whose work is so essential in a wealthy country where citizens throw away so much stuff. Like many others who do fieldwork among wealthy industrial or postindustrial nations, Nagle exposes the complexity of the contributions of workers often taken for granted. One Amazon.com reviewer of *Picking Up*—referring to how the book reveals the importance of these "invisible" jobs—suggested imagining city life without the discard work done by the men Nagle calls "garbage fairies"! Not only does Nagle teach anthropology at New York University; she also is the anthropologist-in-residence for the New York City Department of Sanitation.

Sometimes anthropologists conduct studies of immigrant communities in their own countries. Along with Australia, North America is a continent whose people are mostly descendants of immigrants with diverse ancestral homelands. Some immigrants of the last few decades are largely or partly assimilated, having adopted many of the customs and beliefs of citizens whose ancestors arrived earlier. In other cases, though, they are only partially assimilated. On the job, they act like they are "mainstreamed." But at home and when among members of their own ancestral communities, they continue their language, cuisine, family relations, wedding and funeral customs, and other practices and beliefs.

For example, in the 1970s, the U.S. government relocated thousands of Hmong, a people of highland Southeast Asia, into places like the Central Valley of California and the upper Midwest. Even after two or three decades of living in the United States, some elderly Hmong who were first-generation immigrants speak little English, have large numbers of relatives living together in houses other Americans consider "single-family" dwellings, use their traditional methods of curing, and (allegedly) eat animals that Americans define as pets.

Likewise, many people with Chinese, Japanese, Korean, and South Asian heritages maintain some traditions of their ancestral homelands to a surprising degree. Some African Americans celebrate their origins with Kwanzaa. A large Somali community lives in central Ohio. Many Latinos speak "Spanglish" and continue to celebrate Latin festivals. Citizens whose ancestors came from Italy, Germany, Poland, Greece, and other parts of Europe recognize their national origins with festivals and food. Of course, so do people whose ancestors came from the British Isles, although most fail to recognize that they too have an ethnic heritage and identity. After all, they are not "minorities"!

As anthropologists have focused less on peoples of far away, the boundaries between cultural anthropology and other disciplines (especially sociology) are less clear-cut than they were a few years ago. Most anthropological work, though, is still done in relatively small communities (on the order of a few hundred to a few thousand), where the researcher can interact directly with people and experience their lives firsthand. More than any other single factor, the intense fieldwork experience distinguishes cultural anthropology from other disciplines concerned with humankind. Also, cultural

Globalization brings together people of different cultural backgrounds for international travel, education, and business. Learning about other cultures has increasing practical importance in modern global society.

anthropology remains more comparative in its scope and interests than the other social sciences and humanities. Even today, cultural anthropologists are more likely than sociologists or psychologists to conduct research in a country other than their own.

In the past couple of decades, anthropologists have researched globalization—the process by which citizens of the world's 195 nations participate in a single system that encompasses *all* peoples and nations to varying degrees. Global Challenges and Opportunities presents an overview of the process of globalization in the past several decades.

Scholars in disciplines like economics, political science, history, and sociology have researched and theorized about globalization. Most of their work concerns macro-level studies, meaning that the unit of study is the nation, region, city within the nation, or—even more "macro"—relationships between nations. Cultural anthropologists occasionally work at this level, but mostly our studies involve intensive, firsthand, prolonged fieldwork in local communities, both rural and urban. We study many dimensions of globalization, including markets, forms of global entertainment, ways of dating and getting married, changes in family organizations, how migrant workers adapt to factory life and urban environments, and so on. Such research provides a bottom-up view of globalization that complements the top-down view focused on by most of the media and scholars.

Today, globalization and its consequences are one of the most important areas of anthropological work. What are its impacts on people of all nations? Is a global megaculture developing that will someday make all human cultures pretty much alike? In later chapters, we present many examples of such anthropological studies.

Global markets connect the world's regions by trade in finished consumer products and raw materials. This plant in Recife, Brazil, produces fabrics later dyed and woven into clothing sold on the global market.

Glowimages/Getty Images

Stories about *globalization* appear daily in news media. The parts (continents, regions, nations, cities, towns, small villages) of the global system are interconnected by flows of technology, overseas transportation of resources and products, communications, short-term travel, long-term migration, and market exchanges of raw materials and finished products. Monthly, huge container ships move billions of dollars' worth of products across the Pacific and Atlantic Oceans. North American consumers benefit from the low labor costs of China, South Asia, and other regions when they shop at Walmart, Toys "R" Us, and most clothing and shoe stores. More people than ever before migrate between nations to study and work, affecting their home countries as well as those to which they relocate. The Internet and mobile phones link people together to an unprecedented degree, facilitating the flow of information, ideas, and media between nations.

These interconnections profoundly affect relationships between countries. There are many current issues that lead to political conflicts, including violent ones. Should the rapidly industrializing countries be forced to enact environmental regulations to curb greenhouse gases? If so, by whom and on what authority? What should a democratic government in a developed, free-market economy do when its citizens lose jobs due to factories located half a world away? How much do modernization and Westernization threaten cultural heritages, and does this affect the rise of religious extremism? Should South Asian, African, and Middle Eastern countries do anything about the flow of information from Western nations in order to protect their cultural traditions? Or should the whole world welcome a free market in ideas and beliefs, comparable to the free market in material products? And—perhaps the most important question—who gains and loses most from the globalization process?

It is important to recognize that globalization is a *process* rather than a *state*. In discussing relationships between parts of a system and the whole system, we often say that the whole affects the parts, which in turn affect the whole. The globalization process impacts nations, so nations respond to globalization; then the process of globalization changes to respond to changes in nations. Thus,

Anthropological Perspectives on Cultures

The main difference between anthropology and other social sciences and humanities is not so much the *kinds* of subjects anthropologists investigate as the *approaches* we take to studying human life. We believe it is impor-

tant to study cultures and communities holistically, comparatively, and relativistically. Taken together, these perspectives also make cultural anthropology distinctive.

Holistic Perspective

To study a subject holistically is to attempt to understand all the factors that influence it and to interpret it in the context of those factors. In anthropology, the **holistic perspective** means that no single aspect of a human culture can be understood unless its relationships to other aspects of the culture are explored. Holism requires, for example, that a fieldworker studying the

holistic perspective Assumption that any aspect of a culture is integrated with other aspects, so that no dimension of culture can be understood in isolation.

as globalization transforms nations, it too is transformed. As the global system evolves, some of its parts become more tightly integrated into it, but even localities that most consider isolated or pristine are affected directly or indirectly.

Interconnectedness between world regions is not new, as we will discuss in Chapter 4. Pointing to the half-millennium of contact between regions and peoples, some say there is nothing new about globalization. If globalization is only about the existence of contacts and interconnections between peoples, they are correct. However, both the intensity and the form of contacts and interconnections are different in the twenty-first century. By *intensity*, we mean that the number and importance of contacts and interconnections have increased dramatically in the past several decades; today, the lives of more people are affected more thoroughly than, say, 50 years ago. By *form*, we mean that the ways in which the world's peoples are interconnected are different than in the past. Two differences are especially important.

First, globalization transforms the division of economic activities between nations and regions. Until the mid–twentieth century, some nations and regions specialized mainly in supplying primary products—products extracted directly from nature, such as oil, food, metals, lumber, and other raw materials from wells, plantations, mines, and forests. For example, there were "banana republics" in Central America, "gold coasts" in West Africa, and "sugar mills" in the Caribbean. Generally, these nations and regions were known as "underdeveloped" or "Third World." Of course, there were exceptions, but the pattern was that developed and mostly wealthier countries bought these relatively low-valued raw materials and turned them into higher-valued, profit-making products with their industrial factories and labor force.

Today, factory production itself has globalized. In Latin America, Asia, and other regions, hundreds of millions of factory workers produce finished commodities for sale in international markets. More than ever before, there is an *international* market for industrial labor, meaning that factory workers of the countries we used to call underdeveloped are competing with the labor force of more developed countries. Whole industries have relocated. For example, the American clothing and shoe industries have almost disappeared, their factories replaced by those in China, Bangladesh, Indonesia, Brazil, and other countries with far cheaper labor. Other industries that have moved offshore are toys and consumer electronics. Some say the globalization of factory production is leading to a decline in income among middle-class families in Europe and North America and is largely responsible for the growing disparity of income and wealth in those regions. It also contributes significantly to the discontent and even despair among working-class people who experience wage stagnation and decline and perceive that the chances of better lives for their children are threatened by "others."

Second, international migration, study abroad, tourism, and the Internet are increasing two-way cultural exchanges. Most people think the media are transmitting the "culture" and "tastes" of the West to the rest of the world. One concern is that the North American and European culture (the West) will eventually destroy national and local traditions. However, millennials know that anime, manga, and K-pop have been transmitted in the opposite direction. Will a global cultural melting pot emerge?

In sum, although contacts among peoples and nations is not new, the globalization process has transformed the form and intensity of these interconnections in the last three or four decades. In the remainder of this book, we discuss globalization in feature boxes like this one as well as in the main body of the text itself. We emphasize the effects of globalization on *all* nations and regions, and not just how people like "us" are affecting people like "them," or how "they" threaten "us."

rituals of a people must investigate how those rituals are influenced by the people's family life, economic forces, political leadership, relationships between the sexes, and a host of other factors. The attempt to understand a community's customs, beliefs, values, and so forth holistically is one reason ethnographic fieldwork takes so much time and involves close contact with people.

Taken literally, a holistic understanding of a people's customs and beliefs is probably not possible because of the complexity of human societies. But anthropologists have learned that ignoring interrelationships among language, religion, art, economy, family, and other dimensions of life results in distortions and misunderstandings.

The essence of the holistic perspective may be stated fairly simply: *Look for connections and interrelationships, and try to understand parts in the context of the whole.*

Comparative Perspective

More than most people, anthropologists are aware of the diversity of the world's cultures. The ideas and behaviors learned from upbringing and experience in one's own society may not apply to other peoples with different cultural traditions. This implies that any general theories or ideas scholars might have about humans—about human nature, sexuality, warfare, family relationships, and so on—must take into account information from a wide range of societies. In other words, theoretical ideas about humans or human societies or cultures must be investigated from a **comparative perspective**.

The main reason anthropologists insist on comparison is simple: Many people mistakenly think the customs and beliefs that are familiar to them exist among people everywhere, which is usually not the case. Are humans innately aggressive? Are nuclear families biologically based? Is pair bonding (the nuclear family) rooted in our evolutionary past? Do men inevitably seek more sexual variety than women? Is competition in our genes? Cultural anthropologists are interested in these and other *general* questions about humanity, but we believe that we must consider *all* of humanity to answer them.

Knowledge of cultural variability makes anthropologists suspicious of any general theoretical idea about humans that is drawn from experience of life in only one nation or community. The idea *might* be valid for all people, but we cannot know until we have looked elsewhere. The beliefs and practices of people living in different times and places are far too diverse for any general theory to be accepted until it has been investigated and tested in a wide range of human groups. To state the comparative perspective concisely: *Valid generalizations about humans must take into account the full range of cultural diversity.*

Relativistic Perspective

Fundamentally, **cultural relativism** means that no culture—taken as a whole—is inherently superior or inferior to any other. Anthropologists adopt this perspective because concepts such as superiority require judgments about the relative worthiness of behaviors, beliefs, and other characteristics of a culture. However, such judgments are usually rooted in one's own values; and, by and large, values depend on the culture in

which one was raised. (If you think there must be universal standards for judging cultures, you may be right. However, aside from actions such as homicide, people don't agree on what they are.)

To see why a relativistic approach to studying cultures is important, contrast cultural relativism with ethnocentrism. **Ethnocentrism** is the belief that the moral standards, values, beliefs, and so forth of one's own culture are superior to those of other cultures. Most people are ethnocentric, and some degree of ethnocentrism is probably essential for individuals to have the sense of belonging needed for personal contentment. It may be necessary for the culture itself to persist. Mild ethnocentrism—meaning that people are committed to certain values but do not insist that everyone else hold and live by those values—is unobjectionable and inevitable. But extreme ethnocentrism—meaning that people believe their values are the only correct ones and that all people everywhere should be judged by how closely they live up to those values—leads to attitudes of intolerance and misunderstandings that anthropologists find objectionable.

Clearly, in their professional role, anthropological fieldworkers should avoid evaluating the behavior of other people according to the standards of their own culture. Ethnocentric attitudes and standards make objectivity difficult while doing fieldwork. Like the holistic and comparative perspectives, the essential point of cultural relativism may be stated simply: *In studying another culture, do not evaluate the behavior of its members by the standards and values of your own culture.*

Relativism may seem like a simple concept. However, consider what happened recently among a people called Jarawa. Numbering around 400, they live on South Andaman Island, now a part of India. India wanted to help the Jarawa retain their ancient ways, free from the interference of wealthier and more powerful outsiders. The Indian government set aside a forest reserve of 300 square miles so the Jarawa could continue to gather and hunt the wild products of the forest. Unfortunately, poachers entered the reserve, and one of them impregnated a young woman, who gave birth to a boy who was notably lighter skinned than his tribe mates. (The poacher later was arrested for rape.) Previously, Jarawa had been known to kill "mixed blood" infants born from liaisons with outsider fathers. A Jarawa man killed the infant. Indian prosecutors refused to prosecute the Jarawa killer, saying that he was acting to preserve the purity of his "race" and the cultural integrity of his tribe. In real situations like this one, does the relativistic perspective apply? How far should it be taken?

comparative perspective Insistence by anthropologists that valid hypotheses and theories about humanity be tested with information from a wide range of cultures.

cultural relativism Notion that one should not judge the behavior of other peoples using the standards of one's own culture.

ethnocentrism Attitude or opinion that the morals, values, and customs of one's own culture are superior to those of other peoples.

Because of globalization, people of different nationalities and cultural traditions interact through international travel, transnational education, and business. Learning about other cultures is increasingly important for practical, pragmatic purposes in the twenty-first century.

This example illustrates how easy it is to misunderstand relativism. To anthropologists, relativism is a *methodological principle* that refers to an outlook that is essential for maximum objectivity and understanding when studying a people whose way of life differs from their own. As a methodological principle, relativism recognizes that behavior viewed as morally wrong (perhaps even sinful) in one society may not be wrong in another. Polygamy, women who routinely appear bare-breasted in public, eating grubs, animal sacrifices, and comparable customs and actions are common among some peoples. Unqualified condemnations of such customs or beliefs have no place in anthropological research or in anthropological writings.

However, to many, the term *relativism* means "anything goes" with respect to the behavior of people in another culture or ethnic group. *Moral relativism* (relativism as a *moral principle)* implies that there are no absolute, universal standards by which to evaluate actions in terms such as right and wrong or good and bad.

Some people blame moral relativism for a host of social problems. For example, in the contemporary United States, many worry about not only the morality but also the long-term societal effects of gay and lesbian relationships. When gays and lesbians demanded the equal rights they believe only marriage can grant, in the past several years the legislatures of a number of states passed laws defining marriage as a relationship between a man and a woman. Others worry that society's acceptance of extramarital sex or tolerance for non-heterosexual relationships erodes family values and endangers national unity. Many believe that public schools should teach patriotism and traditional morality. Some blame delinquency and crime on public education that has become too secular. Such arguments and policies imply that there *are* absolute standards and clear rules about right and wrong or moral and immoral behavior. But moral relativism *taken to its extreme* says that few such standards or rules exist.

Newcomers to anthropology often confuse the two meanings of *relativism*, mistakenly believing that anthropologists promote both kinds. Most anthropologists are methodological relativists, but few are moral relativists. Anthropologists are as likely as anyone to consider oppression, slavery, violence, murder, slander, and so forth as morally objectionable. Many anthropologists speak out against the violence that spokespersons for some cultures claim are part of their religion, such as stoning of women found guilty of adultery. When a Pakistani teenager was shot in 2012 for promoting the education of girls, anthropologists did not accept the shooting as part of Pakistani culture. In 2016, when people were killed and injured by attacks in Brussels, Belgium, and in Orlando, Florida, anthropologists were as horrified as most other people.

One of the main ways the relativistic perspective affects anthropological views on such events is that we seek to understand the historical background and cultural context that contributed to them. Another is that we do not simply assign blame to the culture or religion for the actions of the individuals responsible because most members of that culture or believers in that religion do not engage in such actions. A third way is that anthropologists tend to examine practices and beliefs in their own homelands rather than assuming that their own way of life is best.

Unfortunately, the issues are not as simple in practice as the conceptual distinction between methodological and moral relativism implies. An example will illustrate. Most people have heard of the custom of *female genital mutilation* (FGM) (sometimes mislabeled "female circumcision"). The practice is widespread (but far from universal) in some regions of northern Africa and southwest Asia. It varies in severity, ranging from removing the clitoris to stitching shut the labia until marriage. Cultural beliefs about the reasons for the custom also vary. Most often the cultural rationale centers on controlling female sexuality and increasing a woman's desirability as a marriage partner. In many places, a majority of older women support the custom, so it is not unambiguously an issue of male control or oppression of women. Sometimes a girl or young woman herself considers it a symbol of her femininity and of her and her family's honor. In instances in which the girl herself consents, issues of relativism are especially complicated.

How should anthropologists view this custom? Should we think of it as just another age-old tradition—comparable to people eating with their fingers or men covering their genitals with only penis sheaths—that varies from people to people but is *inherently* neither right nor wrong? Surely not: Genital mutilation causes pain, exposes women to the dangers of infection and other complications, and is applied only to women because of their gender. Often, it is forced upon a female at a certain age—even if she objects. Because of its pain, danger, selectivity, and social enforcement, female genital mutilation is not comparable to customs that vary from people to people but are generally harmless.

Then is female genital mutilation a form of oppression? And, if so, by whom? Can culture itself oppress people? If it is oppression, does the anthropologist simply learn and write about it, place it in its local cultural context, compare the cultures that practice it with other cultures that do not, develop an idea about its meaning and why it occurs, and then do nothing? That is what many anthropologists believe we should do *as anthropologists.* Others disagree, believing instead that we should speak out against such practices, both as anthropologists and as human beings.

Then again, exactly what counts as "such practices"? Does eating dogs or cats or horses count? Does female footbinding in 1600s China count? Would tightly binding the waists of women in nineteenth-century Europe count? In the twenty-first century, just how different are surgeries to increase or reduce the size of breasts, hip and thigh liposuction, facelifts, and various piercings from female genital mutilation? Is it that they are voluntary? If so, then when a North African woman consents to her procedure, does her consent make the custom acceptable? If a woman feels so constrained by the ideals of beauty as defined by the culture in which she grew up, is it *unambiguously* true that surgery to make her body conform to ideals of beauty and attractiveness is voluntary?

Along these same lines, why is there so little international concern over the removal of the foreskin of American male infants, who have absolutely no choice when a physician mutilates their genitals? In 2009 in the Eastern Cape Province of the Republic of South Africa, 91 men died from their circumcisions, considered a rite of passage into manhood. Should we regard male circumcision as just as morally objectionable as the deaths and suffering caused by female genital mutilation?

Answers to such questions are not obvious, which is our main point. Most anthropologists would probably be satisfied with the following solution. Relativism as a methodological principle is essential to anthropological research because it facilitates fieldwork and leads to greater objectivity. Moral relativism is a separate matter and depends largely on one's personal standards and values. When a (Western) anthropologist witnesses customs like female genital mutilation that clearly cause harm, it is difficult to remain morally neutral. In such cases, we usually examine the custom holistically and in its historical context, which often helps us understand the conditions that led to it.

We also should consider comparable practices (such as expensive and painful surgeries to improve attractiveness) that might have a similar character or function within our own culture. We might note that "we" sometimes do similar things as "them." Perhaps we have trouble recognizing the similarity because we are familiar with our own practices, so we need also to examine ourselves when we condemn others. Such a critical look at one's own culture is another dimension of the relativistic perspective.

Such considerations do not resolve the essential tension between methodological and moral relativism. Do you believe that human rights are universal? If so, then you are *not* a moral relativist. On the other hand, knowledge of cultural diversity leads some anthropologists to wonder about the assumptions implicit in the United Nations Universal Declaration of Human Rights, found at the United Nations website. For example, Article 16(3) states, "The family is the natural and fundamental group unit of society and is entitled to protection by society and the State." Anthropologists are likely to ask questions like "What is meant by *family*?" and anthropologists are skeptical of the assumption that the family is the "*natural* and *fundamental* unit of society."

Some Lessons of Anthropology

In 2011, the governor of Florida asked whether state-funded universities really need anthropology departments. The governor was interested mainly in saving money for his state. But he specifically targeted anthropology, rather than sociology, literature, economics, or philosophy. Why?

Anthropology does seem esoteric. As we have seen, historically most cultural anthropologists did fieldwork in far-off places, studying "primitive cultures," "tribes," or (more politely) "indigenous peoples." Then we published articles and books that for the most part only anthropologists and their students read—the latter mainly because they were required to. What good is that?

Many political officeholders as well as others do not like anthropology for another reason. The field very often adopts a critical perspective on prevalent assumptions, ideas, and practices. We question common assumptions about human nature. We challenge prevalent beliefs about the causes of inequalities based on socioeconomic and ethnic characteristics. When we hear that families are declining, we look beyond the deterioration of moral standards and alternative sexualities as *the* cause. Most of us do not even apply terms like *deteriorate* and *decline* when talking about change in families. When environmentalists criticize China and India for their pollution of water and air and their rising contributions to global warming, anthropologists ask how such environmental problems look from the perspective of the Chinese and Indians. As a colleague once said, "Anthropologists think otherwise."

What insights does anthropology offer about humanity? What is the value of the information that anthropologists have gathered about the past and present of humankind? We consider these questions in future chapters. For now, we note some of the most general insights and contributions.

First, anthropology helps us understand the biological, technological, and cultural development of humanity over long time spans. Most of the reliable information available about human biological evolution, prehistoric cultures, and non-Western peoples resulted from anthropological research. This information has become part of our general storehouse of knowledge, recorded in textbooks and taught in schools. We easily forget that someone had to discover these facts and interpret their significance. For example, only in the late nineteenth century did most scientists accept that people are related to apes, and only in the last several decades has the relationship between humans and African apes become clear. Although we *Homo sapiens* (modern humans) share over 98 percent of our genes with *Pan troglodytes* (chimpanzees), many people still do not believe that humans are related to apes—another reason that anthropology is unpopular with some public officials.

Anthropology has contributed more than just facts. Anthropological concepts have been incorporated into the thinking of millions of people. For example, in this chapter we have used the term *culture*, confidently assuming our readers know the word and its significance. You may not know that the scientific meaning of this word, as used in the phrase "Tibetan culture," is not very old. Well into the nineteenth century, people did not fully understand the distinction between a people's culture (the *learned* beliefs and habits that made them distinctive) and their biological makeup (their *inherited* physical characteristics). Differences we now know are caused largely or entirely by learning were confused with differences caused by biological inheritance.

Early twentieth-century anthropologists, such as Franz Boas and Alfred Kroeber, provided factual evidence showing that biological differences and cultural differences are independent of each other. Margaret Mead's 1928 book *Coming of Age in Samoa* challenged prevalent beliefs about gender and adolescence. As these examples illustrate, anthropologists have contributed much to our knowledge of the human condition, although most people are not aware that it was mainly anthropologists who developed these understandings.

Another value of anthropology is that it teaches the importance of knowing and understanding cultural diversity. Anthropology urges all of us not to be ethnocentric in our attitudes toward other peoples. Mutual respect and understanding among the world's peoples are increasingly important with globalization's impacts on world travel, international migration, multinational business, and conflicts based on ethnic or religious differences. Reducing ethnocentric opinions will not solve the world's problems, but a more relativistic outlook on cultural differences might help to alleviate some of the prejudices, misunderstandings, stereotypes, interethnic conflicts, and racism that cause so much trouble among people on all continents.

A related point is that anthropology helps to minimize the miscommunications that commonly arise when people from different parts of the world interact with one another. As we shall see in Chapter 2, our upbringing in a particular culture influences us in subtle ways. For instance, English people know how to interpret one another's actions on the basis of speech styles or body language, but these cues do not necessarily mean the same thing to people from different cultures. A Canadian businessperson selling products in Turkey may wonder why her host does not cut the small talk and get down to business, whereas the Turk cannot figure out why the salesperson thinks they can do business before they have become better acquainted. A manager from a German firm may give unintentional offense when he shoves the business card just formally handed him by his Korean or Japanese counterpart in his pocket without carefully studying it. A Vietnamese student attending a California university may come across as a sycophant to her professors because her culture values learning so highly, a value that often manifests itself as deep respect for teachers. A Euro-American tourist visiting the Navajo reservation in Arizona may misinterpret a Navajo's reticence to make eye contact as unfriendliness, when it means something else to the Navajo. Anthropology teaches people to be aware of and sensitive to cultural differences—people's

actions may not mean what we take them to mean, and much misunderstanding can be avoided by taking cultural differences into account in our dealings with other people.

Finally, people can use anthropology's comparative perspective to understand their own individual lives. By exposing you to the cultures of people living in other times and places, anthropology helps you see new things about yourself. How does your life compare to the lives of other people around the world? Do people in other cultures share the same kinds of problems, hopes, motivations, and feelings as you do? Or are they completely different? How does the overall quality of your existence—your sense of well-being and happiness, your family life, your emotional states, your feeling that life is meaningful—compare with those of people who live elsewhere? Anthropology offers the chance to compare yourself to other peoples who live in different circumstances. In learning about others, anthropologists hope that students gain new perspectives on themselves.

SUMMARY

1. **List the four major subfields of anthropology and their primary interests.** Anthropologists usually specialize in one of four subdisciplines. Biological/physical anthropology studies the biological dimensions of human beings, including nonhuman primates, the physical variations among contemporary peoples, and human evolution. Archaeology uses the material remains of prehistoric and historic peoples to investigate the past, focusing on the long-term technological and social changes that occurred in particular regions of the world. Cultural anthropology is concerned with the social and cultural life of contemporary and historically recent human societies. Anthropological linguistics concentrates on the interrelationships between language and other elements of social life and culture.

2. **Describe how anthropology differs from other disciplines that also study humans.** The broad scope of anthropology distinguishes it from other disciplines in the social sciences and humanities. The field as a whole is concerned with all human

beings of the past and present, living at all levels of technological development. Anthropology is also interested in all aspects of humanity: biology, language, technology, art, religion, and other dimensions of human life.

3. **Explain some of the practical uses of anthropology in solving human problems.** Anthropologists apply the insights gained from the concepts, data, methods, and theories of their field to solve real-world problems in areas such as development, business, education, and health care services. Most people who do applied work are trained in cultural anthropology, but the other three subfields also are represented. As an undergraduate major, anthropology trains people in critical thinking and cultural sensitivity, skills that are increasingly useful as globalization brings diverse people together into larger systems.

4. **Discuss how cultural anthropology has changed in the last four decades.** Until around 1970, cultural anthropology concentrated on cultures known as

"tribal" or "indigenous." This is not as true in the globalized world of today. Many anthropologists conduct research in the urbanized, industrialized nations of the developed world. However, firsthand, extended fieldwork in villages or relatively small towns or neighborhoods continues to be a hallmark of cultural anthropology. Also, cultural anthropologists are more comparative and global in their interests and research than other social scientists.

5. **Understand the meaning and importance of the holistic, comparative, and relativistic perspectives.** Holism is the attempt to investigate the interrelationships among the customs and beliefs of a particular people. The comparative perspective means that any attempt to understand humanity or explain cultures or behaviors must include information from a wide range of human ways of life. Cultural relativism urges fieldworkers to try to understand people's behaviors on their own terms, not those of the anthropologist's own culture. Most anthropologists consider themselves methodological relativists, but moral relativism is a separate, though related, matter.

6. **Describe the wider lessons one can learn from studying anthropology.** Anthropology has practical value in the modern world. Anthropologists discovered most existing, reliable knowledge about human evolution, prehistoric populations, and indigenous peoples. Early anthropologists were instrumental in popularizing the concept of culture and in showing that cultural differences are not caused by racial differences. The value of understanding peoples of different regions and nations is another practical lesson of anthropology, one that is increasingly important as global connections intensify. The information that ethnographers have collected about alternative ways of being human allows individuals to become more aware of their own life circumstances.

2 Culture

Hinterhaus Productions/DigitalVision/Getty Images

To anthropologists, culture means the knowledge and behavior patterns that people socially learn while growing up in a particular society or group. This young woman's tattoos and hair are part of her way of defining her identity and communicate meanings to other persons.

LEARNING OBJECTIVES

After reading this chapter, you should be able to:

1. **DEFINE** culture in a way that is useful to compare and contrast different cultures.

2. **UNDERSTAND** the concept of cultural knowledge and five of its key components.

3. **DISCUSS** the evidence for the origins of the human capacity for culture.

4. **ANALYZE** the relationship between cultural knowledge and the behavior of individuals.

5. **DESCRIBE** why cultural and biological differences between human populations vary independently.

The word *culture* is so common that we hear or read it almost every day. Often it means that some individuals are "more cultured" than others. For example, we might think that some people are more culturally sophisticated than other people because they regularly attend symphonies or go to art galleries. Perhaps you have heard someone complain about the popular culture of sitcoms, TV reality shows, action-adventure movies, rap music, tattoos and other body art, such as body piercings. Maybe you use people's speech habits or clothing styles as grounds for thinking that some persons have "more culture" than others because of their ethnic identity, social class, or where they went to school.

Taken in context, these meanings of the word *culture* are fine. However, anthropologists define and apply the term in a different way. In the anthropological conception, it is almost meaningless to claim that one group of people has more culture or is more cultured than another group. Anthropologists believe that judgments about "high culture" and "low culture" are themselves based on cultural assumptions: "High" according to *whom* or according to what *standards*? Phrases like "working-class culture" and "popular culture" do have meaning in anthropology, but that meaning usually does not imply judgments about relative quality or sophistication.

In this chapter, we discuss the anthropological conception of culture. After giving the word a fairly precise definition, we cover some of its main elements, introducing some important concepts and terms along the way. We also consider how anthropologists think about the relationship between cultural differences and biological heredity.

Introducing Culture

The Englishman E. B. Tylor was one of the founders of the field that would eventually become cultural anthropology. In Tylor's 1871 book *Primitive Culture*, he pulled together much of the available information about the peoples of other lands (that is, places other than Europe). His definition of culture is often considered the earliest modern conception of the term. Tylor (1871, p. 1) wrote that culture is "that complex whole which includes knowledge, belief, art, morals, law, customs, and any other capabilities and habits acquired by man as a member of society." Notice the broadness of this definition. Culture includes almost everything about a particular people's way of life, from "knowledge" and "art" to "customs" and "habits." Notice also that culture is something an individual acquires as "a member of society," meaning that people learn their culture from growing up and living among a particular group.

Since Tylor's day, anthropologists have defined culture in hundreds of ways, although the main elements of Tylor's original conception of culture are still with us. Practically all modern definitions share certain key features. Anthropologists agree that culture

- Is learned from others while growing up in a particular human society or group
- Is widely shared by the members of that society or group
- Is responsible for most differences in ways of thinking and behaving that exist between human societies or groups
- Is so essential in completing the psychological and social development of individuals that a person who does not learn some culture would not be considered normal by others

In brief, culture is learned, shared, largely responsible for differences between human groups, and necessary to make human individuals into complete persons.

Anthropologists often use the term *culture* to emphasize the unique or most distinctive aspects of a people's customs and beliefs. When we speak of Japanese culture, for example, we usually mean the beliefs and customs of the Japanese that make them different from other people. How Japanese think and act differs in some ways from how Iranians, Vietnamese, and Indians think and act. The phrase "Japanese culture" concisely emphasizes these differences. To refer to "the" culture of a people is to call attention to all the things that make that people distinctive from others.

There are some things that anthropologists do *not* mean by the word *culture.* We do not mean that Japanese culture is inherently better or worse than, say, French or English culture. We mean only that the three differ in certain identifiable ways. Anthropologists also do not mean that Japanese, French, or English culture is unchanging. We mean only that they remain in some ways distinct despite the changes they have experienced over the years from historical contacts and globalization. Above all, anthropologists do not mean that Japanese, French, and English cultures are different because of the biological (genetically based) differences between the three peoples. We mean only that children born into the three cultures are exposed to different ways of thinking and acting as they grow up. They *become* Japanese, French, or English because of their upbringing in different social environments.

How do cultures differ? At the broadest level, they vary in ways of thinking and ways of behaving. *Ways of thinking* means what goes on inside people's heads: how they perceive the world around them, how they feel about particular people and events, what they desire and fear, and so forth. *Ways of behaving* refers to how people commonly act: how they conduct themselves around parents and spouses, how they carry out ceremonies, what they do when they are angry or sad, and so forth. Obviously, thoughts and actions are connected. How we act depends, in part, on how we think. In turn, how we think depends, in part, on how people around us behave, because our observations of their actions shape our thoughts.

Ways of thinking and behaving interact and are interdependent. But because neither completely determines the other, anthropologists commonly distinguish between them by using the terms *knowledge* and *behavior.* An analogy with language will help clarify why this distinction matters. All the knowledge (information) you have in your head about how to communicate by talking is *language.* What you actually say or talk about in particular situations is *speech.* Although you could not communicate without mastering a language, that knowledge alone does not tell you what to talk about or what to say. Your speech depends on the situation: who is present, your goals at the moment, how you and others define the occasion, and so forth.

Cultural knowledge includes all the information about the world and society that children learn and adults apply during their lives. It is what you know because you were born into a given group at a certain time. Cultural knowledge includes things like

- Attitudes about family, friends, enemies, and other kinds of people
- Notions of right and wrong (moral standards)
- Conceptions about the proper roles of males, females, and other gender identities
- Ideas about appropriate dress, hygiene, and personal ornamentation
- Rules about manners and etiquette
- Beliefs about the supernatural
- Standards for sexual activity
- Notions about the best or proper way to live (values)
- Perceptions of the world, both natural and social

This list could be expanded to include all other knowledge that members of a society or other group learn from previous generations. These and other kinds of knowledge largely determine how the members of a culture think, react, and sometimes feel. In this text, we sometimes use words like *beliefs* and *ideas* as synonyms for *cultural knowledge.*

Behavior includes all the things people regularly do, or how they habitually act. *Regularly* and *habitually* imply that members of the same culture generally adopt similar behaviors in similar situations (e.g., in church, on the job, at a wedding or funeral, visiting a friend, sitting in a classroom). Anthropologists are usually more interested in these regularities and habits—in what most people do most of the time in similar situations—than in the behavior of particular individuals. That is, usually we are more interested in **patterns of behavior** than in the behaviors

cultural knowledge Information, skills, attitudes, conceptions, beliefs, values, and other mental components of culture that people socially learn during enculturation.

patterns of behavior Within a single culture, the behavior most people perform when they are in certain culturally defined situations.

of particular individuals, which might be idiosyncratic. To avoid repetition, we sometimes use the terms *behavior* and *actions* as synonyms for *patterns of behavior.*

Defining Culture

It is useful to have a formal and fairly precise definition of *culture:*

> **Culture** is the *shared, socially learned knowledge* and *patterns of behavior* characteristic of some group of people.

This definition seems simple and perhaps even plain common sense, but in fact each part of it is problematic, as we now discuss.

Shared

Culture is *collective*—it is shared. People brought up in a given culture are mostly able to communicate with and interact with one another without serious misunderstandings and without needing to explain what their behavior means. Individuals who share the same culture usually do not have to explain their intentions or actions to one another so as to avoid cultural misunderstandings.

The characteristic that "some group of people" shares culture is intentionally imprecise. The nature of the group that shares culture depends largely on our interests. The people who share a common cultural tradition may be quite numerous and geographically dispersed, as illustrated by phrases like "Western culture" and "African culture." We use such phrases whenever we want to emphasize differences between Africans and Westerners. However, in this context the hundreds of millions of people to whom *culture* refers are so scattered and diverse that the term *group* has little (if any) meaning. On the other hand, the group that shares a common culture may be small. Some Pacific islands or Amazonian tribes, for instance, have only a couple hundred members, yet the people speak a unique language and have distinct customs and beliefs.

We often assume that people who share a common culture are members of the same nation-state (country). Identifying a cultural tradition with a single nation is sometimes convenient because it allows us to use phrases like "Canadian culture" and "Chinese culture." The identification of culture and country is reasonably accurate for some countries, like South Korea and Japan—although both these nations have immigrants and foreign residents, and Japan has an indigenous culture, the Ainu. However, the giant neighbor of South Korea and Japan, the People's Republic of China,

recognizes 56 minority peoples, some of whom have traditional homelands within China that are labeled "Autonomous Regions" on maps.

Most modern nations contain a lot of cultural diversity within their boundaries. This is especially true for nations with a history of colonialism. For example, the internationally recognized national borders of most African and South Asian countries are a product of their history as colonies, not of their indigenous cultural or ethnic identities. That is, more often than not, colonizing nations created boundaries between their colonies to further their own interests rather than to reflect cultural distinctions and ethnic divisions (see Chapters 4 and 16). Thus, modern India has dozens of languages and cultural identities, as do most sub-Saharan African nations like Kenya and Tanzania.

Modern European nations are also multicultural: Migrants from North Africa, Turkey, South Asia, and other regions now work in European countries like France, Germany, and Great Britain. The immigrants enrich their host countries with new cuisines, festivals, music, and other cultural practices. But they also take jobs and have different beliefs and behaviors. Some "native" Europeans view immigrants as a political threat and as endangering their own way of life. In 2009, the citizens of Switzerland were so anxious about immigrants from Islamic countries that they voted for a law against building more minarets—the towers that identify (Muslim) mosques. France at one point legally banned the headscarves worn by many Muslim women.

European resentments increased greatly in late 2015 when tens of thousands of Syrians fleeing conflict in their homeland became refugees in many European countries. Are a few of them Islamic terrorists? Will they take our jobs or lower our wages? Can our social safety net support them? Will they follow our laws or undermine our culture?

In addition to increasing diversity within most nations today, there are other complexities of the word *shared.* Individuals have a **cultural identity**, meaning that they define themselves partly by the cultural group in which they were raised or with which they identify. Your cultural identity helps define who you are, along with your ideas about your gender, race, and other features.

culture The shared, socially learned knowledge and patterns of behavior characteristic of some group of people.

cultural identity Cultural tradition a group of people recognizes as its own; the shared customs and beliefs that define how a group sees itself as distinctive.

The development of the global economy encourages international migration to seek education, better employment, a more satisfying social life, and even spouses. These men are Muslims praying in the courtyard of the Central Mosque—in London, England.

Yet cultural identity is complicated: If you are African American, you may feel you share a common identity with people born and living in Africa or with people of African heritage living in Haiti or Jamaica or parts of Brazil. Although you are far more likely to be like Euro-Americans in how you think and act, you might still identify with others whose ancestors were Africans. Similar considerations apply to other cultural identities, such as individuals whose parents were born in East Asia and Latin America. Notice that *cultural identity* implies contrast: The traits that define identity such as physical features and historical origins contrast with traits that define other identities (see Chapter 16).

For such reasons, confounding "culture" with "nation" is simplistic: Many cultural groupings and identities coexist within the boundaries of most modern nations. The term **subculture** refers to cultural variations that exist within a single nation. Most obvious are *regional subcultures.* Contrast the American states of Mississippi

and Connecticut; the Canadian provinces of Quebec and British Columbia; or the Great Britain regions of Scotland, Wales, Northern Ireland, and England.

Sometimes people extend the concept of subculture to particular groups that recruit their members from the nation at large, as in phrases like "corporate cultures" or "occupational cultures." Particular religious denominations are sometimes called "subcultures" to emphasize contrasting worship rituals and values between them, like Episcopalians and Southern Baptists. The word *subculture* often is applied to people based on sexual orientation, as in LGBT and straight subcultures. Some people distinguish subcultures based on contrasts like rural and urban, public school and prep school, homemakers and professional women, and even male and female.

These examples show that culture is shared at various levels, which makes the notion of shared culture complicated: At which level shall we speak of "a" culture or of "the" culture of people X? Generally, the words *culture* and *subculture* are useful if they contrast some group with another of the same kind—for example, western Europe with East Asia, English with French, Cherokee with Anglo, North with South, Catholic with Methodist. In most cases, the context of the discussion adequately defines the level contrasted.

subculture Cultural differences characteristic of members of various ethnic groups, regions, religions, and so forth within a single society or country.

The word *subculture* is often applied too loosely, however. It is most useful when it points out distinctions that have many dimensions. For example, if gay subculture refers *only* to sexual orientation, then the word *subculture* is not very useful. It becomes more meaningful if it refers to broader contrasts between straights and gays in values and lifestyles. Also, the more similarities there are between the members of the groups we wish to contrast, the less meaningful the concept of subculture becomes. Not just any difference between groups should be called "subcultural" (otherwise, even families could be subcultures). Distinctions based on criteria like occupation, employment status, or type of school are so vague that they have limited usefulness.

For all these reasons, saying that "culture is shared by some group of people" is not a simple matter. In the global society of the twenty-first century, some people think the entire world is headed toward "sharing" a single culture—a monolithic global culture. This possibility is discussed in Global Challenges and Opportunities.

Socially Learned

Individuals do not invent their culture, no more than each generation invents its own language. Rather, the members of any given generation learn their culture from previous generations. In time, they transmit that culture to future generations, albeit with some changes. Of course, during their lifetimes some people have more influence on their culture than others, but even very innovative and creative people build on the cultural knowledge their group has learned from previous generations.

The process by which infants and children learn the culture of those around them is called **socialization** or **enculturation**. Learning one's culture happens as a normal part of childhood. To say that culture is learned from others seems commonsensical, but it has several important implications that are not completely obvious.

To say that culture is *learned* implies that it is not transmitted to new generations through biological reproduction. Culture does not grow out of a people's gene pool or biological makeup, but is something the people born into that group develop as they grow up. Africans, East Asians, Europeans, and Native Americans do not differ in their cultures because they differ in their genes—they do not differ *culturally* because they differ *biologically.* Any human infant is perfectly capable of learning the culture of any human group or biological population, just as any child can learn the language of whatever group that child is born into. To state the main point in a few words: *Cultural differences and biological differences are largely independent of one another.*

To say that culture is *socially* learned is to emphasize that people do not learn it primarily by trial and error. The main ways children learn culture are

- Intentional instruction by others, such as family members and teachers
- Observation and imitation of the behavior of others, such as peers and role models
- Listening and other forms of communication
- Inference, or figuring out things on their own from what they already know from previous instruction, observation, and communication

Notice that the first three methods depend on social interactions, whereas the fourth results from rational thought, emotional responses, and some degree of introspection and awareness of one's individuality.

As an infant, you did not learn what is good to eat primarily by trying out a variety of things that might be edible and then rejecting things that tasted bad or made you sick. Rather, other people taught you what is and is not defined as food. If you are a North American, you probably view some animals (cattle, fish, chicken) as food and others that are equally edible (horses, dogs, guinea pigs) as not food. You did not discover this on your own but by learning from others what is edible, good tasting, or appropriate. This social learning of what is good to eat spared you most of the costs (and possible stomachaches and health hazards) of learning on your own by trial and error.

Relying on social learning rather than trial and error gives humanity many advantages. First, any innovation that one individual makes can be communicated to others in a group, who thus take advantage of someone else's experience. If you recombine the elements of old tools to develop a more effective tool and share your knowledge, other members of your community can also use that better tool.

Second, each generation socially learns the culture of its ancestors and transmits it to the next generation, and so on to future generations. Thus, any new knowledge or behavior acquired by one generation is potentially available to future generations (although some of it is lost or replaced). By this process of repeated social learning over many generations, knowledge accumulates. People alive today live largely from the knowledge acquired and transmitted by previous

enculturation (socialization) Transmission (by means of social learning) of cultural knowledge to the next generation.

Is Everyone Becoming a Westerner?

As interactions between the world's nations become more frequent, their impacts differ widely. People concerned about these impacts have varied opinions on what the future holds for cultural diversity on our planet.

Some fear (although others hope) that the cultures of the most wealthy and militarily powerful regions will eventually become globally dominant, gradually displacing other traditions. Many North Americans see evidence of this trend when they travel to places like East Asia or India and find businesses like McDonald's or KFC thriving. This is what many Middle Eastern political and religious leaders fear as they ban movies with scantily clad women. Some wealthy European countries like Italy and France are concerned that the American consumer culture is overwhelming their national traditions. Some see the international marketing of products as cultural imperialism, with companies from the United States usually identified as the main perpetrators—although Nokia (Finland), Nestlé (Switzerland), Samsung (South Korea), Panasonic (Japan), De Beers (South Africa), ASUS (Taiwan), and other companies with global markets and advertising also are quite involved.

In short, many believe that what they call Western culture is becoming *the* global culture. Some seem to treat this global cultural future as inevitable—for better or worse.

An alternative is that new cultural forms and understandings will arise out of increased contacts between peoples that result from travel and migration. International travel for tourism and business exposes people to other places and peoples. Many travelers go back home with new understandings and appreciation of the countries that hosted them. Temporary and permanent migration connects peoples and traditions.

Most of the richest countries of Europe were formerly colonial powers, and many of them are now destination countries for migrants. Large numbers of people from former colonies have immigrated to nations like France (Algerians) and Britain (Pakistanis, Bangladeshis, and Indians). In destination countries like Canada, the United States, and recently Australia, immigrants arriving for jobs bring their traditions along with their labor. Some citizens of destination countries worry about being culturally overwhelmed (and eventually outvoted) by immigrants. They wonder whether "those people" can or even want to be culturally assimilated. Those who

CHRIS MARTINEZ/Newscom/La Opinion/Los Angeles

In most modern nations, there are subcultures based on region, ethnic identity, national origin, and many other features that people use to define themselves as distinctive from others. These Korean Americans of Los Angeles are enjoying a festival that educates others about the Korean culture.

generations. Even "innovators," who often receive much credit and reward, build off what previous generations have learned and socially transmitted. They recombine existing things and ideas into something new—no easy task and also not entirely "their" idea.

Third, because culture is socially learned, human groups are capable of changing their ideas and behaviors very rapidly. Biological evolution (resulting from genetic change) is slow because it relies on biological reproduction. In contrast, no genetic change and no biological evolution need occur for the knowledge and behavior patterns of a human population to be massively transformed. Furthermore, your genetic makeup is fixed at conception. During the course of your life, continue to speak their native tongues are especially suspect. Others who are more sympathetic to diversity enjoy the new choices in food, films, and music that immigrants bring with them, believing that immigration culturally enriches their nations.

Globalization has other effects. In some countries, people feel culturally and economically threatened by the frequency and intensity of contacts, which leads them to cling more firmly to what they believe are their traditional values. Globalization can lead to greater attachments to a cultural past perceived as pure or uncorrupted by foreign influences. Outside influences are consciously rejected, sometimes with profound political consequences, including violence. (Most readers will think this paragraph refers to the Islamic Middle East, but they should be aware that similar reactions are occurring in their own nations.)

In countries with large numbers of immigrants, sometimes newcomers are culturally and linguistically assimilated into the majority or so-called mainstream. Future generations may not be recognized as immigrants nor consider themselves such. Or, instead of assimilation, people from a particular national background may establish permanent cultural enclaves in their new homelands. Festivals, cuisines, family and living arrangements, and languages are often preserved in these enclaves. In large North American cities, these include Chinatowns, Koreatowns, "little Mexicos," and so forth. Programmers and software engineers from India work in California's Silicon Valley and other places. To find spouses, many of them go online to connect with people they have never met. They might ask their parents in their ancestral region to set up meetings with suitable husbands or wives for when they go back home.

As these examples illustrate, as people of the past and present have migrated from their original countries, they have kept some of their traditions and maintained communities as ethnic enclaves within the larger society.

Thus, globalization has diverse impacts. There is no point in trying to predict what will happen in the end, mainly because changes will continue in future decades. There will never be an end—in the sense of a final outcome to cultural change once the global system has stabilized—because the global system will never stabilize.

It is worth pointing out, however, that when people discuss the worldwide spread of Western culture, in most cases they are really talking and worrying about the external manifestations of culture. They are concerned with the observable trappings of culture rather than with *culture* as anthropologists usually use the term. For example, McDonald's originated in the United States, but does its presence in Japan and South Korea threaten those cultures? Do Honda manufacturing plants in the Midwest threaten American culture? If you are an American citizen, did you feel your culture was endangered when a Chinese company bought IBM and started producing computers with the Lenovo label? If you are a Canadian resident of Vancouver, British Columbia, did you worry that your traditions were under attack when thousands of immigrants from Hong Kong settled in your city in the 1990s?

In fact, many things that people now believe are "theirs" originated elsewhere. The English alphabet came from the ancient Greeks, who adapted it from the even more ancient Phoenicians. English numerals (1, 2, 3, and so on) are in fact Arabic numerals. The English language originated in northern Europe out of

the Germanic subfamily, which is part of the widespread Indo-European language family. Canadian and American staples such as bread, steak, potatoes, and peas originated in other places. Although corn, tomatoes, beans, and chilies originated in North America, those of us with European ancestry learned about them from the original Native Americans. Many features of most cultures came from somewhere else or arose of various mixtures from various places, so borrowing from foreigners and/or combining foreign features to create new things is more common that most realize.

Finally, it is worth countering the common opinion that the transmission of the material manifestations of culture has been in only one direction—from the West to the Rest. Certainly, Western movies and music are popular in most of the world, as are Western fashions, cosmetics, and a host of other trappings. But similar things have moved in the other direction. Japanese anime and manga, karaoke, sushi, and horror movies have made it big among North American young people. Indian and Chinese movies, shisha or hookah smoking from the Middle East, East Asian martial arts and tai chi, tattoos featuring Chinese characters, and salsa dancing and music also are very popular. In Honolulu, you can visit bars that serve kava (a mouth-numbing drink made from the root of a plant from the pepper family, which originated in Polynesia and other Pacific islands). In most large North American and European cities, you can visit restaurants that will sell you food from practically anywhere. In late 2012, a Korean singer called Psy set a record for the most hits on YouTube with the music video "Gangnam Style." K-pop was all the rage and remains popular in the United States, and even more so in Japan and Taiwan

Are you feeling threatened yet?

however, your ideas and actions are able (and likely) to change dramatically.

In sum, culture is learned, not inborn, which means that cultural differences cannot be explained by biological/genetic differences between groups of people. The fact that culture is *socially* learned gives humanity some big advantages over other animals: Innovations can spread,

knowledge can accumulate over time, and peoples' ideas and actions can change rapidly in a single generation.

Social learning has a downside, too. For reasons no one fully understands, sometimes ideas and beliefs arise that lead some to harm or even kill other people. In 1995, in Japan the members of a "cult" called Aum Shinrikyo released a nerve gas in five trains at rush hour, injuring

Belgian officers inspect the airport in Brussels, where three simultaneous terrorist attacks on March 23, 2016, killed 31 people. Brussels is the headquarters of the European Union and ISIS may have chosen it as part of an effort to weaken the EU.

over 5,000 and killing 12 people. In Oklahoma City in April 1995, Timothy McVeigh bombed the Murrah Federal Building, killing 168 people. McVeigh was influenced by antigovernment, antitax, pro-gun movements. This was the worst terrorist attack on American soil until September 11, 2001. On that date, Al Qaeda terrorists crashed airplanes into the Twin Towers of New York City's World Trade Center, as well as into the Pentagon in Washington, DC. Nearly 3,000 people were killed that day. On December 14, 2012, a 20-year-old man killed 26 people at Sandy Hook Elementary School in Newtown, Connecticut. Even more people died in 2007 when a student killed 32 in a mass shooting at Virginia Polytechnic Institute. In March 2016, 31 people were killed and about 300 injured in an attack at two locations in Brussels, Belgium. ISIS claimed two of its members as the perpetrators. And in Orlando, Florida, in June 2016, 49 people were killed and another 53 were wounded by a man who had pledged allegiance to ISIS.

None of these people simply thought up the beliefs and ideas that led to their violent behavior. They were influenced by the beliefs and ideas of others, perhaps because in their minds these beliefs and ideas made sense of their life experiences. None of the original beliefs necessarily called for violence, but for some individuals violence was justified for revenge for real or imagined past wrongs, or against groups perceived as threatening, or to achieve some greater good. Sometimes, beliefs not only harm other people, but also the individuals who accept them. The men who guided the 9/11 aircraft died, as did the mass murderers in Newtown, San Bernardino, and Orlando. The individuals who commit acts of terror commonly commit suicide.

Knowledge

By *cultural knowledge*, anthropologists do not mean that a people's beliefs, perceptions, rules, standards, and so forth are true in an objective or absolute sense. In our professional role, for the most part anthropologists do not judge the accuracy or worthiness of a group's knowledge. For us, the most important thing about cultural knowledge is that

▪ The members of a culture share enough knowledge that they behave in ways that are meaningful and acceptable to others so that they avoid frequent misunderstandings and usually do not need to explain what they are doing.

- The knowledge guides behavior such that the people can survive, reproduce, and transmit their culture.

In a few words, cultural knowledge generally leads to behavior that is meaningful to others and adaptive to the natural and social environment. We consider some of this knowledge later.

Patterns of Behavior

As everyone knows, individuals brought up in the same culture differ in their behaviors. The behavior of individuals varies for several reasons. First, individuals have different *social identities:* gender identities, old and young, rich and poor, family X and family Y, and so forth. Actions appropriate for people with one identity may not be appropriate for others. Second, the behavior of individuals varies with *context and situation:* A woman acts differently depending on whether she is interacting with her husband, child, priest, or employee. Third, each human individual is in some ways a *unique* human individual: Even when brought up in the same society, we differ in our emotional responses, appetites, interpretations of events, reactions to stimuli, and so forth. Finally, cultural standards for and expectations of behavior are often *ambiguous.* For these and other reasons, the behavior of individuals is not uniform within the same culture.

Despite such complexities, within a single cultural group, behavioral regularities or patterns exist. For instance, in the 1980s had you visited a certain area of the Amazonian rain forest and encountered a people called the Yanomamö, you might have been shocked by some of their actions. By most cultures' standards, the Yanomamö are unusually demanding and aggressive. Slight insults often lead to violent responses. Quarreling men may duel in a chest-pounding contest during which they take turns beating each other on the chest, alternating one blow at a time. More serious quarrels sometimes call for clubs, with which men bash each other on the head. Fathers sometimes encourage their sons to strike them (and anyone else) by teasing and goading, while praising the child for his fierceness.

If, on the other hand, you visited the Semai, a people of Malaysia, you might be surprised at how seldom they express anger and hostility. Indeed, you might find them *too* docile. One adult should never strike another—"Suppose he hit you back?" they ask. The Semai seldom hit their children—"How would you feel if he or she died?" they ask. When children misbehave, the worst physical punishment they receive is a pinch on the cheek or a pat on the hand. Ethnographer Robert Dentan suggests one reason for the nonviolence of the Semai: Children are so seldom exposed to physical punishment that when they grow up, they have an exaggerated impression of the effects of violence.

The contrasting behavioral responses of the Yanomamö and Semai people illustrate an important characteristic of most human behavior: its social nature. Humans are supremely social animals, interacting with others throughout most of our lives in patterned social relationships. Anthropologists give special attention to the regularities of these patterned relationships, including things such as how family members interact, how females and males relate to one another, how political leaders deal with subordinates, and so forth.

The concept of **role** is useful to describe and analyze interactions and relationships. Individuals are often said to have a role or to play a role in some group. Roles usually carry names or labels, such as "mother" in a family, "student" in a classroom, "accountant" in a company, and "headman" of a Yanomamö village. Attached to a role are the group's *expectations* about what people who hold the role should do. Learning to be a member of a group includes learning the expectations of its members. Expectations include rights and duties. The *rights* (or privileges) defined by my role include the benefits the group members agree I should receive as a member. My *duties* (or obligations) include other group members' expectations of my behavior.

Rights and duties are usually *reciprocal:* My right over you is your duty to me, and vice versa. My duties to the group as a whole are the group's rights over me and vice versa. If I adequately perform my duties to the group, then other members reward me, just as I reward them for their own role performance. By occupying and performing a role in a group, I behave in ways that others find valuable, and I hope that some of my own wants and needs will be fulfilled. Conversely, failure to live up to the group's expectations of role performance is likely to bring some sort of informal or formal punishment. Among the Yanomamö, young men who refuse to stand up for themselves by fighting are ridiculed and may never amount to anything. The shared knowledge of roles and expectations is partly responsible for patterns of behavior.

Defining culture as *shared and socially learned knowledge and behavior* seems pretty inclusive. Actually, though, anthropologists do not consider some things to be cultural that most other people do. For example,

role Rights and duties that individuals receive because of their personal identity or membership in a social group.

Component	Brief Definition	Examples
Norms	Standards of propriety and appropriateness	Expected behaviors at weddings and in classrooms
Values	Beliefs about social desirability and worth	Individual rights; work ethic
Symbols	Objects and behaviors with arbitrary and conventional meanings	Interpretations of nonverbal behavior; meanings of sacred objects
Classifications and Constructions of Reality	Divisions of reality into categories and subcategories	Kinds of persons; divisions of nature into kinds of plants and animals
Worldviews	Interpretations of events and experiences	Origin and content of good and evil; fate of soul in afterlife

many anthropologists do not see architecture and art objects such as paintings and sculptures as part of a people's culture. They are, rather, physical representations and material manifestations of cultural knowledge. They are *products* or *expressions* of culture rather than *aspects* of culture. For instance, art expresses a culture's values, ideals of beauty, conflicts, worldviews, and so forth. Houses and public buildings are products of a people's family life, sexual practices, political organization, ideas of beauty and symmetry, religious beliefs, and status distinctions. Many anthropologists do not even see writing as part of culture. Rather, writing is a means of storing knowledge, transmitting information, and—in the case of fiction—telling stories that are meaningful in the cultural group. Thus anthropologists do not agree on whether such material objects—often called *material culture*—are part of culture or only material manifestations of culture.

Notice, though, that these complications depend largely on how we choose to define culture. Different definitions serve different purposes: One or another is useful only for *some* purposes. Here we consider shared knowledge and behavioral patterns as the essence of culture, but we could define *culture* in such a way that it includes material objects (like tools, art, and architecture).

---

norms Shared ideals and/or expectations about how certain people ought to act in given situations.

Cultural Knowledge

Cultural knowledge includes beliefs, attitudes, rules, assumptions about the world, and other kinds of information stored in our brains. In this section, we discuss only five elements of cultural knowledge: norms, values, symbols, classifications and constructions of reality, and worldviews. We cover these elements because they are among the most important components of cultural knowledge and because their anthropological meaning goes beyond that of everyday speech. The Concept Review previews the five major components in a few words.

Norms

Norms are shared ideas about how people ought to act in certain situations, or about how particular people should act toward particular other people. The emphasis is on the words *ought, should,* and *situations.* The fact that norms exist does not mean everyone follows them all the time. Some norms are regularly violated, and what is normative in one situation need not be in other situations. *Norm* thus does not refer to behavior itself. Rather, *norm* implies that (1) there is widespread agreement that people ought to adhere to certain standards of behavior, (2) other people judge the behavior of a person according to how closely it adheres to those standards, and (3) people who repeatedly fail to follow the standards face some kind of negative reaction from other members of the group.

Any culture includes hundreds or thousands of norms. People are not consciously aware of many of them. (For example, the next time you interact with someone, try standing closer than "normal" and observe their reaction.) Sometimes people feel that norms are irrational, arbitrary rules that stifle their creativity or keep them from doing what they want for no reason—other than that society disapproves. In fact, though, norms make social interactions much more predictable and so are quite useful to us as individuals. It is mainly because we agree on norms that we know how to behave toward others and that we have expectations about how others should behave toward us in diverse social situations or settings.

For example, at social gatherings where you do not know many people, you may feel awkward or nervous. But in your culture people know how to introduce themselves, so soon you are telling others who you are and asking other guests what they do, what they are studying, and where they are from. Perhaps you even know subtle ways of figuring out whether someone is available. Here, and in many other cases in everyday life, we do not experience norms as oppressive. Rather, norms are useful guides to how to do something in such a way that others know what you are doing and accept your actions as normal rather than thinking you are strange.

Values

Values refer to beliefs about the way of life that is desirable for society. Values have profound, though partly unconscious, effects on people's behavior. The goals we pursue, as well as our general ideas about the good life, are influenced by the values of the culture into which we were born or raised. At the level of individuals, values affect our motivations and thus influence the reasons we do what we do. Values are also critical to the maintenance of culture as a whole because they represent the qualities people believe are essential to continuing their way of life. One way to think of values is that they provide important standards that people believe must be upheld under most circumstances. People may be deeply attached to their values and, sometimes, are even prepared to sacrifice their lives for them, as suicide bombers illustrate.

Although people may say they cherish their values, it is easy to overemphasize their importance in real people's lives. For one thing, to uphold one value sometimes leads us to neglect others (e.g., people who value career enhancement may be less available to their families, although they value those relationships also). For another, our personal interests can lead us to ignore or downplay some values in some situations (e.g., people who value honesty may still believe that it is acceptable to be less forthcoming in competitive business situations).

Also, our fears, loves, hates, and other emotions can lead us to ignore our values in favor of other concerns.

Here are some North American examples that illustrate such complexities. Most people agree that those accused of crimes have rights to a speedy trial and an attorney. But perceived threats from people accused of terrorism lead many to agree that these values can justifiably be ignored in some situations. As an abstract moral value, prisoners of war should not be tortured. But national security also is important. What should a nation do when national security seems to conflict with upholding human rights? To say that values are shared does not mean that everyone gives them the same importance. And which values apply often depends on situational rather than absolute factors.

Many disagreements about public policy arise from how much weight people place on one of their values as opposed to other values. "Something" should be done about undocumented immigrants, but should 11 million people be rounded up and sent back to their birth countries? To prevent new ones from entering the United States, should the government build a wall across the southern border?

Then there are conflicting values. For instance, there are *family values*. But what constitutes a family? Many do not think gay and lesbian couples count as families. There are values placed on marriage, which some consider the bedrock of society. But recent trends lead to questions about who can marry whom, what rights are involved with alternative marriages, and which unions should be legally recognized. In April 2016, North Carolina legislated that individuals can only use the public restrooms of their birth gender, to deter trans people from using the alternative restroom. Many states have legislated that businesses cannot be forced to provide services in support of acts that violate their religious beliefs, such as making wedding cakes or issuing marriage licenses for gays and lesbians even if same-sex marriage is legal in that state. Perhaps you know of older people who favor only traditional marriage and family but whose opinion changes when one of their children comes out.

Most Americans hold strong values about *equal opportunity*, but if opportunities are to be truly equal, then people should not be allowed to pass much wealth to their children because that provides their children a head start in life. Yet shouldn't people be allowed to give their wealth to their children if they so choose? It

values Shared ideas or standards about the worth of goals and lifestyles.

is their *private property* (another value), but children who inherit large amounts of property have done nothing to earn it—which conflicts with values about working for what you have.

Symbols

Symbols are things (like objects or an actions) that represent, connote, or call to mind something else. Just as we learn norms and values during socialization, we learn the meanings that people in our group attach to symbols. And just as norms and values affect patterns of behavior, so do the understandings people share of the meanings of symbols.

For the most part, people's shared understandings about the meanings of actions and objects are unconscious. Contrast this to values: We can speak to inquiring strangers about our values and explain to them why we believe they are important. But it is nearly impossible to tell someone why a particular gesture, a way of walking, a style of dress, or a certain facial expression carries the meaning it does rather than some other meaning. We "just know." "Everyone knows," for such things are common knowledge and maybe even common sense to people who have shared understandings of the symbols.

Two important properties of symbols are that their meanings are arbitrary and conventional. *Arbitrary* means there are no inherent qualities in the symbol that lead a human group to attribute one meaning to it rather than some other meaning. Thus, the wink of an eye that often means "just kidding" in some cultures is—literally—meaningless in other cultures. *Conventional* refers to the fact that the meanings exist only because people implicitly agree they exist. Thus, at an intersection, a red light means "stop," but only because all drivers agree that it does.

Many symbols are objects that stand for something important or sacred: a flag, a cross, a wedding ring, a religious text. Other symbolic objects have practical uses or functions, in the sense that they are useful in everyday life: not only expensive cars, enormous houses, gaudy jewelry, and clothing styles have practical uses but also are status symbols. Even individual persons can be symbols. The queen of England and the emperor of Japan have little formal power in their nation's constitution.

Rather, they symbolize their people's history, traditions, and values. Many citizens are emotionally attached to them despite the expense of maintaining the trappings of their offices.

Victor Turner's ideas about symbols have influenced anthropology and other disciplines for decades. Writing in 1967 about objects used in rituals among the Ndembu, an indigenous people of Zambia, Turner noted that Ndembu ritual symbols have several properties that make them powerful in the minds of people. Turner called two of these properties *multivocality* and *condensation*.

Symbols represent many qualities and abstract values simultaneously (multivocality). They do so by expressing their meanings in a material form (condensation) that is easy to represent, think about, and become emotionally attached to. National flags, monuments to slain soldiers, public buildings, and religious symbols like statues and crosses are good examples of these two properties. People become emotionally attached to such symbols, which can come to stand for all that is right and valuable. Some feel that flag burning should be illegal and is even treasonous. To many, gun ownership is a symbol for individual rights, and regulation of guns is an infringement of freedom— heartfelt emotions are expressed when governments want to restrict the right to bear arms. The cross represents more to Christians than just the death of Jesus. Menorahs are meaningful to Jews, as are headscarves to Muslims. Some Japanese continue to revere their emperor, even though the emperor himself renounced his divinity in 1945.

Symbols are critical to meaningful social interactions. Our shared understandings of what actions mean allow us to interact with one another without the need to explain our intentions or to state explicitly what we are doing and why. Because you assume that most people you interact with share your understandings, in most situations you know how to act and what to say so as not to be misunderstood. Cultural knowledge includes common understandings of how to interact with one another appropriately (i.e., according to shared expectations) and meaningfully (i.e., in such a way that other people usually are able to interpret our intentions).

Nonverbal communication provides a fine example of these understandings. When you interact with someone face-to-face, the two of you are engaged in a continual giving and receiving of messages communicated by both speech and actions. Spoken messages are intentionally (consciously) sent and received. Other messages—including body language, facial expressions, hand gestures, touching, and the use of physical space—are communicated by nonverbal behavior, much of which is unconscious. Nonverbal messages

symbols Objects, behaviors, and other phenomena whose culturally defined meanings have no necessary relationship to their inherent physical qualities; symbols are arbitrary and conventional.

emphasize, supplement, or complement spoken messages. We are not always conscious of what we are communicating nonverbally, and sometimes our body language even contradicts what we are saying. (Is this how your parents could tell when you were lying?)

One general point is that cultural knowledge conditions social behavior in ways people do not always recognize consciously—at least until someone's behavior violates our understandings. Furthermore, many gestures and other body movements with well-known meanings in one culture have no meaning, or have different meanings, in another culture. On a Micronesian island studied by one of the authors, people may answer yes or show agreement by a sharp intake of breath (a gasp) or by simply raising the eyebrows. One may also answer yes by the grunting sound ("uh-uh") that carries exactly the opposite meaning to North Americans. You would signal "I don't know" or "I'm not sure" by wrinkling your nose, rather than by shrugging your shoulders.

Aside from showing the social usefulness of shared understandings of symbolic actions, these examples illustrate one way misunderstandings occur when individuals with different cultural upbringings interact. Raised in different cultures in which gestures and sounds carry different meanings, individuals (mis)interpret the actions of others based on their own culture's understandings, often seeing the others as rude, unfriendly, insensitive, overly familiar, and so forth.

Consider some examples. Arabs and Iranians often stand "too close" for the Canadian and American comfort zone. In South Korea, it is common to see two young females holding hands or with their arms around each other while walking. But their touching

symbolizes nothing about their sexual orientation, nor does two men holding hands in parts of the Middle East. Japanese are less likely than North Americans to express definite opinions or preferences or to just say no to a request. To outsiders, this reluctance often comes across as uncertainty, tentativeness, or even dishonesty, whereas the Japanese view it as politeness. The common American tendency to be informal and friendly is viewed as inappropriate in many other cultures where outward displays of emotions are not displayed to mere acquaintances.

In a world where the globalization of trade and international travel are commonplace, it is worth knowing that much of what you "know" is not known to members of other cultural traditions, just as what they "know" may be unfamiliar to you. Think before you take offense at their actions. And think before you give it.

Classifications and Constructions of Reality

The members of a cultural tradition share beliefs about what kinds of things and people exist. They have a similar **classification of reality**, meaning they generally share knowledge of the basic kinds of animals, plants, inanimate objects, and humans exist. Another term for this is the **cultural construction of reality**. From the multitude of differences and similarities that exist in some phenomena, a culture recognizes (constructs) only some features as relevant in making distinctions. The cultural construction of reality implies that different peoples do not perceive the human and natural worlds in the same ways.

Natural Reality

How a people divide up plants, animals, landscape features, seasons, and other dimensions of the natural world is culturally constructed. As just one example, the Hanunóo, an indigenous people of the tropical forests of the Philippines, identify 1,600 kinds of plants. They distinguish 400 more "kinds" of forest plants than a botanist would. The Hanunóo make fine distinctions between flora because of the way they use the forest for slash-and-burn farming (discussed in Chapter 7). It is not that the botanist is right and the Hanunóo wrong,

Lane Oatey/Blue Jean Images/Getty Images

Symbols include more than physical objects like religious icons, jewelry, clothing, and cars. When people are socialized, they understand the cultural meanings of behavior as well. Most Koreans and Japanese recognize that these two young women are just friends.

classification of reality (cultural construction of reality) The ways in which the members of a culture divide up the natural and social world into categories, usually linguistically encoded.

but that they use different criteria to construct their plant classification.

How people culturally construct natural phenomena influences how they define and use nature. Plants, animals, minerals, waters, and the like are classified not just into various kinds but also into various categories of usefulness. For example, what one group considers food is not necessarily defined as food by another group. Muslims and Orthodox Jews consider pork unclean. Traditional Hindus refuse to consume the flesh of cattle, an animal that is sacred to them. The fact that a given animal or plant is edible does not mean that people *consider* it edible (otherwise more North Americans would eat dogs, as do many East and Southeast Asians, and horses, as do some French).

Finally, people of different cultures differ in their beliefs about the kinds of things that do and do not exist. Some people believe in witches who use malevolent supernatural powers to harm others. Traditional Navajo believe that witches can change themselves into wolves, bears, and other animals. The Tukano people of the Bolivian rain forest believe that a spirit of the forest controls the animals they depend on for meat. So when meat is scarce, a Tukano shaman makes a supernatural visit to the abode of the forest spirit. He promises to magically kill a certain number of humans and to send their souls to the forest spirit in return for the spirit's releasing the animals so the hunters can find game.

As the Navajo and Tukano examples illustrate, not only do different cultures classify objective reality in different ways, but they also differ on what reality *is:* One culture's definition of reality may not be the same as that of another culture.

Social Reality

Countless generations of people in a particular culture found ways of ordering and classifying phenomena into categories. However, human senses can be misleading: The Earth is not truly flat although it appears to be from ordinary perceptions; the sun only appears to move across the sky; rocks are not completely solid; life forms change, but too slowly for humans to notice in their lifetime. Only in the last few centuries have systematic observations and experiments allowed scientists to realize the limitations of our sensory impressions.

In addition to natural phenomena, human beings also make cultural constructions of human beings, placing them into categories and attributing certain characteristics to those categories. In future chapters, we discuss cultural constructions of families and of gender. Here we consider another cultural construction, that of race.

Most people assume that race is a natural category—determined by an individual's genes, easily visible, and mostly obvious. If people cannot tell which race you are, they probably think of you as "mixed race." "Mixed race" is a tricky concept because people of "mixed racial heritages" are usually assigned to whichever racial category is seen as the minority one. (Figure 2.1 illustrates the complexity and confusion surrounding racial classification.) Thus, President Barack Obama is the first black U.S. president, although his mother was white. (Incidentally, the late Ann Dunham Soetoro was a cultural anthropologist who did fieldwork in Pakistan and Indonesia.) Even if we are born and live in a place that is racially homogeneous, we can observe racial differences by visiting almost any large city. Race certainly seems natural.

Most anthropologists disagree. They argue that race is not, in fact, a natural category but a cultural construction of people based on perceptions and distinctions that arise more from culture than from biology. What does this mean, and why do most anthropologists believe it? (For simplicity, from now on we will use the term *race* without quotation marks with the understanding that the term connotes a cultural construction.)

➤ **NOTE: Please answer BOTH Question 5 about Hispanic origin and Question 6 about race. For this census, Hispanic origins are not races.**

5. Is this person of Hispanic, Latino, or Spanish origin?

- ☐ **No,** not of Hispanic, Latino, or Spanish origin
- ☐ Yes, Mexican, Mexican Am., Chicano
- ☐ Yes, Puerto Rican
- ☐ Yes, Cuban
- ☐ Yes, another Hispanic, Latino, or Spanish origin — *Print origin, for example, Argentinean, Colombian, Dominican, Nicaraguan, Salvadoran, Spaniard, and so on.* ↗

_____

6. What is this person's race? *Mark* ☒ *one or more boxes.*

- ☐ White
- ☐ Black, African Am., or Negro
- ☐ American Indian or Alaska Native — *Print name of enrolled or principal tribe.* ↗

_____

☐ Asian Indian	☐ Japanese	☐ Native Hawaiian
☐ Chinese	☐ Korean	☐ Guamanian or Chamorro
☐ Filipino	☐ Vietnamese	☐ Samoan
☐ Other Asian — *Print race, for example, Hmong, Laotian, Thai, Pakistani, Cambodian, and so on.* ↗		☐ Other Pacific Islander — *Print race, for example, Fijian, Tongan, and so on.* ↗

_____

- ☐ Some other race — *Print race.* ↗

_____

Figure 2.1 In this portion of the 2010 United States Census form—sent to all American households—respondents are asked to identify their race. In item 5, the form correctly does not equate "Hispanic origin" with "race." However, notice that there are 12 "races" specifically listed in item 6, and others are lumped together as "other Asian" or "other Pacific Islander." Presumably, if you fall into one of these two categories, you have lots of "races" with which you can identify yourself. How many of these are "races," in the anthropological meaning?

First, the differences out of which race is constructed are only skin deep. When we say people are the same or different races, we generally focus on selected visible physical traits: skin color, facial features, hair characteristics, and so forth. If we looked beyond observable traits to consider other (invisible or less visible) traits, different racial categories would result. For example, a racial classification of the world's people based on blood groups (ABO, Rh factor, and other characteristics) would produce a different classification than one based on skin color. So would a racial classification based on the shape of teeth or jaws, or on the ability of adults to digest the milk enzyme lactase. Culturally, we define some physical features as relevant (we consider them *significant*) whereas others are unrecognized (unperceived) or irrelevant. In short, the traits we use to define races lead to one kind of racial classification, but we would have a different classification if we used different traits.

Second, how many races are there? Most elderly people raised in North America would say three, which in earlier days were called Mongoloid, Negroid, and Caucasoid. This threefold classification of humanity is based on the history of contacts between Europeans and certain peoples of Africa and Asia. But why only three? Why not 6 or 13 or 40? The so-called Pygmies of Central Africa are quite different physically from their Bantu neighbors, as are the once-widespread Khoisan peoples of southern Africa. The indigenous peoples of New Guinea, Australia, and the surrounding islands are quite different physically not only from many of their neighbors but also from some Africans whom they outwardly resemble in their skin coloration. Many people of southern Asia have skin as dark as some Africans, although in some other physical characteristics they resemble Europeans. What about Malaysians, Polynesians, and Native Americans? Should they be separate races, or combined with others? If so, which others?

Third, along these same lines, different cultures sometimes develop different racial classifications. Brazil is well known for its history of interbreeding among peoples from different continents. Based on his fieldwork, Conrad Kottak reported that in a single village in northeastern Brazil, 40 different terms were used to refer to *race*! The villagers recognized distinctions between themselves that outsiders did not see, not only revealing their cultural constructions but suggesting that other peoples' racial categories might also be constructed.

Fourth, racial classifications change over time even within the same cultural tradition. In the Americas, people who today are seen as racially indistinguishable once were widely viewed as members of different races. When large numbers of Irish immigrated to the Americas after the potato blight struck Ireland in the mid–nineteenth century, they were considered a race by many other Americans whose ancestors had lived here somewhat longer. Further, many viewed Jewish people as a distinct racial group, even though Judaism is a religion. Such distinctions may sound absurd today—to most North Americans, at any rate. Perhaps present-day racial divisions seem will seem equally absurd in the next century.

In sum, most anthropologists believe that race is culturally constructed for the following reasons:

▌ Different racial categories can be constructed by applying different criteria.

▌ There is no objective way to determine whether some population should be considered a separate race or grouped with other populations into a single racial type or how many human races exist.

▌ Different cultures identify different numbers and kinds of races, raising doubts about the biological reality of any given culture's racial categories.

▌ Even within a single society or nation, the definition of race changes over time.

So, do some anthropologists deny that there are physical differences between populations whose ancestors originated in different continents? No. To claim that races are culturally constructed is not to deny biological/genetic realities. However, it does deny that these differences cluster in such a way that they produce categories of people who consistently differ in the same biological ways (i.e., races).

Individual human beings differ from one another physically in a multitude of visible and invisible ways. If races—as most people define them—are real biological entities, then people of African ancestry would share a wide variety of traits while people of European ancestry would share a wide variety of *different* traits. But once we add traits that are less visible than skin coloration, hair texture, and the like, we find that the people we identify as the same race are less and less like one another and more and more like people we identify as different races. Add to this point that the physical features used to identify a person as a representative of some race (e.g., skin coloration) are continuously variable, so that one cannot say where brown skin becomes white skin. Although the physical differences themselves are real, the way we use physical differences to classify people into discrete races is a cultural construction.

For these and other reasons, most anthropologists agree that race is more of a cultural construction than a biological reality. Indeed, the American Anthropological Association recommended (unsuccessfully) eliminating the word *race* from the 2010 U.S. census. The American Anthropological Association has an excellent website that portrays conceptions of human differences: http://www.understandingrace.org/home.html

Why does it matter whether race is a cultural construction rather than a biological reality? As long as people can avoid viewing some races as inferior to others, why is it so important that we see race as a cultural construction?

For one thing, once a culture classifies people into kinds or types, it is difficult to avoid ranking the types according to some measure of quality or inborn talent. Familiar qualities include intelligence, work ethic, athletic ability, and musical talent. Some people believe Asians are naturally smart and work hard, whereas African Americans are better natural athletes, dancers, and musicians. From such seemingly innocent stereotypes, we too easily conclude that it is natural talent that puts many Asians near the top of their class and explains why so many African Americans succeed in athletics, dance, and music.

Another reason to view race as culturally constructed is that doing so helps to avoid confusing race with other kinds of differences that have nothing to do with physical differences. Most North Americans do not distinguish—at least not consistently—differences due to race from differences due to language, national origin, or cultural background. The latter differences, of course, are based on culture and/or language, not on physical characteristics. Too easily, *race* is confused with *ethnicity*. For example, many people view Native American and Hispanic as the same kind of identity as race. But Hispanics may be black or white or brown or any other humanly possible color, and many people who identify themselves as Native Americans based on their origins and culture are indistinguishable physically from Americans with European ancestry.

Last, race is currently a part of the way people identify themselves to one another. It is an important part of an individual's social identity. Another person's perception of you—and your perception of yourself—is affected by your assumed membership in some racial category. Such identities often carry racial pride. Racial pride may be a positive force in the lives of people who have suffered the effects of prejudice and discrimination, as older African Americans who were part of the 1960s Black Power movement will appreciate. Yet racial pride cuts both ways, as those familiar with the beliefs and activities of the Aryan Nation and other such groups dedicated to maintaining racial purity know.

Political leaders and opinion shapers in the popular media can and do manipulate the opinions of one race about other races to further their own political and social agendas. Playing on racial prejudice to win votes needs to be subtle, lest candidates and opinion shapers be charged with racism. But there are code words that may signal true intent: The "welfare queens" of the 1980s have become "people who want free stuff."

Worldviews

The **worldview** of a people is the way they interpret reality and events, including their images of themselves and how they relate to the world around them. Worldviews are affected by cultural constructions of reality, which we have just discussed. But worldviews include more than just the way a culture carves up people and nature into "kinds."

People have opinions about the nature of the cosmos and how they fit into it. All cultures include beliefs about spiritual souls and what happens to souls after bodies become lifeless in this world. People have ideas about the meaning of human existence: how we were put on Earth, who or what put us here, and why. They have notions of evil: where it comes from, why it sometimes happens to good people, and how it can be combated. They have beliefs about what supernatural powers or beings are like, what they can do for (or to) people, and how people can worship or control them. Everywhere we find myths and legends about the origins of living things, objects, and customs. (We have more to say about such topics in Chapter 14.)

These examples all derive from a people's religion. But it is important not to confuse worldview and religion, and especially not to think that *religion* and *worldview* are synonymous. Although religious beliefs do influence the worldview of a people, cultural traditions vary in aspects of worldview that we do not ordinarily think of as religious.

For instance, the way people view their place in nature is part of their worldview: Do they see themselves as the masters and conquerors of nature, or as living in harmony with natural forces? The way people view themselves and other peoples is part of their worldview. Do they see themselves, as many human groups do, as the only true human beings and all others as essentially animals? Or do they see their way of life as one among many equally human but different ways of life? Most modern scientists share a similar worldview: They believe that all things and events in the universe have natural causes that we can discover through certain formal procedures of observation, experimentation, and systematic logic.

Atheists also have a worldview: Nothing supernatural created the universe and our planet, and everything now works automatically and mechanically, with no divine input necessary. Many religious persons claim that such beliefs can lead to disbelief in absolute moral standards—with no divine guidance, "anything goes," they fear. Atheists and agnostics respond that human well-being and social responsibility can serve equally well as a moral compass and that some of history's worst tragedies have been caused by religion and hatreds derived from religion.

Origins of Culture

Like so much else about our early past, when humanity began to depend on culture is uncertain. Most anthropologists think the essence of culture—without which everything else cultural could not exist—is the ability to create and understand symbols. If meanings are arbitrary and conventional, that implies a highly developed ability to distinguish the meanings of objects and behaviors from their outward forms. Dating the development of the ability to understand symbols would then imply that culture was present. But how to determine when humanity developed this capacity?

It is difficult to know whether some long-gone people had the ability to create and understand symbols. For example, artifacts like spear points were made for practical purposes—that is, to provide something useful like food or shelter. Tools are not necessarily symbolic, as shown by the fact that other animals make and use them. Decades ago, toolmaking was seen as the hallmark of humanity, but evidence that apes and other animals make tools debunked this idea (see Chapter 1). Painting or carving representations of nature and people would be evidence of symbol use. Famous caves in France and Spain contain impressive paintings of mammals and human handprints. However, these are no earlier than about 40,000 years ago.

If music making could be identified, that too could be evidence of symbols. In June 2009, a team of archaeologists reported the earliest known musical instrument. About 35,000 to 40,000 years ago, a prehistoric group living in what is now southwestern Germany made a flute from the wing bone of a vulture. The flute had at least five fingering holds that produced different notes, and the makers modified one end of the bone to make it into a better mouthpiece. The technique for

making the flutes seemed highly developed, suggesting that flute-making skills developed even earlier. Why people would make a musical instrument is subject to speculation. One commentator suggests that these early inhabitants of Europe "produced symbolic objects that embodied complex beliefs shared by a larger community of individuals" (Adler, 2009, p. 696). If so, then the instruments, and perhaps music itself, requires the mental ability to create and understand symbols.

From Africa, archaeologists uncovered evidence that strongly suggest even earlier symbolic capacity from at least 80,000 years ago. These discoveries included beads, a form of art, and evidence of sophisticated transmission of knowledge that suggests language.

In 2007, archaeologists reported evidence that early *Homo sapiens* from North Africa created objects that carried a meaning beyond their physical properties. An international team of archaeologists excavated marine shell beads that ancient people of Morocco manufactured around 82,000 years ago. Many beads were perforated and had wear patterns indicating that they had been strung and worn on the body. Some were coated with a mineral, red ochre, showing that the makers altered the natural color of the shells. It is highly probable that people were decorating their bodies with the beads, implying that others understood the beads as symbols of beauty, status, family or group identity, or the like. The beads communicated meanings that were not determined by their appearance or other physical properties. That is, the beads were symbols.

From a site in southern Africa comes more evidence of symbolic capacity. At a cave on the South African coast known as Blombos, prehistoric people incised lines in crisscross patterns on ochre rocks. Archaeologists working there found abalone shells in which remains of processed (ground and powdered) ochre were stored. They also found 70 marine shells that had been perforated and strung on a cord to produce a necklace or similar ornament. These remains are between 70,000 and 100,000 years old.

In 2012, archaeologists published findings about a site on the South African coast dated to about 71,000 years ago. Here ancient people used fire to heat the mineral *silcrete*. Heat-treating made it easier to flake stone stools accurately and finely, allowing the manufacture of tiny stone tools called *microliths*, an inch or less in length. Several microliths were attached to a bone or wooden shaft with cords and/or sticky pitch. When thrown or thrust, the sharp edges of the microlith penetrated the hides of animals more efficiently than a single stone point attached only to the tip of a spear. To manufacture microliths, the prehistoric

Africans chipped small pieces of stone ("flakes") off a larger piece of stone (the "core"). They then reworked the flakes to make effective cutting edges and attached them to a shaft. Thus, 71,000 years ago, a prehistoric people in South Africa used fire not just for warmth and cooking but as a part of a manufacturing process. They skillfully struck sharp-edged tiny flakes from heat-treated stone. The final tool was a composite of several stone flakes, cordage, and a shaft. The technology lasted for tens of thousands of years and was thus a toolmaking tradition, passed down over hundreds of generations. All this implies transmission of sophisticated knowledge using language.

Probably culture as we learn and experience it today originated earlier than its physical manifestations in the form of beads, instruments, art, beads, or other symbolic objects. But so far, hard evidence from Africa suggests that humanity clearly had the capacity for culture by around 80,000 years ago.

Culture and Human Life

Anthropologists believe culture is absolutely essential to human life as it is usually lived—in association with other people, or in social groups. To be sure, living in social groups does not require culture. Many species of termites, bees, ants, and other social insects live in quite complex groups, yet they have no culture. Gorillas, chimpanzees, baboons, macaques, and most other primates are also group-living animals. Primatologists have shown that chimpanzees learn to use and make simple tools, share food, communicate fairly precise messages, have intergroup conflicts in which animals are killed, and form relationships in which two individuals who are physically weaker cooperate to overpower a stronger animal. Yet few anthropologists claim that chimpanzee groups have culture in the same sense as all human groups do. (Some use the term *proto-culture* to emphasize that many animal behaviors are socially learned rather than instinctive.) If other group-living social animals cooperate, communicate, and survive without culture, why do people need culture at all?

The main reason boils down to this: The culture of the society or other group into which people are born or raised provides the knowledge (information) they need to survive in their natural environments and to participate in the life of groups. This knowledge, which infants begin to socially learn soon after birth, is necessary because humans do not come into the world equipped with a detailed set of behavioral instructions inherited genetically from their parents. Rather, people are born with *a propensity to learn the knowledge and behaviors of the group they were born into from observation, interaction, and communication with members of that group.* The title of a 2012 book written by British biologist Mark Pagel phrases the main point concisely: Humans are "wired for culture."

Culture is necessary for human existence in at least three specific ways:

1. Culture provides the knowledge by which we adapt to our natural environment by harnessing resources and solving other problems of living in a particular place. As they grow up, children socially learn skills for tracking game, gathering wild plants, making gardens, herding livestock, or finding a job, depending on how people make their living in a particular society. Current generations are usually wise to take advantage of the adaptive wisdom learned and passed down by their cultural ancestors.

2. Culture is the basis for human social life. It provides ready-made norms, values, expectations, attitudes, symbols, and other knowledge that individuals use to communicate, cooperate, live in families and other groups, relate to people of their own and opposite sex, and establish political and legal systems. As they grow up, people learn what actions are and are not acceptable, how to win friends, who relatives are, how and whom to court and marry, when to show glee or grief, and so forth.

3. Culture provides our views of reality. We socially learn the concepts by which people perceive, interpret, analyze, and explain events in the world around us. Our culture provides a filter or screen that affects how we perceive the world through our senses. Some objects out there in the world are sensed; others are not. Some events are important; others are ignored. Growing up in a given culture thus leads people to develop shared understandings of the world, which are not the same as truth.

In brief, culture is essential to human life as we know it because it provides us with the means to adapt to our surroundings, form relationships in organized groups, and interpret reality. Adaptation, organization, interpretation—these are three of the main reasons culture is essential to a normal human existence. In later chapters, we look at some of the diverse ways various cultures have equipped their members to adapt to their environment, organize their groups, and understand their world.

Cultural Knowledge and Individual Behavior

How are the shared ideas and beliefs of a group of people related to the behavior of individuals—to what real people actually do? This question is important not only for studying other cultures but also for learning how people think about their own lives and their relationship to society.

Is Behavior Culturally Determined?

Some believe that culture largely determines or dictates behavior, a view known as **cultural determinism**. If this idea is strictly true, then the notion of free will might be an illusion. Perhaps culture is pulling our strings, making us *believe* we have free will. In this view, individuals are carriers and transmitters of their cultural heritage. In fact, the belief we have free will might itself be part of some society's cultural knowledge, ingrained in its members by enculturation.

Notice that the cultural determinism view emphasizes some components of culture and deemphasizes others. For example, norms instruct individuals what to do in particular situations: how to act toward friends, coworkers, and mothers-in-law; how to perform roles acceptably; and so forth. The values we socially learn tell us what is important for society as a whole and also provide individuals with a set of goals to pursue. Those who deviate are usually forced to conform, are ostracized, or are eliminated.

Sometimes the relationship between cultural knowledge and individual behavior is as simple as cultural determinism implies, but not usually. Norms are flexible and usually situational. Values provide only rough and sometimes conflicting guidelines for behavior and can be inconsistent. Culture also includes shared symbols with their meanings, constructions of reality, and worldviews. These last three influence our behavior but only indirectly (by affecting how we perceive and interpret the world) rather than directly (as instructions). The effect of cultural knowledge on behavior is more complicated than cultural determinism implies.

It *could* be true that your mind is mainly a vessel that transmits your culture to the next generation, but you probably think you are more complicated than that. Most modern anthropologists agree, recognizing that culture does shape individuals, but it is also shaped *by* individuals.

In most situations, individuals calculate, weigh alternatives, and make decisions. For those actions that are important in their own lives or in the lives of others they care about, they plan ahead and consider the possible benefits and costs before they act. In considering the relationship between knowledge and behavior, we must take into account people's ability to think ahead, plan, strategize, and choose.

Formulating plans and making choices involve rational thought and emotional dispositions, both of which occur in the context of cultural knowledge. Planning and choosing involve the following procedures: deciding on one's goals (ends); determining the resources (or means) available to acquire these goals; calculating which specific actions are likely to be most effective; estimating the relative costs (in time and/or resources) and benefits (rewards) of these alternative actions; and, finally, choosing between alternative courses of action.

Culture affects every step of this choice-making process. Norms force individuals to take into account how others are likely to react to their behavior. Values affect the goals that people have and discourage them from acting in ways that infringe on the rights of others. Choices are affected by the existing cultural constructions of people and things, worldviews, and individuals' anticipation of how others will interpret the meaning of their actions. So important are the effects of cultural knowledge on individual decisions that one influential anthropologist long ago defined culture itself as "standards for deciding what is, . . . what can be, . . . how one feels about it, . . . what to do about it, . . . and how to go about doing it" (Goodenough, 1961, p. 552).

Thus, an important way cultural knowledge affects behavior is by its influences on choices individuals make about what to do in various situations. One way to say this is that cultural knowledge provides boundaries for behavior. Within these boundaries, people are free to choose between alternative actions. Most people do not overstep cultural boundaries because they believe in the moral correctness of norms and values, because they fear negative reactions from others, or because doing so would involve actions that others might misinterpret.

Why Does Behavior Vary?

The complexity of the relationship between knowledge and behavior is the main reason we distinguish knowledge from behavior. Another reason is that shared ideas and beliefs sometimes do not predict

cultural determinism Notion that the beliefs and behaviors of individuals are programmed by their culture.

behavior very well, and what is expected is often not what occurs. There are several major reasons the actions of different individuals vary.

The most obvious reason is that no two individuals have exactly the same life experiences, even though they are brought up in the same cultural tradition. Although we often speak of "the" way children are raised, in fact enculturation practices vary from family to family even within the same community. Different childhoods and life experiences make individuals (even siblings, as most people know) different in their reactions and actions.

Other reasons for variations in behavior are more subtle. Norms do not always provide unambiguous guidelines for behavior. Generally, you should not lie, but sometimes a small lie is necessary to preserve a personal relationship, to avoid hurting someone's feelings, or to avoid greater harms. Often, too, lies are so useful to achieve our personal goals that our private interests take precedence over the norm against lying.

As for values, in many situations pursuing one worthwhile goal or upholding one value conflicts with pursuing another goal or upholding another value, so people must choose between them. You may believe in the work ethic, value success in your career, enjoy sports, and want to be a good parent. You hold these beliefs, values, and goals simultaneously. But holding a job and advancing a career reduces the time we can devote to upholding family values, so we must decide how to allocate our scarce time and energy between activities that are all culturally defined as valuable.

Also, individuals find ways to justify (to themselves and to others) violations of norms and accepted moral standards when such norms and standards conflict with their interests. You may rationalize stealing from your employer by believing you are underpaid. Your boss may justify having you work overtime for no extra pay because he is pressured from his own boss. Your company may lay off its workers and move its operations overseas because it must operate in a highly competitive global environment.

Finally, people receive contradictory messages about what actions are proper and morally right. Sometimes ideal models for behavior are contradicted by the messages and models people receive from the actions of their parents, relatives, friends, political leaders, and the media. Our older relatives might want us to uphold their standards of sexual morality, but when we watch TV and movies or go on the Internet, we are exposed to conflicting messages and values.

The preceding examples are familiar to most readers. Our main point is this: All cultures have abstract public values and norms that distinguish right from wrong, appropriate from inappropriate, and so forth. But real-world situations are complicated. Real-life individuals have personal goals to pursue and sometimes yield to temptation. People have to choose between values and norms that conflict in some circumstances.

In sum, all humans and all groups deal with the complicated conflicts between private interests and public duties. The actions of individuals are often an uneasy compromise between the two. Although our behavior is embedded in the context of cultural knowledge, its relationship to this context is complex and variable. We all recognize this complexity in our own behavior. Rather than simplistically condemning the hypocrisy of others, we should recognize more often that this complexity applies to them as well.

Biology and Cultural Differences

In many ways, humans are like other mammals. Biologically, we must regulate our body temperatures, balance our energy and liquid intake and expenditures, and so forth. But anthropologists say that humans are special mammals because we rely so heavily on culture for our survival.

Do biological, genetic, and physical differences between groups of people have anything to do with the cultural differences between them? To rephrase the question so that its full implications are apparent: Is there any correlation between cultural differences and physical differences between groups of people?

Before the twentieth century, many people believed the physical differences between groups of people explained differences in how they thought, felt, and behaved. That is, they believed racial differences partly or largely accounted for differences in culture. According to this notion, now called **biological determinism**, cultural differences have a biological basis, meaning that groups of people differ in how

---

biological determinism Idea that biologically (genetically) inherited differences between populations are important influences on the cultural differences between them.

they think, feel, and act because they differ in their innate biological makeup.

Biological determinism is a convenient belief about what makes human groups (like ethnicities and races) differ in their beliefs and actions. It is simple to understand. Often, it is a politically or economically useful idea, especially when combined with ethnocentric attitudes about the superiority of one's own culture. If French or Chinese see their culture as superior to African or Native American cultures, that might be because the French or Chinese are biologically superior to Africans or Native Americans. Colonialism, expropriation of land and other resources, slavery, and genocides often were justified by the idea that groups of people differed in their customs and beliefs—and also in their intelligence—because of their physical differences. If biology determines who comes out on top in competition among individuals and groups, then whoever comes out on top and on bottom is justified—and even inevitable. Competition between individuals and groups produces losers as well as winners *due to the natural or inherent characteristics of both*. This notion is usually called **social Darwinism**, although it is a misapplication of Charles Darwin's theory.

Anthropologists of today reject biological determinism and social Darwinism. The diverse cultures of Africa did not and do not differ from the cultures of Europe or Asia because the peoples of these continents differ biologically. Nor do the cultures of different ethnic groups within a modern nation differ because these ethnic groups differ genetically: African Americans, European Americans, and Asian Americans do not differ in their beliefs and actions because of their different genetic makeup.

To claim that physical differences are largely irrelevant as causes for cultural differences seems like a sweeping overgeneralization. Although difficult to prove, evidence for it is familiar to most people. Consider the following three facts, drawn from everyday life:

1. Individuals of any physical type are equally capable of learning any culture. North America now contains people whose biological ancestors came from all parts of the world. Yet most modern-day African, Korean, South Asian, Irish, and Arab Americans have far more in common in their thoughts and actions than any of them have in common with the people of their ancestral homelands.

2. An enormous range of cultural diversity was and is found on all continents and regions. For example, most West Africans are biologically similar, yet they are divided into many dozens of different cultural groupings. The same disjunction between physical characteristics and cultural diversity applies to people of northern Asia, southern Asia, Europe, and other regions. Far too much cultural variability exists within populations that are biologically similar for biological differences to be a significant cause of cultural variation.

3. Dramatically different ways of thinking and behaving succeed one another in time within the same biological population and within the same society. Cultures can and regularly do undergo vast changes within a single human generation, as the changes in countries like China, Brazil, and India since the 1980s so clearly reveal.

Because of these and other kinds of evidence, most cultural anthropologists feel justified in reaching the following conclusion: Physical (including racial) differences between human populations are mostly irrelevant in explaining the cultural differences between them. For the most part, if we want to explain the differences between the Kikuyu culture of East Africa and the Vietnamese culture of Southeast Asia, we ignore the physical and genetic differences between the Kikuyu and the Vietnamese.

However, "for the most part" does not mean "totally." There are features in which differences in behavior can be attributed to biological differences between human groups. One well-understood example is the relation between population-level genetic differences and milk drinking. All infants drink milk, but not all human populations retain the ability to continue consuming milk into adulthood. Milk contains lactose, a kind of sugar, but lactose must be broken down in the small intestine by the enzyme lactase before the body can digest it. Many peoples are lactose-intolerant, meaning that they lose the ability to digest milk as they mature.

For example, most adults of eastern and central Asia and southern Africa cannot digest fresh milk, nor can most Native Americans and African Americans. But the vast majority of Europeans and people with European ancestry (European Americans and European

social Darwinism View that the degree of success in achieving social rewards is determined by the inherent (inborn) characteristics of individuals and groups.

Members of any racial category can and do learn the same culture. Having passed citizenship examinations, these people became American citizens on July 4, 2005.

Visions of America/Getty Images

Australians/New Zealanders) are able to digest lactose, as are most peoples of Central Africa. The obvious reason for the difference in behavior or in taste is genetic: The ancestors of some peoples were able to drink milk, so milk drinking evolved as a behavioral pattern. This seems to be an example of a biological difference "causing" a difference in behavior between groups of people.

Actually, it is difficult to disentangle cause and effect in this case. It is likely that milk drinking and genetic change *coevolved.* After cattle were domesticated several thousand years ago, milk became such a potentially nutritious food that the few people who were able to digest it into adulthood had more children. So, over many generations, natural selection led more and more people to be able to digest milk. At the group level, milk's food value increased, as did the ability to digest it. This much is a biological change. People therefore responded by raising more cattle to provide more milk (as well as other resources provided by cattle). This is the behavioral response to the biological change. As the ability to digest milk increased among the population, more people were able to drink it, so people wanted

more cattle, leading cattle to become more valuable and people to breed more cattle, thus further increasing the supply of a food that led lactose-tolerant genes to increase in the population.

Put simply, cattle domestication led to a human genetic change, which initiated a cultural response, which led to more genetic changes. This kind of coevolution probably also affected other changes in human diets after people domesticated plants and animals beginning around 10,000 years ago (see Chapter 7).

Cultural Universals

Biological factors are relevant to human life in a broader way. Human beings have physiological needs and biological imperatives just like other animals. To persist over many generations, all peoples develop means of meeting biological needs and coping with environmental problems. If any people failed to do so, they are no longer around.

Because humans are both cultural and biological beings, much of what we do is oriented around the

akg-images/Bruce Connolly/Newscom

Whether music and decorative arts help people survive or perform other essential social or cultural functions is not clear, but both are cultural universals. This performance is part of a Chinese festival.

- Organized ways of sharing and exchanging goods
- Games, sports, and other kinds of recreational activities
- Beliefs about supernatural powers and rituals used to communicate with and influence them
- Decorative arts
- Singing and other forms of music
- Standards of modesty
- Customary ways of handling the dead and expressing grief
- Myths, legends, and folklore
- Rites of passage that publicly recognize the movement of people through certain stages of life

Although we could list more cultural universals, our main point is that many of them are not easily explained by the fact that they are necessary for the short- or long-term biological survival of populations. Perhaps many of these universals exist because they are a necessary byproduct of a toolmaking, group-living, culture-bearing, language-speaking, symbol-understanding species. For example, games and singing may bring people together, and decorative arts may be related to status or family differences.

Although we call them cultural universals, the precise forms that these and other universals take vary from culture to culture. For instance, all human societies have beliefs about the supernatural, but the nature of these beliefs varies enormously among cultures, as seen in Chapter 14. Likewise, people in all societies have prohibitions against sexual relations with certain kinds of relatives, but which family members are excluded varies from society to society, as discussed in Chapter 9. Male–female differences are important among all peoples, but how people culturally construct these differences varies quite a lot, as described in Chapter 11. Most of the rest of this book deals with these and other cultural variations.

It is important to understand that the peoples of the world are overwhelmingly similar biologically, no matter how different they might appear to our perceptions, which are based in part on our cultural constructions. As we cover cultural variations in future chapters, it is also important to realize that cultures are not infinitely variable.

satisfaction of biological needs for food, shelter, reproduction, disease avoidance, and so forth. It is partly because of such universal problems that anthropologists have discovered **cultural universals**, or elements that exist in all known human cultural groups.

Some cultural universals are obvious because they are requirements for long-term survival in a species that relies on social learning, material technology, and group living. These universals include toolmaking, building shelters, methods of communication, patterns of cooperation used in acquiring food and other essential resources, family systems, ways of teaching children, methods of social control, ways of regulating who may have sexual relations with whom, and so forth. There is no great mystery about why all human groups have such things.

Other cultural universals are not so obvious. They do not seem necessary for the physical survival of individuals or groups but are nonetheless present in all cultural traditions. Among these are

- Ways of assigning tasks and roles according to age and gender
- Prohibitions on sexual relations (incest taboos) between certain kinds of relatives

cultural universals Elements of culture that exist in all known human groups or societies.

1. **Define culture in a way that is useful to compare and contrast different cultures.** *Culture* is here defined as the shared, socially learned knowledge and behavioral patterns characteristic of some group of people. The term *group* may refer to an entire society, an ethnic group, or some kind of subculture, depending on the context of the discussion. To describe and analyze culture, it is useful to distinguish between cultural knowledge and patterns of behavior.

2. **Understand the concept of cultural knowledge and five of its key components.** Cultural knowledge has many dimensions, some of which are norms, values, shared understandings of the meanings of symbolic objects and actions, constructions of reality, and worldviews. Cultural knowledge is not true in any objective sense, but it must at least allow a society to persist in its environment, and it must enable people to interact appropriately and meaningfully.

3. **Discuss the evidence for the origins of the human capacity for culture.** How and when humanity first developed culture is uncertain. Because of the centrality of symbols for language and culture, evidence that ancient people used symbols is also evidence for culture. Archaeologists unearthed a musical flute in Germany that is around 35,000 years old. Colored beads, which are about 80,000 years old, have been found in southern Africa and were probably strung as jewelry and used as symbols of status of identity.

4. **Analyze the relationship between cultural knowledge and the behavior of individuals.** Cultural determinism is the idea that cultural knowledge determines the actions of individuals, but this view is simplistic. Cultural ideas and beliefs serve as more than just rules or instructions for behavior. A more realistic view is that cultural knowledge affects the choices people make about how to act in particular situations. Cultural knowledge limits and influences behavior but does not determine it in detail because people's actions most of the time are not simply programmed by their culture.

5. **Describe why cultural and biological differences between human populations vary independently.** Biological determinism is the notion that cultural differences between human populations are greatly affected or even determined by the biological differences between them. This idea is generally rejected because convincing evidence exists that biological and cultural differences vary independently. The shared biological heritage of the human species does affect culture, however, because how people meet their biologically given needs is reflected in their culture. The existence of cultural universals also suggests that the shared genetic heritage of all humanity affects the kinds of cultures that are possible in the human species.

3

Culture and Language

People communicate mainly by language, but nonverbal signals also send messages in ways that often vary from people to people, as these Sicilian women illustrate.

After reading this chapter, you should be able to:

1 **EXPLAIN** why language is such a powerful means of communication, using five distinctive properties of human languages.

2 **DESCRIBE** how words are formed from combinations of discrete sounds.

3 **DESCRIBE** how Native American words were incorporated into English.

4 **DISCUSS** the modern-day global forces favoring the survival and spread of some languages and the contraction and possible extinction of others.

5 **DISCUSS** some ways messages are communicated nonverbally, how speech is affected by social context, and the strategic use of language to acquire personal goals.

6 **DESCRIBE** the Sapir-Whorf hypothesis and some of the controversies surrounding it.

As part of enculturation, children socially learn one or more languages of their speech community. **Language** consists of the shared knowledge of sounds, words, meanings, and grammatical rules that people use to send and receive complex messages. Along with our dependence on culture, humanity's ability to communicate complex, precise information is the main mental capability that distinguishes humans from other animals.

Language and Humanity

Although we talk to or text people daily, we seldom consider how remarkable it is that we are able do so. As with culture, we take language for granted, and most of us do not realize how unusual our communication skills are. (If you were a fish, would you know how well your body is adapted to move through water?)

The ability to speak, write, and comprehend the messages of language requires knowledge of an enormous number of linguistic units (sounds, words) and rules for combining them (grammar). Language and culture together are critical to the development of human individuals—without them, our psychological and social development is incomplete. In all probability, without them we would be unable to think, as the word *think* is generally understood. The thinking processes itself

language Shared knowledge used by speakers to send and hearers to understand messages.

depends crucially on the knowledge of some language. In fact, some scholars suggest that knowledge and use of a particular language conditions our minds to perceive nature and people in particular ways, thus shaping how we think about the world and the things in it.

Not only is *Homo sapiens* the only animal capable of speech, but we also are the only animal biologically evolved to speak and understand true language. Other animals certainly communicate. Male birds sing to announce territories and attract mates, as do other animals like frogs and toads. Worker honeybees returning to the hive dance to tell hive mates the direction, distance, and quality of a food source. Other species of social insects like ants and termites have similar capabilities. Elephants, some whales and dolphins, gorillas, bonobos, and chimpanzees likewise perform impressive feats of communication.

However, only humans have language in its fully developed form. To understand the meaning of "fully developed," compare language to the communicative abilities of great apes. With the aid of intensive training from humans, chimpanzees and gorillas have learned to use sign language or to manipulate symbols standing for words and concepts into sentences. With no human interference, one chimp taught sign language to another and later they used it to communicate with one another. Despite these feats, no great ape is capable of answering this simple question: "What are your plans for next week?"

Language shaped humanity's biological evolution. Most obviously, this includes the speech regions of our brain. It also includes our vocal tract. The human *vocal tract* consists of the lungs, trachea (including the vocal cords as well as the windpipe), mouth, and nasal passages. The vocal tract is biologically evolved for speech. The human mouth is a remarkable resonating chamber.

Here are a few examples. You make different vowel sounds by raising and lowering the tongue or parts of the tongue. Changing the position of the tongue modifies the shape of the mouth and produces sounds of different wavelengths that human ears recognize as different sounds. For example, compare where your tongue is for the vowel sounds as you say these words: *sit* and *set, far* and *fur, did* and *dad, teeth* and *tooth, lass* and *loss.* Likewise, you pronounce most consonant sounds by interrupting the flow of air through the mouth. The initial sound of the word *tip* is formed by bringing the tip of the tongue into contact with the alveolar ridge just behind the teeth and then releasing the contact suddenly. You change *tip* to *sip* by blowing air through your mouth while almost, but not quite, touching the tip of your tongue to your alveolar ridge, thus making the initial sound a brief hissing noise. (Try it and see for yourself.)

Your vocal cords interact with your mouth to make distinct sounds. Either they vibrate and produce a buzzy sound (as in "mmmm"), or they remain open and allow air to flow into your mouth freely (as in the first sound "h" in *how*). You change *tip* to *dip* by vibrating your vocal cords with the first sound of the word *dip.* Articulating various parts of the vocal tract in contrasting ways makes other vowels and consonants of English and other languages.

You move all these parts of your vocal tract unconsciously with astonishing speed and precision. Each sound is possible because the vocal chamber formed by the mouth, throat, nasal passages, and the muscles of the tongue and lips are biologically evolved for this purpose. There is a good reason chimpanzees cannot speak human words: Their vocal tract is not evolved to do so. Yet, with training, any human child can utter the sounds found in any language.

Language allows people to communicate about concrete persons, places, things, actions, and events. It allows communication and thought about abstract concepts as well. Among such abstractions are truth, evil, God, masculinity, values, humanity, zero, law, jihad, universal, democracy, ethnicity, space, culture, and hatred. Humans all understand such abstractions. Indeed, without the ability to conceptualize such abstractions, culture as we experience it could not exist. Furthermore, our everyday behavior is greatly affected by contrasts that are abstract, such as friend and enemy, beautiful and ugly, play and work.

The social learning by which children acquire culture would be impossible without language. Because people share language, much of the knowledge in one person's mind can be transmitted into the mind of another person. During enculturation, not only do we learn facts and lessons about the world, but we also hear stories and myths, communicating messages that are often implicit and unstated. These stories, myths, and other narratives become part of our identity, shape our relationships with other people, and help formulate the cultural constructions and worldviews of a people.

The Power of Language

All languages have properties that allow novel and complex messages to be communicated quickly, precisely, and in several mediums; this is possible even if the people or events under discussion are far away in space or time.

In 1960, linguist Charles Hockett identified 13 properties that distinguish language from the communication abilities of other animals. Five of Hockett's properties are especially important to demonstrate the power of language.

Discreteness

Discreteness means that, while speaking, people combine units (sounds and words) according to conventional rules. Knowing a language means knowing both the units and the rules for combining them. Words are composed of discrete units of sound (e.g., "j," "u," "m," "p") that are combined to communicate a meaning (*jump*). Similarly, we apply rules to combine units of meanings (words) to form sentences.

Discrete sounds are the essential units (metaphorically, they are the building blocks) of language. Discreteness makes alphabets possible. In alphabetic writing, people combine the letters of their alphabet to form printed words.

Originally, each sound of the English alphabet was pronounced in a similar way in all the words in which it appeared. For example, the letter (sound) "t" appears in *student, textbook, eat,* and *today.* In English writing, most letters no longer represent a single sound. The letter "a," for example, is pronounced differently in the words *act, father, warden, assume,* and *nature.* Some single sounds in English are rendered in *two* letters, such as "th," "ng," and the "gh" in rough and ghoul. Why doesn't English spelling always reflect the way words are pronounced? One reason is that since the widespread use of the printing press, changes in English pronunciation have occurred faster than changes in spelling.

By themselves, most sounds carry no meaning. The three sounds in *cat,* for example, carry meaning only when strung together. When combined differently, they mean *act* and *tack*. Words, then, are composed of sound combinations that a speech community recognizes as conveying standardized meanings. Not all combinations of sounds are possible in a given language. For instance, in English, "mp," "nt," and "ld" are all possible combinations, but "pm," "tn," and "dl" are not (although these combinations are used by other languages).

Productivity

Just as all languages use a small number of sounds to make a large number of words, so speakers string words together according to grammatical rules to convey the messages carried by sentences. By mastering their language's words and meanings and the rules for combining words into sentences, speakers can send and listeners can understand messages of great complexity with amazing precision (e.g., "From that basket of beefsteak tomatoes, give me the reddest one").

Productivity derives from this ability to put words together to create new sentences to communicate messages. It refers to a speaker's ability to create totally novel sentences and to a listener's ability to comprehend them. Productivity means that a language's finite number of words can be combined into an infinite number of meaningful sentences. The sentences are meaningful because the speaker and listener know what each word means individually and the rules by which the words may be combined to convey messages.

Although people routinely apply them each time they speak and hear, most are not consciously aware of their knowledge of these rules. Unless you have linguistic training, you probably do not know that you form an English plural by adding one of *two* sounds (either "z" or "s") to the end of a noun. For example, contrast the last sounds of *beans* and *beats* or *cobs* and *cots*.

Arbitrariness

The relationship between the sound combinations that make up words and the meanings these words communicate is *arbitrary*. The words and combinations of words (sentences) are symbols (see Chapter 2).

Children learn to match certain sound combinations (words) with their meanings. By the age of 1 or 2 years, most children have learned the meanings of dozens of words. They have mastered words that refer to objects (*ball*), animals (*doggie*), people (*mama*), sensory experiences (*hot*), qualities (*blue, hard*), actions (*eat, run*), commands (*no, come here*), emotions (*love*), and so forth. The child learns to associate meanings

with words, even though the specific sound combinations that convey these various meanings have no inherent relationship to the things themselves.

Because of the arbitrary relationship between meanings and words, our ability to communicate linguistic messages is based on shared conventions. As symbols, words can carry factual meanings ("look at trees") or meanings that are charged with emotion ("save the trees").

Displacement

Displacement refers to our ability to talk about objects, people, things, and events that are remote in time and space. Because language uses symbols (words and sentences) to transmit meanings, objects and people do not have to be immediately visible for us to communicate about them. We can discuss someone who is out of sight

Because of language's displacement property and its symbolic nature, humans can communicate about things, people, and beings remote in space and time. This Hindu pilgrim is praying in Varanasi, India.

because the symbols of language (in this case, a name) call that person to mind, allowing us to think about him or her. We can speculate about the future because, although its events may never happen, our language has symbols that stand for future time and more symbols that allow us to form a mental image of possible events.

We can learn about events that happened before we were born, such as wars in Vietnam, Iraq, and Syria. People can learn of events and things far away in space, such as fighting in Afghanistan, factories in China and India, tsunamis in Japan, mass homicides in Colorado and Connecticut, and nuclear threats from North Korea.

The displacement property also makes it possible to describe things (like ghosts and zombies) and places (like the Shire and Winterfell) that do not even exist. We can share stories about events that might not have really happened and thus create myths, fiction, legends, fairy tales, and folklore. Political leaders can mislead citizens, and be misled themselves, about weapons of mass destruction and terrorist connections in distant lands. Much that is familiar in human life depends on this important property—including the ability to lie.

Multimedia Potential

Another important property of language is *multimedia potential*, meaning that linguistic messages can be transmitted through a variety of media. When you speak, the medium for your message is speech, transmitted to the ears of your listeners by sound waves. Writing is the medium in which the messages of this book are transmitted. When you text relatives and friends, software converts the letters on your phone's keypad into a digital form that is transmitted in cyberspace into

letters they can read and understand. Gestures and body movements are communications media that are received by the sense of sight rather than hearing, and hand and finger gestures are media for the hearing impaired, as illustrated by American Sign Language. Even touching and the resulting nerve signals can be media for language. Helen Keller, both blind and deaf, communicated and received linguistic messages by touch.

Of course, speech was the original medium for language. Beginning about 5,000 years ago, the ancient Sumerians of the Middle East developed writing. Egyptians developed their hieroglyphic system shortly afterward. Chinese writing grew out of symbols incised into cattle scapulae and the hard underside of tortoises. The ancient Mesoamerican peoples known as Zapotecs and Maya carved meaningful symbols into stone pillars and walls, now recognized as yet another independent origin of writing. This means that the Mesopotamians, Chinese, and Mesoamerican peoples did not "learn to write" from some other people but invented their own writing system.

In various ancient civilizations, writing was used to keep records of taxes, labor, oracles, the passage of time (calendars), and military conquests. Over several centuries, writing techniques spread to other regions such as the Greek islands, South Asia, Korea, Japan, and western Europe. We take writing so much for granted that it is hard to imagine life without books and magazines, computers and the Internet, street signs and billboards, cell phones and texting. Although obvious when stated, few people today think about how writing makes modern life possible.

The Concept Review summarizes these five key properties of language. Together, discreteness, productivity,

---

CONCEPT REVIEW   Five Properties of Language

Discreteness	Language is composed of sounds and words that cannot be reduced to smaller units and that are combined to communicate precise messages.
Productivity	A finite number of words may be combined and re-combined into an infinite number of sentences.
Arbitrariness	People who do not speak a given language cannot understand the meanings of words and sentences by their physical properties or how they sound.
Displacement	People are able to discuss things, persons, and events remote in time and space as well as nonexistent things, persons, and events.
Multimedia potential	Messages can be transmitted through many media, including air (sound), print, movement (sign language), and digitally.

arbitrariness, displacement, and multimedia potential make language the most precise and complete system of communication known among living things. If these properties seem obvious—fancy words for "what everyone knows"—that is because, as human beings, we rarely think about what it is that makes our species special.

In brief, language is powerful. It makes abstract thought possible. It allows the fast and precise transmission of information from one individual and generation to another. It makes it possible to speculate about events that could possibly happen tomorrow if another set of events should happen to occur. We can learn about events that happened far away and long ago and events that didn't happen at all. Language allows us to text "I love you" even when we don't mean it, to write and read fictional stories and novels, and to understand myths and legends. All these are things humans do so routinely that we consider them ordinary. And they are—for humanity.

How Language Works

When children learn language, they master an enormous amount of information. **Grammar** refers to all the knowledge shared by those who speak and understand a language: the sounds of the language, rules for combining sounds into sequences, meanings conveyed by these sequences, and how sentences are constructed by stringing words together according to precise rules.

Grammatical knowledge is *unconscious:* Those who share a language cannot verbalize the knowledge that allows them to communicate with one another. It also is *intuitive:* Speaking and understanding are automatic, and we ordinarily do not need to think about how to speak or understand linguistic messages. This scientific use of the term *grammar* differs from the everyday understanding of the word. In everyday speech, some people judge others partly on the basis of whether others use "proper" grammar.

---

grammar Knowledge shared by those who speak and understand a language, including sounds, rules for combining sounds into sequences, meanings of these sequences, and constructing sentences by combining words according to precise rules.

dialect Variation in a single language based on factors such as region, subculture, ethnic identity, and socioeconomic class.

In the English language and most others spoken by large numbers of people, there are several **dialects**, or variations in speech patterns, including in pronunciation and vocabulary. Dialects may be based on factors like region (e.g., England, Wales, the American South, Australia, Jamaica) or ethnic identification (e.g., Louisiana Creole, Black English, Spanglish). But speakers of English all understand one another, although sometimes with difficulty. In the United States, one American dialect, called *Standard American English* (SAE)—and it *is* a dialect, the one common in the national news media—is culturally accepted as most proper. Some of those whose dialect is SAE look down on those with other dialects, often based on differences in class, race, or educational levels.

Members of various ethnic and racial categories often have their own ways of pronouncing words or styles of speaking. Children learn dialects based on ethnic identity at a young age from family and friends. But there may be more to speaking a dialect than simply speaking the way you learned while growing up. In Canada and the United States, many African and Hispanic Americans adopt a speech style as a symbol of pride in their identity. To show they are cool, some young whites adopt phrases they hear from the media or from persons with African or Hispanic heritages. In Hawaii, some Haoles use the word *brudda* to address native Hawaiian males, thus trying to show they are in touch.

Notice that there is no such thing as a superior and inferior dialect (or language) *in the linguistic sense.* That is, each language, and each dialect, is equally capable of serving as a vehicle for communicating the messages its speakers need to send and receive. So long as a person successfully communicates, there is no such thing as bad grammar or people who don't know proper grammar. If Jennifer says, "I ain't got no shoes," you will have a different impression of her than if she says, "I have no shoes." But the first Jennifer's speech is perfectly good English—to members of certain subcultures who speak one English dialect. If speakers communicate their intended meaning to listeners, then the words they use or the ways they construct their sentences are as valid linguistically as any other. The evaluations we make of someone else's grammar or overall style of speech, then, are *cultural* evaluations. They are based on some people's cultural beliefs of correct grammar, conceptions about the kinds of people who speak in a certain way, and so forth. Education systems try to inculcate students in the dialect that is broadly accepted as correct—but it is a dialect.

With this point about the equality of languages and dialects in mind, here we briefly cover two aspects of grammar: (1) sounds and their patterning, and (2) sound combinations (words) and their meanings.

Sound Systems

When we speak, our vocal tract emits a string of sounds. The sounds of a language, together with the way these sounds occur in regular and consistent patterns, make up the *phonological system* of the language. The study of sound systems is called **phonology**.

The particular sounds that speakers of a language recognize as distinct from other sounds are called **phonemes**. Phonemes are individual sounds that make a difference in the meanings of words. Linguists use slash marks / / to show that a particular sound is a phoneme in a given language. Thus, a few English consonants are /f/, /t/, /b/, /n/, /z/, and /1/. Some English vowels are /a/, /i/ (pronounced "ee"), /o/, and /u/. Thus, words consist of a string of phonemes, like /mi/ and /yu/ (although there is an "o" in the way we spell *you*, phonologically the "o" is absent).

Of course, languages have different phonemes, and the phonemes of some do not appear in others. If you know Spanish, then you know that /v/ does not exist in that language, which is why native speakers of Spanish may pronounce *very* as *berry*. Japanese has no /l/ or /r/ sound, which is why Japanese people have trouble distinguishing them when they speak English. On the other hand, the Japanese language distinguishes sounds that English does not. Japanese use double consonant sounds that make a difference in the meanings of words, like /t/ versus /tt/ or /p/ versus /pp/. Thus (using English spelling), *kite* means "come" and *kitte* means "stamp," which is one reason Japanese can be hard for many foreigners to pronounce correctly. Other languages, including Korean, also double up consonants to make different words.

Furthermore, differences that one language recognizes in sounds are not always recognized in other languages. English speakers hear differences between consonants that are voiced (your vocal cords vibrate to make a buzzy sound, as in /v/) and voiceless (your vocal cords do not vibrate, as in /f/). Thus, in English, *vat* and *fat* are different words, as are *bat* and *pat*. But in Kosraean, a language of Micronesia, the sound differences between /v/ and /f/, /d/ and /t/, /b/ and /p/, and /g/ and /k/ make no difference in meaning. It is as if English speakers could not distinguish between *veal* and *feel*, between *dan* and *tan*, between *big* and *pig*, and between *got* and *cot*. In English, whether a consonant is voiced or voiceless makes a different in the meanings of words in which they occur; in Kosraean, it does not.

One of the most interesting ways languages differ in phonology is in how they use the pitch of the voice to convey meaning. (The *pitch* of a voice depends on how fast the vocal cords vibrate: The higher the frequency of vibration, the higher the pitch of the voice.) English speakers use pitch to convey different meanings, as you can see by contrasting the following sentences:

She's going home.

She's going home?

The first statement is turned into a question by altering the pitch of the voice. In the question, the pitch rises with the word *home*.

Speakers of English use pitch changes over the whole sentence to communicate a message; that is, the voice pitch falls or rises mainly between words, rather than within a word. There are many other languages in which a high, medium, or low pitch used within an individual word, or even in a syllable, changes the fundamental meaning of the word.

When the pitch (or tone) with which a word is said (or a change in the voice pitch during its pronunciation) affects the meaning of a word, the language is known as a **tone language**. Tone languages are widespread in Africa and in southeastern and eastern Asia. Chinese, Thai, Burmese, and Vietnamese are all tone languages (Japanese and Korean are not), which is one more reason most Canadians, French, and Germans have trouble mastering these languages. As an example of how pitch can affect meaning, consider these words from Nupe, an African tone language:

bá (high tone) = to be sour

bā (mid tone) = to cut

bà (low tone) = to count

Here, whether *ba* is pronounced with a high, mid, or low tone changes its meaning. Because the tone with which a word is pronounced changes its meaning, the pitch of the voice is a kind of phoneme in tone languages. It has the same effect as adding /s/ in front of the English word *pot*, which alters the word to *spot*.

Words and Meanings

Words are combinations of phonemes to which people attach conventional meanings. Any language contains a finite number of words, each matched to one or more meaning.

phonology Study of the sound system of language.

phoneme Smallest unit of sound that speakers recognize as distinctive from other sounds; when one phoneme is substituted for another in a morpheme, the meaning of the morpheme alters.

tone language Language in which changing voice pitch within a word alters the meaning of the word.

As part of growing up, these children master the four tones of their native language, Chinese.

Morphology is the study of meaningful sound sequences and the rules by which they are formed. Any sequence of phonemes that carries meaning is known as a **morpheme**. Why not just call them "words"? Because in analyzing meanings, morphologists need a more precise concept than *word*. For example, you know the meanings of the following sound sequences, none of which is itself a word:

un	ed
pre	s
non	ing
anti	ist

Both the prefixes in the first column and the suffixes in the second alter the meaning of certain other morphemes when they are attached to them.

Sound sequences like these are detachable from particular words. For instance, adding the suffix *-ist* to *art* and *novel* creates new meanings: "a person who creates art" and "one who writes novels." That *-ist* has a similar meaning whenever it is a suffix is shown by the made-up word *crim;* by adding *-ist* to it, you instantly know that a *crimmist* is "a person who crims."

To analyze such compound words and their meanings, linguists have a concept that includes prefixes and suffixes such as *uni-, -ing,* and *-ly.* There are two kinds of morphemes in all languages. A **free morpheme** is any morpheme that can stand alone as a word—for example, *desire, possible, health, complete, anthropology,* and *establish.* A **bound morpheme** is attached to a free morpheme to modify the meaning in predictable ways—for example, *dis-, bi-, un-, -er, -ly,* and *-ed.* Thus, by adding bound morphemes to the free morphemes in our examples, we get the following:

desires	desirable	undesirable
possible	impossible	impossibility

healthy	healthful	unhealthy
completed	incomplete	uncompleted
establishing	establishment	antiestablishment
anthropologist	anthropologically	nonanthropologist

Just as phonemes are a language's minimal units of sound, morphemes are the minimal units of meaning. Thus, we cannot break down the free morphemes *friend, vocabulary, linguistics,* and *soccer* into any smaller units that carry meaning in modern English. Nor can we break down the bound morphemes *non-, -ish,* and *tri-* into any smaller meaningful units.

We make new compound words by applying a rule of compound word formation, not by learning each compound word separately. For instance, take the English rule for forming a plural noun from a singular noun. It is usually done by adding either the bound morpheme /z/, as in *beads, colors,* and *eggs;* or /s/, as in *lamps, steaks,* and *pots*—all meaning "more than one."

Children learn the rule for plural formation at an early age, but it takes them a while longer to learn the many exceptions. Adults think it's cute when children apply the morphological rules of English consistently to all words, saying "childs," "mans," "foots," "mouses," and "deers" for plurals and using "goed," "runned," "bringed," and "doed" to make a present-tense verb into a past-tense verb. But children are born with the mental capability to deduce rules of sound and word combinations from their speech community, so are merely applying the rules they have deduced from many other words.

Of all linguistic elements, free morphemes are most easily transmissible across different languages. Speakers often do not know how much of their native vocabulary is mutt-like rather than purebred. For example, English has taken lots of words that did not exist in its Germanic origins, as the next section discusses.

Germanics, Romantics, and Native English

When peoples who speak different languages come into contact, one or both groups often incorporate (borrow) foreign words. Incorporation is especially likely to happen if one language's words have no counterparts in the other, as is often the case for nouns and verbs. Because of the spread of world trade and political systems during the last five centuries, English words have spread widely into other languages. Japanese and Korean have incorporated hundreds of English words, many from the realm of technology and commodities. In France, the use of English words became such a hot political issue that the government outlawed the importation of further English words.

However, English speakers should not become too proud of the spread of "their" words. The English language itself is a member of the Germanic subfamily of languages, along with Dutch, German, Norwegian, Icelandic, Swedish, Danish, and Afrikaans. Between two and three thousand years ago, all these languages were a single language, which linguists call "proto-Germanic." As Germanic peoples migrated to different regions, the proto-Germanic languages diverged (became distinctive over centuries) until the speakers of each could not understand the other: Separate languages then existed.

Although English is a member of the Germanic subfamily, over the centuries English adopted hundreds of words from the Romance languages, which include French, Spanish, Portuguese, Italian, and Romanian. These languages originated in Latin. As the Roman empire spread throughout much of Europe, people who spoke a Germanic or other local language incorporated words from their Roman overlords. Many of these words are *cognates,* as English speakers who study modern languages like Spanish and French recognize.

Far less recognized is the fact that early English colonists who settled in the Americas adopted many words from Native Americans—words that are now part of American English. The earliest European settlers of eastern North America came from the British Isles and France. Except for French-speaking Quebec and parts of California, Texas, and the Southwest, most citizens of Canada and the United States speak English as their native language. But few of us realize the impact of the original native languages—those spoken by Native Americans—on English vocabulary. Many familiar English words, phrases, and place names are derived from one or another Native American language.

The earliest Spanish and Portuguese explorers were surprised at how many of the plants and animals in the "New World" (North and South America and the Caribbean) were unknown to them. A few animals, such as deer and wolves, were enough like familiar European fauna that European words were applied to them. Others, however, had no European counterparts. Terms taken from North American Indian languages were adopted for many of these, including *cougar, caribou, moose, raccoon, chipmunk, opossum, skunk, woodchuck,* and *chigger.* Other English terms for animals are taken from the languages of South American peoples: *condor, piranha, tapir, toucan, jaguar, alpaca, vicuna,* and *llama.* Plants, too, were unfamiliar, and Native American words were adopted for *saguaro, yucca, mesquite, persimmon, hickory,* and *pecan,* to name only some of the most common derivatives.

As we discuss in Chapter 7, Indians of the Americas were the first to domesticate numerous food plants that now have worldwide importance. All the following crop names have Native American origins: *squash, maize, guava, hominy, avocado, tapioca* (also called *manioc* and *cassava,* both words also taken from native languages), *pawpaw, succotash, tomato,* and *potato.* European immigrants also adopted Indian words for natural features other than plants and animals: *bayou, muskeg, savanna, pampas, hurricane,* and *chinook.* Terms in various Native American languages for clothing, housing, and other material objects have made it into English: *igloo, tepee, wigwam, moccasin, parka, poncho, toboggan, husky, canoe, kayak,* and *tomahawk. Caucus* and *powwow,* for meetings, are two other English words with native origins. Those who smoke might be interested to learn that the tobacco plant is from the New World, as is the name.

People everywhere name geographic locations. The earliest European settlers often named American places to honor important people in their home countries—for example, Charleston, Albuquerque, Columbus, Carolina, and Virginia (the latter named after the condition of England's Queen Elizabeth I). Other American place names are derived from European geography—Nova Scotia (new Scotland), New Hampshire, Maine (a province in France), and, of course, New York, New Jersey, and New England.

Native American peoples had their own names for places and landscape features, and often these names were the ones that endured and appear on current maps. River names with Indian origins include Mississippi, Ohio, Yukon, Missouri, Arkansas, Wabash, Potomac, Klamath, Minnesota, and Mohawk, to mention just a few of the most familiar. The lakes called Huron, Ontario, Michigan, Oneida, Tahoe, and Slave (pronounced "slaw-vay") have Indian names, as do hundreds of other bodies of water in Canada and the United States. Whole states are named after Indian peoples, such as the Illini, Massachuset, Ute, Kansa, and Dakota, whereas names of other states and provinces are derived from native words, such as Manitoba, Ontario, Saskatchewan, Texas, Oklahoma, Ohio, Minnesota, Iowa, and Nebraska. A few large cities with names derived from Indian languages are Tuscaloosa, Tallahassee, Natchez, Tulsa, Cheyenne, Miami, Chicago, Saskatoon, Ottawa, and Omaha. Seattle was named after a particular Indian leader, Seal'th, of the West Coast.

Finally, the names of two whole countries on the North American continent have Native American roots. *Kanata* (Canada) is an Iroquoian word meaning "village" (although it now is applied to a much larger community).

The area formerly known as New Spain took the word the rulers of the Aztec civilization used for themselves—Mexica—after winning its independence in 1823.

In sum, many English words and place names have Native American origins. More generally, the languages people consider native to their region or country usually are a product of historical contacts and interactions. Our time perspectives—how far into the past we go when we think about language—are too short to recognize connections between our native tongue and other languages.

Growth in the intensity of economic globalization and global contacts in the last several decades have had a multitude of impacts on the world's languages and their survival, as discussed in the Global Challenges and Opportunities feature.

Communication and Social Behavior

Anthropological linguists are interested in how language is related to a people's way of life—their cultural knowledge and behavioral patterns. One topic is how language is used when people with different roles interact with one another. Even when our voices are silent, we send messages by body language and facial expressions, both of which are enormously important in conveying emotions and intentions. Also, language itself is only one of the ways people send messages to one another. We begin with this topic: nonverbal communication.

Nonverbal Communication

People send and receive messages using more than just phonemes, morphemes, and sentences. Facial expressions allow people to read one another. We also routinely send both conscious (intentional) and unconscious (implicit) messages by how we move our bodies or parts of our bodies. *Kinesics* studies the role of body motions in communication. We also can convey feelings and other emotions and messages by touching another person.

Some nonverbal facial expressions convey the same messages across all peoples, so presumably these are part of *Homo sapiens'* biological heritage. Pleasure, sadness, anger, puzzlement, and some other emotional responses are shown by similar facial expressions everywhere and convey similar meanings universally. Notice, though, that people sometimes use facial expressions to deceive, as with phony smiles and feigned anger. Also, frequently a given facial expression is normatively appropriate (like a smile in greeting someone), so the expression occurs regardless of the actual internal emotional state of the person.

People also communicate nonverbally by using space—here meaning how closely persons who are interacting position themselves when standing or sitting or walking. *Proxemics* studies the meanings conveyed by space and distance. Edward Hall, who pioneered the field of proxemics in the 1950s and 1960s, noted that in the United States people communicate messages by how far apart they stand or sit while interacting. There is intimate distance (up to about 18 inches), personal distance (about 2 feet to 4 feet), and social distance (over 4 feet), the latter applying mainly to formal situations. (Try violating these conventions by standing a bit too close to an acquaintance; just be sure to do so in an area where the person can move away from you.) Distance can convey other kinds of social messages: It is usually offensive or a sign of aggression "to get in someone's face," as illustrated by barroom quarrels and player–umpire altercations.

Like speech, most forms of nonverbal communication are symbolic behaviors: A particular body motion or distance does not inherently convey a certain message but does so only because of conventions, or common understandings. Because much nonverbal communication is arbitrary and conventional, there is great potential for misunderstanding when people do not share the same meanings for nonverbal messages—that is, when people have learned different conventions. Probably the potential for misunderstanding is even greater with nonverbal messages than with spoken language. When two people from different cultures converse, both generally know that they do not understand the other's language, so at least each person is aware of his or her own ignorance. However, both are more likely to think they understand nonverbal messages, so they might give or take offense when none is intended.

Miscommunication is especially likely with touching—the unspoken rules for which vary greatly from people to people and even from individual to individual. On one Micronesian island, married, engaged, or romantically involved couples rarely walk hand-in-hand in public, although close friends of the same sex frequently do so (carrying no implication of sexual preference). Touching someone on the head—including what North Americans consider an affectionate rub or friendly pat—is offensive. In Korea and Japan, women often affectionately walk holding hands or with their arms around each other.

Some scholars who study nonverbal communication distinguish *low touch* and *high touch* cultures. Such dichotomies are usually simplistic, but it is true that cultures vary greatly in how they define situations in which touching is normatively desirable or appropriate.

Similar ideas apply to the use of space. Again, the possibilities for miscommunication are great when people with different cultural upbringings interact. Sometimes Middle Easterners or Latin Americans stand too close for North Americans' comfort zones. Simply becoming aware that cultural norms about body motions, touching, distance, and so forth differ from people to people can help us all avoid taking offense when someone violates our norms about space. In a world where international migration, tourism, global business, and other forms of intercultural contact are exploding, awareness of such differences is both personally useful and socially valuable.

Speech and Social Context

During enculturation, children learn how to communicate appropriately in given social situations. Different situations require different verbal and nonverbal behavior because how a person speaks and acts varies according to whom the person is talking, who else is listening, and the overall situation in which the interaction is occurring. Much speech behavior is an aspect of the role a person takes on relative to other people such as friends, bosses, children, siblings, and teachers. For example, when you want to make a good impression at a job or admissions interview, what you say and how you say it matter a great deal.

To speak appropriately, people must take the total context into account. First, they must know the various situations, or social scenes, of their culture: which are solemn, which are celebrations, which are formal versus informal, which are argumentative, and so on. Cultural knowledge includes knowing how to alter one's total (including verbal) behavior to fit these situations. Second, individuals must recognize the kinds of interactions they are expected to have with others with whom they have particular relationships, which is connected to their social roles. Should they act lovingly, jokingly, contemptuously, or respectfully and deferentially toward someone else?

These two elements—the particular culturally defined situation and the specific individuals who are parties to the interaction—make up the *social context* of verbal and nonverbal behavior. The field of **sociolinguistics** studies how speech behavior is affected by social context.

sociolinguistics Specialty within cultural anthropology that studies how language is related to culture and the social uses of speech.

Migrations are significant events. When people move to a new region, they carry lots of baggage—not just their possessions, but also their genes, cultures, and languages. Until several hundred years ago, migration was the main way languages spread to new regions.

The migrations that brought the bodies, cultures, and languages of western Europeans to the Americas was massive. This influx of migrants led to the disappearance of a large number of the several hundred indigenous languages of North and South America between the 1500s and the 1900s. The people who spoke them either died out from new diseases and violence or became linguistically assimilated into whichever European ethnic group dominated them politically. Today, the vast majority of people who live in the Americas speak English, Spanish, Portuguese, or French. Most of those born into some indigenous Native American community also speak one of these four languages as their first or second language.

At the global level, no one knows how many of the languages that existed a few hundred years ago are extinct today. Between 4,000 and 9,000 languages have disappeared since the fifteenth century. In some cases, as among Native North Americans and many Australian Aborigines, the main reason for linguistic extinction was the biological extinction of the speakers as a result of disease and violence. In other cases, although the people whose ancestors once spoke their own language are alive today, the languages have died as the groups became assimilated culturally and linguistically into their nation's majority. For example, in the late nineteenth and early twentieth century in the United States, the federal government opened dozens of Indian Schools. Native American children were removed from their families and reservations (sometimes forcefully) and placed in European American educational surroundings where they usually were forbidden from speaking their native tongues.

To see how a language can wither away over several generations, consider the languages of immigrants. Some second- and third-generation immigrants continue to know the language of their ancestral land, but after that few descendants are likely to speak it. Once a language is no longer spoken in the home, it takes a conscious and dedicated effort to learn it, and over time fewer and fewer children will do so. If children are exposed to only the majority language in formal school settings as well as in peer groups, their chances of learning the language of their ancestors dwindles.

Only if there is an entire community of speakers—who use the language among themselves, who serve as linguistic models for young children, and who reward youngsters for speaking it well—is a language likely to survive. In present-day North America, the Amish are one such community, as are various big-city Chinatowns, Koreatowns, and numerous Latino, Persian, and Arab communities. Cities like Vancouver, San Francisco, and Los Angeles include tens of thousands of Chinese who form enclaves where Cantonese or Mandarin is spoken as the first language. There are other less-known linguistic communities, such as the Hmong (refugees from Southeast Asia who were resettled in the United States in the 1980s), South Asians (in California's Silicon Valley and many other cities), and Somalis (in central Ohio).

A rich source of statistical information on the world's language is SIL International's Ethnologue. com. According to Ethnologue's 2016 website, there are about 7,100 languages in existence, of which nearly 4,500 (63 percent) are spoken in Asia and Africa. The Asian continent—which contains two-fifths of the Earth's land surface and three-fifths of its people—has thousands of languages, but most are very localized and have relatively few speakers. In fact, more than half of Asia's

Globalization has dramatically increased trade, travel, education, media, and other connections between citizens of different countries. Learning a language other than one's native tongue enriches one's knowledge of other peoples and is also economically valuable.

AMR Image/iStock / Getty Images Plus/Getty Images

languages have fewer than 10,000 speakers. In Canada and the United States, about 300 indigenous (Native American) languages are still spoken. This sounds like a high number, but almost 100 of them have only a few elderly speakers and so are likely to be gone soon. Ethnologue currently reports that 360 languages have become extinct just since 1950—a rate of 6 languages per year.

Ethnologue breaks down endangered languages into categories, according the degree to which they are endangered. One category is languages "in trouble," meaning that parents still speak it but increasingly do not teach it to their children. Over 1,500 (21 percent) of world languages are in this category. Another category is "dying" languages, those in which the only living speakers are older than childbearing age. Over 900 (13 percent) of languages fall into this category. Therefore, it is likely that one-fifth or even one-fourth of the world's remaining languages will disappear in the next 50 years.

Few people today are actually forced to give up their indigenous language. However, today's globalization affects the survival of languages. When representatives from companies speaking different languages make deals, either they need to use translators or someone has to learn the other's language. When people on remote Pacific islands or in mountain villages of Southeast Asia search the Internet, they are exposed to new languages and may even learn one. Globalization thus promotes the success of a few languages—namely, those used for communication in the global arena. Over time, communication in one of these languages becomes more and more useful. If, at the same time, the linguistic community that once sustained the local language is disintegrating, the local language is likely to become endangered.

Mandarin has more native speakers than any other language, around 850 million. Spanish has the second-most native speakers (406 million), followed by English (335 million), Hindi (260 million), and Arabic (223 million).

However, English is the language most widely used in worldwide commerce, the international mass media, and globally popular culture. More than any other single language, English is learned as a second language in diverse countries from Japan to Mexico. In fact, far more people now speak English as their second language than as their first language. In places like southern Asia and the Pacific, where are many hundreds of localized indigenous languages, English is usually the *lingua franca*—the language that people learn as their second language so that they can communicate widely with one another. And English nouns are commonly used for modern objects and technology.

Although English is the language most commonly used in international politics and marketing, the English-speaking world also is responding to global changes. In the 1970s and 1980s, the West feared competition from "Japan, Inc.," and American colleges hired more Japanese language teachers. Japanese popular culture—anime, manga, sushi, cosplay, horror films—continues to make Japanese cool to many young people.

In the 1990s and early 2000s, China's annual economic growth rate of around 10 percent and its rising importance in international affairs led to the expansion of Chinese language programs in North America and Europe. In many American colleges, German and French language instruction withered as enrollments in Chinese boomed.

In 2012, the Korean pop artist Psy released a music video that by 2016 received over 2.6 billion views on YouTube. K-pop is big in Japan, China, North America, and Europe. Perhaps Korean will soon become a hot second language.

That English is so widely spoken as a second language is a result of the history of British colonialism and the late twentieth-century economic and political dominance of the United States in world affairs. It is not because English is somehow superior to other languages and certainly not because it is easy to learn as a second language. Some countries known for their strong national identity resent the influx of English words—notably France, which at one point passed laws against the use of certain English words.

Some predict that in the next century or so all indigenous languages will wither and die. They will become less useful in a worldwide system in which participation is virtually mandatory or highly rewarding economically.

But perhaps not. Humans value other things besides money and commodities. In many regions, people want to affirm or reaffirm their national or ethnic identities. Learning to speak the ancestral language of their homelands is one symbolic means of doing so. Most members of the ethnic majority in Canada and the United States have heard that many Native Americans choose to learn their native tongues as part of maintaining their identities as shown by Navajo, Inuit, Lakota, and many other indigenous languages.

Many people who are not minorities in their nation-states feel the same. For example, Wales is part of Great Britain, like Scotland and Ireland. The vast majority of Welsh people speak English as their first language, yet about one-fifth of schools use Welsh as the primary language of instruction, and all require years of instruction in Welsh. The desire to preserve the language of one's native land is a mark of national or ethnic identity. It is a symbol of a political or social commitment to the broader goal of preserving cultural identities.

In such ways, speaking a particular language can communicate more than just the messages encoded in words and sentences. Speaking your native tongue can tell people that you are proud to be who you are. In Europe, many people learn three or more languages because their schools emphasize language instruction, and many Europeans travel widely on their continent. Perhaps more U.S. school districts should realize that learning foreign languages is not a costly luxury in a globalizing world.

Nick Clements/Getty Images

Japanese honorifics include rules about formality and politeness, many of which are related to the relative status of the individuals interacting.

Terms of address are a familiar example of how speech both reveals and reinforces the nature of a social relationship. Whether to address someone by a first name or a title like "Doctor" or "Professor" varies with social context. Higher-ranking people are more likely to address lower-ranking individuals by their first name, or even by their last name used alone. Not only does this nonreciprocal use of address terms reflect social inequality, but it also reminds people of it each time they speak. Spanish speakers have a similar understanding with polite address terms such as "Don" or "Señora." They also have to choose between two words for *you:* the formal (*usted*) or the informal (*tu*), depending mainly on relative status.

Speech style and habits depend on status and rank in other ways. For example, in the old days, the speech of women and men in North America differed more than it does today—as in the use of profanity and words like *adorable* and *lovely.* In modern times, there are fewer differences between the vocabularies of women and men, largely as a consequence of changing gender roles and expectations and the influence of popular media. Even today, though, some people make judgments about a stranger's class background or sexual orientation by how he or she speaks.

Other cultures exhibit customs in speech behavior with which most English-speaking people are unfamiliar. Here are just three examples:

- In parts of Polynesia and Micronesia, traditionally commoners had to use a special *respect language* when they were addressing members of the noble class. On some islands, the respect language had not only a different speech style but also different words. Often there were severe penalties for commoners who erred in addressing a noble, including beatings or worse if the offender was judged to have been intentionally disrespectful or challenging.

- In Korean and Japanese, a complicated set of contextual speech norms (called *honorifics*) governs the degree of formality and politeness people normally use to show respect to those of higher social position. For instance, verbs and personal pronouns have alternative forms that speakers must choose between in addressing others. Relative status is the main determinant of which form to use. In Japanese, one verb form is used when the speaker is of higher status than the listener, another form when the two are of roughly equal status, and yet another when the speaker is a social inferior. Today, to a large extent, knowing how to speak is a matter of politeness and decorum, but in traditional Korea and Japan, honorific speech was socially and sometimes legally enforced.

■ All societies have customs of taboo, meaning that some behavior is prohibited for religious reasons or because it is culturally regarded as immoral, improper, or offensive. There are linguistic taboos also. For instance, the Yanomamö of the Venezuelan rain forest have a custom known as *name taboo.* It is an insult to utter the names of important people and of deceased relatives in the presence of their living kinfolk. So the Yanomamö sometimes give names like "toenail of sloth" or "whisker of howler monkey" to children, so that when the person dies, people will not have to watch what they say so closely.

Norms partly explain why people's use of language varies with social context—you are not expected to act and speak the same way at a party as you do in church or at work, for instance, and you are enculturated to know intuitively and unconsciously how to adjust your behavior to these different contexts.

The choice of speech style, words, and phrases is governed by more than just norms, however. People have personal goals, and speaking in a certain way can help them get what they want. In everyday life, we strive to present the image of ourselves that we want someone else to perceive. The opinions that employers, friends, lovers and hoped-for lovers, coworkers, roommates, and even parents have of us depend partly on how we speak—our use of certain words and avoidance of others, the degree of formality of our style, whether we try to hide or to accentuate regional dialects, and so forth. How we speak is an important part of what social scientists call our *presentation of self.* It is part of how we try to control other people's opinions of us.

Like other ways we present ourselves—including the jewelry we wear, how we sit and walk, how we design our hair or shave our head, where and what tattoos we place on our bodies—the way we speak is part of the way we tell others what kind of a person we are. Almost without knowing it, we adjust our speech style, mannerisms, and body language to manage the impressions other people have of us. Our cultural knowledge of these adjustments is mostly routine and usually unconscious—except perhaps at events like job interviews or public speeches.

The Language of Power

We noted earlier that language is powerful, allowing people to communicate complex messages precisely and efficiently. When used strategically, language is powerful in another sense—to influence or persuade. By controlling *discourse*—what is talked about and how it is discussed in the public arena—individuals and groups attempt to control opinions. Those who control the content of messages potentially control the information available to other people. Because human emotional reactions, thought processes, and behavioral responses depend largely on information, language can be an instrument of power.

Political speech obviously employs language of power. Professional consultants advise politicians on what (and what not) to say and how to say it to increase political advantage. Here are a few recent examples of language use in an attempt to control political discourse:

■ On abortion: Is it "murder," or does a woman have "the right to choose," and how much does this answer depend on whether "human life begins at conception" or somewhere later in pregnancy?

■ On immigrants: You usually know how a politician feels by whether she says "illegal immigrants" (or "illegal aliens") or "undocumented workers."

■ On inheritance taxes: The phrase "death tax" is used by politicians who oppose taxing the enormous estates of wealthy people, while those who favor inheritance taxes speak of creating "equal opportunities" and "leveling the playing field" for the next generation.

■ On gun control: Those who oppose it speak of the "right to bear arms" guaranteed by the "Second Amendment." Others point to massacres—such as ones in Aurora, Colorado; Newtown, Connecticut; and Orlando, Florida—claiming the "gun lobby" bears "partial responsibility." The Second Amendment to the U.S. Constitution reads, "A well-regulated militia, being necessary to the existence of a free State, the right of the people to keep and bear arms shall not be infringed." Yet gun control opponents do not quote the "well-regulated" phrase, mentioning only the "right . . . shall not be infringed."

■ On gender identity: In spring 2016, there was conflict in North Carolina over which public restrooms transgender persons should use. The Obama administration proposed guidelines under which individuals should use the facilities of the gender with which they "identified." Governments of states like Texas and Arkansas refused to follow the guidelines, arguing that the gender on a person's "birth certificate" should be the sole determinant of restroom occupancy.

Strategic use of speech happens most intensively during elections. Candidates and parties choose words that arouse positive emotions and attachments to themselves and their programs. In the United States, phrases like "socialist," "tax and spend," "big government," "national security," "individual responsibility," and "personal freedom" resonate with most conservatives, who say that increasing taxes on the wealthiest will be "job killers." Liberal leaders favor "working people," "environmental protection," and "universal health coverage." They speak of "giant corporations" with their "fat cat CEOs." Climate change legislation is a "job killer" for some and a "surefire job creator" for others. Both parties use the phrase "the American people want (need)" as often as possible, although in reality few Americans want and need precisely the same things as the rest of Americans. Every leader uses phrases like "strengthen the middle class," "protect families," "grow the economy," and "jobs, jobs, jobs."

In the 2016 U.S. presidential primary elections, mainstream Republican leaders were astonished when Donald Trump beat out established conservative candidates. A few of Trump's "outrageous" statements were about

- Immigrants ("rapists and murderers")
- Foreign Muslims ("they can't be allowed to come here—period")
- A female Fox News journalist ("blood coming out of her . . . wherever") and, some believed, women in general
- Free trade, so favored by mainstream Republicans ("China is killing us")
- American decline ("We don't win anything anymore")

And many others. Trump also seemed to know very little about international affairs, the Constitution and the legal system, and even economics. He promised to "make America great again," to "build a great wall and make Mexico pay for it," to abolish Obamacare and replace it with "something great," and to meet with Kim Jong-un (the leader of North Korea).

Despite such speeches, Trump became the Republican nominee. The same words and phrases that alienated party leaders won over citizens who believed their economic standing had been harmed by immigration; who thought that the outsourcing of jobs and wage stagnation were caused mainly by free trade deals; who felt that Islamic extremism was the main national threat; and who viewed themselves as victims of discrimination by companies and governments who gave special breaks to minorities. To many voters, Donald Trump "tells it like it is." Almost all Republican Party leaders declared they would never support Mr. Trump in March 2016. Yet by early June, practically all of them did.

Why are such words, phrases, slogans, and the like so important to political campaigns? One answer is that the majority of voters do not understand most issues or their complexity, so candidates use language that appeals instead to their feelings and values. Another is that effective language use—the kind that arouses emotions, demonizes opponents, calls to mind cherished values, reassures about personal and family security, calls on patriotic impulses, and the like—saves candidates from having to reveal details of what they will actually do should they be elected. Solving a large country's complicated problems is a tough job. Providing details of plans and policies is politically dangerous, but who can be against job creation, improved security, and family values?

Language and Culture

Another interest of anthropological linguists is how the culture a people shares is connected to the language they speak. This topic can be technical, so in this section we focus on only two areas that might tie language and culture together. First, some parts of language reflect social relationships and the importance people culturally attach to different things or categories. Second, it is possible that language shapes a people's perception of reality and even their entire worldview.

Language as a Reflection of Culture

Most anthropological fieldworkers try to learn the language of the community in which they work. For one thing, speaking the local language facilitates interaction and may help create relationships of trust. In addition, fieldworkers also know that learning the language helps them understand the culture because many aspects of a people's language reflect their culture.

For instance, a complex classification tends to develop around things that are especially important to a community. If people frequently communicate about objects, qualities, actions, or persons, they are likely to have many names or labels for them and to divide and subdivide them into many detailed categories. Occupational differences illustrate the point. A professional mechanic or carpenter identifies hundreds of different tools, whereas the Saturday afternoon home mechanic or handy spouse identifies only several dozen. Attorneys must master a complex vocabulary that other people sometimes call "legalese." Numerous other examples could be cited, but there are no surprises here.

What about differences *between* whole languages, spoken by members of *different* cultures? Similar ideas apply. To understand them, the concept of **semantic domain** is useful. A semantic domain is a set of words that belongs to an inclusive class. For example, *chair, table, ottoman,* and *china cabinet* belong to the semantic domain of "furniture."

In a similar way, different languages vary in the semantic domains they identify, in how finely they carve up these domains, and in how they make distinctions between different members of a domain. For instance, tropical lowland peoples are not likely to have semantic domains like "snow" or "ice" in their native language, whereas some Arctic peoples have an elaborate vocabulary about snow and ice conditions. Furthermore, the degree to which some semantic domain has a multilevel hierarchical structure depends on the importance of the objects or actions in people's lives: island, coastal, or riverine people dependent on fish are likely to have many categories and subcategories of aquatic life, fishing methods, and flood and tide stages, for instance. Can we go beyond such fairly obvious statements?

For some domains, we can. Some things or qualities seem natural, meaning that the elements in the semantic domain appear self-evident. Distinctions even seem inherent in the things themselves. We therefore expect that people everywhere construct these domains in similar ways. For instance, the wavelength and amount of light reflected from an object determine its color. In this sense, color is an inherent (natural) quality of a thing. Blue, green, and other colors result from different wavelengths, but not every language recognizes the same wavelengths with separate names for colors.

Likewise, biological kinship is a natural relationship, in the sense that who an infant's parents are determines who will and will not be the baby's genetic relatives. Obviously aunts and uncles are different kinds of relatives from parents. But not all peoples recognize such differences and make them culturally significant, which means that "relatives" is not entirely a natural semantic domain.

Consider the relatives that English-speaking people call aunt, first cousin, and brother. An aunt is a sister of your mother or father; a first cousin is a child of any of your aunts and uncles; and a brother is a male child of your parents. These individuals are all biologically related to you differently, so you "naturally" place them into different categories and call them by different terms.

But other distinctions are possible that you do not recognize as distinctions and that are not reflected in the kinship terms you use. Not all your aunts are related to you in the same way: Some are sisters of your mother; others are sisters of your father. Why not recognize this difference by giving them each their own term? Similarly, your first cousins could be subdivided into finer categories and given special terms, such as terms meaning "child of my father's sister," "child of my mother's brother," and so on. And because we distinguish most other categories of relatives by whether they are male or female (e.g., brother versus sister, aunt versus uncle), why don't we apply the sex distinction to our cousins?

How do we know that the way a people divide the domain of relatives into different categories is cultural rather than natural or strictly biological? Because different cultures divide the domain in different ways. People in many societies, for instance, call their mother's sister by one term and their father's sister by another term. It is also common for people to distinguish between the children of their father's sister and their father's brother, calling the first by a term we translate as "cousin" and the second by the same term they use for their "real" brothers and sisters.

Even stranger to English language speakers are peoples who call the daughters of their maternal uncles by the term *mother* (just like their "real mother"), but not the daughters of their paternal uncles, for whom they use the term *sister*. (These various ways of categorizing kin, by the way, are not random; such labels are related to other aspects of a people's kinship system, as discussed in Chapter 10.) Obviously, the way various peoples divide the seemingly natural domain of biological relatives is not the same the world over.

We could provide other examples, but the overall point is clear. A language reflects how the members of a culture divide up the world by constructing various categories of reality out of the natural properties of things and people (see Chapter 2).

semantic domain Class of things or properties perceived as alike in some fundamental respect; hierarchically organized.

The implications of this point are more important than you might think. If a language has a word for something—an object, a kind of person, an emotion, a natural feature of the landscape—then those who know the language tend to think it is real. Giving something a label predisposes us to think of it as a "thing." These "things" are real in one sense: The word refers to *something* real that people perceive. But this reality might differ for someone who speaks a language that reflects a different culture.

Language, Perceptions, and Worldview

We have seen that many aspects of a language reflect the culture of the people who speak it. Could the converse also be true? Is it possible that knowing a given language predisposes its speakers to view the world in certain ways? Could the categories and rules of language condition people's perceptions of reality and perhaps even their worldview?

Language could shape perceptions and worldviews both by its vocabulary and by the way it leads people to communicate about subjects such as space and time. Any language's vocabulary assigns labels to only certain things, qualities, and actions. It is easy to see how this might encourage people to perceive the world selectively. For instance, as we grow up, we learn that some plants are trees. So we come to think of "tree" as a single kind of thing, although there are so many kinds of trees that there is no necessary reason to collapse all this arboreal variety into a single label. In such cases, language affects our cultural constructions of reality.

Also, language might force people to communicate about time and space in a certain way. The words and rules of language could condition relationships between individuals and between people and nature. Potentially, linguistic constraints on the way people must speak to be understood by others can shape their views of what the world is like.

The idea that language influences the perceptions and thought patterns of those who speak it, and thus conditions their worldview, is known as the **Sapir-Whorf hypothesis** (or the **linguistic relativity hypothesis**), after the two anthropological linguists who proposed it. One of the most widely quoted of all

anthropological passages is Edward Sapir's statement, originally written in 1929:

> [Language] powerfully conditions all our thinking about social problems and processes. Human beings do not live in the objective world alone, nor alone in the world of social activity as ordinarily understood but are very much at the mercy of the particular language which has become the medium of expression for their society.... The fact of the matter is that the "real world" is to a large extent unconsciously built up on the language habits of the group. (Sapir, 1964, pp. 68–69)

Sapir and Benjamin Whorf believed that language influences the worldview of its speakers. It does so, in part, by providing labels for certain kinds of phenomena (things, concepts, qualities, and actions), which different languages define according to different criteria. Language thus makes some phenomena easier to think about than others. The attributes that define them as different from other things become more important than other attributes. These attributes provide a filter that biases our perceptions.

In brief, the linguistic relativity hypothesis holds that people's perceptions, the verbal categories they use to think about reality, and perhaps their entire worldview, are related to the language they learn while growing up. The units of time sequence of the English language are a good example: seconds, minutes, hours, days, weeks, months, years, decades, centuries, millennia. Of these, only days, months, and years are in any sense natural, meaning they are based on natural occurrences (sunrises and sunsets, moon phases, annual cycles of the seasons).

Even these natural occurrences do not correspond with the English language's units of time. Days do not run from sunrise to sunrise but begin at midnight. Months no longer reflect lunar phases. Years begin in January rather than at solstices or equinoxes. Decades, centuries, and millennia are purely linguistic categories with no natural basis. Units used on watches—seconds, minutes, and hours—are linguistic units as well.

How much is our perception of time affected by such arbitrary divisions imposed on our minds by language? Do the units of our language—inscribed on watches and calendars—create our views of time?

In the 1930s and 1940s, Whorf suggested that language does indeed condition a people's conceptions of time. He noted that English encourages its speakers to think about time using spatial metaphors. For example, we say "a long time" and "a long distance," although time is not really long or short in the same sense as distance. Also, English-speaking people talk about units of time using the same concepts with which they talk about numbers of objects. We say "four days" and "four apples," although it is possible to see four objects at once but not four units of time (days in this case). Finally, English-speaking people classify events by when they occurred: those that have happened, those that are happening, and those that will happen.

Whorf suggested that the language of the Native American Hopi leads them to think about time and events differently. With no tenses equivalent to English's past, present, and future and no way to express time in terms of spatial metaphors, Hopi speak of events as continuously unfolding, rather than happening in so many days or weeks. Whorf argued that the Hopi language led the Hopi people to a different perception of the passage of time.

Notice some implications of linguistic relativity. If true, it implies that, unconsciously, the language community into which we happen to have been born shapes our perceptions and thought processes. Therefore, the world is not *directly* perceptible through our ordinary senses because the categories of our language bias our interpretations of sensory inputs. If valid, then it is difficult for anyone to know anything for sure. Following this reasoning, it would mean that objectivity in perception and interpretation are partially an illusion because individuals can perceive and interpret only with the concepts and patterns their language provides. As we cover in Chapter 5, some anthropologists use ideas like this to question the discoveries and theories of science itself.

What shall we make of the Sapir-Whorf hypothesis? Certainly, none of us as individuals creates the labels our language assigns to reality, nor do we create the constraints our grammar places on the way we talk about time and space. Rather, we learn them from our linguistic ancestors, and we must adhere to these labels and rules if we are to be understood. Surely, this necessity biases our perceptions *to some degree*. The question is, how much? More precisely, how important is language as opposed to other influences on perceptions and views of reality?

For decades, the Sapir-Whorf hypothesis was not generally accepted, although most scholars were intrigued by the idea that language shapes thought. One reason for skepticism is that if language significantly shapes the way its speakers perceive and think about the world, then we would expect a people's perceptions and worldviews to change only at a rate roughly comparable to the rate at which their language changes. But worldviews typically change much more rapidly than language. In the past century, the English language has changed little compared with the dramatic alteration in the worldviews of most of its speakers. Despite the enormous economic, political, and ideological changes that have swept Asia in the past several decades, Chinese, Japanese, Korean, Hindi, Vietnamese, and other languages have changed little. The fact that linguistic change or replacement is usually far slower than changes in worldviews suggests that language and worldview are not tightly integrated.

Despite this and other weaknesses, recent empirical research has led to reconsideration of the Sapir-Whorf hypothesis. Researchers at the Max Planck Institute for Psycholinguistics have investigated how speakers of different languages talk about space and location. (Here, we simplify their complicated and technical findings.) Consider how English speakers talk about space. Space can be relative to the location of the speaker or hearer—for example, "on my left" or "above you." We also talk about space using absolute locations, especially when we discuss long distances—for example, "head north to get there" or "south of town." These "cardinal directions" do not depend on which way an individual is now facing. When we provide someone with directions, we often combine relative and absolute references—for example, "turn left on Main Street and go west for about 2 miles."

Some other languages talk about spatial directions in different ways. In southern Mexico, there is a Mayan community who speak a language called Tzeltal. In their language, the important spatial references are "uphill" and "downhill." These are more like cardinal directions to them because the overall slope of the land is consistent, and they are seldom on the other side of the mountaintop or ridge. Tzeltal speakers describe movements in terms of "ascending," "descending," or "going across." If an object is on the ground, a person might say it is "uphill of us." They make no distinction between left and right, so a translation of the location of a house might be "to the downhill of you." Apparently, the Tzeltal language does affect perceptions: When shown two mirror-image photographs, Tzeltal speakers usually say they are exactly the same.

Also interesting is an Australian Aboriginal language called Guugu Yimithirr. It uses only absolute references, comparable to English's cardinal directions. Thus, they might say, "There's a fly on your northern knee" (P. Brown, 2006, p. 109). They have no equivalent to "right," "left," "front," or "behind." A Guugu Yimithirr warned a linguist who was filming him to "look out for that big ant just north of your foot" (Deutscher, 2010, p. 166). If they ask you to move over so they can sit down, they might tell you to move westward. When some older Guugu Yimithirr were watching a TV with a screen facing south, they said that a man on the screen moving toward them was walking northward.

Whether languages like Tzeltal or Guugu Yimithirr cause or even predispose their speakers to perceive the world in certain ways is not proven, of course. However, the Guugu Yimithirr seem always to know their directions even when they are in unfamiliar surroundings, suggesting that they are more attuned to four directions than other people. From wherever you are reading this, can you point to the east?

Recently, economist Keith Chen proposed a provocative argument derived from the hypothesis that language shapes how people think and the behavior that results. This concerns how a language constructs present, past, and future events by modifying or not modifying verbs. English and many other languages use modifiers to denote past and future tense. For example, "you *will* go," "you *are* going," "you *went*." Other languages do not use such modifiers, instead using phrases that translate literally as "you go next week," "you go," "you go yesterday." These languages also communicate about past, present, and future, but don't modify the verb itself to do so. Chinese—the language spoken by Chen's ancestors—is a notable example of such a language.

Chen argues that languages that use verb-tense modifiers subtly lead people to emphasize the *difference* between the present and the future. In deciding whether or how much money to save, languages like English and Spanish predispose people to value present income over the benefits of saving for the future. In contrast, people whose languages use context rather than verb modifiers to denote past, present, and future are not reminded of the difference in benefits gained from present and future. Chen argues that—overall—this leads their speakers to save more. In his TED talk posted in February 2013, Chen stated his point concisely: The two kinds of language lead people to "think more or less about the future every time we speak."

To investigate this idea, Chen looked at many societies from various continents. He chose societies that are similar in most socioeconomic characteristics but that differ in whether their languages use tense modifiers. Similar socioeconomic characteristics should lead to (predict) similar savings rates, but Chen found that savings rates vary significantly between societies that modify and those that do not modify verb forms. That is, language determines how much people save at least as much as their economic conditions. Of course, an idea like Chen's is certain to be controversial not only because its practical implications would be quite important but also because it contradicts so much of what we think we know about economies.

SUMMARY

1. **Explain why language is such a powerful means of communication, using five distinctive properties of human languages.** Along with culture, language is the most important mental characteristic of humanity that distinguishes us from other animals. Five properties differentiate language from other systems of communication. It is composed of discrete units (sounds, words) combined in different sequences to convey different meanings. Language is productive, allowing us to intuitively combine sounds and words creatively to send an infinite number of messages. It relies on the shared, conventional understanding of arbitrary and meaningful symbols. Displacement enables humans to communicate about things, events, and persons that are remote in time and space. Language's multimedia potential allows communication in writing and movements (e.g., signing).

2. **Describe how words are formed from combinations of discrete sounds.** Phonology is the study of the sounds and sound patterns of language. When we speak, we combine sounds in patterned ways to articulate meaningful sound sequences (words). Knowing a language includes mastery of its discrete phonemes, based on the features of sounds that speakers recognize as making a difference in the meanings of words in which they occur. Among many other phonological differences, languages vary in the way they use voice pitch to convey meanings, as illustrated by tone languages.

3. **Describe how Native American words were incorporated into English.** As English settlers visited and colonized North America, they encountered animals, plants, and crops that did not exist in Europe. In many cases, the words they

adopted for these unfamiliar life forms were taken from a Native American language. Native words were also adopted to refer to locations, means of transportation, articles of clothing, and many other objects unknown to European settlers.

4. **Discuss the modern-day global forces favoring the survival and spread of some languages and the contraction and possible extinction of others.** Population gains or losses and assimilation by more powerful societies historically were the reasons for the spread, contraction, or disappearance of languages. Today, increasing interaction and communication in the global arena also is causing language change. Economic trade, popular media, international education, and other forces that create new relationships lead to the favoring of some languages over others. However, national and ethnic pride can counteract such global forces if a language itself becomes a symbol of some larger objective.

5. **Discuss some ways messages are communicated nonverbally, how speech is affected by social context, and the strategic use of language to acquire personal goals.** The meanings of body language and facial expressions used in nonverbal communication vary from people to people and are important sources of cultural misunderstandings. Sociolinguists study how speech is influenced by cultural factors, including culturally defined contexts and situations and the presence of other parties. Speech styles mark differences in rank and status, as between ethnic groups, classes or statuses, and males and females. Speech formality and overall style are parts of a person's presentation of self, so speaking communicates many meanings beyond those in the words themselves. Language commonly is a strategic tool in competitions over political power and government policies.

6. **Describe the Sapir-Whorf hypothesis and some of the controversies surrounding it.** The Sapir-Whorf hypothesis proposes that a people's language shapes their perceptions of reality and thus predisposes them to view the world in a certain way. Vocabulary might influence perceptions by leading its speakers unconsciously to filter out some properties of reality in favor of other properties. The conventions of language also might force individuals to talk about subjects such as time and space in certain ways. The notion that language significantly shapes perceptions and thought processes is not accepted by most modern scholars. Recent research concentrates on how particular language constraints affect perception and thought in specific areas of culture, as illustrated by directional labels among the Tzeltal and Guugu Yimithirr. One recent proposal is that the way a language requires people to speak about present and future is a powerful influence on how much income they save rather than spend.

4

Cultural Diversity and Globalization

We can see one obvious cultural consequence of globalization in urban architecture. Although this is a photo of Mumbai in India, the buildings could easily be in any major city in the world.

After reading this chapter, you should be able to:

1 EXPLAIN why society is dynamic and always changing.

2 DISCUSS how the present diversity of human culture came about.

3 ELABORATE on the development and spread of globalization.

4 DESCRIBE how the industrial revolution gave the European powers economic and military domination in the world.

5 ANALYZE the third and most recent stage of globalization and the global economy.

Humans are social animals; we live in groups. We do this not simply out of desire, but out of necessity. We cannot physically survive as individuals—at least not indefinitely. Thus, we live in groups: societies. A **society** is a socially distinct group of people who share a common identity, language, and culture. The two most critical purposes of a society's culture are to provide its members with the means to gain adequate food and shelter while protecting them from competing members of other societies. To accomplish these ends, a society's members have to act collectively and maintain group social cohesion over time.

The culture of a society, among other things, functions to organize and structure the behavior of individuals—not only to accomplish these necessary economic and political ends, but also to reinforce interdependence of individuals within the society while minimizing personal conflicts that might disrupt or destroy the cohesiveness of the group. Thus every society has an organizational structure that serves to define the rights and obligations of the individual members in regard to their behavior in economic, family, political, religious, and other group activities.

Cultural Change and Diversity

Neither the membership boundaries of a society nor its culture are stable over time. The members of a society may, and frequently do, become geographically separated—usually through migrations. The cultures of these separate groups change independently. The result may be two or more groups that are increasing culturally distinct from one another—in other words, new societies. For example, starting in the seventeenth century,

French settlers came to North America. Today there are Quebecois (primarily in Quebec), Acadians (primarily in the Maritime Providences of Canada), and Cajuns (in Louisiana). Over the last three centuries they have become increasingly culturally distinct from one another as well as from the peoples of France. In other cases, when the members of two or more societies come into contact, the result is a combination of cultural traditions. The people in Haiti are such an example in that their culture combines not only the cultural traditions of various African peoples but also French traditions as well. Sometimes smaller societies might be totally absorbed, socially and culturally, by more dominant societies.

Why does the culture of a society change over time? Culture is dynamic, allowing us, both individually and collectively as groups, to adapt to new natural and social environments. This is critical to our survival as human beings because we acquire, both directly or indirectly from our natural environment, those things we need to meet our most basic biological needs—food, clothing, and shelter—while at the same time we are usually in contact, and frequently in competition, with other human groups for survival; this is our social environment. Because both natural and social environments change over time—due to environmental changes, migrations of people, or other factors—culture has to change to meet new challenges.

Although all aspects of culture are dynamic and subject to change, technological changes have the most profound impact on culture in that they can redefine our relationship to the natural environment as well as

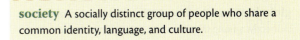

society A socially distinct group of people who share a common identity, language, and culture.

Discovery	New cultural knowledge independently discovered by members of the society through observation, experimentation, or chance
Innovation	The combination of two or more preexisting elements of cultural knowledge in such a manner as to create something totally new to the members of the society
Borrowing	The spread or diffusion of cultural knowledge from members of one society to those of another society

our relationships with other peoples. However, this still does not answer the question of how the culture of a society changes.

There are three major processes involved in cultural change: (1) Members of the society—through observation, experimentation, or chance—independently discover new knowledge, or (2) they create a new cultural trait by combining two or more existing cultural elements to create something different, or (3) they borrow new cultural knowledge from some other group (see the Concept Review feature). Of the three processes, internally generated changes are slower in that they depend upon the size of the group and the existing cultural complexity of the society. Independent discoveries by the members of a society—such as a new edible plant or a new use for a particular type of stone or wood—are rare. Thus, changes within a the culture of a society usually take the form of combining two or more existing cultural elements to produce something new. The simplest example of this is when some individual or individuals (it probably occurred independently more than once) took a sharp stone and mounted it on a wooden club to produce a stone-headed ax. The same is true for most other internally generated changes; a society builds on what it has.

Contact with other societies, particularly societies that are more culturally complex, produces more rapid cultural change. In some cases the members of a society see the cultural alternatives presented by another society, judge them to be superior to their own, and voluntarily borrow and adapt them. This is particularly true with technology. In other cases a society becomes politically dominated by another society; the dominant group physically forces the original society to adopt cultural behaviors to conform to the dominant society's standards. An example of this was when the Spanish, starting in the

sixteenth century, forced Native American peoples under their control to become Catholics.

Finally, it is important to realize that the culture of a society is an integrated system. The introduction of some new cultural element has to be accommodated within the existing culture, thus resulting in the modification or replacement of other aspects of the culture. In the case of Native Americans under Spanish rule, they usually retained many of their preexisting religious traditions and practices while also adopting and modifying Catholic practices. The result was a unique mix—a new religious tradition.

For most of human history, cultural change has progressed slowly because most societies were geographically isolated, which limited the opportunities for learning and borrowing from other societies' knowledge, behavior, and technology. That is not true today. Globalization ended geographic and cultural isolation and allowed for the diffusion of culture among virtually all of the peoples of the world. As a result, we live in a time of rapid cultural change, a time unparalleled in human history. Not only is culture rapidly changing, but also the rate of this change is accelerating.

We sometime speak of "globalization" and the "global economy" as if they are the same thing: They are not. **Globalization** refers to the flow of cultural knowledge, directly or indirectly, among the different peoples of the world. This started about 500 years ago with European expansion. The first phase of globalization, beginning about 1500 and lasting until about 1800, saw the European conquest of the Americas and the establishment of direct trade with Asia and Africa. The second phase, which started about 1800 with the industrial revolution in Europe, ultimately resulted in the division of Asia, Africa, and Oceania into European controlled empires. The *global economy* (discussed at the end of the chapter), an integrated world economic system, started only about 60 years ago with the collapse of these empires; it is the third phase of globalization.

globalization The flow of cultural knowledge, directly or indirectly, among the different peoples of the world.

The World Before Globalization

Contrary to what some people believe, all contemporary humans are fully modern *Homo sapiens,* meaning, among other things, that we all possess the same intellectual capabilities for the learning and development of culture. The present diversity in human culture is the product of 150,000 years or more of localized histories of human groups as new societies and technologies developed, with each adapting to unique social and natural environments. Thus to more fully understand cultural diversity, we have to start with the broad patterns of human cultural change. Over time, the basic economic activities of people have changed dramatically, necessitating the development of new social and cultural institutions to organize and direct their behaviors.

Modern humans evolved in Africa about 200,000 B.P. (Before Present), and between 125,000 and 60,000 B.P. some migrated to Asia and Europe. About 50,000 B.P. the first humans arrived in Australia. Humans started arriving in the Americas by 15,000 B.P., if not earlier. By about 10,000 B.P., humans had occupied all major landmasses except for Antarctica and a few isolated islands. They had accomplished this as hunters and gatherers, with the same basic stone, bone, horn, and wood tool technology—living off wild animals, fish, edible plants, and another food sources that naturally occurred. In doing this their cultures changed as they migrated and adapted to new natural environmental settings—from the Arctic to the tropics; from mountains to plains and islands; from grasslands to deserts to temperate forests to rain forests and swamps.

With each migration, they had to acquire new cultural knowledge of other animals and plants and modify their basic technology and techniques to successfully utilize them. For people who settled along the coast, lakes, or rivers and streams, they had to gain knowledge of the different species of fish, shellfish, or marine animals and how to acquire them. Similarly, they learned about new floral resources available to them—which ones could be eaten and when and where they could be found and which ones were best suited for other purposes, such as for making tools, shelters, as well as for fuel for fires or for curing diseases and injuries. In addition they had to adapt their clothing styles and dwellings to meet the different climatic conditions they were now confronting. Finally they had to modify their social behavior and movements to adapt to the seasonal and geographic variability in the availability of critical food resources and other needs. Localized knowledge of critical natural resources was the key element to human survival during this early period. Thus, although there were broad similarities in basic technologies—in the application and modifications of these technologies and in specialized cultural knowledge and in social behaviors—there was increasing localized cultural diversity among the world's peoples.

Starting about 10,000 B.P., people began domesticating plants. Plant domestication occurred independently in many scattered regions of the world and in each case involved the domestication of different plants. Crops such as wheat and barley were domesticated in the Middle East, wet rice and millet in Asia, dry rice and sorghum in West Africa, corn and beans in Mesoamerica, and potatoes and manioc in South America. Each of these crops required a somewhat different technology for cultivation and was limited to specific environmental settings. Domestication meant that humans were now food producers and able to some degree to control both the location and the quantity of food available to them. No longer were they totally dependent upon the whims of nature for their food.

These first food producers planted only small gardens to supplement their primary source of subsistence—hunting, gathering, and sometimes fishing. Over time, foraging activities declined as garden size increased, and people became more dependent on food production. Associated with this early crop production were a rapid growth in population and an increase in size and permanence of settlements. However, even where these plants were domesticated, only a small portion of the land was actually suitable for their cultivation. This led to migrations as the now more numerous farming peoples began expanding out of their original areas in search of new land—changing, displacing, or absorbing many, but not all, of the neighboring foraging societies.

However, it is important to note that most of the regions of the world were still occupied by foraging peoples. Domestication only added a new level of localized cultural diversity. In Chapter 7 we will discuss hunters and gathers, which we term *foragers,* and these first agriculturalists, which we term *horticulturalists,* in more detail. Here we are just going to note a few characteristics. Among foragers, the group usually collectively owned the land, all families had equal access to natural resources, and group leadership was informal. Among horticulturalists, land was still communally owned, but individuals or families now had "use rights" to the land they cleared for gardens. Leadership in larger social groups became more formalized and structured. However, while all of the horticultural societies were confronting the same basic issues, each developed its own distinct cultural solutions. Thus,

As small groups of nomadic foragers, like the San pictured in this photo, humans spread throughout the world.

between the different horticultural societies there was localized cultural diversity as well.

At some time after the domestication of plants, people began domesticating animals. In Europe, Asia, and Africa, animals such as cattle, horses, asses, camels, sheep, goats, and water buffalo were domesticated. In the Americas there were few animals suitable for domestication and thus few were domesticated—llamas, alpacas, turkeys, guinea pigs being the most important. In both cases domestication of animals gave local populations a new and more reliable source of meat. However, in Europe, Asia, Africa, and South America, it resulted in a new form of economic adaptation: herding. In Chapter 7 we will discuss these people, *pastoralists*, in more detail. Here it is important to note that herd animals gave some people the ability to move into grasslands and deserts, regions unsuitable for growing crops. These migrations resulted in the changing, replacement, or absorption of many foraging peoples. Although the land was still usually owned communally, individuals and families now had

use rights to particular grazing areas and water sources. However, the most important change was in personal property; herd animals were owned individually or by families. They were portable, transferable, and inheritable wealth. Significant inequalities in wealth developed. Once again new localized differences in cultural institutions appeared.

In many parts of the world, horticulture evolved into intensive agriculture, which allowed for the support of even greater numbers of people. In Europe, Asia, and Africa, domestic animals were critical because of their physical strength and ability to pull plows—a new technological development. Lacking suitable animals for plowing, in the Americas intensive agriculture was dependent upon still other new technologies, such as terraced fields, raised fields, and irrigation. Regardless, the cultural effects were basically similar. Fields now became inheritable private property, being worked generation after generation. Villages now became permanent, with houses occupied for multiple generations. Inequalities in wealth became greater, and wealth itself became inheritable, resulting in the development of class and caste systems. Leadership became increasingly formalized and centralized.

Intensive agriculture resulted in increasing the land area suitable for farming as well as greater productivity of the land under cultivation. As a result there was a dramatic increase in the population of intensive agricultural peoples and a territorial expansion at the expense primarily of small horticultural populations, but of some foraging and pastoral peoples as well. Intensive agriculture was the basis for the independent emergence of cities and localized civilizations in the Americas, Europe, Asia, and Africa. Each of these civilizations emerged with its own distinctive cultural traditions—in art and architecture, crafts, religious practices, technologies, and frequently but not always in writing systems. With emergence of cities and civilizations, new cultural diversity began to appear, including craft specialization, markets and market exchange, ecclesiastical religious organization, and state-level political organization.

Thus early human culture was characterized by the migration of foraging peoples followed by scattered, independent, localized cultural developments associated with horticulture, intensive agriculture, and pastoralism. Trade between groups was limited, and diffusion of cultural knowledge was minimal. This began to change with the emergence of civilizations. Civilizations were much larger, politically organized aggregates of peoples. Because of their far more complex technologies and economies, they required a broader range of natural resources than they typically controlled. This led to expansionist warfare, the creation of multisocietal empires, and the development of long-distance trade, which resulted in ever-increasing contact between regional civilizations as well as neighboring foraging, horticultural, and pastoral peoples.

In the **Old World**, most of these regional civilizations had come into contact with each other by early in the ancient period, when they formed an almost continuous band from the western Mediterranean through the Middle East to South and Southeast Asia to China and the Far East. Another group of geographically separate civilizations were found in sub-Saharan Africa. Although members of these civilizations had very little, if any, personal contact with individuals from more distant civilizations, they usually had a vague knowledge of their existence and had some indirect exchange of cultural knowledge and technologies with them through a series of middlemen. Similarly, in the **New World** of the Americas, regional civilizations, each with its own distinct cultural tradition, stretched from Mesoamerica south into the Andes. However, contact appears to have been even more limited than that between civilizations of the Old World.

Thus, prior to 1492, two different groups of more or less interconnected civilizations had developed—one in the Old World and the other in the New World. Although most of the world's population at this time was in some way incorporated into one or another of these civilizations, most of the land surface of the world was still occupied by scattered groups of foragers, pastoralists, and horticulturalists. The general pattern of human cultural development up to this point in history had been one of ever-increasing highly localized cultural diversity.

Globalization

Because globalization was the result of European expansion and because the relative wealth and power of European peoples changed more dramatically during this period than any other region, let's start our discussion with Europe. Late fifteenth-century Europe was a relatively isolated, politically fragmented region with a population of only about 60 million. Agrarian dependent, Europeans relied upon farming: oats, rye, wheat, barley, other crops, and domesticated animals. With most of the population consisting of self-sufficient peasants, specialized craftspeople and artisans were relatively few. Trade both within Europe and with other civilizations was limited, and thus their trade centers and cities were few and small. Compared to the civilizations of Asia, European technology was relatively limited.

Asia at this time is best seen as a series of culturally distinct but more or less adjacent civilizations stretching from North Africa east to China. With a population of about 300 million, collectively Asia was the most technologically and politically developed portion of the Old World. The three main centers of Asian civilization were the Islamic Middle East (which included North Africa), South Asia or India (which was basically Hindu), and China. In addition there were many smaller secondary centers. In contrast to Europe, the cities and trade centers of Asia were larger, with numerous highly skilled craftsmen and artisans. A series of land and maritime trade routes connected the major centers of Asia, and some cultural knowledge, behaviors, and technology diffused between them. Land routes such as the Silk Road connected China and the Middle East. Omani Arabs—whose ships traveled between the ports of China, Southeast Asia, India, the Middle East, and eastern Africa—controlled the maritime routes.

Old World The landmasses of Europe, Asia, and Africa.

New World The landmasses of North and South America.

One of the defining characteristics of civilization was the development of monumental architecture such as seen in the Parthenon of ancient Athens.

The western-most of these Asian civilizations and the one directly bordering Europe was Islamic. The conflict between Muslims and Christian peoples, which started in the seventh century C.E. (Common Era), was primarily responsible for the economic isolation and relative technological backwardness of Europe.

South of the Sahara were the scattered kingdoms of the African civilizations. Except for those kingdoms bordering the Sahara, most lacked indigenous writing systems; thus relatively little is known about these peoples. Their agriculture was based on the growing of millet, sorghum, dry rice, melons, and other crops, some of which had been domesticated locally. Although covering a larger land area than Europe, the population of sub-Saharan Africa was not as dense, probably between 35 and 60 million. Although some of the coastal peoples of East Africa traded with the Omani, the trade of the western kingdoms was by trade routes across the Sahara. Although there were some cities, such as Timbuktu and Gao, they were fewer and smaller than those of Asia and Europe. And although these civilizations produced metalwork in iron and bronze, there were fewer craftsmen and artisans. The civilizations of sub-Saharan Africa were the least technologically developed of those of the Old World, even though they were not that far behind those of Europe.

By 1500, the vast majority of Old World peoples were members of the politically organized states associated with one or another of these agriculturally based civilizations. However, in other regions of Europe, Africa, and Asia—the Arctic, northern woodlands, deserts, grasslands, tropical rain forests, swamps, and rocky or forested mountains—there were still other peoples: foragers relying on hunting or fishing, horticulturalists, and pastoralists. Although some of these peoples were in direct contact with members of one or more of these civilizations, most were not. Figure 4.1 shows the major civilizations and regions of the Old World.

In the Americas the major civilizations were in Mesoamerica and in the Andes. Here there were the largest cities, the most skilled craftsmen and artisans, and the largest politically organized empires and armies. In 1500 the largest empires were the Aztecs in Mexico, with about 25 million, and the Inca in the Andes, with about 12 million. Both were multisocietal empires, meaning that there was cultural diversity within as well as between the two. The Mesoamerican civilizations were based primarily on the cultivation of corn, while the Andean civilizations were heavily dependent on the potato.

Both had a system for writing and/or recordkeeping. In Mesoamerica they used symbolic glyphs, while in the Andes they use *quipus* or knotted strings—systems very different from those of the Old World. New World peoples had some knowledge of metallurgy—working gold, silver, copper, and bronze—but in most cases it

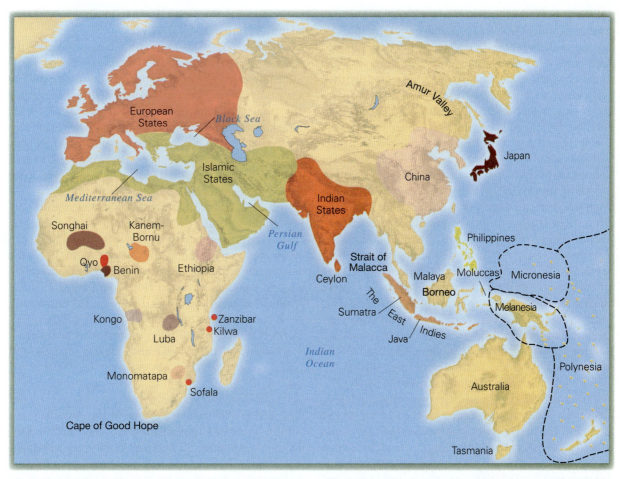

Figure 4.1 This illustration shows the major civilizations and regions of the Old World in Europe, Asia, Africa, and Oceania (ca. 1500).

was used for ritual items or ornaments. For most purposes, even the most technologically advanced Native Americans relied on a stone and wood tool technology.

Other regions were populated with well-developed horticultural societies: the eastern and southwestern United States, islands of the Caribbean, and lowland South America. However, foragers dependent on hunting, fishing, and/or gathering occupied most of the Americas. Unlike the Old World, there were few animals suitable for domestication in the New World, and only in a small portion of South America were there any herding societies. Altogether, the population of Native Americans was probably between 80 and 120 million in 1492, with the majority concentrated in Mesoamerica and the Andes. In comparison, the population of the Americas was about the same as Europe and sub-Saharan Africa combined. However, the comparison of the size of states shows a greater difference. The Aztec empire was far larger in population than any country in Europe at that time—the largest, France, having a population of only about 15 million. The Inca empire was

larger than any European country other than France. Spain, soon the conqueror of both the Aztecs and the Inca, had a population of only about 6.5 million.

The smallest of these major world regions, with a population of only a few million and the most culturally isolated, was Oceania: Australia and the islands of the Pacific. Geographically it was divided into four distinct areas: Australia and Tasmania, Melanesia, Micronesia, and Polynesia. Linguistically and culturally, the peoples of Australia and Tasmania were distinct from neighboring peoples. Nomadic foragers dependent upon hunting and gathering, they had the least complex technology of any people in the world, even lacking the bow and arrow. Politically they were organized into small groups, usually with informal leaders.

To the north and east were island peoples of Melanesia, Micronesia, and Polynesia. Melanesia consisted of New Guinea and several large, mountainous, island groups as far east as Fiji. To the north were the islands of Micronesia, a mix of small volcanic islands and scattered coral atolls. To the east, in the central Pacific, was Polynesia, which except for New Zealand consisted mainly of widely scattered volcanic island groups. The peoples of all three of these regions were horticulturalists, with a heavy dependence upon fishing for the coastal and island populations. Although they varied regionally, their main crops were either root crops such as taro or tree crops such sago, breadfruit, bananas, and coconuts. In addition they raised pigs. With only limited contact with the peoples of Asia, they had only a stone (or shell) tool technology, but it was far more developed than that of the peoples of Australia and Tasmania.

All of the coastal and island peoples made highly sophisticated outrigger and hulled canoes with sails. With these canoes and well-developed navigational skills, these peoples, particularly the Micronesians and Polynesians, were able to travel hundreds if not thousands of miles over the open Pacific between islands and island groups. Although they were politically diverse, most of these peoples were formally organized with hereditary leaders. The islands of the central Pacific were the last land areas settled by humans, with Easter Island and the Hawaiian Islands being discovered and settled after 300 C.E. With the settlement of these islands, the first stage of human expansion had come to an end.

Prior to1492 there had been two major independent lines of cultural development: the Old World and the New World. However, even within the Old World and the New World the diffusion of new technologies, ideologies, and cultural knowledge between the major centers of civilization was usually indirect, extraordinarily slow, and limited by geography. Thus each of these centers retained its own distinctive cultural tradition. European expansion was going to end this isolation. First, it would bring the peoples of the Old and New World into contact, resulting in what Alfred Cosby called the "Columbian Exchange." Just as important, European explorers and traders would provide a conduit that would greatly increase the directness and the speed through which technologies, ideologies, and other forms of cultural knowledge and behaviors could diffuse among all of the regions of the world.

Early European Expansion

European contact with other civilizations had been blocked by Islamic expansion during the seventh century. From ancient literature, Europeans knew of other civilizations to the east: India and China. Some luxury goods—silks, cottons, porcelains, and spices—came into Europe via Islamic middlemen. However, these goods were extremely limited and expensive. In the fifteenth century, first the Portuguese and later the Spanish attempted to make direct contact with the eastern-most civilizations of the Old World: India and China.

In the 1430s, the Portuguese began charting the Atlantic Coast of Africa. The Portuguese moved slowly and cautiously down what was initially the dry coastline of the western Sahara Desert. By the 1450s they had reached the tropics, making contact with non-Islamic coastal kingdoms. Treaties and trade agreements were made with these kingdoms by which the Portuguese acquired gold, ivory, and other local products. They continued to proceed slowly, and it was not until 1488 that they reached the Cape of Good Hope, the southern tip of Africa.

In the 1490s, two world-changing events occurred. In 1492 Christopher Columbus, sponsored by Spain, sailed west across the Atlantic hoping to reach India. Instead he found the Americas. In 1498, the Portuguese explorer and trader Vasco da Gama sailed around the Cape of Good Hope and landed in India. The era of globalization had started. The initial cultural consequences of European contact differed qualitatively from one region to the next, so we will discuss the Americas, Africa, Asia, and Oceania separately.

The Americas

The earliest Spanish settlement in the Americas was on the island of Hispaniola, present-day Haiti and the Dominican Republic. Their initial discovery was disappointing; there were small gold deposits but little else of interest. Still looking for India or China, Spanish explorers and settlers quickly spread to other islands in the West Indies: Cuba, Jamaica, and Puerto Rico. In 1519, Hernán Cortés landed on the coast of Mexico and by 1521 had completed the conquest of the Aztec empire. Cortés sent vast quantities of gold and silver back to Spain, which encouraged others to search for wealth and plunder. In 1532–34, Francisco Pizarro discovered, conquered, and looted the Inca empire. By the late 1500s Spanish conquistadores had explored much of the Americas, from the lower Mississippi Valley to the Amazon and the La Plata rivers, and had located and conquered every major indigenous American state. In little more than half a century, the Spaniards had gained control of the richest and most populous portions of the Americas, which were the West Indies, Mesoamerica, and the Andes. More than half of the native population of the Americas had fallen under Spanish political and cultural domination. The relative ease with which the Spanish came to conquer and control such vast land areas and large indigenous populations with so few people is best explained by the "Columbian Exchange" and its consequences.

The **Columbian Exchange** refers to the diffusion of cultural knowledge, people, and diseases between the peoples of the Old World and the New World. This was an exchange that resulted in the massive destruction of indigenous peoples and their cultures, while ultimately changing the political and economic balance of power among the peoples of the Old World. In the centuries that followed, the culture of virtually every society in the world would either directly or indirectly be changed to some degree by what occurred.

The Spanish conquests, and the later conquests of other indigenous Americans by other Europeans, were not solely the result of the superiority of steel weapons and guns over stone weapons and bow and arrows. European conquest was primarily the result of the introduction of Old World diseases for which indigenous Americans had no natural immunities: smallpox, measles, influenza, bubonic plague, diphtheria, typhus, cholera, malaria, and scarlet fever. The rapid decline in Native American populations started almost immediately at contact. When Cortés landed in Mexico in 1519, there were an estimated 25 million Native Americans. The Spanish were aided in their war by a smallpox epidemic that killed or incapacitated most of the Aztecs. Similarly, smallpox wiped out much of the Incan army, making possible Pizarro's conquest of Peru in the 1530s.

Following these conquests, the native populations collapsed even more. By 1568 the native population of Mexico had dropped to 2.65 million and by 1605 to slightly more than 1 million. In Peru the native population of about 12 million in 1532 had declined to only about 1 million by the late 1550s. Highly contagious, these epidemics spread to indigenous populations well beyond the area of Spanish control and contact. Particularly vulnerable were the powerful and populous farming peoples of South America and the eastern portion of what was to become the United States. It was not a single epidemic of one disease that killed off the native population but a series of epidemics of different diseases. In the first two centuries following European contact, the population of Native Americans had probably declined by 90 percent or more.

The Spanish had taken control of the richest resources of the Americas: gold and silver deposits as well as lands for farming and ranching. At the same time, the Portuguese had taken control of the eastern-most portion of South America: Brazil. From the very beginning, the Spanish and the Portuguese faced a dilemma: Few Europeans were willing to settle in the Americas, and the collapsing native population was inadequate to supply the labor needed for economic development. This labor shortage would result in the African slave trade.

Africa

During the sixteenth century, the Portuguese had a virtual monopoly on the European trade with Africa. Slavery had existed in Spain and Portugal before 1492; however, the number of slaves was extremely limited. A new source had to be found to supply the labor needs of their colonies in the Americas, and Africa was going to become that source. Slavery also existed in Africa, and initially the Portuguese traded for these individuals. However, as the demand for slaves increased, this source was quickly depleted, and the Portuguese then began encouraging the leaders of the coastal kingdoms to raid other, usually interior groups for slaves.

The magnitude of the African slave trade cannot be determined with any exactness. We know that the slave trade grew steadily during the sixteenth and seventeenth centuries as the English, French, and Dutch established ports along the coast of Africa and also became involved in the trade to supply their new colonies in the Americas. It reached its height in the last decades of the eighteenth century and only ended about 1870. Estimates of the total number of African slaves sent to the Americas range from 10 million to 50 million, but the actual number was probably closer to 10 million. The vast majority of these individuals were captured in slave wars. In exchange for slaves, ever-increasing numbers of guns were traded in Africa. During the early eighteenth century, 180,000 guns were being traded annually, and by the height of the trading late in that century, the number was between 300,000 and 400,000 guns. As a result warfare became endemic throughout most of West and Central Africa.

Little is directly known concerning the nature and the consequences of the slave wars on the peoples of Africa during the three centuries between 1500 and 1800 because most African peoples did not have writing systems, and Europeans restricted their movements to the coasts where they traded for slaves. We can only surmise that there must have been a significant displacement of people and that several individuals died for every slave transported to the Americas.

Asia

The Portuguese faced a problem in Asia. The population of Asia far surpassed that of Europe and was divided into numerous highly developed, wealthy, and militarily

> **Columbian Exchange** The exchange of people, diseases, domesticated animals and plants, and other cultural knowledge between the peoples of the Old World and the New World.

powerful states. In almost every aspect of technology, Asian peoples were equal to if not more advanced than Europeans. In economic terms, Asia was a self-sufficient region with only limited interest in outside trade. Although Asians had highly desirable goods such as silk and cotton textiles, spices, coffee, tea, and porcelain, the Portuguese had little to offer in exchange. Realizing that the only significant role they could play in Asia was as middlemen in the inter-Asian trade, particularly between India and China, they turned to the only advantage they had: superiority in naval warfare. In 1509, they defeated the Arab fleet and took control of the Indian Ocean from the Omani traders. Then by entering into agreements with local rulers, between 1509 and 1557 they established a series of trading ports along the coast of southern and eastern Asia. With profits from the Asian trade, during the 1500s an average of 10 ships per year returned to Portugal with goods from Asia to then be traded in Europe.

In 1564, the Spanish established a trading port at Manila in the Philippines to trade with Chinese merchants; Spanish ships—Manila galleons—sailed between Manila and Acapulco in Mexico. From Acapulco goods were transported over land to Vera Cruz and from there shipped to Spain. Unlike the Portuguese, the Spanish had nothing to exchange for goods except silver and gold from their mines in the Americas.

Starting in the 1600s, Dutch, English, and French merchants began sailing around the Cape of Good Hope and establishing small fortified trading ports in India, Ceylon, and the islands of the East Indies. The ports were fortified not to protect them from local rulers, with whom they had trade agreements, but from rival European powers. After Ivan the Terrible fused the Russians into a centralized state in the 1550s, Russia began expanding its territory across northern Asia, conquering the small nomadic pastoral and foraging peoples of Siberia. By the 1630s, the Russians had reached the Pacific coast of Asia and in 1640 signed a treaty with the Chinese allowing them to trade gold and furs for tea.

Early Consequences of Cultural Contact

By the late 1700s, the first phase of European expansion—the initial conquest of the Americas and the establishment of trade with Africa and Asia—was coming to an end. The cultural consequences of European expansion, both direct and indirect, differed from one region of the world to the other. The vast majority of the peoples of Oceania had experienced no effects. The Manila galleons avoided the scattered islands, except for Guam, in Micronesia, where the galleons made their only stop. Otherwise the peoples of Oceania were as unknown to Europeans as Europeans

were to them. Although the Asian trade was extraordinarily valuable and important to Europeans, it was relatively insignificant to the economy of Asia. Whatever cultural effects Europeans had on the peoples of Asia were highly localized and insignificant.

Although direct contact between Europeans and sub-Saharan Africa had been limited to a few coastal areas, the slave trade had greatly changed most of the region. Prior to the slave trade, firearms, if known at all, would have been extremely rare. During the seventeenth and eighteenth centuries, Europeans were trading with African peoples for muskets of ever-increasing sophistication and in ever-increasing quantities. The slave-for-gun trade shifted trade networks and disrupted the existing balance of power among the African societies. As slave-related warfare escalated, new states emerged, and many of the older kingdoms declined. In West Africa, the Songhai empire disintegrated, and the Kanem-Bornu weakened considerably. At the same time, along the coast, many of the small kingdoms and city-states such as Oyo, Ashanti, and Benin were rapidly expanding due to the slave trade. In Central Africa, the Kongo kingdom, refusing to participate in the slave wars, disintegrated, and new slave-raiding states such as Lunda emerged.

At the same time, New World crops introduced by the Portuguese dramatically changed African farming. In the early 1500s, corn, manioc, sweet potatoes, pineapples, peanuts, papayas, and some lesser crops were introduced. In savannas and grassland portions of West Africa—central Angola and the northern and southern extremes of the Congo basin—corn became the dominant staple, which greatly increased the productivity of their farming. In the tropical forest regions, manioc was far superior to existing starchy crops. Few details are known about the effects of these new crops. Some scholars have suggested that the introduction of corn resulted in a population explosion that minimized the demographic impact of the slave trade. It is also clear that corn and manioc allowed for the expansion of farming populations into regions that had been occupied by foragers and pastoralists.

The two regions of the world most directly and dramatically affected during this first stage were the Americas and Europe. After the initial occupation of the major islands in the West Indies and the conquest of the main Indian states and empires of Mesoamerica and the Andes, Spanish expansion slowed. After 1600, the Spanish extended their control to only a few small adjacent areas of the Americas. In the West Indies, due to epidemics of Old World diseases and absorption by European immigrants and African slaves, with few

Ian Murphy/Getty Images

The introduction of New World crops greatly changed the lives of many of Africa's farming peoples.

exceptions Native Americans had vanished; the few survivors were absorbed into the now more numerous European and African populations.

Among the highly civilized peoples of Mesoamerica and the Andes, several things had occurred. The vast majority of native peoples had died in epidemics, taking with them most of their hereditary political leadership, priests, and other cultural leaders. The Spanish reduced the surviving native population to illiterate agrarian peasants who were forced to at least seasonally work in the Spanish-owned mines and on their farms and ranches. They forced upon all of these people at least a veneer of Catholicism, destroying temples, while building churches and assigning priests to their communities. In addition they introduced Western technology as well as crops and animals: plows, steel tools, wheat, oats, horses, donkeys, cattle, sheep, and goats. Despite these changes, most surviving communities still retained their social and cultural distinctiveness: languages, most of their cultural institutions, many of their religious beliefs and practices, and their traditional crafts.

The greater portion of the Americas remained beyond direct Spanish control. However, even among the still politically autonomous groups of Native Americans, dramatic cultural changes had already occurred. The epidemic diseases had also affected these peoples. Most of the populous highly organized agricultural peoples of the eastern United States and lowland South America had been destroyed by disease. Much of the cultural knowledge of these peoples had died with their former political and religious leaders. The remaining population survived as small, politically fragmented groups of widely scattered horticulturists. The peoples least affected by the early Spanish were scattered foragers who still occupied much of the Americas.

The Spanish conquest of the West Indies, Mesoamerica, and the Andes effectively cut the Americas in two: the part north of Mesoamerica and the region east of the Andes (the lowland tropical forests and grasslands of eastern South America). The Portuguese settled the Atlantic coast of North America first, and somewhat later, the English and French settled the Atlantic coast of South America.

Change came most rapidly for the still autonomous indigenous peoples of the tropical forests and

Conversion of native peoples to Christianity was one of the primary interests of the Spanish in the Americas.

grasslands of lowland South America. Having a tradition of keeping domesticated animals (llamas and alpacas), by the mid–sixteenth century the peoples of the grasslands of southern South America started adopting horses, donkeys, cattle, sheep, and goats from the Spanish. By the seventeenth century, many of these groups had became pastoralists, while others had become horse-mounted foragers. In the 1530s, the Portuguese began establishing sugarcane plantations along the coast of Brazil. Although areas of settlement would be limited to the coast for the next three centuries, their effects on native peoples extended well into the interior. Africa was the source of most of the slave labor to work sugarcane plantations, but Native Americans were enslaved as well. By the last decades of the sixteenth century, Portuguese slave raiders were ranging into the interior in search of villages to attack. As the surviving groups withdrew, the slave raiders went farther into the interior, even attacking Jesuit-controlled Indian mission communities in Spanish territory. In the late 1600s, these slave raiders began

prospecting for gold, diamonds, and other minerals; by the late 1700s, they had penetrated virtually every portion of the Amazon Basin.

It was not until the early seventeenth century that the relative isolation of the indigenous North American peoples started changing with the establishment of colonies along the Atlantic coast by the English, French, and, for a short period, the Dutch. Most of these settlers, particularly the English, were not interested in conquering the native peoples but rather in dispossessing them of their land. However, some Europeans became traders, exchanging guns and metal tools for hides and furs. By the mid-1700s, virtually all of the woodland peoples from Hudson Bay to the Gulf of Mexico were actively involved in this trade. In the last decades of the seventeenth century, horses from the Spanish settlements in New Mexico started diffusing among the foraging peoples of the Great Plains and Rocky Mountains. By the eighteenth century, these indigenous peoples had become horse-mounted foragers. Also during the same period, the Navajo in the

Southwest became pastoralists—keeping herds of sheep and goats. During the eighteenth century, the Spanish extended their mission settlements of Indians up the California coast, and in the 1780s, Russians began trading with the peoples of Alaska and along the Northwest Coast.

By 1800, the indigenous civilizations of the Americas had been virtually eliminated; little remained of their cultural achievements other than the ruins of what had been their cities. Their population—once reduced by 90 percent or more—was now recovering. However, they were still under the political control of resident Europeans. The Indian population of most of the Caribbean and Atlantic coastal areas had vanished. Even though most of the land area of the Americas was still occupied by small communities of autonomous foragers and horticulturalists, the lives and cultures of these scattered peoples had, to varying degrees, been changed by European expansion.

The Industrial Revolution

Europe and the Americas

The establishment of overseas colonies and trade ended European isolation and dramatically increased their wealth and knowledge of both the natural and human world. With Gutenberg's invention of movable type and the printing press in the mid–fifteenth century, new knowledge was disseminated on an unprecedented scale. Starting in the sixteenth century, the printing of books increased dramatically. Intellectually, European were the first people to gain a global perspective of the world's geography, peoples, and resources. As a result, Europe entered the so-called Age of Enlightenment with major advances in philosophy, science, and technology.

In the last decades of the eighteenth century, dramatic events affected the relationship between Europe and the other regions of the world and within Europe itself. Starting in 1775, in the English colonies of North America, the resident European population revolted, establishing the United States. In 1804 the African slaves revolted in Haiti and drove out the French. The revolutions soon spread to the Spanish colonies, and by the 1820s the resident Europeans in these colonies had established independent countries. Although some colonies remained, the English, French, and Spanish had lost their most valuable colonies in the Americas.

During this same period, machine-made goods began replacing handcrafted items—the start of the industrial revolution. At first textiles were produced using water wheels to power the machinery in the mills. However, this soon changed to machinery powered by coal-fired, steam-driven technology producing other goods. The steam engine allowed for the production of much greater quantities of goods with less human labor. Thus, these goods were less costly than handmade goods.

This basic change in the production of goods resulted in a wide range of other technological innovations, particularly in the transportation of goods and people. Steam-powered locomotives replaced horse-drawn wagons for long-distance land transport. Wooden sailing ships were first replaced by steam-powered wooden paddlewheel boats and ships, which then were replaced by steel-hulled, propeller-driven ships by the last decades of the nineteenth century. Whether by land or sea, greater quantities of goods, products, and people could be moved much faster and cheaper.

However, what truly changed the world's balance of power were the advances in military technology. In the first decades of the 1800s, European armies were still armed with slow, inaccurate, single-shot, muzzle-loading muskets. Before the end of the century, these forces were armed with rapid firing, highly accurate, cartridge-loading rifles and even machine guns. Similarly, breach-loading artillery pieces with exploding shells replaced the old muzzle-loading cannons. During the same period, European navies changed: Steel-hulled, steam-powered ships armed with breach-loading cannons replaced wooden sailing ships armed with muzzle-loading cannons. Europeans now had overwhelming military superiority over the other peoples of the world on both land and sea.

The industrializing countries of Europe needed markets for the ever-increasing quantities of goods being produced by their factories, as well as new sources of raw materials and food to maintain the production of these industries and feed their workers. Initially, the colonies or former colonies in the Americas were the primary overseas markets and sources of raw materials, resulting in increased economic expansion even after independence. The United States was the main beneficiary. At first a source of timber, cotton, tobacco, whale oil, and a variety of food crops, the United States soon experienced its own industrial revolution while increasing exports of commodities.

The economic expansion of the United States was accompanied by increasing numbers of immigrants from Europe. In 1776, the settled area of the United States was limited to the coastal fringe, east of the Appalachian Mountains. By the 1880s, the entire region from the Atlantic to the Pacific had been settled, and the indigenous peoples had been defeated and placed on small reservations. The change was not as dramatic in Latin America; many of the countries were still relying on gold, silver, and other mineral production as well as plantation crops to pay for imports. There were exceptions; Argentina, for example, became a major supplier of grain and cattle to feed industrial Europe. As a result, the resident European population expanded into the grasslands of the Pampas and Patagonia, displacing the native peoples.

Asia

During the early 1800s, European powers—particularly England, France, and the Netherlands—started expanding their areas of control in Asia. China had successfully resisted making trade concessions. In the Opium War with England (1839–1842) and in a second war with England and France between 1856 and 1858, China saw its navy and army badly defeated and was forced to make humiliating land and trade concessions. During the late 1700s and early 1800s, the British East India Company had expanded its territorial control in parts of India. The crushing of the Sepoy Mutiny (1857–1858), a native uprising, ended any question about England's political domination in India. However, there was still the problem of distance. All shipping to and from Europe and Asia had to pass around the tip of Africa, a long and costly journey.

In 1859, a French company began construction on the Suez Canal, connecting the Mediterranean and the Red seas. Open to the ships of all countries, the canal was completed in 1869, cutting the shipping distance between Europe and Asia by more than half and greatly increasing the European presence in Asia. By the end of the nineteenth century, most of Asia had been brought under the direct or indirect control of European powers. England had India, Burma, Malaya and Sarawak (Malaysia), Hong Kong, and Ceylon (Sri Lanka). The French held Indochina; the Dutch had extended their control over the islands of East Indies; and the Russians controlled most of Central Asia, Siberia, and part of Manchuria. Although still technically independent countries, China, Nepal, Afghanistan, Thailand, and Persia (Iran) were so strongly dominated by one or another European power that some have called them "semicolonial" regions. Only two countries truly retained their autonomy: the Ottoman empire, which at the time included Turkey, Iraq, Syria, Lebanon, Palestine, Jordan, and most of the Arabian Peninsula; and Japan. Japan, adopting a European model, was creating its own empire, including Korea and Formosa.

Africa

The initial impact of European industrialization on Africa was an intensification of the slave trade as plantations in the Americas increased their production of sugarcane, cotton, and other commodities. However, as opposition to slavery and the slave trade increased, during the early and mid–nineteenth century the slave trade declined, only ending in the 1870s. Africa had potential as both a supplier of raw materials and as a market for manufactured goods, a potential that could not be realized under the existing conditions.

The slave trade and resulting warfare had destroyed the political stability of much of the region, and as a result Europeans saw sub-Saharan Africa as a dangerous place in need of control. As late as the 1870s, the French, English, Spanish, and Portuguese claimed and controlled only a few scattered coastal areas. However, other European powers coveted portions of the region, most of which was still unmapped and unknown to Europeans. At the Berlin Conference in 1884–85, Britain, France, Germany, Belgium, Italy, Spain, and Portugal unilaterally divided up the peoples and resources of sub-Saharan Africa among themselves. With these agreed-upon geographic boundaries, the European countries quickly moved to bring the peoples of their new territories under their physical control and to develop their resources. With overwhelming military power, they crushed the few native peoples who attempted armed resistance. Although policies were diverse for the colonies now under the control of Europeans, the peoples of sub-Saharan Africa had their political organizations and economies restructured, while Christian missionaries traveled widely in search of converts.

Oceania

The extension of European domination over the peoples of Oceania was sporadic and slow. In 1668 the Spanish had established the first European colony in Oceania on Guam. However, a hundred years passed before the English established a second colony, a penal colony, at Botany Bay in Australia in 1785.

The pattern of English expansion in Australia and the nearby islands of Tasmania and New Zealand basically followed the pattern of the earlier English expansion in North America. The initially small colony of Europeans grew through continued migration, as the native population declined due to disease and/or warfare. By the mid-1800s, Europeans outnumbered native populations who had or would soon be sent to small reserves. Of little economic value, European countries had little incentive to extend their empires to include the other islands of Polynesia, Melanesia, and Micronesia.

By the mid–nineteenth century, American and European missionaries, whalers, traders, and sailors were frequenting the islands of the still independent peoples of the Pacific. The effects of contact were wide-ranging from island group to island group. Epidemics destroyed much of the population on some islands but had no lasting effects on others. Islands such as Fiji, Hawaii, and New Caledonia, with valuable resources to be developed, found their populations displaced by immigrant workers. Most of these immigrants were not Europeans but Asians: from India, Japan, China, Indochina, and the East Indies. However, most islands saw no influx of immigrants.

In the mid–nineteenth century, the French and English began to slowly incorporate some of the island groups in their empires, usually through agreements with local leaders. In the 1880s, Germany began incorporating other islands into their new overseas empire: portions of Micronesia, Western Samoa, and part of New Guinea. During the Spanish-American War in 1898, the United States took control of Guam and the following year annexed Hawaii and American Samoa. Finally, in 1900 the Tonga Islands became a British protectorate; the political division of Oceania among the Dutch, British, French, German, and Americans was virtually complete.

Cultural Consequences of European Expansion

By the beginning of the twentieth century, European peoples virtually dominated the world, politically and economically. The Americas were political controlled by resident Europeans, the only exception being Haiti, which was African American. Sub-Saharan Africa, with minor exceptions, was divided into European colonial processions. Most Asian countries were under the direct or indirect control of one or another European country. The same was now true of Oceania as well.

The social and cultural consequence of 400 years of European expansion differed greatly from one region of the world to the next. Europe itself had changed dramatically. In 1500, Europe was still basically a feudal society, with an inherited, landowning nobility supported by peasants who worked on their estates. Towns with merchants and craftspeople were small and few. With the conquest of the Americas and the expansion of **global trade**, this began to change.

As the nobility of these countries profited from this expansion, other elements of the society also profited.

Towns began to grow, and an increasing wealthy middle class of merchants and artisans began to emerge. The overseas colonies and possibility for migration presented an opportunity that many poorer people and religious dissidents took advantage of. However, it was not until the industrial revolution that European society, particularly in western Europe, began to change. While the nobility continued to live off of the income from their agricultural estates, the middle class expanded dramatically with the emergence of industrialists: the owners of the new textile mills, coal mines, and manufacturing plants. Many of these industrialists quickly accumulated fortunes that far exceeded the wealth of most of the landed nobility.

Associated with industrialization, there was rapid growth of urban manufacturing and trade centers and a massive migration of families from rural farms to cities. Most workers were now wageworkers—in manufacturing, mining, or commerce—and not tenant farmers or laborers on the estates of the nobility. A modern capitalist economy had emerged, with increasing demands for political and other social rights—not just for the now economically powerful middle class but for the factory workers and miners as well. In addition to the changes in technology and material wealth, the most readily apparent social change was increasingly democratic political institutions and the erosion of the rights and privileges of the nobility.

The Americas had changed more than other region of world. Now the **resident population** came from three distinct groups: Native Americans, Europeans, and Africans. The resident European population was far from homogeneous. During the colonial period, Spanish, Portuguese, English, French, Scots, Scots-Irish, Irish, Dutch, and Germans had settled in various regions of the Americas. The nineteenth century had seen the arrival of immigrants from still other parts of Europe. African slaves, primarily but not exclusively from West and Central Africa, had been brought to the Americas. This African population arrived speaking many different languages and representing a wide diversity of cultural backgrounds.

global trade The economic exchange of goods and other products between the different peoples of the world via established trade networks.

resident population The people who live or lived in a particular region of the world at a specific time; may or may not refer to an indigenous people.

Almost immediately after they were brought to the Americas, African slaves began escaping. Many found refuge among the Native American peoples. Still others escaped in small groups and formed their own distinct societies. During the colonial period, large numbers of free African communities were established in the southern portion of the United States, the West Indies, Mexico, and Central and South America. In language and culture, these new African societies were highly diverse—distinct from one another, from their African ancestors, and from the slave populations from which they had fled. Here we are discuss three of these groups.

Black Carib

The Garifuna, or Black Carib, are predominately African in ancestry with a high degree of Native American ancestry. In 1675, a slave ship was wrecked on a small island near St. Vincent in the West Indies. The surviving Africans, Ibibio men from what is today Nigeria, were rescued by the Caribs who brought them to St. Vincent. The Spanish had avoided these smaller islands, the Lesser Antilles, in part because the Caribs were a highly aggressive and warlike people. Both the words *Caribbean* and *cannibal* are derived from Carib.

The Ibibio men intermarried with Carib women. The descendants of these couples spoke the Carib language, with male and female dialects, practiced Carib-style skull deformation of infants, and in their material culture and most other aspects of their culture were indistinguishable from the Caribs. Like the Caribs they also relied on hunting, fishing, and the cultivation of manioc. This assimilation of Native America culture occurred despite large numbers of other escaped African slaves joining the community. This mixed African/Native American community, the Black Caribs, quickly came into conflict and separated from the Native American community, occupying the windward side of the island while the Red Caribs lived on the leeward side.

In the late 1600s, the French and the British began occupying the Lesser Antilles—both claiming St. Vincent. The French first settled on the leeward or Red Carib side of the island and developed plantations worked by African slave labor. The Black Caribs were extremely hostile to Europeans, and in 1719 they defeated a French military force.

In Peace of Paris, signed in 1763 to end the Seven Years War, the French ceded St. Vincent to the British. The new British governor of the island, wanting to expand the sugarcane plantations, was faced with a problem. Two-thirds of the richest land on the island was on the windward side belonging to the Black Caribs. The British were conflicted over how they should be dealt with. Although some referred to them as "Indians" and argued that they had an "aboriginal claim" to their lands, others saw them as "usurpers of . . . Carib heritage" and thought they should be transported back to Africa. No one seems to have suggested that they be re-enslaved; they were considered far too dangerous for that.

Attempts to negotiate land sales with the Black Caribs failed. A British attempt to build a road on the windward side resulted in armed resistance, and the First Carib War broke out. Lasting from 1769–1773, this war consisted primarily of skirmishes and ended in a peace agreement in which the Black Caribs ceded a very small portion of their land. However, conflict between the British planters and the Black Caribs continued. In 1795, with French support, the Black Caribs attacked the British plantations. The following year, the British defeated the Black Caribs and took about 5,000 captives. About half died in captivity before, in 1797, the surviving Black Caribs were taken to Roatan Island off the coast of Honduras. From

The survival of African cultural traditions among the Maroon peoples of Suriname is readily apparent in this painted Djuka house front.

Ariadne Van Zandbergen/Alamy

Roatan, the Spanish moved the Black Caribs to the mainland where they became known as the Garifuna or "cassava (manioc) eaters." Today there are about 200,000 Garifuna occupying 43 communities along the Caribbean coast from Belize to Nicaragua.

Black Seminole

In 1585, the Spanish established a fort at St. Augustine in Florida and missions among the Timucua and other neighboring tribes. In 1670, the English established Charleston, South Carolina, and began to establish plantations with slaves primarily from West Africa. The English, with the support of the Muskogee (Creek), began raiding Indian-Spanish missions for slaves—not to use on the plantations in South Carolina, but to sell in the West Indies and the English colonies in New England.

By 1700, the missions had been deserted, and most of northern Florida was uninhabited. As early as the 1680s, slaves from South Carolina had begun fleeing to Spanish Florida. In 1693, the king of Spain issued an edict giving these ex-slaves freedom in return for defending Florida against the English. Communities of free Africans quickly developed. Drawn primarily from a number of different West African societies, these communities spoke Gullah, an English-based Creole language similar to that spoken in western Africa. In the early 1700s, small groups of Creek and Hitchiti-speaking peoples, unhappy with the English, also began moving into Spanish Florida where they collectively became known as the Seminole. After the English took control of Florida in 1763, these Gullah-speaking African communities became increasingly associated and allied with the neighboring Seminole communities. This became particularly evident after the United States acquired Florida in 1819.

While there was some inter-marriage, the groups remained separate with their own villages. In material culture, housing, and dress, they became almost indistinguishable, with both groups supporting themselves by hunting, farming, and keeping domesticated animals. Thus these African communities became known as the Black Seminole. However, they retained their own languages—Gullah and Seminole (Creek and Hitchiti)—and their own distinct cultures. This difference was evident in the syncretic religious practices of the Black Seminole, which incorporated "southern plantation," African, and Indian elements together with some Baptist and Catholic characteristics. It was also evident in naming. The Black Seminole used a Kongo naming system in which males were given double names. Some names were of African origin, others were of slave origin, and still others were of geographic origin.

Fearing American slave catchers, starting in 1821, some Black Seminoles moved to Andros Island in the Bahamas. However, with the passage of the Indian Removal Act of 1830, the situation worsened. The government wanted to remove the Seminole to Indian Territory and to re-enslave the Black Seminole. The Seminole War of 1835–42 was the most costly Indian war in U.S. history. It ended with most of the Seminole and 500 Black Seminoles being moved to Indian Territory. By the end of the war the government had decided that the Black Seminoles were far too dangerous to try to re-enslave.

Although most remained in Indian Territory, in 1849 some Black Seminoles moved to Mexico where they were given land at Nacimiento in return for helping to protect Mexico from Comanche and Apache raiders. In 1870, after discussion with U.S. officials, some returned to the United States, with most men joining a new army unit: the Seminole Negro Indian Scouts stationed at Fort Clark, Texas. In 1914, this unit was disbanded, and together with their families they settled at Brackettville, Texas. Although their unit never numbered more than 50 men, during the Indian wars four of them received the Congressional Medal of Honor.

At the turn of the twentieth century, the lands of the Seminole Nation in Indian Territory were allotted to individual tribal members. The Seminoles were listed as either "Indian" or "freedmen" for those who had once been slaves. The Black Seminoles were enrolled as freedmen. When the Seminole Nation was re-organized in 1969, two freedman bands were politically recognized. However, in 1991, when the Seminole were to be paid by the federal government for their lost lands in Florida, the freedmen were excluded. This was based on the concept that they did not actually have title to lands in Florida.

Saramaka

The Guianas refers to the northern coast of South America between the Orinoco and Amazon rivers. Both the Spanish and Portuguese ignored this resource-poor region. In 1605, the Dutch established a small settlement there and in the 1620s began importing African slaves and developing sugar and cotton plantations. Starting in the mid-1600s, the English and French also began competing with the Dutch for the Guianas—a rivalry that would last for 200 years.

The Guianas never became an important region for sugar, cotton, and other plantation crops and thus never attracted many European settlers nor had large numbers of African slaves. Most of the Native American population died during the seventeenth century due to Old World diseases; as a result, the vast jungle areas inland from the coast were lightly inhabited and of little value or interest to the European colonists on the coast. As early as the 1620s, escaped slaves from the coastal plantations began forming communities along isolated river valleys in the interior. Due to their relative isolation from one another, during the colonial period at least six new African societies emerged, each with its own distinctive language and generic African-derived culture. The two largest of these groups were the Saramaka (Saramacca) and the Djuka (Ndyuka). The six societies are known as the Maroon peoples.

From their isolated communities in the interior, these African communities would raid the coastal plantations for weapons, tools, and supplies, freeing other slaves to join them. Periodically Europeans would mount military expeditions to travel into the interior to attempt to destroy these communities and re-enslave their inhabitants. Finally, in 1762, the Dutch negotiated a treaty with the Saramaka and the Djuka; the treaty formally recognized

continues on next page

their independence and allowed them peaceful trade with the European settlers. However, they could no longer give refuge to escaped slaves.

The Saramaka live on the Suriname River in what is today Suriname, formerly Dutch Guiana. Their language is a mixed English-Portuguese Creole with a few words from Dutch and African languages. The traditional economy is based on hunting, fishing, and gardening. They have collective ownership of their land and use rights to the gardens they clear. They live in small, scattered permanent villages and also have smaller farming villages. Descent is matrilineal (through the mother's line), and the core of every village is a group of matrilineal families. They have a paramount chief as well as other formal officials. Their religion is a syncretic blend of various African-derived deities and ritual practices reflecting their diverse African origins. They practice scarification, the African custom of creating designs on the skin by scarring. However, it is in their art where the strength of their African heritage becomes most overtly apparent. Even common domestic items—wooden bowls, combs, spoons, house doors, drums, canoe paddles, and prows—are frequently carved with highly elaborate designs.

For over 300 years, the Saramaka remained relatively isolated and independent of the other peoples of Suriname. In 1975, Suriname became an independent country, and in 1986 fighting broke out between government troops and members of the six Maroon tribes. During the conflict, many Saramaka fled to French Guiana. In 1992, a peace agreement ended the war, but the Maroons lost title to their lands. In the 1990s, the government began granting logging and mining concessions to multinational corporations, some of which are for land in the traditional territory used by Saramaka. The Saramaka filed a case against the government in the Inter-American Court of Human Rights. In November 2007, the court found in their favor, ruling among other things that the Saramaka are a tribal community and have the same legal status as indigenous peoples. However, the government of Suriname has so far ignored this ruling.

All of these various groups of people had experienced changes in their cultures and to varying degrees were culturally influenced by the others. Scattered groups of Native Americans still existed from the Arctic to the tip of South America. All of them had been culturally influenced by Europeans to some degree, and many had been influenced by Africans as well. This influence was different from one part of the Americas to another.

There were some regions where the Native Americans constituted the vast majority of the population. There were other regions where native populations had disappeared altogether, and there were regions were surviving native groups had been reduced to small minority populations. Although the vast majority was under the control of the dominant European population, there were still some autonomous groups, particularly in South America. Some were still foragers, others farmers, and some lived on support from their national governments.

Originally, the major European groups differed from one another in language and culture. However, residence in the Americas forced regionalized adaptations in their cultures. They had to adopt economic behaviors and technologies suitable to environmental conditions that were frequently very different from those of Europe. Depending upon where they lived, they came into cultural contact with other groups of Europeans, Native Americans, and/or Africans.

As slaves, Africans were usually settled in communities of individuals of mixed African cultural heritage. Although all Africans were forced to conform to certain cultural practices imposed by their European owners, what those new cultural practices were and how stringently they were imposed depended on the region. As a result, the culture that developed among the slave population was partly European and, to different degrees, African or even Native American in origin. In addition, even in colonial times, there were free black communities. In some cases, these individuals had gained their freedom and lived among the dominant European population, usually adopting the cultural practices of the prevailing community. In many other cases, escaped slaves, particular in South America and the Caribbean, formed their own separate communities. Some of these communities were basically derived from African cultural traditions. Other communities adopted Native American languages and a culture that was both African and Native American in origin.

Thus, these new "African American" cultures showed an extremely high degree of localized diversity. In addition, through intermarriage, a large number of mixed societies emerged that combined varying degrees of Native American, European, and/or African ancestry and cultural heritage. Although all had greatly changed, by 1900 the peoples of the Americas were far more socially and culturally diverse in 1900 than they had been in 1492. For a closer look at the impact of European expansion on indigenous and resident populations, see the Global Challenges and Opportunities feature.

For the peoples of Oceania, the effects of European expansion had been mixed. The suffering and cultural change of the indigenous peoples of Australia, Tasmania, and New Zealand paralleled what had happened to the native peoples of the Americas. At the other extreme, there were at least several hundred thousand horticultural peoples of highland New Guinea who had not yet had any direct contact with Europeans and who would not until the 1930s. In between were the other peoples whose experience differed greatly from one island group to another.

The direct and indirect cultural effect of European contact and colonial subjugation differed from one area to another in sub-Saharan Africa. The four centuries of the slave trade and internal slave raiding undoubtedly affected the cultures of people throughout much of Africa. The colonial period also had some effects, depending on region and colony. In the Congo Free State (later Belgian Congo and now the Democratic Republic of Congo), the ruthless exploitation of resources and people resulted in the deaths of over half the population within the first 20 years. However, those African peoples who had little if anything that European colonialists wanted barely, if at all, felt the European presence. In the Kalahari Desert and other isolated regions, there were still foraging peoples, such as the San, whose lives had been little touched by Europeans. Throughout the grasslands and desert regions, there were traditional pastoral communities, while in the woodlands and jungle regions most of the farming communities had only indirectly felt the influence of European colonial domination.

Asia was less impacted by European expansion than any other region of the world. With highly organized political, social, economic, and religious institutions, the European colonial officials attempted only to modify and manipulate them to economically benefit the empires, not to destroy or replace them. European influence in Asia was greatest, not in the countries they directly or indirectly controlled, but rather in one of the few that fully retained its autonomy: Japan. In the last decades of the nineteenth century, Japanese leaders began to systematical adopt the latest European technology. While minimizing the effects of this new technology on other aspects of Japanese culture, by the early twentieth century Japan had developed an industrial economy that was competitive with Europe and the United States.

This is the way the world would basically remain for the next half century. With few exceptions, the resident populations of European descent would control the independent countries of the Americas, while most of the countries of Africa, Asia, and Oceania were dominated by one or another of the imperial European powers. There was an increased diffusion of cultural practices; however, it was not balanced. Although Western peoples attempted to impose their cultural beliefs and practices, particularly Christianity, on other indigenous peoples, they were highly protective of their technological knowledge, wanting to sell only finished products. There was global trade but not an integrated global economy. The independent countries of the Americas imposed tariffs and quotas on imported and exported goods to protect their local markets and industries. The European empires had been created for the economic benefit of the "home country," as protected markets for manufactured goods and as sources of raw materials. Trade both within and between empires and independent countries were strongly regulated. It was not until after World War II and the collapse of the European empires that the global economy would start to emerge with free trade.

The Global Economy

The **global economy** refers to an integrated global market in which goods and services are exchanged globally with their prices determined by supply and demand with minimal interference or control of national governments. Before this global exchange could develop, the colonial empires had to disintegrate.

In 1945, there were about 60 fully independent countries in the world. Between 1946 and 1980, 88 newly independent countries were created out of the old colonial empires. In the 1990s, the Soviet Union (the old Russian empire) and Yugoslavia collapsed, resulting in the creation of 18 new countries. Today there are about 200 countries in the world. However, political independence alone did not result in free trade between countries. Taxes (tariffs) and quotas on the importing and exporting of goods were not simply an important source of revenue for most countries; they also served to protect local markets for domestic producers and consumers. In 1947, 23 countries signed the General Agreement on Tariffs and Trade (GATT). This agreement lowered or eliminated tariffs on thousands of goods traded between these countries.

Over the last half-century, other agreements involving still other goods and countries have been signed. In 1957, 6 countries formed the European Economic

---

global economy An integrated global market in which goods and services are bought and sold globally with prices determined by supply and demand.

Container shipping has greatly lowered the cost of shipping of manufactured goods and has played a key role in the development of the global economy over the past 30 years.

Community; today known as the European Union (EU), it includes 28 countries (although in June 2016 the United Kingdom voted to withdraw from the EU). In 1994, the United States, Canada, and Mexico signed the North American Free Trade Agreement (NAFTA). In 1995, GATT was replaced by the World Trade Organization (WTO), which today has 162 member countries. In addition, there are many other trade agreements between particular countries or groups of countries. While there are still tariffs and quotas on the importing and exporting of some goods, today they are minimal.

During this same period, there have been major advances in shipping and communications. Oceangoing ships carry most (almost 90 percent) of international cargo. As late as the 1960s, cargo was usually packed in small boxes and loaded and stored on ships, piecemeal, by hand. Unloading was done in the same manner. Starting in the 60s, a new method came into use: standardized containers, usually 20 to 40 feet in length, and ships designed to carry these containers. Goods were loaded in the containers at the factory, taken to the port, and loaded by cranes onto ships, to later be unloaded by cranes usually onto trucks or trains. Today it takes one-tenth the amount of time to load and

unload cargo ships that it did in 1960. This change has greatly reduced the amount of labor needed, and thus the cost, to handle shipments. It has also significantly cut the amount of time cargo ships spend in port to load or unload, once again reducing cost.

However, the change that has truly integrated the global marketplace has been in information technology—computers, the computer network, and telecommunications. The more recent development of mobile phones that can access the Internet means that this system is now becoming a fully integrated and electronic information and communications system. With this system we can now store, transmit, access, and even manipulate text, photos, videos, figures, drawings, and other data from almost any portion of the globe.

For multinational corporations, this now means that it is irrelevant whether their branch offices or field operations are on the other side of town or the other side of world; they can have virtually instantaneous communication with them. Not only can they be in contact with individual employees by voice calls, text messaging, or e-mails, but also they can have group meetings using Skype. The same is true in communications with suppliers and customers. Not only can agreements be made, but also contracts can be sent and paid for electronically.

These developments in information technology have meant that multinational corporations can act far more quickly and effectively now than in the past; but these changes have benefited smaller specialty retailers as well. For the production and marketing of goods, geographic locale has become increasingly irrelevant. The global economy is in the process of restructuring the economic activities and thus the cultures of peoples throughout the world.

Associated with the development of the global economy has been the globalization of technology, knowledge, and access to information. At the beginning of World War II, the countries of Europe and North America had a virtual monopoly on the production and the distribution of the world's most advanced technologies; through their academic institutions, they controlled not just scientific and other research, but the dissemination of that knowledge as well. It was their de facto control of advanced knowledge and their almost exclusive ability to transform this knowledge into meaningful technological products that gave the Western peoples of Europe and North America economic and political dominance in world affairs. As a rule, not only were non-European peoples collectively ignorant of advanced scientific and technological knowledge, but they also lacked the means of implementing this knowledge.

Today, as in the colonial past, the latest products of modern technology are marketed throughout the world. However, as corporations have becoming increasingly international, they have built and equipped the most modern manufacturing and processing plants in developing countries and trained local workers to operate them. Thus there has been a massive transfer of technology from developed countries to developing countries.

One of the advantages European people had during the colonial period was that they collectively controlled far more knowledge of the world than any other people. It was this knowledge that resulted in their technological achievements. As early as the sixteenth century, the Portuguese brought students from the Kongo kingdom in Africa to study in Portugal. Other countries did the same during the colonial period; however, this opportunity was only available to a small number of these students, and their teachers were European.

In recent decades, the knowledge and research of the academic world have become globalized. Both university student bodies and their faculties have become increasingly diverse. In 2011, there were over 115,000 international scholars teaching and researching in U.S. colleges and universities, and their numbers are increasing. In that same year, the Association of American Universities noted that of their 51 member institutions in the United States and Canada, 11 of the presidents or CEOs of these institutions were foreign born. In 2013–14, there were 4.5 million international students enrolled in colleges and universities throughout world. Of this number, almost 900,000 were enrolled in U.S. institutions, while over 300,000 U.S. students were studying abroad. Following the lead of multinational corporations, colleges—particularly in the United States, the United Kingdom, and Australia—have established campuses in other countries. In 2013, there were a total of 178 such campuses in 53 countries, and 52 different U.S. universities had 82 campuses in 37 different countries. At the same time, there has been an increase in international academic conferences, while academic journals have become international in scope and distribution. Within the academic world, there is an ever-increasing global exchange of academic knowledge as well as students, faculty, and researchers.

However, this global flow of cultural information is not limited to the academic world. In the not-too-distant past, most of the world had extremely limited information concerning peoples who lived outside the region of the country in which they lived, let alone those who lived in other countries or on other continents. For the vast majority of the world, people only obtained information and knowledge about other cultures from movies, TV, radio, and printed materials.

The Internet has had a dramatic impact. In 2005, it was estimated that 16 percent of the world's population used the Internet; by 2014, the number had jumped to 40 percent. Although most users are in developed countries, the percentage of users in the developing world has been increasing rapidly. Between 2005 and 2014, the percentage of users in Africa jumped from 2 percent to 19 percent. In 2015, it was estimated that 300 million new users were added.

We have entered an era in which the majority of the people of the world have unprecedented access to information. With almost 1 billion websites available, individuals have virtually unlimited access to news and data from around the world, and they can view photos, videos, and movies. As a result, we, the world's peoples, are far more aware of technological, economic, cultural, and political alternatives. The direct and indirect consequences of globalization of technology, knowledge, and access to information are just now beginning to emerge. In the first decades of the twentieth century, no one would have thought that China, India, Pakistan, and North Korea would have been capable of independently developing

Human migration is resulting in increasing social and cultural diversity in urban populations. Here Muslims pray outside the mosque in the Barbès-Rochechouart district of Paris.

weapons systems that might possibly threaten Europe or North America.

While the global economy has greatly benefited the peoples of the world, some individuals, countries, and regions within countries have materially benefited far more than others. Economic inequalities in the world are increasing. It is not just that these inequalities are increasing, but that the peoples of the world are, thanks to the advances in information technology, increasingly aware of these inequalities.

Over the past 50 years, the population of the world has grown from 2.5 billion to over 7 billion. Increasing awareness of the world's economic inequalities has resulted in the greatest migration in human history. Most of this migration is from rural to urban centers, with people seeking better economic opportunities. In 1950, the United Nations estimated that 29 percent of the world's population lived in cities. By 2005, the estimate was 49 percent or 3.2 billion. By 2030, they estimate that about 5 billion or 60 percent of the world's people will live in urban settings. In 1950, 6 of the 10 largest cities were in the United States or Europe. Today, 14 of the 16 world's largest cities are in Africa, Asia, or Latin America.

At the same time, there has been a massive migration from developing countries to developed countries: Over 220 million people live in a country other than the one in which they were born. As a result, most cities and most developed countries are becoming increasingly ethnically diverse. One does not have to travel to some remote region or another country or another continent to find "strange" and "exotic" people. Increasingly in cities throughout the world, those "other" peoples whose norms, values, and beliefs are very different from our own are living nearby and are people with whom we interact on a daily basis.

Traditional cultural behaviors—by which we mean preexisting cultural behaviors that are the main focus of most of the following chapters—are being challenged directly and indirectly by the expanding global economy, migration, and access to information and technology. What is going to be the final result? Is a common global culture going to be the result? That is highly doubtful. All we can say with any certainty is that the cultures of the peoples of the world are going to change significantly—some far more than others.

1. **Explain why society is dynamic.** The culture of a society is always changing. Our culture allows us to attempt to change our natural and social environments; it is our adaptive dimension. We act in groups to acquire the food, shelter, and other things we need from the natural environment and to protect ourselves from groups of competing humans. While all aspects of a people's culture change over time, changes in technology have the greatest effect in that a new technology can profoundly change our relationship to our natural environment as well as our social environment. The three main sources of cultural change are (1) discovery: new cultural knowledge independently discovered by members of the society through observation, experimentation, or chance; (2) innovation: the combination of two or more preexisting elements of cultural knowledge in such a manner as to create something totally new to the members of the society; and (3) borrowing: the spread or diffusion of cultural knowledge from members of one society to those of another society.

2. **Discuss how the present diversity of human culture came about.** At first all peoples were foragers sharing the same basic technology. As they migrated to different regions of the world, they modified their technology and other cultural behavior as they adapted to new natural and social environments—from the Arctic to the tropics, and from jungles and woodlands to deserts and grasslands. Later, independently of one another, peoples in widely scattered regions of the both the Old World and the New World domesticated plants and animals. As they became farmers and herders, their cultures became increasingly diverse and localized. However, farming and herding were not suitable for all areas of the world, and foragers continued to flourish. Later, new farming technologies (intensive agriculture) developed that could support increasing numbers of people and required more cooperation between people.

The result was the emergence of civilizations with, among other things, cities, metallurgy, and highly centralized governments. These civilizations developed independently in different regions of the Old World and New World, adding still another level of localized cultural diversity. Eventually the civilizations of the Old World came into contact with one another, resulting in exchanged cultural knowledge. Cultural borrowing between civilizations was limited, and these societies remained distinct from one another. In the New World, a similar process occurred. Thus, in the 1400s there were still two totally independent lines, as well as numerous distinct secondary regional lines, of cultural development; each had its own domesticated plants and animals, technologies, writing systems, religious beliefs, and other cultural knowledge.

3. **Elaborate on the development and spread of globalization.** Globalization began in 1492 with Columbus and can be divided into three stages. The first stage was the conquest of the Americas and the development of a global maritime trade network. During the three centuries that followed 1492, Europeans dramatically changed the world. The Spanish and later the Portuguese, English, French, and Dutch invaded the Americas, conquering or displacing most of the native peoples and gaining control of the majority of the land and resources. At the same time, these same European peoples were establishing a global maritime trade network that soon brought all of the peoples of the world into contact with one another, directly or indirectly. The establishment of this global trade network resulted the Columbian Exchange—the exchange of peoples, diseases, and cultural knowledge between the Old World and the New. Initially the single most important consequence was in the New World. Europeans introduced Old World diseases such as smallpox, malaria, influenza, and cholera, for which the indigenous peoples

of the Americas had no natural immunities. The result was a massive population collapse. This collapse greatly facilitated the conquest of the rich natural resources of the Americas by Europeans, but it also created a labor shortage. The colonists solved this labor problem by bringing in slave labor from sub-Saharan Africa to work the mines and plantations. The slave trade resulted in slave wars throughout most of West and Central Africa. These wars politically destabilized most of Africa. At the same time the introduction of New World crops, primarily corn and manioc, greatly expanded agriculture in Africa, resulting in population growth. Contact with Asia was limited to trade. To Europeans the trade for Asian luxury goods—silks, cottons, porcelains, teas, and spices—was important and desirable. To Asians this European trade was insignificant and had little impact on the vast majority of Asians. Until 1785, European contact with the people of Oceania was limited to a single island group: Guam. Thus while the cultures of many of the peoples of the world were directly or indirectly affected by European expansion during this period, it differed greatly from one region to another.

4. **Describe how the industrial revolution gave European powers dominance in the world.** The industrial revolution in Europe, starting in the last decades of the eighteenth century, dramatically changed the balance of power among the world's people. For the first time Europeans became the most technologically advanced people in the world. At the same time, the resident European populations in the Americas were becoming politically independent of Europe. In search of new sources of raw materials for their industry, as well as markets for the ever-increasing quantities of manufactured goods they were producing, Europeans turned to Asia, Africa, and Oceania. During the mid–nineteenth century, Britain, France, and the Netherlands expanded their political and economic control in Asia. By the end of the century, almost every country in Asia was either a colonial possession or under the political control of one of these countries. In the 1880s, Germany, Britain, France, Portugal, and Belgium

unilaterally divided Africa between their empires. Also in the last decades of the nineteenth century, Germany, Britain, France, the Netherlands, and the United States claimed dominion over the last remaining independent peoples of Oceania. The dominance of European peoples in the world was complete.

5. **Analyze the most recent stage of globalization and the global economy.** At the beginning of the twentieth century, most of the peoples of Africa, Asia, and Oceania were under the direct or indirect control of one or another European empire. The purpose of these empires was to economically benefit the home country. The colonial possessions served as controlled markets for their industrial production as well as sources of raw materials for their industries. The home country regulated the trade within and between these empires by tariffs (taxes) and quotas on goods. Global trade was thus highly fragmented. While there was global trade, the global economy—an integrated global market in which goods and services are sold at prices determined by supply and demand—did not and could not exist. Following World War II, the European empires started to disintegrate. Starting in 1947, a group of countries began negotiating agreements to eliminate tariffs and quotas on imports and exports of goods: free trade. This evolved into the World Trade Organization, which today involves the vast majority of the world's countries. At the same time, technological advances in shipping drastically lowered the cost of shipping goods while developments in communications technology allowed for virtually instantaneous communication between people throughout the world. Associated with the emergence of the global economy has been the globalization of knowledge, particularly in engineering and science, of popular culture and technology. In addition there have been massive migrations of people, both within and between countries, and the increasing integration of people into a Western capitalist economic system. The eventual cultural consequences of these dramatic changes are yet to be seen.

5

The Development of Anthropological Thought

The First Thanksgiving in 1621, a year after the Pilgrim Fathers had left the Old World (colour litho), White, Mike (Michael) (20th century)/Private Collection/© Look and Learn/Bridgeman Images

The field now called anthropology arose out of the encounter of the West with indigenous peoples of Asia, Africa, the Pacific, and the Americas. Not all encounters were as peaceful as shown in this painting of the first Thanksgiving in 1621.

After reading this chapter, you should be able to:

1 **DISCUSS** the global forces that contributed to the emergence of anthropology.

2 **DESCRIBE** the main ideas of the nineteenth-century unilineal evolutionists.

3 **UNDERSTAND** the ways American historical particularism and British functionalism challenged unilineal evolutionism.

4 **DESCRIBE** the mid–twentieth-century rebirth of evolutionary interests (neoevolutionism).

5 **DISCUSS** the main differences between the scientific and the humanistic approaches to modern anthropological thought.

6 **DESCRIBE** evolutionary psychology, materialism, interpretive anthropology, and postmodernism.

7 **ANALYZE** why contemporary anthropology has no single unifying theoretical orientation.

Anthropology developed out of the contact between Europeans and the rest of the world. Even earlier than the four voyages of Columbus in the 1490s, horses and camels took Europeans to the Middle East and parts of Asia. After Columbus's discoveries, ships carried Spaniards, Portuguese, English, French, and Russians to the two Americas and to remote islands of the Pacific Ocean. There, Europeans contacted people who did not look, act, and think in familiar ways.

A few European intellectuals struggled to understand these peoples and their "primitive" ways of living. Between the 1500s and 1800s, most European interpretations were based on their Judeo-Christian worldview. By the last few decades of the nineteenth century, advances in knowledge and the emergence of the scientific worldview resulted in new ways of understanding humanity in all our variability. Only then did anthropology become an independent field of academic study.

When it first emerged, cultural anthropology was distinct from other fields because of its focus on the peoples and cultures of other (non-European) lands and with other (non-Western) cultural traditions. Increasing contacts between Europeans and other peoples brought new knowledge and curiosities, but this alone did not lead to the formation of a new discipline. In the 1800s, the expansion of European colonies in Africa and parts of Asia produced practical reasons to learn about and understand cultural differences.

Many anthropologists of today call faraway peoples with diverse ways of living "the Other" in contrast to ourselves—the cultures of the West, as we say. Although the word is problematic (*Other* is ethnocentric—Other to whom? to us, of course), we use it in this chapter because it is a convenient shorthand for the non-Western peoples on which anthropology concentrated during its first century.

The Emergence of Anthropology

Until a few centuries ago, the vast majority of the world's people had little knowledge of any region or any culture other than the one into which they themselves were born. There were some exceptions. In the fifth century B.C.E., the Greek historian Herodotus wrote about the peoples of Persia (now Iran), northern Africa, and nearby regions. Much later, in the 1200s, the Venetian trader Marco Polo reached China (then Cathay), traveling along the ancient Silk Road that connected Rome and China since before the time of Christ. Marco Polo's descriptions of his adventures in China made his book popular among the European literary elite. However, descriptions like those of Herodotus and Marco Polo were rare and often treated skeptically. Some parts of Marco Polo's account were so surprising to his European readers that many of them did not believe his tales, such as the one about the Chinese burning black rocks as fuel.

In the 1500s, the nations of Europe began to send large numbers of explorers, traders, missionaries, and military personnel to other continents. During the next 400 years, Spain, Portugal, Britain, France, and other

European nations established formal colonies in large parts of Africa and Asia and in most of the Americas (see Chapter 4). European visitors produced hundreds of written descriptions about the customs and beliefs of Native Americans, Asians, Africans, and Pacific Islanders. From such books, articles, and letters sent back home, Europeans learned that previously unknown continents and regions were populated by people who were definitely Other in their customs and beliefs.

Between around 1500 and the mid-1800s, most Western scholars believed in the essential accuracy of the story of creation recounted in the Judeo-Christian Bible. In the biblical account, Earth was only a few thousand years old; one biblical scholar claimed that Earth was created in 4004 B.C.E. Because God created everything in only six days, humanity was the same age as Earth itself. Furthermore, the biblical creation story contained no explicit reference to any land occupied by the kinds of Others that Europeans were encountering. Who were all these people of the Americas and Africa? How could Western thinkers make sense of these peoples and their "primitive" ways of living? Did their existence challenge the worldview derived from Judeo-Christian teachings?

The surprising discovery of two unknown civilizations in the New World across the Atlantic Ocean caused debates. In 1519, Hernán Cortés encountered the Aztec civilization of southern Mexico. Temples placed atop steep-sided stepped pyramids, broad plazas, complicated agricultural fields, and, of course, all the gold and other riches of the Aztec elite classes awed Cortés and later Spaniards. Farther south, the Inca civilization existed along most of the length of the Andes Mountains. When Spaniard Francisco Pizarro and his soldiers entered the Inca capital in the early 1530s, he met a ruler whom people treated like a god. These two civilizations might have challenged ideas that Europeans had about their own superiority, except that both were soon conquered—the Aztec by Cortés in 1521 and the Inca by Pizarro in 1535.

By the mid-1800s, other puzzles had sprung up. For example, people in Europe discovered human bones and stone tools and other evidence suggesting that ancient peoples had lived on their own continent. In Germany's Neander Valley, a partial skeleton of a humanlike creature was unearthed. Were the Neandertal bones human, and, if so, what did they mean for our understanding of humanity and, especially, ourselves?

Europeans in the 1800s noted that many ancient tools were made of chipped stone. They later noticed a regular sequence of toolmaking: the earliest were made of stone, some later tools were smelted of bronze, and still later iron was used. This sequence came to be known as the Three Ages: the Stone Age, Bronze Age, and Iron Age. Each age had a greater variety of tools than the preceding one, and the materials used in each stage seemed superior to those of the earlier stage. It looked like Europe also once contained simpler, cruder peoples.

In North America, in the early 1800s European settlers of Ohio and surrounding states commented on the existence of large earthen mounds, wondering who could have constructed these ancient monuments—certainly not the ancestors of the "Indians" who then lived in these regions! (Of course, future work showed conclusively that Native Americans made the mounds; their cultures proved to be about as complicated as those of Europe itself.)

Until the mid-1800s, the Judeo-Christian worldview framed most interpretations of peoples in other continents and archaeological remains in Europe itself. Perhaps those Others of other lands were the descendants of Noah's wayward son, Ham. Maybe they were remnants of one of the lost tribes of Israel, as some scholars claimed about the Polynesians. Possibly, the Devil buried the Neander bones and prehistoric artifacts to undermine believers' faith. Whatever the specific explanation, the customs and beliefs of people who lived long ago or far away generally were interpreted in terms of the biblical account of world creation and human history.

In the mid–nineteenth century, evidence from geology and biology informed a new understanding of the world. These findings led to a whole new worldview about Earth, life in general, and human life in particular, which is now accepted by the majority of scholars from all continents. Geology and biology helped bring humanity within the grasp of the *scientific* worldview, in which human beings and human cultures are understood to be the result of some process that is entirely natural.

In geology, James Hutton and Charles Lyell demonstrated that Earth itself was not merely thousands of years old, but many millions (today, geologists believe our planet is about 4.5 billion years old). In biology, Charles Darwin revolutionized popular ideas about life on Earth. Rather than each plant and animal being separately made by the Creator, Darwin proposed that one species arose out of another by an entirely natural process. He documented this process in his 1859 book, *On the Origin of Species.*

Darwin's natural process is *evolution.* Evolution means that over long periods of time, one species changes into a new species or into several new species.

Some species die out altogether, leaving no descendants. But often, before its own extinction, a species changes (evolves) into one or more new species. Thus, multiple new species evolve and eventually change into other species. Given enough time, all the diversity of life on Earth can be explained by this process of natural transformation. From simple beginnings, the natural process of evolution created all the forms of life that surround us today. All it takes are the slow accumulation of changes and time—millions and millions of years of time. When geology demonstrated the age of Earth, it showed that our world was old enough for diverse and complicated life forms to evolve from simple beginnings.

Darwin's main impact was on biology and the field now called *paleoanthropology*. Darwin established the possibility that the human species evolved from an apelike ancestor, and his idea was confirmed in the twentieth century (see Chapter 1).

Darwin's ideas about origins and changes in the natural world also influenced how Western intellectuals viewed human *cultural* as well as *biological* existence. If biological life forms evolved, then could cultural forms also have arisen through a process of gradual change? Simple forms of organic life had transformed into more complex forms of life. Analogously, in human existence, some scholars reasoned that more complex ways of life had developed out of earlier, simpler ways of life.

During these same centuries in Europe and North America, the Enlightenment (Age of Reason) and the industrial revolution led to belief in progress—the notion that human life has gotten better and better over the course of many centuries. The idea of progress in the realms of technology and ideas led to optimism about the human future.

In summary, by the nineteenth century a few scholars who wanted to understand human cultures had access to two major kinds of information: (1) written accounts left by Westerners who visited other lands, including colonies of European nations; and (2) tools that ancient, long-disappeared peoples from Europe and North America had left in the earth. Influenced by Darwin's theories and the intellectual climate of the Enlightenment, scholars assimilated ideas about origins, evolution, and progress. They reasoned that there is a relationship between the various peoples in the written accounts and the ancient people who made

the prehistoric tools and monuments. The long-disappeared prehistoric peoples of Europe and the Americas were similar to the peoples described in the accounts of Western visitors to other continents. Just as stone tools were the earliest form of technology, so "primitive" peoples still alive in the nineteenth century were living representatives of earlier forms of culture. They thought that American "Indians" and many Others were still living in the Stone Age.

Nineteenth-Century Unilineal Evolutionism

Interested scholars began to investigate and theorize about how and why cultures had changed over many centuries and millennia. Like plants and animals, cultures had evolved. The earliest simple (so-called primitive) cultures had given rise to ever more complex (advanced) cultures. This cultural evolution represented progress or development: Later cultures were, in some *objective* sense, superior to earlier cultures. (Here, "objective" means that there is a universal standard by which superiority can be judged, an assumption that later anthropologists questioned.)

The approach of these early anthropologists is called **unilineal evolutionism**. At the time, founders of this approach could not have known that future generations of anthropologists would challenge most of their goals, methods, and conclusions.

This theory, briefly stated, holds that as human cultures evolved, they passed through a series of stages. Examples of each stage could be found in the peoples described in all those written accounts of surviving primitives and also in the artifacts that prehistoric peoples had left behind, in or on the ground. Although nineteenth-century Western civilization represented the highest stage of cultural evolution, peoples living on other continents were cultures that had survived from earlier stages. The cultures of these peoples had survived into the present because they had changed at slower rates than the cultures of more advanced peoples. Such peoples were living relics from humanity's distant past. Their cultures were "survivals" of earlier cultural stages—their way of life had not changed much from humanity's deep prehistoric past.

For example, the evolutionists thought that survivals of the earliest stages of cultural evolution still existed in remote places, like Australia and Polynesia. In 1877, the American Lewis Henry Morgan published *Ancient Society*, a book that integrated information compiled from written accounts of peoples from all continents. Morgan defined and labeled the stages.

unilineal evolutionism Nineteenth-century theory holding that all human ways of life pass through a similar sequence of stages in their development.

AUSTRALIAN ABORIGINES, PREPARING A MEAL.

Unilineal evolutionists believed that the world's cultures evolved through sequential stages, with peoples from various regions arrayed along a continuum from simple to more complex cultures. To document their stages, they used written records to find "survivals" of the earliest stages. They placed people like Australian Aborigines in the earliest stage: "Savagery."

He placed the Australian Aborigines and the Polynesians in "Savagery," as he labeled the earliest (simplest) stage. Remnants of later, intermediate stages still existed in the people of the Fiji islands of the Pacific and the Iroquois Native Americans. Both cultures are living representatives of the middle stage of cultural evolution, which Morgan called "Barbarism." Elsewhere, later evolutionary stages exist: the Incas of the Andes, the Aztecs of Mexico, the Chinese, Koreans, and Japanese all had evolved to "Civilization." Thus, Morgan reasoned, the earliest cultures were like the Australians and Polynesians, later ones resembled contemporary Fijians and Iroquois, and the Inca, Chinese, and some other ancient civilizations represented the earliest human civilizations. The highest stage was Western civilization. By comparing peoples who exemplified all the stages, evolutionists believed they could reconstruct the nature of the various stages and figure out what had led one stage to progress to the next.

The unilineal evolutionists are usually considered the first cultural anthropologists. They had a subject matter that was by and large separate from that of other disciplines—the cultures and societies of peoples who lived in foreign lands (the Others). They had a reasonably coherent objective: to reconstruct and understand the stages through which human cultures had traveled along the road to civilization. They used a methodology that was then in its infancy—comparing and contrasting diverse peoples to discover the nature of the stages and the relationships between them. In brief, cultural anthropology became an academic discipline because it had its own subject matter, objectives, and methods.

Consider another example of unilineal evolutionism. In 1871 the Englishman E. B. Tylor published the landmark book *Primitive Culture*. In it, he investigated the origins and development of religious beliefs. Tylor argued that religious beliefs originated out of peoples' attempts to explain certain experiences. For example, immediately after someone dies, the physical body still exists even though the life of the person has ended. What explains the difference between a living and a dead person?

Being ignorant of the actual causes of death, early humans reasoned that living people have a spiritual essence (a soul) that animates or gives life to the physical body. When the soul leaves the body, the person stops breathing and moving and, hence, dies. Also, people experience dreams, trances, and visions in which they see images of all kinds of things and events. Reasoning logically, but falsely, early peoples concluded that the things in dreams and visions are real and that the events actually occurred. Tylor called the form of religion that this reasoning produces *animism*. Peoples of this early stage believe in spiritual beings, including nature spirits living in mountains, trees, water, heavenly bodies, and animals; spirits of deceased persons (ghosts); spirits that cause illness; spirits that possess someone and make them insane; and a multitude of other spirits.

Tylor thought animism was the earliest, primeval form of religion from which all others arose. He reasoned that living peoples who still had animistic beliefs represent survivals of this earliest stage of religion. Therefore, scholars could learn about the earliest form of religion by studying living peoples who were still animistic.

How did animism evolve into later forms of religion? Over time, early peoples reasoned that some spirits were more important or influential than others. Eventually, people came to believe that such spirits held higher positions. They became gods of various things and activities such as gods of sun, moon, sky, rain, earth, clans, war, agriculture, love, fertility, and so forth. There were many such gods, as well known from Greek and Roman mythology and Hinduism of ancient India. This stage of religion is called *polytheism*, meaning religions that include a belief in many gods, each with his, her, or its own sphere of influence.

What about *monotheism*, the belief that there is only one god? This form was represented by the Judeo-Christian heritage of the West. It was also familiar from Islam, which had been known to Europeans for more than a millennium. Tylor argued that monotheism evolved when one of the gods of polytheism acquired dominance over other gods. Eventually, over centuries, the other gods came to be seen as false gods or not to exist at all. Not surprisingly, Tylor believed that monotheism was the most evolved form of religion.

Morgan's and Tylor's stages illustrate the main ideas of unilineal evolutionists. Examples of each stage survived in many scattered places—in fact, on all continents. One stage evolved into another—not just in one region or continent but in many. For example, animistic religions evolved into polytheistic religions among many peoples, and, in turn, polytheism evolved into monotheism several times. The fact that the same sequence of stages occurred again and again among widely scattered peoples seemed to imply that human cultures developed in regular, recurrent patterns. If so, then human cultural evolution followed some sort of law, meaning that similar processes were resulting in similar changes, analogous to Darwinian evolution.

A Science of Culture?

Following this logic, most unilineal evolutionists thought that the new field of anthropology could and should be a science. They believed the development of culture could be explained much as biology explains the evolution of living organisms. Tylor (1871, p. 2) wrote that human "thoughts, wills, and actions accord with laws as definite as those which govern the motion of waves, the combinations of acids and bases, and the growth of plants and animals."

Few anthropologists of today agree with this statement because, unlike waves and chemicals, humans have active minds of their own. Many contemporary thinkers do not believe that Tylor's "science of culture" is possible at all. Some do not think it is even desirable, because one kind of human should not treat other kinds of humans as objects for study.

The unilineal evolutionists made significant contributions to the development of anthropology. Thanks largely to their writings, by the early twentieth century anthropology became a full-fledged academic discipline. Scholarly fields that investigated various aspects of humankind were already established in European and U.S. universities as departments or schools of religion, theology, art, philosophy, classics, history, anatomy, and so forth. But the discipline focusing on the physical and cultural diversity of humanity was not recognized until the last decades of the 1800s. In the United States, the first anthropology course was taught in 1879 at the University of Rochester. In 1886, the first anthropology department was founded at the University of Pennsylvania. It was followed near the turn of the century by university departments at Columbia, Harvard, Chicago, and California (Berkeley).

Anthropological Thought in the Early Twentieth Century

Despite their contributions to the foundation of the discipline now called anthropology, many assumptions of the unilineal evolutionists were mistaken. In the early decades of the twentieth century, most of their ideas were discredited—partly because their methods were flawed, much of their information was erroneous, and their overall theory grew out of ethnocentric views. In the English-speaking countries, anthropologists in America and Great Britain set out in different directions, as we now discuss.

Historical Particularism in the United States (1900–1940s)

At the end of the 1800s and for the next three or four decades, the American anthropologist Franz Boas and his students questioned the methods and the findings of unilineal evolutionism. Boas was so influential in the United States that he is often called the father of American anthropology. In his view, each culture has its own separate past. Because each culture was affected by almost everything that had happened to it during its history, each is unique. The similarities that unilineal evolutionists had used to place various cultures into the same stage are mostly superficial.

This approach is usually called **historical particularism** (or **historicism**). Notice that if it is true that each culture is the *distinctive* product of its *unique* history, then it is difficult to identify any general principles that affect all cultures. Rather, each culture must be studied on its own terms.

Clearly, the unilineal evolutionists did not study each culture "on its own terms." In making their comparisons and formulating their stages, they imposed their own terms (e.g., complexity, progress, stages) on other cultures. Take the notion of complexity, for example. In the realm of technology, most people might agree that guns and bullets are more complex than bows and arrows, which, in turn, are more complex than spears and throwing sticks. But what does "complex" mean when applied to other customs and beliefs, like those about marriage, political organization, or religion? In what sense are the religions Tylor called monotheistic more complex than animistic ones? Boas held that such features are merely *different* from culture to culture. By any *objective* criterion, one form of religion does not represent progress over another.

There were other problems also. For example, Japan ranked as a civilization, but its indigenous religion was Shinto, which would be considered animistic. In a similar fashion, Polynesians had a complex system of governance, but Morgan placed them in "Savagery" because of the names they called their relatives and their marriage practices. The coexistence of "low-stage" traits in "high-stage" cultures, and vice versa, suggests that there was more than one line of cultural evolution.

Furthermore, Boas realized that the evolutionists' stages derived from ethnocentric assumptions: Evolutionists placed their own culture at the top of the (imaginary) cultural ladder; searched writings to find many Others whose cultures represented "earlier stages"; gave the stages labels like "Barbarism"; slotted particular cultures into their own preconceived classifications; and then concluded that they were discovering the laws of cultural development using the methods of science.

As an example of Boas's point, consider Lewis Henry Morgan, who assigned various peoples into stages he called "savages," "barbarians," and "civilized." But many literate, civilized people—including Japanese, Koreans, and Chinese—labeled Morgan's own people as "barbarians." Is monotheism more evolved than animism or polytheism? Perhaps, but you are more likely to think so if your own religion is monotheistic. If your criteria for defining evolution are ethnocentric, then your concept of stages is almost useless. You have not discovered actual stages of progress. You have invented them and then imposed the stages you yourself made up on the cultures of Others. (As a thought-provoking side comment, notice how often you can find unilineal thinking in scholarly writings as well as in popular media.)

The historical particularists also claimed that it is difficult to place the customs and beliefs of *different* peoples into the *same* stage of progress. In most cases, the customs and beliefs of widely scattered peoples only appear to be similar. For example, in Tylor's scheme, the ancient religions of both Greece and Polynesia had many gods and so would be classified as polytheistic. Tylor defined a stage of religion, *polytheism*, and placed peoples who believed in many gods into that stage. What would the ancient Greeks and Polynesians—not

historical particularism (historicism) Theoretical orientation emphasizing that each culture is the unique product of all the influences to which it has been subjected in its past, making cross-cultural generalizations questionable.

to mention Hindus—have said about such comparisons? Likewise, Muslims, Jews, and Christians are all monotheistic, but is this single feature of their religions enough to place them into the same stage? How would members of these faiths feel about this?

In short, to say that the customs and beliefs of two or more Other cultures are the same or similar because they look the same to us is to ignore a host of differences between these cultures. The Greeks and Polynesians had different gods, who did different kinds of things to and for people. For the historicists, this is enough to consider them different forms of religion. Carried to its extreme, of course, this means that every religion has a different form from every other religion, which makes *every* religion unique. You could apply the same logic to individuals, of course: We are all unique, but aren't some individuals more alike than others?

To understand a culture, therefore, Boas thought we must study it *individually*, not as a representative of some hypothetical stage. Anthropologists must free themselves from preconceived ideas and assumptions and give up speculative schemes and the fruitless search for laws of cultural progress.

Boas believed the unilineal evolutionists made errors partly because of their ethnocentrism. He also noted that the ways the evolutionists investigated other cultures—their methods—led them astray. Today, nineteenth-century evolutionists often are called "armchair anthropologists" because they themselves had not lived among any "savages" and "barbarians" themselves. (Louis Henry Morgan, who actually studied the Iroquois Native Americans firsthand, was a rare exception.) Instead, for the most part, they relied on descriptive accounts written by people who too often were untrained, who presented their impressions rather than hard facts, and who were biased in their perceptions of Others.

Boas thought that professional anthropologists must abandon the comforts of their offices and engage in firsthand interactions with members of Other cultures. The main need of the young field of anthropology was more factual information about these cultures, not unsupported speculations made in faculty offices. Anthropologists themselves must conduct *ethnographic fieldwork*. This was the only way they could be somewhat confident that they had their facts correct. And only after anthropologists were sure that their facts were correct should they begin to even try to make general statements or to theorize about cultures. Boas, in brief, wanted more and better descriptions of more cultures.

These descriptions require that fieldworkers remain objective as they observe and record the customs and beliefs of other cultures. Fieldworkers must enter the communities and lives of Others with an open mind. If they go into their research with preconceived notions, their observations and writings are likely to report things consistent with their own preconceptions and not to notice or report on contradictions. While doing their research, fieldworkers should be cultural relativists (Chapter 2). While living among Others, we must temporarily suspend our own values, morality, standards of hygiene, ways of interpreting actions, and so forth. Not only does a relativistic attitude help us fit into the community, but it also minimizes the chances that we will misinterpret or misunderstand people just because we see them through the filter of our own culture's perceptions and biases.

Boas himself conducted firsthand fieldwork among two Native American peoples: the Inuit (Eskimo) and the Kwakiutl of the Northwest Coast of North America. He sent many of his students at Columbia University out for fieldwork experiences, including Margaret Mead, who became famous for her 1928 book, *Coming of Age in Samoa*. For decades, Margaret Mead was the one anthropologist most people knew about. Again and again, she discussed the dramatic differences among the peoples of the world—so much so that the idea that there is a "human nature" became widely questioned. Mead also was one of the intellectual founders of modern feminism, because she emphasized the multitude of differences in how cultures regard relations between the sexes.

Today, living among and participating in the lives of the people under study is the main method by which one becomes a professional anthropologist and acquires a positive reputation in the discipline. The emphasis on ethnographic fieldwork is one of Boas's lasting legacies.

In addition to learning more about cultures and their diversity, fieldwork offers other benefits. The traditional customs, beliefs, and languages of many of the world's peoples had already disappeared because of diseases, genocide, assimilation, and other effects of contacts and interactions. Surviving cultures and languages were vanishing or changing rapidly. Boas believed it was the duty of anthropologists to record disappearing traditions before they were gone forever. Many students of Boas, like A. L. Kroeber and Robert Lowie, did fieldwork among Native American peoples, whose cultures they believed were especially endangered.

Finally, Boas and his students conducted a lot of research to show that biological differences and cultural differences are largely independent of each other; that is, the culture of a human group is a product of social learning and tradition, not of genetic heritage (see Chapter 2).

Margaret Mead was Franz Boas's most famous student. During her long career, she worked in Samoa, Bali (Indonesia), and Manus in the Admiralty Islands, where this photo was taken in 1953.

In sum, historical particularism made four enduring contributions to modern anthropology:

- It discredited the overly speculative schemes of the unilineal evolutionists.
- It insisted that fieldwork is the primary means of acquiring reliable information.
- It imparted the idea that cultural relativism as a methodological principle is essential for the most accurate understanding of another culture.
- It demonstrated and popularized the notion that cultural differences and biological differences have little to do with each other.

These contributions shaped modern cultural anthropology.

Historical particularism gave rise to other movements in the first half of the twentieth century. One of the most influential is called **configurationalism**.

One of Boas's students was Ruth Benedict, whose 1934 book *Patterns of Culture* is considered a classic. Benedict argued that, from the vast array of humanly possible cultures, each particular culture develops only a limited number of "patterns" or "configurations" that dominate the thinking and responses of its members. Each culture develops a distinctive set of feelings and motivations that orient the thoughts and behaviors of its members. These configurations give each culture a distinctive style, and the thoughts and actions of its members reflect its configurations.

configurationalism Theoretical idea that each culture historically develops its own unique thematic patterns around which beliefs, values, and behaviors are oriented.

For example, Benedict wrote that the Kwakiutl of the Northwest Coast of North America are individualistic, competitive, and intemperate. This configuration affects Kwakiutl customs. They stage ceremonies known as *potlatches*, in which one kin group gives away enormous quantities of goods to another. The aim is to shame the rival group, for if the rival is unable to return the presentations on certain occasions, its members suffer a loss of prestige. To avoid this condition, the recipient group is obliged to return gifts of even greater value. The whole complex of behaviors connected to the potlatch reflects the cultural configuration of the Kwakiutl—the Kwakiutl are so caught up in the prestige motivation that groups will give away large quantities of material wealth to achieve the value they place on prestige. To describe the Kwakiutl, Benedict used the label "Dionysian," after the Greek god known for his drinking, partying, and other excesses.

Benedict contrasted the Kwakiutl configuration to the Zuni of the North American Southwest. Zuni control their emotions, she claimed. They are moderate, modest, stoical, orderly, and restrained in their behavior. They do not boast or attempt to rise above their peers but are social and cooperative. This "Apollonian" cultural theme, as Benedict called it, permeates all of Zuni life. Unlike a Kwakiutl leader, a Zuni man does not seek status; indeed, a leadership role practically has to be forced on him. So, according to Benedict, each culture has its unique patterns and themes, which makes it possible for a megalomaniac in culture A to be a model citizen in culture B.

Although modern anthropologists agree that different cultures emphasize different themes or patterns, most believe Benedict overemphasized the effect of culture on the thoughts, feelings, and actions of its members. It is simplistic to characterize whole cultures in such terms, such as that Kwakiutl are prone to excess, whereas Zuni are moderate in all things. Rather, the personality and character of the members of a culture are highly variable, and the relationship between cultural knowledge and the individual behavior is complicated (see Chapter 2).

Historical particularism changed the way anthropologists thought about culture and conducted research, but it has limitations. Think about the claim that each culture is unique—like no other. Certainly, those interested in cultural differences will easily find them and

can legitimately claim that no two cultures are alike. At some level, the view that each culture is unique is correct. However, so is the claim that no two individuals brought up within the same culture are exactly alike. Yet they *are* alike in some ways. Just as it is true that in some ways cultures are unique, in other ways a given culture does have things in common with some other cultures. More generally speaking, there are similarities as well as differences between ways of life. Historical particularists tended to overlook the similarities and to neglect the investigation of factors that might explain them.

Consider also the claim that, because each culture is the product of its particular history, one cannot generalize about the causes of cultural differences. According to historicism, there are no "general" causes of cultures. Rather, there are multiple causes, whose relative importance is difficult to disentangle. Besides, causation varies from people to people, depending on their particular history.

Others disagree. To say that the natural environment is important in culture X, religion in Y, values in Z, and so forth is to say little more than that everything is related to most everything else. However, it is possible that some influences are more important than other influences in all or most human populations. For example, some scholars claim that how people interact with their natural environment is *generally* more important than religion or values in causing people to live the way they do.

By the 1940s and 1950s, the interests of many American anthropologists returned to investigating general principles of human cultural existence. Meanwhile, another way of studying human societies and cultural diversity developed in Europe.

British Functionalism (1920s–1960s)

At about the same time that historicism was popular in the United States, a different approach developed in Great Britain. Generally called **functionalism**, its main tenet was that social and cultural features should be explained primarily by their useful functions to the people and to the society—that is, by the benefits they confer on individuals and groups. Because humans are social beings who live in families, communities, and other kinds of organized groups, most aspects of their culture and society serve to help individuals meet their needs and/ or to contribute to the maintenance of the society itself.

Bronislaw Malinowski was a leading British functionalist. He emphasized the needs of individuals. To Malinowski, the main purpose of culture is to serve human biological, psychological, and social needs. What are these needs? Most biological needs are rather obvious: nutrition, shelter, protection from enemies, maintenance

---

functionalism Theoretical orientation that analyzes cultural elements in terms of their useful effects to individuals or to the persistence of the whole society.

of health, and—if the society is to persist—biological reproduction. In addition, humans also have psychological and social needs such as love and affection, security, self-expression, and a sense of belonging. The purpose of culture is to fulfill these needs. Unlike other animals, humans have few inborn instructions or instincts that tell us how to meet our needs. Instead, as we grow up in our culture, we learn the behaviors, social rules, values, and ways of perceiving the world that guide our actions and our thoughts (see Chapter 2).

Some parts of culture meet individual needs directly, such as knowledge of how to acquire food or make shelter. Other aspects function to raise and socialize new generations of group members, such as enculturation practices and family life. Still others encourage people to adhere to group values and rules that make cooperation possible, such as religious beliefs and practices and creative arts. Thus, even if a given cultural feature does not *directly* serve individual needs, it still *indirectly* contributes to the maintenance of cultural knowledge and behavioral patterns without which human survival would be difficult.

One cannot deny that an important function of culture is to help people meet their needs. However, in some kinds of societies, some individuals and groups have their needs (and wants) met more completely than others. Furthermore, culture itself can create perceived needs (you may think you need something when you merely desire it). And the social and economic conditions under which people live make them need some things that people of other times and places did not need. If you were an attorney in Britain or a college student in India in the 1970s, you would not need a computer, but you would today, if you are to be successful. Finally, it is likely that perceived needs grow as the capacity for meeting them increases, as all economists know. Thus, the idea of needs is more of a problem than it appears: Needs do vary from place to place and time to time.

Also, if we are interested in cultural differences, then the idea that the main function of culture is to satisfy needs does not take us very far. If *needs* do not include *wants*—what we would like to have to make us happy, such as material wealth and social status—then needs are pretty much the same among all peoples. Also, people living in different times and places satisfy their needs in a variety of ways. By themselves, universal needs alone cannot explain cultural differences.

For example, eating beef will satisfy the nutritional need for protein. However, many devout Hindus and Buddhists not only refuse to consume cattle flesh but also maintain an entirely vegetarian diet because of their religious beliefs. Most contemporary vegetarians and vegans do not consume meat because of health or moral considerations and/or because their diet is an important part of their self-identity. A human body does not need meat to maintain health, so the universal need for protein cannot explain the many ways in which people acquire protein. To generalize this point: The basic needs of humans are the same everywhere and can be satisfied in such a variety of ways that needs alone cannot explain cultural diversity. At the very least, differences in the natural environment that provides need-satisfying resources must be taken into account.

A. R. Radcliffe-Brown was another influential British functionalist. Instead of emphasizing the needs of individuals, Radcliffe-Brown focused on the needs of societies. For him, maintaining orderly social relationships—between family members, friends, members of the same village or town, leaders and followers, and the like—is the main function that must be met if societies are to exist and persist. He imagined that a human society is like a living organism in which each organ has a function to fulfill that contributes to the life of the whole body. In studying a body, a physiologist not only looks at each organ individually but also considers its role in the life process of the whole organism. Just as organisms cannot stay alive for long unless their organs function properly, so a society cannot persist unless its various institutions play their proper roles in social life. Radcliffe-Brown felt that most customs and beliefs a people share help their society remain in *equilibrium* (a steady state, with not too much conflict or rapid change).

From today's perspective, it is clear that societies are not analogous to living organisms. Individuals have minds and motives of their own, unlike cells and organs. And few societies are in equilibrium for very long. Societies change constantly. The rate of change and the direction of change vary, and functionalism had relatively little of lasting value to say about change.

Despite these and other shortcomings, British functionalists made enduring contributions to anthropology. Emphasizing the importance of social relationships between individuals and of living in organized groups leads us to pay more attention to how groups are organized and how they relate to one another. Radcliffe-Brown's emphasis on social equilibrium led us to pay more attention to how the parts of a society and culture fit together and therefore made us pay more attention to cultural integration.

The Fieldwork Tradition

Like the American historicists, the British functionalists helped establish the tradition of firsthand

Bronislaw Malinowski was an influential British functionalist. He is best known for his ethnographies about the Trobriand Islanders. Like the American Franz Boas, Malinowski insisted that cultural anthropologists conduct firsthand fieldwork themselves.

fieldwork. Malinowski is famous mainly because of his fieldwork and ethnographic writings about the Trobriand Islanders of the western Pacific. Some of his books, like *Argonauts of the Western Pacific* and *The Sexual Life of Savages,* are ethnographic classics. Not only is fieldwork the best means of obtaining reliable information about a people, but it is also a necessary part of the training of anthropologists, Malinowski believed. We cannot claim to understand people, or the diverse cultures in which people of various places grow up, until we have immersed ourselves in the experience of some culture other than our own.

Malinowski thought the main objective of fieldwork is to see the culture as an insider to the culture sees it. In an often-quoted passage from his 1922 ethnography *Argonauts of the Western Pacific,* Malinowski (1922, p. 25) wrote:

> [T]he final goal, of which an Ethnographer [*sic*] should never lose sight . . . is, briefly, to grasp the native's point of view, his relation to life, to realize *his* vision of *his* world.

This idea of what fieldwork is all about remains influential—though controversial—today.

To "grasp the native's point of view," fieldworkers usually make visits that last at least a year, and they often return to the community many times. Also, fieldwork involves deep involvement in the daily lives of the people. Where possible, fieldworkers should master the native language, live with the local people, participate in games and voyages, become familiar with how members of families relate to one another, observe lots of ceremonies and rituals, record myths and legends, and—generally—learn all they can about a culture from interacting with people and participating in their lives. This way of learning about another culture is generally called *participant observation,* and it is the most important method for many fieldworkers (see Chapter 6).

Because of the influence of early twentieth-century anthropologists like Boas and Malinowski, today the fieldwork experience is an essential part of the graduate training of almost all cultural anthropologists. Fieldwork demonstrates that you can *do* anthropology yourself as well as *study* the anthropological research and theories of your teachers and other scholars. It demonstrates that you can contribute original knowledge about some group of Others; and in most colleges and universities, making new contributions is essential for success in one's academic career.

Until 20 or 30 years ago, most fieldworkers were from either North America or western Europe. So, most ethnographies describing the ways of life of diverse peoples were written by Western anthropologists, who for the most part were trained in Western universities. But anthropology today has gone global. People of many nationalities representing many cultures are now

As we've seen, anthropology arose after western Europeans came into contact with peoples of Africa, Asia, Australia, the Americas, and the Pacific. For nearly a century, the theoretical and field research of most Western anthropologists occurred with little regard for how the peoples among whom we did fieldwork would react to the research and its publication. For the most part, the neglect of local reactions was not because researchers did not care about the people, but because so few were literate enough to read Western writings.

Today, anthropology itself has globalized. Countries whose peoples we traditionally study have universities with their own anthropologists who often write about their own country or even their own people. National or regional governments are sometimes reluctant to allow Western fieldworkers to come in. Many people who appear in our ethnographies now read what we write and are often critical of our findings and, occasionally, of how they are used. Some are resentful because their customs, beliefs, opinions, and voices are represented by outsiders rather than by themselves. Some believe (usually mistakenly) that anthropologists grow wealthy by writing about them, while they are paid relatively little when they assist us.

One issue for a global anthropology is *who benefits*? Until recently, the main readership of most anthropological writing was other anthropologists or students. Anthropology was mainly the study of Others, and such study was valuable for its own sake. Ideally, it taught values of mutual understanding as well as educating people about cultural variations in time and space. This remains an important goal of anthropology today. However, more anthropologists believe that the benefits of their research should be more widespread and should filter out to those whose lives and cultures we research and write about. Among other things, this desire includes an argument for clearer, jargon-free writing, but too often such writing is undervalued in the colleges and universities in which most research-oriented anthropologists work. Also, more work should be translated into more languages, which is very expensive.

Another issue for global anthropology is *representation:* Who is best qualified to describe the culture of a people, to translate their customs and beliefs into a form that is intelligible to outsiders? Some anthropological scholars from the West were reluctant to give up their claim to represent Others, even when educated Others challenge their findings. In his 2004 book *Native Anthropology,* Takami Kuwayama notes that because the most prestigious universities are in western Europe and North America, representations of Others sometimes come from ways researchers are rewarded.

At present, if you are to speak authoritatively (i.e., have others take your views seriously), you must publish. You must write scholarly books and find someone to publish them. Better, you must get your articles published in scholarly journals that are peer reviewed (i.e., the article is critically analyzed by others who are recognized experts in the subject, who decide whether your article is meritorious enough to be published). Many native anthropologists who have jobs in their own countries have less access to the world of publishing than scholars in Western universities. Therefore, the information they gather and the opinions they offer may be underrepresented in the global community of anthropological scholars. The fact that English has become the primary language of discussion does not help the situation.

Finally, in publishing as in other realms of life, sometimes it is who you know rather than what you say that determines whether something you write appears in print. The Internet is widely accessible in most nations, but the general culture of academia tends to devalue information posted there unless it appears in an online peer-reviewed journal. Despite progress in achieving a worldwide anthropology, obstacles to inclusion remain in many parts of the world.

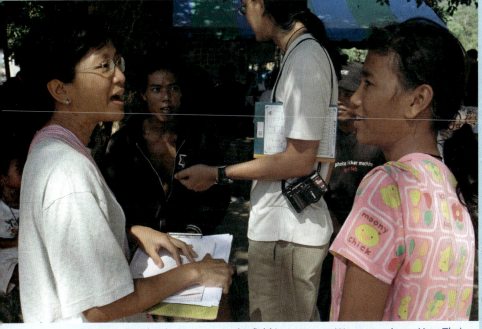

Aroon Thaewchatturat/Alamy

Anthropology has become a popular field in some non-Western nations. Here Thai anthropologist Naruman Hinshiranan talks to a woman in Phang Nga Province in southwest Thailand.

anthropologists, interested in writing about the very people whom Western ethnographers used to monopolize. This has led to new issues, and in the future new ways of representing Other cultures are likely to emerge (see the Global Challenges and Opportunities feature).

For many anthropologists, fieldwork is personally transformative. Even anthropologists have trouble overcoming their own biases and looking at Others relativistically instead of through ethnocentric lenses. After being intensively exposed to another way of living, we often come away with a different perspective on ourselves. Fieldwork is the closest most of us come to dissolving the differences between us and Others. This is another reason most professional anthropologists conduct fieldwork—that, and the fact that most of us like it.

Mid–Twentieth Century: Rebirth of Evolutionism

The objections of the historical particularists to unilineal evolutionism were powerful, but other evolutionary approaches came back into fashion in the 1940s and endure today. The problems with the old (unilineal) evolutionism were its flawed assumptions and inadequate methods. Some mid–twentieth-century scholars thought they had corrected the assumptions and adopted more sophisticated methods. They developed a "new evolutionism," or **neoevolutionism**, so called because their objectives were much the same as the objectives of the nineteenth-century evolutionists, but their methods and specific theories were different. Two North American anthropologists were especially influential.

Writing mostly in the 1940s–1960s, Leslie White thought that the nineteenth-century evolutionists got some things right after all. Some components of human cultural existence have, in fact, improved over the centuries, namely the technologies (tools, technical knowledge, skills) that people use to acquire nature's resources. Improved how? Improved in the sense that people with better technologies are able to harness more energy per person per year. That is, some technologies are more productive or efficient than others, so people can produce more useful products with them. Cultural evolution is an *objective* fact, White argued. It occurs as the amount of energy harnessed

from the natural environment increases. In principle, cultural evolution can be defined without resorting to ethnocentric assumptions. *If true*, White overcame one of historical particularism's main objections.

White took his argument further. Over long periods of time, as humans discovered and invented new technologies that increased the quantity of energy captured, changes in the organization of societies and in the ideas and beliefs of their members followed. To use White's own terminology, improvements in the "technological system" drive changes in the "social system" and the "ideological system." Generally speaking, over time, human social and ideological systems have grown more complex. What does "complex" mean? It means that the scale (size) of societies increases dramatically, occupational specialization develops, large-scale trade and long-distance exchange grow, political centralization occurs, and inequality between classes increases.

White believed that improvements in technology and the resulting increase in the ability of people to harness energy *caused* most important changes in human cultures. For example, he argued that the transition to agriculture *caused* civilization to develop in some regions, and the discovery of how to harness the energy of coal *caused* the rise of industrial society in Great Britain. For this reason, White is often called a *technological determinist*, meaning he believed that technology causes (determines) almost everything else in culture that is important. What causes changes in aspects of culture like family organization and political structures? To White, these were part of the social system, and they largely responded to changes in technology. What about aspects of culture like religion, philosophy, worldview, and art? To White, these were part of the ideological system, and by and large they changed to reflect and justify changes in the social system.

In summary, White boldly generalized that as technology develops, the social system evolves to take advantage of the increased energy available, and new ideologies arise to explain and justify the new technological and social arrangements. So, cultural evolution is in fact a regular, patterned process about which anthropologists can generalize by making objective comparisons and contrasts. Each culture is *not* entirely unique, and we can legitimately provide explanations that do not depend on the "native's point of view." White agreed with E. B. Tylor that anthropology should be "the science of culture," and White made this the title of a book he published in 1949.

Julian Steward was a contemporary of White who agreed that how a people acquire natural resources and cope with their environment is the most important part of their way of life. But, more than White, Steward's theory emphasized the natural environment,

neoevolutionism New evolutionism, or the mid–twentieth-century rebirth of evolutionary approaches to studying and explaining culture.

which provided food, fuel, water, and other necessary resources. In his study of the Numic peoples of the Great Basin, Steward investigated how food resources were distributed seasonally and geographically. He argued that much of the culture of the Shoshone and other Numic peoples could be explained by how they scheduled their work and movements to take advantage of the availability of food. Steward's ideas eventually gave rise to the modern field of *ecological anthropology*, which studies how humans relate to the environment. We discuss the general results of such studies in Chapter 7.

Men like White and Steward made attempts to explain culture in scientific terms respectable again. For White, the general principle needed to explain cultural evolution is technological determinism. For Steward, the complicated interactions between humans and the natural environments are the most important causes of cultural differences and similarities. White and Steward are two of the most important intellectual ancestors of the various scientific approaches in Western anthropology today.

Anthropological Thought Today

Boas's early criticisms of the unilineal evolutionists illustrate a continuing controversy. First, the unilineal evolutionists thought that anthropology should be like the natural sciences in its goals. Their goal was to discover the general principles (laws) that governed cultural development. In contrast, the historicists mistrusted most generalizations, especially broad and sweeping ones like "all cultures pass through similar stages." The closer you come to getting inside another culture, they argued, the more details you perceive, and, hence, the more different it looks from other cultures. Most similarities are only superficial, like the "similarity" between polytheism in ancient Polynesia and Greece. In discovering similarities, you tend to neglect differences.

Second, the evolutionists uncritically placed similar cultures in the same stage of progress (like the Iroquois and the Fijians, both placed in "Barbarism"). But the historicists insisted that the evolutionists' idea of progress was ethnocentric and that therefore stages were artificial creations. If there are no universal stages, or even widespread stages, then the "regularities of cultural development" that the nineteenth-century scholars perceived were not real, but only the result of their ethnocentric assumptions and faulty methods.

Third, the evolutionists compared and contrasted cultures from all parts of the world and found customs they considered the same among widely scattered peoples. But the historicists reasoned that because each culture's history is different from the history of every other culture, it follows that each culture is unique and distinctive. It is misleading to place customs and beliefs from several cultures into the same category because there are in fact subtle differences between them.

For example, if you say that the ancient Polynesians and Greeks have the same form of religion, which *you* label as polytheism, that label is *yours*, not theirs. To call the two religions the same is to misrepresent them—the people believed in different gods, not the same ones, and the gods did different kinds of things for (and to) people. Saying they are the same form denies the religions, and the people who believe and practice them, their distinctiveness. It denies the Others their own voices. It privileges the voice of the anthropologist, meaning that it implicitly assumes the anthropologist's ideas are more valid than the ideas of Others about what they do and how they think.

It is impossible here to discuss all the issues that concern cultural anthropologists in the twenty-first century. Instead, we concentrate on a few major but related questions. Can and should cultural anthropology be a science, in the same sense that biology is a science? What are the most useful concepts and theoretical orientations to use in studying human cultural diversity? When we conduct fieldwork in another culture, should the fieldworker decide what is important—that is, should anthropologists define the questions and propose the answers? Or, should the views of the Others themselves take precedence—that is, should the "native's point of view" take priority? Can an outsider ever grasp the native's point of view? Do the natives even agree on their point of view?

One important division today is between cultural anthropologists whose interests and methods are more similar to science and those whose interests and methods are more humanistic. These two generalized approaches are our focus for discussing anthropological thought today.

Scientific Approaches

Those who adopt a **scientific approach** seek to discover the general forces that make cultures the way they are or were; that is, they want to *explain* human

scientific approach Approach suggesting that human cultural differences and similarities can be explained in much the same ways as biologists explain life and its evolution.

ways of life. As well as researching specific Others, scientifically oriented anthropologists are interested in human culture in general, meaning they want to discover whether there are any general principles ("laws," E. B. Tylor called them) that affect all peoples. They are interested in big questions: What are the primary causes of social and cultural differences and similarities? What makes societies and cultures change and/ or change at different rates? What are the relationships among the major components of a people's way of life such as acquiring resources, family organization, political structure, and religious beliefs and rituals? When two cultures come into contact, what kinds of forces affect the outcome?

Given the complexity of humanity, and even of a single culture, the answer is always going to be "It all depends." Scientifically oriented scholars agree but ask, "On what, mainly?" If the answer turns out to be "On everything else," then the scientific approach probably will not be able to achieve its goals. There can never be a general theory that answers their big questions because the word *theory* implies that only a few general principles or forces are responsible for most of the important differences, changes, relationships, and other phenomena. However, if cultures are indeed products of everything that happened in the past, then there are no general and important processes that operate widely in *most* societies *most* of the time. Human existence would be too chaotic and random to be explained by any general theory.

Scientifically oriented anthropologists agree that cultures are complicated and subject to random forces, but they hold that the most important forces are not random; instead, they operate widely and powerfully. In this respect, they follow the tradition of the unilineal evolutionists and the neoevolutionists.

Here we consider only two scientific approaches.

Evolutionary Psychology

In the late 1970s, some anthropologists adopted a theory then known as **sociobiology**. Social scientists now usually call it **evolutionary psychology**. It emphasizes the similarities between humans and other animals, arguing that humans are subject to the same kinds of processes that operate in other animals.

evolutionary psychology (sociobiology) Scientific approach emphasizing that humans are subject to similar evolutionary forces as other animals; associated with the hypothesis that human behavior patterns enhance genetic fitness.

Harvard biologist Edward O. Wilson was instrumental in developing this theoretical framework in the biological sciences. Wilson was interested in animal social behavior. For example, why do so many animals (e.g., lions, ants, many ungulates) live in herds or other groups whose members help one another by cooperating in hunting or emitting alarm calls that warn the group of a nearby predator?

Why are such behaviors puzzling? Most biologists have long believed that natural selection usually produces organisms that are genetically *selfish*. Unselfish (*altruistic*) behavior in animals is rare, existing only under very special circumstances. For instance, most cooperative social behaviors such as calls to warn others of predators are costly to the individual animal, yet the benefits accrue to the group. A prairie dog calling to alert its neighbors to a predator might call the predator's attention to itself and thus stand a greater chance of getting eaten. How could natural selection produce animals that act altruistically, when altruistic behavior is so costly to the altruistic animal? Natural selection should select against altruism because an altruistic animal will have less chance of survival and reproduction than the selfish ones.

Wilson, along with other biologists such as Richard Dawkins and William Hamilton, solved this puzzle by noting that the beneficiaries of altruistic behaviors are not individual organisms but genes. Because genes are the units that are transmitted to offspring through reproduction, only genes that (re)produce more copies of themselves in the next generation can survive. Sociobiologists argue that genes tend to program the bodies that temporarily house them to act in ways that improve their biological *fitness*—that is, in ways that increase their frequencies in the next generation. To paraphrase Dawkins, a body and its behavior are a gene's way of making more copies of itself.

Some evolutionary psychologists claim that this statement applies to humans as well as to other animals. If taken seriously and applied to humans, potentially this means that *your* body and behavior are your genes' way of making more copies of themselves. Here you can understand why some believe that evolutionary psychology is not relevant for humans, whose thoughts and behaviors are socially learned rather than inherited genetically. On the other hand, almost certainly the genetic makeup of humanity makes some things easier to learn than others. You also can imagine that genes make some things more likely to persist over generations—namely, those things that enhance survival and reproduction. Another way to say this is that genes might bias what people are prone to learn.

The main contribution of evolutionary psychology is the insight that the fitness of an individual animal is enhanced if it aids a relative that shares the gene for altruism. This principle is most apparent in parents aiding (feeding, protecting, teaching) their offspring. However, it also applies to other relatives. For example, a female can potentially increase her fitness if she aids her brother, if that brother carries the same gene. By helping her brother, she herself may reproduce less, but this cost can be more than offset if her help substantially improves her brother's chances of transmitting that gene to his offspring.

Thus, natural selection increases the survival of any gene that programs its body to help a relative if the cost in fitness (to the gene) is lower than the benefit to the same gene housed in the relative's body. So, an individual animal can behave altruistically, but only if the benefit of the altruistic act helps a relative more than it costs the altruist (note that the behavior is not truly altruistic because it increases the fitness of the gene that causes it).

Some anthropologists believe that such ideas contribute to explaining human social behavior. For example, you and I have a genetic interest in the welfare of our relatives. All else equal, the more closely related we are, the more we care for them, and people care most for those individuals who are the main vehicles for transmitting their genes—their own offspring and offspring's offspring. We care little, or less, for nonrelatives and will assist them only if they somehow return benefits to us or to our relatives. They do this mainly by reciprocity; that is, they return our help immediately or at some later time *if* we can count on their presence and help in the future. Evolutionary psychologists claim that selfishness motivates most human actions, although the selfish motive is sometimes disguised when we help family members or friends in expectation of future returns.

More generally, evolutionary psychologists note that, for most of human history, the most important human groups (bands, discussed in later chapters) were composed mostly of relatives who cooperated in foraging, food sharing, child care, and other activities. They also point out that far more human societies allow a man to have several wives than allow a woman to have several husbands, which is consistent with sociobiology (see Chapter 9). They claim that evolutionary psychology helps explain many of the following widespread human mental and behavioral predispositions:

- *Xenophobia*—We may hate or mistrust strangers who belong to other races or ethnicities because, as obvious nonrelatives, we cannot trust them, and any help we give them is unlikely to be reciprocated. (Some say this helps explain ethnocentrism.)

- *Warfare*—Braver or stronger men who protect the group are more likely to attract more wives and/or have more sex and hence more offspring. (Some believe this helps explain why so many cultures reward warriors.)

- *Male unfaithfulness to wives*—Extramarital sexual relationships allow males to have more children and therefore more fitness without the costs of raising the children. (Some think this accounts for why men in most societies are allowed to have more than one wife, while having more than one husband is a rare marriage form.)

- *Female preference for marrying high-status/wealthy males*—Women get access to more resources through such marriages, thus improving the survival chances and ultimately the fitness of their offspring. (Some claim this insight explains why women prefer to marry up the social ladder, in societies where one exists.)

- *Revenge motives*—Someone is less likely to attack you or your group if the person knows you are likely to retaliate, that you are honor bound to avenge the death. (Some believe that the death penalty in many nation-states does not actually deter violent crimes but is really about the retribution that benefited our ancestors.)

Critics of such ideas charge that these and other so-called predispositions are more the product of socialization than of genes because they vary from people to people. Even if evolutionary psychology helps in understanding such widespread patterns, critics say that it tells us little or nothing about the reasons different peoples exhibit them strongly, weakly, or not at all. So the help is minimal at best. It may even be harmful if it makes us erroneously believe we now understand something. And, at any rate, the insights of sociobiology apply primarily if "all else is equal," which is rarely the case. Finally, many self-sacrificial acts of devotion by individuals—such as suicide bombers and Kamikaze pilots who kill themselves out of devotion to their faith, values, or homeland—are problematic for evolutionary psychology (unless their close kin receive some benefits in fitness).

Numerous other arguments exist both for and against evolutionary psychology, some of which we cover in later chapters. For now, note that it is an excellent example of the scientific side of cultural anthropology: It holds that people are subject to the same principles and pressures as other animals—most importantly, to the forces of natural selection.

Materialism

Another modern scientific approach—more popular than evolutionary psychology—is **materialism** (also called **cultural materialism**). Like Malinowski, this approach argues that the satisfaction of human material needs and desires is the most important influence on how societies are organized and on what people think and believe. People face similar material needs as do all animals: We must receive adequate intakes of food and water, regulate our body temperature (by building shelters and wearing clothing), reproduce, cope with organisms that cause disease, compete successfully, and so forth. To satisfy these needs efficiently, people have to organize their societies in certain ways to cooperate or to succeed in competition with other societies. Many other elements of a people's culture are determined by or are greatly influenced by how people organize their activities to survive and persist in their environments, materialists claim.

At root, materialists think that how a people make their living in their environment is the most important influence on the rest of their cultural existence. If relationships with the environment and acquiring material resources are primary, then those aspects of culture that help people acquire resources strongly affect all other aspects. Far more than any other animal, people depend on *technology* to exploit resources, compete with other groups, and cope with other problems of environmental adaptation. Technology includes not just the physical *instruments* (the tools) used to produce food, provide shelter, and generally cope with the environment. Equally important, technology includes the *knowledge* (skills) about the environment, about resources, and about the manufacture and effective use of tools that people have socially learned from previous generations.

Because humans rely on tools and knowledge to acquire food and harness other resources, technology is among the most important aspects of culture everywhere. Materialists believe a people's technology strongly affects other parts of their culture, including family life, political organization, values, and even worldviews, much as White argued in the 1940s. Yet most materialists of today disagree with White's view that increased energy capture made possible by

technological improvements has generally made human life better and resulted in progress. In contrast to White, most modern materialists believe technological changes have improved the lives of *some* people in *some* respects, but that changes in technology have had mixed results overall.

By emphasizing the importance of physical/biological needs, technology, environment, and population size, modern materialists resemble earlier thinkers such as Malinowski, White, and Steward. However, modern materialists emphasize interrelationships between people and environments. For the most part, early theories about causation were linear, meaning that one thing makes another thing the way it is; thus, A "causes" B, or A "determines" B. But materialists of today are more likely to view technology, environment, population, and culture as having feedback relationships with one another. That is, as their numbers increase, people interact with their environment in new ways and so change the environment. In turn, this changes the way the people live, and so on over long time periods.

An important process for many materialists is *intensification*: As human numbers grow in a region, people modify more and more of the natural environment in order to produce greater quantities of food and other material needs. Usually intensification involves greater and/or more extensive modification and/or destruction of some parts of natural environment. For example, as people exploit a resource, they may deplete its supply. Future generations must then work harder to acquire the same resource, develop a new method of acquiring it, or switch to an alternative resource. Other cultural changes accompany this long-term process of intensification, if the process is not halted or reversed.

We discuss some of these processes in Chapter 7. For now, note three of the main arguments of materialists:

1. Many customs and beliefs of a particular culture can be explained by how they help people live in the natural world.

2. Population growth and intensification are major factors that lead to cultural change.

3. Generally, and in the long run, material forces like the natural environment, resources, technologies, and population densities are more important than aspects of cultural knowledge (ideas and beliefs), such as values, symbols, and worldviews.

materialism (cultural materialism) Scientific theoretical orientation claiming that the main influences on cultural differences and similarities are technology, environment, population size and growth, and how people produce and distribute resources.

Humanistic Approaches

Many ideas of both evolutionary psychology and materialism are not seriously questioned. Most people do transmit their genes by having children, and most of us are more likely to help relatives than strangers. But whether the biologically determined predispositions identified by evolutionary psychology really are important causes is debatable. Some deny that such universal human predispositions exist at all. Some say that even if such predispositions do exist, then explaining them has the effect of justifying racial hatreds, violence, sexual inequalities, and the like. The very notion that human beings are innately selfish is odious to many anthropologists.

Likewise, clearly people have material needs. But whether such needs are basic and whether they shape all of human existence is debatable. Some think humans differ from other animals in that these needs can be satisfied in such a multitude of ways that cultural differences cannot plausibly be reduced to material need and want satisfaction. They are skeptical that material factors cause cultural differences and similarities and long-term changes. In fact, they doubt that any *general* explanation applies to human cultures. Many believe that any scholar who tries to explain culture dehumanizes people by treating them as objects.

Most scholars who adopt the **humanistic approach** doubt or deny that any single theory can explain culture in the same way that evolutionary theory explains life or that Einstein's relativity theory explains the physical world. Humanistic anthropologists are skeptical of general theories for many reasons. One is that humanity's social and cultural worlds are just too complicated for one theory to explain them. All those cultures of all those Others cannot be reduced to a single formula, they claim.

Humanistic scholars say that another reason for rejecting general theories is the uniqueness of humanity. *Homo sapiens* is such a special kind of animal that the methods and analysis that biology uses to explain other life forms do not apply to us in any significant respect. Human uniqueness lies mainly in our heavy dependence on social learning and our capacity for complex communication—that is, in both culture and language.

Other animals live in the natural world, with food sources, predators, mates and potential mates, and so forth. Of course, humans also eat, drink, sleep, and engage in sex. But, humanists point out, we also live in a cultural world: What, when, and how we eat, drink, sleep, and have sex are largely determined by the culture into which each of us happens to have been born. People live in the natural world, but we also culturally construct the natural world and have a worldview (see Chapter 2). Our constructions and worldviews are as important in affecting our behaviors, thoughts, and feelings as living in the real world itself, humanists claim.

Language also makes us unique, humanists say. Language provides words with which we classify and categorize objects, people, events, actions, qualities, and so forth. Because of language, we construct categories of events, people, groups, objects, plants, and so on, which vary from culture to culture. Because of its displacement property (see Chapter 3), language even provides us with words for things that have no material existence at all, such as ghosts and demons, and such beliefs affect our behavior—sometimes dramatically. If the Sapir-Whorf hypothesis has any validity and generality, then our language conditions our perceptions of the world itself, so every people exist in a perceived world that is unique to them. These features of language are all unique to humanity, and because of them we create our own reality as well as respond to actual reality.

All of this seems to imply that human reactions to the natural environment and human beliefs about the world are products of culture and language. To humanistic anthropologists, at the most, material factors like environment, technology, and population affect culture only by *limiting* (constraining) how a people act, think, and feel. Material factors cannot *determine* (cause) actions, thoughts, and feelings because these factors themselves are, in part, products of actions, thoughts, and feelings. Neither causes or explains the other, which makes untangling causes and effects pretty much impossible, argue humanistic anthropologists.

To the materialists' claim that nature's resources are important influences on cultures and societies, a critical humanist may respond that resources are not entirely natural. Consider food resources, for instance, which materialists believe are among the most important influences on cultures. Based on religious prohibitions and cultural notions of what is edible and what is not, various peoples refuse to eat cattle, pigs, dogs, horses, and insect larvae. These (including the larvae) are the same flesh considered so delicious by many other peoples. Cultures have food taboos that are based on something besides nutritional considerations.

For example, in 2012 the British people were outraged when it was reported that some beef products also contained horsemeat, although their fellow

humanistic approach Orientation that mistrusts attempts to explain cultural differences and similarities and cultural changes in favor of achieving an empathetic understanding of particular cultures.

Loren Holmes/Alamy

Humanistic anthropologists point out weaknesses of the materialist orientation. For example, a natural resource used by one people may not be used as a resource for another people or may be used for other cultural purposes. Traditional higher-caste Hindus do not eat beef, but they revere cattle and use them in rituals and festivals around temples.

Europeans, the French, freely buy horsemeat. If food and other resources are culturally defined and culturally meaningful as well as biologically nutritious, then in human life food is culturally defined, not "given," by the environment. Long ago, our cultural ancestors built (culturally constructed) the cultural world in which we live our lives. We live within this cultural world as well as within the natural one, humanists point out.

Thus, some humanistic anthropologists think that Tylor's and White's "science of culture" is not possible: Humans and their societies are too complex and too diverse, and humans live partly in worlds that their language and culture construct for them.

Some humanistic anthropologists do not believe that anthropology should even *try* to be scientific. In their view, scientific anthropology objectifies cultures; that is, in its efforts to generalize, science places cultural features into categories (e.g., forms of marriage, types of religions) that are the categories of the anthropologist, not those of the people themselves. Humanists often make this point by saying that scientifically

oriented anthropologists rob people of their voices. They mean that scientific anthropologists are arrogant to the extent that they believe they know better than the Others themselves what is important in their lives and what was important in shaping their culture.

As for research, humanistic anthropologists point out that fieldworkers carry their own culture with them into their research experiences. This culture affects their interactions with the community, including whose stories they believe, which perceptions they consider important, and so forth. Conversely, individuals in the community have their own perceptions, opinions, and biases about the fieldworker. Among the many factors that affect how the community reacts are the fieldworker's physical characteristics, gender, and personality, as well as the historical experience of the community with individuals of the anthropologist's own society. Although most fieldworkers attempt to overcome their own cultural biases and to fit into the community, complete objectivity is impossible. In fact, many humanists think that any ethnography cannot be a simple report on facts about a given group. Rather, it is a "construction," meaning that an ethnography is a product of interactions that another fieldworker would not experience.

You might well wonder, *if* all this is true, how is it that materialists have been so misguided about the importance of environment, technology, adaptation, and so forth? Some humanistic anthropologists claim that materialist thinking is a product of Western cultural values and beliefs. Because the West places such high value on material welfare and consumption, materialists mistakenly impose these same values and beliefs on other cultures. Living in a competitive and capitalistic society predisposes materialists to see "economic man" in cultures where he does not exist. Materialist theory is a kind of ethnocentrism, they claim.

Some materialists respond in kind. They point out that most academics are members of the privileged class—in status, wealth, or both. Because most academics (including humanistic anthropologists) so seldom have to worry about filling their stomachs; or sheltering themselves from heat, snow, and rain; or protecting themselves from enemies, it is easy for them to believe that such concerns are not important in other cultures either. The humanists' failure to realize the broad importance of material factors is related to their own wealth and privilege. The humanistic approach is a kind of ethnocentrism, some claim.

Even more than the scientific approach, it is difficult or impossible to collapse humanistic anthropology into a few schools or ways of approaching Others. Here, we discuss only two. Interpretive anthropology became popular in the 1960s, whereas postmodernism has become influential since the 1980s.

Interpretive Anthropology

Interpretive anthropology emphasizes the uniqueness of each culture. Every culture has its own ways of doing things, its own worldview, its own values, and so forth. Even if two or more cultures look similar, close examination usually shows that the meanings they attach to behaviors, objects, and concepts are different. This uniqueness makes comparisons between different cultures misleading. In this and other respects, interpretive anthropology is similar to historical particularism. And because science attempts to generalize through comparisons and contrasts, it follows that anthropology is more of a humanistic discipline than a scientific one. It has more in common with literature and art than with biology or psychology, according to the interpretive approach.

Interpretive anthropologists emphasize the symbolic dimensions of a particular culture. All social behavior has a symbolic component, in the sense that participants constantly must behave in ways that others will understand. All social interaction, therefore, is symbolic and meaningful. Meanings exist only by virtue of common agreement among the parties to the interaction—whether the interaction involves making conversation, making change in a store, or making an iPhone at a plant in southern China. Neither participant can tell an observer how he or she knows what the other participant "means" by this or that behavior. Yet participants behave in ways that others understand, and they consistently interpret the behavior of others correctly.

The job of the anthropologist is not to *explain* elements of a culture but to *explicate* one element through others. That is, the anthropologist shows how one thing in a cultural system makes sense in terms of other things in the same system, because interpretation is seeing how things make sense when understood in their context. (Analogously, a dictionary explicates the meanings of words in terms of other words. Only if one knows the meanings of many words in the dictionary can one use them to decipher the meanings of unknown words.) We seek to understand a people's way of life as they understand it. The late Clifford Geertz (1983, p. 58), who shaped the interpretive approach, used Malinowski's words when he wrote that anthropologists should seek to grasp "the native's point of view," and "to figure out what the devil they think they are up to." This involves acquiring intimate knowledge of a particular culture so that the ethnographer can make sense of the culture for those who do not know it. Most interpretivists are uninterested in comparisons, because the meanings of actions, objects, events, and social relationships are too diverse for comparisons to be valid.

According to many interpretive anthropologists, the search for generalized explanations of human ways of life is futile. So many factors contributed to the formation of a culture—and these factors interacted in such complex and unpredictable ways—that we must concentrate on understanding the unique elements of each way of life. In this respect, interpretive anthropologists exemplify the humanistic perspective.

interpretive anthropology Contemporary approach that analyzes cultural elements by explicating their meanings to people and understanding them in their local context; generally emphasizes cultural diversity and the unique qualities of particular cultures.

Postmodernism

Postmodernism generally maintains that the methods and assumptions of all science—including fields such as biology—are themselves culturally situated. This means that science, as most people understand it, is not objective in its theories and even in its facts (data). Rather, it is conducted by scientists who are products of a particular cultural upbringing. Like all knowledge, scientific theories are affected by conditions in the scientists' own culture.

For example, a postmodernist might say that evolutionary psychologists are enculturated into a culture that practically celebrates selfishness. In free-market economies, everyone is supposed to be looking out for themselves and consuming commodities and competing. So the evolutionary psychologists raised in this economic system (mistakenly) believe people everywhere act this way and claim that these alleged biological imperatives apply to humanity in general. Such theories are culture bound, in the same way that Boas showed that unilineal evolutionism was culture bound (ethnocentric).

If all this is true, how can the proponents of science be so misguided? Postmodernists point out that scientific thinking and methods became prominent during the Enlightenment period (also called the Age of Reason) of late eighteenth- and nineteenth-century western Europe. Enlightenment philosophers emphasized rational thought as the key to advancing knowledge about the world, from the solar system to humanity. Tradition, and especially religion, were viewed as impediments to discovering truth. Emotions could also get in the way, especially if they keep otherwise rational thinkers from accepting the reality of a fact or principle just because they do not like it or its implications.

For example, you might refuse to accept evidence showing that not all societies are patriarchal. You reject or discount the evidence because it is not consistent with what you learned while growing up or what you think your religion teaches. Your refusal to accept the evidence is not rational, so it gets in the way of improving your knowledge. This would not matter very much for your society unless, of course, men hold the power in that society, and most of them feel and believe as you do. Enlightenment thinkers tried to free thought from the shackles of religion and emotion, so that reason and science could reveal the world to us as it really is.

Postmodernists do not think there is anything very special about the Enlightenment version of rational thought. They say that human knowledge originates in a particular social, economic, and political context. *Scientific* knowledge is no exception. Science is a product of a particular cultural tradition—that of Western civilization—and therefore reflects the economy, family organization, political ideology, worldview, and so forth of Western society. Science is one among hundreds of other systems of cultural knowledge. At the extreme, postmodernists hold that science has little more claim to absolute truth than the ideas and beliefs of other peoples. All are valid on their own terms, but none is privileged or has any exclusive claim to objectivity. If scientists themselves do not realize this, it is because they are inside their own knowledge system and so fail to grasp the implicit assumptions of their rationalistic and mechanistic worldview.

Postmodernists also think the most important thing about the context of knowledge is power relationships. Prevalent beliefs and ideas in a community reflect power relationships, largely because those with power have the most influence on which ideas and beliefs become prevalent. To illustrate with a modern example, most North Americans attach positive value to abstractions like private property, free-market capitalism, the rule of law, and various individual rights and freedoms. These values reflect, and support, the interests of some people over other people. A lot of scholarly knowledge—including much of what is taught in colleges and universities—is like this, postmodernists claim. For example, evolutionary psychology is often taught as a credible or even correct theory in biology courses, although many postmodernists believe its theories support sexism and patriarchy.

In anthropological fieldwork, there is often a power dimension to the relationship between the fieldworker and the local people. Most fieldworkers are able to command more resources and thus can influence people to talk about things they would rather not discuss (despite published ethical standards in fieldwork, covered in Chapter 6). Postmodernists tend to mistrust older ethnographies, and generally they prefer accounts in which the fieldworkers openly discuss their personal relationships with members of the community. They also prefer ethnographies in which the ethnographer gives her or his readers access to local voices.

As mentioned, postmodernism penetrated anthropology in the 1980s and has attracted more converts in our discipline than in any other social science. One

postmodernism Philosophical viewpoint emphasizing the relativity of all knowledge, including science; focus is on how the knowledge of a particular time and place is constructed, especially on how power relations affect the creation and spread of ideas and beliefs.

reason for the popularity of this perspective in anthropology is its apparent consistency with cultural relativism. However, critics of the approach became vocal in the late 1990s. How have their own ideas escaped the influence of power relationships? Why wouldn't *their* ideas be culture bound as well?

Postmodernism reminds us that rationality and science do not provide all the answers and do not ask many relevant questions. It leads us to ask where our ideas come from and who might gain and lose from them. Perhaps most important, it warns anthropological thinkers of the dangers of becoming arrogant about our objectivity. Scientifically oriented theorists might forget that they are cultural beings and that their own ideas about the human world are culturally conditioned.

The Concept Review feature sharply contrasts the main differences between the scientific and the humanistic approaches. Notice that they differ in their conceptions of the primary goals of anthropology, in the significance of humanity's biology for anthropological research and findings, in the validity of conducting cross-cultural comparisons, in whether anthropological research among humans can be objective, and in the appropriate aims of conducting fieldwork.

Like most dualistic contrasts, the ones in the Concept Review are presented starkly, and there is more overlap between the two approaches than shown.

Either, Or, or Both?

The differences between the scientific and humanistic orientations are sometimes presented as conflicting: Humanists often accuse scientists of dehumanizing people in their misguided efforts to explain them, whereas scientists claim that humanists are deceiving themselves if they think they can get inside some Other culture and grasp the native's point of view.

A recent controversy illustrates that many anthropologists continue to have contrasting views of what their discipline is or should be. Until 2010, the American Anthropological Association stated that its long-range plan is "to advance anthropology as the science that studies humankind in all its aspects." At the 2010 annual meeting of the AAA, however, the Executive Board revised the plan to state its purpose as "to advance public understanding of humankind in all its aspects." The replacement of "science" with "public understanding" led to strong reactions from scientifically oriented anthropologists, who felt the official statement undermined their perspective.

CONCEPT REVIEW — Main Contrasts Between Scientific and Humanistic Approaches

	Scientific	Humanistic
Overall Goals of Anthropology	Explain cultural differences and similarities and how and why cultures change.	Describe and interpret particular cultures.
Human Uniqueness	As an animal species, all humans share core motivations, emotions, and behavioral predispositions; food, shelter, security, and reproduction are primary needs.	As a culture-dependent and language-using species, human motivations and behavioral predispositions vary enormously; constructions and symbolic meanings are important.
Role of Comparison	Discover patterns and relationships that apply broadly.	Distort the cultures compared and ignore the complexities of particular cultures.
Objectivity	Systematic observations and cross-checking of individual and group patterns of behavior make objectivity attainable.	Descriptions emerge from interactions between fieldworkers and local people; knowledge of cultures is constructed, not objective.
Fieldwork Emphasis	Research topics are chosen for their relevance to wide issues in the scientific community.	Achieve an insider's view and/or represent the voices of the people themselves

To some extent, different approaches exist because of the differing interests of anthropologists. For example, scholars whose research areas include subjects such as human–environment relationships, economic systems, or long-term changes in societies are likely to find a materialist approach useful. Those who study dimensions such as mythology, art, oral traditions, or worldviews are more likely to fall into the humanistic camp. So, in part, the diversity of modern approaches reflects the fact that human beings and their cultures are complex and multifaceted; the orientation most useful to understand one facet (e.g., subsistence) may not prove very useful to understand another (e.g., worldview).

In the interest of balance, in the remainder of this book, we try to avoid choosing between the two orientations by taking the following approach. Like evolutionary psychologists and cultural materialists, we think *it is important* that people are part of nature. But we recognize that different elements of a culture are influenced to different degrees by material conditions. The way an economy is organized is greatly influenced by the local environment, climate, technology, and the size and density of the human population. But the ways the members of a culture resolve their disputes, raise their children, perform their rituals, or act toward their fathers-in-law are less influenced by material conditions or are influenced by them only indirectly. Details of the legends they recite, the specific objects they use as religious symbols, and the ways they decorate their bodies may have little or nothing to do with material forces. Such elements of a cultural system are only loosely tied to the natural world and to material needs and wants. We cannot account for them without considering people's desires for a meaningful existence, an emotionally gratifying social life, an intellectually satisfying worldview, creative self-expression, and so forth.

Different orientations are useful for studying different dimensions of culture. Still, people who are new to anthropology are often puzzled by the diversity of approaches within the field. We therefore conclude this chapter by suggesting answers to the question posed in the following section.

Why Can't All Those Anthropologists Agree?

Most scholars in the natural sciences generally agree on a set of laws or principles that govern the aspects of the world they study. In geology, for example, processes such as sedimentation, plate tectonics, volcanic eruptions, fossilization, and so forth are fairly well understood and account for the main geological features of our planet. Biologists, likewise, believe that the process of evolution produced the diversity of all life on Earth, although the relative importance of natural selection and random events in this process remain uncertain.

Cultural anthropology lacks a comparable set of general principles. Why can't anthropologists agree more than we do? Several factors contribute to the absence of consensus.

First, humans are conscious and self-aware beings who state a variety of reasons for why we do what we do and think what we think. The zoologist studying an animal's behavior observes and records the behavior and then typically tries to identify the elements of the natural and social environment to which the behavior is adapted. But the anthropologist must listen to the reasons people themselves give for their behavior. People talk back, and anthropologists must take their talk as well as their actions, into account.

Second, for ethical reasons, anthropologists do not set up controlled experiments to study how people respond. Suppose—following Steward's lead—we want to study how the natural environment affects cultures. We cannot hold everything constant except the supply of food, water, or shelter and then see how people react when the supply of food, water, or shelter is varied. Anthropologists do not control the conditions under which different peoples live their lives. The best we can do is look around the world for natural experiments—places where the natural environment is similar and peoples with different histories live. We can choose a sample of peoples who live in environments that appear to be similar and then see whether the peoples who live in these places have similar cultures. For example, we might compare indigenous peoples who live in the world's deserts: the Sahara of northern Africa, the Kalahari of southern Africa, the American Southwest, the Gobi of Central Asia, and so forth. To conduct such a comparative study, we would have to rely on the ethnographic reports written by a multitude of earlier ethnographers, whose reports resulted from their observations and discussions with peoples in the various deserts.

Suppose our comparative study finds, as it will, that the cultures are similar in some respects but different in others. Then other problems arise: Natural environments are only similar, never identical. Did we fail to detect a small but critical difference in the environment that might explain the cultural differences? Or, are the differences due to nonenvironmental factors? Likewise, shall we call customs and beliefs that differ in minor ways between the cultures the same, or are the subtle differences between them sufficient to call them different? Suppose we observe that desert people share food within their villages. But then we discover that people in several of the cultures give different reasons for the behavior—in culture X, people say they want to help one another, whereas in culture Y, they say they give only because they expect to get something back later. Are both of these behaviors still sharing food? Or, should we consider them different because people's stated motivations differ? Such questions are inherently difficult to answer when dealing with human beings, and anthropologists cannot sort them out in laboratories or other experimental settings.

Quite likely a third reason anthropology lacks a common theoretical orientation is because people become anthropologists for a wider variety of reasons than people become, say, physicists. Some of us study anthropology because of our curiosity about why the human species is so diverse culturally. Others go into the field to further the cause of social justice—by educating themselves and others about racism, ethnocentrism, colonialism, or sexism, for example. Some want to immerse themselves in travel and interaction with people who are different from themselves, and they become anthropologists because the field provides them with such opportunities. The very broad scope

of anthropology (see Chapter 1) helps account for the variety of reasons people choose it as a career: You can study agriculture, family life, political organization, medicine, art, religion, folklore, and almost anything else having to do with humankind. Naturally, people who study topics as diverse as these are unlikely to agree on their theoretical orientations to the field as a whole. Indeed, many of them consciously reject any form of theoretical orientation, preferring to concentrate on researching particular cultures.

In sum, there are at least three major reasons modern cultural anthropologists have such varied orientations to the study of culture:

1. Our subjects—other human beings—are conscious beings who are aware of their own behavior and state their own reasons for why they do what they do. Human subjects talk back.

2. Anthropologists cannot set up experiments that enable them to control the conditions under which people live. Anthropologists observe people as they live their everyday lives.

3. The broad scope of the field and the enormous diversity of reasons people study anthropology make it unlikely to achieve theoretical consensus. Cultural anthropologists are among the most diverse of scholars.

SUMMARY

1. **Discuss the global forces that contributed to the emergence of anthropology.** Anthropology originated as a distinct academic discipline in the late nineteenth century, after colonialism intensified contact between peoples of European ancestry and the indigenous peoples of Africa, Asia, the Americas, and the Pacific. Darwin's theory of evolution was one of the main notions that Western intellectuals believed made sense of the peoples and cultures of other lands.

2. **Describe the main ideas of the nineteenth-century unilineal evolutionists.** Unilineal evolutionists applied the ideas of evolution to cultures. Using written accounts as their main source of information about Other cultures, they arranged cultures into a sequence of progressive stages,

from simple to complex, with Western civilization at the pinnacle. Anthropology thus began as the academic field that studied how humankind progressed out of rude beginnings into a more "civilized" cultural existence.

3. **Understand the ways American historical particularism and British functionalism challenged unilineal evolutionism.** In the early twentieth century, both American and British anthropologists developed new approaches. The American historical particularists, led by Boas, demolished the speculative schemes of the unilineal evolutionists by arguing that concepts such as complexity depend on one's point of view and so have little objective meaning. Boas popularized the notion of cultural relativism that

remains a hallmark of anthropology today. In Great Britain, functionalists such as Malinowski and Radcliffe-Brown tried to show how the various parts of a culture and a social system serve to meet the needs of individuals and society. Both the historical particularists and the functionalists emphasized the importance of firsthand fieldwork as the surest path to accurate descriptions of a people and as essential for the training of anthropologists.

4. **Describe the mid–twentieth-century rebirth of evolutionary interests (neoevolutionism).** In the middle decades of the twentieth century, neoevolutionists like White and Steward returned to cultural evolution, avoiding most mistakes of the unilineal evolutionists. White emphasized the importance of technology, and Steward stressed adaptation to the local environment, as factors in making cultures the way they are. Both men thought that a people's methods of acquiring resources (energy, food, and so forth) from nature are the main influences on culture. Both also believed that anthropology should be and can be a science.

5. **Discuss the main differences between the scientific and the humanistic approaches to modern anthropological thought.** One broad controversy among modern cultural anthropologists is whether their field is primarily a scientific enterprise or a humanistic study. Scientifically oriented scholars believe that people are subjected to the same kinds of natural forces as other animals and that genuine explanations of differences and similarities and long-term changes are possible and desirable. Humanistically inclined anthropologists believe that humanity is such a unique kind of animal that special concepts and theories are required

to understand our species. Attempts to explain humans are thus futile and dehumanizing.

6. **Describe evolutionary psychology, materialism, interpretive anthropology, and postmodernism.** Evolutionary psychology (sociobiology) and materialism are examples of scientific approaches. Evolutionary psychology emphasizes that humans are like other animals in that most of our behavior helps us transmit our genes to future generations. Materialists argue that how a given people organize their groups and pattern their activities to acquire energy and materials from their natural environment is the major explanation for other aspects of their cultural system. In contrast, humanistically oriented anthropologists mistrust generalized explanations of cultural phenomena. Interpretive anthropologists emphasize the uniqueness of each culture and favor studying, appreciating, and interpreting each culture individually. Postmodernists think that science in general has no particular claim to truth and that many scientific ideas taught by schools and colleges reflect power relationships in the wider social and cultural context.

7. **Analyze why contemporary anthropology has no single unifying theoretical orientation.** Contemporary anthropologists do not agree among themselves on many fundamental questions, including even the major objectives of their field. Their lack of consensus is understandable, given that their (human) subjects are self-conscious and willful beings; that anthropologists cannot experiment with people's lives; and that anthropology studies subjects that are so diverse that a single theoretical orientation is unlikely to be able to encompass all of them.

AP Images

6

Methods of Investigation

Margaret Mead's highly innovative field studies made her one of the most widely read anthropologists of the twentieth century.

Ethnographic Methods

Ethnographic Fieldwork

Problems and Issues in Field Research

Fieldwork as a Rite of Passage

Ethnohistory

Comparative Methods

Cross-Cultural Comparisons

Controlled Comparisons

117

After reading this chapter, you should be able to:

1 **DISCUSS** the major objectives of cultural research.

2 **UNDERSTAND** that research requires different methods.

3 **DESCRIBE** the methods used to study the culture of a contemporary or living society.

4 **DESCRIBE** the method used to study the past culture of a society.

5 **UNDERSTAND** the purpose of comparative research.

6 **EXPLAIN** cross-cultural comparisons.

7 **DESCRIBE** controlled comparative studies.

Anthropological research has two purposes: (1) to collect and record descriptive data about the cultures of specific peoples (*ethnography*), and (2) to explain the past and present diversity found in cultural systems in the world (**ethnology**). We discussed cultural change in Chapter 4. Recognizing that the culture of a society is constantly changing, we further divide research into studies that describe a culture at one period in time (**synchronic**) and research that studies the changes in culture of a people over time (**diachronic**).

As a result, research can be grouped into four broad categories, each with its own methodologies. However, it is important to note that any particular study may actually involve the use of two or more methodologies. For example, it is very common for ethnographic studies to combine both ethnographic field research and ethnohistoric research, as seen in Table 6.1.

Ethnographic Methods

There are two sources of cultural data about a particular people: the living members of the society and written accounts or other records about that group of people. Collecting cultural data by studying and interviewing living members of a society is called **ethnographic fieldwork**. Studying a people's culture using written accounts and other records is termed **ethnohistoric research**.

TABLE 6.1 Research Methodologies

Ethnography	Ethnology
Synchronic ethnographic fieldwork	Cross-cultural comparisons
Diachronic ethnohistoric research	Controlled comparisons

---

ethnology Study of human cultures from a comparative perspective.

synchronic Describing a culture at one period in time.

diachronic Describing changes in a culture over time.

ethnographic fieldwork Collection of information from living people about their way of life.

ethnohistoric research Study of a people's culture using written accounts and other records.

Ethnographic Fieldwork

Ethnographic fieldwork, the most commonly used research method, involves the collection of cultural data from living individuals. The researcher lives with or close to the people being studied and interacts with them on a day-to-day basis for a long period, usually a year or more. Not infrequently, the anthropologist has to learn the group's language and behave according to the group's social norms. By its very nature, fieldwork fosters a close personal relationship between the researcher and members of the society being studied. This closeness between researchers and the people they study distinguishes anthropologists from most other social scientists.

Anthropologists have always used fieldwork as the primary method for collecting cultural information. Over the past century, the objectives of fieldwork have changed and with it the data-gathering techniques.

Today, a number of techniques are used in the course of any research project.

Interviewing is the most basic method of collecting cultural data. The anthropologist asks questions and elicits answers from members of the society being studied. Interviews may be structured or unstructured. A *structured interview* consists of a limited number of specific questions. It may take the form of a questionnaire the researcher fills in as the questions are answered. This type of interview is best suited for collecting general quantitative data about the group. For example, most research begins with a census of the community: the number of people in each family, their ages and relationships, and basic economic information about the family. In this manner, the researcher constructs demographic and economic profiles of the group. Structured interviews are also used to create genealogies. Most research requires a clear knowledge of how group members are related to one another. Genealogies are important in understanding the social and economic behavior of individuals beyond the immediate family. There are, however, limits to the utility of structured interviews.

In *unstructured interviews*, the researcher asks open-ended questions, hoping that the respondent will elaborate on the answers. The questions may be general, about family life, marriage, a particular religious ritual, or economic activity. Most cultural data are collected through unstructured interviews. In these interviews, the researcher learns the cultural explanations for information collected in the structured interviews.

Although it is the source of most cultural data, interviewing has serious limitations. The problem usually is not with the answers given by the members of the group, but rather with the questions asked by the researcher. What is relevant or irrelevant to the proper understanding of a particular cultural phenomenon depends on the culture of the individuals involved. Initially, the researcher does not understand the cultural context of the data and thus does not know what questions need to be asked and answered. The early stages of a research project are often characterized by "shotgun" questioning as the anthropologist seeks to learn enough about the culture to ask the right questions. Through interviewing, a researcher can gain basic knowledge of a culture's major structural features. However, no matter how knowledgeable and willing the respondents might be, verbal descriptions in themselves are incomplete and do not enable the researcher to gain an in-depth knowledge of the people or an understanding of the true dynamics of their culture.

To understand the limitations of interviewing, ask yourself this question: If an anthropologist from another culture asked you to describe a baseball game, what would you say? How complete would your description be? Chances are, if you are an avid fan, you could relate enough information for the anthropologist to gain a basic understanding of the game. You could tell how many players are on each side and explain the basic rules about balls, strikes, runs, errors, and innings. However, from memory alone, it would be impossible to explain everything that might occur during a game. Every baseball game, like every other cultural event, is to some degree unique. From memory alone, it is impossible for you to explain everything that might actually occur during a game. The best you could do is give the researcher an idealized model of a baseball game. Certain facts would be left untold, not because you were hiding them but because they are either so commonplace or so unusual that they are not part of your consciousness concerning the game. Interviews alone can give the researcher only a simplified overview of a particular cultural phenomenon, an idealized model.

If researchers want to truly understand baseball, they cannot simply talk to someone about it; they need to see a game. In fact, researchers should observe several games and discuss what occurred with a knowledgeable person. It would be even better for researchers to participate, at least in a minor way, in some games. Only by combining interviewing with observing and participating can one begin to more fully understand the rules and dynamics of the game. So it is with the study of any cultural phenomenon.

During the late nineteenth and early twentieth centuries, anthropologists relied primarily on interviews alone to collect cultural data. This technique was well suited to the anthropological objectives of that time. The traditional lifestyles of non-Western peoples were rapidly changing in many parts of the world, and anthropologists were concerned about collecting as much cultural data as possible before knowledge of these ways of life disappeared.

This was particularly true in North America, where Native American groups had already been placed on reservations, and their economies and cultures had drastically changed. Anthropologists wanted to learn about earlier Native American lifestyles before all knowledge of the pre-reservation period was lost. Researchers could not observe, let alone participate in, a bison hunt or the

interviewing Collecting cultural data by systematic questioning; may be structured (using questionnaires) or unstructured (open-ended).

organizing of a war party. The only way the pre-reservation culture of these peoples could be studied was by interviewing individuals who had grown to adulthood before the reservations were created. Today, we refer to this early use of interviewing alone as **recall ethnography**. In a relatively short period, anthropologists were able to collect, and thus preserve, a vast body of general descriptive data on pre-reservation Native American cultures.

In the 1920s, anthropologists' interest began to shift from just recording descriptions of the general culture of a society to attempting to understand the basic dynamics of cultural systems. In other words, anthropologists wanted to see how these systems worked and how their parts fit together. A leader in this change was Bronislaw Malinowski, mentioned in the discussion of functionalism in Chapter 5, who popularized a new data-collection technique called **participant observation**. Anthropologists no longer merely recorded interviews and analyzed people's statements. To a greater or lesser extent, they took up residence with the people they were studying and began trying to learn about the culture by observing people in their daily lives and participating in their daily activities.

Participant observation has often been misinterpreted, even by some anthropologists who have taken it too literally. It does not mean becoming a full participant in the activities of the people—in other words, "going native." The emphasis of this technique is more on observation than on participation. Participant observation usually does require that one live in the community because only by doing so can one observe and record the behavior of individuals as they go about their daily work, visit their friends, interact with their relatives, participate in rituals, and so on. These observations of behavior serve to generate new questions. Why does a family share its food with some families but not with others? Why do some men wear their hair in a particular style? Does a particular color of clothing have any meaning? Some behaviors have significance; others do not. For example, variations in hairstyles may

be merely the result of personal preferences, or they may reflect status differences. Color may or may not have special significance. In American culture, black symbolizes mourning; but in other societies, covering one's body with white clay symbolizes the same emotion. Participant observation allows the researcher to collect more detailed data than does interviewing alone, and thus it makes possible a deeper understanding of interrelationships among cultural phenomena.

Firsthand observations of the members of a community also enable the researcher to see how people diverge from the culturally defined, idealized model of behavior. An incident that occurred while Malinowski was working in the Trobriand Islands illustrates the divergence between cultural norms—the way people say they ought to behave and the way they actually behave. One day, Malinowski heard a commotion in the village and discovered that a young boy in a neighboring village had committed suicide by climbing a palm tree and flinging himself onto the beach. In his earlier questioning of the islanders, Malinowski had been told that sexual relations between a man and his mother's sister's daughters were prohibited. On inquiring into the suicide of the young boy, Malinowski found that the boy had been sexually involved with his mother's sister's daughter and that such incestuous relationships were not rare. So long as such liaisons were not mentioned in public, they were ignored. In this particular case, the girl's ex-boyfriend had become angry and publicly exposed the transgression. Although everyone in the village already knew of this incestuous relationship, by making it public the ex-boyfriend exposed his rival to ridicule, thus causing him to commit suicide. It is doubtful that such behavior could have been discovered by only interviewing individuals.

Problems and Issues in Field Research

Every fieldwork experience is unique. Thus, specific problems differ, depending on the personal characteristics of the researcher, the nature of the community, and the particular questions being studied. There are, however, three difficulties that, to varying degrees and in different ways, affect virtually every field research situation: (1) **stereotyping**, (2) defining the fieldworker's role in the community and developing rapport, and (3) identifying and interviewing consultants.

Ethnic Stereotyping

When we think of stereotypes—preconceived generalizations concerning a particular group of people—we usually think only of their effects on the perceptions of one party of a relationship. Anthropologists ask themselves how they can overcome their own stereotypes and

recall ethnography Technique for reconstructing a cultural system at a slightly earlier period by interviewing older individuals who lived during that period.

participant observation Main technique used in conducting ethnographic fieldwork, involving living among a people and participating in their daily activities.

stereotyping Having preconceived mental images of a group that bias the way one perceives group members and interprets their behavior.

cultural biases about the people they study. Stereotyping, however, is a two-way street. Every society has beliefs or stereotypes concerning members of other societies and of ethnic and racial groups. Thus, although the goal is for anthropologists to put aside their personal biases and beliefs sufficiently to study the cultural system of another people with some degree of objectivity, those with whom the ethnographer will be living and studying will not have put aside their own biases and beliefs about other people.

The situation is rapidly changing, but most anthropologists have been and still are of European ancestry, while most subjects of anthropological research are non-European peoples. Even if a particular anthropologist is of Asian, African, or Native American ancestry, a similar problem exists because anthropologists seldom belong to the local community they study and thus are outsiders. As a result, an anthropologist who enters another community must contend with local stereotypes about the ethnic or racial group with which the anthropologist is identified.

During World War II, many Navajos served as "code talkers" for the Marine Corps in the Pacific, sending and receiving coded messages in Navajo for field communication. The Japanese were never able to break the code because they were unfamiliar with the language. Tom Sasaki, a Japanese American anthropologist, arrived on the Navajo reservation in 1948 to begin his research. The rumor spread that he was possibly a Japanese spy wanting to learn the language so they could break the code. As a result, he did not attempt to learn the language. Even still, mistrusting his motives, many of the Navajo veterans initially avoided him.

In the case of anthropologists of European ancestry, local stereotyping has most frequently been derived from contact with only a limited range of individuals such as missionaries, soldiers, government officials, tourists, or people involved in economic development projects. Regardless of the nature and intensity of this contact, most non-Western peoples have well-developed ideas about the expected behavior of such individuals.

The tendency of local people to attempt to fit the ethnographer into one of their existing stereotypical categories can at times prove a burden for fieldworkers. Anthropologists' behavior seldom conforms to the model that the local people have developed. Thus, an anthropologist attempting to gain social acceptance in such a society is typically met with suspicion, if not at times with hostility. The types of questions anthropologists ask about behavior and beliefs frequently arouse more suspicions and elicit guarded answers. Why does this researcher want to know about our family structure, political organization, and ritual secrets? What is the person going to do with this information?

While the anthropologist is trying to understand the community, the members of the community are attempting to understand the anthropologist's motives. Depending on the nature of previous contacts, some types of questions may provoke more suspicion than others. For example, a minority or tribal group involved in some illegal or illicit activity—such as smuggling, poaching, or growing drugs—may wonder whether the anthropologist will inform government authorities. Members of groups that have been exposed to Western culture frequently assume that the ethnographer's objective is to make money and that researchers become wealthy by publishing books.

In other cases, members of the community may be aware that Europeans and Euro-Americans do not approve of or believe in certain types of behaviors, and few people will disclose information on topics they think will be met with disapproval or scorn. This reticence is particularly evident for certain types of religious beliefs and practices.

As a result of the extensive activities of Christian missionaries, most non-Western peoples are well aware that Westerners usually deny the validity of witchcraft and the existence of werewolves. Members of societies that hold such beliefs are frequently hesitant about discussing these subjects with Westerners. They are understandably reluctant to talk openly about an uncle who they believe can turn himself into a deer or a snake with someone who they think will view what they say as ridiculous. Likewise, they probably would hesitate to say that their father had been killed by a witch if they thought the researcher did not believe in witchcraft. Clyde Kluckhohn found Navajos to be highly reluctant to formally discuss witchcraft in interviews. In his book *Navaho Witchcraft*, he noted that over half of the individuals he "interviewed" for the book were Navajo hitchhikers he picked up driving around the reservation or friends he talked to while driving them to town or to a government agency. In private casual conversations while driving, they were more far likely to discuss witchcraft.

Developing a Role and Rapport

An anthropologist has to develop a rapport with the members of the community, often against a background of suspicion and distrust. **Rapport** in this sense means acceptance to the degree that a working relationship is possible. Although ethnographers are rarely totally accepted

rapport Working relationship between the researcher and the members of the community he or she is studying.

World History Archive/Alamy

In 1897, an invading British military force took over 900 brass plaques from the royal palace of the Kingdom of Benin (now part of Nigeria) and sold them at auction to help cover the cost of the expedition. Today they are scattered among museums in Europe and North America. As early as 1936, the Oba of Benin requested their return. More recently, the Nigerian parliament has requested their repatriation.

The discipline of anthropology is rooted in European colonial expansion. From the very beginning, some individual soldiers, explorers, and missionaries thought that it was important to create a record of the peoples whose cultures they were in the process of destroying.

Four years after the conquest of Mexico, in 1529, Father Bernardino de Sahagún arrived as a Franciscan missionary. His interest in Aztec culture eventually resulted in what some have termed the first ethnography of a Native American society. In 1549, Diego de Landa became the Bishop of Yucatán. While aggressively pursuing a policy of converting the Maya to Catholicism, he also wrote an account of the Maya religious and cultural practices he was attempting to destroy. In 1609, Garcilaso de la Vega, the son of a Spanish conquistador and a member of the Incan nobility, published an account

of the Inca in Peru. Other Spaniards recorded similar accounts, and in the centuries that followed, still other Europeans thought it important to do likewise. By the seventeenth century, members of the European nobility and wealthy merchants had begun collecting exotic ethnographic items from around the world, creating what were called "curiosity cabinets." However, these early ethnographic accounts and collections were not done in a systematic manner.

It was not until the mid-1800s, with the creation of public museums, that the systematic study and collection of cultural materials began to emerge, and it would not be until the beginning of the twentieth century that anthropology would become an academic discipline within universities. What originally distinguished anthropology from other academic disciplines was its focus on non-Western peoples, particularly smaller societies of preliterate, indigenous peoples who hunted, gathered, herded, and farmed. In Britain, early anthropologists initially focused on the peoples in the British empire, while in the United States anthropologists focused on the Native American peoples who by this time lived on reservations. It was widely believed that these small groups of indigenous peoples could not become modern or "civilized" and survive. They were doomed to extinction—if not biologically, then certainly culturally. To the academic world, it was important to preserve a permanent record of these peoples, because they represented an earlier vanishing stage of human cultural development.

To anthropologists, the idea that within a few generations these peoples would be gone meant that they could disregard their cultural sensitivities in collecting and recording the cultures. Archaeologists could excavate their burials. Physical anthropologists could collect and study the remains of their ancestors. Museum curators could collect their most sacred religious objects, even the ones still needed for their rituals. Cultural anthropologists

could research the most private and sacred aspects of their lives and record them in text, photographs, and drawings as well as on film and in audio recordings.

Early cultural anthropologists approached their research and collecting with an almost religious zeal. In regard to their cultural behavior, both past and still existing native peoples had no rights, and many anthropologists went to great lengths to secure cultural data. Leslie White, in his introduction to his study of the Zia Pueblo in New Mexico, notes, "The pueblo . . . takes a firm stand on the question of secrecy [in regard to religious practices]." However, "there are occasional individuals . . . who feel that a record of it [meaning religious practices] should be made and preserved. It is the ethnographer's task to 'scent out' such individuals" (White, 1962, p. 17). He further stated that these individuals had to be interviewed secretly to protect them.

To anthropologists, it was critical to record and preserve as complete a record as possible of the culture of these peoples before they were gone—not for the use of their descendants, if there were any, but for civilized peoples to have a better understanding of their own, uncivilized past. This is not to say that anthropologists totally disregarded their human rights. In fact, anthropologists were among the earliest and most vocal supporters of individual and economic rights for these peoples at a time when most people of European descent argued that they had no rights. At the same time, basic cultural and intellectual property rights were being ignored.

This relationship between anthropological researchers/collectors and the indigenous peoples remained basically unchanged until the last decades of the twentieth century. Early anthropologists were correct, in part. Globalization eventually changed the lives of these peoples—some more than others. Collectively, they have become increasingly educated and literate, with increasing numbers even attending universities to become lawyers, doctors, and other professionals. In other words, many members of these societies have become fully "modernized." However, early anthropologists were incorrect in their assumption that these descendants would lose their identities and their cultural heritage. As they became more integrated into and aware of the "modern" world, they became increasing hostile not only to the economic and political domination and exploitation by the societies that controlled them, but to what they viewed as the cultural exploitation by members of these dominant societies as well.

Initially, their concern was with the repatriation of their tangible cultural properties: human remains, burial goods, sacred objects, and objects of cultural patrimony. Western societies had applied a different legal standard to the cultural properties of indigenous peoples. Had these same cultural properties belonged to members of the dominant society, there would have been no question as to the illegality of having taken them. Anthropologists and museums had in fact stolen them.

Many governments have adopted laws and policies in attempts to remedy this situation. In 1984, Australia passed the Aboriginal and Torres Straits Islander Heritage Act, which gave protection to indigenous areas and objects of significance. In 1990, the U.S. Congress passed the Native American Graves Protection and Repatriation Act (NAGPRA), which called for the repatriation of human remains, funerary objects, sacred objects, and objects of cultural patrimony to Native American groups, including native Hawaiians, held by museums and federal agencies. In the 1990s, Canada adopted a policy, not a law, to encourage the repatriation of cultural properties to its native peoples, and many Canadian museums have voluntarily done so. In 2000, the Working Group on Human Remains, a governmental advisory committee, was established in Great Britain to study the issue of human remains in publicly funded museums. Many British museums have already repatriated human remains. In 2007, the United Nations passed the Declaration on the Rights of Indigenous Peoples.

Among other things, the declaration states that indigenous peoples have the right to "the access and/or the repatriation of ceremonial objects and human remains." However, this policy is not legally binding. Regardless, the repatriation of the tangible cultural properties of indigenous people has increasingly become a global issue.

The question of tangible cultural properties only affects some forms of cultural anthropological research. It is the related issue of intellectual property rights that is most directly relevant to cultural anthropologists' research. Most developed countries in the world today have laws protecting intellectual property rights. Literature, songs, music, art, logos, and knowledge are or can be the property of individuals or groups in the form of copyrights, patents, or trademarks. Also legally recognized, but not as clearly defined, are the rights of individuals and groups to privacy and even secrecy as well as protection against slander and libel. The earliest anthropologists recognized that individuals and groups within these indigenous societies owned and controlled the use of certain oral traditions, songs, music, artistic designs, and knowledge. They also noted that certain (usually religious) activities were not public but private, the knowledge of them being restricted to certain groups within these societies. Yet they, like White, worked diligently to record them—in writing, in photographs, and on film and tape recordings. Even worse, still other members of the dominant society ignored the intellectual property rights of indigenous peoples, freely using them for commercial purposes in popular literature, movies, television programs, advertising, and countless other ways, while frequently demeaning the members of the society as being childlike, savages, or worse.

Near the time of his death in 1976, Charles Mountford, an Australian anthropologist, published *Nomads of the Australian Desert*, using photographs of and other materials he had collected from the Pitjantjatjara people in the 1930s and early 1940s. The Pitjantjatjara sued, claiming a breach of confidence and that the publication had made available to uninitiated men as well

as women and children information that harmed the social and religious stability of the Pitjantjatjara. The Australian courts agreed, blocking sales of the book in the Northern Territory where they live. In 1982, Mountford's photographic collection was to be sold at auction. However, the Pitjantjatjara Council again sued in court and was able to remove those photographs that its members considered potentially harmful from the auction.

Intellectual property rights, the rights of privacy, and control of public images have become increasingly contentious issues. The 2007 UN Declaration states that indigenous peoples "have the right to maintain, control, protect and develop their intellectual property over . . . cultural heritage, traditional knowledge, and traditional cultural expressions" as well as "privacy to their religious and cultural sites." However, as noted, this is a moral position that lacks the force of law.

Increasingly, indigenous peoples throughout the world are themselves attempting to control cultural access to members of their societies, related archival materials, and the public dissemination of information relative to their cultural heritage. In 1997, the Working Group of Indigenous Minorities in South Africa (WIMSA) announced that from now on they would require payments from the media and from researchers wishing to document or study San life and that legal action would be taken against companies for the unauthorized use of San photographs in books, postcards, advertisements, and tourist promotions. However, the San were concerned about other intellectual properties as well. Based on traditional San knowledge and use, the South African government agency the Council for Scientific and Industrial Research (CSIR) was able to study and isolate the active chemical properties of the hoodia cactus. CSIR sold their now patented discovery to a pharmaceutical company to be used in diet pills. The San sued in court, and in 2003 the CSIR agreed to share in the royalties.

In 2006, a group of Native and non–Native American academics drafted a set of "Protocols for Native American Archival Materials," which, among other

continues on next page

things, calls for restricting access to and use of certain culturally "sensitive" materials found in archival collections.

Many indigenous groups and societies throughout the world have developed their own formal protocols for the researching and recording of members of their society. Probably none are as comprehensive as the one adopted by the Hopi in Arizona, entitled "Protocol for Research, Publication and Recordings: Motion, Visual, Sound, Multimedia and Other Mechanical Devices." The stated reason and purpose of this policy is to protect the Hopi people's rights to privacy and to intellectual property, due to the continued abuse, misrepresentation, and exploitation of the Hopi. All projects or activities involving intellectual property have to be reviewed and approved by the Hopi Cultural Preservation Office. It further defines projects or activities as, "but not limited to, research, publications recording-motion, visual sound whether oral, written, via multimedia or other mechanical devices discovered or yet to be discovered." Research is defined as including, "but not limited to, ethnology, history, biogenetic, medical, behavioral, ethno-botany, agronomy, ecology, anthropology, archaeology, and microbiology." The Hopi tribe furthermore

> reserves the right to: (1) Prevent publication of intellectual resources which is unauthorized, sensitive, misrepresentatives or stereotypical of the Hopi people. . . . (2) May require deposit of raw materials or data, working papers or products in a tribally designated repository, with specific safeguards to preserve confidentiality.

Finally, it states that the Hopi tribe will

> review and have input into the product or results before publication. The purpose of this step is to assure that sensitive information is not divulged to the public or misrepresentations can be corrected.

The importance of the Hopi statement on protocols is that they are voicing the concerns of indigenous peoples throughout the world. Survival of a people depends on being able to have some control over their own cultural traditions and the outside world's perceptions of those traditions— an almost impossible task for smaller, relatively powerless peoples alone.

Globalization has changed all peoples in the world, including smaller indigenous societies. All peoples have become increasingly aware of other societies and their cultural differences, particularly over the past hundred years. This has dramatically changed the relationship between cultural researchers and the people they study. Anthropologists have long held that their research should "do no harm" to the people they study, either individually or collectively. It was implicit in the first formal Code of Ethics adopted by the American Anthropological Association (AAA) and explicitly stated in later codes, together with the recognition of their rights to privacy. In 2009, the AAA code specifically recognized the need to "protect cultural heritage or tangible or intangible cultural or intellectual property." However, the new Code of Ethics, adopted in 2012, changed the phrasing from "intellectual property" to "intangible heritage" and "privacy" and emphasized "do no harm" and "freely granted consent." The difficulty is that *harm* is a culturally relative term. Mountford did not think that publishing photographs and descriptions of rituals would "harm" the Pitjantjatjara, but later it was acknowledged that these practices could be harmful. Only the people themselves can or should judge what is or might be harmful. As to a society's right to privacy, as White discovered, a researcher can always find someone who will freely grant consent.

In large part, the changes in the AAA's Code of Ethics are a public acknowledgment that a professional organization does not have the authority to control its members' behavior. Indigenous peoples have to protect themselves by developing formal or at least informal protocols for research, such as those of the Hopi. Increasingly, out of necessity, cultural research will focus on the study of issues that both the researcher and the people being studied see as being of mutual value, not just of some abstract academic importance.

Both the nature and the focus of field research in cultural anthropology have changed dramatically over the past 30 plus years. No longer a colonial enterprise, both cultural anthropology as a discipline and the peoples we study should greatly benefit from the change.

by the people among whom they work, over a period of time, most anthropologists succeed in gaining some degree of trust and friendship among members of the group.

The particular role or roles that anthropologists eventually define for themselves within a society vary greatly with the circumstances of the particular situation. Depending on the amount and nature of research funding, an anthropologist may be an important economic resource for the community, paying wages to interpreters and assistants or distributing desirable goods as gifts. Anthropologists who have a car, truck, or other means of transportation frequently find themselves providing needed transportation for members of the community. Ethnographers may also provide comic relief by asking "silly questions," behaving in a funny manner, making childlike errors in speaking the language, and generally being amusing to have around. Researchers may also be a source of information about the outside world, disclosing information to which local people would not otherwise have access. Sometimes community members are as curious about the anthropologist's society as the anthropologist is about theirs. Or the anthropologist may be considered just a harmless nuisance. During the course of research, the typical fieldworker adopts most of these roles, plus many others (see Global Challenges and Opportunities).

Identifying and Interviewing Consultants

Ethnographers learn a good deal about people simply by living among them and observing and participating in many of their activities. However, observation and participation alone are insufficient. We want to know not only what people are doing but also why they are doing it. Because certain realms of culture are not observable (e.g., religious beliefs, myths, stories, and social values), the researcher has to interview members of the group.

An individual who supplies the ethnographer with information is called a **consultant** or an **informant**. Field research involves the help of many consultants, who sometimes are paid for their services. Just as no one individual is equally well informed about every aspect of our own cultural system, so no single individual in another society is equally knowledgeable about every aspect of his or her society's way of life. Women are more knowledgeable than men concerning certain things, and vice versa. Shamans and priests know more about religious rituals than other people. The elderly members of the community are usually most knowledgeable about myths, stories, and histories. Thus, the anthropologist has to attempt to identify and interview those most knowledgeable about the particular subject or subjects being studied. An individual whom the local community considers to be expert in some particular area is known as a **key consultant** or **key informant**.

A number of factors affect the quality and accuracy of the data collected through interviewing. It is important to always remember that the members of the community are just like any other group of people. Whether they are fully cooperative or not, individuals differ in their abilities to recall specific facts. Still other individuals are actually misinformed, or for various reasons they deliberately misinform the researcher. There is a widespread belief among many younger Native Americans that their ancestors frequently and deliberately gave anthropologists misinformation about their culture. Did this happen? It undoubtedly did occur. Also, Native American people in particular love to joke, and a naive researcher would be a likely victim of their humor.

The first summer I was working on the Navajo reservation, I was interviewing a talkative local man who suddenly remarked that the valley in back of his house was called "No Fat Valley" after a cow they had butchered there was found to have no fat on it. I had never met the man before, and he seemed to have good sense of humor and liked to joke. Although I made a note of his remark, I was thinking that he was joking with a naive anthropologist and forgot about it. Several years later I was driving by this valley with another local man with whom I had become a close friend. To pass the time, I casually asked if the Navajo had a name for this valley. He told me that in the 1930s he was working on digging the irrigation ditch near the mouth of the valley. There had been a bad drought on the mesa, and the workers saw a skinny stray cow coming down the valley. The workers caught it and killed it. When they were butchering it, they were surprised. It was so skinny that it had no fat on it, so they started calling the valley "No Fat." In this case I was initially wrong. However, undoubtedly in others cases many cultural researchers have probably been victims of local humor.

Cultural barriers also make it difficult to collect certain types of data. For example, collecting genealogies is not always as easy as it might seem because in many societies it is customary not to speak the names of the dead. Among the Yanomamö in Venezuela and Brazil, not only is it taboo to speak the names of the dead, but it is also considered discourteous to speak the names of prominent living men, for whom kinship terms are used whenever possible. When ethnographer Napoleon Chagnon persisted in his attempts to collect genealogies, the Yanomamö responded by inventing a series of fictitious genealogical relationships. Only after five months of intensive research did Chagnon discover the hoax. When he mentioned some of the names he had collected during a visit to a neighboring village, the people responded with uncontrollable laughter because his informants had made up names such as "hairy rectum" and "eagle shit" to avoid speaking the real names. Sometime misinformation has undoubtedly worked it is way into the academic literature. However, to avoid these and other difficulties, anthropologists try to interview a number of individuals separately about specific points to gain independent verifications.

Fieldwork as a Rite of Passage

Fieldwork is important to cultural anthropologists not just because it is our primary source of data on human cultures but also because it is a key aspect of the anthropologist's education. It is one thing to read ethnographies

consultant (informant) Member of a society who provides information to a fieldworker, often through formal interviews or surveys.

key consultant (key informant) Member of a society who is especially knowledgeable about some subject and who supplies information to a fieldworker.

about other ways of life, but it is something quite different to live among and interact with individuals from another cultural tradition daily for a year or longer.

As we have noted, anthropologists usually live in the native community, submerging themselves in the social life of the people, living in native dwellings, eating local foods, learning the language, and participating as fully as an outsider is allowed in daily activities. Living as social minorities, usually for the first time in their lives, anthropologists depend on the goodwill of people whose norms and values they neither totally understand nor completely accept. Under these conditions, the researcher has to adjust his or her behavior to fit the norms and behavior patterns of the people under study. Modifying the fieldworker's own behavior is necessary to learning about the community. During the course of their research, anthropologists will violate, or at least be perceived as violating, some of the societal norms of behavior. Such incidents may destroy the rapport gained with some key consultants or result in the researcher being ostracized. In serious cases, the fieldworker may become the target of physical violence.

When in the field, except on rare occasions, the anthropologist is the uninvited guest of the community. Regardless of how researchers may rationalize their work as being for the long-term good of the community, science, or humanity in general, they are basically there to serve their own needs and interests. If a serious problem develops between the anthropologist and members of the community, the fieldworker must bear the primary responsibility and blame.

The fieldwork experience tests and taxes the attitude of cultural relativity (as discussed in Chapter 1) that anthropologists teach in their classrooms. It is easy to discuss cultural relativity in a university setting, but it is more difficult to apply this concept when actually living with another group of people. Regardless of which society it is, certain cultural behaviors will offend one's own cultural norms and values. For example, according to the anthropologist's own social norms, some local people might "abuse" certain family members or certain powerful leaders might "exploit" lower-ranking members of the society. As the fieldworker develops friendships, this abuse or exploitation frequently

becomes personalized. Under what circumstances, if ever, should an anthropologist attempt to intervene and try to impose her or his cultural standards on the members of another society? This question poses a real and personal dilemma. In theory, such intervention is never permissible, but in real-life situations, the answer is not always so clear.

Many people experience a kind of psychological trauma when surrounded by people speaking a language they cannot fully understand and can speak only imperfectly, eating foods that are strange, seeing architecture that is alien, and observing people using gestures and behaving in ways they either do not comprehend or do not approve of. The strange sounds, smells, tastes, sights, and behaviors result in disorientation. Out of their normal cultural context, fieldworkers do not understand what is happening around them, yet they realize that their own actions are often misunderstood. The symptoms of **culture shock** are psychological and sometimes even physiological: paranoia, anxiety, longing for the folks back home, nausea, hypochondria, and, frequently, diarrhea.

The attempts by ethnographers to maintain their relativistic perspective and objectivity in their daily interaction with members of the other society usually compound the normal trauma of culture shock. Socially isolated and unable to release their frustrations and anxieties through conversations with sympathetic others, they often have to cope with their psychological difficulties alone.

For many anthropologists, much of their time in the field is extremely traumatic, and as a result, most anthropologists view fieldwork as a rite of passage. More than any other aspect of their training, fieldwork transforms students of anthropology into professional anthropologists. Although many overemphasize the importance of fieldwork, it is undeniably a significant educational experience. Most individuals return from their fieldwork with a different perspective on themselves and their own culture. Fieldwork often teaches us as much about our own culture as about the culture of the peoples we are studying.

Ethnohistory

The study of past cultural systems through the use of written records is called **ethnohistory**. Since the late nineteenth century, anthropologists have used historic written materials in their studies, but the importance of this research has been widely recognized only since the 1970s. The growing interest in ethnohistory had come with the realization that non-Western societies

culture shock Feeling of uncertainty and anxiety an individual experiences when placed in a strange cultural setting.

ethnohistory Study of past cultures using written accounts and other documents.

have changed far more dramatically over the past few hundred years than had previously been thought.

Like historians who study their society's past, ethnohistorians make use of materials such as published books and articles, newspapers, archival documents, diaries, journals, maps, drawings, and photographs. Not surprisingly, many scholars treat *history* and *ethnohistory* as if they were synonymous. There are, however, critical—yet frequently overlooked—differences:

- An ethnohistorian is primarily interested in reconstructing the cultural system of the people. The actual historical events themselves are of interest only because they cast light on the cultural system or changes in the system.

- Historical events have little significance outside the cultural context of the peoples involved. Ethnohistorians study nonliterate peoples. Thus, whereas historians can use accounts recorded by members of the society being studied, ethnohistorians have to use accounts recorded by members of other literate societies. As a result, the problem of interpreting accounts is far more difficult for the ethnohistorian than for the historian.

The problem of interpretation raises an additional question about the validity of particular reports. Not only do we have to ask about the accuracy of the account, but we also have to ask how knowledgeable the recorder was about the cultural context of the events. Ethnohistorians use certain criteria to evaluate the potential validity of an account. How long did the writer live among these people? Did the observer speak the language? What was the observer's role? Soldiers, missionaries, traders, and government officials have different views, biases, and access to information.

The difficulty with ethnohistory is that no hard-and-fast rules can be used in evaluating these data. The longer an individual lived among members of a particular society and the better the person spoke the language, the more reliable the account should be; however, this cannot be automatically assumed. In some cases, the writer may have had little interest in the people, perhaps because the contacts were only job related. This attitude is evident in the accounts of many traders and government officials. In other cases, the account may be self-serving, with individuals attempting to enhance their careers. Thus, sometimes soldiers and government officials falsified their official reports.

Ethnocentrism is still another factor. Missionary accounts, in particular, often demonstrate overt bias against local customs and beliefs; one has to remember that individuals become missionaries because they are avid believers. Nevertheless, missionaries, who were scholars themselves, wrote some of the most objective accounts of other societies.

Thus, in ethnohistoric research, there is no simple way to evaluate a particular document or account. At best, a single event may be recorded in several independent accounts that can each be used to verify the accuracy and interpretation of the others. Unfortunately, multiple observations are the exception, not the rule.

A good example of the problem of the cultural interpretations of historic events is the case of Captain James Cook. In January 1778, Cook discovered the Hawaiian Islands. He stayed for only three days before sailing for the North Pacific. The next winter he returned and sailed among the islands for seven weeks before landing on the large island on January 19, 1779. This second landing was greeted by thousands of Hawaiians, including King Kalani'opu'u. Cook was presented with a feathered cloak and cap while thousands of people prostrated themselves chanting the name "Lono," a Polynesian god. On February 4, he left with a great celebration by the people. However, problems with one of his ships forced him to return. On this third landfall, he was killed on the beach. Why?

For a long time scholars have argued that Cook was identified as the god Lono. Studying the written accounts of English seamen who accompanied Cook and ethnographic descriptions of Hawaiian religious beliefs and practices, Marshall Sahlins reexamined the case. Lono was a mythical god-king who periodically returned to the islands and ruled in human form, usurping the power of earthly kings who were representatives of the rival god Ku. Every year a series of rituals were performed dedicated to Lono's symbolic returns. Cook's movements and his first two landings in 1778 and 1779 corresponded with the timing of these rituals. However, his third landing did not. It was interpreted as Lono's return to take the power of the earthly kings and the priests of the god Ku. Thus, the priest of Ku killed Cook, viewing his killing as sacrifice of the rival god-king Lono, a ritual that they reenacted every year. Is Sahlins correct in his interpretation?

Gananath Obeyesekere, a Sri Lankan anthropologist, challenged Sahlins's analysis. He could not think of a single example of Sri Lankans or any other South Asian people seeing the newly arrived Europeans as gods. To him this was an example of European myth building in which the European explorer/civilizer becomes a god to the natives, as well as exemplifying the implicit assumption among Western academics (meaning Sahlins) that non-Western peoples are prelogical or mystical. However, neither Sahlins nor Obeyesekere nor the early English who accompanied Cook were Hawaiian. Ethnocentric bias is a problem not just with interpreting ethnohistoric accounts but in the academic interpretations of these accounts as well.

A final limitation on the use of ethnohistoric materials is that seldom are all aspects of a particular society evenly reported. For example, data on economic activities may be the most abundant, whereas information on religious ceremonies and beliefs may be absent or limited. As a result, ethnographic studies based on ethnohistoric research alone usually lack the depth and balance of studies gained from field research.

Despite its problems and limitations, ethnohistoric research provides us with the only clues we have to the past culture of many societies. It is also the key to a vast store of previously untapped cultural data.

Comparative Methods

So far, we have discussed only how anthropologists collect cultural data on peoples, past and present, using fieldwork and historical materials. We have some cultural data available on more than 1,200 societies. As shown in the following chapters, anthropologists have used these data to demonstrate a wide range of cultural variability among human populations. However, we are not interested in merely describing particular cultural systems and the range of variability they display. We are also interested in attempting to explain why these differences exist. In other words, anthropologists want to make generalizations concerning cultural systems. Generalizations cannot be made based on the study of a single society; we need **comparative methods** by which many societies can be explored in a systematic way. The objective of comparative studies is to test hypotheses.

Comparative research dates back to the earliest day of anthropology. The research of the unilineal evolutionists of the late of the nineteenth century, Tylor and Morgan (discussed in Chapter 5), was based on comparative studies. However, there were some serious methodological problems in these early studies. In 1937, a group of

---

comparative methods Methods that test hypotheses by systematically comparing elements from many cultures.

cross-cultural comparison Methodology for testing a hypothesis using a sample of societies drawn from around the world.

---

social scientists at Yale University led by George Peter Murdock produced the Outline of Cultural Materials, the first universal systematic scheme to topically classify cultural variables. This led to the establishment of the Human Relations Area Files (HRAF) in 1949. HRAF created the "Collection of Ethnography," which consisted primarily of published books and articles on about 400 different societies in the world, indexed for 710 subject categories. This setup allowed for quick retrieval of relevant cultural material on specific topics. Later, between 1962 and 1967, Murdock complied his "Ethnographic Atlas," in which he coded cultural variables on 100 topics for 1,167 different societies, allowing researchers to analyze the correlations between a limited range of cultural variables without consulting the ethnographic literature. HRAF and the "Ethnographic Atlas" revolutionized comparative studies (see http://hraf.yale.edu/).

Cross-Cultural Comparisons

By far, the most frequently used comparative method is **cross-cultural comparison**. In this method, hypotheses are tested by examining the statistical correlations between particular cultural variables, using synchronic data drawn from a number of societies. Historical changes in the societies examined are ignored; the societies are compared at whatever period they were studied or on which relevant cultural data exist. The HRAF, for example, allows one to compare variables not just between twentieth-century peoples throughout the world, but with imperial Romans, sixteenth-century Aztecs, and many other earlier societies as well.

This research method involves three steps. First, the researcher must state the idea as a hypothesis—that is, state it in such a way that it can be supported or not supported (tested) by data drawn from a large number of human populations. Second, the ethnologist chooses a sample of societies (usually randomly) and studies the ethnographies that describe their way of life. Third, the data collected from these ethnographies are classified and grouped in such a manner that the correlations between variables may be shown statistically. What the researcher is attempting to find is the pattern of association: Do two or more cultural variables consistently occur together or not? In most cases, these tasks are far more difficult than they may sound.

To illustrate how the cross-cultural method is used to test a hypothesis, we shall examine the relationship between sorcery and legal systems within a group of societies. Sorcery is discussed in some detail in Chapter 13. Here, it is sufficient to know that sorcery is the belief that certain people (sorcerers) have power, either supernatural or magical, to cause harm to others. Some anthropologists believe that sorcery serves as a means of social control in societies that lack a formalized legal apparatus—courts, police, and so forth—to punish wrongdoers. They argue that people will be reluctant to cause trouble if they believe that a victim of their troublemaking has the ability to use supernatural power to retaliate against them. Overall, societies without a formal legal system should have a greater need for a mechanism such as sorcery to control behavior. So, if the hypothesis that sorcery is a mechanism for social control is correct, we ought to find that sorcery is more important in societies that have no formal means of punishment than in societies with a specialized legal system.

To see whether this hypothesis is true across a variety of societies, we use the cross-cultural method. We determine for many societies (1) the relative degree of importance of sorcery and (2) whether the society has a formal apparatus for punishing wrongdoing. We make a table in which all the possible combinations of the two cultural elements are recorded:

Sorcery	Specialized Legal Apparatus Absent	Specialized Legal Apparatus Present
Important	A	B
Unimportant	C	D

In the cells of the table, we record the number of societies in which the four possible combinations are found. If the hypothesis is supported, we should find that cells A and D contain the greatest number of societies. If the hypothesis is not supported, we should find that the distribution of societies in the cells is random, or that cells B and C contain the greatest number of societies, or some other distribution.

In 1950, Beatrice Whiting conducted such a study by surveying the ethnographic literature for 50 societies. Her results were as follows (Whiting, 1950, p. 87):

Sorcery	Specialized Legal Apparatus Absent	Specialized Legal Apparatus Present
Important	30	5
Unimportant	3	12

On the basis of this comparison, we might conclude that the hypothesis is supported because most of the societies fall into the cells predicted by our hypothesis. We would not worry about the eight societies (the "exceptions") that appear in cells B and C. The hypothesis did not claim that social control was the *only* function of sorcery, so the importance of sorcery in the five societies in cell B might be explained by some other factor. Nor did we claim that sorcery was the *only* way that societies lacking a specialized legal apparatus had to control their members, so the three societies in cell C might have developed some alternative means of social control. (However, outside the scope of this text, statistical tests are available that show how confident a researcher can be that such associations did not occur by chance.)

Some confusion is caused by cross-cultural tabulations such as this. One of the most common is to mistake correlation for causation: Simply because two cultural elements (X and Y) are usually found together does not mean that one (X) has caused the other (Y). Y could have caused X, or both X and Y could have been caused by some third element, W. In the preceding example, it was assumed that the absence of formal legal punishments "caused" many societies to need some other social control mechanism, and that sorcery became important to meet this need. On the basis of the data in the table, we might also conclude that societies in which sorcery is important have little need for a formal legal apparatus, so they fail to develop one.

This approach suffers from several disadvantages, the most important of which is the problem of bias by the researcher, who must decide, for example, whether sorcery should be considered important or unimportant among some people. Borderline cases might get lumped into the category that supports the researcher's hypothesis.

Using cross-cultural methods to see whether some specific hypothesis applies to a large number of societies is thus easier today than ever before, but some difficulties still exist. One seems to be inherent in the method itself, which dissects whole cultures into parts ("variables") and assigns a value (or "state") to each part. In the preceding example, the variables were sorcery, which had two states (important, unimportant) and specialized legal apparatus, which also had two states (present, absent). To test the hypothesis that the states of these two cultural elements are consistently related, we ignored everything else about them. We also ignored everything else about the societies in the sample, such as their family systems and their economies.

A more familiar example makes the point clearly. One element of cultural systems is the number of gods in whom people believe. For purposes of some specific hypothesis, the possible states of this variable might be

Christianity, Judaism, and Islam are all monotheistic and have common historical roots. But Christians and Jews do not pray by prostrating themselves toward Mecca, as these Muslims are doing. Should cross-cultural researchers consider all of them one kind of religion or not?

monotheism (belief in one god), *polytheism* (belief in many gods), and no gods. Any researcher who included modern North America in the sample would probably consider our primary religion—Christianity—as monotheistic. Most of the Middle East also would be considered monotheistic. But, can we consider North American monotheism equivalent to the monotheisms of the Middle East? If we consider them the same, we ignore the differences between the worship of the Christian God, the Jewish Yahweh, and the Islamic Allah. When we lump these three varieties of monotheism together into a single kind of religion, we distort them to some degree.

Cross-cultural studies examine data ahistorically, or without reference to time. In other words, the cultural system of a particular society is treated as timeless or unchanging. Thus, in cross-cultural studies and the "Ethnographic Atlas," there is "a" cultural system coded for the Cheyenne: Cheyenne cultural system circa 1850. However, the culture of a society is constantly changing. For example, today the Cheyenne live in houses, drive cars and trucks, and participate in a wage-money economy. In 1850, the Cheyenne lived in hide-covered

tepees, rode horses, and hunted buffalo. In 1650, the Cheyenne lived in permanent earth lodge villages, traveled by foot or canoe, and depended on farming and hunting for their subsistence. Although Cheyenne cultural systems have continuity, all aspects of their culture have changed, to some degree, over the period just described. Thus, in reality, there is no Cheyenne culture but an ever-changing system. The ahistorical studies used in cross-cultural research create an artificially static picture of the cultural system of a society.

Controlled Comparisons

In contrast to cross-cultural comparisons, controlled comparisons make use of diachronic data—comparisons of known changes in certain cultural variables, while controlling for historical and environmental factors. This allows the researcher to define general cultural patterns and test hypotheses. Although a number of early researchers produced such studies, it was not until 1954 that Fred Eggan formally defined controlled comparisons as a distinct research method. Controlled comparisons, like cross-cultural studies, can be extremely complex. We illustrate this method with a simple example.

As we discuss in Chapter 9, people organize their family lives in various ways. Two common ways are matrilineal descent and patrilineal descent. In matrilineal societies, family group membership is inherited through your mother; you belong to your mother's family. In patrilineal societies, group membership is inherited through your father; you belong to your father's family.

Anthropologists have long attempted to explain why some societies are matrilineal and others patrilineal. Cross-cultural research has shown that a relationship exists between matrilineality and patrilineality and the relative economic importance of females and males in the society. However, cross-cultural studies can show us only correlations between descent and other synchronic aspects of the cultural system. For example, these studies can tell us what types of economic systems are most frequently found with matrilineal or patrilineal societies. Cross-cultural studies cannot measure the long-term effects of external changes on matrilineal or patrilineal societies. Is matrilineality or patrilineality more adaptive in some situations than in others? If so, what types of situations favor matrilineal societies and which favor patrilineal societies? To examine this question, we must turn to controlled historical comparisons.

Michael Allen has asserted that matrilineal societies in the Pacific were more successful than patrilineal societies in adapting to European contact. Is there a way to test Allen's assertion? First, we must restructure this statement as a testable hypothesis. What do we mean by success? The term *success* is subjective and cannot be directly measured. We have to convert this term into some measurable quantity. One quantifiable measure of the success of a particular system is the relative ability of a society to maintain or expand its population over time. Thus, our hypothesis would be "Given the same disruptive external pressures, matrilineal societies maintain their population levels better over time than patrilineal societies."

Now we need to find groups of matrilineal societies and patrilineal societies that experienced a comparable intensity of external contact over a period of time and compare their relative populations at the beginning and end of the period. If Allen is correct, the matrilineal societies should have a larger population at the end of the period than the patrilineal societies.

The farming Native American tribes of the eastern United States present an almost ideal case for testing Allen's assertion. They had similar cultural systems, except that some were matrilineal and others were patrilineal. Their collective histories of contact with

Europeans were also basically the same. During the historical period, all these societies suffered the effects of epidemic diseases, warfare (with Europeans as well as each other), severe territorial dislocation, political domination by Europeans, and social discrimination.

Now the problem is determining an appropriate time frame to examine and finding comparable population data. One problem with ethnohistoric research is that the researcher is forced to use the data available in the records. It was not until about 1775 that sufficient population data were available in missionary, military, and explorer accounts to estimate the populations of all these tribes with any accuracy. In 1910, the U.S. Bureau of the Census conducted a special Native American census, which was the first truly comprehensive survey of Native American societies in the United States. Thus, the time frame we will use is from 1775 to 1910. Using ethnographic data, we can then classify particular societies as either matrilineal or patrilineal and determine their populations at the beginning and end of this period:

	1775	1910	Percent
Matrilineal Societies	88,590	82,714	93
Patrilineal Societies	36,400	13,463	37
Totals	124,990	96,177	77

From this table, we can see that during this 135-year period, the matrilineal societies declined by only about 7 percent of their total population, whereas patrilineal societies lost 63 percent of their population. If maintenance of population is a measure of a society's success, then matrilineal societies in the eastern United States were more successful than patrilineal societies.

As is the case with all comparative studies, findings such as these raise more questions than they answer. Are these population figures and the historical experiences of these societies truly comparable? If they are comparable, what is the significant factor? Descent form or some other cultural factor we have not considered? We need to add at this point that not all matrilineal societies in this study were equally successful in maintaining their population levels, and that a few patrilineal societies studied increased in population during this period. There is room, then, for argument. If, in the final analysis, however, we decide that our findings are valid and that matrilineal societies are, under certain conditions, more adaptive than patrilineal societies, we still cannot directly say why.

Cross-cultural comparisons and controlled comparisons give us distinctly different measures of cultural phenomena. They address different questions and

Ethnographic Methods	The collection of cultural data on a particular society or group of societies; the primary purpose is the collection of descriptive data.
Ethnographic Fieldwork	The collection of cultural data from living individuals; this usually requires that the researcher live with or close to the people being studied.
Ethnohistoric Research	The study of the past cultural system of a people through the use of written records.
Comparative Methods	The comparative study of the cultural systems of a number of different societies; the objective is to test hypotheses so that we can explain why differences exist.
Cross-Cultural Comparisons	The testing of hypotheses by using synchronic data drawn from a number of different societies.
Controlled Comparisons	The comparative use of historically documented changes in particular groupings of societies over time to define general cultural patterns and to test hypotheses.

test different hypotheses. They are complementary, not competitive, methodologies.

Some anthropologists believe that both types of comparative studies distort each cultural system in the sample so much that the whole method is invalid. They think that ripping each element out of the particular context in which it is embedded robs it of its significance because each element acquires its meaning only in its unique historical and cultural context.

Despite these and other problems, comparative methods are the only practical means available for determining whether a hypothesis is valid among human cultural systems. Those who use these methods are aware of the difficulties, yet they believe that the advantage of being able to process information on large numbers of societies outweighs the problems. The Concept Review outlines the various research methods we have discussed in the chapter.

SUMMARY

1. **Discuss the major objectives of cultural research.** Cultural research has two objectives. One objective is to record as complete a description of the culture of a particular society as possible. These descriptive studies are termed *ethnographies*. As you will discover in the following chapters, there is tremendous cultural diversity among the peoples of the world. Why? The other objective, therefore, is to attempt to explain this diversity in cultural behavior. These studies are called *ethnologies*. Not surprisingly, the research methods used differ greatly.

2. **Understand that ethnographic research requires different methods of study.** Remembering that the culture of a society changes over time, there are

two sources of cultural data: the living members of the group and historical materials—such as earlier published accounts, manuscripts, drawings, maps, photographs, and the like describing or relating to their past culture. The ethnographic method used by researchers depends on whether they are studying the contemporary culture or the past culture of the society. Studies of the past culture of a society can be either *synchronic*—a description of the culture at a particular time in the past, such as during the 1700s or in the 1870s—or *diachronic*—a description of the changes in the culture over time, such as from 1700 to 1890. These two different approaches to the study of a particular culture involve the use of very different methods and very different research problems.

3. **Describe the methods used to study the culture of a contemporary or living society.** Fieldwork—or, more correctly, ethnographic field research—is the primary method of collecting data concerning the culture of a living people. Fieldworkers usually live among those they study for at least a year, conducting formal interviews and surveys and engaging in participant observation. The difficulties of conducting fieldwork vary with the personality and gender of the fieldworker and with the people and specific topic being studied. All fieldworkers must address four problems. First, not only must fieldworkers fight against their own ethnocentrism and tendencies to stereotype the people they study, but they must also overcome the stereotypes local people have developed about outsiders. Second, it is often difficult to establish a rapport with local people because they may have had no previous experience with the kinds of questions fieldworkers ask. Third, it may be challenging to identify reliable consultants/informants and find people willing to participate in intensive study. Fourth, sometimes people deliberately deceive anthropologists because they mistrust their motives, do not want certain facts to become public, or are culturally forbidden to give away secrets of their culture. Thus, researchers have to attempt to interview several members of the society to gain independent verification of the interpretation or description of a particular event or behavior.

4. **Describe the method used to study the past culture of a society.** Research into the past way of life of a people involves the analysis of written accounts, published and unpublished, and any other materials that shed light on their past culture. This research is called *ethnohistoric research*. This method requires considerable interpretation by the researcher. In almost all cases, these individuals—because they belonged to different societies and came from different cultural backgrounds and traditions—had at best an imperfect understanding of the cultural traditions they were describing in ethnohistoric research. How well did they understand what they were describing? Did they know the language, or did they depend on interpreters? How long did

they live there and in what capacity? In addition, the contents of these accounts are to some degree affected by the ethnocentrism as well as by the personal interests of their authors. Just as in the case of ethnographic fieldwork, the research has to attempt to find two or more sources to independently verify a particular cultural interpretation or description of an event.

5. **Understand the purpose of comparative research.** The purpose of comparative research is to test hypotheses in order to attempt to explain cultural diversity. Comparative methods involve ways of systematically and reliably comparing massive amounts of ethnographic information. The use of comparative methods presents many difficulties, including stating the research hypothesis in such a way that is testable, reliably defining and measuring the variables of interest for many societies, deciding whether similar cultural elements from two or more societies are the same or different, and contending with unintentional researcher bias. The results of comparative studies can be difficult to interpret. Correlation is often confused with causation.

6. **Explain cross-cultural comparisons.** Cross-cultural comparisons involve the systematic comparisons of synchronic cultural data to determine correlations between particular cultural variables. By "synchronic," we do not mean that the cultures of all of the peoples compared were contemporaneous, but only that these descriptions were for a single period of time in the history of a particular people. What the researcher is attempting to do is discover correlations between different aspects of cultural behavior. The only important factor is that they occurred within the same society at the same time.

7. **Describe controlled comparative studies.** Controlled comparisons involve the systematic comparisons of documented changes in a limited number of cultural variables and societies over time. In addition to the problems noted with comparative studies in general, the ethnographic literature needed for these studies is extremely limited.

7

Culture and Nature: Interacting with the Environment

Scientifically oriented anthropologists believe that the way people harness nature's resources—for food, drink, shelter, fuel, and other uses—is the most important influence on their way of life. These wet rice terraces in Vietnam illustrate one form of intensive agriculture, which led to dramatic changes in human existence.

LEARNING OBJECTIVES

After reading this chapter, you should be able to:

1 **DISCUSS** how relationships between humans and the environment differ from those of other animals.

2 **DESCRIBE** hunting and gathering and analyze its major impacts on cultures.

3 **DESCRIBE** horticulture and analyze its major consequences for cultures.

4 **DISCUSS** how intensive agriculture led to the emergence of civilization.

5 **DISCUSS** nomadic pastoralism and its benefits in certain environments.

6 **ANALYZE** industrialization and how it affects human lives, globalization, and worldwide environmental problems.

Anthropologists who follow the materialist orientation (Chapter 5) believe human–environment interactions are important causes of cultural differences and similarities. Materialists also argue that changes in human–environment relationships are prime movers of long-term cultural changes.

In this chapter, we follow the materialist orientation by describing the major ways human groups interact with the natural environment. Besides describing interactions between humans and nature, we analyze their main cultural consequences—how they affect or shape other aspects of human life. We also discuss how long-term changes in human–environment interactions led to major changes in human life. Later chapters deal with other dimensions of cultural diversity, including forms of exchange, marriage and family life, kinship systems, gender relationships, political organization, religion and worldview, and artistic expression.

Understanding Interactions with Nature

In the biological sciences, *adaptation* refers to how organisms survive and reproduce in their environments. To emphasize that human groups—to greater or lesser degrees—alter their environments in the process of living in them, for humans the term *interaction* is more accurate than *adaptation*. Of course, other animals also alter their environments, as when beavers construct dams, birds build nests, prairie dogs dig burrows, and earthworms aerate and create new soil with their casings.

But, to a much greater extent, humans intensively and intentionally modify nature as they interact with it, as when farmers clear land for crops, families cut forests for houses and fires, civilizations build cities, and industrial economies produce greenhouse gases. Both prehistorically and historically, humans altered nature in the process of adjusting to it. *Interaction* both emphasizes these alterations and calls attention to how humans and nature mutually affect each other.

As with other species, the environment affects humans physiologically and genetically. For example, bacteria, viruses, and parasites kill or sicken susceptible individuals, but those who are genetically resistant survive, reproduce, and pass more of their genes along to the next generation. By means of natural selection, over many generations human populations become more resistant to the life-threatening microorganisms to which they are exposed—even as the microorganisms evolve better means of attacking us. Natural selection acting on our genes helps us to adjust to the environments where we live.

The most important way humanity differs from other species is that we adjust to changes in our environments mainly—not exclusively—by means of cultural changes rather than genetic ones. If the climate grows colder or if a group migrates to a colder area, humans cope primarily by lighting fires, constructing shelters, and making warm clothing, not generally by evolving physiological adaptations to cold. Humans hunt animals by making weapons and mastering techniques of cooperative stalking and killing, not by physically evolving the ability to run faster than prey. Group cooperation and technology (including both the tools themselves and the knowledge required to make and use them) allow humans to adapt to a wide range of environments without undergoing major alterations in their genetic makeup.

The transmission of socially learned knowledge and behavior (that is, culture) enabled humanity to colonize all of Earth's terrestrial habitats, from tropical rain forests to Arctic tundra, from the vast grassy plains of Central Asia to tiny Pacific atolls. Our ability to live in diverse habitats by means of technology and group living is mainly responsible for the success of the human species. Humanity is by far the most abundant mammal for our size—in 2016 around 7.4 billion—and our numbers continue to grow.

Of the many dimensions to human–environment relationships, two are most important for our purposes. First, the natural environment in which a people live provides *resources* that they extract to meet their material needs and wants. From their natural surroundings, people harness energy to nourish their bodies (food), to keep themselves warm and cook their foods (fuel) and to put to other uses. People mine raw materials like stone and metals to make tools and cut trees to provide shelter. Harnessing energy and harvesting materials takes technology (tools and skills) and requires that people expend their own time and energy (in labor, or work). As they use their technology and expend their labor, people transform resources into *products* that help meet their needs and wants.

Second, the environment poses certain *problems* that people strive to solve or overcome: resource scarcity, excessively high or low temperatures, parasites and diseases, rainfall variability, deficient soils, and so forth. Solving these and other problems of living in a particular time and place sometimes leads a group to modify their surroundings. For example, hunters can set fire to woodlands or grasslands to attract more game animals to their territories. Farmers can produce more food by clearing new lands, fertilizing soils, and irrigating crops. Industrialized nations construct highways, shopping malls, factories, and housing developments.

There are other dimensions to human–nature interactions as well. Humans are social animals (see Chapter 2) who live in groups of various sizes and compositions. Groups have to organize their members to acquire resources and solve problems efficiently. First, individuals have to know what to do and what they can expect others to do. So groups allocate different tasks to different people, resulting in the *division of labor.* Second, many tasks are more efficient if people work together for common goals. For example, several hunters may have a better chance of spotting, tracking, and killing large game than a single hunter. Because cooperation is often more efficient (and enjoyable) than working alone, human groups develop *patterns of cooperation.* Third, it is helpful if people know when and where to apply technology and labor so they do not conflict with others or get in one another's way. Groups therefore develop patterned ways of *allocating resources* among individuals, families, and other kinds of social units.

Materialist anthropologists prioritize human–environment interactions in their efforts to explain cultural differences and to account for long-term cultural changes in our species. Humanistic anthropologists tend to disagree that material factors should be given this priority, for reasons described in Chapter 5. Even if materialists are correct, always keep in mind that how a people interact with nature affects some aspects of their life more than other aspects.

At the broadest level, anthropologists place human–environment relationships into four major categories, based largely on how people acquire products—especially food—to meet their material needs and wants:

- **Hunting and gathering** (also called **foraging**), in which people exploit the wild plants and animals of their territory for food
- **Agriculture** (or **cultivation**), in which people intentionally plant, care for, and harvest crops (domesticated plants) for food and other uses
- **Herding** (or **pastoralism**), in which people tend, breed, and harvest products of livestock (domesticated animals) for food, trade, and other uses
- **Industrialism**, in which people discovered ways of harnessing the energy in fossil fuels (coal, oil, natural gas), resulting in a dramatic increase in levels of material consumption and profits for private industries

hunting and gathering (foraging) Harvest of wild (undomesticated) plants and animals.

agriculture (cultivation) Purposeful planting, cultivation, care, and harvest of domesticated food plants (crops).

herding (pastoralism) Tending, breeding, and harvesting the products of livestock, which are taken to seasonally available pasturelands and water.

industrialism Development of technology to harness the energy of fossil fuels to increase productivity, profits, and the availability of consumer commodities.

The first three categories are *preindustrial*, applying to how all of humanity acquired food before the industrial revolution of the late 1700s. Even after the origins and spread of industrialism, many of the world's people remained preindustrial. "Preindustrial" thus refers to a *cultural condition* rather than to a period of time. In a few places, preindustrial societies still survive, which does not mean they are unaffected by the industrialized portion of humanity.

This listing does not faithfully depict the complex realities of human–environment interactions. It is very important to recognize that the categories are not mutually exclusive. For example, until contact with Europeans after 1492, many Native Americans cultivated crops like corn, beans, and squash, yet relied on wild game and/or fish for most of their fleshy food because most people kept no livestock. Many African people today farm some of their lands, but they also raise cattle and other livestock on lands less suitable for agriculture. Since agriculture began several thousand years ago, most peoples have adopted a combination of production strategies, depending on their technologies, local environments, and what their neighbors are doing. Finally, even in industrialized nations, various occupations engage in hunting, fishing, agriculture, and livestock husbandry. However, nearly all citizens pursue these activities for wages and profits rather than for their own subsistence.

Hunting and Gathering

Hunter-gatherers—also called *foragers*—acquire food from collecting (gathering) the wild plants and hunting (and/or fishing for) the animals that live in their regions. On current evidence, *Homo sapiens* has existed as a separate species for around 100,000 years. But no people farmed crops or herded livestock until about 10,000 years ago, and most peoples continued to live off wild plants and animals until a few thousand years ago. Hunting and gathering thus supported humanity for roughly 90 percent of our existence as a unique species. Figure 7.1 shows where hunters and gatherers lived at the time of their first contact with Europeans. Even after Western colonialism incorporated so many indigenous people into larger systems, many hunters and gatherers survived in a few places even into the twentieth century.

Although foragers do not grow crops or keep livestock for meat and other products, many attempt to increase their food supply in other ways. For example, some Native Americans periodically burned forests

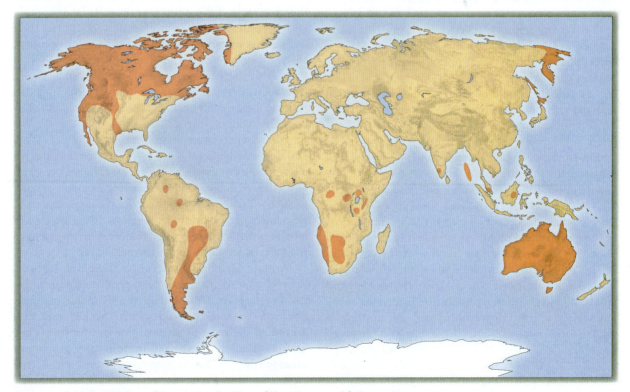

Figure 7.1 **Principal Regions of Foraging at the Time of First Contact with Europeans**

and grasslands to attract game or increase the supply of sun-loving wild berries or other plants. However, compared to farmers and herders, hunters and gatherers do not modify their natural environments very much but instead take what nature offers. If edible wild plants are available only in particular places during particular seasons, foragers move to those places at those times to harvest them. If important game animals live in large migratory herds, hunters must follow them or else hunt other animals when the herds have left their region. A brief general principle helps understand the foraging way of life: To acquire resources efficiently, foragers must organize themselves to be in the right place at the right time with the right numbers of people.

Foraging and Culture

Anthropologists classify hunting and gathering as a single type of adaptation, and in the minds of many people, all foragers seem pretty much alike. (This is why you may have heard, "When humans were still hunters and gatherers on the African savanna …") But foragers living in different habitats differ, partly because environments vary in the kinds and quality of food resources they contain. For example, fishing peoples of the resource-rich environment of the American Northwest Coast lived a fairly sedentary existence in large permanent settlements, whereas the Shoshone of the arid and resource-sparse American Great Basin roamed in small bands or individual families. Despite such differences, most—but not all—foraging peoples share certain cultural similarities. Our main goal in this section is to describe how hunter-gatherer interaction with the environment affects their cultures.

Division of Labor by Gender and Sex

Among foraging peoples, gender and age are the major basis for the division of labor. Of course, in any group, special knowledge and skill also are a basis for assigning tasks. In the vast majority of foraging peoples, men do almost all hunting and women most of the gathering of plants. However, it is not unusual for either gender to lend a hand with the activities of the other. For example, among the BaMbuti of the tropical forest of Central Africa, the women and children help the men with hunting by driving game animals into nets. However, in general, hunting is men's work.

Seasonal Mobility

Most foragers move frequently to cope with seasonal changes. None of Earth's environments offers the same kinds and quantities of resources year-round. Most places experience seasonal differences in precipitation. Outside the humid tropics, marked seasonal variations in temperature occur as well. Ordinarily, game animals are only available in some places at different seasons, and most nuts and fruits are available at only certain times of the year.

Foragers migrate to where food or water is most plentiful or easiest to acquire during a given season. For example, the Hadzabe people of Tanzania live in an arid region with distinct wet and dry seasons. In the rainy months, the Hadzabe disperse around the many temporary waterholes that form, living on the wild plants and animals in the immediate vicinity. At another time of the year, when these ponds evaporate, they live in large camps clustered around the few relatively permanent water sources.

Seasonal Congregation and Dispersal

To gather plants and hunt animals efficiently, foragers adjust the sizes of their living groups to adapt to the seasonal availability and abundance of their food supply. At some times of the year, it is most efficient to disperse into small groups, which cooperate in the search for food. During other seasons, these groups come together in larger congregations.

The Western Shoshone live in the arid Great Basin in parts of the states we now call Nevada, Utah, and Wyoming. Until white settlers disrupted their indigenous way of life in the mid–nineteenth century, the Shoshone lived off wild plants and animals. Most of their meat came from deer, antelope, and small mammals such as rabbits and squirrels. Plant foods included roots and seasonally available seeds, berries, pine nuts, and other wild products.

For most of the year, Shoshone roamed the dry valleys and slopes of the Great Basin in tiny groups consisting of a few families or even single families. Families occasionally gathered for cooperative hunting of antelopes and rabbits, which they drove into corrals and nets. But a more permanent aggregation of families was difficult because a local area did not have enough resources to support large numbers of people for more than a few days.

Around October, the cones of the piñon trees on the high mountains ripened and produced large, nourishing pine nuts. During their travels in late summer, Shoshone families noticed which specific mountain areas had the most promising pine nut harvest. They arranged their movements to arrive at these productive areas in early fall. Ten to 20 families arrived in the same region, harvesting and storing pine nuts, which sometimes lasted throughout most of the winter. In spring the families split up again, reliving the pattern of dispersal into small groups until the next fall.

Bands

To hunt and gather efficiently, in most environments foragers live in small, mobile groups of 50 or fewer. To distinguish these living groups from the settled hamlets, villages, towns, and cities found among other peoples, anthropologists call these mobile living groups *bands*. (Chapter 12 discusses the political aspects of band life.) All or most members of a single band are relatives or are married into the band. Kinfolk or not, members cooperate in acquiring the wild resources of a given territory. In most foraging communities, the size of bands is flexible, with the numbers adjusted to the availability of the food supply.

The Ju/'hoansi (also known as the !Kung) of southern Africa illustrate band organization. Living in what is now southeast Angola, northeast Namibia, and northwest Botswana, the Ju/'hoansi are the most thoroughly studied of all hunter-gatherers. The northern part of their environment is an arid tropical savanna,

which turns into the Kalahari Desert in the south. Into the twentieth century, most Ju/'hoansi exploited this habitat entirely by foraging. They gathered more than 100 species of plants and hunted over 50 kinds of animals, including mammals, birds, and reptiles. Plant foods consisted of nuts, fruits, berries, melons, roots, and greenery. A particularly important and nourishing food was the mongongo nut, which ripens in April and provided about half the people's caloric intake.

Because their habitat received so little rainfall and then only seasonally, the availability of water greatly affected the seasonal rhythm of the Ju/'hoansi. From about April to October (winter in the southern hemisphere), there was little precipitation. Practically no rain fell between June and September. During this dry season, water for people and animals was available only at a few permanent waterholes, around which many families congregated into relatively large settlements of 50 or more individuals. When summer rainstorms created temporary waterholes between November and March, Ju/'hoansi traveled in smaller camps to exploit the more widely distributed wild resources. But rainfall

Eric Baccega/AGE Fotostock

Among most hunter-gatherers, women contribute significantly to the daily food supply by gathering and processing plant foods. This Ju/'hoansi woman is peeling a plant root containing valuable liquid as well as calories and nutrients.

in this part of southern Africa is not reliable from year to year or place to place. In some years, up to 40 inches of rain falls during the wet months; in other years, as little as 6 inches. Precipitation is also spatially unpredictable: One local area may receive severe thunderstorms, while 20 miles away there is no rain at all.

Aridity, seasonality, and variability in precipitation influenced how the Ju/'hoansi organized their bands. During wet months, people spread out among the temporary waterholes in camps with about 10 to 30 persons. When they moved to a waterhole that had not been occupied recently, game was relatively plentiful, and a wide variety of plant foods were easily available. But the longer a band remained, the more its members exhausted the resources surrounding the waterhole. The men had to roam farther away from their camps in their hunts, and the women had to travel longer distances while collecting plants.

After several weeks, the people at the camp would judge that the costs of continuing to forage in the area were not bringing adequate returns in food. They then moved to a new wet-season camp. One ethnographer, Richard Lee, succinctly noted that the Ju/'hoansi "typically occupy a camp for a period of weeks or months and eat their way out of it" (1969, p. 60). If the Ju/'hoansi stayed in larger groups during the dry months, they would have had to move more often, consuming more time and energy. As the months passed and the land dried up, people made their way back to the permanent waterholes, where several dozen people congregated, and the lower quantity and variety of food made life a bit harder.

Reciprocal Sharing

It is mutually beneficial for foragers to share food and other possessions, both within and between families. The sharing is more or less on the basis of need: Those who have more than they can immediately use share with others. For example, among the Ju/'hoansi, on any given day only some people actually go out gathering and hunting. Sharing applies especially to meat. Successful hunters returning to camp share the kill with other families, including those who have not participated in the day's hunt.

One reason for the special emphasis on the sharing of meat is the uncertain returns of hunting compared to gathering. Among the Ju/'hoansi, on most days women return to camp with their carrying bags full of nuts, roots, fruits, and other wild plants. Men's chances of capturing game, however, are smaller: Only about two out of five hunting trips capture animals large enough to take back to camp. Men who are successful one day

may be unsuccessful the next, so they give today in expectation of receiving tomorrow or later.

Sharing is *normatively expected behavior;* people who regularly fail to share are subjected to ridicule or other kinds of social pressures. Going along with the expectation of sharing is a positive cultural value placed on equality of personal possessions (property) and even of social status. Families who attempt to hoard food or other products may be ostracized. Men who try to place themselves above others socially by boasting about their hunting skills or other accomplishments are soon put in their place. The result is that—compared to many other peoples—there is both economic and social equality between the families of most hunting and gathering bands.

Resource Allocation

It is useful to have familiar, patterned ways of allocating natural resources among individuals, families, and other kinds of groups—property rights, in some form. Many hunters and gatherers have developed similar ways of allocating such rights: who can harvest which resources, where, and when.

One possible way to allocate rights over a territory and its resources is for each group to establish and maintain exclusive claims to particular territories. Cultural ideas about the relationship between people and territory might be, for example, that this area is mine or ours, whereas that area is yours or theirs. Among foragers, exclusive access would mean that each band has rights to remain in a specific area during a particular season. One benefit of allocating rights in this way is that the members of each band would know they alone can harvest the foods found in particular places at definite times. Another advantage is that bands would not interfere in one another's hunting and gathering activities.

Despite these (apparent) benefits, most foragers allocate rights to resources differently. Among the Shoshone during the hot months when nuclear or extended families were sparsely distributed, rights to resources were "first come, first served," meaning that whichever group arrived at an area first was free to harvest its plants and animals. No family had exclusive access to any particular territory in any season.

Among the Ju/'hoansi, rights were a little better defined. People recognized particular individuals as the "owners" of places where food and water resources were found. Commonly, the reliable waterholes together with the wild resources around them were "owned" by a set of siblings whose rights grew stronger as they grew older. But by merely asking permission—seldom refused—anyone with a kinship relationship to one of the "owners" could come, visit, and use the area's food and water. Because most Ju/'hoansi had many relatives and in-laws who were "owners" of various places, each family had many options about where and with whom they would live, work, relax, and socialize.

Thus, who was living and foraging together fluctuated radically, and each band received visitors several times a year. Instead of establishing exclusive claims to particular places, Ju/'hoansi families were attached loosely to territories; for the most part, they came and went according to their preferences and circumstances. If a quarrel or dispute occurred, one of the parties could simply leave to join another group temporarily. Most other known hunter-gatherers had similar ways of allocating rights to resources.

To sum up, most foraging peoples were similar in the following respects:

▌ Division of labor based mainly on gender and age

▌ Frequent movement based on seasonal changes

▌ Congregation and dispersal of groups, especially from season to season

▌ Living in small bands of varying size and flexible composition

▌ Strong values of reciprocal sharing and of equality in personal possessions and social status

▌ Loose attachment of people to territory and flexible rights to resources

You can see how these similarities helped foragers harness resources and cope with problems. But, although these characteristics describe most hunter-gatherers reasonably well, we must keep in mind that foragers are diverse. Not all have these cultural features.

In fact, in some environments, foragers lived quite differently. Along the Northwest Coast of North America (roughly from northernmost California into the Alaskan panhandle), food resources—especially fish—were exceptionally abundant, and the Native Americans who lived there were able to smoke and preserve a supply of fish that lasted for many months. Also, salmon and other fish were more reliably abundant along this coastline than in most other environments where foragers lived— in most years, people could count on fish swimming up the rivers to breed in the fall, and in the bays and estuaries year round. Because of abundance, reliability, and long-term food storage, there was not much need for seasonal mobility or small living groups.

Most Northwest Coast peoples settled in villages, where many families lived in spacious and often elaborately decorated wood-plank houses. Resource abundance and

reliability also affected property notions along the coast. If a food resource is so abundant and reliable that you can usually count on its availability, then it makes sense for you to stay close to it and defend it against other groups that might desire it as well. So, people of the Northwest Coast developed more defined property rights: Particular groups along the coastline were more closely associated with particular locations than were some peoples, such as the Hadzabe, Shoshone, or Ju/'hoansi.

Foraging cultures also varied on the North American Great Plains after about 1700, when the Native Americans acquired horses. Plains peoples were hunters and gatherers—they did not farm—but the horses introduced by Europeans allowed them to effectively hunt the tens of millions of bison that once grazed North America's tall grass prairies. Although they hunted antelope and other mammals, bison was Plains peoples' main food resource. During the spring and summer, the bison gathered in huge herds that were most effectively hunted cooperatively by dozens of mounted men. In most areas of the Plains, grasses grew luxuriantly in the spring and early summer, leading the bison to congregate in herds of tens of thousands. As the summer progressed, the land became drier and the grass patchier, so the bison broke up into smaller herds for the fall and succeeding winter months. The people most Americans know as the Cheyenne followed this pattern after acquiring the horse in the 1700s.

What Happened to Hunters and Gatherers?

For tens of thousands of years, living from wild foods worked well enough to allow the human population to grow to several million. Furthermore, foraging is a flexible strategy to acquire food that historically has supported people in rain forests, grasslands, savannas, high mountains, and northern tundra. For example, the Netsilik are an Inuit (formerly called "Eskimo") people who traditionally spent the winters in igloos erected on the surface of Arctic ice in the Hudson's Bay region. Here in their winter camps, Netsilik lived largely on the meat and blubber of seals that they captured by ingenious methods. As the seasons changed, Netsilik moved to rivers and lived off fish and in summer and in fall off migratory herds of caribou. Many people of the South American Amazon also lived by hunting and gathering, hunting forest animals in the treetops as well as on the ground. Ingenuity and rapid communication by social learning allowed hunter-gatherers to migrate into all the continents except Antarctica by around 13,000 years ago. Even by that early date, humanity was a successful species.

Amazonian hunters are amazingly skilled at making bows and arrows from local woods as well as using them to kill forest animals on the ground and in trees.

In fact, most research suggests that hunter-gatherers enjoyed a relatively high quality of life. Richard Lee's quantitative studies of the Ju/'hoansi in the 1960s show that they worked only about two and a half days per week to acquire their food supply. Even adding in time spent in other kinds of work, such as toolmaking and housework, the Ju/'hoansi worked only about 42 hours per week. Most adults in modern industrial nations would be happy with such a short total workweek! Furthermore, the Ju/'hoansi's relatively modest work efforts were sufficient to keep them well fed most of the time: Adults consumed an average of 2,355 calories and 96 grams of protein per day, more than sufficient for their bodily needs. Robert Kelly compared figures on other foragers living in various environments. He found that working hours similar to those of the Ju/'hoansi were common in reasonably productive environments, but quantitative studies are few and have uncertain reliability.

Most evidence also indicates that foraging peoples enjoyed a diverse diet and were healthy compared to farmers. Hunters and gatherers live on plants and animals that

naturally occur in their habitats, and their cultural heritage taught how to cope with periodic droughts and other hazards. In most places, their diets were diverse compared to those of farmers and herders, who focused their attention and efforts on only a few crops and livestock. Foraging bands were small and moved often, which reduced the incidence and spread of infectious diseases. There are, of course, exceptions, but generally hunter-gatherers did not have a hard life if adequate nutrition and low workloads are the standard.

Once plant and animal domestication developed, however, agricultural and herding peoples increased in numbers and expanded their territories. Over several millennia of expansion, cultivators and herders pushed most foraging peoples into regions that were ill suited to crops and livestock. As a result, when European contact with people of other continents intensified after about 1500, hunters and gatherers lived primarily in regions too cold or arid to support agriculture (see Figure 7.1). In the last two or three centuries, even more foragers have lost their lands as they died from diseases and warfare, yielded their territories to outsiders for plantations and mines, relocated onto reservations, and/or gave up foraging voluntarily for other ways of making a living.

By the beginning of the twentieth century, most foragers had died out altogether or had become assimilated into some other society. Contact was especially hard on Native Americans, who lived on lands highly coveted by Spanish, French, English, and Portuguese settlers. Because of their isolation from Old World populations, Native Americans were susceptible to a host of diseases brought by Europeans and the Africans they enslaved. Most scholars who have looked seriously at the impact of diseases on Native Americans estimate that 80 to 90 percent of Indians died from epidemics. Europeans did indeed conquer and subdue many native peoples, but not in the way most imagine: Bacteria and viruses were more important than guns and bullets. The indigenous foraging peoples of Australia and Tasmania suffered in similar ways and to similar degrees.

Only a few foragers preserved their way of life into the twentieth century. In the twenty-first century, the hunting and gathering way of life is almost gone. The Ju/'hoansi have been surrounded by herders, and many have taken up raising livestock. Governments have curtailed their old freedom of movement by fencing off lands. Some have left the Kalahari to work for wages in mines or, in the 1960s and 1970s, to serve as trackers for the military in South Africa. Some have voluntarily settled down at government-funded stations, where they have begun eating large quantities of corn porridge, drinking alcohol, and catching new diseases (including HIV). Recently, governments have realized they could earn money from tourists by turning much of the Ju/'hoansi territory into game parks. Even the people themselves have become tourist attractions: Outsiders come to watch them perform "traditional" dances and curing ceremonies.

The Hadzabe, discussed earlier, are one of the few remaining East African people who still get a lot of their food from foraging. In 2006, the royal family of the United Arab Emirates offered large payments to the government of Tanzania to lease part of Hadzabe land for hunting safaris. The international press publicized the lease offering, and international pressure led the U.A.E. to cancel the plan, but the Hadzabe had already lost some of their hunting grounds to another game park and to encroachments by neighboring peoples. In 2011, the government of Tanzania recognized the legal rights of the remaining 1,500 Hadzabe to remain on their lands. However, as long as national governments can grant rights, such rights can be revoked. Just as foragers lost numbers and territories in the past, so today forces arising from the global economy endanger their ways of living.

Some indigenous peoples of the Americas continue to hunt and gather. Ojibwas in Minnesota harvest wild rice in lakes. Inuits hunt sea mammals in Alaska and the Canadian Arctic. Northwest Coast peoples still fish for salmon and other fish along the coast and in rivers. Some Native Americans of the Great Plains and Southwest still hunt bison for ceremonial purposes. However, none of these Natives make their living off the land. Too much of their land and resources have been lost. Incorporation into nations has led them to make new adaptations to cope with new problems brought about by contacts with wealthier and more powerful people. By force and/or choice, most Native Americans now live off of new resources, such as jobs and market sales. The total environment in which they live is more a product of their historical interactions with other peoples than of the natural world.

Domestication of Plants and Animals

Domestication is the purposeful planting, cultivation, and harvest of selected plants and the taming and breeding of certain species of animals. People who live by domestication of plants (farmers) increase the supply of their foods by replacement of the natural vegetation with edible or useful crops. Those who make part of their living from livestock (herders, although most farmers also keep livestock) control their location, breeding, and numbers. Controlling part of the environment for farming requires new technologies and, in most circumstances, additional labor inputs compared to foraging.

With respect to plants, in this book we are concerned with *food crops*, or those species that people intentionally select, plant, care for, harvest, and propagate for purposes of eating. People also grow plants for other purposes, such as for fibers (cotton, flax, hemp) or for drugs (tobacco, coca leaf, opium poppy). With animals, we are concerned with *livestock*, or those species that people raise, control, and breed to provide food (meat, dairy products) or other useful products (hides, wool), or for performing work (pulling plows

domestication The purposeful planting, cultivation, and harvest of selected plants and the taming and breeding of certain species of animals in order to increase their usefulness to humans.

and wagons, carrying people and possessions). People also keep animals for other reasons, such as companionship (pets).

Origins of Domestication: Wheres and Whens

The "wheres and whens" of domestication are fairly well established by archaeologists, botanists, and other scholars. Most people alive today do not know that many or most of their meals contain foods that were domesticated in other continents. A Canadian meal consisting of potatoes, squash, and beef contains foods that originated in three continents. Spicy dishes in Sichuan province of China might contain tofu, green beans, chili peppers, sweet potato, and noodles made from wheat. Only one of these was domesticated in China. Knowing the original places where the food on our plates was domesticated perhaps will help us appreciate the contributions of our long-dead ancestors to how we live.

Domestication of both plants and animals occurred independently in the Old World (Europe, Asia, and Africa) and the New World (the Americas and the Caribbean). Before Columbus's voyages initiated contact between the two worlds, the crops grown in the two hemispheres were completely different.

Old World Crops

The earliest plant domestication occurred about 10,000 years ago in the region around what is now Jordan, Israel, Syria, eastern Turkey, western Iran, and Iraq. This region is known to prehistorians as the *Fertile Crescent*. Wheat, barley, lentils, peas, carrots, figs, almonds, pistachios, dates, and grapes were first grown here. Oats, cabbages, lettuce, and olives were first domesticated along the Mediterranean fringe. West African peoples domesticated sorghum, finger millet, watermelons, and African rice between 6,000 and 4,000 years ago. Sorghum and finger millet still feed millions of people on the African continent. Eggplants, cucumbers, bananas, and coconuts originated in southern Asia and Southeast Asia. Soybeans, Oriental rice, two varieties of millet, citrus fruits, and tea were domesticated in ancient China at various times—rice around 7,000 years ago and millets as early as 10,000 years ago. Taro and Pacific yams (root crops widely grown in Southeast Asia and the Pacific) and bananas were probably first cultivated in New Guinea or the islands around it, perhaps as early as 9,000 years ago. Sugarcane may have originated in the same area. We get our morning caffeine from coffee, first domesticated in the Ethiopian highlands.

New World Crops

Maize (corn), tomatoes, several varieties of beans, peppers, avocados, and cacao (now used in the making of chocolate) originated in Central America and Mexico, in either the highlands or the coastal lowlands, or both. Various members of the squash family (squash, pumpkins, and gourds) were first intentionally grown in the same region, although squash probably was also grown in eastern North America. The earliest evidence for domestication of these crops is between 10,000 (for maize and squash) and 4,000 (for common beans) years ago. From northern and western South America came numerous crops that are still important to the region and to the world, including potatoes, sweet potatoes, and lima beans, dating from about 6,000 years ago. Between 8,000 and 6,000 years ago, lowland South American peoples were planting manioc (cassava), peanuts, and pineapple. Chili peppers originated in South America also, but Europeans took them back to the Old World and then to Asia during the colonial era. Chili peppers then began to spice up food in southern China, India, Thailand, and other parts of the Old World.

In the 1980s, researchers discovered that the Native Americans who inhabited the eastern United States 5,000 to 4,000 years ago domesticated several crops, including sunflower, gourds and squash, marshelder, and goosefoot. The indigenous peoples apparently abandoned the last two, grown for their tiny seeds, when maize and beans from Mesoamerica became available, with their larger seeds and better yields. A couple of crops that were important in the diet of other Indians at the time of contact with the Spanish were amaranth and quinoa, but the Spanish outlawed them because of their use in pagan ceremonies. They are becoming more popular in recent years.

Some plants were domesticated not just once but several times in various parts of the world. Squash may have had independent origins in Mesoamerica, the Andes, and eastern North America. Separate species of rice were domesticated in Africa and Asia, apparently independently. Cotton was domesticated independently in three places: South America, Central America, and either India or Africa. Three yam species were grown in West Africa, Southeast Asia, and tropical South America. Apparently, when conditions were right, peoples of all world regions were quite capable of transforming wild plants into domesticated crops—a good point to keep in mind when next you hear someone claim that some cultures (usually their own) are more inventive or creative than others.

The chili peppers used in southern Chinese cooking were domesticated by prehistoric Native Americans of southern Mexico. After contact with Europeans, chili peppers and many other foods that originated in the Americas spread to other continents, where people may be unaware of their origins.

Old World Livestock

In the Old World, the earliest animals were domesticated at about the same times and in the same places as the first crops. Dogs probably were the earliest domesticated animals. Genetic studies comparing dogs with gray wolves (their wild ancestors) suggest that people first domesticated dogs about 20,000 years ago, probably in the Middle East and/or in East Asia. In the Middle East, the wild ancestors of the most important livestock lived in large herds, including sheep, goats, and cattle. These animals were and are kept for their hides, wool, meat, and milk. Another large mammal, the horse, was first domesticated and ridden on the Asian grasslands around 3,500 years ago.

New World Livestock

Compared to ancient Old World peoples, Native Americans domesticated few livestock. In the Andes, llamas, and alpacas (related to camels) were used for meat and transportation. Ancient Andean peoples also wove and dyed the thick, long hair of these animals into beautiful clothing. In South America, people still raise guinea pigs for their meat. Elsewhere in the Americas, turkeys and Muscovy ducks were the only animals domesticated for food—and these only in a few areas. Dogs, present also in the Old World, were used in hunting and often as food.

Why did American Indians domesticate so few animals compared to Middle Easterners and Asians? The answer is uncertain, but one important reason may be that so many of the large herd animal species in the Americas became extinct shortly after the end of the Pleistocene epoch, about 11,000 years ago. Members of the horse and camel family, in particular, all disappeared (except in the Andes). Horses did not return to the Americas until the Spanish brought them in the 1500s. Jared Diamond argues that the large herd mammals, such as bison and caribou that remained after the New World extinctions, were not amenable to human control. Certainly, it was not the capabilities or the intelligence of the prehistoric Indians that explains why they domesticated so few animals.

What's for Dinner?

Soon after Spain, Portugal, France, Britain, and the Netherlands began exploring and establishing colonies on other continents, crops and livestock spread from continent to continent. During the centuries of this Columbian Exchange (see Chapter 4), many New World crops were taken to various parts of the Old World, where they became important foods for millions of people. Manioc (cassava) from Amazonia became a staple in tropical Africa and Asia. Mexican corn spread widely, especially in Africa, Mediterranean Europe, and eastern Asia. In China, corn and South American sweet potatoes grew well in lands and climates that were marginal for other crops and probably alleviated or even prevented some famines. After initial resistance, the Andean potato became a staple food in Russia, northern Europe, and—especially—Ireland. Imagine modern Italian food without the Mexican tomato! Over the centuries, Native American cultivators had become master farmers, and food crops are one of the greatest gifts they bestowed upon the rest of the world.

Crops and livestock also moved across the Atlantic Ocean in the other direction. European colonists took Old World wheat, oats, barley, grapes, and other crops to temperate zones of the Americas. In parts of the Americas with more tropical climates, rice, bananas, and coconuts became important foods.

Livestock was one of the main resources taken from the Old World to the New. Pigs, cattle, sheep, and horses were introduced very soon after the European encounter with the Americas. Over the next couple of centuries, they multiplied rapidly and spread widely, becoming feral in many places. Pigs and cattle thrived and multiplied in the Americas and became enormously abundant by the time European settlers began spreading over the landscape. Abundant and familiar, cattle, pigs, and sheep helped attract European colonists to the Americas in the 1700s and 1800s. Plows pulled by horses, mules, and oxen turned over heavy soils and broke up the matted roots of grasses, enabling settlers to farm the rich earth of the American Midwest and Plains for the first time and making this region the breadbasket for the rest of the country.

Few of us alive today recognize our debt to the prehistoric Middle Easterners, Asians, Africans, Andeans, and Mexicans who domesticated the plants and animals we eat daily. Yet most North American meals include foods brought to the New World centuries ago from other continents. In the stereotypical all-American meal of steak, potatoes with sour cream or butter, broccoli, and spinach or lettuce salad, only the potatoes are truly American—and they came from well south of the border. If you live in southwestern China or southern India, your cuisine would be much different without the chili peppers and sweet potatoes that originated in South America.

Today, there is an ecological movement to "eat local" because a lot of energy can be saved from transportation costs if people in New York eat, say, apples from their own state rather than those grown in Washington. But in eating local, remember that many foods now locally grown originally came from other parts of our planet. The next time you enjoy bread and beef, think of the Middle East. As you bite into the corncob or relish the tomato in the salad, remember the ancient Mexicans.

Advantages and Costs of Cultivation

Most prehistoric hunters and gatherers lived fairly well, so why humans took up farming does not have a self-evident answer. In trying to account for why agriculture developed at all, many archaeologists point to two factors that led prehistoric foragers to begin cultivating crops. The first is climate change: In the eastern Mediterranean, where agriculture developed earliest—about 10,000 years ago when the last ice age ended—the climate became warmer at about the same time people began domesticating plants and animals.

The second factor is growing human populations. Although prehistoric hunters and gatherers lived well, once their numbers began to increase substantially, wild plants and animals could no longer support the population size in a region. Growing crops gives a group greater control over the numbers of *edible* plants that exist in their environment, raising the ability of the land to support people. If a field is planted in wheat or rice or corn, then nearly all the plants growing there produce foods that humans can digest. If the field is left in its natural state, only a fraction of the wild plants are digestible and, hence, edible. Thus, agriculture nearly always supports far more people per unit of territory.

How these two factors interacted, and the importance of other factors, is one of the most controversial issues in modern archaeology. However, most agree the single greatest and most widespread advantage of agriculture over foraging is that agriculture supports far more people—10 or even 100 times more than gathering and hunting.

Farming the land does entail costs, however. Creating and maintaining the community of plants that make up a garden or farm require labor, time, and energy. First, the plot must be prepared for planting by removing at least some of the natural vegetation, whether it be forest or grasses. In some kinds of agriculture, people modify the landscape itself by constructing furrows, dikes, ditches, terraces, or other artificial landforms. Second, the crops must be planted, requiring an investment of labor that foragers do not make. Third, natural processes continually invade the artificial plant community and landscape that people have created: Weeds invade and compete for light and soil nutrients, animal pests are attracted to the densely growing crops, and floods may wash away physical improvements. Periodically, cultivators must beat back nature by removing weeds, protecting against pests, rebuilding earthworks, and so forth. Fourth, the act of farming itself reduces the suitability of a site for future harvests, by reducing soil fertility if nothing else. In future years, the farmers must somehow restore their plots to a usable condition or their yields will fall. All these necessities require labor and other kinds of energy expenditures.

Once plants and animals were domesticated, over the next several thousand years many foraging peoples took up cultivating crops and raising livestock. Even though they did not develop farming themselves, most people who lived in European, African, and Asian environments that could support reliable farming became farmers by 4,000 or 3,000 years ago. However, this probably did *not* occur primarily because hunters and gatherers witnessed the benefits of farming, and so they adopted crops and took the opportunity to work less and be better nourished. One reason for the spread of agriculture was because farming people lived in denser settlements and outnumbered foragers, so they tended to spread into regions suitable for cultivation, displacing or depopulating the hunter-gatherers who had been living there.

In parts of the Old World, having livestock was an efficient complement to farming. Having these animals meant that most men eventually gave up hunting, putting their labor into farming, crafts, warfare, metallurgy, ruling, and other activities instead. When mounted, horses greatly increased the speed of long-distance travel and, of course, increased the mobility of warriors and soldiers. Horses, donkeys, South Asian yaks, and camels enabled people to carry heavy loads long distances, increasing the possibilities and benefits of trade, especially when the animals pulled wagons and carts. For thousands of years, camels made it possible for people and products to cross vast stretches of arid lands in Central Asia and North Africa's Sahara. When harnessed to plows, cattle, horses, mules, and Asian water buffalo supplemented human labor in farming. Their dung added nutrients to agricultural fields and gardens. Finally, pigs—first brought under human control in Southwest Asia and perhaps eastern Asia—are an outstanding source of protein and today remain the major source of meat in China and non-Muslim Southeast Asia.

In the New World, except for residents of the Andes, farming peoples continued to acquire all or most of their meat from deer, antelope, small mammals, fish, and other wild animals. Most New World peoples got the bulk of their meat from wild, not domesticated, animals, even though many of them were farmers.

Plant and animal domestication probably had more long-lasting and dramatic effects on cultures than any other single set of changes in peoples' relationship with nature—except industrialization. For example, once certain plants evolved by human selection into crops, people produced more food in a given area of land. Increased production allowed them to remain in one place for long periods—over time, groups became more *sedentary*. They could also live in much larger settlements than the bands of most foragers; groups settled in *villages* and, later in some places, in *towns* and *cities*.

Preindustrial farming systems are conveniently divided into two overall forms, based partly on the energy source used in farming and on how often a garden or field is cultivated. The forms are usually called *horticulture* and *intensive agriculture*. Both have many, many varieties—far too many for us to even mention most of them.

Horticulture

In **horticulture**, people use mainly or entirely the energy (power) of their own muscles to clear land, turn the soil, plant, weed, and harvest crops. There are no plows pulled by horses, oxen, or other draft animals to

horticulture Methods of cultivation using hand tools powered by human muscles and in which land use is extensive.

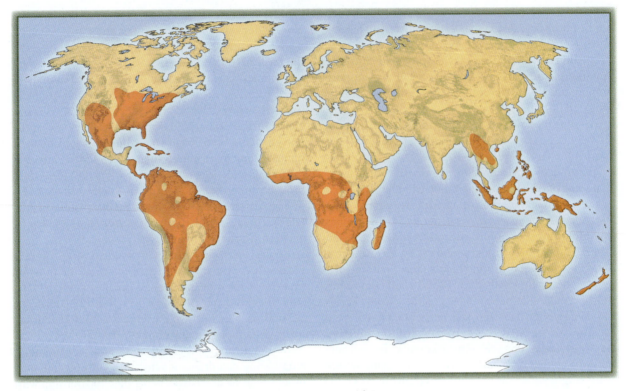

Figure 7.2 Principal Regions of Horticulture at the Time of First Contact with Europeans

help prepare the soil. Instead, hand tools such as digging sticks, shovels, and hoes are used for most tasks. Some people clear new fields by burning the natural vegetation and fertilize their gardens with animal or human waste or with other kinds of organic matter. If irrigation is necessary, horticulturalists usually hand-carry water from nearby rivers or streams. Figure 7.2 shows the most important regions where horticultural adaptations existed at the time of contact by the West.

Varieties of Horticulture

One type of horticulture is *shifting cultivation* (also called *slash and burn*). Once widespread, in the modern era it occurs in small pockets of tropical rain forests in Central and South America, Southeast Asia, and Central Africa. Shifting cultivators farm the forest in a cycle. Using axes, knives, and other hand tools, they first cut down a small area of forest. After the wood and leaves dry out, they burn them to recycle some valuable plant nutrients in the form of ash. Generally, a given garden plot is cultivated for only two or three years before its fertility declines, and it is gradually abandoned. Then a new area of forest is cleared and burned, and a new garden is planted, tended, and harvested. After a few

years, its yields also fall. That plot too is left for the forest to regrow until the land can again produce an adequate harvest, which typically takes 10 or more years.

Shifting cultivation works well as long as population density (the number of people who live in an area of a given size) does not grow too large. For every plot of land under cultivation at any given time, several plots are *fallowed*—they have been left alone for the forest to regrow and the land to recover. If, for every acre of land being cultivated, 10 acres are under fallow, then far fewer people could be supported per acre than if only half the land were fallowed at any one time.

Environmentalists often blame shifting cultivators for cutting and burning the tropical forests that are carbon sinks and that protect the land from erosion. To some extent, this is true. However, shifting cultivation has been practiced for many centuries, whereas large-scale deforestation is a more recent phenomenon. Perhaps the blame for deforestation lies elsewhere.

Dry land gardening is another form of horticulture. It is defined by the main climatic factor with which cultivators have to cope: low, erratic, and unpredictable rainfall. Dry land gardening occurs in the American Southwest, in arid parts of Mexico, in some of the Middle East, and in much of sub-Saharan Africa. In the more arid regions

Getting food is perhaps the most important way that people interact with their environments. This Somali woman is hoeing her field. Cultivating the soil is only one way of producing food.

of Africa where rainfall is too low and unpredictable to depend entirely on crops, people complement dry land gardening with livestock such as cattle and goats.

Cultivation in arid lands is risky: Even if rainfall and harvests are adequate in most years, there is a chance that in any given year not enough rain will fall. Therefore, people who cultivate in dry regions have developed various gardening strategies and techniques to cope with the possibility of drought.

In most parts of the American Southwest, annual rainfall averages only about 10 inches, concentrated in the spring and late summer. Over centuries, Western Pueblo peoples such as the Zuni, Hopi, and Acoma learned to cope with the risk of drought by planting some of their crops in those areas most likely to retain soil moisture, as around seeps and springs. Yet, in some years, the unpredictable rains are so torrential that runoff washes away the crops. To cope with such natural hazards, Pueblo diversify both the place and the time of their planting. They plant the seeds of corn, squash, beans, and other crops in several locations so that, no matter what the weather, some fields usually produce a harvest. Staggering the time of planting likewise lowers the risk of cultivation. Thus, by mixing up where and when they plant, Pueblo peoples reduce the risk of cultivation in an arid, highly seasonal environment, and in favorable years, they stored corn in ceramic pots placed inside adobe and wood houses.

Cultural Consequences of Horticulture

The productivity (yield for a given amount of land) of various horticultural methods is much greater than that

of foragers. Some people think horticulture is rudimentary agriculture because the physical tools are so simple. However, horticultural peoples developed sophisticated knowledge of what, when, and where to plant to handle environmental problems. Their tools may be simple, but their knowledge is not at all rudimentary. In fact, agricultural scientists study indigenous horticultural systems to learn how some traditional peoples have farmed their lands sustainably for hundreds of years.

At a general level, how do the cultures of horticulturalists differ from those of foragers? Subsequent chapters address this question more thoroughly. For now, we note only two of the most important ways in which horticultural adaptation shapes the way of life of people who live by it.

First, most horticulturalists live in larger and more permanent settlements. Rather than bands or camps of 20 to 50, most horticulturalists aggregate into *hamlets* or *villages*, sometimes with hundreds of residents. Also, rather than moving every few weeks, people become more sedentary, remaining in the same location for years, decades, or sometimes even longer. Settlements are more permanent because effective adaptation does not require people to move frequently, and families who have cleared and planted plots want to stay around at least long enough to recoup their labor investment.

Second, resource allocation differs from most hunter-gatherers: Particular individuals, families, and other groups are more attached to specific, fairly bounded places where they or their ancestors established a claim. When a family invests its labor in clearing, planting, and improving plots or fields, over time that investment establishes the family's *claim* to the land. Families pass those claims (rights) on to their children, most of whom transmit the rights to their own children. Over several generations, families—and/or family lines—become the recognized owners of particular plots of land.

In turn, these two factors have other effects. For example, if people remain in one place for years or decades, it is easier to store possessions, which raises the potential for wealth accumulation. More definite land rights raise the possibility that some families will inherit or otherwise acquire more productive resources than others. Because the land itself becomes valuable, *within* a settlement rights to parcels may be disputed, and people who cultivate the land are not likely to be willing to abandon their ancestral lands without some kind of argument or conflict. *Between* settlements, potentially some larger, stronger hamlet or village will want to take over the lands of smaller, militarily weaker groups. Intergroup violent conflict is more likely among horticulturalists than foragers.

Intensive Agriculture

In the farming system anthropologists call **intensive agriculture**, farmers keep their fields under cultivation far longer than horticulturalists. Indeed, some intensive agriculturalists have maintained their lands under almost continuous cultivation—the same fields are farmed year after year, with only brief fallow periods. This is what is meant by using land more *intensively:* To produce higher yields, farmers work the land (and usually themselves) harder. This motivates them to develop new technologies to ease their workloads and to keep a farm productive for a long time. Figure 7.3 shows the major regions where intensive agriculturalists lived at the time of first contact with Europeans.

With shifting cultivation, people rely mainly on natural processes to restore land productivity, which

works but takes a long time. Intensification is possible only if people use their own labor and knowledge to maintain the yields of their land for long periods. In various regions, people fertilize (generally with the dung of livestock), rotate crops, weed carefully, turn over the soil prior to planting, add compost (organic matter) to the soil, and irrigate their crops. For some of these tasks, a new tool (the plow) and a new source of energy (the muscle power of draft animals) are useful. Using plows pulled by horses, mules, oxen, water buffalo, or other draft animals, a farmer can more quickly prepare the soil. In addition to traction for the plow, livestock provide many other useful products: meat, milk and other dairy products, manure, hides, and transportation. After harvest, livestock may be turned loose to graze on the residue of crops, fertilizing fields with their dung.

For all these reasons, intensive agriculture is substantially more productive per area of land than horticulture. An acre of land produces greater yields; hence, it is capable of supporting far more people—5, 10, and even 20 times the numbers of most horticultural peoples. Supporting more people is almost certainly the main advantage of intensive agriculture over horticulture.

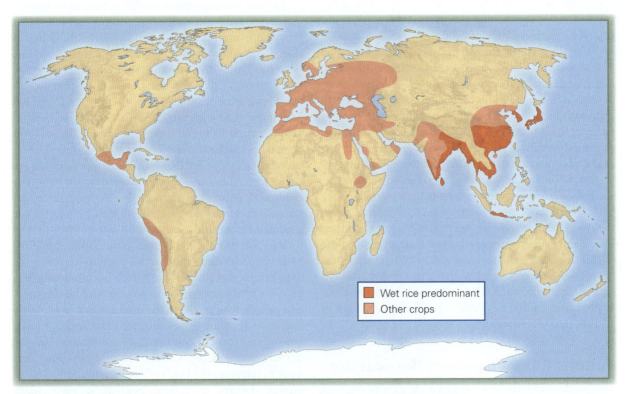

Figure 7.3 Principal Regions of Intensive Agriculture at the Time of First Contact with Europeans

Varieties of Intensive Agriculture

In the Old World, especially in parts of Asia and Europe, intensive agriculturalists plowed the land by harnessing oxen, horses, or other draft animals to plows. This allowed them to farm more land than if they used only human labor. Another method of increasing yields is to augment the water supply by artificial means. Farmers around the world use many irrigation methods. Some construct low dams along streams and rivers to conserve runoff and dig ditches to transport water to the fields. In many Asian river valleys, ditches transport water and fertile silt to fields during the annual monsoons, when rivers overrun their banks. In many mountainous regions of Southeast Asia and China, the level of water in hillside rice fields is controlled with an elaborate system of terraces. Rice is produced through a highly coordinated system to supply water in these *wet rice* regions. Along China's northeastern plain, the emperor controlled floods along the Yellow River by organizing citizens to construct and maintain levees. Visitors to the region may be surprised to find the river level is higher than the surrounding plain, thanks to the labor of millions of Chinese peasants over many centuries.

Although indigenous Native Americans had no animals suitable for plow agriculture, they developed other ways of improving yields and keeping land under prolonged cultivation. Native Americans in places such as the Valley of Mexico (land of the Aztecs) and the Andes (homeland of the Inca) had large cities and high population densities, so their farming classes had to produce a lot of food. In the Valley of Mexico, people transformed swamps and the margins of lakes into productive fields called *chinampas* by constructing raised fields in which they planted crops like tomatoes, squash, and corn. By continually adding new organic materials from the lake bottoms, they kept gardens under cultivation for several years. In the Andes, the citizens of the Inca empire constructed stepped terraces to reduce erosion, growing an incredible variety of potatoes and other crops during the summer. Andean peoples also developed a variety of methods for coping with frost in their mountain homelands.

In sum, compared with horticulturalists, intensive agriculturalists produce more food per unit of land. Its high productivity is due to factors such as short or no fallow periods, preparing the land more thoroughly prior to planting, removing weeds, adding manure and other organic matter to preserve fertility, and manipulating the supply of water. These and other inputs give people greater control over conditions in their fields, leading to higher yields per unit of land—assuming all goes well in nature.

Cultural Consequences of Intensive Agriculture

Intensive farming eventually had dramatic cultural consequences in many regions, most of which resulted from the relatively high productivity of agricultural lands. A farm family using intensive methods can usually feed many more people than just its own members. Intensive farmers can produce a **surplus** over and above their own subsistence (food) requirements. This surplus can be used to feed other people, families, and groups who no longer need to produce their own food.

What happens to this surplus? Many things, depending on circumstances. Farmers can trade excess food for other useful products like pottery, tools, wood, and clothing. If the community has money (see Chapter 8), families may produce excess food to sell and use the money to buy other goods. If the village or other settlement has a strong political leader, such as a chief, he can collect the surplus as *tribute* from his subjects and use the food to pay laborers who work on public projects such as trails, temples, and irrigation facilities. If the community is part of a larger, more encompassing political system, with a ruler and a governmental bureaucracy, then the government may collect part of the surplus as a *tax*. Political officials then use the tax for public purposes (e.g., support of armies, the judiciary, and the religious hierarchy) and/or to further its own political interests.

These possibilities illustrate a central fact about preindustrial farmers who relied on intensive agriculture: Most were not politically independent and economically self-sufficient communities but were incorporated into some kind of larger system organized at a higher level. Their villages or towns were part of a more inclusive political system that dominated or ruled them in some way. The surplus they produced was traded, sold, or taxed (or all three) to support people who did not themselves do farmwork—people such as rulers, aristocrats, bureaucrats, priests, warriors, merchants, and craft specialists.

Intensive agriculture, then, in preindustrial times was strongly associated with large-scale political and economic organization; local-level farmers in villages produced food and other products for people who lived elsewhere, and they in turn received things (products,

surplus Amount of food or other goods a worker produces in excess of the amount consumed by the individual or the individual's dependents.

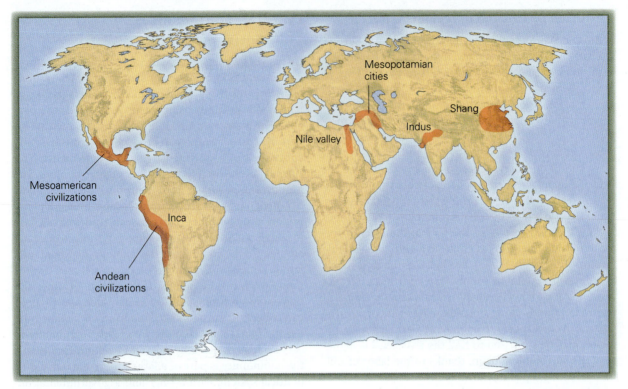

Figure 7.4 Ancient Civilizations

services) from the larger system. The association of intensive agriculture with large-scale political organization is ancient, going back more than 5,000 years in parts of the Old World and more than 3,000 years in two regions of the New World.

Within a few centuries or millennia after the development of intensive agriculture, **civilization** emerged in these regions. These civilizations were socially and politically complex societies, including, among other things, the first cities. Civilizations have a form of government known as the *state* (discussed in Chapter 12), which contrasted markedly with the egalitarian groups of foragers. *States* are large-scale political units that include a ruler, a governing bureaucracy, class distinctions between the elite and common people (see Chapter 13), and methods of extracting labor and surplus products from those responsible for farming the land.

In ancient times, intensive farmers were incorporated into the four major civilizations of the Old World: the valley formed by the Tigris and Euphrates rivers of Mesopotamia, the Nile Valley of Egypt, the Indus

River Valley of Pakistan, and the vast empire of China. In the New World, too, agricultural peoples were part of large-scale political units, such as the Maya, Toltec, and Aztec of Mesoamerica and the Inca of the Andean coast and highlands (Figure 7.4).

Intensive farmers supported other classes and occupations in these early civilizations. They produced the food and paid tribute or taxes to support the rulers, priests, armies, and officials who staffed the government; armies who protected the city; priests who organized the worship of gods; craftspeople who specialized in pottery, masonry, carpentry, weaving, and other tasks; merchants who bought and sold products.

So far as we know, intensive agriculture is virtually a prerequisite for civilization. No civilization ever developed out of a foraging or horticultural adaptation. However, there was *positive feedback* between intensification of agriculture and civilization: As the people in civilizations grew in numbers and as the civilization/state became more complex, more food was needed, which led farmers to work the fields even harder— resulting in further intensification of agriculture.

By about 2,000 years ago, other states developed in Old World places like Korea and Japan (both influenced by China), southern India, much of Southeast Asia, parts of Africa, and most of Europe. In later centuries,

> **civilization** A level of cultural complexity characterized by intensive agriculture, cities, monumental architecture, writing systems, metallurgy, and craft specialization.

the entire world was dramatically affected by states, which tended to expand to incorporate more people and resources to supply necessities for ordinary citizens and luxury goods for elite classes.

Intensive farming methods survive even in the twenty-first century—especially in the developing regions of southern Asia and Southeast Asia, Latin America, and Africa. Economically, farming communities often fit into their nations as **peasants**, a term anthropologists apply to rural people who live by a combination of subsistence agriculture and market sale. Peasants are integrated into a larger society both politically (they are subject to laws and governments imposed by their nations) and economically (they exchange products of their own labor for goods produced elsewhere). In many developing countries, peasants are a numerical majority of the population and produce much of the food consumed by town and city dwellers. Peasants produce goods that are sold for money, traded or bartered, paid to a landlord as rent, and rendered to a central government as taxes.

So far as we know, there were no peasants until the emergence of the ancient civilizations, so one byproduct of civilization was the development of peasant classes. The farmwork of prehistoric and historic peasants fed the craft workers, the merchants, the state-sponsored priests, the political elite, the warriors, and the builders of palaces and temples. Peasants paid tribute or tax (in food, crafts, labor, and/or money), and these resources provided for the maintenance of the society as a whole as well as of the elite classes. The peasantry of feudal Europe, for example, eked out a meager living, paying a substantial portion of their annual harvest to their lords or working many days a year on their lord's estate.

Civilization is usually viewed as a good thing, leading to progress as it spread to other world regions. True, the high productivity of intensive agriculture allowed the specialized division of labor that led to writing, metallurgy, monumental architecture, cities, and the great religious and artistic traditions we associate with civilization. But what about the peasants who produced the food that made such progress possible? For them, writing meant that more accurate records could be kept of their taxes or the number of days they worked for overlords. Iron and other metals meant that peasants had better farming tools; yet for the most part they were not allowed to use them to ease their own work but instead only to produce more surplus for others to appropriate. Metal also meant that weapons became more deadly and armies more dangerous, allowing one state to make war against other states more effectively. Most peasant families continued to live in hovels, even while engineers designed great palaces, religious structures, and walled cities and towns that were built using peasant tax labor. Throughout history, most peasants the world over were denied the benefits offered by technological progress, although the food they produced made much of this progress possible.

In his 2007 book *A Farewell to Alms,* economic historian Gregory Clark argues that agriculture and civilization did not improve human life for the majority of people at all. Not until well after the industrial revolution of the late 1700s did the quality of life for most ordinary people improve, as measured by nutrition, longevity, health status, and consumption levels. The situation is more diverse than Clark implies, but for decades anthropologists have questioned the notion that human life has steadily improved since the "discovery" of agriculture. The increased food supply of agriculture *could* have improved life for ordinary people, and sometimes it did. But often the secondary effects of agriculture on societies and polities made the majority of people worse off. Surpluses benefited mainly elite classes much more than those who actually produced the food. Perhaps there is a broader lesson: In most cases, people who own resources and make important decisions for others tend to gain most when something is said to improve.

Pastoralism

Most farmers keep domesticated animals. Southeast Asian and Pacific horticulturalists raise many pigs and chickens. Intensive agriculturalists raise livestock like horses, mules, oxen, water buffalo, and cattle. Livestock pull their plows, fertilize their fields, provide leather and wool, and yield meat and dairy products (milk, cheese, yogurt, and other nutritious foods). Livestock are more than supplementary to farming: Because of the meat, eggs, milk, hides, wool, transportation, fertilizer, and horsepower they provide, domestic animals are usually critical to the nutritional and economic welfare of cultivators. The income earned by selling livestock or their products is often the main source of cash for many peasants and other farmers in developing countries.

However, cultivators do not depend on their livestock to the same extent or in the same way as *pastoralists,* or

peasants Rural people who live by a combination of subsistence agriculture and market sale, integrated into a larger society politically and economically.

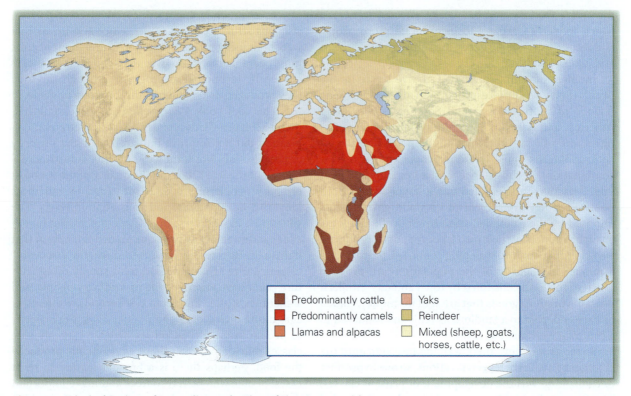

Figure 7.5 Principal Regions of Pastoralism at the Time of First Contact with Europeans

herders. Herders acquire much of their food by raising, caring for, and subsisting on the products of domesticated animals. With few exceptions, these livestock are gregarious (herd) animals. Cattle, camels, sheep, goats, reindeer, horses, llamas, alpacas, and yaks are the common animals kept by herders in various parts of the world.

Agriculture and keeping livestock often coexist among the same people. However, when identifying a people as pastoral, we mean more than that they keep livestock. When farmers raise livestock, they generally grow crops especially for their animals or maintain fallowed fields on which their animals graze. In contrast, among pastoral peoples, livestock rely on grassy pasturelands that grow naturally in their territories. The key phrase is "grow naturally": The needs of their animals for naturally occurring food and water greatly influence the seasonal rhythms of their lives. Most often, the best natural grasslands are seasonally available, either because of altitude (generally more grasslands exist in the mountains during summers) or because the herds themselves deplete the grasses by feeding on them. So, most pastoralists migrate two or more times a year. This seasonal mobility, called **nomadism**, is the defining feature of the pastoral way of life.

Contrary to what some people think, pastoralists do not wander aimlessly, but migrate in organized seasonal and spatial patterns. Most herders take their livestock to highland areas or mountain pastures to graze during the hottest season of the year. Seasonal movements up- and down-slope according to the productivity of pasturelands is called **transhumance**.

For the most part, herders live in only certain kinds of environments (Figure 7.5 shows the primary areas where pastoralists lived prior to European expansion). Pastoralists live mainly in deserts, grasslands, savannas, mountains, and Arctic tundra. Although diverse, these environments do share a common feature: Cultivation is impossible, extremely difficult, or highly risky because of inadequate or great yearly fluctuations in rainfall (as in deserts or savannas) or very short growing seasons (as in mountains and tundra).

> **nomadism** Seasonal mobility, often involving migration to high-altitude areas during the hottest and driest parts of the year.
>
> **transhumance** Pastoral pattern involving migration to different elevations to respond to seasonal differences in the availability of pasturelands.

As always, there are exceptions to our generalizations, but most pastoralists live in regions not well suited to cultivation.

In such arid or cold environments, keeping livestock offers several advantages. First, most vegetation of grasslands and arid savannas (grasses and shrubs) and tundra (lichens, willows, and sedges) is not edible for humans. Livestock such as cattle, sheep, goats, and reindeer can digest this vegetation and transform it into milk, blood, fat, and muscle, all of which are drunk or eaten by various pastoral peoples. The Sami people (formerly called Lapps) of northern Europe keep reindeer that eat the sparse tundra vegetation and transform it into flesh and milk that is eaten by their owners. The Turkana of Kenya and many other East African peoples who live in arid lands maintain enormous herds of cattle, drinking their milk and blood almost daily and eating their flesh only on special occasions. After all, a living cow produces products continuously, so often it is worth more alive than dead. As these examples illustrate, in some regions livestock allows people to exploit indirectly certain wild plant resources not directly available to them. In brief, livestock converts inedible plants into edible products.

A related advantage of herding is subsistence risk reduction. In areas of low and unreliable rainfall, in some years crop yields are inadequate because of drought. In Tibet, Peru, and other high-altitude regions, crops may fail because of low temperatures or short growing seasons. Livestock provides insurance against fluctuations in the food supply from unpredictable droughts and cold periods.

The Karimojong of Uganda traditionally lived by a combination of horticulture and cattle herding. In the central, wetter part of their lands, Karimojong women tended gardens of sorghum (an African grain) and a few other crops. Crop yields fluctuated unpredictably with rainfall. Boys and young men took the family's cattle to pasturelands away from where the women lived and worked. While living in these small mobile cattle camps, the men lived largely by drinking the milk and blood of their herds, supplemented by the sorghum beer that the women sometimes brought when they visited. Not only did cattle add animal products to the Karimojong diet, but they also provided insurance against low sorghum yields. In brief, livestock helps people cope with risky environments.

A third advantage of livestock is their mobility. Not only do animals store meat on the hoof, but they also can be traded or sold to neighboring peoples. Herds can be moved to areas where the pasture is most lush or where the water supply is abundant. People can move their herds and themselves away from neighbors who have grown too aggressive. In some regions, like Africa's Sahara or Central Asia's ancient Silk Road, caravans of camels moved products produced in one place across hundreds of miles of relatively barren land, where they were traded or sold. Two thousand years ago, the elite of the Roman empire enjoyed the translucent, flimsy garments made from Chinese silk that had been transported across Asia. The Romans had no idea that the fine fibers came from the larval stage of the silk moth. All along the cold, arid route were trading stations and towns where traders were serviced and where products were sold to be transported and sold again at the next station or town.

Aridity, temperature, short growing seasons, and other ecological and climatic factors go a long way toward explaining why pastoralists live where and how they do. However, the natural environment does not totally explain the geographic distribution of pastoral peoples. Some herders live in areas where the environment can support crops; although they certainly know how to cultivate the soil, they choose not to grow crops.

Many decades ago, British anthropologists defined a culture area known as the *East African cattle complex*. In this complex, widespread in East African savannas, cattle are more than an ordinary source of food. The East African man loves his cattle like some North Americans love their SUVs and pickups. Cattle represent wealth and manliness. They are the source of prestige and influence in tribal affairs, and they are bridewealth for wives. When sacrificed ritually, cattle are religious symbols and are the source of blessings from the ancestors and gods.

The cattle-herding Maasai of Kenya and Tanzania are a famous example of the East African cattle complex. In some parts of Maasai territory, cultivation is possible; in fact, most Maasai neighbors combine cattle herding with cultivation of sorghum and other crops. However, the proud Maasai look down on cultivation because their cattle represent wealth and are the main symbol of their cultural identity relative to their neighbors. Maasai, therefore, live largely off the products of their cattle—blood, milk, meat, curds—and trade with their neighbors for cultivated foods.

The reasons so many Maasai continue their pastoral way of life are, therefore, cultural as well as ecological. Their pastoral way of life helps define their cultural identity relative to neighboring peoples.

The main benefit of pastoralism is that it allows large numbers of people to live well in regions unsuitable or marginal for farming. It therefore is informative

Nomadic pastoralists move their herds to areas of fresh pasture, usually following seasonal variations in rainfall and heat. The Maasai of Kenya and Tanzania are among the most famous African cattle herders.

to compare how most indigenous herders raise and feed livestock with how livestock are raised and fattened in nations with an industrialized food system.

Traditional pastoralists might teach us that livestock are most efficiently used as converters of inedible plants into edible meat and other animal products. If you feed foods that people can eat to livestock, you lose most of the energy, vitamins, and protein to the bodily functions of the animal.

Yet consider livestock use in North America and other nations where agricultural production is mechanized. In such nations, government policies provide subsidies to certain farmers, high yields produce an excess of low-priced agricultural commodities, and most citizens have little knowledge of livestock (What farm animal has life stages called "gilt" and "shoat"?) or about how their food is produced. In North America, most soybeans and corn are grown as fodder for cattle, pigs, and fowl. When you eat a pound of flesh, indirectly you consume several pounds of corn and soy. You also consume (and pay for) the energy used to grow and process the corn and soy into animal fodder. You support the industries that produce the fertilizers, herbicides, and insecticides used to produce the crops that make grocery-bought meats so tender and juicy—that is, so fatty.

Nature and Culture in Preindustrial Times

So far, we have synthesized an enormous amount of information, although we have not covered many complications and exceptions. Recognizing these, we emphasize one major point: *The ways a people harness the resources and cope with the problems of living in a particular environment are important influences on many dimensions of the group's culture.* (See the Concept Review for a summary of these influences.)

Just how important these influences are, of course, is debatable, as the scientific and humanistic theoretical approaches illustrate (see Chapter 5). Nonetheless, few anthropologists question the following generalizations about the relationship between the main forms of human interaction with nature and cultural systems:

- In most environments, foraging is most efficient when people live in small, seasonally mobile groups that maintain flexible rights to the natural resources of large territories.

- Horticultural people settle in hamlets or villages in which land and other productive resources are owned by families or other kinship or residential groups.

Form of Adaptation	Means of Acquiring Food	Basic Organization of Communities	Rights to Resources	Internal Differentiation
Hunting/Gathering	Collection/gathering of wild plants; hunting of animals; sometimes fishing	Small, mobile bands of 10–50, usually varying in size according to season	Flexible access to resources over large territories	Division of labor based on sex and age; social equality based on sharing
Horticulture	Cultivation of crops using hand tools and mainly human muscle power	Scattered hamlets or villages of 100 or more, largely but variably sedentary	Ownership of land and productive resources by kin groups and/or residential groups	Variable social differentiation but little specialization and inequality
Intensive Agriculture	Cultivation of crops with animal-powered plows or other means of using land intensively	Central administrative places, with cities and towns surrounded by rural peasant communities	Rights vested in or controlled by multilevel administrative officials responsible to the state	Craft and service specialization with social distinctions and major inequalities
Pastoralism	Tending of livestock that provide products (meat, milk, hides, wool) to eat, trade, and sell	Seasonally nomadic living units of varying size and composition	Grazing rights based on membership in families, kin groups, or the tribe itself	Variably complex differentiation based on age, sex, and often hereditary distinctions

- Intensive agriculture resulted in the development of towns and cities occupied by elites and specialists and surrounded by rural peasant communities that contribute labor, tribute, and/or tax to support the government and public projects.

- Pastoral peoples are seasonally nomadic, with grazing rights to pasturelands vested in families or other kin groups or in the tribe as a whole.

In future chapters, as we cover various aspects of culture, we sometimes discuss the ways in which human–environment interactions affect family life, gender relationships, political organization, and other dimensions of cultural systems.

Industrialism

Thus far, we have focused on preindustrial peoples. Before the domestication of animals and the development of plow farming in parts of Asia, Africa, and Europe, humans used their own muscle power and hand tools to interact with their environments. Once intensive agriculture developed in some regions, farmers took advantage of the muscle power of their cattle, oxen, horses, and other livestock. In addition to using their own energy to do agricultural work, humans worked their livestock to acquire additional energy. Notice that both these energy sources were living organisms. Another source of energy was dead trees (wood), which provided fuel for warmth and cooking, but those trees had died recently.

Industrialism is the most recent—and not necessarily the final—major way in which humans interact with nature. Industrialism shelters the world's more affluent persons from the environment and provides them with their means of survival without them having to engage nature directly—except under tightly controlled conditions like sea cruises, hunting trips, and fishing vacations. Heating and air conditioning keep us warm or cool indoors, and we no longer need to butcher our own meat or gather firewood for cooking. Machines and the energy needed to power them substitute for human labor, allowing people who 200 years ago would have been producing food, wood, pottery, metals, and other material things to find other jobs in factories and services. In fact, one of the hallmarks of industrialization is that few people work in activities that extract natural resources like farming, fishing, lumbering, and mining. This is a new condition in human history.

Energy and Society

Industrialization began in Great Britain in the late 1700s and in the next several decades spread to the rest of Europe and North America. At first, British textile mills (and later those in New England) were powered by falling water. Around 1800, efficient ways were found to burn coal to produce compressed steam, which powered looms that could turn out textiles of cotton and wool in massive quantities. Later, people figured out ways to harness the energy stored in oil and natural gas.

There is a reason that coal, oil, and natural gas are called *fossil fuels*—each of these energy sources derives ultimately from long-decayed plants and animals. While living, these organisms took in carbon, concentrating it in their bodies, where most of it still exists in the form of mineral deposits or natural gas released by decay. Once combusted, coal, oil, and natural gas release enormous quantities of energy.

Physicists often say that energy is the capacity to do work. With vast quantities of energy, vast quantities of work can be done—thanks to machinery and fossil fuels more than to human work. Therefore, vast quantities of products can be manufactured. Electricity generated from coal- or oil-fired power plants, falling water (hydroelectric), and most recently nuclear sources provides power for private industries and private homes. In the long time frame of human prehistory and history, these are all very recent developments, no matter how normal they seem to people alive today.

Way back in the 1940s, the neoevolutionist Leslie White (see Chapter 5) theorized that energy capture is the most important factor in powering cultural change. Some numbers White would find important are worth mentioning. Kilowatt-hours are one measure of power, defined as the rate at which energy is converted to work. Every week, the muscles of a man who is fairly fit can generate about 3 kilowatt-hours of power. A gallon of gasoline contains about 12.3 kilowatt-hours of power, which is equivalent to about four weeks of human muscle power. If you spend $3.00 (U.S.) on a gallon of gas, that $3.00 buys about four weeks of equivalent human power.

In terms of ability to get work done without having to do it with our own muscle power, think of energy from fossil fuels as comparable to the human power that slaves provided to their masters. One slave provided power (work), two slaves provided about twice as much power, and so on. As Thomas Love points out metaphorically, fossil fuels are our *energy slaves*: The energy output of $3.00 worth of gasoline is equivalent to having one slave working for us for four weeks.

Except during periodic energy crises, citizens of industrialized nation-states take the energy derived from fossil fuels for granted, seldom thinking about what happens when they turn on light switches, car engines, air conditioners, and stoves. When the world market price of crude oil rises to over $100 per barrel, we become more aware of the monetary costs of energy and are sure "they" are price gouging us. Energy to move around as we wish and to heat and cool our living space is so important that we usually give up something else if its price increases.

But fossil fuels are very cheap. If you drink bottled water, you pay more per gallon to slake your thirst than you do to power your car when the price of gasoline skyrockets to $3.00 per gallon. Giving up bottled water will help you weather the next energy crisis.

Consequences of Industrialism

Acquiring energy from fossil fuels was the key development of the **industrial revolution**. It was more than a revolution in how products were made. As just one component of the dramatic consequences for human life, consider what happened to food production and distribution.

As factories developed, over time more and more people migrated to cities to work for wages. Urban factory workers and their families needed food, and industrial products had to be moved around, so roads and transportation networks became more extensive. Markets expanded to supply food to city people and factory products like clothing and tools to farmers. Some farmers out in the countryside continued to grow their own food, but eventually most farmers specialized in selling food to others. The more farmers can produce, the more they can sell, so farmers were motivated to invest in technology that made their land more productive. By the early twentieth century, new companies specialized in supplying the demands of farmers for equipment (e.g., tractors), chemicals (e.g., fertilizers, insecticides), water (e.g., pumps), and similar products. By the mid–twentieth century, *factory farming* was common in the developed world. Around 1950 an American factory farmer could produce enough to supply food for 20 or 30 nonfarmers. In 2015, that production was closer to 50 nonfarmers.

Changes in food production and distribution are only one consequence of the industrial revolution. Most people take their lifestyle for granted. Think about a few

industrial revolution Historical period in the eighteenth and nineteenth centuries during which predominantly agrarian societies became industrialized and urban through the harnessing of energy in fossil fuels.

other implications of industrialism for your life. Most readers would be hungry without supermarkets or some other kind of retail outlets that used to be called *grocery stores*. Even if you know how to hunt, fish, and garden, you probably don't have access to enough land to support yourself—unless you are wealthy, in which case you might have or be able to get the land but don't want to support yourself in *that* way.

Most likely, your individual workday is (or some day will be) tightly scheduled. The same applies to your week—but at least there's the weekend. Perhaps you think you are burning up when you go outside into 95-degree heat and freezing if your living space goes down to 55 degrees. If you are not already a homeowner, someday you probably hope to become one. You will feel lucky to have your own place and probably do not know that most people in humanity's past have had a place to live without having to buy it at all.

You are far more likely to have one or two children than six or seven. Having only a child or two won't hurt you much because you don't need children to help around the farm or to support you when you get old. Besides—kids cost a lot: all that day care, new outfits, sport fees, college educations, and the rest. You hope Social Security and other forms of assistance will still be there when you retire. Chances are you will live long after your retirement, at least if you have enough discipline to control your diet and exercise more often.

If none of this seems like the result of a revolution, contrast how we live with the ethnographic examples of foragers, farmers, and pastoralists described earlier in this chapter. Remember that industrialism has only been around for about two and a half centuries.

Industrial technology opened up all kinds of possibilities for humanity. It has improved the material living standards of 2 to 3 billion people in the last two or so centuries. Like other ways of extracting nature's resources, industrialism has social and cultural consequences. And like the others, it is not free of costs.

Transportation provides an example of these possibilities and costs. By the mid-1800s, steam engines powered the locomotives that made train transportation both rapid and cheap. One cost of this progress was that most wagon makers had to find new ways of making a living. Trains greatly facilitated the settlement of the American West. Boxcars moved Western products east, and vice versa, helping integrate the American economy and eventually forming a single market where the beef from cattle grazed in Colorado sold at about the same price in Oregon and North Carolina.

Later, when a way was found to manufacture internal combustion engines powered by gasoline, automobiles were invented. After Henry Ford introduced the assembly-line production of automobiles in the early decades of the twentieth century, increased efficiency of production brought the costs of autos down so much that ordinary families could afford one. In the United States in the 1950s, the federal government responded by constructing tens of thousands of miles of new roads, including the interstate highway system. By using income tax revenues to do so, the feds subsidized the auto industry and car owners. (This is ironic given the present widespread outcry over proposed federal and state subsidies for public transportation!) Passenger travel and freight transport by rail declined as a consequence, even though trains are far more efficient in energy terms than cars and trucks. By the late 1900s, middle-class families could afford two, three, or more motor vehicles, including the minivans that facilitated hauling kids and purchases.

In the last half of the twentieth century, two new methods of freight transportation grew rapidly: trucks and container ships. Both modes of transporting freight had worldwide consequences and caused rapid changes in how millions of people live their everyday lives, although most of these consequences were unknown or not thought about.

The long-haul trucking industry moves products rapidly and cheaply from factories and fields to retail stores and supermarkets. In January, residents of Ontario and North Dakota can enjoy produce grown on irrigated mega-farms in Southern California's Imperial Valley and tomato fields in northwestern Mexico. Should global energy prices increase significantly, increased costs for growing and transporting the veggies will rise, and northerners will pay more for southern foods. The same will occur should the federal government eliminate the huge subsidies it now pays for the irrigation water necessary to transform California's Imperial Valley from semi-desert to agricultural paradise.

Globalization of Industrialism

Obviously, the growth and spread of industrial society have global impacts. It encouraged colonialism, as richer nations sought natural resources to supply their factories to seek control over natural resources in other continents (see Chapter 4). Although the colonial centuries have passed, today most nations participate in the global industrial system in which richer nations establish factories offshore. Many forces encourage the globalization of factory production. One that most people overlook is the cost of ocean transportation.

By lowering costs of transporting freight to overseas destinations, giant container ships helped integrate the global economy. The places and people that produce manufactured commodities are different places and people than where the company is registered and where most of its stockholders reside. Of course, profits are the reason so many manufacturing jobs have moved offshore. It is cost effective for American companies to ship computer components to China where Chinese workers assemble them into a Mac or a PC, then send them back to the United States. But computer makers still make more profits and consumers enjoy lower costs than if computers were assembled by American or Canadian workers. Should global energy prices rise enough, then higher shipping costs will curtail or slow the **globalization of production**. The consequences of such a slowdown would be global and serious.

Most people explain the relocation of assembly and other production facilities to newly industrialized countries in Asia and other continents mainly by low labor costs. Labor is inexpensive in countries like

China and India for several reasons. They have millions of people migrating to cities looking for factory jobs, so the labor supply is plentiful. (Chinese factories, though, began complaining about labor shortages in 2012.) For many reasons, most unskilled labor is not organized by unions. One reason is that governments and local managers want to keep wages low so their workforce is competitive in the global labor market. Another is that there are plenty of unskilled laborers to accept work that others refuse because of its low wages.

Also, India and China are often said to be overpopulated, meaning they allegedly have too many people to be supported by their nation's resource and economic base. Globalization of factory production provides their people with more resources—mainly with jobs, which have become the resources (no longer natural ones) that most people in industrialized nations need for survival and well-being. Conversely, factory globalization has taken away resources (jobs, wages) from many factory workers in North America, Japan, and Europe. If factories close or if workers in general have not had pay raises in a decade or two, those workers have done nothing to decrease their resources.

> **globalization of production** Process of corporations that are headquartered in one country relocating their production facilities to other countries to reduce production costs and remain globally competitive.

These people in Guangdong province of China are manufacturing toys that accompany McDonalds' Happy Meals. As globalization provides resources (jobs) for some workers in the world economy, it removes resources from other workers. What, then, are the net benefits of the globalization of factory production?

At the same time, globalization has indirectly increased resources available to consumers in the wealthier nations whose corporations have exported jobs overseas. If you pay lower prices for electronics, clothing, shoes, and a host of other goods because they are produced in countries with low wages, your money will buy more commodities. You now have more resources, although you have done nothing to create them but have simply benefited from global market forces.

Globalization and the Environment

Low labor costs alone do not account for the explosive growth of what some call the *global factory* since the 1980s. Other costs of offshore production for corporations also are low, because factory health and safety and environmental regulations are more lax than in the corporations' home countries. When European, Japanese, North American, and Australian governments passed far-reaching environmental regulations in the 1970s, they increased the production costs of their industries. But to the extent that governments applied the regulations evenly and fairly, no particular company in an industry received a competitive advantage. Companies adjusted by lowering expenses in other areas and increasing what they charged consumers. They "adapted to the new regulatory environment."

Most scientists and many ordinary citizens recognize the heavy environmental costs of industrialization. Natural resources are harvested from all over the world to supply raw materials for factories. Extracting resources leads to depletions, landscape destruction, soil erosion, and other deteriorations of environmental quality. As a byproduct of burning fossil fuels like coal and oil, factories pollute the air, making government regulation mandatory for environmental and health reasons. Coal mines dig out earth and rock to uncover seams of coal. Without regulations to curtail them, factories would release toxic chemicals that pollute waterways. Modern agriculture usually is more factory-like than farm-like, relying on machinery for most operations. Runoff from agricultural chemicals and modern livestock feedlots pollutes rivers and streams.

Government regulation of mines, industries, farms, auto emissions, and the like have significantly reduced many environmental impacts in South Korea, Japan, Australia, North America, and Europe. If it were not for these regulations and their enforcement, the environmental consequences of industrialism would certainly be far worse than they are. Anyone who lived in the Los Angeles basin in the 1960s and 1970s has experienced these consequences. Anyone living today in Beijing, Rio de Janeiro, or Mumbai is experiencing them now.

Why don't farms and businesses just act in environmentally responsible ways? A few do, of course. However, in a market economy, if an environmentally responsible company voluntarily decides to clean up its wastes and reduce its harmful emissions, then that company will suffer in the competitive marketplace because its production costs will rise. That would be economically foolish, and competitive markets do not reward this kind of foolishness.

Ever since factory production boomed in countries like Brazil, Russia, India, and China (the BRIC countries) their citizens experienced the negative environmental effects of factory production. Consider the People's Republic of China (PRC). With several hundred million rural peasants and relatively low factory wage rates, China is still not a rich country. China has a huge population of nearly 1.4 billion (four times that of the United States), a government that seems committed to development, a cultural tradition infused with a work ethic, and a large pool of workers. In August 2010, China surpassed Japan as the world's second-largest economy, now trailing only the United States.

China's industries have grown so rapidly since the 1980s that it now has serious air and water pollution problems. China uses about half of the world's cement for its new roads and buildings. It imports about half of the world's iron ore, which it manufactures into steel for use in construction and in products like motor vehicles and ships. Tap water is unsafe to drink in most large Chinese cities. According to the World Bank in 2007, China had 16 of the world's 20 most polluted cities. One day in January 2013, the air pollution index in Beijing was 755—measured on a scale of 0 to 500! In late 2012, 16,000 dead pigs were found floating in the river that supplies water to Shanghai, the PRC's largest city. For 2010, a ministry of the Chinese government estimated the monetary cost of the environmental damage caused by rapid industrialization at $230 billion, which is 3.5 percent of China's gross domestic product. China's slowing pace of economic growth since 2013 led to reduced construction of new coal-fired power plants. China is building massive new wind farms and solar panels so perhaps in the next couple of decades it will no longer be the world leader in emissions.

China and India together have about 2.5 billion people—40 percent of the world's total population. When countries this large pollute, other countries notice because some kinds of pollution easily cross national borders. Air pollution from Chinese factories wafts over to the Koreas and Japan. Sometimes, upper

Climate change is an environmental problem recognized widely only in the past few decades. Combustion of fossil fuels releases carbon dioxide into the atmosphere, which traps solar radiation and leads to global warming, changes in rainfall patterns, and other results. Some believe that climate change is not a serious problem and, even if it is, doubt that human activities are its main causes. (Some politicians are correct when they say cattle and other livestock pass methane, a potent global warming gas.) However, there is very broad consensus among credible scientists that climate change is real and is a *global* problem, meaning that the carbon dioxide that one country puts into the atmosphere harms or will harm all other countries. Global warming therefore requires international agreements and cooperation.

However, agreements at the global level are difficult to reach. In July 2009, there was a meeting in Italy of the 17 nations that generate about 80 percent of Earth's greenhouse gases. In a draft agreement, the wealthiest eight nations offered to reduce their emissions by 80 percent by 2050, primarily by means of government mandates and regulations. However, India, China, Brazil, Mexico, and the other less developed countries refused to agree to even the indefinite goal of reducing their emissions significantly to achieve a worldwide greenhouse gas reduction of 50 percent by 2050.

In December 2009, representatives of 193 nations met in Denmark, aiming to reach a binding agreement on reductions in greenhouse gas emissions. Environmentalists hoped countries would agree to cut emissions by a certain percentage, depending on their level of development, by a given date like 2030 or 2050. However, there was no international agreement because countries could not agree on issues like the scale of reduction, the timetable, or financing. Finally, in December 2015, representatives of 195 nations reached the Paris Accord by signing an agreement committing nearly every country to reduce its greenhouse gas emissions. If the agreement is actually implemented, about half of global greenhouse gases will no longer go into the atmosphere.

Why are international agreements about climate change so difficult? Greenhouse gases are "public bads." It does no good if richer countries cut their emissions by half if the less-rich nations continue to increase their emissions

China's economy has grown remarkably since the 1980s, but this growth has side effects, including pollution of air and water, as this photo of a Beijing street illustrates. China now contributes more to global warming than any other nation.

Hung Chung Chih/Shutterstock.com

atmospheric winds carry sulphur dioxide from China's coal burning clear over to North America's Pacific coast. Countries like India and China are experiencing car booms, which increases global oil prices and hastens the time when the price of oil will rise high enough to really threaten the standard of living of the middle class in many countries. The newly industrializing regions also contribute significantly to global warming, raising world issues such as who should pay most to reduce greenhouse gas emissions in the interest of future generations. The Global Challenges and Opportunities feature discusses this issue.

Media give a lot of press to coastal and island people, who will be most directly affected by rising sea levels caused by global warming. However, greenhouse gases alter worldwide precipitation patterns as well as of greenhouse gases. Citizens of richer nations would pay the costs of reducing their emissions only to have their efforts undone by other nations that refused to agree. By 2008, China emitted more carbon dioxide and other greenhouse gases than the United States, becoming the world's single largest contributor to global warming (although not in per capita terms). Without cooperation from the Chinese and other emerging industrial economies, any agreement on global warming would not matter. An agreement between all major emitters is necessary. Why don't the leaders of emerging nations sign agreements that are in the global interest?

Political leaders in some countries claim—understandably and truthfully—that industrialization in the West historically caused the most depletions and pollutions and brought the planet dangerously close to irreversible climate change. Among large nations that are growing rapidly are Brazil, Russia, India, and China, which are commonly referred to as *BRIC nations*. Why should citizens of BRIC countries be forced to pay the costs of damage already done by the countries that became wealthy by not attending to the environmental damage their economies caused? Why should their people have to sacrifice their recently rising standards of living to protect the global environment? Their citizens still consume far less than those of the rich nations and contribute less to climate change than the developed world.

Leaders of many newly industrialized countries also point out that European and North American companies have relocated some of their most hazardous and polluting industries in poorer regions in order to avoid costly government regulations in their home countries. Western companies and governments therefore are responsible for part of the pollution generated by global factories that produce commodities for export to highly developed countries. The richer countries export some of their dirtiest industries to the newly industrialized countries and then expect those countries to clean up their pollution and reduce their harmful emissions. Consumers in Europe and North America also benefit from the global factory by significantly lowered retail prices of clothing, shoes, consumer electronics, and other offshore products. Therefore, consumers in the developed countries should do their part to reduce global warming by paying the higher prices that tighter and enforced regulations would bring.

These are some of the arguments of those who think it is unreasonable for newly industrialized nations to pay the costs of reducing greenhouse gas emissions. Richer countries point out that there is nothing they can do about their past environmental records and that cooperation from all nations is needed. The issue is one of equity: Which countries should reduce their emissions by how much?

Perhaps it will help if people realize that there are nations whose people contribute almost nothing to climate change, yet they will be most affected. Two such impacts are rises in sea levels and changes in temperature and precipitation.

Thermal expansion of seawater and melting glaciers led to a rise in sea level of about 2 inches between 1993 and 2009. This rise appears to be accelerating as glaciers melt faster. By 2100, sea levels are likely to increase by 1 to 6 feet, depending on the rate of glacial melting. North Americans hear that low-lying areas like southern Louisiana and much of Florida will be seriously affected by land losses and storm surges if sea levels rise only 8 to 20 inches in this century. This would be a tragedy that should be avoided. But theoretically most Florida and Louisiana people can be relocated. The United States now emits about one-fourth of the world's greenhouse gases. Factories in low-lying Bangladesh produce a lot of clothing for export. Yet Bangladesh contributes only about 0.1 percent of all greenhouse gases. A sea-level rise of 20 inches would inundate the living space of about 20 million mostly impoverished people. In densely populated Bangladesh, there are few other places for people to move. How will they cope with a global problem not of their own making?

Other regions would be even more affected by climate change. We seldom hear about the fate of Pacific Island nations composed entirely of low atolls, such as Kiribati, Tuvalu, and the Republic of the Marshall Islands. The *highest* elevation of most atoll nations is around 20 to 30 feet. A significant rise in the sea level would flood most of their living spaces. Equally seriously, their staple crops, like taro (an edible root) and breadfruit (a tree crop), are intolerant of salt water and are already being killed as ocean water that lies just below the land surface reaches their roots through the permeable limestone. The coral reefs on which coral atoll people depend for fish are already affected by bleaching and acidification, which dissolves the calcium carbonate of shells and reefs. Again, atoll peoples contribute essentially nothing to climate change, but their lives may be most seriously affected.

temperature. Climate scientists cannot predict the severity or location of the most serious impacts. Some regions will experience a more favorable climate for crop production than at present because the length of growing seasons will increase or more rainfall will occur. Some climate models suggest that the tropics and subtropics will experience the most severe agricultural impacts. About 3 billion people still get most of their food from subsistence farming. For many of them, global warming will reduce their ability to support themselves.

The advantage the recently industrializing nations have is their ability to deliver products to the global market at extremely low costs. If they do not do so, other countries will. Viewed in this context, serious and enforced environmental and safety regulations like those adopted by today's rich countries would threaten the constant creation of new jobs and the rise in consumption. China's growth since around 2010 has been slowed by competition from other nations as well as by the fact that it has created newer, more lucrative, high-status jobs because of that growth itself. Should China impose costly regulations on its factories, prices for its products would rise, and the continual growth of Chinese employment and living standards would be further threatened. The Chinese government is legitimately worried about the impacts on social stability and what Chinese leaders call a "harmonious society." China has an active environmental movement, and its national government is making efforts to clean up its manufacturing, but officials at the local level too often profit by not enforcing regulations. After all, "The country is large and the emperor is far away."

All the above is not meant to excuse Brazil, Russia, India, China, and other rapidly industrializing nations for their inability or unwillingness to pass and enforce environmental regulations. Rather, our point is to propose that environmentalists and self-righteous citizens in the more affluent parts of the world make more of an effort to "grasp the native's point of view," to borrow Malinowski's phrasing (see Chapter 5). How much harm would be done to ordinary citizens of the newly industrializing nations if their production costs rose substantially? China already is offshoring some of its own production to still poorer nations, who, in turn, are likely to contribute to global environmental problems. If the Chinese central government should

lose control because the country cannot provide jobs for 200 or 300 million people, what would be the global consequences? If the richer nations enjoy cleaner air and water partly because they export some of their most polluting industries overseas, what are their obligations in regard to environmental protection in the overseas nations?

One consequence of globalization is the globalization of consequences. When industrial production globalizes, so do its negative global environmental impacts. We began this chapter by saying that two of the most important dimensions of human–nature interactions are extracting resources and handling environmental problems. Industrialism extracts resources from all over the world, and these resources are bought and sold on the world market. The scale of this buying and selling also is new.

Global industrialism has created environmental problems that are worldwide. That also is new. In the last few decades, new international institutions have been created, such as the Organization of American States, the Association of Southeast Asian Nations, the Organization of African Unity, and the European Union. Nations have signed agreements that promote free trade, such as the North American Free Trade Agreement. Members of the European Union buy and sell to one another using a new currency, the euro. Countries usually find ways of negotiating and enforcing agreements when it is in their economic interest. Perhaps it's time to do the same for the global environment.

SUMMARY

1. **Discuss how relationships between humans and the environment differ from those of other animals.** Humans adjust to their environments by cultural changes in technology and organization more than by changes in their genes. One important way people interact with nature is by productive activities, which require labor, technology, natural resources, and group organization. People also find ways to cope with the problems of living in a particular habitat, which occurs mainly by means of group-level accumulated experiences.

2. **Describe hunting and gathering and analyze its major impacts on cultures.** Hunters and gatherers,

or foragers, live exclusively from the wild plants and animals available in their habitats. Foragers organized their activities so that at the proper season, they could be at the places where wild foods were naturally available. Most exhibited the following characteristics: (1) a division of labor based mainly on sex and age; (2) high mobility; (3) congregation and dispersal of groups, usually based on seasonal changes; (4) small living groups or bands; (5) reciprocal sharing; and (6) loose and flexible rights to the resources of a given territory. These features are well illustrated by cultures such as the Hadzabe, Shoshone, and Ju/'hoansi. However, there are many exceptions to these generalizations such as fishers of the Northwest Coast and the Cheyenne of the Great Plains.

3. **Describe horticulture and analyze its major consequences for cultures.** Domestication increases the productivity of an environment by planting and cultivating selected plants (crops) and taming and breeding certain animals (livestock). Horticulture is one form of plant domestication. Horticulturalists use only hand tools in planting, cultivating, and harvesting their plots or gardens, as illustrated by shifting cultivation and dry land gardening. Horticulture produces more food per acre than foraging, and it requires that people make a labor investment in particular pieces of land (their plots). Broadly, this leads to two cultural consequences: (1) People remain in one place for a long time (sedentism) as the size of their settlements increases (villages), and (2) particular families establish their own claims to certain pieces of land, producing cultural beliefs that land is the property of specific groups.

4. **Discuss how intensive agriculture led to the emergence of civilization.** Intensive agriculturalists use various methods to keep yields high, including fertilization and irrigation. Intensive farming eventually raises productivity enough that a single farm family is able to produce a surplus over and above its own food needs. Out of this surplus potential a new form of culture, called *civilization*, arose in several regions of both the Old World and the New World. Supported by intensive agriculture, civilization changed human life profoundly, leading to new developments such as writing, specialization, huge architectural structures, roads, and familiar artistic traditions. But it is doubtful that the peasant class enjoyed very many of these benefits.

5. **Discuss nomadic pastoralism and its benefits in certain environments.** Nomadic pastoralism is most beneficial in regions unsuitable for agriculture due to aridity, extreme temperature, or inadequate growing seasons for crops. In these kinds of habitats, herding offers several advantages: It allows people to convert indigestible grasses and other vegetation into edible flesh and dairy products; and it reduces the risk of living in an unreliable environment, both because livestock provide a way of storing food on the hoof and because the food supply (herds) can be moved to more favorable places when times are hard.

6. **Analyze industrialization and how it affects human lives, globalization, and worldwide environmental problems.** Industrialism exploits the energy contained in fossil fuels like coal, oil, and natural gas. By vastly increasing the amount of energy available to humanity, industrialism transformed most aspects of human life—from the number of people working in extractive industries to family sizes. To reduce the costs of production, corporations in the richer nations relocated many factories overseas, providing jobs for citizens there and greatly impacting the workforce and consumers in their own nations. Because of the globalization of production, environmental problems like water and air pollution and climate change have accelerated, generating international issues about which nations should bear the costs of environmental cleanup.

8

Exchange in Economic Systems

Peasants who sell products at marketplaces like this one in Chichicastenango, Guatemala, make money, but they do not depend on market sales for their entire livelihood. In this and other ways, their lives contrast with those of people who live and work in countries with fully market economies.

Economic Systems

Reciprocity
  Generalized Reciprocity
  Balanced Reciprocity
  Negative Reciprocity
  Reciprocity and Social Distance

Redistribution

Market
  Money
  Market Exchange
  Market Economies and Capitalism
  Productivity

Globalization and Markets

After reading this chapter, you should be able to:

1. **DESCRIBE** the three main forms of exchange in economic systems.

2. **ANALYZE** how the form of reciprocity between people varies with social distance.

3. **DISCUSS** the relationship between redistribution and political organization.

4. **DESCRIBE** the properties of money.

5. **DISTINGUISH** market exchange and market economies (capitalism) and the differences between neoliberalism and social welfare capitalism.

6. **DISCUSS** the globalization of markets and its costs and benefits to corporations, consumers, and workers.

In September 1958, San Francisco-based Bank of America mailed small plastic cards to its 60,000 customers in Fresno, California. Those who received the card must have been surprised to see the bank was giving them a $500 line of credit, allowing them to purchase $500 worth of merchandise without paying cash. The bank had previously persuaded around 300 Fresno merchants to accept the cards rather than cash for merchandise. Bank of America itself would pay the merchants for the purchase, then bill their cardholding customers for all their purchases in a given month. With its $500 line of credit, in effect each card was a small loan.

This, of course, was the origin of the first general-purpose credit card, called BankAmericard. It was not the first credit card. Since 1949, affluent residents of New York City could use the Diner's Club card—but only at selected restaurants. Particular chain stores, like Sears and J. C. Penney, had charge cards that were accepted at their stores but nowhere else. Before credit cards, people who wanted to make expensive purchases that they could not afford from their wages or salaries either had to save up or go to a bank, fill out a form, and persuade the bank to approve a loan for household goods like refrigerators, TV sets, and new furniture. With the BankAmericard, cardholders received revolving credit, in which they did not have to pay their entire bill within a specific time period but could pay whenever they wished as long as they did not exceed their limit. However, late payments did carry interest charges, which over the years increased greatly. The bank expected to make most of its money from small transaction fees it charged merchants, and

merchants expected to make money as more people became customers and spent more at their stores.

Eventually banks and merchants were proved correct. But at first, the bank lost money with the BankAmericard. Some stores did not accept the card, preferring to avoid transaction fees. And because in the beginning the cards were sent out indiscriminately (there were no credit scores in those days), about one out of four cardholders did not pay their bills. Some cards were pilfered, including out of mailboxes, so fraud was widespread. Soon the bank began mailing applications for cards rather than actual cards, allowing it to select which recipients qualified. Additional banks begin offering the card, and in 1976 the bank changed the name of the card to VISA, a term that was chosen because it connoted acceptance. By then there were many competing California banks that associated together and issued a card called Master Charge—now MasterCard.

Credit cards are a recent form of exchange in economic systems and have some consequences most people do not think about, as we shall discuss. This chapter describes the main forms of exchange that have existed historically and cross-culturally and some of their social and economic effects. We also discuss changes in exchanges that helped create the modern world.

Economic Systems

The word *economics* has many meanings, but here we use its everyday one: Economics is how people make their living by satisfying their needs and wants. At the societal level, three processes are involved in making a living.

First, people work and use technology to transform nature's resources into useful *products.* In modern *postindustrial* economies, most people—in their roles as employees—do not produce any tangible (material) product but work in *services.* For example, they produce or process or transmit information, post blogs, nurse or doctor their patients, wait on restaurant diners, manage the activities of others, and so forth. Service industry workers do not produce any material products with their own labor, but their jobs allow them to earn money that satisfies their own material wants and needs.

Second, someone *consumes* the products. We consume material products by eating them, living in them, driving them, wearing them, and so forth. Many material products are valued for their practical use: Food nourishes, houses shelter, motor vehicles transport, and clothes cover. In addition to their material usefulness, many products also are valued *symbolically.* For example, in addition to their practical value, food choices may express identity, houses demonstrate wealth, motor vehicles display income and may earn status, clothes flatter. These products send social messages about who we are, as well as satisfying material needs and wants. Many products and services are bought largely or entirely for their symbolic significance, such as jewelry, cosmetics, haircuts, tattoos, and sometimes club and fitness center memberships.

Third, between the time they are produced and consumed, many material products are *exchanged.* In economies like those of foragers or horticulturalists, often the producers and the consumers are the same people (usually, family members), but nonetheless exchange exists in these and in all economies. In modern market economies, the producers and the consumers are nearly always different people or groups, so practically every product is exchanged (marketed) before it is consumed. Most people make their living by working for firms or public agencies in exchange for money in wages, salaries, tips, commissions, and the like, which they then use to buy goods and services.

reciprocity Exchange of products or objects between two or more individuals or groups.

redistribution Collection of products or money from an organized group or society, followed by a reallocation to the group by a central authority.

market Exchange by means of buying and selling, using money.

In industrial market economies, nearly all products are produced entirely for sale. Once the value (money) acquired from the market exchange has been gained, the companies or persons who produce and sell the product have little further interest in it, except insofar as its quality affects future sales or reputation. However, markets are only one way of organizing exchange. In subsistence-based economies, families or other kinds of kinship groups produce mainly for their own needs, not for sale on the market. And rather than exchanges based on supply, demand, and prices, exchanges are organized around other principles.

Anthropologists usually classify forms of exchange into three major modes or types:

- **Reciprocity**, in which individuals or groups pass products back and forth, with the aim of helping someone in need by sharing with him or her; creating, maintaining, or strengthening social relationships; or obtaining products made by others for oneself.

- **Redistribution**, in which the members of an organized group contribute products or money to a common pool or fund that is divided (reallocated) among the group as a whole by a central authority.

- **Market**, in which products are produced and sold for money, which in turn is used to purchase other products, with the ultimate goal of acquiring more money that can be spent on more products, or saved, or invested.

The Concept Review illustrates the three forms of exchange. Notice the key differences. With reciprocity, generally speaking products pass between individuals who already know one another or wish to establish or strengthen a relationship. With redistribution, people who contribute to a central pool or fund may or may not have relationships with one another, but all have a relationship to the authorities who collect and reallocate. With markets, no party needs to know any of the others outside the context of the exchange itself. With a few qualifications, market transactions are *impersonal,* and one person's money is worth the same as anyone else's.

Most products (including land and labor) are exchanged through the market mode in modern industrial economies, but reciprocity and redistribution also exist. Examples of reciprocity are various gifts we give and receive on holidays, birthdays, weddings, baby showers, and other culturally special occasions. If you are employed, every pay period you participate in redistribution because federal, state, and local governments collect a portion of your wage or salary as taxes. They spend these public

Reciprocity	Back-and-forth exchange of products, gifts, and objects; symbolizes relationships as well as satisfies material needs and wants
Redistribution	Collection of products and valuables by a central authority, followed by distribution according to some normative or legal principle
Market	Free exchange of products (P_1, P_2) and services (S_1, S_2) for money ($) at prices determined by impersonal forces of supply and demand

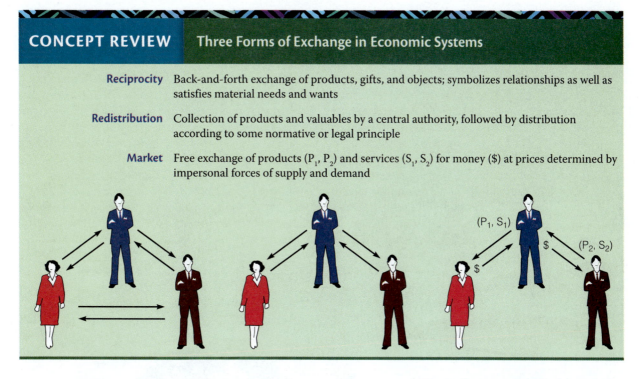

monies on public purposes, like wars or roads, or transfer money to other members of society, like the elderly, the poor, and subsidies for corporations and farmers.

All these exchange forms thus exist in modern societies, but not all preindustrial peoples have all three. Reciprocity in one form or another occurs in all human populations. But redistribution implies a central leader(s) whose role(s) carries authority to organize the collection of resources from the group and to make decisions about how they will be reallocated. Redistribution, therefore, is an insignificant exchange mode in societies that lack strong leaders who make decisions on behalf of the group. The market mode of exchange requires money, private property, and certain other features that are absent in nonmarket economies.

Reciprocity

In subsistence-oriented economies such as those based on foraging, horticulture, and pastoralism, most families and households are capable of producing most of the food and other products they consume. That is, most families are *potentially* self-sufficient in the sense that they own or have access to the land, labor, tools, and other resources necessary for survival.

However, in no known society are families, households, or other kinds of social groups self-sufficient *in fact.* Everywhere, such groups exchange products with other groups. Most anthropologists say this is because

families and other groups need or want to maintain relationships with other families and groups, and exchange is necessary to create and sustain these relationships. For one thing, most groups need help from time to time, so they keep up relationships with others to increase their long-term economic security. Other reasons include acquiring spouses, maintaining political ties, strengthening military alliances, and gaining new social contacts.

The form of exchange used for such purposes is *reciprocity*, defined as the transaction of objects without the use of money or other media of exchange. Reciprocity takes several forms, including sharing with those in need, providing hospitality, giving gifts, engaging in mutual feasting, and bartering. Various forms are motivated by different considerations and values, so anthropologists distinguish three forms of reciprocity: generalized, balanced, and negative.

Generalized Reciprocity

The defining feature of **generalized reciprocity** is that those who give objects do not expect the recipient to make a return at any definite time in the future.

generalized reciprocity Giving of products or services without expectation of a return of equal value at any definite future time.

Each member of this Inuit (Eskimo) whaling crew will receive a share of the whale meat and blubber. Sharing the fruits of cooperative efforts is one form of generalized reciprocity.

Generalized reciprocity occurs between individuals who are (or at least are normatively expected to be) emotionally attached to one another and therefore have an obligation to help one another on the basis of relative need. Parents who provide their children with shelter, food, vehicles, and college educations are practicing generalized reciprocity that sustains younger generations. Giving without expectation of definite return also should occur between parties to certain other kinds of social relationships, such as wives and husbands, siblings, and sometimes close friends. Other familiar forms include donating objects to Goodwill and Salvation Army and giving money to United Way or your alma mater. However, in these latter cases the possibility of taking tax deductions for your gift complicates the concept of generalized reciprocity.

balanced reciprocity Exchange of products or services considered to have roughly equal value; social interests or goals usually motivate the exchange.

Because it includes various forms of sharing with relatives and other people culturally defined as close, generalized reciprocity is found in all societies. However, among some peoples it is the dominant form of exchange, meaning that more resources are distributed using this form than any other form.

For example, most hunter-gatherers expect their band mates to share food and be generous with their possessions, partly because most members of a band are relatives of some kind (see Chapter 7). Among the Ju/'hoansi, the band is a social group within which food sharing is culturally expected or even mandatory. Those who are stingy with possessions or who fail to share food with others are ridiculed or socially punished in some other way. Generalized reciprocity ensures an equitable—if not entirely equal—distribution of food among the band's families.

Balanced Reciprocity

In **balanced reciprocity**, products are transferred to the recipient, and the donor expects a return in products of roughly equal value. Over the long run, the value of the products exchanged should be approximately equivalent.

The return may be expected soon, or whenever the donor demands it, or by some specified time in the future. With balanced reciprocity, the giver tries to apply some kind of sanction against the receiver if the latter does not reciprocate within the appropriate time period. Donors may become angry if there is no reciprocation, may complain or gossip to others, may try to force a return, or may suspend all relations until things of appropriate value are returned.

Although the value of the objects exchanged is supposed to be about equal, balanced reciprocity is characterized by the absence of bargaining between the parties. In some preindustrial economies, the exchange of objects without having to negotiate for each transaction frequently is organized by a special relationship between two individuals known as a *trade partnership.* Individuals of one tribe or village pair off with specific individuals (their "partners") from other regions with whom they establish long-lasting trade relationships.

For instance, in the Trobriand Islands off the eastern tip of New Guinea, there was a form of balanced reciprocity called *wasi.* Residents of coastal villages traded fish for yams and other garden crops produced in the mountainous interior. The exchange was formalized: A coastal village paired off with an interior village, and within each village individuals formed trade partnerships. The rates of exchange between the garden produce and the fish were established by custom, so there was no haggling at any particular transaction.

In *wasi,* each trade partner received foods not readily available locally, so parties to the transaction gained a material benefit. In other cases, trade partnerships have social as well as material benefits. For example, the Ju/'hoansi have a gift exchange custom called *hxaro.* In *hxaro,* the gift exchange is delayed—those who receive an object are not expected to return anything for an indefinite and often long period of time. Hxaro partners rely on one another for mutual support in other contexts, such as when one partner asks to forage in the territory of another. The social relationship created and reinforced by *hxaro* matters more to people than the objects given and received.

In *hxaro,* gifts make friends and vice versa, illustrating that gifts have *symbolic value.* More generally, when two people exchange gifts, ideally both gain something more than the sum total of the economic worth of the objects. On your friend's birthday, instead of giving her earrings in exchange for a gift of about equal value on your own birthday, you both could save the cost of wrapping paper and cards by buying the objects yourselves. However, neither of you would gain the symbolic value added when the exchange of objects becomes an exchange of gifts on culturally appropriate occasions. As material symbols of good relations, gifts both create and sustain feelings of solidarity and relations of mutual aid between individuals and groups.

Gifts show that the giver has expended some resources and taken some trouble because she or he cares about the recipient. Perhaps this is one reason why so many people prefer not to receive cash or gift cards: They take too little effort, are too generic to be personal, and the nature of the gift does not express the character of the relationship. To many people, gifts of cash or cards dilute the symbolic value of the gift.

Gift exchange communicates warm feelings, perhaps even better than words, both because talk is cheap and because some of us never know the right words to say. Conversely, failure to present objects of the socially appropriate value also can communicate feelings, although less warm ones.

On the other hand, gifts are used to obligate people from whom the giver wants something. Receiving gifts tends to make someone feel indebted and therefore can be used to create an obligation to return a favor if not a material object. Political lobbyists and sales representatives know that contributions and gifts can serve one's self-interest.

Among many preindustrial peoples, balanced reciprocity takes the form of mutual exchanges of gifts or invitations for political purposes. The Maring are a horticultural people of the mountainous interior of Papua New Guinea. In the 1960s, when Roy Rappaport worked among them, the Maring lived in settlements composed of clusters of kin groups. Each settlement was periodically at war with some of its neighbors and formed political alliances with other neighbors. When warfare occurred, the warriors of each settlement relied on their allies for military support and, in the case of defeat, for refuge.

To express continued goodwill, every few years, whenever they accumulated enough pigs, the members of a settlement invited their allies to an enormous feast, appropriately called a pig feast. At the pig feast, which was attended by hundreds of people, allies brought large quantities of wealth objects to exchange and pay off debts; they consumed enormous quantities of pork provided by their hosts; they were on the lookout for potential spouses and sexual partners; and they aided the host settlement in the ceremonial dancing that the Maring believed ritually necessary for success in the fighting that would soon occur. The host group also used their pig feast to gauge the amount of military support they could expect from their allies: The more people who attended the feast, the more warriors the host settlement could put on the battleground. Later, the

Gift exchange is a familiar form of reciprocity. Here in Narita, Japan, two men formally exchange gifts before an important festival.

guests accumulated enough pigs to reciprocate by hosting a pig feast of their own.

Reciprocal feasting was essential to the military success and continued survival of a Maring community. Here, and among many other peoples, the back-and-forth flow of products, invitations and return invitations, and other forms of give-and-take are essential for well-being and sometimes military survival.

In the contemporary world, too, balanced reciprocity in the form of foreign aid creates and sustains relationships between communities—in this example, between nations. In anthropological jargon, foreign aid seems like more of an example of generalized reciprocity conducted on a massive scale. However, to the extent that it influences relationships between donors and recipients it is more than aid. American aid promotes political stability in another country (Iraq), maintains potential sites for military operations

(Pakistan), and assists allies in warding off perceived or actual enemies (Israel, South Korea). Moreover, foreign aid is a relatively cheap way to look out for the interests of one's own nation, requiring less than 1 percent of the federal budget.

Negative Reciprocity

In **negative reciprocity**, both parties attempt to gain all they can from the exchange while giving up as little as possible. Negative reciprocity is usually motivated largely by the desire to obtain material goods at minimal cost. Insofar as it is motivated by the desire for material goods, negative reciprocity is like market exchange; it is different mainly because no money changes hands.

In economies with no money, negative reciprocity is an important way for individuals and groups to acquire products that they do not produce themselves. Few communities are entirely self-sufficient: Some foods the community likes to eat may not be found where the people live; some materials the group needs to make tools may not be found locally; and the people in the group may lack the skills

negative reciprocity Reciprocal exchange motivated largely by the desire to obtain products or services.

needed to produce some of the objects they use. To acquire these things, people produce other goods to exchange for "imports."

Barter is the most common form of negative reciprocity. In the interior highlands of Papua New Guinea, many indigenous peoples manufactured money or wealth objects by stringing shells together into long chains or belts. Because these shells did not occur naturally in the interior, they were traded from people to people until they reached their final destination. Salt was also a trade object because it was found in only a few areas. Similarly, in western North America, the obsidian (volcanic glass) used to make stone tools was found in only a few areas; other peoples acquired it through trade. In some cases, these trade routes stretched for hundreds of miles, with the obsidian passing through the hands of numerous middlemen before finally being made into a tool.

Reciprocity and Social Distance

Each type of reciprocity tends to be associated with certain kinds of social relationships. Marshall Sahlins first distinguished the three varieties back in 1965. He noted that the form of reciprocity that occurs between individuals or groups depends on the **social distance** between them. Social distance is the degree to which cultural norms specify persons should be intimate with or emotionally attached to one another. A given mode of reciprocal exchange is normatively appropriate only with certain kinds of social relationships.

North American social norms illustrate the idea. We expect people to practice generalized reciprocity with children and perhaps with siblings and elderly parents. Others may judge those who refuse to offer to help family members as uncaring or selfish. Well-off grandparents may help with their grandkids' higher education, with cars, or with down payments on a house. But middle-income persons who repeatedly give or lend money to a deadbeat cousin might be seen as foolish.

As our social relationships with other people change, so does the kind of reciprocity we practice with them. As we mature, we go from being the recipients of generalized reciprocity to a more balanced reciprocity as we become more independent. Near the end of our parents' lives, most of us provide generalized reciprocity, for most parents need or appreciate the assistance of children in spite of government aid by Social Security and Medicare.

Finally, changing one form of reciprocity into another can be a way of changing the nature of a social relationship. Because the form of reciprocity two people practice is related to the degree of social distance between them, one party can increase or decrease the social distance by initiating a new form of exchange. Or someone can signal his or her wish to draw another person closer by tentatively initiating a relationship of balanced reciprocity.

If we are work colleagues, I can let you know that I want to become friendlier by giving you an unexpected gift or inviting you to dinner. In turn, you let me know whether you share my feelings by returning my gift on an appropriate occasion, or repeatedly finding reasons to refuse my dinner invitation, or coming to dinner several times at my place without reciprocating. If we both use this strategy of reciprocity, neither of us needs to be put in the potentially embarrassing position of verbalizing our feelings. I signal my wish by my initial gift or invitation, and you decline or accept my offer of friendship by your response.

Here again reciprocity is symbolic, conveying messages about ideal social relationships, hoped-for relationships, and even rejected relationships. Because we routinely use reciprocity as a way of conveying feelings and sending social messages, anthropologists commonly view reciprocal exchanges as a form of communication.

Redistribution

The major difference between reciprocity and redistribution—the second major form of exchange—is how the transfer of products and other resources is organized. With reciprocity, resources pass back and forth between two participants, with no third party acting as intermediary. With redistribution, resources collected from many individuals or groups are taken to a central place or put into a common pool or fund. Some overarching authority (empowered to make decisions on behalf of those who contributed) later draws from this pool or fund and returns public goods and services to allegedly benefit the group as a whole.

In the preindustrial world, a common form of redistribution is **tribute**. The subjects of a chief or other

social distance Degree to which cultural norms specify that two individuals or groups should be helpful to, intimate with, or emotionally attached to one another.

tribute Rendering of products (usually including food) to an authority such as a chief.

titleholder contribute products (usually including food) into a common pool under chiefly control. Often tribute is culturally viewed as a material symbol that continues to acknowledge the chief's authority. The chiefs and their relatives consume some of the accumulated products, some are distributed to support the work of crafts specialists (e.g., weavers and potters), and some are redistributed to the whole population at public feasts, celebrations, and ceremonies.

Examples of redistribution systems using tribute payments existed on the islands of Polynesia and Micronesia in the Pacific Ocean. On most islands, the entire population was divided traditionally into two ranks or classes: noble and commoner (Chapter 13 has more about rank and class). Nobles themselves did little agricultural or other manual work, but instead managed the political system and organized religious ceremonies. Commoners produced the food for themselves and their families and performed most physical labor, giving products and services to nobles.

On some islands, the king or principal chief was culturally perceived as the ultimate owner of the land and its resources. Nobles generally had ritual functions, including prayers and sacrifices to deities and ancestors. On most islands, commoners paid periodic tribute to families of noble rank, whether in return for their use of the land, or as a sacred obligation, or both. Tribute fed the nobility and their families and supported specialists. The tribute rendered by commoners was used partly for public purposes—such as feeding people who worked on trails and public buildings, providing relief from temporary food shortages, and publicly celebrating special events. On a few of the larger, resource-rich islands such as Hawaii, Tahiti, and Kosrae, the nobles were sufficiently powerful to become materially wealthy from tribute: They lived in the best houses, slept on the softest woven mats, wore special clothing, had numerous servants, and ate only the finest foods.

In modern nations, the main resource (money, in this case) collected is taxes on wages, profits, retail sales, property, interest, and other income and assets. Consider how national tax systems are supposed to operate in most modern nations. The national government redistributes tax revenues in two main ways. First, revenues are distributed in such a way as to benefit the whole country. Citizens receive police protection, law enforcement, national defense, infrastructure (like roads and bridges), regulation of polluting industries, and so forth. Here, resources collected from the citizenry are expended on public goods and services, although

often unequally between regions and neighborhoods. Second, taxes provide assistance for individuals in need. In the United States, these are *transfer payments* in the form of Social Security, Medicaid and Medicare, disaster relief, child welfare, and so forth. Such public expenditures are based on moral norms and cultural values about social justice, equal opportunity, and helping those in need. Redistribution systems generally are used for similar purposes: to provide public goods and services and to provide assistance to individuals and groups in need.

There are other sides to redistribution, which also are familiar. First, there is often conflict over who should provide the public resources, how the resources should be expended, and how much of a share should be given to those who collect and distribute them. One common social and political problem with redistribution is political disagreement: When many individuals and groups have contributed to the public pool or fund, not everyone is likely to agree on how of the public resources should be spent for the public good. Much of the conflict between political parties in modern industrial democracies is rooted in disagreements over who should be taxed, how much they should be taxed, and how government revenues should be spent. Parties and various interest groups are, in many cases, quarreling over redistribution: Who pays? Who gets what? And how much? People and parties labeled "conservatives" and "liberals" regularly fight over such issues.

Second, elected officials and other officeholders who make important decisions about redistribution sometimes use public resources to further their own interests and ambitions, rather than to benefit the entire country or to help those in greatest need. In the United States, for instance, elected officials make "pork barrel" deals to allocate federal tax dollars to finance highway construction in their own districts. Congestion might be reduced for a while, but the real purpose is to provide jobs for their constituencies or to serve special-interest groups who contribute to their reelection. Balanced reciprocity between members of Congress often integrates well with redistribution: "You vote for my district's highway project; I'll vote for your wetlands reclamation."

In the United States, health care continues to cause bitter conflicts. It is widely agreed that American health care is both too expensive and inadequately distributed and needs reform. Around 18 percent of the U.S. gross domestic product is spent in the health care industry, far more than any other industrialized nation. Until the passage of the Affordable Care Act ("Obamacare"), the United States was nearly alone among developed nations in not providing subsidized coverage for all its citizens. Subsidized health insurance or socialized medicine (depending on one's political views) raises many issues about redistribution: Is health care a right that all citizens have? Is providing health insurance a legitimate function of government—that is, should the government redistribute tax dollars to provide health care?

Market

For our purposes, the word *market* has two uses. In one, market is one of the main forms of exchange, alongside reciprocity and redistribution. In another, market is a set of organizing principles, as in the term *market economies.* The two uses are related but not identical. Market exchange can exist even in economies that are not based on the market's organizing principles. Here we define market exchange as requiring a medium of exchange, so we begin with money.

Money

Money is another of those things we take for granted—so much so that it seems like a simple thing. However, the idea of money presupposes a lot of other ideas and institutions, so money actually is rather complicated.

At root, money is objects that serve as *media of exchange* in a wide range of transactions of goods, services (perhaps including labor), or both. With money, person A can acquire something from person B without having to return an object desired by B—that is, without having to barter. B can then use the money to buy a chosen object or service. If people sell their time and skills for money, the value of the labor is expressed in terms of money (wages and salaries). This facilitation of exchange is the main function of money.

Other characteristics of money are derived from its function as exchange media. For example, money serves as a *standard of value:* We can compare the values of goods and services because money serves as a common measure of how much things are worth. Having a common standard makes it a lot easier to compare the values of alternative products; for example, if you buy that new 4K, you can calculate what you are giving up by your purchase: You could buy other things with that amount of money.

Money is also a *store of value:* Because you can use it any time to purchase a wide range of goods, it stores your wealth, often in a portable form that can be carried in pouches or pockets. If you want to defer immediate consumption so that you can get something really expensive later, just save your money, because it stores your resources indefinitely. If inflation is high, though, and you store your wealth in a low-yielding bank account, then your money becomes worth less without you doing anything at all.

Money also has *symbolic significance.* Money is one way to evaluate people, especially if we don't already know them. Clothing, jewelry, cars, houses, and so forth are not indicators of moral worthiness, but they are still signals about how much individuals or families are "worth." How you spend your money also tells others a lot about you. Money can even symbolize national identity or independence: For years, many English citizens resisted adopting the pan-European currency (the euro) because they viewed it as a threat to their sovereignty. In June 2016, Great Britain voted to withdraw from the European Union. A narrow majority did not like the rules the EU imposed on its members, including ones about accepting immigrants as well as economic regulations.

These and other characteristics mean that not just any object can be used as money. Obviously, money objects must be *durable.* This is why hard objects such as modified stones, shells, and metals often serve as currency.

The supply of the money object must be *controllable* because if people can get all they want of it, its value inflates, and it becomes worthless as an exchange medium: Who would give you anything in exchange for it? The monetary supply can be controlled by a government, which manufactures the only "legal tender" in the society. Or the supply can be controlled by using only imported or rare objects as money. Shells imported from far away frequently serve as money because of their scarcity and durability. The money supply can also be controlled by using a currency that requires a lot of labor to make. Minerals or shells can be ground into precise shapes, drilled with holes, and strung into necklaces. In such cases, money remains scarce because it takes a lot of time to make it.

Money is more useful as an exchange medium if it is *divisible.* Often different kinds of objects serve as denominations of money—equivalent to nickels,

---

money Objects that serve as exchange media in a wide range of transactions of goods, services (including labor), or both.

quarters, $1 bills, and $1,000 bills. Among the Kapauku—a people of the rugged interior of Papua province, Indonesia—small cowrie shells imported from the coast serve as money. As the shells circulate, their natural polish wears off. Older cowries are scarcer, so they are worth more than newer ones. Thus, among Kapauku the age of the money serves as a kind of denomination.

For convenience, most money is *portable.* In different cultures, you can stick it in your pocket, carry it around your neck or waist, wrap it in a bundle, roll it up, or wear it around your arm. Chinese and Korean coins had holes in the center so the owner could store them on a cord. On the island of Yap in Micronesia, however, huge stone discs weighing hundreds of pounds serve as a kind of money. Yapese stone money is seldom moved; rather, the ownership of it is transacted so that the money stays in one place even when its owner changes.

As the stone money of Yap illustrates, an enormous variety of objects serve as money in various regions around the world. In preindustrial economies, the kinds of monetary objects are surprisingly diverse. In Africa, for example, the following objects served as money in some part of the continent: iron, salt, beads, cowrie shells, cloth, gin, gold dust, metal rods, brass bracelets, and livestock. Among the ancient Aztecs, cacao beans served as currency.

We began this chapter by describing the first general-purpose credit card. Credit cards are not money. Rather, they are a promise to a business that the issuing financial institution will pay the business money for some object or service the cardholder receives. With actual money, in most cases you must have the cash with you to make a purchase; with credit cards you only have to plan (or hope) to have the cash later. If something costs $100 (and even though you know how much other stuff $100 will buy) and you use the card, you still have the actual $100 in your wallet or elsewhere. Are you more or less likely to decide to purchase it with $20 bills or by scanning a plastic card? Financial institutions that issue the cards and the merchants who pay the fees to accept the cards learned the answer in about 1960.

One of the more unusual forms of money is the stone money of Yap in the Federated States of Micronesia.

Market Exchange

To say that objects or services are exchanged by markets means they are bought and sold at a price measured in money. Person A possesses products that person B wants to acquire; B acquires the products by giving A whatever amount of money both A and B agree on; A then uses the money to acquire more products from other people.

Most readers are so familiar with money and markets that the preceding sentence is just a convoluted way of stating common sense. If it seems that way to you, perhaps it is because you are so accustomed to the conditions market exchange requires that you do not realize that these conditions did not exist in the past or even in the present of many peoples. These conditions include:

■ Some objects that serve as media of exchange—that is, *money.* Notice that money itself potentially earns more money, as when it is lent for interest, which is the price of money.

■ Rates at which particular products and services exchange for money or at which money itself can be purchased for a fee—that is, *prices* and *interest* are determined by *supply and demand.*

■ Parties to exchanges have choices about alternative buyers or sellers and are free to make the best deal they can. Market exchange implies the absence of coercion: Neither party to a transaction can be forced to buy or sell from the other party. This is the *free market.* No third party (a government, for example) sets prices or forces anyone to buy or sell from anyone else. No single supplier of a good (a monopolist) controls enough of the market to force people to buy from him, her, or it (in the case of firms).

Some people have trouble grasping the full significance of differences between market exchanges and balanced reciprocal exchanges. As we have seen, there is often an element of selfishness in balanced reciprocity, making some think that reciprocal exchanges would become market exchanges if only the people had a form of money. If only they had money, they would have markets, goes the logic.

However, the difference is real and significant. It lies in the form and degree of selfishness in the total context of the exchange. Acting in your own self-interest is more than just tolerated in markets. In the free-market context, selfish acts are expected and positively valued because selfish choice making is believed to lead to an efficient economy. Selfish behavior is a *market norm,* so in the market context lawful selfishness is expected. You are foolish if you pay more than you need to. With balanced reciprocity, the two parties expect something from each other, but the return cannot be precisely judged to be equivalent and can be largely symbolic. Returns can be material objects, mutual help when needed, invitations and hospitality, or even just a well-communicated sense of gratitude. It is crass to measure such returns in money. Reciprocity is a *social norm.*

This difference between market and social norms is why you might worry or feel anxious about buying a used car from a friend, as will your friend. If the car is a lemon, how will it affect the friendship? In contrast, when you buy a used car from a dealership, you worry about other things besides damaging your relationship with the salesperson.

To further clarify the difference, consider this example. When you go to a friend's house for dinner, to be polite you might take a small gift, like a drink, a dessert, or a plant. Later you might invite your friend over for a meal to reciprocate. Next time, show up empty-handed. At the end of the meal, pull out your wallet and tell your friend you kept track of what you ate and estimate the cost of the meal at about $17. Tell your host you'd like to pay your share now rather than inviting her or him over to your place later. Or, the next time you exchange gifts, if someone has clearly shorted you, tell the person that she owes you about $6, your estimate of how much more your gift cost than hers.

If doing this makes you uncomfortable or if the very idea of doing it seems wacko, then you recognize the difference between social norms and market norms. On the popular TV show *The Big Bang Theory,* one of the many reasons Sheldon Cooper's behavior is humorous is that he seems oblivious to such distinctions, often treating other people as means to his own ends.

Market Economies and Capitalism

It is possible, and formerly was common, for societies to have money and markets without also having a market economy. For centuries, peasant classes in various places have sold foods they produce themselves at local markets. People make baskets, pottery, leather goods, art objects, cloth and clothing, and other goods to sell locally or, sometimes, in distant places. The Aztec civilization of Mexico had enormous marketplaces and even had traveling merchants who went around buying and selling products. The ancient silk routes connected the civilizations of China and the Middle East along trading stations and towns in Central Asia, where traders bought and sold Western and Eastern products like glass and silk. Even today, peasant marketplaces remain important in West Africa, southern and Southeast Asia, the Caribbean, and Central and South America.

However, marketing products and going to marketplaces does not imply that the entire economy is organized by market exchanges. Most peasants and other indigenous peoples grow most of their food using family labor and are not employed for wages in the impersonal labor market. They go to the market (in the sense of *place*) to buy something they need but cannot or do not want to produce themselves, but they do not depend on the market (in the sense of *system*) for their livelihood.

A **market economy** is one organized on *market principles.* Here are the most important of these principles and a short example of each:

- *Practically all privately owned goods and services have a monetary price and can be bought and sold on the free market.* Families live in houses and on the land on which they are built. This "real" property is the main asset of most families. Many change houses every few years, depending on their economic circumstances and the housing market.

- *Most people make their living by selling something on the market.* Some people make a living by selling goods or services to consumers. But most people are workers: They make their living by selling their labor time and skills to an employer (such as a firm or public agency). Workers have to do this because most of them do not own the resources nor have the capital to enter the market in any way other than as workers.

- *The market allocates productive resources, such as labor, land, equipment, and technology.* The supply of and demand for these resources determine

the uses to which they are put. If a company is producing products that consumers are not interested in or is charging prices consumers refuse to pay, the company will go out of business, or change what it produces, or find ways to lower prices by lowering its production costs. All companies adjust to market realities. In the 1970s, the American auto industry adjusted to Japanese competition and rising global oil prices by reducing car sizes and improving gas mileage. Resources were reallocated toward smaller cars because car companies made new choices to remain globally competitive.

- *The economy is self-regulating.* Impersonal forces of supply and demand set prices and therefore regulate the kinds of economic activity that occur. No individual, corporation, industry, or other entity controls a market economy because it is inherently decentralized. The "invisible hand," as early economist Adam Smith called this principle of self-regulation in 1776, is impersonal.

Capitalism is organized on these four market principles. As companies produce products or services, they earn profit through sales. Profits may be distributed to owners (often dividends to shareholders), saved in a financial institution, given as bonuses to top managers or workers, and/or reinvested in the company in hope of future profits to make the company grow. Through accumulating capital, companies expand and hire more workers, benefiting them. If a company is profitable, its profits go to owners and investors, who may save or spend them, creating additional demand for goods and services and thus stimulating more business activity. In this way capitalism is an economic growth engine.

In the economies of industrialized nations, people often sharply contrast socialism and capitalism. Ignoring many complications, in essence **socialism** means that the government makes decisions about product prices, wages and employment, what is produced and how, and the accumulation of income and wealth. Under socialism, the government sets prices for products and wages, which means that product prices and wages are not determined by supply and demand. The government, not market forces, decides what and how much is produced and thus allocates productive resources.

Each economic system has strengths and weaknesses. Again setting aside numerous complexities, it is commonly said that the strength of capitalism over socialism is *efficiency*: Overall, capitalist economies outperform socialist ones in the quantity of goods and services produced per person. This is because the incentives built

market economy Economy organized by market principles: prices determined by supply and demand; individuals and families rely on the market for livelihood; free-market allocation of resources, products, and services; self-regulation and decentralization of decision making.

capitalism Market economy; emphasizes capital accumulation through profitmaking as the key to economic growth and maximum material welfare.

socialism Economy in which government makes decisions about product prices, wages and employment, what is produced, and accumulation of income and wealth.

At the closing bell, traders on the New York Stock Exchange applaud the best day for stock prices in 2014. Rising prices of stocks are often interpreted as a positive indication for the American economy as a whole, although a small percentage of Americans own the majority of stocks.

into capitalism better encourage and reward hard work and training. (Notice that if one is an evolutionary psychologist, one might claim that capitalism is more consistent with human nature.) On the other hand, capitalism automatically and regularly produces losers as well as winners: Some individuals are better off than others, often because of inheritance from parents or because of educational and other advantages they have from living in a particular place or because of their ethnic identity or gender. Capitalism also has business cycles (booms and recessions), which occasionally are economically disastrous for workers and businesses (the Great Depression) and often require government bailouts (the 2007–2011 financial crisis). Finally, capitalism automatically produces *social and economic inequalities*, discussed in Chapter 13.

It is both easy and convenient for someone who believes in capitalism to give credit to the winners and disparage the talents and efforts of the losers. (Notice that if you are a postmodernist, you are likely to believe that such beliefs reflect wealth inequalities and power

relationships.) It is especially easy for someone to believe this if that person is winning—unless that person later becomes a loser. Then previously unsuspected complications become apparent.

The ideas justifying socialism are that it provides better for the poor by heavy taxation on the well-off and thus produces greater equality and more of what some call *social justice*. However, this has not always happened in real socialist economies, which critics say is why so few socialist economies remain today. In theory, socialism is friendlier to workers than capitalism with respect to wage laws, regulations about factory conditions, parental leave, unemployment compensation, and similar policies. But theory often conflicts with reality—with socialism as with capitalism.

Economies organized by market principles have many advantages for individuals. You can shop around until you find the best deal available, now especially easy with your smartphone and QR codes. You can change jobs if you are dissatisfied with the work or your employer. In the twenty-first century, many people carry hardly any money but have deposited "it" some-where and use those small cards that are a promise to pay when they want to buy something—not only a convenient practice but also one that allows people to spend money they have not yet earned and thus invites indebtedness. Furthermore, an economy organized on free-market principles is tremendously productive, as Karl Marx—the nineteenth-century archenemy of cap-italism—recognized. The People's Republic of China has experienced tremendous economic growth since its government introduced market reforms in 1978.

After the industrial revolution (Chapter 7), capitalism emerged and expanded in western Europe and North America. Its philosophical basis—the cultural ideas that provide its legitimacy—was and is that free markets serve as an invisible hand that efficiently regulates what is pro-duced and consumed. For example, saying that the market "allocates resources" means that if some industry is declin-ing (like textiles or shoes), then the profit made by compa-nies in that industry fall. Companies in that industry will go bankrupt or choose to go into some other industry. As a result, companies that produce products (like computer software) or services (like Internet advertising) will profit and grow, producing value for their owners. This process can be hard on the families of workers in declining indus-tries but benefits those in growth industries, and overall it is beneficial because it is efficient.

Capitalism is a "system," not a "thing," and how its prin-ciples operate vary from place to place and time to time. People—including economists—have different ideas about which version of capitalism works best. One set of ideas is called **neoliberalism** (or **laissez-faire**, roughly translated as "leave them alone"). People who believe in it are not lib-eral in the political sense. Rather, they believe in what they call "economic freedom": In market situations, leave peo-ple and corporations alone to do what they think is best for themselves and those they care about. This results in the best results for society as a whole. Governments can inter-fere with free markets with the best of intentions, but usu-ally there are unintended consequences that result in less growth and public benefit than would otherwise occur.

neoliberalism (laissez-faire) Belief that economic freedom results in the best results for society as a whole; mistrust in government interference with free markets.

social welfare capitalism Capitalist economy in which a legitimate function of government is protection of workers and society from the harmful impacts of free markets; involves extensive regulations of business and worker protections.

For example, when governments intervene to protect workers, they interfere with the workings of free mar-kets. Examples of intervention are minimum wage laws, safety regulations, requiring employers to provide health insurance, and allowing labor unions to require workers to pay union dues. These kinds of government interfer-ence might help the few (the workers in a given industry) but hurt the economy overall, because government in-terference reduces the efficiency of the overall economy.

In short, neoliberals place a lot of trust in free mar-kets. But even they agree that some forms of government interference is legitimate. It should protect property rights, construct infrastructure (e.g., roads, ports), and provide defense, police, and some form of public schools. It should regulate industries by minimizing external costs, which are things companies do that harm individ-uals, communities, or the environment. Forcing factories to reduce the amount of air and water pollution is a famil-iar example. Mandating auto safety equipment is another.

However, neoliberals argue against other kinds of government actions. Governments should not sup-port, by tax breaks or subsidies, companies that gov-ernment officials judge are in the public interest, such as alternative energy technologies. That would lead to the government picking winners and losers rather than the market allocating resources. Governments should not impose heavy taxes on corporate profits, because then corporations are less motivated to make as much profit as they can, which reduces growth and ultimately harms the economy. Governments should be only minimally involved in redistribution of income from wealthier people to poorer people—both because most of the wealthy have earned their income and because redistribution discourages work effort.

In contrast to neoliberal ideas is **social welfare capitalism**. This form of capitalism is based on free mar-kets, although many people incorrectly consider social welfare capitalism to be a form of socialism. People who champion social welfare capitalism point out that free markets generate a lot of bads along with their goods. One important task of elected governments is to minimize the negative consequences of capitalism without seriously compromising the value of free markets and the capitalist system. This involves heavy regulation of external costs ("heavy handed," neoliberals believe); extensive legal or regulatory requirements about worker safety, wages, and benefits; and taxation of the wealth and income of indi-viduals to fund social programs benefiting the poor and unemployed. When North American political candidates and officeholders talk about European-style socialism, they actually are referring to social welfare capitalism, because no European country is socialistic today.

However, most European countries do have socialized medicine: Governments pay for preventative medical care and for treating the sick and injured. To neoliberal thinkers, this is not a legitimate function of government and results in long waits for treatments and high costs: They believe health care services should be subject to the "discipline of the market," which they think will make medicine more effective as well as efficient.

Productivity

For a society or nation as a whole, some believe the main benefit of capitalism is *productivity*: Compared to socialism, market economies allocate resources more efficiently, which leads to higher productivity.

Think about the cultural meaning of the word *productivity*. When you say you have a productive day, you mean you have done a lot of work in some period of time. In economics, though, factory productivity is measured by the cost of producing goods compared to the market value of the goods when they are sold. Costs are measured by money, as is the GDP (gross domestic product) of a nation. Many economists worry when factory productivity falls, because it means that factories are using more input to produce the same level of output. Because labor is a cost, companies can reduce their costs by finding ways to employ less labor by automation, reorganization, or moving production to places where labor costs are lower. This leads to layoffs and firings, which is good for the company's productivity, however hard it is on unemployed workers and their families.

In a capitalist economy, companies do not and should not care about things such as whether firings and layoffs harm their workers or the general economy. By "companies," we do not mean the individuals in the company or even its managers or board, all of whom have a diversity of ethical and moral views. We mean what is in the interest of "the company," or what it should do to maximize its . . . what?

Most readers will answer "profit." In her 2009 book *Liquidated: An Ethnography of Wall Street,* anthropologist Karen Ho provides a slightly different answer: "shareholder value." On the basis of her ethnographic interviews in 1998–1999 with investment bankers working for Wall Street firms, Ho describes the *corporate culture* of the financial industry. One thing investment bankers do is use money (much of it borrowed) to buy stock in underperforming (undervalued) companies. Typically, they then break the company up and sell parts of it to other companies, thus liquidating the company. Ho's study is too complex to summarize in its entirety, so here we present some of her main findings.

First, investment bankers judge the success of a company by shareholder value (roughly, the price of its stock). According to Ho's interviews, in the culture of Wall Street, a company owes nothing to its employees aside from the provisions of their contract. Nor is it obligated to consider the impacts of its actions on the national welfare. For example, in a great many cases, soon after a company has fired or laid off a large number of its "excess" employees, its stock price rises. This increases its shareholder value because it has shed excess capacity. The management is responsible to the company's shareholders, so if shareholder value increases after layoffs and firings, management has done what it is supposed to do: increase the wealth of its shareholders.

Second, Ho writes, the high-level employees of Wall Street firms consider themselves as among the smartest people around. Most have degrees from elite business schools and rarely underestimate their own abilities. This does not imply they think their decisions are perfect, but a relative lack of humility makes them more likely to allocate money—usually the money of other people who are looking to achieve high returns on investments—toward risky investments because they think they have the brainpower and skill to assess risks accurately. Once hired, they work very long hours, often 70 or 80 hours a week, and are under constant stress because of pressures to perform.

Third, in addition to salaries, investment bankers earn annual bonuses, often far exceeding their salaries. Usually, senior managers make decisions about bonuses in secret and without justifying them to their subordinates. More often than one might expect, mid-level analysts themselves are "liquidated" (fired). The world of finance changes so rapidly that a division of a firm that was profitable last year may not be this year, so whole divisions are often let go. Wall Street culture instills the belief that that most assets must be liquid—they must be able to be reallocated very quickly. Labor is such an asset. Because of bonuses and the real possibility of not working for a company very long, employees are incentivized to raise the shareholder values of companies they buy and sell as rapidly as they can.

Like you and me, investment bankers are natives. To grasp their point of view, suppose you work as an investment banker in a Wall Street firm. Your compensation is tied to your performance, which depends on what happens to the shareholder value of the companies you advise your firm to invest in or take money out of. You are not always sure whether your performance meets expectations, which makes you work even harder to become more productive. Your firm believes that the financial sector changes so often that you and your entire division might be liquidated at any time. You and your colleagues can play it safe and allocate money in relatively safe but low-return investments. But you and your colleagues are the smartest of the smart, so you are able to evaluate the risks of investments. If the future works out, you will make loads of money for the company and for yourself through annual bonuses. If not, you might be downsized, but that could happen anyway.

Karen Ho's Wall Street research has many implications for understanding financial markets. Here we call attention to only one. Many people blame greedy bankers for the financial collapse that began in 2007. These critics seem to assume that the crisis was caused by the actions of individuals who were so intent on making money that they set aside their ethical standards or morality or found some other way of justifying their actions. Ho's work provides an alternative: It was not greed but the way that the financial industry is "structured"—the corporate culture that guides decisions, how rewards are allocated, expectations placed on people working in a highly competitive industry, and the like. Without a change in industry structure and corporate culture, a new group of less greedy bankers would soon appear to be equally greedy.

Remember the difference between market norms and social norms? In a capitalist economy, a corporation that acts altruistically toward its own workers or the general society raises its own costs and so reduces its competitiveness. Because of globalization, in the twenty-first century the companies of one nation's economy are competing with the companies of other nations, whose governments impose fewer or different regulations. There are few enforceable international regulations that level the playing field for corporations active in the global economy.

Therefore, the desire/need to remain globally competitive becomes an argument for a political strategy. A nation's corporations claim that things like government overregulation and unreasonable demands of labor unions are reducing their international competitiveness. In this and other ways, the global economy affects national elections, political debates, and programs that are enacted or not enacted. Public policies in all nations are affected by how nations are integrated into the global economy. In the United States, neoliberal ideas have been around for a long time but became influential in the early 2000s. Perhaps globalization has helped to promote the influence of the neoliberal agenda in political decision making.

Globalization and Markets

The most important food crop domesticated by prehistoric Native Americans was maize, usually called corn in the United States. As the ancient Mexicans learned, corn provides nourishing food, especially when mixed with complementary crops like beans (see Chapter 7). However, in today's United States, the nourishment it provides is not mainly food for people. About one-third of corn is processed into feed for livestock, including pigs, poultry, and cattle.

Corn also is a source of energy. This energy formerly fueled the bodies of people. However, today about 40 percent of U.S. corn is manufactured into ethanol and mixed with gasoline to fuel engines. In addition, corn is a good source of carbohydrates. Today most of the remaining corn crop that is not processed into ethanol or livestock feed is processed into high-fructose corn syrup that people consume in soft drinks, beverages, and canned foods. However much you enjoy summer's corn on the cob, in fact that corn is a tiny fraction of your total corn consumption. The rest is hidden from you in the form of animal products, fuel in your gas tank, and beverages.

Since the mid-1970s, many in the United States have worried about rising world prices of energy (mainly oil), too much of which is produced in foreign countries where Americans have little influence and where there is great hostility towards the West. Americans are overly dependent on foreign oil. To increase energy independence, some U.S. states instituted hydraulic fracturing ("fracking"), although its long-term environmental effects remain uncertain.

Another way to reduce foreign dependence on energy is ethanol. In the United States, ethanol is made mainly from corn. Once processed into ethanol, mixed with actual gasoline, and pumped into automobile fuel tanks, corn can both reduce prices at the pump and free Americans from becoming too dependent on foreign oil. U.S. family farmers and giant agricultural corporations produce enormous quantities of corn, as you would see if you drove through the country's farm counties. So much U.S. land was diverted to corn for ethanol that production fell for crops that once were agricultural mainstays, like wheat.

To reduce foreign energy dependence, as well as to earn support from farm states, U.S. federal legislators subsidize both corn production and ethanol processing plants. Rising demand for corn from ethanol plants contributed to a tripling of the market price of corn between 2005 and 2013 (however, corn prices vary from year to year). Because corn products (especially fructose) are used in so many processed foods and drinks, the prices of these consumer products rise concurrently when corn prices rise. Although people saved some money on fuel for their cars from ethanol, some of the savings went toward increased prices for snack foods, soft drinks, and other fructose-loaded products. Twenty years ago, the energy used to manufacture ethanol was barely greater than the energy gain from the fuel. A 2016 U.S. Department of Agriculture study reports that the energy gained from ethanol is about twice the energy used to grow and process the corn used to produce it.

There is a global market for corn. Increased American demand for corn made into ethanol contributed to a global rise in the price of corn. In a three-week period in early 2007, the price of corn tortillas in Mexico rose by a third. When there are shortages and anticipated shortages, speculators on commodities tend to bid on them, and competition among them further drives up prices—as seen repeatedly in world petroleum prices. Poorer Mexicans eat a lot of corn tortillas and beans, which for many are staples of their diet. They now pay more for their major dietary staple because Americans have diverted part of their production of a food (and feed) crop to energy. In Mexico, popular protests in 2007 against high prices were later called the "corn riots."

The Maya and other prehistoric Mesoamericans invented the process called *nixtamal* or *nixtamalización*. Derived from the language of the Aztec, nixtamalización involves boiling maize kernels with calcium hydroxide (lime as in limestone, not citrus) and ash (sometimes volcanic). After soaking in this alkaline solution, the kernels absorb valuable nutrients, and the soaking makes the niacin available for absorption by digestion. When the processed kernels are ground into tortillas and eaten with beans as tamales or another food, a nearly complete diet results, which prevents pellagra (a protein-deficient disease caused by lack of niacin) and rickets (a disease caused by lack of calcium). One Mexican nutritionist reported that rising corn prices led many poor Mexicans to switch to eating instant noodles, a much cheaper but far less nourishing food than the maize and beans that have nourished them for centuries.

Maize also is intimately tied into Mexico's history and culture. Corn was first domesticated in southern Mexico. It is a meaningful as well as a nutritional food—like rice in Japan or lamb in Iran—and it is a symbol of Mexico's national identity.

The impact of U.S. ethanol on Mexican corn prices is an example of **market globalization**. Market globalization affects almost everyone to some degree, including people who seem remote and relatively isolated from global forces. In the last five centuries, colonialism, disease, resource extraction from the land,

and (in some cases) slavery have dramatically impacted indigenous peoples. In the modern global economy, many of these peoples have found a small market niche that is uniquely theirs, as the Global Challenges and Opportunities feature explains.

Global markets go back to the colonial centuries beginning about 1500 (see Chapter 4). However, their size and geographic reach expanded dramatically in the last half of the twentieth century. In the 1960s, for example, an agreement between the United States and Mexico allowed U.S. corporations to set up factories (called *maquiladoras*) in Mexico along the Texas border region. The plants produced clothing and consumer electronics for American consumers. U.S. garment companies sent cloth to the maquiladoras to be cut and sewn into clothing sold to American consumers. Electronic firms sent components south to be soldered and assembled. Products were then brought back to the United States for final finishing and sale. There were no tariffs (import taxes) on the finished products, and Mexico allowed U.S. companies to retain ownership of assembly plants on its soil in return for the jobs and training received by its citizens. Most Mexican employees of these multinational firms were unmarried women. U.S. and European corporations made similar arrangements with Asian countries like Taiwan, Singapore, and South Korea.

Since the 1980s, wage levels in the countries mentioned above have climbed, and their governments have instituted more workplace and environmental regulations. To remain competitive by controlling labor and other production costs, corporations relocated production facilities to other countries that had even fewer regulations and lower prevailing wages. In addition to India, China, and Brazil, countries in Southeast Asia (like Malaysia, Indonesia, and the Philippines), the Caribbean, and Africa invited foreign companies to establish factories to provide jobs for their people and tax revenues for their governments.

News media, government officials, labor unions, corporations, and consumers debate the impacts of market globalization. Most important questions focus on its costs and benefits, especially the question of who loses and who gains. Four principal metaphorical interests participate in globalization: corporations who lower costs by outsourcing production, consumers in the more developed nations, workers in richer nations, and workers in developing nations and regions.

market globalization Process through which the world's national economies become integrated into a single exchange system organized by market principles.

Globalization of Indigenous Products

Indigenous peoples are groups whose ancestors lived in a particular region until they came into contact with outsiders who were more powerful and wealthy than themselves. Most often, indigenous peoples lost land, population, and resources as a result of the contact. Nearly always, their traditional ways of living were affected due to exposure to new beliefs and customs as well as loss of resources, land, and participation in a wider economic system. In the Americas, Australia, New Zealand, and most of the Pacific, the indigenous peoples suffered from Old World diseases that resulted in population declines, usually estimated at 80 to 90 percent. As we use the term, *indigenous* refers to peoples like Native Americans, Pacific Islanders, native Africans, and Asians who are ethnic minorities (see Chapter 17).

Today's worldwide economic system affects indigenous peoples in many ways. Economically speaking, one positive way is that the global market connects consumers in the more affluent nations and regions with producers of indigenous arts and crafts. Most of the world's large cities have small stores that sell "tribal" products made by the world's diverse indigenous peoples. Here, you can buy things marketed on the basis that they are indigenous. They are handmade (rather than mass produced), traditional ("just like their ancestors used to make it," although usually this is not the case), authentic (made by an indigenous person who is Other), and different (few people you know have anything like it). The object's appeal is further enhanced if buyers can become the expert among their family and friends, because the object traditionally was used in a cultural context that the educated buyer has taken the time to master.

In the American Southwest, stores in cities like Santa Fe, Albuquerque, Gallup, and Phoenix sell Native American products. Pottery made by Pueblo peoples sells for hundreds or even thousands of dollars. Navajo, Hopi, Zuni, and other Native Americans make bracelets, necklaces, belt buckles, conchos (silver ornaments), and other jewelry from silver and turquoise. Thousands of members of the Navajo nation in the Four Corners region maintain herds of sheep, whose wool they dye and hand-weave into rugs sold to tourists. Visitors who travel to one of the more than two dozen Southwest reservations have the opportunity to buy pots, jewelry, rugs, and other crafts directly from the Native Americans, enhancing their sense of an authentic experience.

Around 2000, jewelry produced by Southwest Native Americans became popular in Japan, which has 127 million people and is the world's fifth largest economy. Japanese tourists visit reservations in New Mexico and Arizona to buy directly from Native artists. Retailers also attend to buy in bulk to sell in their shops and galleries. Many Japanese go to Santa Fe in August to buy at the city's enormous Indian Market. Hopi silver jewelry is especially popular—so much so that shops selling indigenous products in Santa Fe and Albuquerque now have trouble finding Hopi silversmiths who will sell to them.

By moving people as well as things and messages around more than ever before, globalization makes it easier for this Western woman to buy a tapestry from someone on the island of Sulawesi, Indonesia.

John & Lisa Merrill/DanitaDelimont.com "Danita Delimont Photography"/Newscom

Corporations

Corporations in the richer countries were the main originators of globalization, mainly because of reduced labor costs and less restrictive environmental and workplace regulations; practically everyone agrees their top managers and stockholders are the biggest winners. The owners and managers of businesses in what we used to call the Third World also gain new income by producing for the export markets. Americans who criticize offshore production blame it for most of the increase in economic inequality in the United States in last 20 or 30 years.

Most pastoral peoples (see Chapter 7) have marketed their products for centuries, relying on such exchanges for much of their livelihood. They sell or trade wool, hides and leather, milk, and meat to neighboring farmers or at local marketplaces. Many use the hair of their animals to make carpets, garments, carrying bags, and other kinds of tapestries. Herders in Persia (Iran) and many Arab countries shear the wool of sheep, dye it in beautiful colors, and use the fibers to weave carpets, bags, and clothing on hand looms. Ethnic groups in northwestern China and Tibet, the Caucacus in Europe, parts of South Asia, and northern Africa do the same.

Outsiders have long recognized the craftsmanship and beauty of such woven products. The expansion of global markets in recent decades has increased consumer demand for pastoral products, which have become global commodities that fetch high prices among more affluent people of the herders' own country and others. People in the richer countries with enough money can buy carpets—both new and antique—that are hand-woven by herding peoples.

Carpets, hats, coats, tapestries, and other woven products sell for high prices on global markets because they are certified to be "authentic," meaning they were hand-woven by an indigenous ethnic group using fibers sheared from local livestock. The price may be even higher if the dyes are made from local plants and minerals rather than chemically manufactured in factories. If you can't make it to Amsterdam, London, Vancouver, or New York, you can find one on eBay, perhaps even offered by the indigenous person who made it. If you live in Asia, you can buy almost anything in Seoul, Shanghai, Tokyo, Mumbai, Karachi, Kuala Lumpur, or Manila. In all the world's cities, beware of knockoffs and counterfeits. You don't want to buy a rug or serape that looks indigenous but isn't really.

Buying material products is only one way to make a connection to indigenous peoples. For a fee, small companies organize groups of tourists to visit "primitive" places like New Guinea and Vanuatu where native peoples allegedly still follow the ways of their ancestors. Like its companion known as *ecological tourism*, cultural tourism has become popular as an alternative way to visit and learn about other places without so many modern amenities.

Sometimes, people who feel their nations are sacrificing their values and traditions as they grow richer seek connections with a less adulterated, authentic cultural past. The government of the People's Republic of China has built roads and provided public services that have opened up many of the nation's remote mountainous southwestern regions, making it easier for China's emerging middle class to spend a few days in the "backward" areas where minority peoples live. This is one way to transfer money from China's more affluent citizens to regions that have not experienced the boom in the export economy. In Yunnan province in China's far southwest, there is actually a cultural park where Chinese and foreign tourists can witness traditional dances and other "authentic" practices.

In the West, as in some other areas, many people live in houses full of things but feel their lives are empty of meaning. They want authentic experiences, feelings of belonging and identity, spirituality in their lives, and other intangibles. Most people find these within their own cultural traditions. However, some prefer to connect more directly with "native cultures." Familiar examples include Eastern practices like Zen, yoga, meditation, tai chi, and prophylactic acupuncture.

In their quest for meaning and search for new experiences, some Euro-Americans turn to Native American cultures. They think they know enough about shamanistic worldviews (Chapter 14), vision quests, holistic healing, and steam baths to think such Native beliefs and customs will help them find their own spiritual path. Santa Fe, New Mexico, and Sedona, Arizona, are among their favored destinations. Entrepreneurs have established businesses to provide metaphysical services in return for fees in the thousands of dollars. Among other issues, such practices raise questions about whether it is disrespectful to borrow just a little bit of someone else's religious traditions during a week-long sojourn to acquire meaning or spiritual power.

Occasionally, tragedies result. In October 2009, two men died and three people were hospitalized during a sweat lodge ceremony held near West Sedona, a place where vortexes release spiritual energies with healing powers. According to the *New York Times*, the overcrowded sweat lodge was wrapped in blankets and plastic tarps; then water was poured over hot rocks to release the heat and steam needed for the experience. A member of the Klamath-Modoc Native American tribe—who organizes such events—commented, "We would never use plastic to cover our lodges. The lodge has to breathe, that steam has to go someplace." A man who is part Mescalero Apache noted that this event was a good example of "why it is extremely dangerous to conduct sweat lodge ceremonies without proper training."

Consumers

Depending on what they buy, consumers in the richer nations benefit from lower retail prices because so many products are made so cheaply. Go to your closet and try to find a garment or pair of shoes manufactured in your own country. Check out your gaming console, TV, smartphone, tablet computer, and other electronic equipment. What do you suppose you would have paid for such products if they were manufactured in Toronto, London, Tokyo, or Chicago?

On the downside, in recent years some pet foods imported from China contained an additive that harmed animals; Chinese-made drywall contained toxic chemicals and often disintegrated; and a lumber substitute manufactured in China contained hazardous amounts of formaldehyde. It is easy to blame the Chinese—or whomever—but factories are located there because lowered production costs lead to more profits, so corporations who outsourced the production share responsibility.

Workers in Richer Countries

Other players in the global market are workers who lost factory jobs in developed countries, replaced by people who live half a world away. From a market perspective, they are the victims of restructuring and increasing efficiency; their employers must lower costs to compete in the global market to be responsible to their stockholders and increase shareholder value. Kannapolis, North Carolina, was once the home of Cannon Mills, the company that supplied a large percentage of textile products like sheets and towels. Cannon's buildings were demolished into enormous piles of brick rubble, and the American workers were "let go."

Those who favor globalization point out that most laid-off and fired U.S. workers have found other jobs. At any rate, in their role as consumers, workers benefit from the lower prices made possible by lowered overseas production costs. Critics of globalization claim that most of these new jobs are lower-paid jobs in various service industries and that the alleged decline of the American middle class and increasing economic inequalities (see Chapter 13) are due largely to globalization. Certainly the global labor market forces millions of workers—many of whom do not have higher education or professional training—to compete in a wider, global arena.

Workers in Developing Countries and Regions

Views also diverge on the welfare of workers who work in industries producing commodities for the global market. Critics of globalization claim they are exploited. Rich foreign and domestic companies take advantage of their poverty and lack of alternative economic opportunities by offering low wages and deplorable work conditions in terms of hours, health, and safety.

Those who favor the expansion of global markets respond that these workers are being paid more than they would otherwise be paid, they are getting job experience and training, their governments receive the taxes paid on their wages, and local businesses receive the capital needed for investment and future growth. In China, India, Brazil, Mexico, and many other countries, tens of millions of rural people who would otherwise remain peasants migrate to cities to work in factories. Why should we think they are too ignorant to judge whether they and their families are better off taking wage work in cities?

It is difficult for most people to decide which opinion is correct about workers in the global factory. Compared to wages, safety regulations, and general labor welfare standards in Western nations, no doubt the critics are right. Yet compared to the living conditions many factory workers would otherwise face, those who claim that offshore production helps those who work in factory production for export have a case.

Wage rates can be argued either way: If factory workers choose factory work, perhaps outside critics whose life conditions are very different should not be so quick to second-guess their choices. However, whether workers suffer health effects from their jobs—or die—is about as clear a criterion as can exist.

When wage rates in China began rising in the early 2000s, clothing companies from rich nations began relocating factories to countries with even lower production costs to stay globally competitive and to make higher profits. Bangladesh is one such country. Today factories located in Bangladesh produce more clothing for global markets than any other nation except China. International businesses outsource production to 3,500 garment factories in Bangladesh that employ around 4 million people, most of them female. Bangladesh's garment industry provides about 80 percent of the nation's exports. Despite paying the world's lowest minimum wages, the factories receive credit for helping to lift some families out of poverty. At the national level, factories provide foreign exchange, helping Bangladesh earn money to buy products like oil and technology from other countries.

In an industrial suburb of Dhaka, the capital of Bangladesh, until 2013 there was an eight-story building called Rana Plaza. Garment factories owned by five separate Bangladeshi owners and employing about 2,500 people were housed on the four upper floors of the building. Investigation showed that the top four stories had been constructed with no building permits and with substandard materials and disregard for building codes. Because of frequent power failures, to keep machines operating factory owners installed large electric generators in the upper stories, which shook the whole building when switched on. A visit by inspectors revealed large cracks in the walls. For safety's sake, a bank and several retail shops on the first floor closed, but managers of the garment factories on the upper stories ordered their workers to show up the next day.

On April 24, 2013, a generator turned on, and Rana Plaza collapsed from the vibration. For several days

palash khan/Alamy

The costs and benefits of market globalization are difficult to determine, because whether workers gain and/or lose depends on complicated circumstances. However, the 2013 deaths of 1,127 Bangladeshi factory workers due to the collapse of five factories in a single unsafe building leaves no debate about who lost here.

rescue personnel and ordinary citizens worked to free people trapped in the collapse and to clear away the rubble to search for more. After more than a week of rescue attempts, it was determined that 1,127 people died, the deadliest disaster in the known history of the garment industry.

In evaluating this and other human tragedies, many people blame national- or local-level owners, managers, and officials. Local building codes are too lax or are not enforced. Corrupt officials are often bribed to ignore violations. Greedy owners do not care about their employees. Such factors certainly contribute. However, the responsibilities of corporations and consumers in richer nations should not be underestimated. If a global corporation is searching for a place with low production costs to remain competitive, then it should be assumed that suppliers in a particular place know that a lower bid is more likely to win a contract than a higher one. They know that large international corporations are able to look elsewhere, whereas their own options are more limited.

What do you think those suppliers are likely to do to earn the contract?

Odds are, you own some garments that say "Made in Bangladesh" on their labels. Perhaps you don't even know where Bangladesh is. Probably you have no knowledge of conditions in its garment factories, because it would take a lot of moral commitment to do the research necessary to find out. Supply chains in a global economy are very complex, and you cannot see how your choices as a consumer impact workers on the other side of the planet. Consumer demand for a particular product is typically a combination of price and perceived quality, as affected by advertising.

Is it too much to ask global companies to tell us more about a product than where it was made? Suppose you could use your smartphone to scan the QR code that now accompanies many products sold at retail stores. What if, instead of finding out more about the nature of the product itself from that scan, you could learn whether the company stands behind the working conditions that produced it? Would you do that?

SUMMARY

1. **Describe the three main forms of exchange in economic systems.** Anthropologists classify exchange into three major modes or forms: reciprocity, redistribution, and market. Reciprocity is the giving and receiving of objects or services without the transfer of money. Motivations and social effects distinguish three subtypes: generalized reciprocity, balanced reciprocity, and negative reciprocity. In redistribution, the members of a group contribute products, objects, or money into a pool or fund, which a central authority reallocates or uses for public purposes, as exemplified by taxes and tribute. Market exchange involves buying and selling commodities and requires money, prices determined by supply and demand, and privately owned property.

2. **Analyze how the form of reciprocity between people varies with social distance.** The kind of reciprocity that exists between individuals and groups depends on the normative social distance between them. Exchange relationships alter as social relationships change. Conversely, one party can attempt to alter a relationship by offering an object (or invitation), and the other party can signal acceptance or rejection by a particular response. Reciprocal exchanges can communicate messages about feelings and relationships, so they often have symbolic as well as material content.

3. **Discuss the relationship between redistribution and political organization.** Redistribution is a major form of exchange in societies that have formal political leaders, who in preindustrial cultures anthropologists most commonly called "chiefs." As part of their status, chiefs have the right to receive tribute from their subjects, in the form of labor or products. Chiefs organize labor for public projects and reallocate the products among the community. Chiefdoms vary in the proportion of tribute kept by the chief's family versus redistributed back to the community.

4. **Describe the properties of money.** Money makes the exchange of goods and services more convenient and facilitates the making of profit and accumulation of wealth. Money functions as a medium of exchange, a standard of value, and a store of value. These functions mean that money objects usually have the characteristics of durability, divisibility, limited supply, and portability. Credit cards tend to increase purchases by pushing the cost of products into the future.

5. **Distinguish market exchange and market economies (capitalism) and the differences between neoliberalism and social welfare capitalism.** Market exchange involves the buying and selling of products or services using money. Market economies exist wherever market principles organize the entire economy of a people. Capitalism refers to economic growth by the accumulation and investment of capital. Neoliberals place great trust in the invisible hand of markets to regulate economic activity and produce optimal outcomes. In social welfare capitalist economies, governments exercise a lot of control over the free market to benefit workers and the poor.

6. **Discuss the globalization of markets and its costs and benefits to corporations, consumers, and workers.** Because of market globalization, most of the world is integrated into a single-market system. Global markets impact all categories of people. There is wide agreement that corporations who export production facilities benefit from lowered production costs and generally make more profit. Consumers also benefit from prices that are lower than they otherwise would be. The impacts on working-class people in all countries are more complicated, variable, and debated. However, worker health and safety is one issue on which both critics and promoters of globalization agree.

9 Marriages and Families

Popular ideas about whether legal marriage should be limited to opposite-sex persons are changing very rapidly in many nations. Anthropology has some insights on this issue.

189

After reading this chapter, you should be able to:

1 **DISCUSS** the primary theories of incest taboos.

2 **ANALYZE** why marriage is difficult to define cross-culturally.

3 **DESCRIBE** the forms of marriage and some of the ways cultures use marriage relationships for wider purposes.

4 **LIST** the main patterns of marriage exchanges and the cultural rationales behind them.

5 **EVALUATE** changes in attitudes toward same-sex marriage and why the issue is so controversial.

6 **DISCUSS** patterns of postmarital residence and some major influences on them.

7 **EXPLAIN** how postmarital residence patterns produce various household forms in human communities.

M any political leaders proclaim that they want to promote family values because "the family is the backbone of the nation" and is now "under threat." However, when these politicians call families the nation's backbone, they mean the "traditional" nuclear family, consisting of a married couple and their unmarried children. They do not mean families like the gay couple with the adopted daughter on the TV show *Modern Family*. What is a family, anyway? How many forms of family are there? And how many ways are there of creating them?

It is true that the bonds of marriage and family are among the central social relationships of most societies. Because families help support their members and society at large, leaders and many citizens grow concerned when family life and marriage practices change rapidly. According to the PEW Research Center, in the United States close to half of American marriages end in divorce; over a third of children live in households with only one parent present; 40 percent of children are born to unmarried women; and over one-sixth of children are living in a household that includes a stepparent.

Such statistics lead many people other than politicians to think that something has gone wrong with families, which could result in dire consequences. Will broken homes and single-parent families cause harm to children, communities, and even the whole nation? Worrying that marriage between people of the same sex will erode the sacred institution of marriage, in 2004 the American president and some members of Congress attempted (unsuccessfully) to amend the Constitution to enforce the one man–one woman marital norm.

Ethnographic studies and anthropological ideas have something to contribute to such contemporary issues. We look at some of the main ways cultures differ in their marriage practices and in the organization of their families and households. Before doing so, though, we need to define some terms used in this and later chapters.

Some Definitions

An organized, cooperative group based on kinship relationships between the members is what anthropologists call a **kin group**. The **nuclear family**, which consists of a married couple together with their unmarried children, is one kind of kin group. Typically its members live together, share the use of family wealth and property, rely on one another for emotional support, pool their labor and resources to support the family, and so on.

Among their many functions, nuclear families usually have primary responsibility for nurturing and enculturating children. North Americans usually think of

kin group Group of people who culturally view themselves as relatives, cooperate in certain activities, and share a sense of identity as kinfolk.

nuclear family Family consisting of a married couple and their unmarried children.

Term	Meaning
Kin Group	A social group formed on the basis of recognized (including fictive) kin relationships between its members
Nuclear Family	A married couple and their unmarried children
Extended Family	Culturally recognized kinship relationships between nuclear families
Household	A domestic group consisting of people who live in the same place and share assets and certain responsibilities

each nuclear family as living in its own dwelling such as an apartment, condo, townhouse, or house. In fact, some Euro-Americans look down on immigrants from Latin America, Africa, and Southeast Asia for housing too many nuclear families in one "single-family" dwelling.

People everywhere keep track of distant relatives who are part of their **extended family**. In North America, cousins, aunts and uncles, and other distant relatives gather periodically for holidays, family reunions, weddings, and funerals. However, we recognize how hard it can be to "get the whole family" together for such events. Extended families do not have clear social boundaries; rather, people's recognition of relationships wither and are forgotten as relatives become more and more distant. You may know and occasionally interact with your first and second cousins, but beyond that range, whether you even know their names depends mostly on circumstances such as whether they live in your town or state.

In contrast, in many preindustrial societies, extended kinship ties define the most important relationships in people's lives. Extended families are far more important in the lives of individuals: Members live in the same household, rely on one another for help with work and access to resources, share religious duties, and so forth. Some of these groups are enormously large, consisting of hundreds of members, as we see in the next chapter.

A **household** refers to people who reside in the same physical location. In the United States, most people continue to believe that typical households consist of a married couple plus any children still living with them. Yet the 2010 census revealed that only 48 percent of households were "husband–wife households," either with or without children. A third were "nonfamily households,"

meaning that no family members lived in the same space. Popular ideas about what families and households are like often are inaccurate, partly because people tend to confuse cultural norms with social realities.

In some societies, nuclear families live in separate dwellings on land they own jointly with families who are related to them. For example, women who are sisters may live on land given to them by their parents and bring their husbands to live there also. So long as the families use common property like land and tools, cooperate in work, share income or wealth, and recognize themselves as having distinctive identities, they belong to a single *household* even though they live in separate *houses.*

The preceding terms referring to groupings based on family and kinship seem simple enough. But it is easy to use one term when technically you mean another, which can lead to confusion. The Concept Review may provide clarification.

Households are not always formed exclusively by family or marital ties, as gay and lesbian couples, heterosexual unmarried couples living together, and various other roommates and housemates illustrate. In a great many societies, people incorporate unrelated people into their household, acting and feeling toward them in the same way as they do biological relatives.

extended family Set of nuclear families related through culturally variable kinship ties.

household Dwelling or compound inhabited by biological relatives or fictive kin who cooperate and share resources; in some contexts, a kin group of one or more nuclear families living in the same physical space.

This practice is widespread enough that there is a term for it, **fictive kinship**, in which individuals who are not actually biological relatives act toward one another as if they were kin. Adoption is a familiar example. In many islands of the Pacific, it is very common for a couple to adopt (or foster) one or more children, whether or not they have parented children themselves. Unlike in most Western nations, usually adopted children in the Pacific also maintain relationships with their biological parents, who are often relatives of their adopted parents. For many purposes, such children in effect have two sets of parents to support them emotionally and economically.

This chapter mainly concerns the diversity in marriage and family among humanity. We begin with the point that every people have rules that govern who may and may not marry. The most universal of these rules are *incest taboos*, which are so basic that we discuss them first.

Incest Taboos

Rules against sexual intercourse between relatives are called **incest taboos**. Although incest taboos are cultural universals (see Chapter 2), there are many complexities. For one thing, the specific relatives to whom taboos apply vary from people to people. Some societies prohibit sex and marriage between all first cousins, whereas others not only allow but also prefer marriage among certain cousins. But nearly every society prohibits sex between nuclear family members.

However, there are three documented cases in which sexual intercourse between siblings was permitted: the ancient Hawaiians, the prehistoric Incas, and the ancient Egyptians. Among the Hawaiians and Incas, incest was allowed only to members of the royal family and existed to preserve the purity and exclusiveness of the royal ancestral bloodline. In ancient Egypt, elite people sometimes married (and presumably had sex with) their own siblings. Everywhere else in the known world, sexual intercourse between siblings and between parents and children is culturally forbidden (which is not the same as saying it does not occur). In most cultures, the incest taboo is extended beyond the nuclear family to prohibit sex between uncles and nieces, aunts and nephews, and some kinds of cousins.

fictive kinship Condition in which people who are not biologically related behave as if they are relatives.

incest taboos Prohibitions against sexual intercourse between certain kinds of relatives.

Other than the widespread (not universal) extension to these relatives, cultures vary in the categories of kinfolk with whom sex is taboo.

Anthropologists have wondered a lot about why nuclear family incest is almost universally taboo. This wonder sometimes surprises people who are not anthropologists, who usually think that intercourse within the family is universally prohibited because inbreeding is genetically harmful to the children. Indeed, in Euro-American societies, many people believe that incest is illegal because science has demonstrated that the offspring of incestuous matings have a significantly higher chance of exhibiting harmful recessive alleles. But in the West and other human societies, laws or norms against incest existed long before genetic science arose, so clearly biomedical knowledge is not the primary explanation for the universality of the incest taboo.

What, then, are some other reasons for the nuclear family incest taboo? There are four major explanations.

The first two explanations begin with the assumption that many or most people have sexual desire for their close relatives. Because acting on these desires would somehow harm others in their family or other group, the incest taboo exists to help groups control such behavior. In many cultures, adults teach children that incest is among the most reprehensible crimes, and this culturally imposed prohibition discourages people from acting out their desire. Several specific hypotheses make these assumptions, but we discuss only two of the most credible.

"Marry Out or Die Out" is the idea first proposed by E. B. Tylor, one of the nineteenth-century evolutionists mentioned in Chapter 5. Tylor noted that a rule prohibiting marriage between close relatives forces people to seek their mates outside their domestic groups. Such marriages encourage families to establish relationships with one another—relationships that widen the scale of economic and political cooperation. Over time, groups that marry out had an advantage over those that did not, so eventually all groups developed incest taboos.

As we note later, Tylor's idea contains an important insight: Outmarriage offers advantages to those family groups that practice it. Unfortunately, this insight does not pertain to the incest taboo. There is no necessary reason a successful family could not allow sexual relations between its members but forbid them to marry one another. This hypothesis thus confuses the incest taboo ("Thou shalt not have sexual intercourse within thine own domestic group") with outmarriage rules ("Thou shalt not marry within thine own domestic group").

The "Peace in the Family" hypothesis, also called the *family disruption hypothesis*, argues that nuclear family incest would lead to sexual rivalry and competition within the family unit. It would interfere with the normal and essential functions of the family, such as economic cooperation and enculturation. It also might undermine the authority of the parental generation, which would often be challenged by the children. Brothers might be brought to blows over their sisters, and vice versa. Imagine the role confusions. For example, if a man had children by his daughter, the daughter's children would also be her half-siblings, and the father's children would simultaneously be his grandchildren.

This hypothesis is certainly plausible but difficult to evaluate. We do not know whether sexual relations in the family would threaten the family peace because the nuclear family incest taboo is nearly universal. Most likely, families would be seriously disrupted, but we have no way of testing the hypothesis. At any rate, the incest taboo is sometimes extended to very distant relatives who hardly know one another, and family disruption cannot explain these extensions.

The other two explanations both assume that the majority of people have little sexual desire for their close relatives. The two hypotheses are closely related and, indeed, complementary. Also, the same objection applies to both: If there is so little sexual desire between close relatives, then why do people need a taboo at all?

"Inbreeding Avoidance" is the cultural rationale for the taboo familiar to most readers. Both genetic theory and animal experimentation have established that offspring of sexual unions between close relatives have a significantly higher probability of inheriting homozygously recessive harmful alleles that show up phenotypically; that is, incest is bad not only for the children but also for the gene pool. The inbreeding avoidance explanation simply states that the incest taboo exists to reduce the incidence of mating between close relatives.

Why, then, are many anthropologists not completely satisfied with this explanation? One reason has already been mentioned: Many peoples are unaware of these harmful genetic effects, so these effects cannot consciously be the reason for the taboo. This objection, however, does not invalidate the inbreeding avoidance idea because the hypothesis does not require conscious awareness that inbreeding is potentially harmful. Nonhuman primates do not know that inbreeding increases the expression of harmful alleles, but they act as if they know: They generally do not mate with close genetic relatives.

We need only assume that throughout humanity's evolutionary history, those individuals who mated with their close relatives left fewer surviving and reproducing offspring than those who did not. The genes of those who did not interbreed with their close relatives would have spread within the population. Evolution thus built in a lack of sexual desire for close relatives over a long time span. If so, our knowledge is instinctive rather than conscious. This idea about the incest taboo is consistent with evolutionary psychology (see Chapter 5), the general theory that humanity's behavior has been shaped by genetic evolution. (Notice that evolution would also have had to build in knowledge of who one's close relatives are, or who they are most likely to be.)

Another objection to the inbreeding avoidance hypothesis is more serious: Many peoples do not apply the taboo to the kinds of relatives that the hypothesis predicts they should. For example, some peoples allow or encourage marriage between one set of cousins but prohibit both marriage and sexual intercourse with another set of cousins who are equally closely related genetically. Among certain populations, it is quite common for a man to marry his mother's brother's daughter, but for his father's brother's daughter to be prohibited as both a sexual and marriage partner. Yet among other peoples, a man is encouraged to marry his father's brother's daughter. Now why should some populations prohibit sex with one kind of cousin and others encourage it? In other words, the inbreeding avoidance theory alone does not explain the cross-cultural variability in the kinds of relatives to whom the taboo applies. It predicts (or seems to predict) that all peoples ought to prohibit the same relatives.

The "Familiarity Breeds Disinterest" explanation holds that males and females who are closely associated during childhood have little sexual desire for one another once they grow up. Also called the *childhood familiarity hypothesis*, this hypothesis was first proposed by a nineteenth-century scholar named Edward Westermarck. It was rejected for decades but became popular again in the 1970s because of some ethnographic studies that seem to support it.

One study is from the *kibbutzim*, the agricultural collectives first established in Israel in the 1950s. Most kibbutzim have disbanded, but in the past children were not raised by their parents but in communal peer groups by child-care specialists. Several infants of similar age were placed in a common nursery soon after birth. They were nourished and enculturated as a group, with more children joining them later around 5 or 6 years of age. A peer group of 10 to 20 children was raised together until adolescence, more or less as if they were siblings. Boys and girls raised in the same peer group were not forbidden to marry, and in fact adults often encouraged them to get together. But

On Israel's kibbutzim, children raised in communal nurseries and classrooms tend not to be interested in one another as sexual partners, supporting the "familiarity breeds disinterest" theory of the incest taboo.

B. Anthony Stewart/National Geographic Creative

people raised together almost never married, although they had lots of opportunities to get to know one another. Their behavior seems to support the familiarity breeds disinterest idea.

Arthur Wolf's 1960s study of marriage in Taiwan also supports the childhood-familiarity theory. Some Taiwanese couples with male children recruited girls, mainly from poor families, to be reared and trained in their households as future wives for their sons. In such families, a boy and girl grew up together in the same household—in most respects just like brother and sister—and were expected to marry. If it is true that children raised together have little sexual interest in one another, then there should be less sexual activity and greater marital difficulties for these couples than for other Taiwanese. Wolf found that these couples had fewer children, higher rates of divorce, and more extramarital sexual activity than other couples.

Evidence from an Arab village in Lebanon studied by Justin McCabe also supports Westermarck's hypothesis. For a variety of reasons, it is fairly common in the Middle East for a man to marry one of his father's

brother's daughters. In the village McCabe studied, about 20 percent of all marriages were between men and women whose fathers were brothers. These cousins were in constant childhood association with one another because of the sibling relationship between their fathers. If childhood familiarity does indeed produce adult sexual disinterest, then it should be revealed in these marriages. In fact, it is: These cousin marriages had three times the divorce rate and produced fewer children than other kinds of marriage.

So, some ethnographic research suggests that individuals who are raised in the same household tend to be less interested in one another as adult sexual partners. This sexual disinterest cannot be universal, or there would never be any nuclear family incest, but such incest is likely more common than publicly recognized. However, the childhood familiarity hypothesis does explain why most people do not commit incest within the nuclear family—they have little sexual desire for one another.

Furthermore, if childhood familiarity leads to erotic disinterest as adults, then the inbreeding avoidance explanation is also supported. To avoid inbreeding, people must have some way of recognizing their close relatives. In general, my close relatives are likely to be those with whom I was raised, so if I avoid mating with my childhood associates, I generally will not be inbreeding. Both these hypotheses taken together are capable of explaining why nuclear family incest is uncommon.

Some scholars have used the very existence of a taboo on incest to argue against both the inbreeding avoidance and childhood familiarity explanations. Their argument is that if people generally do not have erotic feelings toward close relatives, then cultures do not need an incest taboo. The fact that there is a taboo at all proves there is sexual desire for close kin, for why prohibit an action that people have no desire to commit? But this objection is unfair because neither explanation denies that some people desire close relatives sexually. There is merely evidence suggesting that *most* people do not. We can see why this objection is unfair with an analogous legal prohibition: Few people argue that laws against murder or assault prove that most people would commit these acts without the laws.

Notice that three of the four hypotheses account mainly for incest prohibitions within the nuclear family. They therefore cannot explain everything about incest taboos because in most human populations incest prohibitions are extended to more distant relations. For example, in a great many societies, members of the same clan (see Chapter 10) are subject to the taboo, and many clanmates are very distantly related. Therefore, it is plausible to conclude that the incest taboo has a biological basis, but that some peoples extend it beyond close relatives to achieve other social and cultural objectives.

Marriage

Biologically speaking, procreation creates the family relationships of an individual: Who your parents are determines your grandparents, your aunts and uncles, your cousins, and so forth. Assuming the woman and man are married, marriage and its resulting family relationships seem pretty basic. How many ways can people marry and have families? Several, it turns out. We begin with marriage.

Defining Marriage

What is marriage? Some Westerners with little knowledge of cultural diversity might say that marriage is a relationship between a woman and a man involving romantic love, sexual activity, cohabitation, childrearing, and shared joys and burdens of life. People trained in law

might also note that marriage has legal aspects, such as joint property rights and obligations to share support of children. Religious people may want to include their beliefs that marriage is a relationship sanctioned by God, a relationship that should last until the parties are separated by death. Gay, lesbian, and bisexual people will add their own provisions, which we address later.

These provisions are broadly applicable in many modern nations. However, they obscure the diversity in marriages that anthropologists have uncovered. For example, choosing one's spouse is not always a private matter decided by the couple. In many cultures, marriage is likely to be a public matter that involves a broad range of relatives who must consent to or even arrange the marriage.

Also, as often as not, romantic love is not considered necessary for marriage, and sometimes it is not even relevant to the relationship. Couples do not marry because they fall in love. For example, in traditional China, Korea, and Japan, a man and a woman seldom had a chance to fall in love before they married because they usually hardly knew each other and often had not even met. Sometimes boys and girls were betrothed at birth or as children.

Even when people married as adults, most marriages were arranged by their parents with the aid of a matchmaker, usually a female relative of the groom's family or a woman hired by them. She tried to find a woman of suitable age, wealth, status, and disposition to become a wife for the young man. The matchmaker would match not only the couple to each other, but also the woman to the husband's parents. This was important because the new wife would be incorporated into her husband's family. Her labor would be under the control of her husband's parents, especially her mother-in-law. She was expected to revere the ancestors of her husband's family more than those of her own parents. Her behavior would be closely watched lest she disgrace her husband and in-laws; often she would stay inside the family compound and not be allowed to interact with outsiders without supervision. Her children would become members of her husband's family, not her own. Love and affection might come after a marriage, but duty and procreation were more important than romantic love in China, Korea, Japan, as among many other peoples.

Even cohabitation in the same house does not universally accompany marriage. In many villages in Melanesia, Southeast Asia, and Africa, the men sleep and spend much of their time in a communal house (called, appropriately, the *men's house*), while their wives and young children live and sleep in a separate dwelling.

Other Western cultural notions of and customs about marriage do not apply elsewhere. Sex is not always confined to the marriage bed (or mat). There may or may not be a formal ceremony (wedding) recognizing or validating a new marriage. The marital tie may be fragile or temporary, with individuals expecting to have several spouses during the course of their lives. Or the tie may be so strong that even death does not end it. For example, in parts of old India, there were strict rules against the remarriage of a higher-caste widow, and such a widow often followed her husband to the grave by throwing herself onto his cremation fire (a practice now illegal in India).

Finally, there are culturally legitimate marital relationships that are not between a man and a woman. Among the Nuer of South Sudan, sometimes an older, well-off woman pays the bridewealth needed to marry a girl. The girl then takes male lovers and bears children, who are incorporated into the kin group of the older woman. The pastoral and horticultural Nandi of Kenya allow marriage between women. Some men have more than one wife, and at her husband's death surviving wives normally receive a share of his cattle, which they, in turn, pass along to their own sons. When a married woman grows too old to bear children and happens to have no sons to inherit the cattle given her by her husband, she may take a younger woman as her wife, thus becoming a female husband. She picks a sexual partner for her young wife, whose male children then become the heirs of the female husband. The two women, however, are not supposed to be sexually active after the birth—with other men as well as with each other. Regina Smith Oboler, who worked among the Nandi, reported that the relationship was almost identical to that between a married woman and a man.

Because of such diversity, defining marriage to encompass all the cross-cultural variations in the relationship is hard because there will always be some people who do not fit the definition. As you can imagine, numerous characterizations have been offered, but there is still no agreement on the best one. Most anthropologists agree, however, that marriage in *most* human societies involves the following:

- A culturally defined and variable relationship between a man and a woman from different families, which regulates sexual intercourse and legitimizes children
- A set of rights the couple and their families obtain over each other, including rights over children born to the woman

- An assignment of responsibility for nurturing and enculturating children to the spouses and/or to one or both sets of their relatives
- A creation of variably important bonds and relationships between the families of the couple that have social, economic, political, and sometimes ritual dimensions

If we define marriage in this way, do all societies have some form of marriage?

This question is tricky, and not just because defining marriage is problematic. However, the answer appears to be no. Consider the Musuo (also called Na and Naxi), an ethnic group of Yunnan province in the south of China. The Musuo are ethnically distinct from the Han, who are the majority ethnic group in China. Among traditional Musuo, a typical adult woman remains at the home of her mother and siblings. Men visit her at night for sexual intercourse, but such visits carry no commitment or obligation. Both people have multiple sexual partners without stigma, normatively speaking. The man does not spend the night and seems to have no obligation to his children, or even to recognize them as his. Children are raised by their mother and her own family, which means that Musuo have no nuclear families. Either the woman or her male visitor may initiate the communication that leads to their sexual relationship, but it is always the man who visits at night. The Musuo thus lack all four aspects of the definition of marriage given earlier. Therefore, they have no marriage as we define the term, nor do they have marriage as most people understand it. Cai Hua, the Han Chinese ethnographer, says that the Musuo demonstrate that marriage and nuclear families are not universal human institutions. (It seems that Musuo society has no "backbone.")

Some Han find Musuo relationships so exotic that many of them visit Yunnan province to see them. Han people often view Musuo women as promiscuous and the Musuo people as matriarchal. (If this were true, in these two respects, Musuo would contrast strongly with traditional Han practices, which perhaps is why so many Han are interested in visiting them.) The Chinese central government has a policy of speeding the development of the country's more remote, poorer regions, including the rural areas of Yunnan province. So the government encourages Han visits and has even helped establish parks where Musuo perform their allegedly traditional songs and dances.

However, the Musuo are very unusual. Nearly all other peoples have some institution that is recognizably "marriage."

Functions of Marriage

The near universality of marriage suggests that marriage does important and useful things for individuals, families, and/or society at large. Four functions are among the most important:

1. Marriage creates the social relationships that provide the material needs, social support, and enculturation of children. Most cultures recognize that forming a (variably) stable bond between a woman and her husband to raise children is an important reason to marry. In the human species, one reason the bond between human mates is more important than in most other animals is the lengthy dependence of children on adults. Until age 10 or older, children are largely dependent on adults for food, shelter, protection, and other bodily needs. Equally important, children need adults for the social learning that is crucial to complete their psychological and social development. It is theoretically possible that children *need* only one adult: the mother. But generally children benefit from multiple caretakers and supporters, and marriage helps to create and expand relationships that help children.

Children depend on the care of adults for many years, as this photo of a Vietnamese woman and her two children reminds us. Providing for the physical and emotional needs of children is everywhere a major function of families.

John Bill/Shutterstock.com

2. The marriage bond reduces (but does not eliminate) potential conflicts over sexual activity by constraining adult sexual access. Of course, extramarital sex is not prohibited to the same degree in all cultures, but some kinds of limitations are usually placed on it, often varying by gender. In traditional Korea, Japan, and China, married men were allowed to take concubines or have mistresses without punishment or stigma, but normatively and sometimes legally they had to continue to support their primary wife and her children.

3. All known societies divide up work like getting food and household tasks according to age and gender (see Chapters 7 and 11). Men do some kinds of tasks, women other kinds. Although the work usually overlaps, there is enough differentiation in most communities that the products and services produced by women must be shared with men, and vice versa. Marriage establishes the household unit within which family members do things for one another. The division of labor also means that most mothers need the assistance of *some* male to help provide food and other necessities to her young children. Most commonly, this male is her husband, although in many cultures the mother's brother and other relatives help out (see Chapter 10).

4. Marriage creates new relationships between families and other kinds of kin groups. In a few societies, nuclear families are physically able to produce what they need to survive with their own labor and resources. But the incest taboo forces individuals to marry someone other than their closest relatives. Every such marriage creates a potential new set of relationships between the relatives of the couple. The importance attached to these relationships varies from people to people. At the very least, the families of the wife and husband have a common interest in the children. In addition, a great many societies use the relationships created by intermarriage to establish important trade relationships or political alliances, as we see later.

Because marriage—and the new nuclear family each marriage creates—is useful to individuals and to societies in these and other ways, a relationship like marriage and a group like the family are almost universal among the world's cultures. However, no particular form of marriage or type of family is universal. Cultures evolved various marriage and family forms that performed these functions. To illustrate the diversity of these forms, we now describe two unusual systems.

Two Unusual Forms

Marriage Among the Nayar of Southern India

Before Great Britain assumed colonial control over their part of India in 1792, the Nayar were a warrior caste (see Chapter 13). Because many Nayar men served as soldiers for surrounding Indian kingdoms, they were away from their homes and villages much of the time. Frequent male absence affected marriage and family life. The Nayar lacked nuclear families, in the sense of a couple and their offspring living together and sharing responsibilities. Depending on how we define it, they may not have had marriage either. Yet Nayar people managed all the functions of marriage listed earlier. How did sexuality and provision for children work among Nayar?

Each Nayar village contained several kin groups. At birth, most children became members of the kin group of their mother. Each kin group was linked for certain ceremonial purposes to several other groups, either from its own or from neighboring villages. Nayar women and men who engaged in sexual relations with anyone in their own kin group were put to death because such behavior was considered incest. Restrictions on Nayar women were severe: Under penalty of death or ostracism, women had to confine their sexual activity to men of their own or a higher subcaste (see Chapter 13 for an explanation of Indian castes).

Every few years, all the girls of a kin group who were nearing puberty gathered for a large ceremony, the purpose of which was to ceremonially marry these girls to selected men from the linked kin groups. At the ceremony, each "groom" tied a gold ornament around the neck of his "bride." Each couple then went to a secluded place for three days, where they sometimes had sexual relations. Afterward, the grooms left the village, and none had any further responsibilities to his bride. He might never even see her again. For her part, the bride and the children she would later bear had only to perform a certain ritual for her ceremonial husband when he died. The ritual tying of the ornament by a man of a linked kin group served to establish a girl as an adult, able to have sexual liaisons with other men when she matured.

After her ceremonial marriage, each girl continued to live with her own family. When she reached menarche, she received nighttime male visitors from other kin groups. She established long-lasting relationships with some of her partners, who gave her small luxury gifts periodically but did not live with her. None of her partners supported her or her children in any way other than these occasional gifts. In fact, they also visited other women and fathered other children. A woman's brothers and other members of her own family supplied the food, clothing, and other needs for her and her children.

A Nayar woman's early marriage, then, did not establish a nuclear family, nor did her later sexual partners live with her or support her children. There was only one other thing a woman required from her partners: When she got pregnant, one of them had to admit that he could have been the father of her child by paying the fees for the midwife who helped deliver the baby. If none of her partners did so, it was assumed that she had sexual intercourse with someone of a lower caste. She, and sometimes her child, would be expelled from her kin group or killed.

Nayar marriage, then, was mostly symbolic. There was a ceremonial acknowledgment of a bond between wives and husbands, but other people performed the duties that are usually done by a married couple.

Cross-Generational Marriage Among the Tiwi of Northern Australia

In most societies, people who marry are comparable in age. Often the husband is older—sometimes significantly so. The Tiwi, who traditionally lived on the Bathurst Islands just off the coast of northern Australia, were unusual because both sexes frequently married people of markedly different ages—in fact, most spouses belonged to different generations. Ethnographer C. W. M. Hart worked among the Tiwi in the late 1920s, and Arnold Pilling worked there in the early 1950s. Jane Goodale's later work in the 1960s focused on Tiwi women.

Like other aboriginal peoples of Australia, the Tiwi were hunters and gatherers. Male elders made most of the important decisions in a band, including decisions about foraging activities and the distribution of food. Many elderly men were polygynous—that is, they had more than one wife. Polygynous men had access to lots of food from their wives' gathering and fishing, and they could acquire prestige and allies by distributing the food widely to other families. Tiwi prized meat, but as men reached their 50s and 60s, they were unable to hunt effectively. To hunt meat for food and distributions, they needed sons, which they generally had, and sons-in-law, which they could get by marrying off their daughters.

Tiwi marriage was unusual because of two rare customs. First, when a girl was born, she was almost immediately promised as a wife to some other man. This is *infant betrothal*, with the girl's husband selected by her father. Second, Tiwi norms required that all females be married virtually all their lives. So after she was betrothed, an infant girl was considered already married. And when a woman's husband died, she remarried almost immediately. This is known as *widow remarriage*.

An astute Tiwi father did not marry his infant daughter to just anyone: He used her marriage to win friends and gain allies. The allies who were most valuable were men about his own age, so he tended to marry his daughters to such men. But the relationship created by such a marriage was often reciprocated: If you married your daughter to a friend, you would likely receive his daughter, sooner or later. So a man might gain a wife in return for his daughter.

If a man's wives had daughters when he was in his 40s and 50s (which was common because wives were so young), then he married some of them to men his own age. Not all of them, though, because a man also wanted young sons-in-law to come live in his band and help supply meat. An elder would look around for a man in his 20s who seemed like a diligent and skillful hunter and a promising ally. He married some of his daughters to these younger men. When his daughters grew up, his sons-in-law would supply him and his household with meat.

A girl growing into womanhood would already have a husband, most likely one 20 or 30 years older than herself. Of course, this meant that most wives outlived their husbands but did have children by them. By Tiwi custom, widows had to remarry. But to whom? Some young men in their 20s had failed to attract the notice of elders and therefore had no wives of their own. But they still could be friends and useful allies of the sons of these widowed women. So at the death of a man, her sons (usually with her consent and approval) married their mother to a man 20 or 30 years her junior. That way, she would have the support of a strong hunter as she aged, and her sons would strengthen a friendship and gain an ally. (Tiwi wives might seem like "pawns," but in fact they were active participants in marital machinations, as Goodale documented in her book *Tiwi Wives*.)

If you had visited the Tiwi during their traditional life, here's what you might have observed: Many elderly men had several wives, most of whom were 20 to 30 years younger than themselves. Young men had either no wife at all or only one wife, and that one wife was probably around 20 years older than her husband. Elderly men were married to women who were in the prime of their lives, whereas many younger men in their prime had wives who were old enough to be their mother. Looked at from the point of view of a typical female's life cycle, she was first married to a much older man. Then after he died, she married a man who was young enough to be her son.

We emphasize again that both the Nayar and the Tiwi had unusual marriage systems. (Both systems are no longer operating.) Of course, neither people viewed their own marriage practices as unusual. It was just what they did. Perhaps they even thought it was natural. Maybe they considered it the backbone of their societies.

Variations in Marriage Beliefs and Practices

As the Nayar and Tiwi exemplify, marriage relationships vary between cultures. For one thing, most traditional cultures allow multiple spouses. For another, the nature of the marital relationship—living arrangements, what wives and husbands expect from each other, who decides who marries whom, authority patterns, how the relatives of the couple relate to one another, and so forth—differs from people to people.

Marriage Rules

Everywhere, norms identify members of some social groups or categories as potential spouses and specify members of other groups or categories as not eligible for marriage. One set of norms for marriage are **exogamous rules**. Exogamy ("outmarriage") means that a person is prohibited from marrying within her or his own family or other kin group or, less commonly, village or settlement. (Recall that the incest taboo prohibits *sex,* whereas rules of exogamy forbid *intermarriage.*) Because the incest taboo applies to those people whom the local culture defines as close relatives, members of one's own nuclear family and other close kin are almost everywhere prohibited as spouses.

Other kinds of marriage rules are **endogamous rules**. Endogamy ("inmarriage") means that an individual must marry someone in his or her own social group.

exogamous rules Marriage rules prohibiting individuals from marrying a member of their own social group or category.

endogamous rules Marriage rules requiring individuals to marry some member of their own social group or category.

The classic example of an endogamous group is the caste in traditional Hindu India (see Chapter 13). Other kinds of endogamous categories are found among communities of orthodox Jews, blacks and whites in the American South during the slavery era, and among noble classes in many ancient civilizations and states.

Endogamous rules have the effect of maintaining social barriers between groups of people culturally defined as having different social statuses or ranks. Rules of endogamy maintain the exclusiveness of the endogamous group in two ways. First, they reduce social contacts and interactions between individuals who are culturally believed (often, by widely accepted worldviews) to belong to distinct social categories. Intermarriage creates new relationships between the families of the wife and husband and potentially is a means of raising the status or rank of oneself or one's offspring. Endogamy keeps marriage within the caste, class, ethnic group, race, or whatever. Over generations, this reinforces ties *within* the endogamous groups and decreases interactions *between* the groups.

Second, endogamy symbolically expresses and strengthens the exclusiveness of the higher-ranking endogamous group by preventing its contamination by outsiders. Contamination may refer to higher-ranking families symbolically losing prestige when a member marries beneath his or her rank. It may also refer to beliefs about physical or spiritual (ritual) contamination due to physical contact and relations or even proximity. This is most apparent with India's old castes because the cultural rationale for caste endogamy was to avoid ritual pollution: The Hindu religion holds that physical contact with members of lower castes places high-caste individuals in a state of spiritual danger, precluding the possibility of marriage between them (see Chapter 13).

Technically, endogamy applies only to cultural norms (sometimes laws) about confining marriage to those within one's own group, but it is important to note the existence of *de facto endogamy*, meaning that

although no formal rules or laws require inmarriage, most people marry people like themselves. De facto social class endogamy exists in most modern nations, including North America, partly because opportunities for members of different classes to get to know one another are often limited. For instance, members of different classes usually go to different kinds of schools and hang out with different sets of friends. Such practices decrease social interactions between classes and thus reduce the possibility that people of different classes will meet and want to marry.

De facto endogamy also exists because of beliefs about the dangers of marrying outside one's own kind. Members of elite classes (and parents and other relatives of young people) may worry that would-be spouses of lower-class standing would not fit in with their social circle (to phrase their objection politely). Likewise, interracial couples are warned about the social stigma attached to their relationship and about the problems they and their children will encounter. Of course, these problems exist largely because some people continue to believe that interracial marriages are problematic. Millennials know that this belief and such norms have eroded in recent years.

Racial, ethnic, and religious barriers to intermarriage are breaking down in many regions due to improved education and increased interactions among peoples due to globalization. By expanding the range of nationalities people get to know, international and intercultural marriages are becoming commonplace. Globalization is changing popular attitudes in this obvious way, but it is also impacting marriage and family in more subtle ways (see the Global Challenges and Opportunities feature).

How Many Spouses?

One way cultures vary in marriage practices is in the number of spouses an individual is allowed to have at one time. There are four logical possibilities:

1. **Monogamy**, in which every individual is allowed only one spouse at a time
2. **Polygyny**, in which one man is allowed multiple wives at the same time
3. **Polyandry**, in which one woman is allowed multiple husbands at the same time
4. **Group marriage**, in which several women and men are allowed to be married simultaneously to one another

The last three possibilities are all varieties of **polygamy**, or multiple spouses. It is important to

monogamy Each individual is allowed to have only one spouse at a time.

polygyny One man is allowed to have multiple wives at one time.

polyandry One woman is allowed to have multiple husbands at one time.

group marriage Several women and several men are married to one another simultaneously.

polygamy Multiple spouses.

recognize that the three types of polygamy refer to the number of spouses *allowed* to a person, not necessarily to how many spouses most people have. In polygynous cultures, men are permitted more than one wife, but few men actually have more than one.

It may surprise members of monogamous societies to learn that most of the world's cultures historically allowed polygyny. In the past, before colonialism affected most of the world's peoples, about two-thirds of known societies allowed a man to have two or more wives. Today, polygyny is allowed in many nations in the Middle East, and it also exists among some indigenous peoples of Africa, Southeast Asia, Melanesia, and Amazonia. American news stories give the impression that many Mormons still practice polygyny, but in fact the church outlawed it in the nineteenth century, and the vast majority of Mormon faithful disavow the practice.

Polyandry is rare. It is documented in fewer than a dozen societies—less than 1 percent of the world's cultures. Group marriage, so far as we know, has never been a characteristic form of marriage in a whole human society. Indeed, group marriage, where it has occurred, has been a short-lived phenomenon brought about by highly unusual circumstances.

Many Westerners misunderstand the nature of polygamous marriages. We fail to recognize the social and economic conditions that make these forms of marriage advantageous. We now look at these conditions for polygynous and polyandrous societies.

Polygyny

Many people who view their nations as modernized believe that polygyny is an outmoded form of marriage. Commonly polygyny is interpreted as a manifestation of patriarchy (men force women into the relationship); as reducing female marital happiness (what woman wants to be part of a harem?); as harmful to children (wouldn't the kids of each wife be better off if they had their *own* father?); and as a way to provide men with additional sexual partners (at the expense of each wife). There is some truth to each of these opinions, but they do not tell the whole story of polygyny.

Because so many societies known to anthropology formerly allowed polygyny, many explanations have been offered. Many polygynous peoples practice sexual abstinence for several years after marriage, a custom called the *postpartum sex taboo*. The taboo commonly lasts two to four years. If followed, it reduces the birthrate, which might be beneficial, and also allows each newborn to nurse longer, leading to better child nutrition and health. Because of the taboo, polygyny allows husbands a legitimate sexual outlet, protecting new mothers and their children from having children too close together.

Some suggest that polygyny is a response to a shortage of adult males, because of hazardous male activities like warfare and hunting. If more adult females than males are usually present, then polygyny increases the chances that all women will find husbands and therefore helps provide her and her children with resources and an inheritance.

Disparity in the age of marriage might contribute to the frequency of polygyny. Typically, males are quite a bit older than their wives, partly because they need time to accumulate resources for bridewealth, as discussed later. So, the number of women of marriageable age increases relative to the number of men, allowing some men to have more than one wife and all women to have husbands. Polygyny, then, might solve a social problem caused by a discrepancy in marriage ages for women and men.

Notice that each of these explanations emphasizes the benefits of polygyny—to someone or to some group. Notice also that it is difficult to disentangle effects and causes. For example, does the postpartum sex taboo help cause polygyny? Or do polygynous men not demand sex from their wives with young children because they have other wives, making the taboo more likely to develop as a means of increasing childhood survival and health? Does the fact that men marry later in life than women make polygyny more likely? Or do men marry later because they need resources to acquire a wife, *because* of the fact that polygyny makes wives in such short supply that women's fathers demand resources for them? Whether these sorts of factors, or other factors, account for polygyny is debatable, and most humanistic anthropologists distrust them (see Chapter 5).

However, it is generally agreed that men acquire many benefits from plural wives. Men themselves commonly recognize the benefits. In societies that allow it, polygyny ordinarily is the preferred form of marriage for most men. Generally, men of high rank and status or wealthy men are the ones who have plural wives, although there are exceptions.

Men usually have both social and economic incentives for marrying several women. Socially, a man's status commonly is related to the size of his family and, hence, to the number of his wives and children. Also, when a man marries more than one woman, he acquires a new set of in-laws—fathers- and brothers-in-law whom he can call on for support, reciprocal relationships, and/or political alliances.

Marriage and Family in Global Society: The Case of Japan

As interactions among people of diverse nationalities and cultural traditions increase, people from different regions have more chances to get to know one another. Students cross national boundaries in search of better educations or new cultural experiences. Employees of multinational companies fly all over the world buying and selling. Migrants settle in new homelands. Tourists go abroad to see the world or just to increase their stock of travel stories and photos to show and tell their friends. Sometimes intimate relationships develop from these and other kinds of contacts.

In the old days, when discussing international, intercultural, or interracial relationships, many people talked about the importance of "sticking to your own kind." More polite people discussed all the problems such marriages would have because of society's attitudes. These attitudes are still around, of course, but such marriages are becoming so common that soon almost everyone will know someone who has married inter-someplace or inter-someone. Perhaps we will someday live in a world where most people consider everyone their "own kind."

Some effects of globalization on marriage and family are less direct and more subtle. Take Japan, for example. Japan has been buying from and, especially, selling to the global marketplace since the late nineteenth century, when the nation was opened up by the Americans under threat of force. After losing World War II and having two cities destroyed by the only nuclear weapons ever detonated against civilian targets, Japan recovered within two decades. It already had many advantages over countries that Westerners then called *underdeveloped*. It was predominantly urban. Most of its citizens were well educated. It had been industrialized for decades and was reindustrialized in the 1950s and 1960s. It was comparatively homogeneous linguistically and culturally as well as racially, so most Japanese agreed on important values and goals. It was politically stable with little crime.

After World War II, Japan was the first non–Euro-American nation to develop its economy from global trade. By the 1970s, Japan was such an economic powerhouse that American carmakers and electronics manufacturers justifiably felt threatened. As it grew wealthy by exporting autos, motorcycles, consumer electronics, and other high-tech products, more and more of Japan's rural people left the family farm in search of a better life in the city. This is a common, predictable effect of development: People migrate from farms to cities because of job opportunities and other attractions of city life. Urban households buy their food from farms, theoretically increasing the income of rural people with their purchases.

But marriage and family problems developed in the Japanese countryside. There was an ancient custom known as *primogeniture*, in which the eldest son inherited the family farm, including the farmhouse, equipment, any livestock, and the land. Younger sons made their own ways, perhaps working for their eldest brother on the family estate, joining a Buddhist monastery, or moving to another region. As for daughters, if a woman's parents were able to arrange her marriage to an eldest son, she moved in with her husband's family, to live with her father- and mother-in-law. Usually, marrying an eldest son was a desirable match for a woman with rural parentage. Although she would have to work hard serving her husband's parents as well as helping with farmwork, she had considerable economic security for herself and her children, and eventually *she* expected to become the mother-in-law of her eldest son's wife. Then she could take life a bit easier.

As Japan's industrial production grew rapidly in the 1960s and rural-to-urban migration picked up, younger sons left for the cities. There was still considerable family pressure on eldest sons to remain behind on the family farm. Many Japanese value what is left of their countryside and rural life. Parents, grandparents, and other relatives did not want land that had been in their family to be sold off. Japanese people

Most farmers in Japan are elderly and a great many men in rural areas remain unmarried. Most Japanese women believe that farm life is too difficult and prefer the attractions of city life.

MIXA/Getty Images

There are also short- and long-term economic benefits, especially in horticultural and pastoral adaptations, where a woman's labor is important in providing food and wealth to her family. The more wives and children a man has, the larger the workforce available to his household. In pastoral societies in Africa and elsewhere, polygyny enables a man to increase the size of his herds because he has more herders love rice for its symbolic value as well as for its bodily nourishment. Rural Japanese influence national political policies more than their numbers warrant, and the dominant political party did not want to see the country become even more dependent on imported foods. So the Diet (Japan's national legislature) passed measures limiting rice imports by various means and subsidized Japan's rice farmers. It might appear that the eldest sons were doing well.

Unfortunately, few Japanese women were interested in marrying one. Farmwork is hard, and farming towns are less exciting than the country's vibrant cities. Many Japanese city women have never been to a farm, and most who have would never dream of moving there. A farm wife probably lives with her husband's parents, with little privacy, and usually will have to care for them as they grow old. In the countryside, changing marriage norms eroded the ability of parents to control the marriages of their daughters, so most young, rural women were unwilling to marry a farm boy. Better to marry a *salaryman*—a professional man with a reliable and well-paying job in Tokyo or Kawasaki or Osaka or another city where work is easier and payoffs higher. In cities, salarymen work long hours and sometimes do not come home until midnight, but until recently Japanese wives expected much less socially and romantically from their husbands than Western wives. Odds are, a Japanese husband will turn control over his salary to his wife, who can use it for household expenses and save for their children's education.

By 1980, the shortage of wives for farmers had become a rural crisis. In one village in the late 1980s, there were 120 unmarried men and only 31 unmarried women between the ages 25 and 39. Some Japanese villages organized to find wives for their aging bachelors. One mountain village placed newspaper ads, promising free winter skiing vacations to young women who visited and agreed to meet its men. Over a five-year period, 300 women responded, but not a single one married into the village. In another mountain village of 7,000, there were three bachelors for every unmarried woman. To save the village, the local government became a marriage agent. It brought in 22 women from the Philippines, South Korea, Thailand, and other Asian countries to marry its men, many who were already in their 40s and 50s. Some marriages endured, but others ended in divorce because of the labor demands of farm life, the burden wives bore in caring for their husband's elderly parents, and cultural differences. Small businesses developed that offered counseling services for bicultural couples and served as marriage brokers to match Japanese men with foreign women.

Farming in Japan is now primarily a part-time occupation—farmers find off-season jobs in construction or other tasks, unable to make an acceptable living even with government subsidies. And older persons are now performing most farmwork. In one important rice-growing area, between 1980 and 2003, the number of people making most of their money from farming fell by 56 percent, and the number of people between the ages 15 and 59 fell by 83 percent. There was one increase, though: There were 600 more farmers older than 70 in 2003 than in 1980.

In the 1990s, many Japanese began to worry about another marriage and family problem: More and more women began postponing marriage into their 30s or choosing not to marry at all. Many continue to live with their parents long past the age when formerly they would have married and had children. Some Japanese refer to these women as *parasaito* ("parasite singles"), because they reside with parents even though many have well-paying jobs. Stereotypically, *parasaito* are first-class consumers of luxury goods, buying such expensive purses, shoes, and clothing that they seem overly self-indulgent in a culture that still values humility and submission to authority.

However, the choices these young women make are understandable, given their circumstances. Rents in Japanese cities are among the world's highest. Companies have a tendency to phase women out once they have children. Women know that when they are mothers, much of their time will be spent seeing that the kids get the high grades and test scores that are so important for their future careers. Many Japanese women have good reason to believe that their future husbands will be inattentive to them and their children because of job pressures.

Still, such choices will only worsen one of Japan's most serious problems. For three decades, Japan's birthrate has been falling. In 2015, an average Japanese woman had only 1.4 children over the span of her life. A mean fertility rate of about 2.1 children is required just to replace the population. As a consequence, since 2007 Japan's population has actually been declining. While a fourth of Japan's people are over the age of 65, only around 40 percent are in the prime working years of 20 to 55. Japanese have the highest mean life spans in the world: 81 years for men, 88 years for women. After leaving the labor force, most Japanese live two or three decades. How will the country support so many aged persons in the future?

(wives and children) to tend livestock. Similarly, in those farming societies in which female labor is important, a polygynous man has more family members to tend fields and harvest crops. As he grows older, he will have more children and grandchildren to look after his herds or work his fields and care for him. Thus, as long as he has the resources to support them, a man usually tries to acquire additional wives.

Polygyny is allowed as a form of marriage in many of the world's cultures. This is a Maasai man with his wives and children. Maasai are a cattle-herding people of Kenya and Tanzania.

What determines whether a particular man is *able* to acquire more than one wife? The answer is usually wealth: Only well-to-do men are able to afford more than one wife. "Afford," however, does not mean what Westerners might think; it is often more a matter of being able to *acquire* additional wives than of being able to *support* them. Most polygynous peoples have the custom of bridewealth (discussed later), which requires a prospective groom and his relatives to give livestock, money, or other wealth objects to the kin of the bride. Although fathers and other relatives are typically obliged to help a young man raise bridewealth for one wife, only a minority of men can amass sufficient resources to provide bridewealth for additional wives.

From the female perspective, in many societies polygyny has the beneficial effect of ensuring that virtually all women find husbands. Becoming married is often important for a woman's welfare because marriage legitimizes her children, and in many cultures children are her main or only source of social security—they are the people she depends on for support in her elderly years. There is another reason a woman wants to marry: to ensure that her children are well provided for. In the vast majority of polygynous societies, inheritance of land, livestock, and other wealth and productive property passes from fathers to sons. A woman need not marry to bear children, but she does want a husband to ensure that her sons have an adequate inheritance (her married daughters usually acquire their resources from their own husbands). Thus, in societies in which for some reason there are more adult women than men, polygyny provides a means for almost all women to gain the benefits of husbands for both themselves and their children.

Surprisingly to those who ignore context, there often are social and economic advantages for the co-wives of a polygynous man. Contrary to the view that no woman would want to share a husband with another woman, in many cases wives do not mind having co-wives. Often the most beneficial marriage for a woman is to a man of wealth and status—the type of man most likely to have married other women. Not only will the woman herself be better provided for, but her children may also receive larger inheritances of land, livestock, wealth, or other property. In addition, co-wives may lighten a woman's workload. Co-wives usually work together and cooperate on chores such as producing, processing, and preparing food, tending livestock, and caring for children. Thus, in many societies, it is not unusual for a wife to encourage her husband to take additional wives to assist her in her chores.

However, polygynous marriages have inherent problems. A common one is rivalry between co-wives and favoritism by husbands. Several strategies are used in polygynous societies to minimize friction. One way is for a man to marry women who are sisters, a widespread practice known as *sororal polygyny*. The rationale for sororal polygyny is that sisters are raised together, are used to working together, have preexisting emotional bonds, and are likely to be less jealous of each other. Sisters are, therefore, likely to be more cooperative than wives who are not related to each other—a point consistent with evolutionary psychology (see Chapter 5).

In most cultures in which a man marries a number of women who are unrelated, each wife usually has her own separate dwelling, which helps to minimize conflict among the co-wives. Also, co-wives are usually allocated different livestock to care for, and they may have separate gardens to tend and harvest. The effect of such practices is that each wife, together with her children, is semi-independent from the other wives. Despite such practices, rivalry and jealousy among co-wives are problems in many polygynous marriages.

Polyandry

Polyandry, the simultaneous marriage of one woman to two or more men, is a documented practice in only about a dozen societies. Much has been written about this unusual form of marriage, but we have not yet satisfactorily explained it. In the past some argued that female infanticide is partly responsible, reasoning that the death of large numbers of girls would produce a shortage of adult women, which would lead some men to be willing to share a wife. All else being equal, female infanticide does indeed have the effect of decreasing the number of marriageable women, but there are far more human groups that allow many of their female infants to die than those that practice polyandry. Female infanticide is not a *general* explanation for polyandry.

Rather than discussing general explanations, we note that wherever polyandry exists, it does so as an alternative form of marriage. Like polygyny, polyandry is culturally *allowed*, but it is not the *predominant* form of marriage; most couples are monogamous even where polyandry is allowed. Therefore, to understand the reasons for polyandry, we indicate some of the special conditions that lead some people (namely, husbands and their joint wife) to choose to join in a polyandrous marriage.

The insufficiency of a family's land to support all its heirs is one such condition. Many families in farming communities have faced the following dilemma: Our land is barely adequate, and all available farmland is already owned by another family or by a landlord, so we cannot provide all our children with enough land to support them and their families. In Ireland and some other parts of Europe and in Japan, one solution was *primogeniture*, or inheritance by the eldest: The oldest son inherited the farm and most of its property, and the younger sons had to find other ways of supporting themselves. Younger sons served in the army or became priests or found some other occupation. Daughters who did not marry usually either remained at home or joined a nunnery.

Some peoples of the Himalayas developed another solution—polyandry. The rugged topography and high altitude of Tibet and Nepal sharply limit the supply of farmland. A farm may be adequate to support only a single family, but many couples have three or more sons. If the sons divide their inheritance by each marrying a wife, over time the land would become so fragmented that the brothers' families would be impoverished. To solve this problem, sometimes all the sons marry one woman. This form of polyandry, called *fraternal polyandry*, helps to keep the farm and family intact and limits the number of children in the family. Although the eldest son usually assumes primary responsibility for the wife and children, the joint wife is not supposed to favor him or his brothers sexually. When children are born, ideally each brother treats them as if they were his own, even if he knows that a particular child was fathered by one of his brothers.

What are the benefits of fraternal polyandry? For the brothers, sharing a wife preserves the family property, keeping the land, the livestock, the family house, and other wealth together. Also, one brother can stay in the village and work the family land during the summer, while another brother takes the livestock to high mountain pastures and a third brother (if present) visits towns in the lowlands to sell the family's products. This system also has advantages for the wife, who has multiple husbands to work for her and help support her and her children. Her life is usually less physically strenuous, and she usually has a higher standard of living than a woman married to only one man.

Although Himalayan polyandry has economic advantages, problems can arise. A younger brother can decide at any time to end the arrangement, claim his portion of the family property, marry another woman, and establish his own family. The eldest brother does not have this option because, as head of the family, he bears primary responsibility for supporting the wife and children.

Marriage Alliances

Cultures vary in the importance they attach to the bond between wives and husbands. In some cultures, there is no formal wedding ceremony. Instead, a couple is socially recognized as married when they regularly live together and as divorced when one of them moves out. Each partner retains her or his separate property, so the separation or divorce is not messy. The Native American Zuni of New Mexico are one of several examples. In contrast, in the contemporary United States, the wedding ceremony is often an expensive affair; marriages are supposed to endure; and couples usually own houses, furniture, and other property jointly. Yet about half of all new American marriages will end in divorce—many quite messy because of conflicts over property and custody of the children. For many Americans, monogamy turns out to be *serial monogamy*, meaning only one legal spouse at a time.

Many cultures consider marital relationships to be far more serious. In some, marriage establishes lasting social relationships and bonds not just between the couple but also between their families and other relatives. The relationships between kin groups created by intermarriage are frequently important not only socially but also economically, politically, and often ritually. Marriage establishes an alliance between the members of two kin groups, and in many cultures **marriage alliances** are critical for the well-being and even survival of the intermarried groups. This appears to have been the case among the ancient Israelites. As Moses says in Genesis (34:16): "Then we will give our daughters unto you, and we will take your daughters to us, and we will dwell with you, and we will become one people."

marriage alliances Relationships created between families or kin groups by virtue of intermarriage between them.

levirate Custom whereby a widow marries a male relative (usually a brother) of her deceased husband.

The Yanomamö (introduced in Chapter 2) are a horticultural and hunting tribe of the Amazon rain forest. Most Yanomamö villages justifiably feared attacks by enemies, so a village had to be prepared to defend itself. Men of a village periodically went on raids intended to capture the women and resources of their enemies. All villages therefore needed to establish and maintain military alliances for mutual defense and offense, because the more men a village could mobilize as warriors, the more likely it was to be successful in conflicts. Having allies was also helpful in case of military defeat: A defeated village could take refuge with one of its allies, whose members would feed and protect the refugees until they could establish productive gardens in a new location. Intermarriage was a key strategy in creating and maintaining these alliances. If two or more villages had intermarried, their alliance was as strong as a Yanomamö alliance could be.

The Yanomamö illustrate how intermarriage creates and helps maintain important political relationships between villages or other kinds of groups. Among many peoples, these relationships are important to families or entire communities. If marriages are a means of establishing ties that are critical to a group's material well-being or survival, then the choice of which group to marry into may be too important to be left entirely up to the younger woman and man whose marriage creates the relationship. Older, wiser, and more responsible people should be making such critical decisions.

Understanding the importance of who marries whom to families and even larger groups helps to explain one widespread custom—*arranged marriages*—that many Westerners view as an infringement on a person's freedom to choose. Try looking at it from a different perspective: Under certain conditions, a young couple's freedom to choose their own spouse is an infringement on the freedom of their parents and other relatives to form advantageous relationships with other families. How serious this infringement is, and whether the freedom of one party or another takes precedence, is not absolute but depends on circumstances. Perhaps some readers will find arranged marriages less offensive when they realize that in many societies a poor marriage choice puts more people at risk than just the couple themselves.

The importance of the intergroup ties created by intermarriage is also revealed by two other widespread customs. In one, called the **levirate**, if a woman's husband dies, she marries one of his close kinsmen (usually a brother). The relationships between the intermarried kin groups are too valuable for a woman to be returned to her own family because then she might marry into another kin group. Therefore, a male relative of her deceased husband takes his place. Notice also that the levirate provides most widows with a new husband, which generally enhances her life. As seen in Deuteronomy (25:5–10), ancient Semitic peoples practiced the levirate.

The converse custom, the **sororate**, also preserves ties between kin groups. If a woman dies, her kin group is obliged to replace her with another woman from the group. The Zulu of southern Africa, as well as many other African peoples, practiced both the levirate and the sororate. In societies with these customs, marriages—and the relationships they create—endure even beyond death.

Marital Exchanges

In most cultures, the marriage of a man and a woman is accompanied by some kind of transfer of goods or services. These *marital exchanges* take numerous forms, including the North American custom of wedding showers and wedding gifts. In these, the presents given by relatives and friends help the newlyweds establish an independent household. Generally the gifts are useful to the couple jointly, with food preparation and other household utensils a common type of gift. Most couples today even register at stores so that their relatives and friends will provide the items they want.

Comparatively speaking, the most unusual feature of North American marital exchange is that practically nothing is transferred between the relatives of the groom and bride: The couple treats the gifts as their private property. Like most of our other customs, this seems natural to us. Of course, the gifts go to the couple—what else could happen to them?

Lots of things. For now, notice that the pattern of couples receiving gifts fits with several other features of Euro-American marriage. First, each marriage creates a new nuclear family, which usually results in the establishment of a new independent household. The couple needs their own stuff. In contrast, if the newlyweds moved in with one of their relatives, they would not have as great a need for the local equivalent of pots and pans, wine glasses, dishes, and other household items.

Second, North American marriage-gift customs fit with cultural values about the privacy of the marital relationship: It is largely a personal matter between the couple, and their relatives should keep their noses out. If the in-laws get along and socialize, that's great, but marriages generally do not create strong bonds between the families of the bride and groom. (In fact, the two families often compete for the visits and attention of the couple and their offspring.) As we saw in Chapter 8, gifts make friends, and vice versa. The fact that the in-laws do not exchange gifts with one another is a manifestation of the absence of a necessary relationship between them after the wedding. If, in contrast, the marriage created an alliance between the two sets of relatives, then some kind of an exchange would probably occur between them to symbolize and cement their new relationship.

Third, wedding gifts are presented to the couple, not to the husband or wife as individuals, and are considered to belong equally and jointly to both partners. But there are marriage systems in which the property of the wife is separate from that of her husband; if divorce should occur, there is no squabbling over who gets what and no need for prenuptial legal contracts. Among some Western Pueblo Native Americans of the Southwest, men usually went to live with their wives, so sisters often stayed together their whole lives. A woman might let her husband know he was no longer welcome by placing his personal belongings outside the door. Children stayed with their mothers, of course.

With this background in mind, what kinds of marital exchanges occur in other cultures?

Bridewealth

Bridewealth is the widespread custom that requires a man and/or his relatives to transfer wealth to the relatives of his bride. It is easily the most common of all marital exchanges, found in more than half the world's cultures. The term *bridewealth* is well chosen because the goods transferred are usually among the most valuable symbols of wealth in the local culture. In sub-Saharan Africa, cattle and sometimes other livestock are the most common goods used for bridewealth. Peoples of the Pacific Islands and Southeast Asia usually give their bridewealth in pigs or shell money and ornaments.

Bridewealth is mentioned in the Old Testament. In Genesis, a man named Shechem defiled a young woman and then asked her fathers and brothers to give her to him: "Ask me for as great a bride price and gift as

sororate Custom whereby a widower marries a female relative of his deceased wife.

bridewealth Custom in which a prospective groom and his relatives are required to transfer goods to the relatives of the bride to create or validate the marriage.

you will, and I will give whatever you say to me. Only give me the young woman to be my wife" (Genesis 34:12, English Standard Version).

One of the most common rights a man and his relatives acquire when they transfer bridewealth to his wife's family is rights over the woman's children. Reciprocally, one of a wife's most important obligations is to bear children for her husband. This is exemplified by the Swazi, a traditional kingdom of southern Africa. A Swazi marriage is a union between two families as well as between the bride and groom. The payment of bridewealth—in cattle and other valuables—to a woman's relatives establishes the husband's rights over his wife. A woman's main duty to her husband is to provide him with children. If she is unable to do so, her relatives must either return the bridewealth they received for her or provide a second wife to the husband, for which he need pay no extra bridewealth. Reciprocally, a man must pay bridewealth to gain rights of fatherhood over the child of a woman, even though everyone knows he is the child's biological father. If he does not do so, the woman's relatives will keep the child; if the woman herself later marries another man, her new husband will not receive rights over the child unless he pays bridewealth.

Brideservice

Brideservice is the custom in which a husband is required to spend a period of time working for the family of his bride. A Yanomamö son-in-law is expected to live with his wife's parents, hunting and gardening for them until they finally release control over their daughter. Among some Ju/'hoansi bands (see Chapters 7 and 8), a man proves he can provide by living with and hunting for his wife's parents for 3 to 10 years, after which the couple is free to camp elsewhere.

Like bridewealth, the brideservice custom was known to ancient Israelites. In Genesis 29, Jacob agreed to work for seven years for the foreign father of Rachel in return for the privilege of marrying her. But by the custom of the foreigners, Jacob first had to marry Leah, the eldest daughter, before her father would give him Rachel. So, Jacob worked 14 years for both his brides. As you

now realize, in addition to his brideservice obligations, Jacob practiced sororal polygyny (Genesis 29:1–30).

Brideservice is the second-most common form of marital exchange. It is the usual compensation given to the family of a bride in roughly one-eighth of the world's cultures. Sometimes it occurs in addition to other forms of marital exchange, however, and occasionally it can be used to reduce the amount of bridewealth owed.

Dowry

Dowry occurs when the family of a woman transfers a portion of its own wealth or property to the woman (their daughter) and/or to her husband and his family. The main thing to understand about dowry is that it is *not* simply the opposite of bridewealth; that is, it is not "groomwealth." The woman and her family do not acquire marital rights over her husband when they provide dowry, as they would if dowry were the opposite of bridewealth; rather, the bride and her husband receive property when they marry, rather than when the bride's parents die. By providing dowry, parents give their female children extra years of use of the property and also publicly demonstrate their wealth and their caring for their daughter.

Often dowry is the share of a woman's inheritance that she takes into her marriage for the use of her new family. Dowry may represent an occasion for a family to display their wealth publicly by ostentatiously moving furniture and clothing from their house to that of their daughter's husband. Among some peoples, the family of a man will not allow him to marry a woman unless she and her family are able to make a dowry payment. A common cultural rationale for dowry is that women do not contribute as much to a family as do men, so a family must be compensated for admitting a new female member. (Interestingly, this rationale is usually found among societies in which the domestic labor of the female is both onerous and valuable.)

Historically, dowry transfers were common in Eurasian (Europe, southern Asia, and the Middle East) cultures. Most peoples who practiced it were intensive agriculturalists and had significant inequalities in wealth. It is a relatively rare form of marital exchange, occurring in only about 5 percent of the societies recorded by anthropology.

Although a minority of societies practice dowry, some of these societies are quite populous. Dowry is common today in parts of southern Asia (India, Bangladesh, and Pakistan), where payments include jewelry, household utensils, women's clothing, and money. Much of the dowry is presented to the bride on her wedding day, but her parents and maternal

---

brideservice Custom in which a man spends a period of time working for the family of his wife.

dowry Custom in which the family of a woman transfers property or wealth to her and/or to her husband and his family upon her marriage.

In most societies with the dowry custom, a woman's family provides wealth for her to take with her into marriage. This is a bride from Pakistan.

uncle—often provide gifts—periodically throughout the marriage.

In recent decades, the demands of Indian families for dowry have led to thousands of tragic deaths. Rather than a one-time marital exchange, some Indian families demand additional, continual payments from the parents of a woman who has married one of their sons. They ask for large sums of cash, household appliances like refrigerators and televisions, motorbikes, and other consumer goods. If the wife's family refuses, their daughter may be severely injured or even killed by burning (in "accidental kitchen fires"), beatings, withholding food, falls, or other retaliations.

There are other forms of marital exchanges, including some in which both sets of relatives exchange gifts as a material symbol of the new basis of their relationship. And the three forms just discussed are not mutually exclusive. For example, in parts of traditional China, both bridewealth and dowry occurred at most marriages between well-off families. The groom's family made a payment to the bride's, and the bride's family purchased some furniture and other household goods for their daughter to take with her when she moved into her husband's household. For wealthier families, dowry was usually displayed as it was transported ostentatiously through the streets between the houses of the bride and groom. Dowry thus became a Chinese status symbol. Sometimes, if the bride's family was substantially poorer than the groom's, part of the bridewealth payment would be spent on purchasing goods for the woman's dowry. This was legal and common until after the Communist Revolution in 1949, when Communist Party leaders outlawed both bridewealth and dowry, with only partial success.

Although the preceding information about marriage rules, forms, alliances, and exchanges has barely introduced these complicated topics, enough has been presented to glimpse both the cross-cultural diversity of marriage customs and the societal importance of marriage. Marriage is tied up with economics, politics, and religion. Similar interrelationships among marriage, politics, and religion are seen in the contemporary United States, as the recent culture wars over same-sex marriage illustrate.

Same-Sex Marriage and the Culture Wars

In the early 1990s, some Americans became concerned that love relationships between gay and lesbian persons might be formally recognized by laws allowing same-sex marriage. A 1993 court case in Hawaii ruled that the state had to show a compelling reason to prohibit same-sex marriage. This raised the possibility that Hawaii would allow marriage between same-sex couples, and then other states would be legally obliged to recognize same-sex couples who married in Hawaii. In response to this threat to traditional marriage norms and values, the U.S. Congress passed the Defense of Marriage Act (DOMA), and President Bill Clinton signed the act into law in September 1996. Section 2 of DOMA provided that no state or territory was required to recognize marriages between same-sex partners made in another state. Section 3 stated "the word 'marriage' means only a legal union between one man and one woman as husband and wife, and the word 'spouse' refers only to a person of the opposite sex who is a husband or a wife." The law thus defined marriage as opposite-sex monogamy.

In the view of many Americans and their political representatives, DOMA did not go far enough. In early 2004, the newly elected mayor of San Francisco issued marriage licenses to gay and lesbian couples. In May of the same year, Massachusetts became the first state to legalize same-sex marriage. A few months later, in a Saturday radio address, President George W. Bush said, "The union of a man and a woman in marriage is the most enduring and important human institution." Alarmed at the prospect of other states passing legislation like that of Massachusetts, President Bush and conservatives in the U.S. Congress pressed for an amendment to the U.S. Constitution. After several rewrites, when brought to a vote on July 14, 2004, the amendment read:

> Marriage in the United States shall consist only of the union of a man and a woman. Neither this Constitution, nor the constitution of any state, shall be construed to require that marriage or the legal incidents thereof be conferred upon any union other than the union of a man and a woman.

In the vote, the proposal failed to gain even a majority vote in the U.S. Senate, where a two-thirds vote is required for passage of a constitutional amendment. Liberals saw it as a manifestation of intolerance comparable to racism and an attempt to deny some people the same rights enjoyed by others.

Many who continue to object to same-sex marriage hold that the major function of marriage is nurturing and successfully enculturating children, to make them into responsible, contributing adults. They insist that children need both a mother and a father, and no substitutes will work as well. Strong opponents of same-sex marriage also hold that marriage between one woman and one man is the bedrock of human society, so changing it is likely to endanger social order in lots of unpredictable ways. Many Christians oppose it because of biblical scriptures. The Catholic Church and conservative Protestants remain opposed to adoption by lesbians and gays, with one Protestant leader arguing that it is harmful to children because it purposely creates motherless or fatherless families.

Supporters of same-sex marriage make several arguments. One is that same-sex marriage is the most recent battle for equal rights under the law: The 1960s had the civil rights movement, the 1970s and 1980s had the women's movement, and in the early 2000s the comparable issue is legalization of same-sex marriage. Another argument is that there is no evidence that same-sex parenting harms children, whether they be adopted or born to female partners. There also is no reason to think that same-sex marriage will harm traditional marriage institutions, thus creating a slippery slope that will lead to who-knows-what. Legal arrangements allowing for *domestic partners* do not include the full spousal rights of married couples, such as freedom from inheritance taxes and Social Security or veterans' survivor benefits.

Since 2013, the U.S. Supreme Court has made several decisions supporting same-sex marriage. For example, in 2008 the California State Supreme Court ruled that same-sex couples have the right to marry. But the very next November, voters passed a ballot initiative that amended the state constitution to recognize only heterosexual marriages. The initiative was

challenged in a California court by a gay couple, and the court decided in favor of the couple. In June 2013, the U.S. Supreme Court allowed the lower court's decision to stand. In effect, this decision allowed same-sex marriage in California, making it the thirteenth state to give gay couples the legal rights of marriage.

In that same ruling, the U.S. Supreme Court struck down the 1996 Defense of Marriage Act, the federal legislation providing that only opposite-sex monogamy is legal marriage. In June 2015, the Supreme Court issued a 5 to 4 ruling on an Ohio case declaring that state laws banning same-sex marriage violated the Equal Protection Clause of the Constitution. This seemed to allow lesbian and gay couples the same legal right to marry as heterosexual couples.

Like many court rulings, many citizens did not accept a decision that they considered would promote sexual immorality and violate their religious beliefs. Almost immediately, a county clerk in Arkansas made national news when she refused to issue marriage licenses to lesbian and gay couples, claiming it violated her religious principles. Many private businesses publicly refused to provide services for same-sex couples, such as wedding cakes and photos. Such people felt that the Court's decision about rights to marry violated their own rights. Arguments included that the Court was usurping powers that rightly belonged to states and that the decision was contrary to democratic ways of making decisions. Recently, transgendered persons have encountered similar problems despite legal recognition of their gender (see Chapter 11).

Same-sex marriage became so politicized because it is a major skirmish in the American culture wars. Among other battles are whether there are absolute standards of right and wrong based on what some call traditional values; the role that Judeo-Christian teachings should have in schools, courtrooms, and other public institutions; whether various behaviors and attitudes are symptoms of moral decline; too much tolerance of pornography and sexual permissiveness; and how much multicultural diversity "one nation under God" can absorb without tearing itself apart from within.

Same-sex marriage and the sexual preferences of gays and lesbians provide ammunition for culture warriors: Are they immoral or just another alternative lifestyle? Are homosexual desires, like heterosexual desires, rooted in genes and hereditary, or is being gay a choice? Is being lesbian or gay a mental disorder, and, if so, can it be cured? Would gay marriage have undesirable consequences for the family, children, and the nation as a whole? If so, what, exactly? Would same-sex marriage be a slippery slope, leading to other forms of marriage, like polygamy?

Polls reveal a large shift in American public opinion about same-sex marriage since the 1990s. The first (slim) majority support for same-sex marriage appeared in 2011 polls. By 2016, nearly two-thirds of citizens supported the legalization of same-sex marriage. Although younger and elderly people vary in their support levels, many elderly persons have changed their views. Same-sex marriage has gained remarkable public support since 2000: On the cover of its April 8, 2013, issue, *Time* had a photo of two men kissing with the words "Gay Marriage Already Won."

There are many reasons for any large-scale change in popular opinion. In this case, one reason is that some national figures who ordinarily fight on only one side of the culture wars changed their opinions when their children came out, such as Dick Cheney (secretary of defense under George Bush) and Rob Portman (an Ohio senator). Another is that most people have realized that preferences for same-sex partners are neither a choice nor a disease but largely based on genetics, with a complicated means of inheritance. Third, medical technology has provided new ways of making babies, leading to gay nuclear families in which children are biological offspring of one partner. Finally—and perhaps most importantly—the majority of people now have relatives or know someone who is gay or lesbian, and most of them seem pretty normal rather than posing some kind of threat to society. If a preference or behavior once rare or hidden becomes more common or open, norms, values, and worldviews generally alter to accommodate it.

No matter how fiercely culture wars are fought to preserve the normative marriage practices of the moment, we can be sure that these practices will change and then change again. Aside from the cultural diversity in marriage norms and practices already covered, let's consider American history. Whether people can marry outside their race or ethnicity, what goes on during courtship, how people choose their spouse, what to expect from marriage, what obligations wives and husbands have in marriage, how enduring marriages will be, how the children resulting from the union of a man and a woman are raised—all these and most other features of marriage as we know it today would be viewed with consternation and even horror by North Americans of a century ago. Just a few decades ago, some people would have foretold the negative effects on society and children if blacks and whites were permitted to marry, if premarital sex were to become commonplace and generally accepted, if many wives/mothers were the main family breadwinners, if half of all marriages ended in divorce, and if large numbers of couples entrusted their preschool-aged children to something called day care centers for 40 hours a week.

We've seen in previous sections of this chapter that marriage forms and practices are explicable once we understand the conditions that provide their context. Like practically all other once-cherished institutions and beliefs, marriage patterns in the past and in the future have and will change to adjust to other kinds of changes.

Postmarital Residence Patterns

In modern European and American societies, most newly married couples establish a new domestic group (household) in their own apartment, condo, or house. Among other peoples, it is common for couples to move into an existing household—that of either the husband or the wife. Where most newly married couples in a society establish their residence is known as the **postmarital residence pattern**. Comparative work shows that the Western pattern, in which most couples form new households separate from their parents, is uncommon.

What are common postmarital residence patterns? By splitting enough hairs, it is possible to identify a dozen patterns, but here we present only five (in order from most to least frequent):

1. **Patrilocal**—Couples live with or near the parents of the husband.
2. **Matrilocal**—Couples live with or near the wife's parents.
3. **Ambilocal**—Couples may choose to live with either the wife's or the husband's kin; roughly half of all couples choose each.
4. **Bilocal**—Couples move back and forth between the households of both sets of parents according to preferences and circumstances.

postmarital residence pattern Household in which the majority of newly married couples establish their residence.

patrilocal residence Residence form in which couples live with or near the husband's parents.

matrilocal residence Residence form in which couples live with or near the wife's parents.

ambilocal residence Residence form in which couples choose whether to live with the wife's or the husband's family.

bilocal residence Residence form in which couples move between the households of both sets of parents.

5. **Neolocal**—Couples live apart from both parents, establishing a separate dwelling and independent household.

If this seems like a lot of terms, that's because there are a lot of residence patterns! About 70 percent of all societies have patrilocal residence as the predominant pattern. Thirteen percent have matrilocal residence. Bilocality, ambilocality, neolocality, and other far less common forms together account for the remaining 17 percent.

Influences on Residence Patterns

What sorts of factors affect postmarital residence patterns, such as whether newly married couples live separately or move in with some other relatives? And, in societies in which most couples co-reside with some set of relatives, what affects which set of relatives?

Although there is no simple answer, property rights and inheritance forms are important influences on postmarital residence. In societies in which men own the most important productive property and inheritance passes from fathers to sons, brothers have good reason to join their fathers (and each other) in a common household to cooperate in work and protect their interests in land, livestock, or other wealth. When the sons of most families in a community bring their wives and children into their father's household, this behavior leads to the residence pattern anthropologists call *patrilocal.* Where important resources are controlled or owned by women, and especially if female labor is important in supplying food for their families, then sisters tend to live and work together. *Matrilocal* residence develops when sisters bring their husbands to live with them.

Ambilocal and bilocal patterns are most common in societies in which inheritance of important resources passes through both sexes, and the labor of both women and men is important to household subsistence. Most hunter-gatherers have one of these two patterns. As explained in Chapter 7, most families in a foraging band find it useful to maintain access to several territories, so the rights to gather and hunt in a particular area are flexible. Nuclear families may live off and on with the husband's and wife's bands, depending on sentimental ties or short- or long-term availability of resources. If all or most couples do this, the result is bilocal residence. Or, the couple may settle with whichever parental family has the most resources or with whichever they have good relations, leading to ambilocality.

neolocal residence Residence form in which a couple establishes a separate household apart from both the husband's and the wife's parents.

Industrialized nations are usually neolocal for two major reasons. First, job availability forces many couples to move away from the place where they were born and raised. This is especially true for upwardly mobile couples seeking higher incomes, better opportunities, and the more materially rewarding lifestyle valued by many. Second, in capitalistic industrialized countries, most workers do not rely on their family connections for access to their livelihood but instead sell their labor on an impersonal market to an employer they have never met. In other words, most ordinary citizens do not inherit *productive* property from their parents and do not rely on their parents for their livelihood. This leads most couples to establish independent domiciles free from parental control and interference. The result is neolocal residence and a cultural emphasis on nuclear family ties, making some students wonder what is causing all those other weird residence patterns—once they know of their existence.

Although control over resources and form of inheritance are important overall influences, no single factor determines postmarital residence. For instance, if most couples rely on the wife's family for access to the resources they need to survive and raise children, then most couples will live with the wife's family, and matrilocal residence will be the pattern. But a multitude of other factors also affect residence choices. In fact, in some societies, even though women have much control over land, residence is not matrilocal because these other factors are locally more important than keeping sisters together in a common household. Similar complexities apply to the other residence patterns, so there is no simple explanation.

Other complications also make generalizations difficult. For one thing, a great many peoples do not have a single residence pattern; rather, where people live varies over time. Among some Inuit (Eskimo) peoples, often couples lived neolocally in the summer and patrilocally in the winter. For another, even within a single society, different families make different choices. For example, China's industrial economy is growing at a staggering rate, and its residence pattern is transforming from the pre–twentieth-century patrilocal pattern to a neolocal pattern. Yet many rural couples live with the husband's family, and even many young urban couples live with relatives because of housing shortages and the (weakening) obligation to support elderly parents.

Lest the subject of postmarital residence seems trivial, notice that patrilocal residence tends to socially isolate a woman who has married into her husband's household. She lives with her husband's parents, his brothers, and their wives and children. Conversely, notice that matrilocal residence keeps sisters together. It is husbands who leave their parental house and home and move into a household where they are outsiders. What effects might these two patterns have on women's abilities to control their own lives and make their own choices?

Other reasons exist for our interest in residence patterns. A major one is that they affect the kinds of family relationships that are most prevalent in a human community.

Residence and Households

Both matrilocal and patrilocal residence place a new nuclear family with one set of relatives—either that of the husband or the wife. In turn, whom a newly married couple lives with influences whom they will cooperate with, share property with, feel close to, and so forth. If postmarital residence is patrilocal, for instance, then the husband lives with and works with his own blood relatives (his father and brothers, paternal uncles and cousins *through his father*). The wife is likely to cooperate in household chores, gathering, gardening, and doing other tasks with members of her husband's family more than with her own.

Postmarital residence also affects the relatives with whom children are most likely to develop strong emotional bonds. For example, if residence is matrilocal, the children of sisters (who are cousins *through their mothers*) live together in a single household, much like biological sisters and brothers. Their relationships with their cousins through their mothers are likely to be similar to those with their biological siblings. The children of brothers, on the other hand, will live in different households and are less likely to play together and develop strong emotional attachments.

Most important, the prevailing pattern of residence affects the kinds of household and family units that exist among a people. Consider neolocal residence. If all or most newlyweds set up their own households, distinct from and independent from that of either of their parents, then a new household and family unit is established with each new marriage. This pattern emphasizes the social and economic importance and independence of nuclear families because mothers and fathers—and not more distant relatives—are most likely to be the main teachers of their children and breadwinners for the household. Of course, most couples maintain ties with their parents, siblings, and other relatives, but neolocal residence tends to lead to an emphasis on nuclear families as the most culturally important and stable family unit—sometimes seen as the backbone of society.

In North America, most members of the ethnic majority think the normal—and preferred—way families live is wife, husband, and children in the same dwelling. Therefore few people think about its economic consequences. Most young couples aspire to live in a single-family dwelling, preferably sooner rather than later. In the last half of 2007, falling real estate prices and homeowner defaults on their mortgage payments contributed to a severe recession. Many homeowners fretted that they would not make as much money when they sold their houses as they had anticipated from past experience or expert forecasts. This was the housing crisis, which also affected the construction industry.

Suppose large numbers of newly married couples stopped living neolocally and moved in with one set of parents. What would happen to homeowner property values and the construction industry then?

Kinship Diagrams

Some notational symbols are needed in the remainder of this chapter and the next. They allow us to show diagrammatically how any two persons are related by bonds of kinship. The symbols are shown in Figure 9.1,

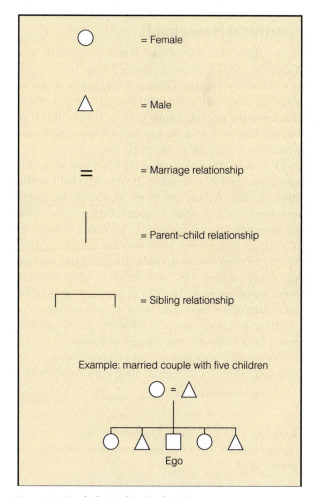

Figure 9.1 Symbols Used in Kinship Diagrams

along with how they are used to show a married couple with five children.

By stringing a number of symbols together, we can make a complete chart—called a *genealogy*—that shows all the relatives of a given individual and how they are related to that individual. In these charts, or *kinship diagrams*, it is useful to have a reference individual, or a person to whom everyone on the chart is related. It is customary to call this reference individual "Ego." In Figure 9.1, Ego is symbolized by a square to show that his or her gender is irrelevant for the purposes of the genealogy. (If Ego's gender mattered, we would symbolize him or her with either a triangle or a circle.)

Family and Household Forms

People use relationships created by marriage and family ties to create different kinds of households, some as small as a mother and her children, others composed of many dozen members.

Matrifocal Households

Many believe that the nuclear family is the basic unit of kinship. (Notice that individuals cannot be the basic unit of kinship because kinship is inherently about *relationships* among individuals.) Possibly, though, those who think the nuclear family is basic believe this only because they live in a society in which a couple and their offspring are the most visible family form.

There is another view—that the basic unit of kinship is a woman and her offspring. People who believe this point out that fathers are more frequently separated from their children than mothers. Fathers may separate temporarily or permanently for many reasons. In subsistence economies, men may be absent for long periods hunting, herding, trading, raiding, or carrying out other duties. In communities and modern countries where most families depend on wage labor, husbands/fathers may take jobs in distant cities or countries for many months or even years, sending money back to their home villages or towns.

Historically, male absence for extended periods was especially common in regions that were colonies of a major world power. In sub-Saharan Africa, especially, European colonial powers imposed taxes on men or introduced new commodities that soon became virtual necessities, such as kerosene lanterns, nails, metal tools, and cooking utensils. In order to earn money to meet expenses, men left to work for foreign companies on distant diamond or gold mines or to work on plantations owned by Europeans. This pattern continues in much of Africa and other regions even today. For the families left behind, the result often is the **matrifocal family**, where a mother (with or without a husband) bears most of the burden of supporting her children economically and nurturing them emotionally and intellectually.

Matrifocal families occur in modern industrial societies as well, whenever households are "female-headed," as the U.S. Census Bureau calls them. Some say that matrifocal families are an important cause of poverty, crime, and other social problems today. Adult men would act more responsibly if they had jobs that supported their nuclear families, they say. Sons need male role models and supposedly find them elsewhere if their fathers are not around. Mothers would be much better mothers if they didn't have to struggle so hard to pay the bills.

In modern nations, it is true that poor families are more likely to be headed by a woman than affluent families are. But this does not mean that matrifocal households are a significant cause of poverty and other social ills. Matrifocal families are also a *consequence* of poverty: Lack of job skills and a multitude of social factors lead to high unemployment among men, causing many women to decide that having a permanent male presence is too costly. Female-headed households in the United States and elsewhere are not necessarily the result of men's refusal to act responsibly or of women's moral choices: They also are adaptations that people make to their economic and social environment.

Extended Households

Extended families are made up of related nuclear families. Because the related nuclear families usually live in a single household, here we use *extended family* and *extended household* as synonyms. Extended households typically include three and sometimes four generations of family members.

Many anthropologists think that the form of family/household that is prevalent in a society depends on its

---

matrifocal family Family group consisting of a mother and her children, with a man only loosely attached or not present at all.

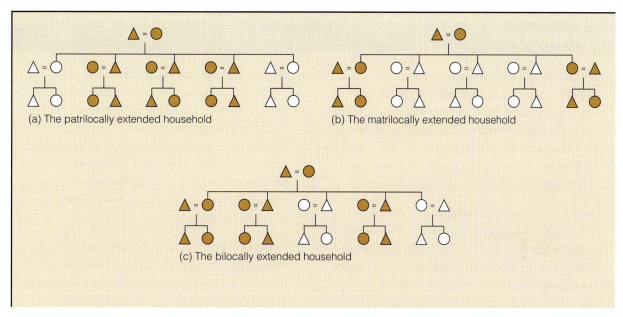

Figure 9.2 **Household Forms.** The shaded individuals are members of a single household.

(a) The patrilocally extended household

(b) The matrilocally extended household

(c) The bilocally extended household

postmarital residence pattern. For example, with patrilocal residence, the married sons of an older couple remain in the household of their parents. Sometimes, each son builds his own house on his parents' land, near their dwelling, and brothers cooperate with one another and pool or share resources. As they grow up and marry, daughters leave to live with their husbands' parents. If all the sons and daughters of a couple do this, the resulting household type is called *patrilocally extended*—brothers live in a single household with their own nuclear families and parents (Figure 9.2a). If all families in the village, town, or other settlement follow this pattern, then the settlement consists of patrilocally extended households. In Figure 9.2a, notice that the residents of each household are related to one another through males. The married women of the community live scattered in the households of their husbands. Often many of them have married out of the village or community.

The converse occurs with matrilocal residence. Mature sons leave their own mothers and fathers as they marry, and the daughters bring their husbands to live with them in or near their parents' households. The household type formed by the co-residence of daughters and sisters with their parents is called the *matrilocally extended household* (Figure 9.2b). The sons of an elderly couple are scattered in the households of the women they have married. If most people follow this residence pattern, then the community consists of households lived in by

women related through females, plus their husbands and children.

The same relationship between residence and prevalent household form applies to the other residence patterns. With bilocal and ambilocal residence, there is no consistency in whether households are made up of people related through males or females. Some couples live with the husband's family, others with the wife's family. The household type is *bilocally* (or *bilaterally*) *extended* (Figure 9.2c). The community's households are a mixture of people related through both sexes, in roughly equal frequency.

With neolocal residence, the settlement—be it rural village or modern suburb—consists of relatively small domestic units made up of nuclear families, each living in its own apartment or single-family dwelling.

We can now see another reason postmarital residence patterns are important: They give rise to various household and family forms. The kinds of family and domestic groups found among a people result from where newly formed families go to live. Stated differently, the prevalent household type in a human community represents the crystallization of the pattern of postmarital residence. And who lives with whom—the household type—is important because households so often hold property in common, cooperate in production and other economic activities, enculturate children together, and sometimes even worship the same ancestral spirits.

SUMMARY

1. **Discuss the primary theories of incest taboos.** Incest taboos are rules or norms that regulate who may have sex with whom. The taboos are more puzzling than they seem. Four main hypotheses try to account for them: "Marry Out or Die Out," "Peace in the Family," "Inbreeding Avoidance," and "Familiarity Breeds Disinterest."

2. **Analyze why marriage is difficult to define cross-culturally.** The wide diversity in marriage customs and beliefs makes marriage difficult to define, but there is some agreement on its major functions for both individuals and societies. Some type of marriage is nearly universal, although the particular form of marriage, the kinds of rights and duties it establishes, and many other aspects of the marital relationship vary. The Nayar and Tiwi illustrate unusual forms of marriage, and the Musuo of southern China have no marriage at all.

3. **Describe the forms of marriage and some of the ways cultures use marriage relationships for wider purposes.** Marriage systems are commonly classified by the number of spouses an individual is allowed: polygyny, monogamy, polyandry, and group marriage, although the last is very rare. No single explanation of marriage forms seems sufficient. Marriage is often the cornerstone of alliances between families or larger kin groups, as illustrated by the Yanomamö. The levirate and sororate are customs that preserve relationships between intermarried kin groups even after the death of a spouse.

4. **Describe the main patterns of marriage exchanges and the cultural rationales behind them.** New marriages are usually accompanied by the exchange of goods or services between the spouses and the families of the bride and groom. The most common forms of marital exchange are bridewealth, brideservice, and dowry. These exchanges are used to create new or maintain old relationships, compensate a family or larger kin group for the loss of one of its members, provide for the new couple's support, or endow a daughter with an inheritance that helps her attract a desirable husband.

5. **Evaluate changes in attitudes toward same-sex marriage and why the issue is so controversial.** In the United States, polls reveal that the percentage of people expressing support for laws allowing same-sex marriage has increased markedly since the 1990s. Despite increases in support and the 2015 Supreme Court decision legalizing this form of marriage, the issue remains a major battle in today's culture wars.

6. **Discuss patterns of postmarital residence and some major influences on them.** From most to least common, postmarital residence patterns are patrilocal, matrilocal, ambilocal, bilocal, and neolocal. There are many influences on which of these forms will be most prevalent in a given community, including economic forces and inheritance patterns. But no single factor is adequate to explain the cross-cultural variation in residence patterns.

7. **Explain how postmarital residence patterns produce various household forms in human communities.** Prevalent forms of family and domestic groups in a community arise out of many couples living with one or another set of relatives. In turn, household forms influence which kinship relationships are most emphasized among a people.

10

Kinship and Descent

WILLIAM ALBERT ALLARD/National Geographic Creative

All peoples recognize and keep track of relationships among family members, but they do so in several ways. This is an extended family in Mumbai (formerly Bombay), India.

Introducing Kinship
Why Study Kinship?
Cultural Variations in Kinship

Unilineal Descent
Unilineal Descent Groups
Descent Groups in Action

Nonunilineal Descent
Bilateral kinship
Cognatic Descent

Influences on Kinship Systems

Cultural Construction of Kinship
Logic of Cultural Constructions
Who's an Aunt? Varieties of Kinship Terminology
Why Do Terminologies Differ?

Where's Our Backbone?

LEARNING OBJECTIVES

After reading this chapter, you should be able to:

1 **DISCUSS** why kinship is important in creating relationships, forming groups, and organizing activities in preindustrial cultures.

2 **DESCRIBE** the two main forms of unilineal descent and the kinship groups that result from them.

3 **DESCRIBE** the two primary forms of nonunilineal descent: bilateral and cognatic.

4 **ELABORATE** on the cultural construction of kinship and explain the wider associations of four of the major terminological systems.

Humans are among the most social mammals. We are born into, live with, and die among other people. Young children rely on parents and other adults for the food, shelter, protection, and socialization needed to raise them to social maturity. Even as adults, we rely on cooperation with others for survival, economic well-being, and emotional gratification. When we die, relatives, friends, and coworkers mourn our passing.

Social groups based on kinship are those whose members recognize themselves as biologically related, but in a greater variety of ways than you might think. In this chapter, we cover how kinship relationships are used in various ways by different peoples to organize relationships and create kin groupings. We also describe the main ways that members of different societies culturally construct their kinship systems and kinship terminologies.

Introducing Kinship

If this text dealt only with relationships created by marriages that create new nuclear families, this chapter would not be necessary. However, historically many peoples culturally emphasized kinship relationships and groups that extended well beyond nuclear and even extended families. These relationships and groups defined by kinship ties organized a variety of tasks and activities. The kinds of tasks and activities, and the kinds of relationships and groups, vary from people to people, as by now you have come to expect.

Why Study Kinship?

In Western societies and developed nations, kinship relationships are important in the lives of individuals. However, compared to many other peoples with

whom anthropologists work, in the West kinship is not an important *organizing principle* of society as a whole. Instead, in the West different kinds of specialized groups organize different kinds of activities. For example, there are economic groups (small businesses, corporations), religious groups (churches, synagogues, mosques, temples), and educational groups (schools, colleges). Each of these groups is relevant to different realms of our lives, and individuals belong to several such groups and associations.

Some groups are *formal*, meaning their members are organized as a group—with officers, membership criteria, explicit goals, rules, and so forth. You might belong to formal groups such as a university, conservation organization, church, sorority or fraternity, political party, and company. Alongside your membership in such groups, you are active in informal *networks* made up of fellow students, neighbors, friends, and coworkers if you socialize with them after work. The members of your social network do not necessarily have any relationship to one another, but you have personal relationships with each of them as individuals.

Notice two important characteristics of these groups and networks. First, they are *voluntary:* If your interests change, or if you find another group or network that satisfies you, you are free to change jobs, churches, neighborhoods, and friends. Second, for the most part, the groups have *nonoverlapping membership:* Each typically consists of a different collection of people. We cooperate and interact with different individuals in the various groups to which we belong. Members of each group have varying and sometimes contradictory expectations about how we should behave because we perform different roles in each. Our behavior differs according to the identity and expectations of the particular persons (the *social context*) we are associating with at the moment—we act one way at home, another at religious services, and yet another at work. People at our place of worship seldom observe how we act on the job, which often is a good thing for us.

In contrast, among many indigenous peoples, one lives with, works with, socializes with, and often worships with the same people, most of whom are relatives. Kin groups and kin relationships are *multifunctional*, meaning that the same groups organize many aspects of people's lives, such as who cooperates in work, who owns which lands, who carries out rituals together, and who quarrels with whom. We could not understand modernized nations without knowing about businesses, schools, churches, governments, and laws. Similarly, we cannot understand kinship-based societies without understanding their kinship groups and relationships.

Cultural Variations in Kinship

In over a century of studying kinship systems and analyzing their functions in diverse cultures, anthropologists have discovered surprising variations. Here are three of the most important.

Ways of Tracing Kinship Relationships

In most of North America and Europe, people believe they are related equally and in the same way to the families of both their mother and father. Particular persons develop closer ties with one or another side of their family according to circumstances and personal preferences, such as which set of grandparents lives nearby. But there is no systematic *cultural pattern* of feeling closer to or socializing with relatives according to whether they are relatives of one's mother or father.

In many other parts of the world, people place primary importance on one side of the family—either the paternal or the maternal side—in preference to the other. For example, in many cultures, individuals become members of only their father's kin group. In such systems, relatives through one's mother are considered relatives, but of a different and less important kind than paternal relatives. There are also systems in which kin groups are organized around maternal relationships, and paternal kin are culturally deemphasized.

Normative Expectations of Kin Relationships

The kinds of social relationships a people believe they should have with various kinds of relatives are part of the norms of kinship. Kinship norms are surprisingly variable from people to people. There are societies in which brothers and sisters must strictly avoid one another after puberty; in which sons-in-law are not

James Peoples

One way kinship systems vary is in whether the most important relationships are traced through males, females, or both sexes. On this Micronesian woman's home island, relationships through females are emphasized.

supposed to speak directly to their mothers-in-law; in which a boy is allowed to joke around with his maternal uncle but must show respect toward his paternal uncle; and in which people are expected to marry one kind of cousin but are absolutely forbidden to marry another kind of cousin. In brief, many social behaviors toward relatives that members of one culture regard as normal are different in other cultures.

Cultural Construction of Relatives

Except for fictive kinship (see Chapter 9), all biological kinship relationships are created through reproduction. When a woman gives birth, her relatives and those of her mate become the biological relatives of the child. The kinship relationship between any two people appears to depend on how these individuals are related biologically.

Yet anthropologists claim that kinship is a culturally constructed—as opposed to a biologically determined—phenomenon. Peoples differ in how they use the biological facts of kinship to create groups, allocate roles, and classify relatives into various kinds. In North America, whether a woman is our maternal or paternal aunt makes no difference: We still call her "aunt" and think of both our maternal and paternal aunts as the same kind of relative. But the side of the family makes a difference in some other kinship systems, in which the father's sisters and mother's sisters are considered to be different kinds of relatives and are called by different terms.

Keeping this overview of kinship diversity in mind, let's look at kinship in more detail.

Unilineal Descent

Consider what it means if people are biological ("blood") relatives. Defining kinship in strictly biological terms, someone is your relative because you and that person share a common ancestor in an earlier generation. Thus, your sister is the female child of your parents; your parents, aunts, and uncles are the children of your grandparents; your first cousins are the grandchildren of your grandparents; and your second cousins have the same great-grandparents as you. Stated differently, people are biological relatives if they are *descended* from a common ancestor who lived some number of generations ago.

Notice that you are descended from 2 parents, 4 grandparents, 8 great-grandparents, 16 great-great-grandparents, 32 great-great-great-grandparents and 64 great-great-great-great-grandparents. Everyone alive today who is descended from these 64 people is related to you to some degree. Going back in time, the number of your ancestors doubles every generation. So, even if you count back only four or five generations, you have an enormous number of living biological relatives descended from those ancestors. It is not as unusual as you might think if your family tree includes George Washington or James Madison or another founding father or mother. Hundreds of thousands of people might also have this person as their ancestor, although most of them do not know it.

Obviously, no people keep track of all their biological kin. From the total range of potential relatives, all cultures consider some to be more important than others. The number of relatives is reduced in two main ways: (1) by forgetting or ignoring more distant kinship relationships, and (2) by emphasizing some kinds of kinship relationships and deemphasizing others. All peoples use the first method, or they would recognize tens of thousands of relatives. In the West, most people have little reason to keep track of relatives more distant than second cousins because they have little interaction with them. (As an exercise, try to name all of your second cousins.)

Many peoples also use the second method: They place more importance on some relatives than on others. The most common way to do this uses the sex of connecting relatives as the basis for defining which kin are close or most socially important. For example, if a given culture places more importance on relatives traced through males, then individuals will think that their father's relatives are more important than their mother's relatives—for some purposes, at least. Relationships through females will be deemphasized and perhaps forgotten after two or three generations. If you lived in such a culture, your second cousins on your father's side might be quite important relatives, but you might barely know your second cousins through your mother.

Culturally speaking, then, kinship relationships are defined by how people trace (keep track of) their descent from previous generations. How people in a given culture trace descent is called their **form of descent**. Descent can be traced through males, females, or both sexes.

Cultures that trace relationships through only one sex have **unilineal descent**: People place importance on either their mother's ancestral line or their father's ancestral line, but not both. The two main categories of unilineal descent are these:

▪ **Patrilineal descent**—People trace their primary kinship connections to the ancestors and living relatives of their father. In cultures with patrilineal descent, a person's father's relatives are likely to be most important in his or her life. Individuals are likely to live among their father's kin, and most property is inherited by sons from fathers.

▪ **Matrilineal descent**—People trace their most important kinship relationships to the ancestors and living relatives of their mother. In matrilineal descent, the mother's relatives are most important in a person's life. People are most likely to live with or near their mother's relatives and usually inherit property from their mother or her brothers.

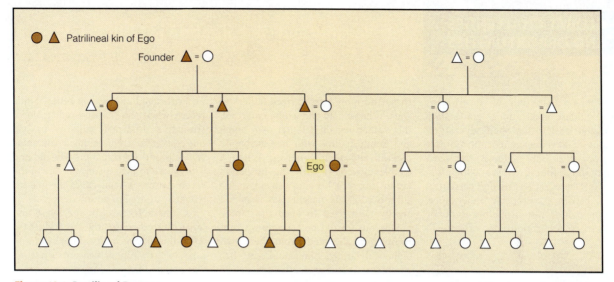

Figure 10.1 Patrilineal Descent

Of these two forms of unilineal descent, patrilineal is the most common. In the most frequently used way of comparing descent, 41 percent of societies are patrilineal, and 17 percent are matrilineal. The remaining 42 percent combine relationships through females and males in tracing their familial connections.

Let's look at each form of unilineal descent more closely to see which relatives are considered most important for an individual. In Figure 10.1, the patrilineal relatives of the person labeled "Ego" are shaded. The kinship diagram shows that Ego's patrilineal kin include only those relatives related to Ego through males. For instance, Ego's father's brother's children are related to Ego through males, whereas Ego's other first cousins (through Ego's mother or father's sister) are not.

Looking at patrilineal descent another way, we see that Ego's patrilineal kin include all the people descended *through males* from the man labeled "Founder" in Figure 10.1. In fact, any two individuals shaded in the diagram are related to each other through males. Women as well as men are patrilineal kin. However, because incest taboos and exogamy rules usually prohibit sex and marriage between patrilineal relatives, the children of two sisters are never patrilineal kin.

How does patrilineal descent affect relationships and behavior between different relatives? In all sorts of culturally variable ways, but the most widespread and important effects are the inheritance of property and obligations to relatives. In patrilineal societies, property is passed down through the male line or, in other words, from fathers to sons. We can see the significance of this effect by contrasting it with inheritance

in North American society. You probably think of both your grandfathers as the same kind of relative and call both "Grandpa" or "Gramps," or whatever. But if you lived in a patrilineal society, your father's father would play a far more significant role in your life, and it would be from him and your father that you would expect to inherit wealth or receive land rights. Your mother's father would pass his property on to his sons and sons' sons—not to you because you are related to him through his daughter, not his son. A similar distinction would exist between paternal and maternal uncles; paternal uncles would be far more important.

In patrilineal societies, individuals have greater obligations to relatives through their father. People know their mother's family, of course, and often have close emotional ties with them, depending on residence and individual circumstances. But one's primary duties are to relatives through the father, not through the mother. For example, if you are a man, you mainly work the land or care for the livestock of your father's family, generally you remain with or near your father's household through most of your life, you are obligated to care for your parents in their older years, and so forth. Because most patrilineal peoples are also patrilocal, most often a woman leaves her own family when she marries to join her husband's family. In East Asia and most of South Asia, families with daughters raised them only to have them leave upon marriage. So a great many families preferred sons to daughters. The Global Challenges and Opportunities box discusses some consequences of the preference for sons in China's recent history.

China has one of the world's oldest civilizations, going back at least to the Shang dynasty of about 3,500 years ago. For most of this history, the Han Chinese, the most numerous cultural/ethnic and linguistic group, were rather rigidly patrilineal and patrilocal. Property inheritance, family names, responsibilities to honor ancestors, obligations to others—all

As a result of China's economic growth since 1990 and its one-child policy, Chinese parents make great efforts and incur high expenses to educate their child through college. These parents celebrate their daughter's graduation.

these and more passed from fathers to sons. When a man and woman married, the woman usually left her own home and family to live with her husband's parents and their relatives. When a couple moved in with the husband's family, the wife became subject to the authority of his parents (as was he) and worked hard to keep the family prosperous (as did he). A wife was not completely alienated from her own biological family: She could visit her parents and brothers, provided it was not too often, she didn't remain too long, and she was properly chaperoned.

However, a woman's main duty was to her husband's family. After a couple married, a wife bowed before the ancestral shrine and tablets of her husband's family, symbolizing the transfer of duties to her in-laws. If a man was wealthy enough to support them, he could take concubines, often even moving them into his household. His wife was not supposed to object provided he lived up to his obligations to support her and her children. All these practices and beliefs were reinforced by the philosophical tradition called Confucianism. Some scholars even call the above characteristics the "Confucian family."

Going along with the patrilineal and patrilocal system was a strong cultural preference for sons. Girls were expensive to raise and could not carry on the family name. The resources and time expended

on a girl's childhood usually brought little return when she married out. Chinese strongly desired male children. In fact, one reason for a man taking a concubine was to produce a son, if the wife did not. The failure to bear a son was one of the seven reasons a man could divorce his wife if he desired to do so.

Chinese trade with the West and Japan intensified in the 1800s and 1900s. After decades of political disorder and poverty for Chinese peasants, in 1949 Chairman Mao Zedong's communist forces won a civil war. The Chinese Communist Party soon instituted government ownership of land and most other productive property. Chairman Mao's reforms helped China break free from Western dominance. He also helped restore law and order and undertook specific policies to improve the lives of women. To aid the goal of socialist development, the Chinese government placed great emphasis on public education for both sexes.

In the last half of the twentieth century, the lives of women (relative to those of men, at least) improved substantially. This happened even in rural areas. Young women have a stronger voice in choosing their husbands and now usually make the final decision about whom they will marry, if only by vetoing their parents' selections. Couples can go out together, which means that marriages are more

In contrast, if you lived in a matrilineal society, your most important relatives would be your mother, your mother's mother, your mother's mother's mother, plus the daughters of all these women and their children. In Figure 10.2, Ego's matrilineal relatives are shaded. Note that only one set of cousins—Ego's mother's sister's children—is shaded in the diagram. They are all related to Ego through female links, and therefore Ego is likely to have closer relationships with them than with other cousins. Property is most likely to be inherited from

one's mother and maternal grandmother and from the brothers of these women. In matrilineal societies, men usually leave most of their property not to their own children but to their sister's children. As a result, maternal uncles (mother's brothers) are important figures in one's life, and in some respects they assume the rights and duties more commonly associated with one's father.

In unilineal descent systems, relationships such as aunt, uncle, and cousin differ from those to which likely to be based on romantic feelings and personal compatibility rather than formal arrangements. Women's education exposes them to new ideas and gives many of them new economic opportunities by helping to level the playing field in the job search.

After Mao's death in 1976, Deng Xiaoping began the economic reforms that led to China's phenomenal growth since the early 1980s, achieved by exporting factory goods to the global economy. China's leaders had long realized that they had to do something to reduce the rate at which the nation's population was growing if China was to avoid a food crisis and develop its economy. In 1979, they instituted a law that became known as the *one-child policy*. Under it, couples who lived in cities could have only one child. Generally, in rural areas, couples were allowed two children. The law was further relaxed for China's 56 minority peoples. Officials in rural regions—cognizant of the continued cultural preference for sons—allowed a couple to try again for a boy if the first child was female. But there were penalties for having extra children: Employers penalized people in pay and promotions, extra fees were imposed for health care and education, fines could be imposed, and extreme social pressure was applied to encourage conformity.

Still, the old preference for sons remained. Beginning in the 1980s, many couples found ways of getting around laws restricting family size: eliminating unwanted female fetuses, abortions, hiding second pregnancies from officials, and leaving one's community during pregnancy to have a secret baby that, if female, was sometimes placed in an orphanage. Between the 1980s and 2010, significantly more boys than girls were born; in many years, the sex ratio at birth was 117 boys to 100 girls, which is only possible by selective female infanticide. As a consequence, projections suggest that by about 2020, China will have approximately 30 million more males than females. Where these men will find their spouses is a problem that receives little Western media coverage, but it is potentially important to China's future stability.

The one-child policy helped lower China's population growth, although other factors also contributed heavily to couples' choice to have fewer children. The policy also resulted in tens of millions of Chinese who have no sisters or brothers. The publicity (some say propaganda) campaign that accompanied the policy, along with a multitude of other factors, significantly raised the status of females in China.

Today, whether a Chinese couple has a boy or girl matters much less than it used to: What matters most now is that their only child receives the education that will allow her or him to get ahead in a career. Many parents, along with grandparents, are quite attentive to their only son or daughter. Only children are sometimes called "little emperors," especially if they are boys, because of what some people view as extreme parental indulgence.

Unlike real emperors, children are under a lot of pressure to succeed in school and to pass the national exams that lead to placement in Chinese colleges. Obligations to live up to parental expectations generally are greater among Chinese than among North Americans, and this extends to parents' wishes about colleges and careers. Some Chinese call the result of the one-child policy "4-2-1": one child is the center of attention of two parents and four grandparents. But 4-2-1 cuts both ways: The same six adults have such high expectations for success that many children who don't measure up feel terrible about disappointing their older relatives. Parents care about their children's success because they love them, of course, and also because they expect that their children will become their main source of support in their later years. As Vanessa Fong discusses in her 2004 book *Only Hope*, rising expectations for upward mobility by both parents and children results in intense competition in schools, and also in new frustrations when rising hopes are not realized.

As is also true in Japan and South Korea, Chinese parents make enormous sacrifices to improve the life chances of their children. Some spend many hours a week going over school lessons. They try to get their 6-year-olds into the best elementary schools so they will have a head start. They pay big bucks to send their children to cram schools, which offer extra lessons after the regular school day. These extra classes are aimed at helping their children in the intense competition of college entrance exams. Furthermore, learning English is viewed as one key to a successful future, so the Chinese government emphasizes English in schools. Private companies, both Chinese and foreign, sell English educational materials to affluent Chinese families.

most of our readers are accustomed. For example, not all cousins are culturally perceived as the same kinds of relatives in unilineal societies. Some cousins are more important relatives than others: father's brothers' children in patrilineal systems, mother's sisters' children in matrilineal systems. This fact leads anthropologists to distinguish between *parallel cousins* and *cross cousins.*

Two sets of cousins are parallel cousins if their parents are siblings of the same sex, so your parallel cousins are your mother's sisters' children and your father's brothers' children. People are cross cousins if their parents are siblings of the opposite sex, so your cross cousins are your father's sisters' children and your mother's brothers' children. If this difference is hard to grasp, notice that in unilineal descent systems, one set of parallel cousins always belongs to the same kin group as Ego. In patrilineal systems, the children of your (Ego's) father's brothers are in your kin group. In matrilineal systems, the children of your mother's

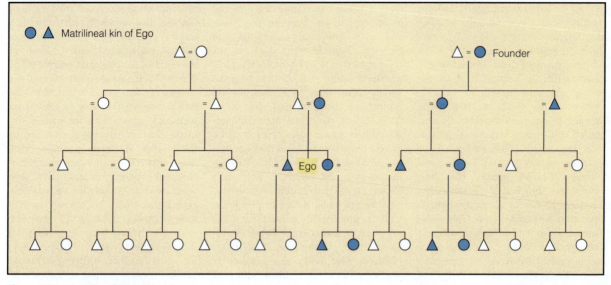

Figure 10.2 Matrilineal Descent

sisters are in your kin group. This is shown by contrasting the cousins shaded in Figures 10.1 and 10.2. Notice that no cross cousin is ever in Ego's kin group in a society with a unilineal descent form.

Unilineal Descent Groups

In Chapter 9, we saw how various peoples form extended households by associating nuclear families together in patterned ways. A much larger group of people—known as a **descent group**—can be established on the basis of kinship ties.

Take matrilineal descent, for example. A matrilineal descent group exists when people who are descended from the same woman through females recognize their group identity and cooperate for some purposes. When a matrilineal rule of descent establishes a group of people all related to one another through females, we say that the group is created using the *matrilineal principle.* We can state the matrilineal principle as "Everyone joins the descent group of his or her mother." Alternatively, we can say, "Only children of the female members of a group become members." Looking back to Figure 10.2, we see that all the shaded individuals in the diagram

are members of a single descent group. The children of the group's men join the descent groups of their own mothers because of incest and exogamy rules.

Conversely, groups can develop by repeated application of the *patrilineal principle*: In any given generation, only males transmit their membership in the group to their offspring. The result of applying this principle for several generations is a group of people related to one another through males, as you can see in Figure 10.1. Assuming the patrilineal kin group is exogamous—and it almost always is—the children of the group's women become members of their father's patrilineal group.

A **unilineal descent group** is a group of relatives all of whom are related through only one sex. A *matrilineal descent group* is a group whose members are (or believe themselves to be) related through females. Stated in another way, all members trace their descent through female links from their common female ancestor. A *patrilineal descent group* is made up of people who trace their descent through males from a common male ancestor.

Unilineal descent groups can be small or enormous, depending mainly on the genealogical depth of the group. A small matrilineal kin group with a few dozen members might consist of people descended matrilineally from a woman who lived four or five generations ago. A large matrilineal group with many hundreds of members might consist of people who trace their ancestry back to a woman who lived 9 or 10 generations ago. Anthropologists often use genealogical depth as a way to define different kinds of unilineal groups. From shallowest to deepest, these groups are called unilineally

descent group Group whose members believe themselves to be descended from a common ancestor.

unilineal descent group Group of relatives formed by tracing kinship relationships through only one sex, either female or male, but not both.

In patrilineal societies, kinship relationships through males are emphasized. These Indian men are celebrating a holiday.

extended families, lineages, and clans. (There are other types not discussed here.)

A **unilineally extended family** consists of people who cooperate and have mutual obligations based on common descent from an ancestor who lived three or four generations ago. Extended families may be defined either patrilineally or matrilineally. Such families may or may not live in the same household (see Chapter 9), but they recognize their close ties, may hold common property, may cooperate in work, and may have shared ritual responsibilities.

A **lineage** is a unilineal group composed of several unilineally extended families whose members are able to trace their descent through males or females from a common ancestor who lived five or more generations in the past. By the conventional definition, the extended families that make up the group must be able to state how they are related to one another for anthropologists to call the group a lineage. Lineages may be either patrilineal (*patrilineages*) or matrilineal (*matrilineages*).

A **clan** is a named unilineal descent group whose members believe they are descended from a common ancestor through either the male line (*patriclan*) or the female line (*matriclan*). The major difference between

a clan and a lineage is generational depth. With clans, the common ancestor lived so far in the past that not all the members of the clan are able to state precisely how they are related to one another. In fact, the common ancestor is sometimes mythical. Like lineages, clans are usually exogamous. Members of the clan think of themselves as relatives and frequently refer to one another as "clan brother" or "clan sister." In many societies, clans own or control land and other forms

unilineally extended family Group of nuclear families formed by tracing kinship relationships through only one sex.

lineage Unilineal descent group larger than an extended family whose members can actually trace how they are related.

clan Named unilineal descent group, some of whose members are unable to trace how they are related but who still believe themselves to be related and who periodically associate or cooperate.

of property. Most often each clan is further subdivided into several lineages.

Among many peoples, clans are *totemic*, meaning that their members are symbolically identified with certain supernatural powers. Most commonly, these powers are identified with particular animals, plants, and natural forces such as lightning, the sun, and the moon. Clans often take the name of their primary totemic symbol, and so have names such as bear clan, sun clan, reed clan, water clan, and eagle clan. Commonly the association with particular supernatural powers entitles specific clans to organize particular religious rituals. Although the functions of clans vary from people to people, they are usually among the most significant economic, social, and political units in the society.

Often people need to call upon different numbers of relatives for different purposes. A woman may need help with gardening chores and will ask her extended family members for help. Or a group may mobilize dozens or even hundreds of men to serve as warriors, so they call upon their lineage mates or clanmates for aid. Unilineal descent is a useful organization for these and many other purposes because it allows people to mobilize varying numbers of their relatives when they need assistance. Using one of the unilineal descent principles, smaller kin groups can be nested inside larger ones.

For example, in a patrilineal society, a nuclear family is a part—a segment—of a patrilineally extended family. In turn, the extended family is a segment of a larger group (a small patrilineage), while the small patrilineage is a segment of a larger patrilineage, which in turn is a segment of a patriclan. Using this *segmentary organization*, dozens, hundreds, or even thousands of relatives can be mobilized, depending on the circumstances. The flexibility of segmentary systems makes them useful for many political purposes, including warfare.

Descent Groups in Action

The preceding description is abstract. But like families, descent groups are made up of living people who work in gardens, own common property, conduct rituals, teach their children, construct their dwellings, and carry out innumerable other activities together. When people work together for common purposes, they have ways of ensuring the continuity of social relationships over time, assigning members to roles and allocating duties and rights to them, making decisions that affect the members, and expressing their group's identity. In a word, they are *organized*. In many regions even today, descent groups and kinship relationships organize a variety of cooperative activities.

Two examples illustrate this. One is the Tikopia, a patrilineal people of an island in the Pacific; the other is the Hopi, a matrilineal Native American people of the Southwest.

Tikopia: A Patrilineal Society

Tikopia is a western Pacific island with only 2 square miles of land. In the late 1920s, when Raymond Firth studied them, about 1,200 people lived on the island. Tikopians viewed their people as belonging to one of four patriclans, each with its own name. Each patriclan is subdivided into several patrilineages, averaging 30 to 40 members. The members of each patrilineage trace their descent back to a common ancestor—the founder of the patrilineage—who lived four to six generations ago. The oldest male member of a patrilineage is usually its head. Lineages are exogamous, so the children of a lineage's women are not members of it.

Tikopian lineages control rights to land and some other kinds of property. Each lineage owns house sites and several parcels of land planted with the four major crops—Pacific yams, taro, coconut, and breadfruit. A lineage's families have the right to plant and harvest crops on lineage land, but they sell, trade, or give it away to members of other lineages. Thus, patrilineages own land and allocate use rights to parcels among their members, and each family acquires most of its food through farming the land of their lineage.

Even after they marry, female members of a patrilineage retain the right to use their own lineage's land to feed themselves and their family. A woman may not, however, pass any rights to this land along to her children, for it belongs to her patrilineage as a whole, not to her as an individual.

The social rank of individuals is also determined largely by their lineage membership and their status within their patrilineage. One lineage of each clan is considered the senior lineage, which makes it the highest ranking in the clan. Because of its superior rank, the senior lineage also has the right to select one of its male members to serve as the chief for the whole clan. Tikopian kinship thus has a political dimension because authority over others is gained largely through lineage membership and rank.

Tikopia beliefs about supernatural powers also are tied into the kinship system. Each clan has specific ritual duties to perform. Each of the four clan chiefs serves as the clan's religious leader and organizer of important religious ceremonies. Each clan has its own ancestral spirits, who were the deceased chiefs of the clan. Each clan also has its own deities, with whom its chief acts as intermediary.

One religious duty of clan chiefs is to carry out rituals that ensure the availability of food for the whole island. Tikopians believe that each of the four major subsistence crops is mystically associated with a particular clan, and so the gods of this clan control the crop. The chief of that clan performs the rituals that ensure the continued supply and fertility of whichever crop "listened to" (as the Tikopia phrase it) the gods of his clan. Thus, each clan—in the person of its chief—has ritual responsibilities toward the other three clans. A patrilineage, too, has an ancestral home with sacred shrines where its members gather to honor their deceased ancestors.

Tikopia exemplifies the diverse functions that are commonly assigned to descent groups. Patrilineages control use rights to land other kinds of property. Lineage membership influences an individual's social rank and privileges. Patriclans have political functions and their chiefs carry out rituals that Tikopians believe are essential for the well-being of all islanders. In brief, lineages and clans organize a wide range of social activities, serving many functions for individuals and the islander community.

Hopi: A Matrilineal Society

The Native American Hopi have a reservation in northeastern Arizona, which they consider part of their ancestral homeland and where many of them continue to live. Hopi traditionally recognized about 50 exogamous matriclans, some of which are now extinct. Their clans are not residential groups; rather, most clans have members who live in more than one of the Hopi's nine villages, or *pueblos*. Each clan is subdivided into several matrilineages. A Hopi pueblo often is a single large apartment-like building divided into many rooms in which families reside. The female members of a Hopi matrilineage usually live in adjoining rooms within a single pueblo.

Traditionally the Hopi are matrilocal, so after marriage a man usually joins the extended household of his wife. Most matrilocally extended households consist of one or more older women, their daughters

Bettmann/Getty Images

The unmarried status of these young Hopi women is shown by their hairstyle. In Hopi villages, traditionally husbands worked the land of their wives' families and moved into their wives' households. Hopi matrilineages and matriclans also organize many other economic and ceremonial activities.

together with their husbands, and sometimes even their granddaughters and their husbands. Because of lineage and clan exogamy and matrilocal residence, husbands are outsiders to their wives' families, and—as Hopi say—their real home is with their mother's extended family.

The women of a matrilineage usually live close to one another throughout most of their lives, whereas the married men of the matrilineage live scattered among the households of their wives. Even while living with the families of their wives, Hopi men remain members of their mother's lineage and frequently return to their matrilineal home for seasonal religious ceremonies and other responsibilities or in case of divorce.

Most property, including ceremonial objects, is inherited matrilineally. Living space in a pueblo, for instance, passes from mothers to daughters. Traditionally, the Hopi were a horticultural people, skillfully working their arid land to produce corn and other crops. Each lineage has use rights over particular parcels at any one time. When a husband moves in with his wife and her relatives after marriage, he brings little property other than his clothing and a few personal items. The house, its furnishings, the food stored there, and other goods remain the property of his wife's family. A man provides food for himself and his family by working in the fields of his wife, but the products of his farm labor belong to his wife.

Membership in a matriclan also establishes one's relationships with the supernatural world. Each clan is mystically associated with a number of supernatural powers called *wuya*. Clans usually take their name from their principal *wuya*, such as bear, rabbit, corn, badger, snake, cloud, sun, and reed. In prayers to their *wuya*, members of a matriclan ask for protection and for bountiful harvests.

Hopi religion features a ritual calendar that includes a large number of annually required ceremonies. In most cases, each ceremony is "owned" by the members of a certain clan, meaning in Hopi culture that this clan has primary responsibility to see that the ceremony is performed on time and in the proper manner. Clans represented in a particular village have a *clan house*, in which the masks, fetishes, and other sacred items used in the ceremonies it owns are kept when not in use. The clan house usually consists of a room adjoining the dwelling of the senior female member of the clan. This woman, the *clan mother*, is in charge of storing ritual objects and seeing to it that they are treated with the proper respect.

There is also a male head of each clan with religious duties. He is in charge of organizing the men of the clan to perform the clan ceremonies. The male head of a clan teaches his younger brothers or sister's sons the ritual knowledge they will need to know to perform the ceremonies properly. In this way, culturally important ritual knowledge is kept within the matriclan. The ritual knowledge of each clan helps make the clans interdependent, because clans need one another to perform ceremonies to bring rain, to help crops grow, to cause the seasons to change, and to ask supernatural powers to provide other kinds of benefits.

Finally, the combination of matrilineal descent and matrilocal residence affects relationships between fathers and children. A child's relationship with her or his father is usually close and tolerant. A father seldom punishes his own children. Culturally, this is not considered his appropriate role because, after all, children and fathers belong to different matrilineages and matriclans. The father's sisters and brothers likewise exhibit warm feelings for their nieces and nephews, often providing them with gifts and affection. The main disciplinarians of children are their mother's brother and other members of their mother's kin group. This is partly because a child's behavior reflects well or poorly on the kin group of her or his mother, so members of this group have the primary duty of monitoring and correcting children.

Hopi illustrate how the matrilineal principle recruits people into kin groups in which they perform various economic, political, and religious roles. They also show how the form of descent found among a people influences interpersonal relationships, including between fathers and children and maternal uncles and their nieces and nephews.

Neither the Tikopia nor the Hopi typify patrilineal and matrilineal kinship. A wide range of diversity occurs in patrilineal and matrilineal systems. The two peoples do illustrate some of the main differences between patrilineal and matrilineal peoples with respect to recruitment into groups, allocation of roles, nature of emotional attachments, and organization of important activities.

They also illustrate than kinship is more than a biological relationship. For example, both Tikopia and Hopi—and everyone else—is related to their biological mother's sister's children in the same genetic way. But the nature and importance of this biological relationship varies between the two people. Some of the biological facts of kinship are downplayed or ignored in tracing how people are related, while others are socially emphasized and carry a lot of weight in peoples' lives. This is why anthropologists commonly say that kinship is *culturally constructed*, not biologically determined.

In bilateral societies, kindred are Ego focused and usually come together only on special occasions, such as weddings, funerals, and, as here in Maine, family reunions.

Nonunilineal Descent

Anthropologists used to say that one advantage of unilineal descent is that everyone belongs to only one family or larger group. So, unilineal rules result in discrete kin groups in which everyone knows who belongs, who has rights to resources, whom they may not marry, and so forth.

In reality, social life is rarely this rule governed. In real societies where either unilineal principle is the norm, the actual membership of lineages and clans is not as well defined as the principles make them appear. For instance, in matrilineal systems, relationships vary and circumstances change: Adoptions, childless women, inability to get along with one's matrikin, insufficiency of land owned by the matrigroup, and other factors make it likely that some individuals will join a group other than that of their mother. More generally, even in unilineal systems, there is some degree of choice about which group to join, depending on personal preferences and circumstances. Still, there is a norm or rule about what should happen.

In societies with **nonunilineal descent**, individuals do not regularly associate with either matrilineal or patrilineal relatives, but they make choices about whom to live with, whose land to use, and so forth. There are different forms of nonunilineal descent, two of which are most common: bilateral and cognatic.

Bilateral Kinship

In **bilateral kinship** (two-sided descent), relationships are traced through both genders, and relatives

nonunilineal descent Form of descent in which individuals do not regularly associate with either matrilineal or patrilineal relatives, but make choices about whom to live with, whose land to use, and so forth.

bilateral kinship Form of kinship in which individuals trace their kinship relationships equally through both parents.

through both parents are about equal in importance. As you recognize, bilateral kinship exists in most contemporary Western countries, but it is also common in other parts of the world. In contrast to unilineal descent, bilateral peoples have no large property-holding kin groups like lineages. Rather, tracing kinship relationships bilaterally produces associations of relatives anthropologists call kindreds. A **kindred** consists of all the people that a specific person recognizes as related to himself or herself.

To understand bilateral kinship and kindreds, imagine a Canadian woman named Liz. Liz recognizes her relatives through her father and mother as pretty much equal and interacts with them in much the same way (unless she has established strong bonds with some people because they live close by or for some other personal reason). The more distant the relationship, the less likely Liz is to interact with or even know who her relatives are. She is likely to see many of her kindred in the same place only at events such as weddings, funerals, and occasional family reunions. Many of Liz's relatives do not know one another (e.g., her cousins on her mother's side are unlikely to know her cousins through her father). All the members of her kindred do not consider themselves relatives, and they certainly do not own any common property. How could they? Their common connection to Liz is what defines them, not their relationships to one another.

As this hypothetical example shows, a kindred is *Ego focused*; each individual is the center of his or her own set of relatives. Only you and your siblings share the same kindred; your mother has a different kindred, as do your father and all your cousins. In contrast, unilineal descent groups are *ancestor focused*; people are members of a descent group because they recognize descent from a common ancestor.

Cognatic Descent

In societies with **cognatic descent** (also called **ambilineal descent**), people are members of several kin groups simultaneously and have options about which of their kin relationships to activate. Cognatic descent has elements of both unilineal and bilateral systems. Individuals are potentially members of both their mother's and their father's kin groups, and they make choices about which of several kin groups they join or associate with. Choices are commonly based on factors such as chances of inheriting rights to land use or other forms of property or wealth, the desire to associate with a relative of high status or rank, childhood residence, and emotional ties. For example, you might decide to reside and cooperate with your mother's relatives if her kin group has a lot more land available for you to cultivate than does your father's group. Or if a coveted political office or honorific title is about to become vacant in your father's group, you might decide to try to acquire it by moving in and working with his relatives.

A *cognatic descent group* consists of all people who can trace their descent back to the common ancestor (founder) of the group through *either* male or female links. Thus, some people are members because of a female ancestor, others because of a male ancestor. The existence of organized groups is a main difference between cognatic descent and bilateral kinship: You and all members of your kindred could never hold property or wealth in common because the social boundaries of your kindred are too indefinite.

Cognatic descent is especially prevalent among Polynesians, such as the Samoans, Hawaiians, Tahitians, and Maoris of New Zealand. Details vary from island to island, but generally speaking people can join any cognatic group to which they can trace ancestry. Membership in the group bestows rights to agricultural land, house sites, and some other kinds of property.

In cognatic societies, most people are members of several groups simultaneously. However, they only activate some options by, for example, contributing labor and foods to feasts sponsored by the groups to demonstrate their interest in and commitment to the groups. The islands of Samoa provide an example. Each Samoan village has a council that plans communal activities, levies fines, and performs other functions for the whole community. Each village includes several cognatic kin groups known as *'aiga*. Although each *'aiga* has branches represented in several villages, every *'aiga* has an ancestral village that its members consider their homeland. In its homeland village, each *'aiga* has the right to select one or more of its men to hold important titles. These titleholders serve as the *'aiga*'s representatives to the village council. Acquisition of a title carries great honor as well as authority to regulate use of the *'aiga*'s land, resolve disputes among the *'aiga*'s

---

kindred All the bilateral relatives recognized by an individual.

cognatic descent (ambilineal descent) Form of descent in which relationships may be traced through both females and males.

members, organize feasts and ceremonial gifts, and assess the members for contributions to marriages, funerals, and other events.

When a title becomes vacant because of death or some other reason, all members of the 'aiga have a voice in choosing the new holder of the title, whether they live in the homeland village or not. Because people belong to several 'aiga at the same time, they have a say in choosing the new titleholder for several groups, although they do not necessarily exercise their rights in every 'aiga to which they belong. Because men belong to several groups, they have the right to compete for and gain a title in these groups. A young man might anticipate a future title vacancy in one of his 'aiga and decide to move to the village where that 'aiga is represented on the council to concentrate his energies on acquiring that particular title. This general kinship and village-level political organization persists in much of rural Western Samoa to this day.

The Samoan 'aiga illustrates some common functions of cognatic kin groups: They can hold property and regulate access to land, organize cooperative activities, and serve as the basis for acquiring honored and authoritative political roles. But in cognatic systems, the range of individual choice about group membership is much wider than in unilineal descent. Individuals have several options to form strong relationships, only some of which they activate.

The Concept Review box will help you keep track of the various forms of descent and the kinds of groups associated with each form.

Influences on Kinship Systems

Anthropologists have wondered for decades why cultures have the form of kinship they do. Why are the Tikopia patrilineal, the Hopi matrilineal, the English bilateral, and the Maori of New Zealand cognatic? Are there any general explanations? So far no one has identified a single factor or even a small number of factors that account for why different cultures develop different kinship systems. There is some agreement, however, on the *influences* (as opposed to the *causes*) on the form of kinship a people will have.

One influence is how people relate to their environment. For example, about 60 percent of foraging peoples are nonunilineal, mostly bilateral. Why? Nonunilineal kinship gives individuals and nuclear families a lot of choice about which of their many kin relationships to activate at any given time. The Ju/'hoansi, Hadza, Shoshone (see Chapter 7) and most other foragers must adapt to seasonal, annual, and spatial fluctuations in wild food availability. This makes it beneficial to keep your options open by maximizing the number and range of people to whom you can trace kinship connections, which is facilitated by nonunilineal kinship. This influence is consistent with materialist approaches (see Chapter 5).

Relationships with the environment affect other descent forms, too. About three-fourths of pastoral societies are patrilineal. According to one hypothesis,

CONCEPT REVIEW	Forms of Descent and Kinship	
Forms	**Defining Characteristics**	**Associated Kin Groups**
Unilineal		
(a) Patrilineal	Descent through male line	(Patri)lineages and (patri)clans
(b) Matrilineal	Descent through female line	(Matri)lineages and (matri)clans
Nonunilineal		
(a) Cognatic	Descent traced through either male or female line	Cognatic descent groups
(b) Bilateral	Kinship reckoned equally through both parents of Ego	None: Members of Ego's kindred associate only temporarily and situationally

nomadic herding is associated with patrilineal descent because men most commonly own livestock, although among many peoples wives and daughters actually care for the herds or flock on a daily basis. To conserve labor in protecting and moving animals to seasonally available pastures, brothers often combine their animals into a single herd. This is one reason ownership of animals typically passes from fathers to sons. Brothers tend to stay together to cooperate in herd management and look after their common inheritance. Therefore, brothers live together with their father. Over generations, this leads to an emphasis on relationships between males—that is, to patrilineal descent.

Patrilineal descent has also been viewed as a way to improve success in intergroup warfare. Examples include the Maring of New Guinea (see Chapter 8) and the Yanomamö of the Amazon (see Chapter 9). Patrilineal descent encourages male solidarity (bonding) and thereby increases male willingness to cooperate in battle, as well as decreasing the chances of male relatives becoming antagonists. Evolutionary psychology (see Chapter 5) might explain patrilineal descent in these terms. Several cross-cultural studies have found an association between patrilineal descent and warfare frequency. But exactly why this correlation exists is a subject of much dispute, especially because war also is important among many matrilineal peoples.

A comparative study of central and southern African societies presented evidence that many peoples who were formerly matrilineal became patrilineal after they adopted cattle herding. The argument is that owning cattle tends to benefit sons over daughters, because cattle are so often used to pay bridewealth. Sons, not daughters, therefore inherit cattle, which potentially they use to acquire more wives, which in turn gives them advantages over other men. Also, many African herders must defend their livestock against raids by neighboring pastoralists. This makes it advantageous to keep related men together, encouraging patrilocal residence and dispersing female relatives. Over generations, patrilineal descent develops as a consequence because men who stay together through most of their lives tend to form close relationships and to pass ownership along to sons.

What sorts of factors influence the formation of matrilineal descent? Many materialist anthropologists think it is connected to how people acquire food. Matrilineal descent is more likely to be found among horticultural peoples than among foragers or intensive agriculturalists (see Chapter 7); 56 percent of matrilineal cultures are horticultural, but only 8 percent are pastoral or combine herding with farming. This association is probably related to the fact that women perform so much of the daily subsistence work in most horticultural populations, as we discuss in Chapter 11.

For evolutionary psychology (sociobiology), a puzzling aspect of matrilineal descent is that most men give more material support to their sister's children than to their own children. This is puzzling because ordinarily men are more closely related to their own children than to the children of their sisters, and evolutionary psychology predicts that people are more likely to help closer genetic relatives than more distant ones. Back in 1974, Richard Alexander suggested that matrilineal descent can be explained in terms of genetic relatedness. Under some conditions, a man is more likely to be more closely related to the children of his sister than to the children of his wife.

When will an average man be more closely related genetically to his sister's children than to his own? The answer: when the probability of paternity falls below about 25 percent—that is, when an average man is only about 25 percent sure that the children of his wife are, in fact, his children. The mathematics of this response is outside our scope. But the idea is that a man and his sister are certain they have the same mother, so they automatically have some genetic relatedness even where there is a good chance they have different fathers. Therefore, a man knows that his sister's children are related to him. But if there is about a 75 percent chance that he is not the father of his wife's children, then few of his own children are genetic relatives. Therefore, it pays off genetically to support his sister's children rather than those of his wife.

Around one-sixth of human societies are matrilineal. Is it likely that there are this many societies with a paternity probability lower than 25 percent? No, because this assumes that in the matrilineal one-sixth of all societies, a woman is roughly three times more likely to be impregnated by a man other than her husband. Although sexual behavior, and especially extramarital sexual behavior, is difficult to research, this number is unrealistic.

However, evolutionary psychology can *potentially* help us understand why there are so many societies whose social organization is based on kinship. Groups that own resources, cooperate in labor, raise children together, go to war together, and the like are most often relatives in preindustrial societies. Generally, this is consistent with evolutionary psychology because relatives should be more altruistic toward one another than nonrelatives. Critics of the approach argue against this idea in several ways, most notably that humans are more likely to cooperate with people they trust. We tend to trust people we know well, and whom do we know better than those we were raised with, regardless of whether they are our biological relatives?

To conclude, a lot of controversy surrounds what causes kinship systems, and most anthropologists doubt that any universal explanation exists. It may be that cross-cultural variations in kinship systems are influenced by so many kinds of factors that no generalized explanation is possible. As a simple example, and all else equal, chronic warfare might tend to favor patrilineality; horticulture might tend to favor matrilineality. However, many horticultural societies also have serious warfare, and other factors certainly influence the form of descent. Therefore, the processes that influence are complicated, and the outcomes are variable.

Cultural Construction of Kinship

In Chapter 2, we noted that a major component of cultural knowledge is the way a particular people construct the world, both the natural world and the social world. Kinship relationships and groups are an important part of the social world in all human cultures. Just as cultures differ in the ways they trace their descent and form social groupings of relatives, so do they differ in how they identify kinds of relatives, using labeled categories to do so. The labeled categories are called **kin terms,** and the way a people classify their relatives into these categories is called their **kinship terminology**.

The simplest explanation is that kin terms reflect the way those relatives are related biologically (genetically). In English, this is true for some terms: *mother, father, sister, brother, son,* and *daughter* all define individuals related to you in distinct (unique) biological ways. For example, no other female relative other than your sister shares your parentage (setting aside considerations of fictive kinship, such as adoption, foster parenting, and step relatives).

However, other English kin terms do not faithfully reflect genetic relatedness. Consider *uncle* and *aunt.* They refer to siblings of your parents, distinguished only by their gender. But the individuals you call "aunt" and "uncle" are related to you in four different ways: your father's siblings, your mother's siblings, your father's siblings' spouses, and your mother's siblings' spouses. The same idea applies to some other terms; a particular term may group together several individuals related to you in different ways. Thus, *grandfather* and *grandmother* includes both your mother's and your father's father. *First cousin* refers to a wide range of people connected to you biologically in different ways.

Even terms with seemingly unambiguous biological referents like *sister* and *brother* are treated in varying ways. In old China and Korea and many other places, terms for siblings were modified by birth order, producing distinctions like *first brother, fourth brother,* and *second sister*. The Chinese and Koreans applied the Confucian respect for elders to sibling terminology: The fact that elder brothers outranked younger ones was reflected in how they addressed one another.

Thus, a people's kinship terminology reflects biological relationships only imperfectly. More fundamentally, kin terms reflect the norms, rights and duties, and behavioral patterns that characterize social relationships among kinfolk. Speaking broadly, collapsing relatives with different biological relationships into a single term reflects the cultural fact that people think of them as the same kind of relative. In turn, and in general, people conceive of them as the same kind of relative because they have similar kinds of relationships with them.

As already described, peoples vary in the ways they trace their main kin ties, in the kinds of relationships and groups created by those ties, and in how they classify relatives into labeled categories. These variations do not perfectly reflect the degree of genetic relatedness between relatives, so anthropologists commonly say that kinship is *culturally constructed.* The **cultural construction of kinship** implies two things: (1) As children grow up in a certain community, they socially learn the logic by which their culture classifies relatives into categories, and (2) those categories do not simply reflect biological/genetic relationships. (If they did, we might be justified in saying that kinship is *biologically determined.*) In fact, as we'll see in a moment, the labeled categories of kinship sometimes hardly match up at all with biological relationships.

Logic of Cultural Constructions

Before we discuss particular kinship terminologies, we need to understand the logic by which they are culturally constructed. By "logic," we mean the principles

kin terms Labels that individuals use to refer to their relatives of various kinds.

kinship terminology Logically consistent system by which people classify their relatives into labeled categories or kinds of relatives.

cultural construction of kinship Fact that the kinship relationships a given people recognize do not perfectly reflect biological relationships; revealed in the kinship terminology.

that people use to distinguish one kind of relative from others. There are many principles, but only five are relevant for our purposes.

First, every kin term has a reciprocal term. For example, the reciprocal term for *grandfather* is either *granddaughter* or *grandson.* If you call a woman "mother," she will call you "son" or "daughter." (In English, the reciprocal term for *cousin* is *cousin.*)

Second, for some terms, the gender of the individuals to whom the term applies makes a difference. In English, gender matters for terms like *brother* and *sister, uncle* and *aunt,* and *grandfather* and *grandmother.* Indeed, gender is the only criterion that distinguishes the relatives just mentioned from one another. Gender is irrelevant, however, for *cousin.*

Third, kinship terms usually reflect whether the individual referred to is of the same or a different generation than Ego's. In English, specific terms are used for relatives in Ego's own generation (like *cousin*), in Ego's parents' generation (*aunt*), and in Ego's children's generation (*niece*). In describing kinship terminologies, we term Ego's parents' generation *the first ascending generation* and Ego's children's generation the *first descending generation.* Although the terms used in most kinship terminologies reflect generational differences, some systems use terms that transcend generations.

Fourth, the sex of the relative who connects Ego to another relative often matters. The distinction between cross and parallel cousins illustrates this logical principle: Among many peoples, a mother's brother's daughter is called by a different term than a mother's sister's daughter. Often, too, a father's sister and a mother's sister have different labels.

Side of the family is a fifth criterion used by some peoples to construct kin terminologies. In English, side of the family is irrelevant: Your relatives through your mother receive the same terms as relatives through your father. As we know, many other cultures place special emphasis on relationships through females

(mothers—matrilineal) or males (fathers—patrilineal). As you suspect, this emphasis is reflected in terminological systems.

These five principles are among the ones that various peoples use to culturally construct kinship. The most general point is that different peoples combine these logical principles—as you can see, they actually are logical *possibilities*—in various ways to form categories or kinds of relatives.

Who's an Aunt? Varieties of Kinship Terminology

The world's diverse peoples have developed many ways of classifying relatives into labeled categories. The classification systems have names like Eskimo, Hawaiian, Sudanese, Iroquois, Omaha, and Crow. Don't be misled by the names of these systems. The American anthropologist Lewis Henry Morgan developed the classification system for kinship terminology in 1871. He named each system after the first people among whom he encountered it. In fact, all the systems are found on many continents, although four of them were named after the Native American peoples that Morgan studied.

Here we cover only four systems: Eskimo, Hawaiian, Iroquois, and Omaha. We further simplify things by considering only terms used for relatives in Ego's generation and in Ego's first ascending (parental) generation. To make these systems easier to understand, we translate the terms into their closest English equivalents. Keep in mind that these translations are only rough approximations and that some terms have no exact English equivalents.

Eskimo Kinship Terminology

Eskimo terminology is the easiest for English speakers to understand because this is the system with which most of us are familiar (Figure 10.3). In this system,

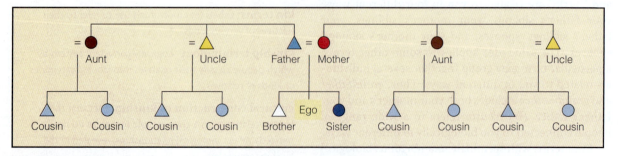

Figure 10.3 Eskimo Kinship Terminology

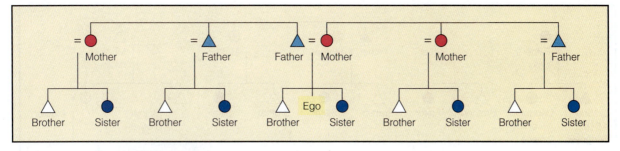

Figure 10.4 Hawaiian Kinship Terminology

Ego's biological mother is called "mother," and Ego's biological father is called "father." These are the only two persons to whom these terms apply. The term *aunt* is used for both Ego's father's sister and Ego's mother's sister, and the term *uncle* is used for Ego's father's brother and Ego's mother's brother. The terms *brother* and *sister* are used for only the children of Ego's mother and father. The term *cousin* is used for all children of Ego's uncles and aunts.

Hawaiian Kinship Terminology

Hawaiian terminology uses the fewest terms (Figure 10.4). All of Ego's relatives in the first ascending generation are called either "mother" or "father." *Mother* is extended to include Ego's mother's sister and Ego's father's sister, and *father* is extended to include father's brother and mother's brother. In Ego's own generation, all relatives are called either "brother" or "sister." Thus, Hawaiian terminology includes no terms equivalent to the English terms *uncle, aunt,* and *cousin.* Although the Hawaiian system extends the terms *mother* and *father,* this does not mean that individuals are unable to distinguish their biological parents from their other relatives of the parental generation.

Iroquois Kinship Terminology

People who use the Iroquois terminology categorize relatives very differently than the Hawaiian and Eskimo systems (Figure 10.5). The term *father* includes the father's brother but not the mother's brother. *Mother* includes the mother's sister but not the father's sister. The mother's brother and father's sister have their own unique terms. Looking at Ego's own generation, we also see a difference. The children of the father's brother and mother's sister are called "brother" and "sister." The children of the mother's brother and father's sister are called by a term that might be translated as "cousin." This is how we label it on the diagram, because of its familiarity, but it could also be labeled "child of father's sister" or "child of mother's brother."

Although the distinctions of the Iroquois construction may seem unusual to us, they also exist in the Omaha system so we need to understand their logic. Peoples who use the Iroquois system distinguish between parallel and cross cousins. They give their parallel cousins the same terms they use for their own brothers and sisters. They distinguish cross cousins from parallel cousins, calling cross cousins by a unique term (here we translate the term as "cousin," although obviously it has no exact English equivalent).

To understand the logic behind calling parallel cousins "brother" and "sister" and cross cousins by a different term, go back to the terms used for Ego's parents' siblings. Ego's father's brother and mother's sister are called "father" and "mother," respectively. Thus, it is logical to call their children "brother" and "sister."

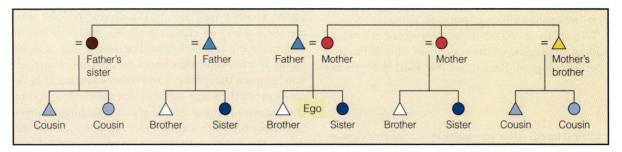

Figure 10.5 Iroquois Kinship Terminology

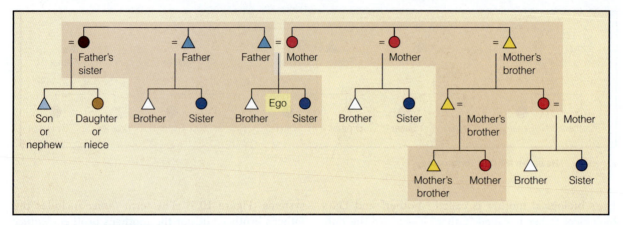

Figure 10.6 Omaha Kinship Terminology

(What do you call the children of the people you call "mother" and "father"?) Ego calls his father's sister by a term that might be translated as "aunt," although the indigenous term is sometimes close to "female father." Ego's mother's brother is "uncle" (or "male mother"). So, it is logical to call their children (Ego's cross cousins) by another term we might translate as "cousin."

Omaha Kinship Terminology

Omaha terminology is difficult for English speakers to grasp (Figure 10.6). The terms used in the first ascending generation are identical to the terms in the Iroquois system, and parallel cousins are called "brother" and "sister." The difference between Iroquois and Omaha is how cross cousins are treated. Omaha terminology has no term similar to English *cousin*. In addition, in Omaha terminology, a distinction is made between cross cousins on the mother's side (the children of mother's brother) and cross cousins on the father's side (the children of father's sister). The mother's brothers' daughters are called "mother," and the mother's brothers' sons are called "mother's brother." Thus, Ego's maternal cross cousins are grouped with individuals in Ego's parents' generation. For Ego's paternal cross cousins, the term depends on Ego's sex. If Ego is a male, he calls his father's sisters' children "niece" and "nephew." If Ego is a female, she calls her father's sisters' children "son" and "daughter." Yikes.

Why are there two separate terms for father's sisters' children, depending on the sex of Ego? This distinction is perfectly logical. Remember that kinship terms are reciprocal and that Figure 10.6 shows only the terms used by Ego. To understand why the sex of Ego matters in this relationship, ask: What would father's sisters' children call Ego? In Figure 10.6, you see that Ego is their mother's brother's child. Thus, if Ego is female, they would call her "mother," and she would reciprocate by calling them "son" or "daughter." If Ego is male, they would call him "uncle," and therefore he would call them "niece" or "nephew."

There are other systems, but these four are the most common and widespread. This diversity is surprising, and some of these cultural constructions of relatives are puzzling. How can we understand them?

Why Do Terminologies Differ?

In previous chapters, we emphasized that cultures are integrated: One aspect fits with others and sometimes makes sense only when understood in context. Kinship terminology systems are a revealing example of **cultural integration** and illustrate that things that seem obvious and natural often are not.

First, notice that the four terminologies described can be separated into two types. In the Eskimo and Hawaiian, the side of the family does not matter in classifying relatives; in the Iroquois and Omaha, it does. Stated another way, among the diverse peoples who use the Eskimo or Hawaiian system, the principle of distinguishing relatives according to the side of Ego's family is irrelevant; they *could* recognize the distinction between the mother's and father's kin, but they do not. Among the many cultures that use the Iroquois or Omaha system, the principle of distinguishing relatives according to family side *is* relevant. Why should the side of the family matter in some terminological systems but not in others?

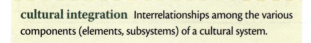

cultural integration Interrelationships among the various components (elements, subsystems) of a cultural system.

As you've guessed, the side of the family matters in some terminologies because in these systems people trace their descent through only one of their parents. The side of the family makes no difference in other systems because these populations trace their kin connections equally through both parents. *In general*—there are exceptions—the way a people trace their descent affects the relationships between kinfolk, which affects the terms used to refer to these kin.

Consider the Eskimo classification. Contrasting to other terminologies, it differs in two main ways: (1) It makes no distinction between Ego's father's and mother's relatives, and (2) no other relatives of any kind are lumped together with nuclear family relatives. Assume that these two features mirror people's ideas about how various kin are related. We might conclude that people think (1) that both sides of the family are equally important to an individual (more accurately, there is no systematic *social pattern* of importance through one side over the other) and (2) that nuclear family relatives are somehow special and thought of differently than are other kinds of relatives.

In the case of North America, traditionally our surnames are inherited mainly through males, but other than this, we are no more likely to have special relationships with relatives through our fathers than through our mothers. And, generally, the members of our nuclear families *are* special: We do not expect to inherit much, if anything, from other relatives; we usually do not live in extended households; kin groups larger than the nuclear family do not usually own property in common; and so on.

More generally, we expect the Eskimo classification of relatives to be associated with cognatic or bilateral kinship. And usually it is: About 80 percent of all societies that use the Eskimo terminological system have a nonunilineal kinship system. This is because neither side of the family is consistently emphasized, so people do not think of their mother's or father's relatives as being any different. The absence of a special relationship with kin through either parent is reflected in the terminology.

What about the Hawaiian system? As in the Eskimo system, family side is irrelevant. Logically, then, it ought to be associated consistently with cognatic or bilateral kinship. The fact that it lumps other relatives with nuclear family members seems to indicate that the nuclear family is submerged or embedded in larger extended households. Ego should have important relationships with the siblings of his or her parents and with their children. Despite this logic, the Hawaiian terminology is not as consistently associated with cognatic or bilateral kinship as is the Eskimo terminology;

in fact, about 40 percent of societies with the Hawaiian classification are unilineal. The Hawaiian system is apparently also compatible with unilineal descent.

And the Iroquois? Ego's father and father's brother are assigned a single term, which is different from mother's brother. Ego calls mother and mother's sister by the same term, which is not the same term that Ego uses for the father's sister. Thus, Ego distinguishes between maternal and paternal aunts and uncles in the first ascending generation. The fact that the side of the family matters in this generation seems to imply unilineal descent. And, the Iroquois system is usually found among peoples who trace their descent unilineally: About 80 percent of all Iroquois terminologies occur in unilineal descent forms. If you look back at Figure 10.5, you will see that Ego uses "brother" and "sister" to refer to the children of relatives Ego calls "mother" and "father." This certainly makes logical sense—if you call someone "mother," it follows that you will call her son "brother" and her daughter "sister." The cross cousins have a separate term (here translated as "cousin") because Ego does not call their parents "mother" and "father."

The Omaha system carries the distinctions between the mother's and father's side into Ego's generation and the generation younger than Ego. If you compare Figures 10.5 and 10.6, you will see that the Omaha system differs from the Iroquois by distinguishing cross cousins according to whether they are related to Ego through Ego's mother or father. The mother, mother's sister, and mother's brother's daughter are called by the same term although they are members of different generations. The mother's brother and mother's brother's son likewise are lumped together under a single term.

What can explain this way of classifying relatives? The fact that these relatives are all related to Ego through Ego's mother must mean something, and the fact that they are classified together and distinguished only by their gender must be significant. Indeed, both these features are clues to the logic behind the Omaha terminology. It is nearly always found among peoples who are patrilineal.

How does patrilineal descent make sense of the Omaha system? In Figure 10.6, we have shaded the background around those relatives in the diagram who belong to Ego's own patrilineal group. Notice that the cousins in Ego's group are called "brother" and "sister," which reflects the social fact that they are in Ego's own lineage. We have also shaded the background of those relatives who are members of Ego's mother's patrilineal group. Notice that all the members of this latter group are assigned only two terms—one for the male members of the group and one for the female members of the group. The two terms have no English translation, but they mean roughly "female member of my mother's group" and "male member of my mother's group." The relatives' common *social identity* as members of Ego's mother's kin group overrides the *biological fact* that they are members of three generations. If you have followed the argument, you will agree that the Omaha system makes perfect sense, provided it is associated with patrilineal descent forms. And, indeed, more than 90 percent of all cultures that use the Omaha terminological system are patrilineal.

Another system, the Crow, is essentially the mirror image of the Omaha. You will not be surprised to learn that the Crow system is strongly associated with societies that have the matrilineal form of descent.

Thus, kin terminologies make sense once we understand that they reflect the prevalent relationships and groupings produced by various ways of tracing kinship connections. The ways people culturally construct and label their relatives reflect the social realities of their kinship system. These ways look mysterious until we understand these classifications and labels in the context of the kinship systems that give rise to them. The Eskimo terminology used by Americans would probably look strange to people who use, say, the Omaha terminology. Our failure to distinguish between relatives through one's mother and father would be strange because to them these relatives are clearly different kinds of relatives, given the way their kinship systems place people into different kin groups.

The various peoples who use one or another of these kinship classification systems cannot state the logic of their classifications in the same way we just did. For instance, people who use the Omaha terminology cannot tell you why they label their relatives as they do because they lack a comparative perspective of their own kinship system. Presumably, to them, their mother, mother's sister, and mother's brother's daughter are called by the same term because all these women are the same kind of relative, just as aunts and cousins are all the same kind of relative in some other cultures. They do not realize that in Eskimo systems these females all have separate terms, nor do they know that their terminology reflects the groupings and relationships of their kinship system.

Then again, people who use the Eskimo system cannot account for their kin terms either, until, of course, they become aware of the diversity in human kinship systems discovered in the past century by anthropologists. The way we classify kinfolk seems quite natural—biologically based—until we learn that other people do it differently.

Where's Our Backbone?

In the last two chapters, we described four forms of marriage: monogamy, polygyny, polyandry, and group marriage. We've also seen that there are a few peoples who might not have any marriage system at all, depending on how marriage is defined. We've outlined four ways in which married couples arrange their residence after they marry: patrilocal, matrilocal, neolocal, and ambilocal. There also are other, rarer forms of postmarital residence not considered here. We've seen how nuclear families are commonly embedded in extended families of several types: Among one people, sisters stay together and bring their husbands to live with them, whereas among another people several brothers bring their wives in to live with them in one household. We've seen that diverse peoples around the world have traced kinship relationships through their fathers, their mothers, through both parents, and through either parent according to choice and circumstances. We've shown that various peoples culturally construct their kinship categories in ways that look mysterious—even incomprehensible—to people who construct their kinship categories in some other way.

Piercing through all the complexities and the key terms needed to understand them, this knowledge has two wider lessons for people living in the twenty-first century. The first is that diverse human groups have developed a wide range of ways of marrying, forming families, living together, and keeping track of their relatives. There is no single right way to run a marriage system, to organize family life, or to reckon which distant relatives are most important. There is variability. Anthropologists have not—and perhaps never will—explain this variability in the scientific meaning of *explain*. But consider how many ways human beings have organized marriage and kinship relationships—relationships that many modern people think are "only natural" or "based on biology" or "morally correct" or are the "backbone" of their nation.

The second lesson is also a simple one: change. Marriage and sexual and family practices have changed throughout humanity's history, and we can be certain that they will change more as circumstances continue to evolve. Perhaps you cannot imagine what other ways of thinking about and organizing marriage, family, and kinship will emerge in the future. However, it is good to keep in mind that in the 1970s the idea that people could acquire cash from a machine called an ATM by inserting a piece of plastic seemed far-fetched, as did personal computers, mobile phones, large numbers of unmarrieds living together, females outnumbering males in higher education, and presidential candidates trashing China because of the absurd possibility that it threatens Us.

SUMMARY

1. **Discuss why kinship is important in creating relationships, forming groups, and organizing activities in so many preindustrial cultures.** In modernized, urbanized societies, many functions and activities are organized by specialized groups, whereas these functions and activities are organized by kinship groups in many premodern cultures. Kinship groups often organize economic, political, military, ritual, and other activities. Kinship ties also help form a person's social identity and often determine one's social rank.

2. **Describe the two main forms of unilineal descent and the kinship groups that result from them.** Although kinship derives from biological relatedness, societies vary in their kinship systems. One variation is how people trace their relationships back to previous generations—in how they trace their *descent*. Peoples with unilineal descent emphasize relationships traced only through one sex. The matrilineal or patrilineal principle forms descent groups composed of people related through females and males, respectively. In order of increasing inclusiveness and genealogical depth, the main kinds of descent groups are extended families, lineages, and clans. The island people of Tikopia exemplify patrilineal descent, and the Native American Hopi exemplify matrilineal descent.

3. **Describe the two primary forms of nonunilineal descent: bilateral and cognatic.** People who trace their kinship relationships bilaterally have no kin groups larger than extended families because the kindreds of different individuals overlap so much. Kindreds are Ego focused, and large numbers of Ego's relatives are likely to get together only on certain occasions, such as weddings, funerals, and family reunions. In cognatic descent, people have options of tracing their ancestry through men or women, or both. Individuals can join any of the groups to which they trace ancestry and can choose those groups with which they want to associate closely, as illustrated by the Samoan ’aiga.

4. **Elaborate on the cultural construction of kinship and explain the wider associations of four of the major terminological systems.** A people culturally construct their kinship system by applying logical principles in various ways. This application produces several systems of kin terminology, of which we discuss four: Eskimo, Hawaiian, Iroquois, and Omaha. Generally speaking, the ideas people have about how they are related to one another are strongly influenced by how the kinship system of their society sorts people into groups and establishes relationships of certain kinds between kinfolk.

11 Gender in Comparative Perspective

Although gender is a significant distinction among all peoples, cultures vary in gender constructions, relationships, roles, rewards, and other dimensions of gender identity. In 2016, Hillary Clinton became the first American woman to be nominated for President.

After reading this chapter, you should be able to:

1 **DESCRIBE** how male–female physical differences affect gender roles and relationships.

2 **EXPLAIN** the phrase "cultural construction of gender" and its importance.

3 **ANALYZE** the relevance of the cultural acceptance of multiple gender identities for understanding gender.

4 **DISCUSS** the factors that influence the widespread patterns and the cross-cultural diversity in the gendered division of labor.

5 **ANALYZE** why it is so difficult to determine whether any societies have complete gender equality.

6 **DESCRIBE** the three most important influences on gender stratification from a comparative perspective.

Human beings feel, think, and act within a cultural framework that affects our private lives, interests, attitudes, worldviews, social behavior, and other aspects of how we define themselves. The feminist movement is one of the most powerful social and political forces of recent times. In addition to radically transforming societies, it affected scholarly interests and research in many disciplines. Anthropologists conducted a lot more field work about gender beliefs, roles, and relationships. We also tried to understand and explain the reasons cultures differ in these beliefs, roles, and relationships.

Today issues connected to gender are one of the most popular research and teaching specializations. Even anthropologists who do not conduct research in gender as such now take gender into account in our research on other subjects. We recognize that many human relationships are permeated by people's cultural knowledge about gender.

Gender and gender identity also are universal bases for organizing group activities and allocating roles to individuals. Your identity as a male or female or as a member of another gender makes a difference in who you are, how you are rewarded, how you interact, and what you can become. In different cultures, gender matters to different degrees and in varying ways. These cultural variations and the factors that affect them are the subjects of this chapter.

Research in gender is so vast that we must focus on only four of the main issues to which anthropologists have made important contributions: the cultural construction of gender, multiple (as opposed to dual) genders, the gendered division of labor, and gender

stratification. Where relevant, we suggest ways in which anthropological findings and perspectives help us and perhaps explain gender roles and beliefs about gender in contemporary societies.

In any society, gender is a key dimension of a person's *social identity:* How other people perceive you, feel about you, and relate to you is influenced by the gender to which they assign you and by how your culture defines gender differences. Less obviously, an individual's *self-identity* is affected by cultural beliefs and ideas: Your conception of yourself depends partly on how your culture distinguishes masculinity and femininity, allocates roles based on gender, and uses symbols (such as dress, behavior, speech style, and sexual preferences and practices) to help define gender differences. Even when interacting with someone of your own gender, your actions are affected by your culture's norms, categories, worldviews, symbols, and other ideas and beliefs that influence conceptions about gender. Finally, just as gender identity affects interactions between individuals, so do beliefs about gender affect behavior in a variety of social settings and contexts: in the workplace, home, school, church, and political arenas, to name a few.

Sex and Gender

The world's peoples vary in the significance they attach to whether a person is female or male and in what specific behaviors they expect from females and males. To emphasize such cultural variations, we make a conceptual distinction between *sex* and *gender*. Most people think that visible sexual features are determined by the X and Y sex chromosomes. In reality, the visible and behavioral expression of sex chromosomes are influenced by embryonic development, how physiology transmits hormones to cells and tissues, and other biological processes. A person's genetic makeup and physiology—in interaction with factors in the environment—form physical characteristics like genitals, hormones, and secondary sexual characteristics (breasts, pelvis, body size, musculature, and the like). Of course, not all individuals can be identified as a member of a *dichotomous* (female–male) category on the basis of their genes. Various peoples treat this ambiguity in different ways, as we shall see.

Females and males differ genetically in many ways. However, a couple of biologically based differences have special importance in comparative studies of various cultures.

First is **sexual dimorphism** At maturity, *most* males are physically larger and stronger than *most* females. Sexual dimorphism is a product of our evolutionary past and is a trait we share with our evolutionary cousins—gorillas and chimpanzees. This difference in size and strength has many implications, two of which are that men are more likely than women to win physical fights and are better able to handle tasks that involve a lot of strength. Sexual dimorphism is often considered to be a given condition, determined by humanity's evolutionary past. Indeed, all human populations exhibit dimorphism, but comparative research suggests the sex-based differences in size are less in societies in which females contribute most to food production.

Second are differences in reproductive physiology: Only women become pregnant, carry children until birth, and produce the milk that their newborns and infants require. Men do contribute sperm in one way or—with in vitro technology—another. *Biological* fatherhood may end there, but almost all peoples assign the role of *social* father to the biological father or another man. *Social* fathers support their partners before, during, and after pregnancy. In most cultures, fathers and other men help to greater or lesser degrees with the care of infants and children, although this varies a lot from people to people.

---

sexual dimorphism Physical differences based on genetic differences between females and males.

cultural construction of gender (social construction of gender) Idea that the characteristics a people attribute to males and females are culturally, not biologically, determined.

For anthropological interests, sexual dimorphism and reproductive physiology are the two most important ways females and males differ biologically. We do not agree on the overall significance of such differences for human cultures. We do agree, though, that various cultures also construct differences and similarities between males and females other than those based on biological differences.

Cultural Construction of Gender

The phrase **cultural** (or **social**) **construction of gender** means that different cultures have distinctive ideas about males and females and use these ideas to define manhood/masculinity and womanhood/femininity. The word *construction* evokes the act of building—from the raw materials provided by biological differences; different cultures build up their ideas and beliefs about how the sexes differ and what these differences mean. How males and females perceive and define themselves and each other, what it means to be a woman or a man, what roles are appropriate for men and women—these and many other dimensions of femaleness and maleness are culturally variable, not universal to the human species or constant across all cultures.

The notion that gender is culturally constructed is too easily and often misunderstood. Some scholars (especially those in the biological sciences) mistakenly believe that anthropologists do not think that genetic (physical) differences between the sexes matter. They think that anthropologists believe that differences in male and female behaviors are determined by culture, not genes.

Some anthropologists do make this claim, especially those whose theoretical orientation is more humanistic than scientific (see Chapter 5). But most accept that biological differences between females and males "matter"—are relevant for both ideas and behaviors—in all cultures.

However, anthropology's focus on cultural diversity makes us aware that human groups define and make use of these differences in a multitude of ways. In *symbols*, various peoples attach cultural meanings to female–male differences that go well beyond biological/anatomical distinctions. In constructions of *social reality*, some cultures minimize the significance of male–female physical differences, whereas others exaggerate them. In *values*, "patriarchy" crudely describes some groups, "sexual equality" others. In *behavior patterns*, some groups fairly rigidly differentiate between female and male activities and roles, whereas others allow both sexes to participate in similar kinds of activities according to individual preferences and circumstances. Our interest in such variations does not imply that we deny biological realities.

One implication of the cultural construction of gender is that there are no cultures that are "natural" with respect to their beliefs about gender. (This includes your own culture, by the way.) This fact makes it very difficult to determine the impact of biological (sexual) differences on the behaviors of females or males because everywhere cultural (gender) constructions obscure and complicate the impacts of genes. Notice, though, that this does not mean that genetic differences are not important: It means only that their effects are difficult to determine.

The Hua of Papua New Guinea

The Hua of Papua New Guinea are a people whose cultural construction of gender differs markedly from that familiar to most of our readers. Studied by Anna Meigs in the 1970s, the Hua are a patrilineal, horticultural people who live in mountain villages of 100 to 300. As we shall see, Hua culture constructs gender on the basis of female–male differences that most other people do not recognize as real. Because of this cultural construction, Hua believe that later in life a woman can become like a man, and a man can become like a woman.

How does Hua culture construct gender categories and characteristics? They believe that bodies contain a life-giving substance (like a vital essence) that they call *nu.* They think of *nu* as a real, physical substance—not a mystical or magical power—that can be transferred from one person to another and gained and lost in various ways. Symbolically, *nu* is associated with growth and maturity. Female bodies contain lots of *nu*, which in Hua belief not only makes women grow faster and age more slowly than men but also makes them moister. On the other hand, males naturally contain a smaller amount of growth-inducing *nu,* so they need extra to help them grow up. Hua explain many of the differences between men and women by the amount of *nu:* Men are stronger and fiercer because they are drier, for example.

Nu is both gaseous (breath) and liquid (blood, sweat, semen, female sexual secretions). A transfer of *nu* from one person to another can be harmful or helpful, depending on the nature of the relationship between the giver and the recipient. *Nu* can be transferred during eating, sexual intercourse, and other kinds of direct and indirect contact. For example, a woman can transfer her *nu* to people when she serves food to them. *Nu* from her bodily secretions and under her fingernails adheres to the food and gets ingested by her children and her husband.

A woman also transfers *nu* to a man when she has intercourse with him. Giving *nu* to a man in the act of intercourse is harmful to the man because it pollutes and debilitates him. Intercourse is also damaging to a man because he contributes his own scarce *nu* (in the form of breath and semen) to a woman during sex. She gains strength and vitality at his expense through sexual intercourse.

People can regulate *nu* by the kinds of food they eat. At different times in their lives, people need more or less *nu*. Women need extra *nu* during pregnancy, so they eat lots of foods considered rich in *nu*. (Broadly speaking, these are fast-growing foods with high moisture content.) During menstruation, though, women have too much *nu*, so they avoid the same kinds of food.

In contrast, young males do not have enough *nu* for full growth and maturation, so during certain periods of boyhood, they are encouraged to eat foods with lots of *nu.* At other times, when they are undergoing the initiation ceremonies that make them into strong men able to fight to defend the village, they are supposed to avoid *nu*-rich foods because such foods will weaken and sicken them. During male initiation ceremonies, there are strict taboos against eating not only these foods but also foods from gardens tended by women or foods prepared by women. Because *nu* makes women polluting to males, the food taboos help protect boys from pollution caused by contact with women.

In Hua belief, the greater the difference in *nu* between a woman and a man, the more dangerous that woman is to that man. But both men and women can and do lose or gain *nu*, depending on their activities, their diet, and their age. After decades of engaging in sexual intercourse with women and eating foods touched by their wives and other women, middle-aged and elderly men have taken lots of *nu* into their bodies. They become invulnerable to further contamination by contact with females and therefore may eat *nu*-rich foods and participate in sexual intercourse with less anxiety than younger men. Gaining *nu* over the years makes them become "like women." Hua call such individuals *figapa*, which Meigs interprets as a third gender category. *Figapa* are "like women" because their bodies contain lots of substances that the Hua symbolically consider feminine.

For their part, women lose *nu* whenever they menstruate, handle and prepare food, and have babies. Over their life course, *nu* leaves a woman's body. Therefore, Hua believe, women become less and less dangerous to males as they grow older. Women who have given birth to more than two children have lost enough *nu* that they are no longer polluting. They therefore become "like men." Hua say these individuals are *kakora,* which is a fourth gender category. People who are *kakora* are eligible to live in the men's house, partly because they are no longer hazardous to men.

Thus, Hua culture recognizes two bases for gender distinctions. One is a person's genitals, which make most people either male or female. The other is the quantity of *nu* in the body, which is affected by a person's stage of life and previous life events and activities. The latter criterion gives rise to the two additional nondiscrete or nonbinary (more or less) gender categories of *figapa* and *kakora.* Although the *figapa–kakora* distinction is relevant in only certain ritual contexts, it is significant that people whose genitals are male or female are classified with the opposite gender for certain purposes.

Hua clearly illustrate the cultural construction of gender. The objective physical distinctions between the sexes—genitals, beards, breasts, and so on—are recognized and relevant in all known cultures. But, as Meigs shows for the Hua, cultures use the (metaphorically) raw material of these differences to construct varying beliefs about the ways in which females and males differ. To Hua, men and women differ not only in observable physical ways but also in the quantity of *nu* each has, and this varies through life cycles. These beliefs in turn affect the attitudes each sex holds about the other and the behavior each sex adopts toward the other. Hua men fear the possibility of feminine pollution and therefore try to minimize their contact with women, their intake of food prepared by women, and their sexual relations with women.

Although readers may not believe in a substance like *nu,* they should still notice that Hua beliefs about *nu* make a large difference in the behavior of both genders and how they relate to each other. The more different some culture's beliefs are from your own, the more obvious it is that those beliefs are a cultural construction rather than biologically determined. Because Hua beliefs pertaining to male–female relationships seem exotic to most Westerners, the fact that gender is culturally constructed among these people is readily apparent.

All people's ideas about gender are culturally constructed, however, including yours and mine. To stimulate thought, we briefly present some ideas on the construction of gender in Euro-American culture.

---

gender roles (sex roles) Rights and duties individuals have because of their perceived identities as males, females, or another gender category.

North American Constructions

Speaking generally, many North Americans see females as compassionate, emotional, socially skilled, physically fragile, and family oriented. Males are taken to be more selfish, rational, tolerant of physical discomfort (tough), coordinated, and individualistic. Of course, these dichotomous characteristics are simplistic and stereotypical, and increasingly people no longer hold these opinions at all.

Consider the possible effects of these cultural conceptions on the uneven distribution of occupational roles between women and men in the modern American economy. Given the cultural construction of gender, men and women tend to find jobs for which they believe they are best suited. If this seems obvious, notice that it happens for more than the obvious reason. First, individual men and women more often *seek* those jobs that they find appropriate for their sex or that they think they have the best chance of getting or succeeding in; the jobs most people apply for are based in part on their beliefs about **gender roles** or **sex roles**.

Second, employers tend to *hire* people according to their own cultural conceptions of which gender is likely to do well in a particular job; the employment market (the market for labor) allocates men and women into certain kinds of jobs by influencing employers' beliefs about relative compatibility and suitability.

Third, people tend to stereotype other people's constructions: Even if you don't think you are best suited for a traditional female role, you may believe that other people think you are. Your *perceptions* of other people's constructions might encourage you to limit your options to what you think their constructions are. Thus, the market for labor responds to job seekers' constructions, employers' constructions, and everyone's perceptions about other people's constructions.

Constructions of which occupations are suited for a specific gender are changing rapidly, yet many jobs remain disproportionately female or male. Women predominate in jobs that involve nurturing (e.g., nursing, day care, elementary school teaching, social work, pediatric medicine), routine interactions with the public (e.g., receptionists, clerks, restaurant waiters, bank tellers), repetitive use of fine motor skills (word processing, sewing and stitching), and cleaning and housekeeping. A few of the jobs in which men predominate are those involving outdoor activity (equipment operation, driving, carpentry, and construction), high-level decision making (management, administration), and knowledge of mathematical principles (science and engineering).

Although constructions of gender are different now than they were even a decade ago, women still far outnumber men in jobs as receptionists, secretaries, and file clerks.

Multiple Gender Identities

Most North Americans today are familiar with the phrase "gender identity." Most—especially millennials—have friends or relatives who are gay or lesbian or who identify as a member of some other gender. Many people think these gender categories developed only recently, as modern nations became more tolerant of gender diversity. They are wrong.

Native American Two Spirits

Many of the world's peoples tolerate and even institutionalize diversity in gender identities, roles, and sexual orientation. Biologically male or female individuals are allowed to adopt aspects of the role or behavior of the other sex with little or no social stigma or formal punishment. In such cultures, a boy who cannot or does not wish to conform to male roles is not forced to follow norms nor is he socially ostracized; instead, he is allowed to act like a female in certain respects or

contexts. Conversely, a girl who shows an affinity for activities culturally defined as male is allowed to participate in manly roles when she becomes an adult. In short, in many cultures, people can adopt the identity and roles typical of the other sex in features such as clothing, work, and sexual preference, with little or no social stigma or legal punishment from other members of their communities.

These practices or customs are often called **gender crossing**. In many cultures, it is expected that a certain number of people are born who, when they mature into adulthood, will become like the other sex in some ways. Rather than stigmatizing such persons or trying to force them to live up to the group's standards of femininity or masculinity, they are accommodated and integrated into social life. Their nonbinary sexual identity is *institutionalized.*

Most North Americans interpret institutionalized gender crossing as a way that cultures accommodate lesbians, gays, and bisexuals. This interpretation is generally correct; however, there is much more to gender crossing than sexual orientation, as we shall see. First, let's consider briefly how anthropological thinking about gender crossing has changed in recent decades.

Until the 1970s or 1980s, most anthropologists viewed gender crossing in the following way. In any society, some individuals are born who do not fit into sexual identity categories of "male" or "female." There are some boys who do not want to go to war, hunt, or compete in politics but instead prefer to hang out with girls, do domestic work, tan skins, or otherwise act in ways culturally considered feminine. Likewise, some girls display an affinity for actions culturally associated with masculinity, preferring to play boy games, use weapons, dress like males, and so on. In many human societies, such persons eventually learn to outwardly conform to the normal sex roles. If they do not conform, they are considered deviant and punished or stigmatized throughout their lives. In some societies, though, there is a legitimate role and identity that allows them to satisfy their inclinations while serving the group in various ways. Institutionalized gender crossing is a cultural mechanism that provides a legitimate outlet for people who otherwise might be unhappy or cause problems in the social life of the community.

gender crossing Custom by which a person of one sex is allowed to adopt the roles and behavior of the opposite sex, with little or no stigma or punishment.

Comparatively speaking, this is a favorable image of cultures that allow gender crossing. Anthropologists often view the institutionalization of gender crossing as a lesson we can learn from Others. Some human groups do not insist on rigid conformity to their sexual stereotypes; instead, they allow diversity, in contrast to chauvinistic cultures like the anthropologists' own. Unlike us, these Others normalize individual variation in aspects such as dress style, sexual orientation, work activities, mannerisms, and the like, rather than rigidly insisting on uniformity. And unlike many of us—who view men who act like women and women who act like men as morally degenerate, dangerous to society, or somehow abnormal—the Others do not despise or ostracize such individuals but provide them with legitimate roles in the community's social life.

The usual lessons are: (1) We ought to be more like those Others by tolerating variation and accepting people as individuals whom we value and who can contribute in various ways, and (2) not all peoples in the world require conformity to their society's normative gender roles, so there is no reason to think our intolerance is universal and, therefore, inevitable. These two lessons are well worth pondering.

Still, some anthropologists today think this view disparages gender-crossed individuals because it assumes they cannot live up to the expectations of their "real" sex, so they are allowed to alter their sex. Furthermore, the view assumes that, in all cultures, people classify individuals as belonging to one of only two genders (female and male), so that a woman who doesn't want to be completely a woman must become partly like a man, and vice versa.

Many peoples recognize more than two gender identities by culturally constructing **multiple gender identities**. To the extent that gender can be culturally constructed, there is no necessary reason to assume that people will define only two genders. Some people define a third or even a fourth gender of man-woman or woman-man (or "not woman-not man" or "half man-half woman," as some indigenous terms often translate). These third- or fourth-gender identities go beyond Euro-American definitions of homoeroticism, transvestism, transgendered, or other concepts familiar in the Western cultural tradition.

multiple gender identities Definitions of sexual identities beyond the female and male duality, including third and fourth genders such as man-woman or woman-man.

Multiple gender identities are well documented for many Native American peoples. In his 1998 book *Changing Ones*, Will Roscoe reports that more than 150 Native American cultures recognized multiple gender identities for males, or females, or both sexes. Males adopted the dress, tasks, family roles, or other aspects of womanhood. Females took on activities usually associated with manhood such as warfare or hunting. By doing so, they took on alternative third or fourth gender identities. Far from being ridiculed, ostracized, despised, or otherwise socially stigmatized, such individuals in most cases were treated with respect and valued for their contributions to their families or group.

Native American tribes had their own word for such roles in their language, but gender identities varied so much from people to people that applying a single English word is problematic. The preferred modern term is *Two Spirits*, derived from a Siouan language phrase referring to persons who had both female and male spirits. We use Two Spirits here, along with man-woman, woman-man, or third- or fourth-gender identity, depending on context.

Among the Navajo of the Southwest, for example, families and local communities generally welcomed third-gender persons. An anthropologist in the 1930s quoted a Navajo elder:

> If there were no *nadle* [men-women], the country would change. They are responsible for all the wealth in the country. If there were no more left, the horses, sheep, and Navaho would all go. They are leaders just like President Roosevelt.

> (quoted in Roscoe, 2000, p. 43)

The elder surely exaggerated, but his statement indicates the Navajo's recognition of the contributions of men-women. They often managed their family's property, supervised work, and became medicine men or took on other ritual responsibilities. On the other hand, we should assume that Navajo (like other people) vary in their opinions, so there was unlikely to have been unanimous approval or tolerance of *nadle*.

People born with female genitals could adopt alternative roles as well, which also were valued in many Native American communities. A Crow family adopted a girl who came to be known as Woman Chief during the nineteenth century. Like boys, she hunted deer and bighorn sheep while growing up. When the man who raised her was killed, she took responsibility for the family, acting as both father and mother. Later in life, she helped save her camp from an attack by the Blackfoot and went on horse-raiding parties. Eventually, Woman Chief took four wives and participated in council deliberations in her band, a role usually reserved for men.

As you might expect, most early Euro-American observers of Two Spirits misunderstood these individuals and their roles in society. They overemphasized the sexual orientation of these persons, whereas in fact their sexual behavior varied from tribe to tribe and from individual to individual within the same tribe. In most cases, even when Two Spirits had homosexual orientations, sexual behavior was not the aspect of the role that was considered overwhelmingly important by the people themselves. Furthermore, Two Spirits rarely engaged in homosexual activity with *each other*. Where homosexuality was an aspect of the role, the people with whom relations occurred often were not considered homosexuals.

A more accurate portrayal of third and fourth genders defines the roles as multidimensional, thus recognizing that practices varied not only from tribe to tribe, but also from individual to individual within the same tribe. Nonetheless, certain patterns are apparent. Serena Nanda identifies several features of gender variants that were widespread (not universal) among Native American peoples. Here are four of the main characteristics:

▪ *Cross-gender occupation or work activities:* A preference for the work of the opposite sex and/or for work set aside for their third- or fourth-gender identity

▪ *Transvestism:* In most cultures, a dress style different from the style of men and women—most commonly cross-dressing but sometimes a combination of female and male garments

▪ *Associations with spiritual powers:* Granting of special powers derived from spiritual forces, often combined with a personal experience interpreted by the group as a calling

▪ *Same-sex relationships:* The formation of sexual and emotional bonds with members of the same sex, who were not themselves men-women or women-men

These four widespread characteristics of third-and fourth-gender identities provide a convenient way to organize our discussion, but the variability of the role must always be kept in mind. No single dimension is typical.

Cross-Gender Occupation or Work Activities

Adopting the work roles of the opposite sex was a widespread feature of Two Spirits. This aspect often received special attention in various Native American communities. Probably more than any other single dimension, occupation/work best defines the role.

A famous Navajo *nadleehi* who died in the 1930s was unusually skilled in weaving blankets, a typically female task. In many tribes, individuals who performed the tasks of the opposite sex often excelled at the work, in the opinions of their communities. Sioux Two Spirits (called *winkte*) dressed like women and lived in their own tepees at the edges of camps. The quill and beadwork of a *winkte* were often highly valued because of their fine quality.

Among the matrilineal, matrilocal Zuni of the American Southwest, a *lhamana* (man-woman) was looked upon favorably by the women of his family because he stayed with the household of his birth rather than leaving upon marriage. Matilda Coxe Stevenson, a nineteenth-century ethnographer, wrote that Zuni *lhamana* would do almost double the work of a woman because they were not burdened by childbirth or the heaviest duties of child care. In spite of such examples, to say that all gender variants exhibited "sex role reversal" in work performance is simplistic; the most famous Zuni man-woman was We'wha, who participated in both female and male tasks.

Commonly, a child who showed an inclination for the work of the opposite sex was considered by others to be chosen or suited for an alternative gender role. For example, girls who acted as though they wanted to go hunting or use weapons were seen as potential women-men. A Mojave adult told a 1930s ethnographer that adults "may insist on giving the child the toys and garments of its true sex, but the child will throw them away" (Roscoe, 1991, p. 139). A child could not control such behavior, in the Mojave view, for the kinds of dreams a child had affected whether the child would become a man, a woman, a man-woman, or a woman-man.

Among the Zuni, as children grow up, they experience several rites of passage that initiate them into ceremonial groups and instruct them in the ceremonial and work duties appropriate for their sex. While a child, one Zuni man-woman underwent the first male initiation ceremony but not the second, making him an "unfinished male" (Roscoe, 1991, p. 144), who could participate in some male activities but not others, such as warfare and hunting.

Transvestism

Wearing the clothing of the opposite sex was especially common and culturally significant among the tribes of the Great Plains, including the Arapaho, Ankara, Blackfoot, Cheyenne, Crow, Gros Ventre, Hidatsa, Iowa, Kansa, Mandan, Omaha, Osage, Oto, Pawnee, Ponca, and speakers of the Siouan language. Although common, transvestism was not found in all cultures with gender crossing. Sometimes men-women dressed like men, sometimes like women, and sometimes their choice of clothing depended on the situation. Among the Navajo, some *nadleehi* (men-women) wore women's clothing; others did not or only sometimes did so. Woman Chief, the adopted Crow woman, did not wear men's clothes, although she adopted many other aspects of the male role.

After whites began settling the West, most regarded men-women (whom many simplistically categorized as "sodomites") as disgusting or sinful. Because it was a visible manifestation of the Two Spirit role, transvestism was especially abhorrent to Euro-American government officials, missionaries, educators, and settlers. Due to formal punishments and white ridicule, this symbol of alternative gender identity had largely disappeared by the early twentieth century.

Associations with Spiritual Powers

Usually, communities perceived Two Spirits as having some sort of unusual powers or abilities derived from spiritual sources. The Cheyenne of the Great Plains used a term that translates "half man-half woman." These people served as masters of ceremony for the important Scalp Dance that followed a successful raid by a war party. They also possessed powerful love medicines, so young men and women sought their services to attract heterosexual partners. Lakota believed that *winkte* could predict future events and bestow lucky names on children. Osh-Tisch (whose name translates as "Finds Them and Kills Them"), of the Crow people, had a vision as a youth and became a powerful medicine person. One Navajo man-woman memorized numerous curing chants and learned to construct dozens of the intricate sand paintings used in curing rituals (see Chapter 14). He was widely credited with near-miraculous healing powers.

Same-Sex Relationships

The sexual orientation of Two Spirits varied from people to people, as well as from person to person within a single tribe. Understandably, reliable information on the sexual orientation of third- and fourth-gendered persons is rare. Some seem to have refrained from sex. But the most common pattern was for men-women to be sexually active with men and sometimes women, but not with other men-women. These relations (most Euro-Americans or Canadians would culturally categorize them as "homosexual relations") in most cases were an expected aspect of the role. Thus, a (genitally) male Two Spirits would engage in sex with men of his group, without stigma or punishment for either party. The man would not be considered homosexual because he had not had relations with *another man* but with a *man-woman*. In some tribes, a man would take a man-woman as a second wife—again apparently without stigma.

Even less is known about the sexual practices of women-men, and often early observers just stated that they were women who avoided marriage or refused to marry. It appears, though, that they most commonly had relations with females. The complications of characterizing a person's sexual orientation are shown by a Mojave woman-man who had three wives (sequentially). All three eventually left her, and later in life, the woman-man became active sexually with men.

As a result of contact with Euro-Americans, Two Spirit identities were suppressed in most regions where Native Americans still lived, especially after the confinement of so many Native Americans on reservations in the 1800s. The majority of whites—settlers, traders, government agents, missionaries, and others—found the existence of a *legitimate* role such as man-woman or woman-man abhorrent. Because most viewed the custom as sinful, as harmful to Indian character, or as an obstacle to assimilation into Euro-American society, they often imposed legal or social punishments for third and fourth genders. For example, in the 1920s, large numbers of Indian children were taken away from their families and communities—by force, when necessary—and placed in on- or off-reservation government-run boarding schools. In these Indian Schools (as they are known today), the explicit goal was to socialize and educate Indian children into Euro-American culture. By separating Native American children from their families and traditions, the theory was, they could be more quickly and thoroughly assimilated into white society. Of course, at Indian Schools young people who showed signs of assuming alternative gender identities were punished.

Through such educational and legal mechanisms, multiple gender identities were suppressed. Even some tribes that had once accepted third and fourth genders came to reject such persons. For instance, in the 1940s, some Winnebago told an ethnographer that "the [Two Spirit] was at one time a highly honored and respected person, but that the Winnebago had become ashamed of the custom because the white people thought it was amusing or evil" (quoted in Roscoe, 1991, p. 201).

Hijra of Hindu India

With 1.2 billion people and dozens of languages and ethnicities, India is one of the world's most diverse countries. Hinduism, the predominant religion, believes in the existence of multiple gods, many of whom are androgynous (having both female and male characteristics). Many Hindu sects are devoted to the worship of specific deities, such as Rama, Vishnu, and Shiva.

In the Hindu parts of India, there is a category of persons called *hijra*. Most are people born with male genitalia who have chosen to undergo an operation that removes their testicles and penis. The operation is a rite of passage that transforms them into "neither man nor woman," in the phrase of ethnographer Serena Nanda. *Hijra* thus are members of a culturally constructed third gender.

Hijra form communities in urban areas of India, especially in the north. In part, these are religious communities, for they worship Bahuchara Mata, one of the avatars of the Hindu Mother Goddess. *Hijra* also identify with Krishna and Shiva, two other deities with anomalous genders. Because of their status as a third gender and their identification with these gods, other Hindus view *hijra* as spiritually powerful, able to bless people and events.

In the neighborhoods where they live, these spiritual powers lead Hindu families to call on *hijra* to perform various services. They dance at temple festivals and perform at life crisis ceremonies, such as childbirth and weddings. After a child is born, *hijra* dance and sing to bless the baby. After a wedding ceremony, *hijra* are called in to pray, sing, and dance to ensure that the couple will be prosperous and bear sons. The families pay them for these ritual services. *Hijra* also are potentially dangerous because of their ability to issue powerful curses. *Hijra* do not discourage this belief, for it helps them if they have problems collecting their fees.

The majority of *hijra* are born with male genitals. The rite of passage that emasculates them is translated as "rebirth," for it is viewed as transforming the person from an "ordinary, impotent male" (Nanda, 1999, p. 26) into the *hijra* identity. Emasculation is culturally interpreted as a religious obligation of a would-be *hijra*, for sacrificing one's genitals shows dedication and sincerity of intent. It is witnessed by other *hijra* and makes it difficult for "fake *hijras*" (Nanda, 1999, p. 37) to join the community just so they can take advantage of the opportunity to receive payment for ritual services.

After the surgery, which is surrounded by lengthy ceremonies and taboos, feminine pronouns (*she, her*) are usually applied to the person. Most of the time, *hijra* dress as females and assume female gestures, postures, gaits, and hairstyles, even when not working in ceremonies.

Becoming a *hijra* provides security—both social and economic—for persons whose lives might otherwise be difficult. *Hijra* residents of a town or city form households with people like themselves, although many maintain relationships with the families they were born into. Many people refer to one another using fictive kinship terms (see Chapter 9) like "sister" and "granny." There is a well-developed social system, including a hierarchy, but most *hijra* eventually rise to the top of the hierarchy. The health and old-age needs generally are managed.

Economically, *hijra* occupy a legitimate niche in Hindu society, which provides them with some economic security. The leaders of a *hijra* community in a particular neighborhood constantly investigate whether Hindu families are about to give birth or have a wedding. When a family is identified, the group marks their distinctive sign on the house with chalk as a signal that no other *hijra* house should show up for the birth or wedding ceremony. *Hijra* perform in groups of three to five or more persons—singing, dancing, drumming, and clowning, often with sexually suggestive themes and movements. Payment is in money and items like rice, candy, and clothing. Typically, *hijra* are dissatisfied with the amounts and may threaten to curse or shame the families. In addition to ritual performances, some *hijra* make their living by acting as prostitutes and live in "houses" of a different kind. Others go out begging for alms.

It is uncertain whether most male and female Hindus accept *hijra* as a legitimate and nonstigmatized third-gender category. Serena Nanda, who worked extensively with *hijra*, seems to think other Hindus view their gender identity with ambivalence. Certainly, Hindus hold diverse opinions about them. Nonetheless, the wider society allows them to live in their midst and provides payment for their ceremonial performances.

Changes in Gender Identity Attitudes and Language

Native American Two Spirits and Indian *hijra* show that attitudes of intolerance, anxiety, fear, and even hatred of transgendered people and other gender identities are not universal among humanity. Realize, though, that there are many peoples whose attitudes toward homoeroticism and multiple genders are highly negative. Acceptance and institutionalization vary among cultures, and many peoples stigmatize gender identities other than female and male. Nonetheless, knowing that lots of cultures accept alternative gender roles is relevant for attitudes in twenty-first-century societies.

When your authors (and the grandparents of most readers) were in high school in the 1960s and 1970s, few of us knew about multiple gender identities. There were males, females, and others—although most of us had only a couple of terms for the Others, depending on whether their gender assignment at birth were male ("queer") or female ("dyke"). If any of our male friends were gay or any of our female friends were lesbian, certainly we would have recognized them as such. Their sexual preferences would have been apparent in their behavior, or so we thought. Guys would have exhibited "feminine" mannerisms and speech. Girls would have had deep voices or broad shoulders or "manly" personalities. Of course, for the most part our ideas were mistaken, as we learned when we met up with some friends a decade or two after graduation and were surprised to learn their actual gender identities. More recently, surely people who still carried old attitudes and beliefs were startled when Olympic gold-medalist Bruce Jenner became Caitlyn Jenner.

Historically, in the United States any sexual act other than male–female intercourse was illegal. In some states, premarital sex was outlawed. Sodomy laws existed in some states into the 1990s, although almost never enforced. In 1969, police raided Stonewall, a gay bar in New York City. Police arrested patrons and assaulted some of them. The riots that ensued, known today as the Stonewall riots, are now viewed as the beginning of the struggle for civil rights for the lesbian and gay communities. However, single events alone do not create movements unless there are preexisting conditions and discontent that lead to social action, as the Black Lives Matter movement illustrates.

In contemporary North America, European nations, and many other regions, nonbinary gender identities have become more open and increasingly accepted normatively and legally. The acronym LGBT now is widely known, and LGBTQIA—lesbian, gay, bisexual, transgender, queer, intersexual, and asexual—is familiar to many older people as well as millennials.

Although practically everyone knows the word *heterosexual,* and it suffices as a purely descriptive term, *cisgender* (often abbreviated to *cis*) recently has come into use. It refers to people whose personal gender identity matches their biological sex—the one that appears on their birth certificate. Why begin using a term that most people have never heard before when one that almost everyone is familiar with already exists? Mainly because *cisgender* acknowledges that heterosexuals also have a gender identity, like LGBTQIA persons.

Many think this proliferation of gender labels results from political correctness, just as many felt (or still feel) about terms like *African American* and *Native American.* Proliferation of gender labels also is associated with identity politics, meaning that those adopting the label want others to acknowledge their gender identity, which (perhaps) connotes acceptance.

There is some validity to these points, but there is more to gender labels. Remember that gender identities other than female and male formerly were far more widely stigmatized than today. Male "homosexuals" commonly were called "queer"—the same term that now has legitimacy among LGBTQIA persons. As more people have openly acknowledged their gender identity, more such identities are publicly known, so why should they not have special terms? As you may recall from Chapter 3, such terms are another example of language reflecting larger cultural changes. Labels proliferate as culturally recognized gender identities do—but remember that "recognized" does not necessarily mean "acceptance."

In addition to labels referring to gender identity, more millennials are giving *gender-neutral* (unisex) names to babies, according to an August 2016 story in the *New York Times.* A particular name is considered gender neutral if less than 65 percent of infants of either sex have the name. Among such names are Hayden, Emerson, Rowan, Finley, River, Phoenix, Royal, Casey, and Tatum—all frequently given to both girl and boy infants.

The baby-naming website Nameberry.com reports that the popular trend for 2016 is the increased use of more gender-neutral names on birth certificates. Scrolling across the top of the website is a list of names that users are currently searching, and unisex names have a specific listing on the site. Like unisex clothing and unisex colors, the increase in gender-neutral names is a linguistic sign of the times. However, the *Times* reports that only 1.7 percent of the 3.9 million babies born in 2015 received unisex names. Perhaps this means that times have not changed all *that* much. Or perhaps it means only that new parents fear reactions from their own parents and family members, or that they worry that their kids will be teased when they enter school.

The Gendered Division of Labor

The **gendered division of labor** (also called the **sexual division of labor**) refers to the patterned ways productive and other economic tasks are divided between women and men. Each gender has access to the products and/or services produced by the other, making the tasks of males and females, to some extent, complementary. This is one of the major dimensions of a people's gender (or sex) roles—the rights, duties, and expectations one acquires by virtue of one's membership in a gender category.

We must correct one misconception about this topic immediately: that it is only natural for men to be the breadwinners for their family. Hundreds of field studies provide all the data needed to discredit this

gendered division of labor (sexual division of labor) Kinds of productive activities and tasks assigned to women versus men in a culture.

idea. Breadwinning—broadly, producing the food and other material needs and wants of domestic groups—is definitely not an activity of men exclusively, or even largely. In many societies, men produce most of the food, but in others women's contribution to daily subsistence equals or exceeds that of men (see Chapter 7).

This finding contradicts the opinion of those who think that patriarchy is rooted in the "fact" that men's work is more important to physical survival and material well-being than women's work. Those who hold this view argue that women are usually economically dependent on men, which in turn makes women socially subordinate to men. But where patriarchy exists, it is not because the tasks men do are somehow more important to family and group survival than women's tasks. This ethnocentric idea probably comes from the way most modern industrial economies worked in the mid–twentieth century: By and large, men earned the money that allowed their families to purchase the goods they needed to survive. It is falsely concluded that the same economic dependence of wives on husbands characterized human prehistory and history.

Besides, who can say whether male or female activities, taken in their totality, are more or less important?

Bearing and nursing children seem pretty significant. Often, if a task is performed by males, it is *symbolically* considered more important, but whether it is *objectively* more important is ambiguous.

These are the anthropologist's usual warnings about confusing the beliefs and practices of one's own cultural experience with those of all humans. Most people's ideas about what is and is not natural for humans to think and do are products of a specific culture at a particular time. Unless we become educated about the cultural diversity of humanity, we consistently—and usually mistakenly—conclude that the ideas and practices of our own society are universal or are a product of human nature.

So, Man the Breadwinner and Woman the Homemaker do not accurately describe the gendered division of labor. Humanity is too diverse for that. Despite cultural variations, however, there are cross-cultural regularities and patterns in the gendered division of labor. What are the main patterns, and can they be explained?

Understanding Major Patterns

Table 11.1 summarizes a vast amount of comparative work on the gendered division of labor. The specific

TABLE 11.1 Patterns in the Gendered Division of Labor

	TASKS THAT ARE PERFORMED BY				
General Category of Activity	**Exclusively Males**	**Predominantly Males**	**Either or Both Genders**	**Predominantly Females**	
Extracting Food and Other Products	Hunting Trapping	Fishing	Gathering small land animals	Gathering shellfish, mollusks	Gathering wild plant foods
		Clearing land Preparing soil	Planting crops Tending crops Harvesting crops		
		Tending large animals	Milking animals	Caring for small animals	
	Woodworking Mining Lumbering			Gathering fuel Fetching water	Fetching water
Manufacturing, Processing, and Preparing Goods for Consumption	Butchering				Processing, preparing plant foods Cooking
	Boat building Working with stone, horn, bone, shell Smelting ore Metalworking	House building Making rope, cordage, nets	Preparing skins Making leather products	Making clothing Matmaking Loom weaving Making pottery	

Source: Adapted from Murdock and Provost (1973).

tasks toward the left of the table are more likely to be performed by males; those to the right are more likely to be done by females. The nearer a task is to the left, the more likely it is to be performed by males, and vice versa.

A few comments are needed to clarify the table. First, it does not portray the division of labor among any specific people. Rather, it represents a composite of information drawn from hundreds of societies in various parts of the world. For example, the tasks listed in the column "Predominantly Females" should be interpreted as those done by women in most societies; however, among a particular people, men perform one or another of these tasks. Tasks listed in the column "Exclusively Males" are those carried out by men in all or nearly all societies, with few exceptions.

Also, the table includes only those activities that produce some kind of material product. Omitted are other activities that are predominantly or exclusively male, such as holding political office and fighting in wars. Also absent are some activities, such as caring for infants, that are predominantly or exclusively women's work in all cultures. Our discussion is limited to activities usually considered economic tasks.

Table 11.1 reveals two patterns. First, all human groups divide *some* kinds of labor by gender in similar ways. That is, some tasks are done mainly or nearly exclusively by one gender in most societies. For instance, hunting, clearing land, preparing the soil, working with hard materials, and cutting wood are exclusively or predominantly men's work in the great majority of societies. Gathering wild plants, processing plant foods, and cooking are mainly the work of females in most cultures. In short, although the table shows that groups vary in the kinds of tasks allocated to women and men, there are *widespread* (although not *universal*) patterns; consistently, some tasks are more likely to be done by men, others by women. The first question is, Why are some tasks done mostly by women, whereas others are done mainly or entirely by men?

The second pattern concerns the tasks in the column headed "Either or Both Genders." These tasks are about equally likely to be performed by men or women, depending on the particular society. Members of either gender may do them, or both may work cooperatively on them. For example, whether men or women plant, tend and harvest crops, milk animals, or work with skins or leather varies from people to people, with no clear pattern apparent. These tasks are so variable cross-culturally that we cannot generalize; whether they are done by women, men, or both depends largely on local circumstances. Our second question is, What determines the cross-cultural variability in the division of labor by gender? Why are women more heavily involved

in agriculture (planting, tending, and harvesting crops) in some societies than in others, for example?

This section focuses on hypotheses that deal with the first question. The next section discusses some reasons for variation.

Why are some tasks nearly always done by men, whereas others are performed by women in most cultures? Biological/physical differences between the sexes—such as sexual dimorphism—provide one possible explanation. Perhaps tasks are assigned in such a way that the members of each gender do what they are physically able to do best.

This possibility seems like biological determinism. If understood properly, though, it is not. Physical differences between men and women are only *relevant* in explaining the sexual division, not *determinative*. To say that physical differences are relevant is to say the following: Because of biological differences, men can perform certain kinds of tasks more effectively than women, and vice versa, and these differences are reflected in widespread cross-cultural similarities in the sexual division of labor.

Consider an example. Anthropologists used to say that men everywhere did one task: hunting. Hunting seems to require certain biological capabilities—such as speed, strength, and endurance—that give men an advantage over women. Furthermore, hunting also was thought to be incompatible with certain responsibilities universally borne by women for biological reasons: pregnancy, lactation (breastfeeding), and child care. Pregnant women would have a hard time chasing game. Lactating mothers would have to quit the hunt several times a day to nurse their infants. Because men could hunt more effectively than women, in foraging populations men hunted. In contrast, gathering required less strength and endurance. Because men had to spend so much of their time hunting, which women couldn't do as efficiently, gathering is largely women's work.

These arguments are partly valid, but female and male biological differences do not make it physically mandatory that males are the hunters and females are the gatherers in foraging populations. For one thing, not all kinds of hunting—and not all tasks connected to hunting—require superior strength, speed, and endurance. For another, there are questions about whether males typically have more endurance than females. Finally, there is no necessary biological reason a woman could not give up hunting only during her pregnancy and lactation and leave her older children in camp under the care of someone else.

At any rate, it is just not true that hunting is *universally* a male activity. When BaMbuti Pygmies of the

Fertility Maintenance	Strenuous, prolonged physical exercise by women leads to lowered body fat and hormonal changes that reduce female fertility, so most strenuous tasks are done by men.
Reproductive Roles	Populations need relatively few adult men to sustain numbers, so societies protect women by assigning most hazardous tasks to men.
Physical Strength	Most men are stronger than most women, so tasks requiring greater strength generally are performed by men.
Child-Care Compatibility	Women are universally bearers and primary caregivers of young children, so women tend to perform those tasks that can be combined most effectively with child care.

Democratic Republic of the Congo rain forest hunt animals with nets, women help by driving game into the nets held by men. In another part of the world, Agnes Estioko-Griffin describes hunting by women among the Agta, a mountain tribe of the Philippines who live on the island of Luzon. Agta men do most of the hunting, but women often accompany them in teamwork efforts, and women frequently hunt together without the company of men. Interestingly, sometimes women take their infants with them on the hunt, carrying the children on their backs. People like the Agta and BaMbuti show that the "man the hunter" image is oversimplified.

But such cases do not make the image entirely wrong. The great majority of peoples in which hunting is a significant means of acquiring food are foragers or horticulturalists. In most foraging cultures, women do most wild plant gathering. Men also contribute plant foods among most foragers, which makes images of "woman the gatherer" also oversimplified. For horticultural peoples, the *pattern* is for women to do most of the planting, weeding, and harvesting of cultivated plants, whereas men hunt to provide meat. These patterns are not *universal* but are *widespread* enough that many anthropologists believe there must be some physical differences between men and women that are relevant in explaining them.

What specific female and male biological differences are likely to be most relevant in explaining similarities? Anthropologists have proposed four main arguments, which are summarized in the Concept Review: (1) the possibility that regular heavy exercise depresses female fertility, (2) the fact that women and men have different roles in reproducing the population, (3) the relative overall strength of the two sexes, and (4) the biological fact that only women give birth to and nurse infants and young children. We discuss each factor, although the first two do not seem very plausible in our view.

Fertility Maintenance

One potentially relevant physical characteristic is that heavy exercise can reduce a woman's fertility. Modern female athletes—especially swimmers and long-distance runners—often do not menstruate or ovulate monthly. This is because of a combination of a low body fat ratio and hormonal changes in women who engage in prolonged physical exercise. Some anthropologists suggest that work activities requiring heavy exertion would reduce women's fertility. For example, hunting often requires wielding weapons such as bows and spears that are powered by muscle energy, locating and tracking prey, and running down animals once they are shot. Lumbering and clearing land for planting also involve physical exertion such as swinging heavy axes for hours at a time. Conceivably, female fertility would be so decreased by such strenuous activities that the population would not be sustained over the course of many generations.

However, hunting among most foragers and horticulturalists is not as strenuous as portrayed, nor are many other activities that are exclusively or largely done by men. In fact, women commonly do many tasks just as physically demanding as those done by men, such as hauling water, gathering firewood for fuel, and planting and harvesting crops. Although fertility maintenance could be relevant among a few peoples, it is unlikely to be a widespread factor and certainly does not account for the widespread patterns in the division of labor by gender.

Reproductive Roles

Another possibility arises from the fact that fewer men than women are biologically necessary to maintain population size. A man produces enough sperm to father many thousands of children (theoretically),

As these Mexican women making corn tortillas illustrate, processing foods once they are harvested is a female task in most cultures.

whereas a woman can bear a child only every year or so. Because only a few sexually active men can impregnate a large number of women, the size of the population seemingly depends more on the number of women than the number of men. Also, in all known societies, women are far more involved than men in the care of infants and young children.

For these reasons, the argument is that fewer males than females are needed to sustain a population. For the gendered division of labor, this difference in reproductive roles might imply that men are more expendable, which helps explain why so many hazardous roles (like hunting and fighting battles) are male roles: The group can afford to sacrifice some of its men but must protect its women as much as possible. If men "must" perform such dangerous roles, then many other tasks are left to women by default.

However, men are expendable only theoretically, and if all else is equal. In those societies—and there are a great many of them—in which warfare is a serious threat, large numbers of men are needed to protect the entire group. In fact, among many peoples, group survival itself depends on the ability to mobilize many warriors and to make political/military alliances with friendly neighbors. Only in their reproductive role are men expendable; in other respects, large numbers of men are essential for group survival. *If* there is a biological explanation for men performing more hazardous activities, it is not because a group finds many of its men to be expendable.

Relative Strength

Another biological factor is the average difference in physical strength between men and women, which allows men to perform tasks requiring great strength more efficiently. In Table 11.1, superior average male strength is *relevant*—once again, it is not all-important—in many tasks under the heading "Exclusively Males" and in some of the tasks labeled "Predominantly Males," such as clearing land and preparing soil.

On the other hand, strength has no obvious relationship to other "Exclusively" or "Predominantly" male tasks, such as trapping, butchering, and working with fibers. Note again that some female tasks also require significant

Despite cultural diversity in the gendered division of labor, widespread patterns exist. For example, men are more likely than women to construct substantial buildings. These Micronesian men are installing the roof on a structure to be used as a cookhouse.

strength, like gathering fuel, fetching water, and even processing food, often using heavy stone pounders or grinders. Relative strength does influence patterns in the sexual division of labor, but other factors also matter.

Compatibility with Child Care

A fourth biologically based difference is that in all cultures women are the bearers, nursers, and primary caregivers of infants and young children. This reproductive fact means that women are most likely to perform those tasks that can be combined with pregnancy and child care. Back in 1970, Judith Brown argued that such tasks have four characteristics:

▌ They are fairly routine and repetitive and do not require a lot of concentration; attention can be diverted with minimal effects on task performance.

▌ They can be interrupted and resumed without significantly lowering their efficient performance.

▌ They do not place the children who accompany their mothers to the site of the task in potential danger; female tasks do not usually risk the welfare of children.

▌ They do not require women and children to travel very far away from home.

The gathering of various products and the domestic work listed in Table 11.1 are highly compatible with child care. In addition, among horticultural peoples, women usually perform garden tasks (such as planting, weeding, and tending crops) and harvesting; these activities, too, generally are relatively compatible with caring for children. Notice that child-care compatibility is most likely an important factor among peoples with high fertility. Of course, for societies in which most couples have few children, this factor becomes less relevant as a basis for allocating productive work.

In sum, biological factors help explain cross-cultural patterns in the division of labor by gender. Gendered differences in strength and child-care roles have the most widespread relevance, although the other two factors might matter among specific peoples.

Notice, though, that even if all four factors in combination totally explain the widespread patterns shown in Table 11.1 (which they do not), none of them can explain the *differences*. In fact, no biological difference between males and females alone can explain the diversity in the sexual division of labor. Biological differences in strength, reproductive physiology, and ability to care for infants are roughly constant in all human

Chris Hellier/Getty Images

Whether or not a task is compatible with caring for young children seems to be an important influence on the gendered division of labor. This woman from the Malagasy Republic is looking after her baby and harvesting rice at the same time.

populations. But a condition that is constant in all groups cannot, by itself, account for things that vary between the groups. Constants cannot explain variability and diversity. We need other hypotheses to account for the cross-cultural variations in the gendered division of labor.

Understanding Variability

Here we discuss only one of the most important variations—that among horticulturalists. Among horticultural peoples, much—and in some societies nearly all—of the everyday garden work is done by women. For example, in traditional cultures in parts of the Pacific, the Amazon Basin, and tropical Africa, women do most of the planting, weeding, tending, and harvesting of crops. Men participate in farming by clearing new land and preparing the plots or fields for planting. In contrast, among peoples who rely more heavily on intensive agriculture, women's actual work in the fields and direct contribution to the food supply are less important. To phrase the general relationship in a few

words: Women are more likely to be involved *directly* in food production in horticultural than in intensive agricultural communities. This difference in the type of farming helps explain variations in the agricultural tasks labeled "Either or Both Genders" in the middle column of Table 11.1.

There are several reasons for this general pattern. First, in the New World, horticultural Native Americans had few or no domesticated animals (see Chapter 7), so men's contribution to the food supply usually focused on hunting. Most routine garden work fell to women because such work is generally compatible with pregnancy and child care. In contrast, most intensive agriculturalists relied on livestock for meat, dairy products, hides, wool, and other products derived from animals. So, men spent relatively little time hunting and so had more time for farming.

Also, prior to the twentieth century, in Europe and Asia nearly all intensive agriculturalists used the animal-powered plow to turn the earth prior to planting. Some researchers have suggested that most women are not strong enough to perform the heavy work of

256   **PART III**   The Diversity of Culture

plowing efficiently. You might remember, though, that draft animals provide most of the muscle power for plow agriculture, which makes this suggestion difficult to evaluate. Also note that men are stronger than women only on average.

There is another reason women are less involved in direct cultivation in intensive agricultural societies. In Europe and Asia (Eurasia), the horticultural and intensive agricultural adaptations tend to involve the farming of different kinds of crops. Roughly half of horticultural societies grow *root crops* like yams, sweet potatoes, manioc (cassava), or taro. In contrast, about 90 percent of intensive agriculturalists rely on *cereal crops* like rice, wheat, corn, barley, and millet.

Why would this matter? Root crops can be stored in the ground for variable periods after they first become ready to eat, so they typically are harvested continuously during the growing season (think of familiar root crops like carrots or potatoes, which gardeners pull or dig up as needed). Either daily or a few times weekly, a woman goes to the garden and returns with root crops for herself, her children, and her husband. In contrast, cereals (which are the seeds of annual plants) tend to ripen at about the same time each year, usually near the end of the growing season. They have to be harvested in a short period of time, dried and processed, and stored for the rest of the year.

How does the type of crop affect the work of men and women? Cereal crops—grains—generally require a lot of labor to process (e.g., seed drying and grinding) before cooking. Plant processing is women's work in most cultures (Table 11.1). Also, people who rely on wheat, rice, barley, or other cereal grains usually face periods of intense labor requirements. At the beginning of the growing season and at harvest time, there is a need for laborers who can do a lot of heavy work in a short period that is best not interrupted by other tasks. Men generally do such work (see the preceding section). In contrast, root-growing horticultural peoples tend to spread cultivation tasks out more evenly over the entire year, making gardening a day-in, day-out, repetitive task that requires less strength and that is more compatible with child care.

A third reason is warfare. Where war was frequent and serious, men in horticultural communities defended the local village, neighborhood, or kin group from enemies. In regions such as highland New Guinea and parts of the Amazon, group survival depended on the ability to defend land and resources from attack. Community welfare often was improved by taking over the land of enemy neighbors, so offensive as well as defensive warfare was common. Men were not actually

fighting their enemies most of the time, of course, but maintaining community defenses and guarding against surprise raids did require significant amounts of (predominantly male) time.

Further, for most peoples, making alliances with other groups improved the odds of success in warfare. Forming and maintaining alliances required a lot of politicking, mutual visiting, and exchanges, requiring substantial male time and energy, as the Maring (covered in Chapter 8) illustrate. Also, male solidarity (male bonding) was useful in enhancing cooperation in fighting, so in many groups where warfare was prevalent, there were elaborate male-only rituals or social events that strengthened ties between men and helped socialize boys into manhood and the warrior role. All these pressures related to defensive and offensive warfare led men to concentrate much of their time and resources in fighting, preparing to fight, or maintaining the political relationships needed for success in organized fights. Routine garden tasks were left to women, partly by default.

In sum, comparative research shows that women usually spend less time in direct food production among intensive agricultural than among horticultural peoples. Here are three of the most important factors that influence female involvement in cultivation tasks:

- Among horticultural peoples, men spend more time hunting than they do in intensive agricultural societies, so horticultural men have less time available for cultivating crops.

- Compared to horticultural communities, intensive agriculturalists tend to grow cereal crops, making it more likely that women spend more time on domestic work, including processing foods before cooking and storing.

- Horticultural peoples tend to be subjected to pressure from hostile neighbors, so men are busier fighting, guarding, politicking, exchanging, and creating bonds and relationships with other men.

In brief, as agricultural systems become more intensive, other factors change that usually lead to reduced women's involvement in direct food production.

It is important to emphasize that these relationships are *generalized*, meaning that they may not hold for any particular people. Horticultural peoples "tend to" be more affected by warfare pressures, intensive agriculturalists are "more likely to" grow cereals than roots, and so forth. Obviously, there are many exceptions to the general patterns.

Consider the Kofyar of Nigeria, for example. They construct terraces on hillsides, spread goat manure over their fields, use compost, and practice other methods of increasing yields that lead anthropologists who observe them to call their farming "intensive." Yet quantitative studies in the 1990s reveal that Kofyar women work about as much as men in agriculture. The Kofyar and many other peoples do not have the relationship between cultivation intensity and male labor that comparative research says they "ought to have" or "predicts they will have."

The Kofyar and other exceptions to the general pattern illustrate two other points. First, the existence of a general relationship established by comparative research does not tell us what any particular group of people is doing or thinking. The culture of any people is a product of the complex interaction of history, adaptation, beliefs, and other factors. In any particular group, factors *unique* to that group may be more important than factors that are generally important. So, the fact that Kofyar women work the land about as much as men does not disprove the general pattern that women's labor becomes less important as agriculture becomes more intensive.

Second, the existence of exceptions does not invalidate a generalization—provided, of course, that the general pattern is well established. If we are interested in the factors that influence the cultural variations in the gendered division of labor, then we must do comparative work to look for general patterns. The fact that particular cultures do not fit the pattern does not invalidate the generalization—at least not until the number of exceptions becomes large enough to make us suspicious of the existence of the general pattern.

As you realize by now, the preceding discussion is an example of the materialist theoretical approach discussed in Chapter 5. How a people acquire food (by horticulture or more intensive methods) influences the kinds of tasks women and men do (given differences in physical strength and reproductive roles). So, the material conditions of life interact with biological differences between women and men to produce the overall pattern of the division of labor along gender lines. That, at least, is the materialist argument.

gender stratification   Degree to which men and women are unequal in dimensions such as status, power, or influence; access to valued resources; eligibility for social positions; and ability to make decisions about their own lives.

Gender Stratification

A fourth main issue in the anthropological study of gender is **gender stratification** or the degree to which human groups allocate material and social rewards to women and men based on their gender. Other sources of unequal rewards include class, caste, family origins, and race (covered in other chapters). Here, we discuss only rewards based on whether one is male or female and ignore complications such as multiple gender identities.

Gender stratification is sometimes referred to as the *status of women*, which can range vaguely between relatively high and low. Whatever we call it, gender stratification is difficult to define because it includes many components that interact in complex ways. Some dimensions that are useful indicators for comparing the degree of gender stratification cross-culturally are listed in Table 11.2.

Of course, gender stratification is more complicated than this (or any) table can summarize. But the table does show some of the main features that constitute the overall pattern of gender stratification in particular cultures. It also is helpful in comparing the degree of gender stratification across cultures. Obviously, gender stratification is *multidimensional,* which makes it difficult to categorize gender stratification among any particular people as "high," "moderate," "low," or "nonexistent." Why is it so difficult?

For one thing, some dimensions are not consistent with other dimensions. Studies of family life often report that women have a great deal of control in making decisions about childrearing and about the allocation of domestic resources, even though they have little independence outside the domestic context. For instance, in two Andalusian towns of southern Spain, David Gilmore's fieldwork showed that wives have great autonomy in managing household affairs. He believes this is because many women are able to live near their own mothers, so that wives and their mothers frequently gang up on a husband. Even in male-privileged societies like traditional Korea, Japan, and China, the eldest female in a household usually managed household affairs with a fair degree of autonomy. Yet in these countries, and in many other societies, women hardly participated in public affairs, had little property entirely their own, usually had little or no choice about whom they married, and were clearly subordinate to their fathers, husbands, and husband's fathers socially and even legally.

Another complicating factor is that, in most cultures, a woman's status changes over the course of her

TABLE 11.2 Important Components of Gender Stratification

Dimension of Gender Stratification	Specific Questions for Societies
Kinds of social roles men and women perform	Are some roles limited to men or women? If so, which roles and how are they rewarded?
Value placed on contributions to groups	Are men's contributions viewed as more important—symbolically and/or practically?
Women's deference to men	Do women defer socially to husbands or male relatives? How much, and in what contexts?
Access to positions of power and influence	Do women hold offices in the political arena? Who controls household and domestic tasks?
Control over personal lives	Do women make marital, sexual, childbearing, work, and other important decisions for themselves?
General beliefs about the sexes	Are men and women viewed as equally capable intellectually and psychologically?

life. In traditional East Asia and South Asia, most families were patrilocally extended (see Chapter 9), so when women married, they left their own family and moved into or near the house of their husband's parents. A young wife was subjected to the authority of her husband's mother and was duty bound to work extremely hard. But, as a woman settled into the household, had a son, and aged, her status improved, and she gradually took over control of the household from her mother-in-law. Eventually, she became the everyday manager of the household and was an authority figure over her own daughters-in-law after her sons married. The same pattern of women's status improving with age appears in numerous other cultures.

Finally, in more complex societies like modern nations, distinctions of rank or class (considered in Chapter 13) or of ethnic affiliation (see Chapter 16) often outweigh male–female distinctions. That is, wealth and/or perceived membership in a racial or ethnic category are other bases of inequality that may be difficult to disentangle from gender stratification.

For these reasons, gender stratification has many dimensions, which are not always mutually consistent. Like other social relationships, male–female relationships are complex. This is not surprising. Concepts like gender stratification are used by contemporary social scientists. The people whose lives anthropologists study may not have this cultural concept at all. Nor are women's and men's lives in any community so simple that an anthropologist (or anyone else) can categorize them unambiguously by statements like "Women have low status in culture X," although many people continue to do so based on incomplete, misunderstood, and ethnocentric or stereotyped information.

Is Gender Stratification Universal?

In spite of complexities, there are significant variations in gender stratification. Even humanistic anthropologists who often mistrust comparisons and objective measurements recognize that there is much less gender stratification among the Native American Hopi, Zuni, Lakota, and Iroquois than among the Yanomamö or Tukano of the Amazon Basin. Gender stratification is a meaningful concept to use for answering certain questions, such as these: Are there societies in which women and men are completely equal? Do matriarchal societies actually exist?

The answer to the second question is a qualified no. The qualification is due to disagreement over the meaning of the term *matriarchy*. Logically, matriarchy should be defined as the mirror image of patriarchy: For a people to be *matriarchal*, women should enjoy all the unequal rights and receive the same kinds of rewards that men have among peoples most would agree are *patriarchal*.

However, *matriarchy* is not always used this way. Anthropologist Peggy Reeves Sanday worked among an Indonesian people, the Minangkabau, who by her definition are matriarchal. She writes, "Defining a female-oriented social order as the mirror image of a male form is like saying that women's contribution to society and culture deserves a special label only if women rule and act like men" (Sanday, 2002, p. xi). Sanday argues that this definition led early twentieth-century anthropologists to search the world for "primitive matriarchies," without success. They did not find any because of the way they defined *matriarchy*, she argues.

So, the popular definition of matriarchy as the mirror image of patriarchy is not the only way to conceptualize the concept. However, if we choose to think of matriarchy as control by females—as the mirror image of patriarchy—then despite fictional stories and the occasional adventure movie in which "Amazons" capture the hero, not a single instance of clear female domination over men has ever been found by ethnographers. Clearly, there have been individual women who hold great power, control great wealth, and are held in high esteem. Certainly, there are queens, female chiefs, and individual matriarchs of families and kin groups. But if we define matriarchy as a social system in which women have the rights and receive the material, social, and symbolic rewards that only men receive in a host of societies, then such a social system has not been documented. To be precise, the privileges granted to men in societies that most agree are patriarchal are not granted to women in any well-documented known society.

The first question—whether there are cultures in which men and women are equal—has a more complex and less certain answer. Some scholars believe that women are never considered fully equal to men. They interpret the ethnographic record as showing that gender hierarchy—inequalities based on gender—exists among all peoples.

Those who believe that male dominance/female subordination is universal point to two fairly well-established generalizations. One applies to the realm of political institutions. In political life, gender hierarchy always exists. In no known society are the primary political authority roles available only to women. But, in many societies, all women are denied the right to succeed to political office, making officeholding a male prerogative. Among most peoples, even kin-group leadership roles are monopolized by men. Male elders of a lineage or clan decide how the group's land and other resources are to be used and allocated, how the group's wealth objects are to be disposed of, whether the group is to engage in a battle to avenge a wrong, and so on. (As we shall see, however, women often do have significant influence over these matters, especially in matrilineal societies.)

The other realm of life with gender hierarchy is religion. In many societies, women are excluded from holding major religious leadership roles. To be sure, there are societies—lots of them, in fact—in which *particular rituals* are performed by and for women, as in female initiations (see Chapter 14). But in most societies females are forbidden to participate in the most important *public* rituals. Even among matrilineal peoples like the Hopi and Zuni of the American Southwest, traditionally men wore the masks and costumes in public dances that benefit the whole community.

According to some anthropologists, then, the activities of men are universally regarded as more important than those of women. Women as a social category are everywhere culturally devalued relative to men as a social category. Complete gender equality does not exist.

Recalling the complexity of such questions, there is another interpretation. Perhaps most fieldworkers—and hence most of the ethnographic information available to shed light on the issue of gender hierarchy—have been biased, in two ways. The first is the *androcentric* (male) bias. Most fieldworkers were men until the 1970s, and most of them were not very interested in the lives of local women. Also, simply because they were themselves men, fieldworkers had little access to female points of view, so they often unwittingly took local males' values, attitudes, and opinions as representative of the entire group. Female points of view were largely unreported, so reports were not objective and were likely incomplete. Contemporary fieldworkers have largely corrected this situation—of course, with many exceptions.

The second possible source of fieldwork bias is the tendency to *essentialize* other peoples. Basically this means that, first, we simplify the complexities of their lives in our own minds and writings, and, second, we have an ethnocentric tendency to impose outside concepts and standards (e.g., inequality) on Others. For example, look again at Table 11.2, specifically the list of dimensions of gender stratification. Whose list is this? Ours, of course. If we claim that some people have gender stratification based on our criteria, then we are deemphasizing Other's criteria. In fact, we might come to one conclusion using our criteria, but this conclusion might vary from their criteria. As you realize, this objection is especially likely among humanistic anthropologists, who often are skeptical of generalized attempts to measure what they consider individual cultures.

In short, some scholars—especially humanistic ones—think that many fieldworkers and theorists have been biased. Because of this bias, the ethnographic record is not objective. Those ethnographers and comparative researchers who say that there are no societies with total gender equality have been misled. Or perhaps they are misleading themselves.

Some anthropologists have found examples of what they consider gender equality. Those who believe that female–male equality exists in some cultures can point to particular people who they think document their belief. Here we consider two such peoples.

Cross-cultural work on gender stratification shows that women have more influence on decision making and higher status if they control important resources. This painting of Iroquois women storing food around longhouses owned by their matrilineage illustrates this general pattern.

The Iroquois

The Iroquois, a matrilineal and matrilocal political confederation of northeastern North America, are a well-documented case of female–male equality (or only near equality?). Iroquois women produced most corn and other cultivated foods, put foods in storage in the residential longhouses, and largely controlled how the foods were distributed from the storehouses. Iroquois men were away from their apartments in the longhouse much of the time, engaged in warfare or cooperative hunting expeditions.

After the introduction of the fur trade into northeastern North America in the seventeenth century, men often were away searching for beaver pelts or raiding their neighbors for pelts. The matrilineally related women of a longhouse influenced their inmarried husbands' behavior by withholding provisions from their hunting trips and war parties.

Only men had the right to hold the most powerful political offices because only men could be elected to the great council of chiefs. But it was the older women of the various matrilineages who selected their groups' representatives to the council. These women also had the right to remove and replace men who did not adequately represent the group's interests. Also, women had a voice in the deliberations of the council itself. They could veto declarations of war and introduce peacemaking resolutions.

The Vanatinai

Across the Pacific from the Iroquois are a people called the Vanatinai. Living in a small island off the southeast coast of Papua New Guinea, the Vanatinai are a matrilineal people. Maria Lepowsky, who worked among Vanatinai in the late 1970s, reports considerable gender equality among them. Women own and inherit gardens and other property, including wealth in pigs and valuables made of shell. Women choose whom they will marry and their husbands render brideservice, but divorce is easy and many people marry several times. Polygyny is possible, but the consent of the first wife is required.

There is much overlap in the division of labor: Both men and women garden, fish, and care for pigs. Men do a lot of child care also, and gender distinctions are not symbolically marked by initiation rituals (see Chapter 14) as in many cultures.

Symbolically, Vanatinai view men as "life takers" (although warfare is not very intense), and women as "life givers." Warfare earns men some prestige, but women also are seen as dangerous and powerful, based on Vanatinai knowledge of witchcraft. Women play important roles in most public rituals, know powerful magical spells, and can communicate with ancestors and other spirits.

Perhaps most indicative of equality is the possibility that a woman can achieve the status of *gia* ("giver"), the most prestigious and influential position. They do so by actively engaging in reciprocal exchanges, both among their own people and on overseas trading expeditions in which they give and receive shell valuables. Women may even organize these expeditions. Lepowsky, unfortunately, does not provide information on the relative numbers of female and male *gia*.

Why This Might Matter

So, is gender hierarchy in favor of men a cultural universal or not? Certainly, some ethnographers have been and are biased—but does this bias account for all reports of female subordination? Certainly, the Iroquois, Hopi (see Chapter 10), Vanatinai, Minangkabau, and many other peoples demonstrate that women in some cultures have achieved considerable control over their own lives and over public decision making—but do such cases represent full equality of men and women?

Indeed, would we know total equality if we saw it in a society? What would it look like? Would men and women have to carry out the same kinds of economic tasks before we can legitimately claim they are completely equal? Is monogamy necessary, or can a society be polygynous and still qualify? How should family life be organized before we can say that husbands in culture X do not dominate their wives? Shall we require that women occupy 50 percent of all leadership roles before we say they have equal rights? (If so, neither Iroquois nor Vanatinai would have gender equality.)

Why are questions about gender stratification important? Those who believe in and promote gender equality think that the more cultures anthropologists discover with female–male equality, the greater the chances that modern societies can achieve the same condition. At the very least, if there are lots of peoples with gender equality, they would show that patriarchy is not inevitable because so many peoples are not patriarchal. Feminist psychologists, sociologists, historians, biologists, and other scholars have examined ethnographic descriptions of various Other cultures, looking for equality or even matriarchy. Their hope is that there are many such cultures.

Although not silent, the ethnographic record on gender equality is filled with ambiguity and uncertainty. It is ambiguous both because gender stratification is so multidimensional, making total equality difficult to recognize, and because of the problem of whose standards and criteria should be applied to actual cultures.

At any rate, how much does it matter *today* if women in other cultures are universally or nearly universally subordinate to men? What matters most is that women and men are a good deal more equal in some societies than in others, which allows us to study the conditions under which future equality is likely to be possible. To argue that because women have always been or have usually been subordinate, they will forever be subordinate is invalid. In the United States, women could not vote until 1920, when the Nineteenth Amendment passed after decades of agitation. Until 2008 the United States had never elected an African American president. Until 2016 neither major American political party had nominated a woman to run for president. Just because no human group has achieved some state in the past does not mean that none will achieve it in the future. It does not mean that we should despair of trying to achieve it today and for the future.

Influences on Gender Stratification

What influences the degree of gender stratification in a society? As the preceding discussion implies, no one has shown that a small number of factors cause some degree of gender stratification. Here, we discuss a few generalizations that point to the kinds of influences that are most widespread and important.

Women's Contributions to Material Welfare

Some materialists argue that women's role in production strongly influences their property rights, their role in public affairs, their degree of personal freedom to make choices for themselves, and other dimensions of their overall status. One idea is that, where women produce a high proportion of the food, shelter, clothing, and other necessities of existence, women tend to acquire influence, property, prestige, dignity, and other benefits. In other words, the gendered division of labor and the proportion of valued goods women produce are strong influences on gender stratification.

Such ideas apply well to some foraging and horticultural peoples, among whom women's gathering or gardening contributes much of the food consumed by their households. Women's productive labor gives them a status closer to equality with men than they have among peoples in which women's subsistence contributions are not as great. For example, among the BaMbuti and Aka, two foraging Pygmy groups of the Central African rain forest, women's labor is critical for success in net hunting. Ethnographic studies on both BaMbuti and Aka report male–female equality or near equality. Among the Ju/'hoansi, too, considerable equality exists between women and men. Both the Iroquois and Vanatinai are horticulturalists. This fits the general idea about the importance of female contributions to material welfare. Yet numerous other horticultural peoples, such as most of the Amazon Basin and Melanesia, also practice horticulture, and women there are quite subordinate.

But everyone's status is closer to equality in most hunter-gatherer and many horticultural populations (see Chapters 7 and 13). So, perhaps the relative lack of gender stratification in these adaptations results not from women's importance as food providers but from some other factor or influence that reduces inequalities of all kinds.

Women's Control over Key Resources

A more complex materialist proposal is that women's contribution to production, by itself, is not enough to earn them relative equality. It is *necessary* for women to contribute heavily to material welfare to gain resources, rights, and respect, but this alone is not *sufficient*. (Analogously, consider enslaved persons.) One specific hypothesis is that women must also own productive resources (land, tools) or have considerable control over the distribution of the products of their labor, or both. If women own productive resources and have a great deal of say over what happens to the goods they produce, then they can have some influence on the activities of men. Overall, this gives them more equality. Peggy Reeves Sanday found some support for this hypothesis in a cross-cultural study done in the 1970s.

This hypothesis seems to account reasonably well for some peoples. For instance, Iroquois women controlled the production and distribution of important resources. They used this control to nominate their male relatives to chiefly positions and to influence public decision making despite holding no formal position on the council. Likewise, Hopi women (Chapter 10) owned land and had considerable control over the distribution of its products. Women had relatively high status in both these societies, as they did among many other Native American peoples.

Vladimir Zhoga/ShutterStock.com

In parts of West Africa, some women earn significant income for themselves by marketing food and other products.

Bridal Photos in Taiwan: Globalization and Localization

Taiwan, South Korea, Singapore, and Hong Kong are sometimes called East Asia's Four Little Dragons. (The big dragon, of course, is China.) In the 1970s, the Little Dragons developed rapidly by exporting clothing, consumer electronics, toys, and automotive accessories to North America and Europe. Hong Kong and Singapore have been financial centers for decades. South Korea is now the ninth-largest economy in the world, producing ships, motor vehicles, TVs, DVDs, and other high-tech equipment for the global marketplace.

Like the other Little Dragons, Taiwan is about as modern as any place on our planet. Its employment structure is about the same as North America and Europe: Only 5 percent of its people work in agriculture, 37 percent are employed in industry, and 58 percent make a living in services. Taiwan has three cities with populations greater than 1 million; the largest is the capital, Taipei, with nearly 3 million people. Annual income per person in Taiwan is over $30,000. Of its 23 million people, 96 percent can read and write. Its people are mostly healthy and long-lived. There are around 30 million cell phones. Taiwan, and especially Taipei, is developed, urban, connected, cosmopolitan—global.

Its marriages and weddings look global, too. Or, rather, they look global if by "global" you mean "modeled after those of the West," which is exactly what "global" means to many people. Taiwanese young people meet and date, and if they fall in love and marry, their wedding ceremonies are familiar to the eyes of Westerners—at least, to Western secularists. Most weddings include white gowns, tuxedos, flowers, and lots of photos.

What is not familiar is that most couples go to an expensive photo salon before their wedding banquet to have pictures taken. Ordinarily, these pictures are displayed at the wedding ceremony itself. And, according to Bonnie Adrian, who studied Taiwanese weddings, in the photos the bride is hardly recognizable as herself. At great expense, she visits a professional makeover stylist in a salon. The stylist shapes the bride's eyebrows with a razor, often removing them entirely only to reapply new ones later with an eyebrow pencil. Next she applies foundation makeup to cover any blemishes; usually this is a light color because fair skin is desirable. Then the stylist attacks the eyes, applying shadow, liner, and false lashes. The goal is to produce a round-eyed look. The lips are next. The foundation makeup has already made the facial features indistinct, so the bride's natural lip color and shape are barely visible. New lip shapes are

Outwardly, most weddings in Taiwan mimic those in the United States and most of Europe. However, Taiwanese attach meanings to wedding photos that most Westerners do not.

Christopher Pillitz/Getty Images

Along the same lines, in many West African and Caribbean societies, women are more active than men in market trade in foodstuffs, handicrafts, textiles, and other goods they produce themselves. Sometimes market-trading women are able to transform their independent control over exchangeable resources into more equitable relationships with men. Wives commonly maintain a separate income from that of their husbands, which they are free to spend on themselves and their children.

Among the Yoruba of Nigeria, women are active in market trade and in craft production, which gives them access to income and economic security independent of their husbands and other men. Many women purchase houses in urban areas and use the rent to improve their own and their children's economic well-being and social autonomy. According to Sandra Barnes (1990, p. 275):

> Property frees the owner from subordinating herself to the authority of another person in domestic matters. It places her in a position of authority over others and in a position to form social relationships in the wider community that are politically significant. Property owning legitimates her entry into the public domain.

The economic independence that some Yoruba women acquire translates into increased participation applied with a brush, depending on the look the stylist wishes to impart, and the lipstick color is added. Finally, the nails are fixed and the hair styled. Typically, all this takes three hours or longer.

What about the groom? He will have his hair cut and styled so that nothing looks out of place, and he may wear a bit of makeup to ensure that his facial features show up properly under the photographic lights. But overall, he is recognizably himself. In the wedding and photos, at least, his appearance is secondary.

Next, the couple visits a photographer who specializes in prewedding photos and takes hundreds or even thousands of pictures. By the time the photographer has finished, usually a whole day has passed—and several thousand dollars have changed hands. The prints are huge, and on the day of the wedding banquet, they are prominently displayed so that all can admire the beauty of the bride.

One interpretation of all this "framing the bride" (as Adrian titles her 2003 book) is that Taiwanese wedding customs have taken on a Western flavor. Consciously or not, it looks like Taiwanese couples have chosen the Western model. Is this an example of cultural diffusion or even cultural imperialism—the makeover of indigenous customs based on the foundation of the West?

Adrian believes this interpretation is simplistic. In old Taiwan, women viewed marriage not as the fulfillment of romantic dreams, but as the beginning of a life of hard work for her husband's family and for the welfare of the children she would soon bear. This attitude carries over into contemporary Taiwan. Today women and men in love have plenty of opportunities to be intimate before they marry. So, they often postpone marriage until they feel ready to have children and undertake the responsibilities of parenthood. When a modern Taiwanese woman marries, she feels she is sacrificing a lot of freedom in the interest of her husband and their offspring. The photo, usually hung in the bedroom, will remind her and him of how beautiful and free she was before the tasks of family responsibility wore her down.

Weddings, banquets, and photographs also reflect implicit competition—what Americans used to call "keeping up with the Joneses." The more photographs and the more work the photographer must do to make them perfect, the greater the expense, and the groom and his family pay for most of this expense. The groom would be embarrassed if the photos were not up to standards, and his wife might remind him of his failure to live up to cultural expectations in future quarrels. At the obligatory wedding banquet, the amount and quality of food must also be up to normative expectations—and

so must the quality of the wedding photos. The groom's family would suffer a loss of face if they did not honor their son's marriage and welcome their new daughter-in-law with an ostentatious banquet and expensive photographs.

These kinds of photographs made before the wedding itself in Taiwan do not primarily document the events of the marriage. They are not records of the ceremony. Rather, they are commemorations of the bride; Adrian (2003, p. 235) says, "they construct brides," meaning that they build an image of the woman before her marriage so that, later her family can see an idealized depiction of the woman she once was.

What are the wider lessons of bridal photos in contemporary Taiwan? Consciously or not, Taiwanese take something from the realm of global culture and use it for their own culturally meaningful purposes. To say it differently, they *localize the global* by shaping the photos to fit their own traditions and reconfiguring what comes in from the outside world to mesh with their own cultural attitudes and beliefs and social practices. Many nations have accepted ideas and practices from the outside, remaking them to fit their own traditions. Humanity does not need to become all alike just because we interact with one another in new global settings.

in neighborhood associations and other public affairs and allows them much freedom from male authority. A wider generalization would be that control over resources increases women's independence from men and allows women to form associations with other women that act like mutual support networks.

Thus, many ethnographic and comparative studies suggest that controlling resources is an important means for women to gain independence from husbands, brothers, and other men. The ability to acquire some measure of control over family resources helps to account for why so many North American wives have received more independence from their husbands. Especially since the 1970s, married women in increasing numbers

have acquired wage- and salary-earning jobs. Between 1970 and 2014, in the United States, the percentage of all married women who were employed doubled.

Even the presence of young children does not keep most American women from entering the workforce: Between 1975 and 2014, the percentage of married women with children under age 6 who were working for a wage rose from 39 percent to 64 percent. Among the reasons for increases in married women's employment are the inadequacy of one person's income to support the family at an acceptable living standard, structural changes to a more service-oriented economy (less goods producing, with a decline in factory employment), the increasing value women place on personal fulfillment through career advancement (partly because of the feminist movement), and the fact that women with college degrees more than tripled between 1970 and 2014 (from 11 percent to 40 percent).

Women also are earning higher percentages of household income: Between 1970 and 2013, women's contribution to household income rose from 27 percent to 38 percent. From 1987 to 2013, among two-earner households the percentage of wives who earned more than their husbands increased from 18 percent to 29 percent. However, although wage and salary equality are improving, in the aggregate women still receive only 83 percent of men's compensation (an increase from 62 percent in 1979).

As a result of entering the workforce and increasing their share of family income in recent decades, many married American women are less dependent on their husbands for resources to support them and their children. Husbands have lost economic leverage in the household relative to wives. And, increasingly, wives have psychological ammunition against their husbands' domestic indolence—they've put in a full day's work on the job just like their husbands.

The legal system has also helped by increasingly considering family violence more than just a private matter as well as by prosecuting or garnishing the wages of "deadbeat dads." Unhappy wives are more able to support themselves economically after divorce or separation, reducing the need for a husband to support them and their children.

In the twenty-first century, increasing numbers of North American couples are "role reversed." Husbands-fathers stay at home with young children while wives-mothers are the breadwinners. Some believe this pattern reverses the natural order of male–female family roles and thus is ultimately harmful to children, who look up to their parents as role models. Others hold that the feminist movement has helped liberate men as well as women from old cultural attitudes: As economic or familial circumstances warrant, or as couples prefer, parents can reverse, switch, or alternate caretaking and breadwinning roles. Perhaps feminism has given both genders more freedom of choice.

With most women now out in the labor force, and with the families of so many women/wives increasingly dependent on their income to pay the bills, more women are demanding equal pay for equal work, equal treatment and opportunity in the workplace, equal legal rights, and equal respect. As anthropological research in other societies suggests, in North America, women's success in obtaining control over important resources empowers them relative to men.

Descent and Postmarital Residence

The form of descent and postmarital residence (see Chapters 9 and 10) influences the degree of gender stratification. Women in matrilineal and matrilocal societies have greater equality in many areas of life. What is it, specifically, about matrilineality and matrilocality that gives relatively high status to women? It is not usual that "women rule" in these societies, in a political or legal sense.

As the matrilineal peoples discussed earlier illustrate, one reason there tends to be a high degree of gender equality is that women have a lot of control over life-sustaining and life-enhancing resources. Where land, wealth, and other property pass mainly from mothers to daughters, wives have more independence from husbands, and some matrilocal peoples view husbands as working for their wives and their wives' families. Commonly—but not universally—in matrilineal, matrilocal societies, husbands are rather loosely attached to their wives' households, and divorce and remarriage rates are relatively high. It may be easier for dissatisfied husbands to leave and remarry than to deal with lots of conflicts with their wives and her relatives (including her brothers).

Other elements of matrilineality and matrilocality also benefit women. Two factors contribute to their equality. First, because husbands live with the families of their wives, sisters remain with or close to one another throughout their lives. A typical wife thus has her mother, sisters, and other female relatives around to support her in domestic quarrels. Second, in many matrilineal and matrilocal societies, domestic authority over a married woman is divided between her husband and her brother. Alice Schlegel long ago suggested this arrangement increases her freedom because each man acts as a check on the other's attempts to dominate her.

This situation contrasts markedly with patrilineal and patrilocal societies, such as old China, Korea, Japan, the Middle East, and most of India and Pakistan. In these societies, when a woman married into a family, she was given household tasks to perform or had child-care duties for most waking hours. Only when she herself bore sons and heirs to her husband's family did her status improve, and only after she herself became a mother-in-law to her sons' wives could she relax a bit. In East Asia, the Confucian social and moral philosophy, which held that women must be submissive to men, affected the way wives and daughters-in-law were treated. Even in modern times, many women feel that marriage results in a loss of freedom and that the heavy duties of family life are burdensome, which in Taiwan affects even wedding practices (see the Global Challenges and Opportunities feature).

In the Islamic parts of southern Asia and in the Middle East, the teachings of the Quran generally supported a woman's subordinate status in the home as well as in public. Also important were the social facts that wives became members of the households of their husbands' parents, and the lines of authority over them were clearly and legally redrawn upon their marriage. Socially, a wife had few viable alternatives to submitting to her husband's family and relatively few sources of support when she was treated poorly. In contrast, in most matrilocal and matrilineal cultures, women do have alternatives to suffering the dominance of their husbands, and they are more likely to receive support from their own birth families.

Gender Stratification in Modern Societies

We conclude by bringing together some of the information and ideas in this chapter and briefly suggesting how they might be relevant to women living in modernized or modernizing nations.

Anthropological research on gender stratification reveals that women's roles, rights, privileges, and the restrictions placed on them, vary substantially from place to place and from time to time. Although it is impossible to determine definitively whether gender stratification is totally absent in some culture somewhere,

clearly the degree of gender equality varies significantly among humanity. There is reason to think that modern societies can move further toward eliminating barriers to female opportunity and achievement. Patriarchy does not seem to be part of the human genome.

Some of our discussion suggests that any change that improves women's independent access to material resources and to social support will have positive impacts on their status in other realms of life. If married women have their own source of income independent of their husbands, then they are better able to become empowered within their families and to escape relationships with men who are physically or psychologically abusive. If, as in matrilineal and matrilocal societies, women are able to maintain relationships of sisterhood (i.e., support from other women) and/or of extended family ties (i.e., aid from their own relatives), then they can mobilize these supportive relationships in times of hardship. If women have legal recourse to sue discriminating employers and would-be employers, then their opportunities and compensation on the job will be improved by the threat of monetary damages.

Going back to the very first point in this chapter: The knowledge that ideas and beliefs about gender are culturally constructed rather than biologically given should—*if taken seriously and understood properly*—lead women and men alike to realize that at least some gendered differences are differences of our own culture's making. It is a biological *reality* (with some qualifications) that women have the physical tools to bear and nurse children and that men on average are larger and stronger than women. But the degree of importance of these biological realities varies from people to people.

SUMMARY

1. **Describe how male–female physical differences affect gender roles and relationships.** Physical differences between men and women are relevant to social behavior in all known cultures, but these differences matter in different ways and to different degrees. For anthropological interests, the two most important genetically based differences are sexual dimorphism and reproductive physiology, which affect who performs economic tasks and child-care responsibilities.

2. **Explain the phrase "cultural construction of gender" and its importance.** A person's sex is determined biologically (by genes), but gender is a cultural construction. The cultural construction of gender means that cultures vary in how they perceive the physical differences between the sexes, in the significance they attribute to those differences, and in the way those differences are made relevant for self-identity, task and role allocation, access to property and power, and

so forth. The Hua people of Papua New Guinea illustrate the cultural construction of gender.

3. **Analyze the relevance of the acceptance of multiple gender identities for the understanding of gender.** Cultures differ in their tolerance of individual variations in gender identities. Many peoples allow gender crossing, in which males are allowed to enact female roles, and vice versa. Others recognize multiple gender identities, in which there are three or four genders, roughly corresponding to man-woman or woman-man. With their acceptance of Two Spirits, many Native American peoples seem especially tolerant of gender crossing and to allow for multiple gender identities. The *hijra* are a socially recognized third gender in India, which further suggests that alternative genders are legitimate roles in many human societies. In contemporary times, the multiple gender identities of LGBTQIA persons are recognized by the proliferation of terms, including *cisgender*.

4. **Discuss the factors that influence the widespread patterns and the cross-cultural diversity in the gendered division of labor.** Despite cultural variations, widespread patterns exist in the gendered division of labor. Four biological factors that influence the broad cross-cultural similarities are (1) the depression of fertility that seems to occur when a woman engages in heavy exercise; (2) the possibility that women are more necessary than men to maintain population size; (3) superior male strength; and (4) the degree of compatibility of a particular task with the care of infants and young children. No biological difference between men and women can account for cultural diversity in the gendered division of labor. Generally, female labor is more important in subsistence tasks in horticultural populations than among intensive agriculturalists. The reasons for this difference are related to the types of crops grown (root crops versus cereal grains), the amount of time needed for food processing, and the greater prevalence of warfare in horticultural groups.

5. **Analyze why it is so difficult to determine whether any societies have complete gender equality.** The nature of gender stratification and the reasons why it varies are controversial, due to problems of definition and the possible biases outsiders bring to their work. Anthropologists have yet to discover any peoples who are matriarchal, as the term is commonly used. People like the Iroquois and Vanatinai have been viewed as examples of equality between the genders. But even specialists in gender studies cannot agree whether gender hierarchy is universal or whether there are societies with complete equality between men and women. This is mainly because gender stratification is multidimensional and because gender equality is so difficult to define.

6. **Describe the three most important influences on gender stratification from a comparative perspective.** Many forces affect gender stratification. Among the most important widespread influences are women's relative contributions to subsistence, women's ability to control key resources, and the pattern of descent and postmarital residence. These influences are relevant for gender equality in the twenty-first century.

12

The Organization of Political Life

Bridgeman/Getty

In many state-level societies, political authority is vested in formally elected bodies, such as the parliament of the United Kingdom.

Forms of Political Organization
  Bands
  Tribes
  Chiefdoms
  States
  Inca Empire

Social Control and Law
  Social Control
  Law

Legal Systems
  Self-Help Systems
  Court Systems

LEARNING OBJECTIVES

After reading this chapter, you should be able to:

1 **EXPLAIN** what is meant by political organization.

2 **LIST** the four main types of political organization and how they structurally differ from one another.

3 **EXPLAIN** what is meant by social control.

4 **DISCUSS** legal systems and how they differ from other forms of social control.

5 **DISCUSS** the two major forms of legal systems and the variants within the two forms.

6 **EXPLAIN** the relationship between the legal system found in a society and the political organization of that society.

Every society has some form of political system—those institutions that organize and direct the collective behavior of the population. In the preceding chapters, we discussed the diversity in family and kinship organization. Among other things, these systems serve to define the economic and social obligations and privileges of the members of the society relative to one another. The political organization of the society, on the other hand, is the overarching institution that directs the collective economic activities and relations to other societies. In the smallest and earliest societies, this distinction between individual and group behavior is virtually imperceptible. In these societies, political leadership and organization is informal and even ad hoc. Only when a specific need for leadership arises does some individual assume an overt leadership role. However, in larger and more complex societies, this distinction is readily apparent. In general, the larger the population, the more formalized the leadership and the more complex the political organization.

Likewise, as mentioned in Chapter 2, all societies define certain behavioral patterns that are approved or acceptable and others that are disapproved or unacceptable. There are always some individuals who will not conform. Therefore, all societies develop mechanisms of social control by which the behaviors of individuals are constrained and directed into acceptable channels.

By means of social control, a society encourages normatively proper behavior and discourages unacceptable actions; the objective is to maintain harmony and cooperation. The most serious deviations from acceptable behavior, which threaten the cohesiveness of the group, fall under that aspect of social control known as *law*, also discussed in this chapter. In the least organized societies, law and political organizations exist independently. As political organization becomes increasingly formalized and structured, governmental institutions take over legal institutions, until legal institutions become part of the formal political structure.

Forms of Political Organization

When we speak of the political organization of a particular society, we frequently are left with the impression that political boundaries and cultural boundaries are the same. But the boundaries of a *polity*, or a politically organized group, may or may not correspond with the boundaries of a particular way of life. For example, the Comanche of the Great Plains, who we will discuss later, shared a common language, customs, and ethnic identity, yet politically they were never organized above the local group. Thus, the term *Comanche* refers to a people with a common language and culture who never united to carry out common political objectives.

At the other extreme, we find highly centralized polities that incorporate several culturally and socially distinct peoples. The United States is unusual in this regard only in the degree of cultural heterogeneity in the population. France, though predominantly "French," also includes Bretons and Basques as well as numerous recent immigrants from Africa, Asia, and elsewhere. India has

Form	Characteristics	Associated Equalities and Inequalities
Bands	Local, economically self-sufficient residence groups	Egalitarian
(a) Simple	Single extended family, usually numbering 25 to 50 people; family head with leadership based on influence	
(b) Composite	Several extended families, usually numbering from 50 to several hundred individuals; big man leadership based on influence	Egalitarian
Tribes	Several economically self-sufficient residence groups; usually numbering between 1,000 and 20,000 people; a few formal leadership positions with limited authority, with access based on inheritance and/or achievements; group cohesion maintained by sodalities	Primarily egalitarian with some societies showing the traits of ranking
Chiefdoms	Several economically interdependent residence groups; usually numbering from a few thousand up to about 30,000; centralized leadership, with a hereditary chief holding full, formal authority	Ranked societies
States	Usually numbering from the tens of thousands up to hundreds of millions, if not more; centralized leadership, with full, formal authority, supported by a bureaucracy	Stratified societies

several hundred different ethnic groups. Russia, China, Indonesia, and the Philippines also integrate highly diversified populations into a single polity. In fact, every large and most small countries in the world today politically encompass several ethnic groups.

In this discussion of political organization, we are taking an evolutionary perspective. By this, we mean that the known political systems of the world are going to be grouped based on the degree of increasing organizational complexity. On this basis, political systems may be divided into four basic forms: bands (simple and composite), tribes, chiefdoms, and states. However, it is important to note that political systems actually exist along a continuum of increasing complexity. As a result, the political systems of many societies do not clearly fall into one category or another. (The Concept Review box outlines different forms of political organization.)

to compete for resources. Thus, bands survived until the modern period only in regions of the world with limited natural resources. Most known band-level societies were found in the deserts and grasslands of Australia, Africa, and the Americas. A few others are or were in the tropical forests of Africa, Asia, and South America and in the boreal forest and tundra regions of North America and Asia.

Bands consist of a number of families living together and cooperating in economic activities throughout the year. Band-level organization most frequently has been found among peoples with foraging economies, which usually dictated low population densities and seasonal mobility. As a result, only a relatively small number of people could stay together throughout the year. Bands ranged in size from only a dozen to several hundred individuals. The adaptive significance of the band's size

Bands

As the least complex form, the **band** is the earliest human political structure. As more complex political systems developed, band-level societies were unable

band Small foraging group with flexible composition that migrates seasonally.

and seasonal mobility is described in Chapter 7. In this chapter, we are concerned with leadership statuses and the political organization of bands.

The smallest type of band, called the **simple band**, is actually an extended family. Leadership is informal, with the oldest or one of the older male or female members of the family serving as the de facto leader. Decisions are usually arrived at through consensus and involve both adult males and adult females. Because all members of the band are related either through descent or by marriage, they are exogamous units, and members of the band have to seek spouses from other bands. Thus, although an autonomous economic and political unit, every simple band was or is, by social necessity, allied through intermarriage with other bands, usually territorially adjacent ones. Simple bands usually have names, although the names may have been informal and may have simply referred to some prominent geographic feature associated with the band's usual territory.

Resource availability influenced the formation of such small groups. Simple bands often were associated with the hunting of nonmigratory game animals, such as deer, guanaco, moose, or small mammals, which occupy a limited territory on a year-round basis and are found either singly or in small herds. The foraging activities of simple bands usually did not generate any significant surpluses of food, which necessitated the year-round hunting of game animals. Effective hunting required only a few male hunters who had intimate knowledge of the seasonal shifts in range of these animals within their territory, while successful gathering

of wild plants required only a few females who had intimate knowledge of local plant resources. A small and highly mobile population was the most efficient way to exploit the natural resources of such areas.

A **composite band** consists of a larger aggregate of families, sometimes numbering in the hundreds. In contrast to simple bands, composite bands encompassed unrelated extended families. Although leadership in composite bands was still informal, it had to be more defined because the leader was not related to all of the members of the group.

Such a leader frequently has been called a **big man**. The big man does not hold a formal office, and his leadership is based on influence rather than authority over band members. **Influence** is the ability to convince people that they should act as suggested. **Authority** is the recognized right of an individual to command another person to act in a particular way. Thus, a big man leader could not, by virtue of his position, make demands or impose rules on the members of the band, and his decisions were not binding on others. Because big man status did not involve a formal office, no prescribed process existed for attaining leadership status. A man might emerge as the leader through a variety of personal accomplishments or qualities such as his proven ability in hunting or warfare, the supernatural powers he possessed, or merely his charisma. There was no set tenure for the position, which was filled by a man until some other leader informally replaced him.

Like simple bands, many composite bands were nomadic groups that moved within a relatively well-defined range. Because of their greater size, composite bands were not as cohesive as simple bands and were politically more volatile. Disputes between families could result in some members joining another band or even the band splitting into two or more bands.

Composite bands formed because economic pressures facilitated or necessitated the cooperation of a larger number of individuals than found in a single extended family. As in the case of simple bands, the behavior of the principal game animals was an important influence. Composite bands were associated with the seasonal hunting of migratory animals that form large herds, such as bison and caribou. Migratory herd animals usually appeared only seasonally in the range of a particular composite band as the herd moved between its summer and winter ranges. Because bison and caribou migrated in herds that sometimes numbered in the tens of thousands, there was no difficulty in locating the herds on the open grasslands and tundra. Unlike the hunters of nonmigratory animals, who secured game steadily throughout the year, hunters of

simple band Autonomous or independent political unit, often consisting of little more than an extended family, with informal leadership vested in one of the older family members.

composite band Autonomous (independent) political unit consisting of several extended families that live together for most or all of the year.

big man Political leader who does not occupy a formal office and whose leadership is based on influence, not authority.

influence Ability to convince people they should act as suggested.

authority Recognized right of an individual to command another to act in a particular way; legitimate power.

migratory animals frequently took most of their game only twice a year, as the herds passed through their territories during seasonal migrations.

Successful hunting of big herds of animals requires maneuvering the herd into situations where large numbers could be slaughtered. Herds might be run over a cliff, into a holding pen, or into a lake where hunters in boats could kill them. Regardless of the method used, all these strategies required a larger group of hunters than was available in a simple band. Thus, composite bands were formed to bring together a sufficient number of hunters to control the movements of large herds of animals.

The Comanche of the southern Great Plains of the United States illustrate the nature of composite bands. These horse-raising, bison-hunting people were politically autonomous until the 1870s. During the early and middle years of the nineteenth century, the Comanche numbered about 6,000 to 7,000, divided between 5 and 13 composite bands. Comanche bands had only vaguely defined territories, and two or more composite bands frequently occupied the same general area or had overlapping ranges. Membership in bands was fluid: Both individuals and families could and did shift from one band to another, or a number of families might join together to establish a new band.

A band consisted of a number of families, each headed by an older male member who was "peace chief" or "headman." One of these family heads also served as the peace chief for the entire band. There was no formalized method of selecting either the family heads or the head of the band. As the Comanche say, "No one made him such; he just got that way." A Comanche peace chief usually was a man known for his kindness, wisdom, and ability to lead by influencing other men. Although a war record was important, peace chiefs were not chosen from among the most aggressive or ambitious men. Such men usually remained war chiefs—great warriors who periodically recruited men to raid neighbors—but frequently had little influence outside war and raiding.

A band peace chief was responsible for the well-being of the band. Through a consensus of the family heads, he directed the seasonal movement of the band and the bison hunts. He did have men who voluntarily assisted him. In the morning, the peace chief usually sent out two men to scout the area around the camp for the presence of enemy raiding parties. He also sent a crier through the camp periodically to announce plans for the movement of the camp, an upcoming hunt, or some other cooperative activity. During the bison hunts, the peace chief called on a number of men from the camp to police the hunt and restrain overly eager hunters from scattering the herd and thus spoiling the hunt for others.

In an extraordinarily individualistic and egalitarian society, the leader of the band had to strive for and maintain consensus. If a dispute arose and a consensus could not be reached, individuals and families were free either to shift residence to another band or even to form a new band under another leader.

Comanche composite bands were economically and politically autonomous residence units. Seldom did two or more bands come together for any unified action, and rarely did leaders of the bands come together to discuss issues. At the same time, there was a strong consciousness of common identity—of being Comanche. The Comanche freely traveled between bands to visit, marry, and even shift residence. There was an informally reached general consensus on whether relations with a particular neighboring group were friendly or hostile.

Thus, on the band level of political organization, populations are fragmented into numerous independent political resident units that operate only at the local-group level. These various residence groups share a common cultural identity and usually attempt to maintain harmonious relations with one another, but they lack any political structure capable of organizing all the various residence groups into a single unit for collective actions.

Tribes

The **tribe** is different from the band in that it has formally organized institutions that unite the geographically scattered residence groups, to give the society greater cohesiveness and make possible a more united response to external threats. Such an institution is called a **sodality**. Sodalities take various forms: they may be based on large kin groups, such as clans and lineages; on non-kinship units, such as age sets; or on voluntary associations, such as male and female

tribe Autonomous political unit encompassing a number of distinct, geographically dispersed communities held together by sodalities.

sodality Formal institution that cuts across communities and serves to unite geographically scattered groups; may be based on kin groups (clans or lineages) or on groups that are not based on kin (age grades or warrior societies).

societies. Regardless of their exact nature, sodalities served to unify the geographically dispersed communities. Although tribal-level societies usually are egalitarian, with leadership dependent in part on the persuasive abilities of individuals, there are formalized political offices with some institutionalized authority. Tribes vary greatly in structure; here we examine one tribal-level society.

The Cheyenne of the Great Plains numbered between 3,000 and 3,500 during the early 1800s. The Cheyenne, like the neighboring Comanche, were horse-mounted bison hunters. They were divided into 10 main nomadic local groups or villages, which averaged between 300 and 350 persons. Village membership was not based on kinship, although the members of a particular village usually were related either by blood or by marriage. Village membership was relatively stable, and marriages between villagers were common. Although a particular village usually frequented a certain range, there was no sense of village territoriality. Periodically and seasonally, family camps and sub-village camps broke off from the main village.

The only time the entire tribe came together was in early summer, when all the widely scattered villages gathered into a single camp at a predetermined location. This crescent-shaped encampment stretched for several miles from end to end, with the open portion facing east. Within the tribal encampment, every village had a designated location; while camped together, they performed tribal ceremonies, such as the Sun Dance. At least one and possibly two rituals were performed, depending on the particular ritual needs of the tribe at that time. After the performance of the ritual, the tribe as a unit staged the great summer bison hunt. After the hunt, the tribe again scattered into smaller village camps.

Politically, the Council of Forty-Four and the warrior societies controlled the tribe. The leader of the Council of Forty-Four, who had both political and religious duties, was the Sweet Medicine chief—the keeper of the most sacred of the Cheyenne religious bundles. Second to him in importance were four other sacred chiefs, each representing specific supernatural beings. Under these five sacred chiefs were 39 ordinary chiefs.

Chiefs served in their positions for 10 years and could not be removed for any reason. Serving as a chief placed a burden on the individuals. Chiefs usually were selected from among the older men, all of whom had war records. When an individual was chosen as a chief, he was to act like a chief, not an aggressive warrior. A chief was to be generous, kindly, even tempered, and

aloof from everyday disputes. In short, he was expected to display ideal human behavior at all times. He was to take care of the poor, settle disputes between individuals, and be responsible for the ritual performances that protected the tribe.

The major sodalities were the warrior societies, of which there were five. These were formal voluntary associations of men, each with its own style of dress, dances, songs, and formal leaders. As young warriors, men were recruited by the different societies until all had joined one or another of the societies. The term *warrior societies* is slightly misleading. The heads of the various societies were what some call the "tribal war chiefs." Although this group planned and led attacks on their enemies, the different societies did not fight or operate as military units in battles. In battles, men fought as individuals, and members of several societies may have been present in a particular raiding party.

Subordinate to the council of chiefs, the warrior societies cooperated as a group only in policing the camps. During the summer tribal encampment, the Council of Forty-Four appointed one of the societies as camp police. Later, when the village scattered into separate camps, the members of the council who lived in the village appointed one of the warrior societies to police the camp. After being appointed, the warrior society usually carried out its function with little direction from the chiefs. Its members scouted the area around the camp to check for the presence of any enemy raiding parties and intervened in any serious disputes between village members.

There are two points to be emphasized about the political organization of tribal societies in contrast to those of simple and composite bands. First, there were now some formalized political and religious offices that bequeathed some limited authority and prerogatives. However, on the whole, tribal societies were still basically egalitarian (see Chapter 13). Few positions were hereditary, and most leaders were selected on the basis of personal qualities and individual merit.

Second, like bands, little economic specialization existed; except for cooperation in communal hunts, families produced their own food and manufactured their own clothes and other material goods. From an economic perspective, each of the scattered residential groups or villages was capable of sustaining itself without support from others; therefore, it was not economic necessity, convenience, or efficiency that led to this higher level of tribal political organization. Although sodalities unite tribes at a higher level of cohesiveness than bands, the mere existence of sodalities is not sufficient to generate or maintain the cohesiveness of a tribe. It is likely that external threats, either real or perceived, necessitated the cooperation in warfare of a large group of people and were the major factor that united geographically dispersed groups.

Thus, warfare—the existence and activities of hostile human neighbors—was an important force in creating the political integration of separate communities. The conflict over hunting territories between Cheyenne and Comanche during the early nineteenth century illustrates the advantage of tribal over band organization in competition over resources. The Cheyenne and Comanche were equally well armed and adept at warfare. However, although numerically smaller, the Cheyenne were able to militarily force the Comanche southward out of the central portion of the Great Plains. The difference was that the tribally organized Cheyenne were able to mobilize greater manpower for conflicts than the politically fragmented bands of the Comanche.

Chiefdoms

Like the tribe, a **chiefdom** also consisted of multiple residential groups or villages. However, unlike tribes, chiefdoms had a highly formalized and centralized political system. A chiefdom was governed by a single chief, who usually served as both political and religious head of the polity. The chief had authority over members of the chiefdom, and the position often was hereditary within a single kin group, which based its rights primarily on supernatural powers. Thus, a chiefdom was not an egalitarian society but a ranked or stratified society (see Chapter 13) with access to resources based on inherited status. With authority and power conferred by the supernatural, governing was not by consensus but by decree.

Most chiefdoms were associated with horticultural societies in which craft or regional specialization in production had emerged. There was a need for regularized exchanges of goods either between geographically dispersed communities or, at times, within a single community. This economic exchange was managed through redistribution, with the chief occupying the central position in the flow of goods (see Chapter 8).

In earlier historic periods, chiefdoms probably were found throughout much of the Old World. During more recent periods, such political systems were primarily concentrated in Oceania (Polynesia, Micronesia, and Melanesia) and in the Americas (the Caribbean and coastal portions of South America and the Northwestern Coast of North America).

PA Images/Alamy

A Samoan chief is pictured here in traditional dress.

The Polynesian-speaking people of Tahiti, an island in the southeastern Pacific, illustrate many characteristics typical of a chiefdom. This relatively large, mountainous, volcanic island had a population of about 100,000 at the time of European discovery. Tahiti was divided among about 20 rival chiefs. Although most of these chiefdoms were about the size of the average tribe and significantly smaller than the largest tribes, their political organization differed significantly.

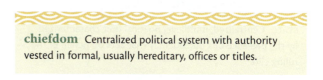

chiefdom Centralized political system with authority vested in formal, usually hereditary, offices or titles.

The economy of Tahiti was based largely on farming, with taro, breadfruit, coconuts, and yams being the main crops. The Tahitians raised pigs and chickens, and fish and other seafood supplemented the food supply. Food production was sufficient not only to meet the needs of the population but also to produce surpluses for export to other islands. Although sufficient food was produced in all regions, there were significant regional differences in the types of food produced because Tahiti varied ecologically.

Tahitian society had at least three and possibly four distinct classes, depending on how finely one wants to divide the units. *Arii*, or chiefs, and their close relatives formed the ruling elite. The *arii* were divided into two groups: the *arii rahi*, or sacred chiefs, and the *arii rii*, or small chiefs. Under these chiefs were the *raatira*, or subchiefs, and the *manahune*, or commoners. The sacred chiefs were viewed as descended from the gods, whereas the commoners were merely created by the gods for their use. The subchiefs were the offspring of intermarriage between the sacred chiefs and commoners, whereas the small chiefs were the products of still later intermarriages between sacred chiefs and subchiefs. Once these four classes were established, class endogamy became the rule.

The sacred chiefs, viewed as gods on Earth, evoked both reverence and fear. Whatever the highest-ranking sacred chiefs touched became *tabu*, or sacred, and could not be used for fear of supernatural punishment. Such a chief had to be carried on the back of a servant, lest the ground touched by his feet became *tabu*. He could not enter the house of another individual for the same reason. The lifestyle of the chief's family differed from that of others, with larger and more elaborate houses, the largest canoes, insignia of their rank, and particular clothing.

Unlike in band and tribal societies, resources in chiefdoms were individually owned. Mainly the chiefs and subchiefs owned land, but ultimate authority rested with the sacred chiefs within the polity. Although sacred chiefs could not withhold the title to lands from the families of subchiefs, they could banish an individual subchief. Crafts were specialized, and craftspeople were attached to particular sacred chiefs and produced goods for them. Thus, the sacred chiefs directly controlled craft production and communal fishing. The chiefs could make demands on the property of the subchiefs and commoners. If someone refused, the chief could have the recalcitrant banished or make him or her a sacrificial victim. Theoretically, the sacred chief was the head judicial figure in the polity, but some believe that the chief seldom intervened in disputes between individuals; the chief usually used these powers only against people who challenged his authority.

The sacred chief in each polity was the focal point for redistributive exchanges (discussed in Chapter 8). The chief periodically demanded surplus production from all his subjects for a public redistribution. Such events were associated with a number of occasions: a rite of passage for a member of the chief's family, the organizing of a military attack, religious ceremonies, or the start of the breadfruit harvest. During such ceremonies, the chief distributed the goods collected to all his subjects.

States

Although they had a centralized political system, chiefdoms were still kinship-based structures. Even in Tahiti, the authority of the sacred chiefs rested in large part on their control over families of subchiefs, each of whom had his own inalienable rights to lands—and thus families—of commoners. As a result, the number of people who could be effectively integrated into a chiefdom was limited. In Polynesia, most chiefdoms ranged from only a few thousand to 30,000 persons. Polities with larger populations require a political structure based on institutions other than kinship.

A **state**, like a chiefdom, has a centralized political structure. States are distinguished from chiefdoms by the presence of a bureaucracy. A chiefdom is basically a two-level system: (1) the chiefs (which in Tahiti included the subchiefs), who have varying levels of authority and power, and (2) the commoners, or the great mass of the populace. A state has three levels: the ruling elite, a bureaucracy, and the populace.

In states, as in chiefdoms, the highest authority and power reside in the ruling elite, the formal political head or heads of the polity. States vary greatly in the types of political leaders present and in the basis for the leaders' authority and power. Leaders in the earliest states frequently were considered to be the descendants of gods, and thus themselves gods on Earth. The Inca of Peru and the pharaohs of Egypt were leaders who ruled as gods. Other political leaders, although not claiming to be gods, have legitimated their positions with claims of having been chosen by God. Early European kings legitimated their claims to leadership on such a basis; and as English coins still proclaim, the queen rules *Dei*

---

state Centralized, multilevel political unit characterized by the presence of a bureaucracy that acts on behalf of the ruling elite.

gratia—"by the grace of God." Other states have evolved political leadership that uses strictly secular ideas to justify their authority. In countries where leaders are elected by a vote of the populace, rule is legitimated by the internalized acceptance of such ascendance to office. Even leaders of strictly secular kingdoms, dictatorships, and oligarchies can, if in power for a sufficient time, have their rule accepted by the populace as "legitimate." We have more to say about legitimization in Chapter 13.

Although they differ greatly in political leadership, states all share one characteristic: a bureaucracy that carries out the day-to-day governing of the polity. In simple terms, a *bureaucrat* is a person to whom a political leader delegates certain authority and powers. The bureaucrat thus acts on behalf of the political leader. Lacking any inherent authority or powers personally, bureaucrats depend on the continued support of political leaders. Using bureaucrats as intermediaries, political leaders could expand the size of their polities both geographically and demographically, while strengthening their political control over the population. Bureaucrats could engineer such expansion without threat of revolution and political fragmentation because they lacked any personal claims to independent political legitimacy.

In addition to differences in their political structure, state-level polities differ from bands, tribes, and chiefdoms in two other important ways. First, they can and usually do have multiethnic populations, including members of a number of ethnic groups who not only have distinct cultural traditions but frequently speak different languages as well. One of these ethnic groups is usually the politically dominant group. Second, with few exceptions, states have market economies (see Chapter 8) and depend to varying degrees on external trade with neighboring groups. (The Global Challenges and Opportunities feature offers an in-depth look at an outgrowth of states today in the global economy: multinational corporations.)

Inca Empire

The Inca empire of ancient Peru was typical of a state-level organization. From the capital of Cuzco, the ruler, or Sapa Inca, controlled a multiethnic empire of between 6 and 12 million subjects who spoke dozens of different languages and extended over 2,500 miles from modern-day Ecuador to central Chile. Dissected by some of the highest mountain ranges and most inhospitable deserts in the world, the Inca empire existed without a writing system for communication, a monetary system for exchange, or wheeled vehicles for transporting goods. Despite this limited technology

Spaces Images/Blend Images/Getty Images

The Inca were able to construct cities such as Machu Picchu despite mountainous terrain.

In Chapter 4 we discussed the recent development of the integrated global market economy. In the spring of 2016, the leak of the "Panama Papers"—over 11 million documents from the files of Mossack Fonseca's office in Panama—greatly increased public awareness of a new dimension of the global economy. The business of Mossack Fonseca was to legally create "shell companies"—companies that have the appearance of a business but do nothing but manage money. These companies are registered in offshore financial centers, which are usually, but not always, small island countries without any taxes on corporations.

The sole purpose of these shell companies is tax evasion. The actual owners of these corporations are in most cases keep secret. The Panama Papers disclosed the names of the secret owners—wealthy individuals and even political leaders from throughout the world. How many shell companies exist and how much money these companies shelter from taxes are not known. The British Virgin Islands is one of the largest of these centers. With a population of only 33,000, the BBC reported that it is the "home" for about 500,000 shell companies. Gabriel Zucman recently estimated that over $7 trillion is hidden from taxation in these tax havens throughout the world. Some think that Zucman's estimate is low; suggesting that the total may be in the $20 to $30 trillion range.

While multinational corporations do not keep the ownership of their subsidiaries secret, they do make use of the same laws to create shell companies and register them in tax havens to avoid paying corporate taxes on profits. It is estimated that U.S. multinational corporations have over $2 trillion in untaxed profits in offshore accounts.

Governments and corporations serve two very different purposes. The purpose of government is to maintain the cohesion of a population that is socially, economically, and, increasingly, culturally differentiated. To accomplish this, they enact regulatory laws that define the rights and duties, obligations and privileges of individuals and groups to minimize conflict and provide for the general welfare. Governments enact regulatory laws concerning wages, labor safety, environmental, and health standards. They enact laws to maintain market competition, which is a critical aspect of a market economy.

In addition, among other things, governments construct and maintain roads and bridges, dams and reservoirs and port facilities, and they fund educational programs, health programs, court and criminal justice systems, and the military. All of these, as well as many other, governmental functions are paid for through taxes. Governments are answerable to the people, and if a significant portion of the population feels that the government is no longer acting in their best interest, the result may be revolution. Most recently we have seen this happen in Tunisia, Libya, Egypt, and Syria.

The purpose of a business or corporation, on the other hand, is extremely limited. A business or corporation exists solely to produce goods, commodities, or services that can be sold for a profit to benefit its owner or owners. They are amoral, impersonal institutions that have no defined duties or obligations to their workers, to their consumers, or to the governments of the countries in which they operate except for those that are imposed by regulatory laws.

Not surprisingly, friction has always existed between governments and corporations. Ideally, governments attempt to regulate and tax corporate activities so as to increase the economic and social benefits to their citizens. Corporations, on the other hand, attempt to minimize governmental constraints or regulations on their activities and taxes so as to maximize profits. As long as they are basically "domestic corporations"—with economic production and/or marketing of goods, commodities, and/or services confined to a single country—there is no question that the national government has the ability to regulate their behavior and tax their profits. However, the emergence of the global economy has resulted in the development of a qualitatively different form of corporation: the multinational corporation.

Although both forms of corporations are legally incorporated in a specific country, multinational corporations, unlike domestic corporations, produce and/or market goods, commodities, or services globally. They are able to do this because of free- trade agreements that allow for the goods, commodities, or services produced in one country to be marketed in another free from tariffs (import or export taxes) or quotas. Not all goods, commodities, and services are covered by free-trade agreements, but most are covered under one agreement or another.

The most comprehensive of these agreements are those between the 162 member countries of the World Trade Organization (WTO). In essence, any goods, commodities, or services covered by the agreement produced in any of the 162 WTO member countries may be sold in another country without being subject to tariffs or quotas. In addition, member countries cannot enact laws that restrict or prohibit the marketing products produced in another member country. If a dispute arises between two countries, it is heard by a WTO tribunal in Geneva. Any existing law in any of the member countries may potentially be considered a restraint of trade, and thus illegal. The authority to determine whether the law of a particular country is "protectionist" rests solely with panels of appointed bureaucrats of the WTO.

If the WTO finds against a country, that country has one of only three options: (1) change the law, (2) pay compensation, or (3) have trade sanctions imposed. There is no appeal of a WTO decision.

In 1995 Venezuela filed a complaint with the WTO saying that the U.S. Clean Air Act, which regulates gas emissions to prevent air pollution, discriminated against the importation of Venezuelan gasoline. The WTO agreed. More recently the European Union (EU), for public health concerns, banned the sale of beef containing artificial hormones. The United States challenged this ban, and the WTO ruled against the EU, saying that a country cannot ban the import of a food as a precautionary health measure. The EU has to present scientific proof that artificial hormones are unsafe. Since 1995, over 500 restraint of trade complaints have been filed with the WTO.

What this means, for example, is that while EU farmers cannot raise or sell beef containing artificial hormones, they have to compete with such beef imported from the United States. Countries still have the right to regulate the production of goods, commodities, and services within their borders but cannot impose these regulatory standards on those imported from other countries.

Not surprisingly, corporations that are fully resident in high-cost developed countries—those with higher taxes; higher wages; and more stringent labor, environmental, and other regulatory laws—are at a competitive disadvantage with corporations resident in lower-cost (less-developed) countries.

Corporations have developed several different strategies to take advantage of existing free-trade agreements: (1) They can close portions of their business operations in their resident high-cost country and contract with overseas corporations in lower-cost countries to supply goods, commodities, and/or services; (2) they can open subsidiary operations overseas to provide them with particular products, which can then be imported and marketed in their resident country; and (3) they can become a fully multinational corporation, producing their products in lower-cost countries and marketing them throughout the world while

remaining legal resident of one of the higher-cost countries.

In these three strategies, the transfer of production to lower-cost countries means the loss of jobs in higher-cost countries—one of which is usually the resident country of the corporation. For example, we have seen this in the United States. Since 1995, 60,000 manufacturing plants and almost 6 million manufacturing jobs have been lost as U.S. corporations have outsourced jobs.

A fourth, more comprehensive strategy is for the corporation to legally structure itself as a corporation with varying numbers of full owned subsidiary corporations scattered throughout the world. The primary reason for this is the avoidance of corporate taxes. Subsidiary corporations are created in countries with either low taxes or even no taxes; foreign profits of corporations are then transferred to these subsidiaries. These tax avoidance schemes may be very complex legally involving multiple subsidiaries.

Apple Inc., a company that produces and markets its products throughout the world, is a good example of how such corporations avoid taxes. As a U.S.-based corporation, all Apple profits are subject to a 35 percent corporate tax rate, even on the estimated 60 percent of its profits that are generated overseas. One of the strategies Apple uses to avoid U.S. taxes is what many call the "double Irish." For tax purposes, Ireland recognizes two types of corporations: resident corporations, which have an actual presence in Ireland and pay a 12.5 percent tax, and nonresident corporations, which although tied to a resident corporation, do not have a physical presence in Ireland and pay no corporate taxes. Apple's "Irish" companies include Baldwin Holdings Unlimited, a nonresident Irish corporation in the British Virgin Islands, and Apple Distribution International in Cork, Ireland, which is a resident corporation that markets Apple products throughout Europe and elsewhere.

Baldwin Holdings "leases" the international intellectual property rights of Apple Inc., for which it pays a small fee. Baldwin, in turn, "leases" these rights to Apple Distribution International, which entitles Apple Distribution

International to most of the profits from their international sales. Revenue from international sales are managed by and paid to Apple Distribution International. After expenses, Apple Distribution International, per the lease agreement, pays most of its profits to Baldwin Holdings for their use of Apple's intellectual property rights. The relatively small amount that remains is the profit for Apple Distribution International, on which they paid 12.5 percent to Ireland. The bulk of these funds, which are paid to Baldwin Holdings, are Baldwin's "profits," on which they pay 0 percent in corporate taxes to the British Virgin Islands: They only pay a small registration fee.

Thus, Baldwin Holdings generates most of Apple's international profits, yet it has no physical presence in the British Virgin Islands: no office, no phone, no address, no employees; it is a shell company that exists solely for the purpose of avoiding U.S. corporate taxes. As long as these profits are held in the name of Baldwin Holdings, they are not subject to U.S. corporate taxes.

Baldwin Holdings is far from unique; there are numerous fully owned subsidiaries of U.S. multinational corporations holding profits offshore. In 2015, Citizens for Tax Justice reported that of the 500 largest U.S.-based multinational corporations, 358 of these companies owned 7,622, if not more, tax-haven subsidiaries.

According to *Fortune* magazine in 2014, the 500 largest companies in the world had a combined revenue of over $31 trillion—an amount equal to almost half of the total GDP (gross domestic product) of all of the countries in the world. If the revenue of the largest of these companies, Walmart, was equated with the GDP of countries, Walmart would be the twenty-third largest economy in the world, ranking just behind Sweden.

Not only are these multinational corporations large, but they also are getting ever larger by acquiring or merging with smaller multinational and domestic corporations. These 500 corporations differ greatly: Some are traditional energy or manufacturing businesses, and others are involved in

continues on next page

If the annual revenue of corporations is equated to the gross domestic product of countries, the United States would rank first, but Walmart would rank as the twenty-third largest economy in the world.

information technology or financial services. Some have existed for a century or more, but most, such as Walmart, are recent in origin. In 1962 Walmart consisted of a single retail store in Rogers, Arkansas. Today it has over 11,000 stores in 27 countries and over 2 million employees.

No company more clearly demonstrates the degree to which free trade has changed the economic structure of the world. It was not until the 1970s that Walmart started expanding when Sam Walton, the founder, noted that if he could import lower-cost merchandise, he could undercut his competitors. Small manufacturers in China became his main source. By 2004 it was estimated that Walmart was purchasing $18 billion annually from Chinese suppliers. By initially opening stores in small towns and small cities in the United States and marketing low-cost imported goods, Walmart was able to quickly eliminate its small, family-owned retail competitors. Once well established in the more rural areas, it moved into the larger cities and finally began competing internationally with large retail chains.

In the United States alone, Walmart has destroyed tens of thousands of small retail businesses and been a major contributor to the loss of manufacturing jobs. However, before blaming Sam Walton for these losses, we have to remember that had he not taken advantage of these new trade agreements, someone else would have created such a mega retailer. His store in Rogers, Arkansas, might have gone bankrupt, and instead of becoming a billionaire, he may have died living on his Social Security checks.

Thanks to the WTO and other trade agreements, the global economy and the multinational corporations that inhabit it have separated themselves from the political world. In the global economy, geography and political boundaries no longer inhibit the flow of goods, commodities, services, and money. The regulatory and tax laws of national governments only effectively apply to individuals and businesses that operate within their geographic boundaries, not multinational corporations. As a result, national governments are losing their ability to provide for the well-being of their populations. These governments have less capability to manage and direct economic development for the overall benefit of their people, and the income of the middle class in most developed countries has eroded. At the same time, the increasing loss of tax revenue due to the "offshoring" of profits by multinational corporations has undermined critical infrastructures—schools, roads, bridges, dams, and ports—while these governments have struggled to provide health, protective, and social services for their populations.

Many scholars have noted that one of the consequence of the global economy has been the increasing transfer of de facto political power from national governments to multinational corporations. Important decisions that directly affect the long-term well-being of the world's peoples are increasing being made by the boards of directors and executives of multinational corporations and not by the political leaders of their national governments. The emergence of the global economy has created, for the first time in human history, global economic activity that is unregulated by any national government or even by an international coalition of governments. These multinational corporations exist in a world without regulatory laws or taxation. With more economic power than many countries in the world, they are primed to play the poorer countries against richer ones in order to gain economic advantage. This raises the question: What is the future of present state-level national governments and the people whose well-being depends upon them?

and hostile terrain, the central government was able to organize human labor for massive public works projects, ranging from buildings and terraced fields to a 9,500-mile highway network that stretched the length and breadth of the country.

The Sapa Inca was also able to mobilize and supply armies numbering in the tens of thousands for extended periods of time. The Inca empire was a state created through the military conquest and incorporation of smaller neighboring states. However, it was the administrative abilities of its leaders—more than their military might—that gave the empire its political cohesiveness.

The Sapa Inca was believed to be the direct descendant of the Sun God. Thus, the Sapa Inca was a divine being, with absolute authority and control over all the people and resources of the empire. Succession was not clearly defined. Any son of the Sapa Inca had a legitimate claim to his father's position. To avoid conflict, the Sapa Inca usually chose one of his sons as his successor before his death, but the death of the Sapa Inca usually resulted in conflicts between potential heirs.

The empire was administratively divided into four geographic regions, each with its own head. The regions were split into provinces with governors and regional capitals. The provinces were, in turn, organized on the basis of what some have called a "decimal administration" of hierarchically nested administrative units based on population size. The largest, with a population of 10,000 households, was called a *huno*, which was divided into units of 5,000 households, 1,000 households, 500 households, 100 households, 50 households, and finally 10 households. Each unit had an official head responsible to the person above him. Periodically, the Inca conducted a census and made adjustments. This was the ideal administrative model; the actual structure varied somewhat from province to province due to local demographic and ethnic factors.

Regional heads were members of the Incan royal family. In some provinces, relatives of the Sapa Inca also filled the position of governor. However, in most cases provincial governors and other provincial officials were drawn from local elite families, and these families even held hereditary rights to these offices. Beneath these officials and their families was the great mass of people—the commoners.

The Inca divided land into plots for use by individual families and households and land for the support of public functions. Every household in the empire was given sufficient land to meet its economic needs. Households and local communities were basically self-sufficient. Food and other goods produced on their land and within the family belonged to the family.

The government of the empire was supported by a labor tax, not a tax on production. Every household was required to supply labor for state purposes. Some assignments were for a number of days per year, others were yearlong, and still others lifelong. The major function of provincial officials was to assign tasks, organize work parties, and oversee the work.

The majority of commoners paid their labor tax by working part of the year farming public fields, tending herds of state-owned animals, weaving cloth, making pottery, repairing public buildings, working on public roads, or performing some other local task. In every province, food, clothes, and other utilitarian goods produced by state-tax labor were stored in public buildings. State-owned food, clothes, and other goods were used to support the army, visiting government officials, and commoners who had been assigned long-term labor tasks that made it impossible for them to be self-supporting. In return for their services, all provincial officials in charge of 100 households or more were allowed to use tax laborers to farm their fields, tend their herds, build their houses, and make their clothes and other goods.

In the 1530s, the Spanish conquered the Inca empire and murdered the last Sapa Inca. However, the provincial governmental structure and the decimal administrative system were incorporated into the government of colonial Peru.

The emergence of states increased the complexity of political units. Bureaucracies not only allowed for specialization in governmental functions but also made possible the effective integration of large land areas and populations into political units. For example, chiefdoms seldom exceeded 30,000 persons, whereas modern states have populations in the hundreds of millions, and in the cases of China and India, over a billion.

Social Control and Law

All societies have clearly defined rules of behavior that govern the relationships between members. Not all individuals in any society will conform to these rules. There will always be some who behave in a socially unacceptable manner. Thus, among all peoples, there are formal and informal ways to correct the behavior of individuals. In general, we call these mechanisms *social control*. One form of social control is the law.

Social Control

Social control refers to the diverse ways in which the behaviors of the members of a society are constrained into socially approved channels. All cultures have certain behavioral norms that most people learn and begin to conform to during enculturation. But all societies have individuals who, to one degree or another, deviate from those norms. Violations of norms usually result in sanctions or punishments for the offender, which serve both to correct the behavior of particular people and to show others the penalties for such deviance. The severity of sanctions and the process by which sanctions are imposed differ greatly, depending on the seriousness culturally attached to the violated norm, the perceived severity of the violation, and the overall political and legal system of the people.

Parents usually correct their children when they misbehave. In our U.S. society, parents may impose sanctions ranging from scolding to spanking to withdrawing privileges. By correcting children at an early age, individuals are trained in proper behavior.

The community as a whole also applies informal sanctions against children and adults who are not behaving properly. Gossip, or fear of gossip, serves as an important method of social control in many societies. Most people fear the contempt or ridicule of their peers, so they try to conform to acceptable behavioral norms. People attempt to hide behavior that would be the subject of gossip, scandal, and ridicule. Individuals whose known behavior consistently violates social norms may even find themselves ostracized by friends and relatives (the severest of informal punishments). Informal economic penalties also may be imposed. A family may withdraw economic support in attempts to modify the errant behavior of a member.

A wide variety of supernatural sanctions may assist in controlling individual behavior; in some cases, these supernatural sanctions are automatically imposed on particular types of behavior. Whether the commission of these acts becomes public knowledge or not, and thus regardless of whether other punishments are in-

---

social control Mechanism by which behavior is constrained and directed into acceptable channels, thus maintaining conformity.

law Type of social control characterized by the presence of authority, intention of universal application, obligation, and sanction.

---

flicted on the individual, the commission still endangers one's immortal soul. Supernatural sanctions can be more specifically directed. In many societies, including some Christian ones, an individual may place a curse on another person by calling on a supernatural being. Fear of sorcery or witchcraft (see Chapter 14) frequently serves as another important form of social control. Most victims are people who offended a witch or sorcerer in some way, often through a breach of social norms.

Law

Law is the highest level of social control; legal punishments usually are reserved for the most serious breaches of norms. The question of how law can be distinguished from other forms of social control is not easy to answer. In societies that have court systems, the distinction is formalized, but in societies with no such formalized legal systems, the distinction is not so clear-cut. E. Adamson Hoebel (1954, p. 28) defined law in the following way: "A social norm is legal if its neglect or infraction is regularly met, in threat or in fact, by the application of physical force by an individual or group possessing the socially recognized privilege of so acting." Law so defined was and is present in virtually every society.

In a legal action, some individual or group must have publicly recognized authority to settle a case or punish a violation. In societies with courts, the authority is obvious; however, in societies that lack courts, the authority becomes less clear. What emerges frequently is an ad hoc authority; that is, because of the peculiarities of the case, a particular individual or group becomes recognized by the community as the authority responsible for its resolution. In some cases, the victim may be the recognized authority. In the victim's absence (as in the case of murder), the victim's family, clan, or kin group may be placed in the role of authority. Such ad hoc authority is discussed later in some of the examples.

Implicit in all legal actions is the intention of universal application, which means that in identical cases, the sanction imposed is the same. Although one might argue that no two legal cases have been or will ever be identical, the notion of universal application requires that the law be consistent and thus predictable; the arbitrary imposition of sanctions is not law.

Hoebel limited legal sanctions to physical sanctions; however, other scholars have argued that this definition is too narrow. A legal sanction does not have to be some form of corporal punishment, nor does it have to involve the loss of property. Based on

Form	Characteristics	Associated Political Organization(s)
Self-Help (a) Familial	Legal concepts based on accepted social norms and behaviors of the society; ad hoc sanctioning authority limited to victim and/or victim's family, with implicit support of other community members	Band
(b) Mediator	Legal concepts based on accepted social norms and behaviors of the society; ad hoc sanctioning authority limited to victim and/or victim's family, with implicit support of other community members; use of a third-party mediator, with limited if any authority, to negotiate a settlement	Composite bands and most tribal peoples
Courts (a) Incipient	A council of leaders discusses the event among themselves to determine the appropriate action that needs to be taken	Some tribal peoples
(b) Mediation	Legal concepts based on the reasonable-person model; formal judges who have the authority to hear cases and impose sanctions	Some tribal peoples have rudimentary court systems; however, true court systems appear with chiefdoms and smaller states
(c) Regulation	Laws and sanctions are formally codified; formal judges who have the authority to hear cases and impose sanctions	States

his work with the Kapauku of New Guinea, Leopold Pospíšil contended that the impact of psychological sanctions can be more severe than that of actual physical punishment. For this reason, he stated, "We can define a legal sanction as either the negative behavior of withdrawing some rewards or favors that otherwise (if the law had not been violated) would have been granted, or the positive behavior of inflicting some painful experience, be it physical or psychological" (Pospíšil, 1958, p. 268).

Legal Systems

On the basis of procedural characteristics, two main levels of complexity and formality can be defined: self-help legal systems and court legal systems. The Concept Review outlines the various forms of legal systems.

Self-Help Systems

A **self-help legal system**, also called an *ad hoc system*, are informal and exist in the absence of any centralized or formalized legal institutions capable of settling disputes. Such systems are associated with band-level societies and most tribal-level societies. In such systems, there is only civil law. All legal actions concern

only the principal parties and/or their families. The reason for terming the legal procedure in these societies *self-help* will become clear.

Self-help legal systems may be divided into two main forms: familial and mediator. In *familial* systems, all actions and decisions are initiated and executed by the families or larger kin groups involved. *Mediator* systems add the formal presence of a neutral third party—the mediator—who attempts to negotiate and resolve the dispute peacefully.

In familial systems, the families involved handle the legal actions. A legal offense only indirectly concerns the community as a whole. When an individual or a family determines that its rights have been violated, the imposition of the proper sanction falls to the plaintiffs; in other words, the offended party assumes the role of authority. Such a system has some problems in implementation, but not as many as one might anticipate. This is not a

self-help legal system Informal legal system in societies without a centralized political systems in which authorities who settle disputes are defined by the circumstances of the case; also called *ad hoc system*.

system of "might makes right." Certainly cases arise in such societies in which the weak are victimized by the strong. In cases of legal redress, however, there is a community consensus in support of the victim and usually a recognized means by which even the weakest members of the community can gather support adequate to impose appropriate sanctions on the strongest.

The Comanche exemplify how a familial legal system operated and how victims weaker than their opponents could nonetheless obtain redress. One of the most frequent Comanche offenses was "wife stealing." Most older Comanche men were polygynous, and some of their wives were significantly younger than their husbands. Among young Comanche men, it was considered prestigious, though illegal, to steal the wife of another man. Under Comanche law, the injured husband could demand either his wife back or some property, usually horses, in compensation. The husband had the responsibility of imposing these sanctions. In such actions, the community played no direct role, but a husband could not ignore the loss of a wife. If he did ignore it, the community would ridicule him, and his prestige would decline. Thus, not only did the community support the husband in pressing his claim, but also they informally pressured him to act.

In imposing these sanctions, the husband was allowed to use whatever physical force was needed, short of killing the offender. In cases in which the men involved were physically about equal, the two met to negotiate and discuss the husband's demands. Behind these negotiations was the potential threat that the husband might physically assault the defendant.

In cases where the husband presented little or no physical threat to the defendant, institutionalized means existed whereby the husband could gain physical backing. Although it lowered his prestige in the community, he could call on his relatives for support; with his male relatives present and prepared to support his demands physically, the husband could then negotiate with the defendant. The defendant always had to stand alone. Even if he had asked his kinsmen for support, they would not have responded for fear of community ridicule.

In cases where the husband was an orphan or lacked kinsmen, he could call on any other man he wanted to prosecute his case. He usually asked for the assistance of one of the powerful war leaders in the band. Such a request was so prestigious that a war leader could not refuse. At the same time, such a request was demeaning to the man asking for help and greatly lowered his prestige. As a result, it usually required a great deal of social pressure to force a man to ask for assistance.

Once the request was made, the issue was between the defendant and the war leader alone. On approaching the defendant, the war leader would call out, "You have stolen my wife," and then proceed to exact whatever demands the husband had requested. For his action, the war leader received nothing in payment other than the increased admiration of the community; the husband received the settlement. Although this process was used most commonly in wife-stealing cases, it could be used for other issues as well. Thus, Comanche legal institutions gave any individual the means to marshal overwhelming physical force to protect his rights.

A more formalized type of legal procedure is found in the mediator system. In this system, disputes are still between individuals and families, and the offended party or the person's family has the position of authority. However, a third party is called on, usually by the offending individual or his or her family, to attempt to negotiate a mutually agreeable solution. The mediator has no authority to impose a settlement. The aggrieved party and/or family must agree to accept the compensation negotiated.

The Nuer, a pastoral society of Sudan, provide an example of how mediator systems operate. The Nuer live in small villages of related families. Although villages are tied together through lineages and clans, there is no effective leadership above the village level. The only formalized leaders who transcend the local units are *leopard-skin chiefs*, who wear a leopard-skin cloak to indicate their positions. These men have no secular authority to enforce their judgments but only limited ritual powers to bless and curse.

The most important function of leopard-skin chiefs is mediating disputes between local families. The Nuer are an egalitarian, warrior-oriented people. Disputes between individuals frequently result in physical violence, and men occasionally are killed. The killing requires that the kinsmen exact retribution. Any close patrilineal kinsman of the murderer may be killed in retaliation, but at least initially the kinsmen of the victim attempt to kill the murderer himself. Immediately after committing a murder, the killer flees to the house of a leopard-skin chief. This dwelling is a sanctuary, and as long as the man stays in the chief's house, he is safe. The victim's kinsmen usually keep the house under surveillance to try to kill the murderer if he ventures out.

The leopard-skin chief keeps the murderer in his house until a settlement is arranged. The chief will wait until tempers have cooled, which usually requires several weeks, before he begins to negotiate the case. First, he goes to the family of the murderer to see if they are willing to pay cattle to the victim's family in compensation. Seldom do they refuse because one of them might be killed in retaliation. After the murderer's family has agreed to pay, the chief proceeds to the family of the victim, offering so many cattle in compensation. Initially, the victim's family invariably refuses, saying that they want blood, that cattle cannot compensate them for the death of their kinsman. The leopard-skin chief persists, usually gaining the support of more distant relatives of the victim, who also pressure the family to settle. The leopard-skin chief may even threaten to place a curse on the family if they continue to refuse to settle for a payment rather than blood. The family finally agrees and accepts cattle, usually about 40 head, as compensation. Even though the matter is formally settled, the killer and his close patrilineal kinsmen will avoid the family of the victim for some years so as not to provoke spontaneous retaliation.

Up to this point, we have examined legal systems that operate without a formalized or centralized political structure capable of resolving disputes. In many of these societies, law, not subordination to a common set of formal political institutions, defines boundaries. To see what we mean, consider the Nuer. The Nuer distinguish among a *ter*, a feud within local Nuer groups that is a legal action subject to arbitration; a *kur*, a fight between members of two distant Nuer groups that cannot be arbitrated; and a *pec*, a war with non-Nuer people. Nuer believe that disputes within a localized group should be resolved by legal means (i.e., peacefully), whereas disputes between individuals who are not members of the same local group should be resolved by extralegal means, including organized warfare. Legal processes serve to repair and maintain social relations between families; thus, law serves both to maintain the cohesiveness and to define the boundaries of the society.

The Jívaro, a horticultural and foraging people of eastern Ecuador, also illustrate how law defines social boundaries. By the 1950s, the Jívaro had been reduced to slightly more than 2,000 persons settled in more than 200 scattered family households. Such households usually consist of a husband, his wife or wives, their children, and possibly a son-in-law or other relatives. Households are grouped into "neighborhoods," which consist of a number of households living within a few miles of one another; the membership of a neighborhood is fluid. Poor hunting, a dispute with other households, or other factors might result in a family's moving away. Neither corporate kin groups nor formalized leadership positions exist. Except for household heads, only a few men are called *unta*, or "big," but their informal leadership role is limited and transitory.

Politically, the Jívaro are organized at a band level. Although they have only limited political institutions, the Jívaro have a strong sense of common cultural identity and territorial boundaries. Living in adjacent or nearby territories are four other Jívaroan groups, who speak mutually intelligible dialects, share the same basic customs, and at times trade with Jívaro households. Despite their minimal political integration, there is no question about which households are Jívaro and which belong to the other four groups.

With this political organization, the methods used to settle disputes define the effective boundaries of the society. Disputes between Jívaros are resolved by legal means, whereas disputes with members of other societies are resolved through extralegal means. Like the Nuer, the Jívaro make a sharp distinction between a feud and a war. A **feud** is the legal means by which a sanction is imposed on another family for the murder of a kinsman. As a legal procedure, a feud proceeds in a manner quite different from a war.

As in most societies, murder is the most serious offense. According to Jívaro beliefs, few deaths are attributable to natural causes; most are the result of physical violence, sorcery, or avenging spirits. Deaths caused by physical violence and witchcraft are considered murders, which have to be avenged by the kinsmen of the deceased. In most cases of physical violence, the murderer is readily identifiable. In cases of poisoning and witchcraft, divination is used to determine the guilty party.

Determination of the guilty party and whether they are Jívaro or non-Jívaro affect how the victim's kinfolk avenge the death. If the guilty party is Jívaro, the kinsmen of the victim attack the household of the murderer with the goal of killing the man himself. If they are not successful in finding him, they may kill a male relative of his, even a young boy. They normally will not harm women or little children, except when the victim was a woman or a child. Even if they have the opportunity to kill more, only one individual will be killed. This is a legal action, and Jívaro law allows only a life for a life.

If the guilty party is determined to be a non-Jívaro, the relatives of the murdered person attack the household of the guilty party, trying to kill as many people as possible. They attempt to massacre the entire family,

feud Method of dispute settlement in self-help legal systems involving multiple but balanced killings between members of two or more kin groups.

with no regard for either sex or age. In some cases, they attack nearby households as well, attempting to kill even more members of the group. This is a war, not a legal action.

The Jívaro, the Nuer, and other peoples who lack a centralized and formal political structure nonetheless have definite means of maintaining social control. To those of us who have formal governmental institutions that are supposed to handle our grievances and right the wrongs done to us, self-help systems look rather anarchic. However, rules govern such systems.

Court Systems

A number of factors distinguish a **court legal system** from a self-help legal system. First, authority resides not with the victim and his or her family but with a formalized institution—the court. The court has the authority and the power to hear disputes and to unilaterally decide cases and impose sanctions. Authority in legal matters is a component of political authority; thus, fully developed court systems can exist only in societies that have centralized formal political leadership— that is, chiefdoms or states. Second, most court systems operate with formal public hearings, presided over by a judge or judges, with formally defined defendants and plaintiffs. Grievances are stated; evidence is collected and analyzed; and, in cases of conflicting evidence, oaths or ordeals may be used to determine truthfulness. Finally, only in court systems does one find substantive law clearly divided into criminal law and civil law.

Court systems in turn may be divided into three categories: (1) incipient courts, (2) courts of mediation, and (3) courts of regulation. All court systems mediate disputes as well as regulate behavior; however, as societies become increasingly complex, the primary focus of the court shifts from mediating disputes to regulating behavior. This shift results in a qualitative

difference not only in courts but also in the nature of the law itself. Associated with this shift is an increasing codification of the laws. Laws and their associated sanctions become standardized and rigid, and civil laws are steadily transformed into criminal laws. Court systems begin to emerge with the concept of "crime against society"—the need to control individual acts that might endanger the society as a whole, as opposed to acts that threaten only individuals. Herein lies the distinction between criminal law and civil law.

Incipient Court Systems

True court systems can be found only in societies that have centralized political systems—chiefdoms or states. However, some tribal societies have what might best be termed an **incipient court**.

Although the Cheyenne, as described earlier, are a tribal-level society, they demonstrate the development of an incipient court system. At times, both the Council of Forty-Four and the warrior societies assumed the role of de facto judges and courts. The Cheyenne recognized that certain individual actions threatened the well-being of the group and thus had to be controlled. Some of these actions were purely secular, whereas others were religious. Designated warrior societies were formally empowered by the council to enforce secular laws and regulations. For example, in preparation for a communal bison hunt, camp members would be told to refrain from independent hunting. A single hunter could disturb the herd, thus spoiling the hunt for the group. To prevent this, one of the warrior societies was designated by the council to police the area around the village. If the members of the warrior society discovered someone hunting illegally, they became the de facto judges and court and immediately imposed sanctions on the offender, often beating him with whips, shooting his horses, and slashing his tepee with knives.

Other secular criminal violations were handled just as swiftly. The Council of Forty-Four was responsible for the religious, or sacred, well-being of the tribe; thus, any action that endangered the supernatural well-being of the Cheyenne was their concern. The murder of a Cheyenne by another Cheyenne was the most heinous of crimes. Such a crime was said to bloody the sacred arrows, the most sacred of Cheyenne tribal medicine bundles. The arrows were symbolic of Cheyenne success in hunting (their main economic activity) and warfare. Murder within the tribe polluted the arrows and thus made the Cheyenne vulnerable to their enemies and less successful in their hunting.

court legal system System in which authority for settling disputes and punishing crimes is formally vested in a single individual or group.

incipient court Court system in which judicial authorities meet, frequently informally, in private to discuss issues and determine solutions to be imposed. Evidence is not formally collected, and the parties involved in these cases are not formally consulted.

When a Cheyenne died at the hands of another Cheyenne, the Council of Forty-Four became a de facto court. Although there was no formal hearing, the council met and discussed the case by themselves. In small societies like the Cheyenne, there was no need for a formal hearing with witnesses—the members of the council knew all of the relevant facts concerning the events. There were two issues they had to decide. First, they needed to determine whether the act was a murder. If so, then the sacred arrows had to be "renewed," or ritually purified. Second, they had to decide on the sanction to be imposed—usually exile for a period of years. For the Cheyenne, there could be no capital punishment without again polluting the sacred arrows.

Another matter the Cheyenne had to deal with was determining when a suicide was a "murder." There were several cases of Cheyenne women committing suicide for what the council determined to be trivial reasons. These were not considered murder, and so the arrows were not renewed. In other instances, however, suicide was treated as murder. In one case, for example, a mother became infuriated when her daughter eloped with a young man of whom she did not approve. The mother found the girl and beat her with a whip while dragging her home. Once inside the tepee, the girl seized a gun and shot herself. In another case a young girl divorced her husband and returned to her parents' home. Sometime later, the mother found the girl participating in a young person's dance and beat her; the girl hanged herself. The council decided in these cases that these girls' deaths were murder on the basis that the mothers had driven the girls to suicide. In both cases, the sacred arrows were renewed and the mothers banished from the tribe.

In other cases, the council had to determine when the murder of a Cheyenne was justified. In one case, a man attempted to rape his daughter; she resisted and killed him with a knife. While the council had the sacred arrows renewed, the girl was not banished, and the people did not treat the girl as a murderer. In still another case, a man named Winnebago took the wife of another man, who retaliated by taking one of Winnebago's other wives. Enraged Winnebago killed the man and was banished by the council. After returning from his banishment, which lasted five years, Winnebago argued with and killed another man. Again the council banished Winnebago, who took up residence with the Arapaho tribe. Later a Cheyenne named Rising Fire became involved in a dispute with Winnebago. Knowing Winnebago's reputation, Rising Fire shot and killed him. The council took no action.

Courts of Mediation

The key difference between court systems is not how the legal hearings are conducted but the manner in which breaches of the law are determined and suitable sanctions imposed. In a **court of mediation**, few laws are codified, and the judges follow few formalized guidelines as to what constitutes a legal violation or the sanction that should be imposed.

This is not to say that judges act arbitrarily in these matters, but that they have tremendous latitude in their actions. What they apply is a **reasonable-person model**. Using prevalent norms and values, they ask the question: How should a reasonable individual have acted under these circumstances? To determine the answer, they must examine an individual's actions within the social context in which the dispute occurred: What were the past and present relationships between the parties involved? What circumstances led up to the event? Thus, judges attempt to examine each case as a unique occurrence. Although some sanctions are imposed as punishments, other sanctions are designed to restore as fully as possible a working, if not harmonious, relationship between the parties involved.

One difficulty in attempting to describe courts of mediation is our limited knowledge of such systems. Polities that had courts of this nature were some time ago brought under European colonial rule. Their courts were soon modified by and subordinated to European colonial courts, which were more regulatory in nature. The example we use is the Barotse judicial system, as described by Max Gluckman. The Barotse made up a multiethnic state in southern Africa that at the time of Gluckman's study in the 1940s had been under British rule for 40 years. The British had removed more serious offenses from the jurisdiction of this court. Despite these factors, the basic Barotse legal concepts aptly illustrate a mediation type of court system.

The Barotse state had two capitals: a northern capital, where the king resided, and a subordinate southern

court of mediation Court system in which judges attempt to reach compromise solutions, based on the cultural norms and values of the parties involved, that will restore the social cohesion of the community.

reasonable-person model Model used in legal reasoning that asks how a reasonable individual should have acted under these circumstances.

capital, ruled by a princess. All villages in the state were attached to one or the other of these capitals. The capitals were identical in structure; each had a palace and a council house. Courts of law were held in the council house.

The titular head of the court was the ruler; in practice, the ruler seldom was present at trials. In the center at the back of the house was the dais, or raised platform, where the ruler was seated if present. There were three ranked groupings of judges. The highest-ranking group of judges was the *indunas*, or councilors, who sat to the right of the dais. The second-highest-ranking group was the *likombwa*, or stewards, who sat to the left. These two groups were divided into senior members, who sat in the front, and junior members, who sat behind. The third group consisted of princes and the husbands of the princesses, who represented their wives. This group sat at a right angle to the *likombwa*.

The plaintiff introduced the case, stating his or her grievance at length with no interruption; the defendant was then allowed the same privilege. The statements of witnesses for both sides followed. There were no attorneys for either side; the judges questioned and cross-examined the witnesses. After all the testimony had been heard, the judges began to give their opinions, starting with the most junior *indunas*, followed by the others in order of increasing seniority. The last judge to speak was the senior *induna*, who passed judgment on the case, subject to the ruler's approval.

In judging a case, the Barotse judges used a reasonable-person model. The reasonableness of behavior was related to the social and kinship relationships of the individuals involved. Also, a breach of the law usually did not happen in isolation, and many individuals could be at fault; so one case frequently led to a number of related cases.

In passing judgment and imposing sanctions, the judges considered numerous factors. One of the most important was the kinship relationship between the parties. The judges attempted to restore the relationship and reconcile the parties—but not without blaming those who had committed wrongs and not without imposing sanctions. The judges' opinions frequently took the form of sermons on proper behavior. As Gluckman (1973, p. 22) noted:

> Implicit in the reasonable man is the upright man, and moral issues in these relationships are barely differentiated from legal issues. This is so even though . . . [they] distinguish "legal" rules, which the . . . [court] has power to enforce or protect, from "moral" rules which it has not power to

enforce or protect. But the judges are reluctant to support the person who is right in law, but wrong in justice, and may seek to achieve justice by indirect . . . action.

Courts of mediation have great potential for meeting the basic social purpose of the law, which is the maintenance of group cohesiveness. There is one serious drawback: Such a system is workable only in a culturally homogeneous political unit; that is, it works only if the judges and the parties involved share the same basic norms and values.

Courts of Regulation

In the second millennium B.P., King Hammurabi of Babylon created the earliest known set of written laws, known as the Code of Hammurabi. The code covered a variety of laws. One section dealt with physicians. It set the prices to be charged for various types of operations, based on the ability of individuals to pay. It also decreed, among other things, that if a surgeon operated on an individual using a bronze knife and the patient died or lost his eyesight, the surgeon's hand was to be cut off. The laws defined in the Code of Hammurabi reflect the emergence of regulatory laws. The role of the court was no longer to merely arbitrate disputes and strive

In courts of regulation, the authority of judges is usually limited.

for reconciliation but to define the rights and duties of members of an increasingly heterogeneous community.

The **court of regulation** was a natural outgrowth of state-level polities, which evolved socially and economically distinct classes and encompassed numerous culturally distinct peoples. As relationships between individuals in the population became depersonalized, the law, too, became increasingly depersonalized. This change in the nature of law was compounded by the political incorporation of diverse peoples who frequently had conflicting cultural norms and values.

The use of a reasonable-person model is workable only as long as there is a general consensus on what is reasonable. In increasingly complex and stratified societies, the possibility of such consensus declined. Mediation of disputes works well in small, kinship-based societies, where all parties recognize the need for reconciliation through compromise. In sharply divided societies, the need for mediation is not as great because reconciliation in itself is not seen as a gain. Compromise is viewed only in terms of what is lost. Laws were thus created to bring order and stability to the interactions between individuals who were not social equals. With law divorced from social norms and values, justice was no longer simply a moral or ethical issue, but came to be viewed in terms of consistency, or precedent.

The separation of law from social norms and values also opened the door for the *politicization* of the laws. Laws were created to serve political ends, as various groups vied with one another for the creation of laws that would protect, express, or further their own goals, interests, and values. This situation is particularly evident in multiethnic and religiously and economically diverse state-level systems such as that of the United States. Given the cultural pluralism, religious diversity, and economic inequality of the United States, it would be impossible to create a code of laws that could equally protect the interests of all classes and that would be consistent with the norms and values of all groups.

As a result, many people find themselves subject to laws and sanctions, some of which they judge either immoral or unethical; at times, people find that laws violate their own cultural values. We see this with groups who think that abortion is murder and thus should be made illegal, and with groups who oppose capital punishment on the grounds that the state does not have the right to kill individuals. During the Vietnam War, we saw it with draft resisters who argued that the state did not have the right to order men to fight in a war they considered immoral. Less obvious is the manner in which numerous ethnic minorities, notably Native Americans, subordinate their cultural norms and values to comply with the legal system. With the emergence of states and courts of regulation, law ceased to be an expression of the social norms and values of the society; instead, it frequently imposes on the population new standards of behavior that many people feel are unjust, if not immoral.

court of regulation Court system that uses codified laws, with formally prescribed rights, duties, and sanctions.

SUMMARY

1. **Explain what is meant by political organization.** Collective action—in economic and social activities as well as relations with other groups of people—is a prerequisite for the survival of a group of people. To be effective, group activities must have leadership and organization, which are the basis for political structure. All societies have some form of political organization.

2. **List the four main types of political organization and how they structurally differ from one another.** The four major categories of political organization are bands, tribes, chiefdoms, and states. Found among foraging societies, the band is the simplest and least formal level of political organization. The two forms of band organization are simple bands and composite bands. In simple bands, the highest level of political organization

is the extended family, with the highest level of political leadership being the heads of the various families. These simple bands are economically self-sufficient and politically autonomous. Because a simple band has as its core a group of related individuals, band members are forced to seek spouses from outside the band; they are exogamous units. Thus, kinship ties through marriage serve as the primary link between bands. Composite bands are larger than simple bands and include a number of unrelated families. Leadership in composite bands is vested in "big men," or informal leaders, who have influence but not authority. The key element in tribal societies is the sodality, which transcend local residence groups and bind the geographically scattered members of the society into a cohesive unit. Sodalities may be either kinship based, as in the case of clans, or non–kinship based, as in the case of warrior societies or age grades. Leadership in such groups is more structured, with formal political offices. Chiefdoms have formal, hereditary leadership with centralized political control and authority. The associated redistributive economic exchange system focused on the chief economically integrates the various communities within the political unit. The state is the most complex level of political organization. States have centralized power and control, but the key characteristic of a state is a bureaucracy—individuals acting on behalf of the political elite, thus enabling the centralized power figures to maintain control of a greater number of individuals.

3. **Explain what is meant by social control.** Individual differences, conflict, and competition within the group must be controlled and channeled in such a manner that the internal cohesiveness and cooperation of the individual members of the group are maintained—thus the need for social control. Social control consists of the various formal and informal methods used to control and channel the behavior of individual members of a society into approved behavior.

4. **Discuss legal systems and how they differ from other forms of social control.** Law and legal systems are merely the highest level of social control. Law is defined as having three attributes: (1) authority, (2) intention of universal application, and (3) sanction. By this definition, all societies have law.

5. **Discuss the two major forms of legal systems and the variants within the two forms.** There are two major forms of legal systems: self-help systems and court systems. In self-help systems, the responsibility and authority for determining a breach of the law and imposing the proper sanction fall to the victim or victim's family (or both). In court systems, formal judges determine where a law has been violated and impose sanctions against the violator.

6. **Explain the relationship between the legal system found in a society and the political organization of that society.** In societies with no centralized political systems, bands, and some tribes, legal systems are self-help. As discussed, this system is not as arbitrary as we might think. In the case of murder or killing, the result may be a feud between families, but a feud—sharply distinguished from a war—is part of the legal process. In societies with centralized political systems, chiefdoms, states, and some tribes, violations of the law are handled by courts. Court systems usually can be categorized as either courts of mediation or courts of regulation. In relatively homogeneous societies, most court systems take as their primary objective the mediation of disputes between individuals and the restoration of harmonious social relationships. In more heterogeneous groups, courts usually become more regulatory in nature, with formally defined laws and sanctions.

13 Social Inequality and Stratification

Desperately poor families coexist with middle class and wealthy classes in nearly all nations today. This photo was taken in the region around Sao Paulo, Brazil.

Equalities and Inequalities

Three Systems
  Egalitarian Societies
  Ranked Societies
  Stratified Societies

Castes in Traditional India

Class in the United States

Maintaining Inequality
  Ideologies
  American Secular Ideologies

Theories of Inequality
  Functionalist Theory
  Conflict Theory
  Who Benefits?

After reading this chapter, you should be able to:

1 **EXPLAIN** the terms *egalitarian*, *ranked*, and *stratified*.

2 **DISCUSS** the primary differences between castes and classes.

3 **DESCRIBE** how ideologies are important in maintaining inequalities in stratified societies.

4 **EVALUATE** the functional and conflict theories of stratification.

In the United States 2016 presidential primaries, two candidates from different political parties talked a lot about inequality issues in the United States. On the Democratic side, Bernie Sanders described how the 1 percent has received almost all the gains in national income in the last couple of decades. Republican candidate Donald Trump railed against free-trade deals that the federal government negotiated—like the North American Free Trade Agreement (NAFTA)—that took American jobs and lowered wages. Sanders mostly blamed Wall Street greed, the inadequately regulated financial sector, and the political influence of corporate elites. Trump laid the guilt on immigrants (undocumented and otherwise), other countries (especially Mexico and China), and expensive and failed wars (Iraq and Libya). Whereas the core of Sanders's support was millennials of all ethnicities, Trump appealed primarily to working-class white men. Both candidates agreed that the "system is rigged." Despite their profound differences, Trump and Sanders appealed to the same feelings—average people are getting screwed by somebody.

In this chapter, we consider yet another dimension of cultural diversity: the allocation of culturally valued rewards. The essence of this topic is "Who gets what and why?" (Race, gender, and ethnicity are three other bases for allocating rewards, as covered in Chapters 2, 11, and 16.)

Equalities and Inequalities

Inequality refers to the degree to which culturally valued material and social rewards are received disproportionately by individuals, families, and other

~~~~~~~~~~~~~~~~~~~~~~~~~~~~~~~~

inequality Degree to which individuals, groups, and categories differ in their access to culturally valued rewards.

kinds of groups. To the extent that inequality exists in a group or whole society, its members receive varying levels of benefits. Although specific rewards vary by culture, in comparing societies, anthropologists commonly distinguish three reward categories.

The most tangible reward is *wealth*—ownership of or access to valued material goods and to the natural and human resources needed to produce those goods. The national economies of modern nations measure wealth in money (total GDP or GDP per capita). Preindustrial peoples who do not use money may value tangible products like shelter and beads and resources that can be used to produce such products.

The second kind of reward is *power*—the ability to make others do what you want based on coercion or legitimate authority (see Chapter 12). Wealth and power go together among some peoples, each mutually reinforcing the other. But not always: Esoteric (secret) knowledge often enhances the power of men and women who have little wealth. On the Micronesian island of Pohnpei, people believe that many elderly people possess secret knowledge that they often do not disclose until just before their death, if at all. Sorcery and witchcraft also can make people powerful (see Chapter 14).

The final type of reward is *prestige*—the respect, admiration, and overt approval other group members grant to individuals they consider meritorious. Prestige (*respect, status*) is a social reward, based on judgments about an individual's personal worthiness or the contributions the individual makes to others in the group. Norms, values, worldviews, and other cultural knowledge affect prestige. For instance, many North Americans admire self-made persons who have succeeded (or who convince others they have) by their own talents and efforts. However, such individuals would be looked down on as self-centered and ungenerous in many other cultures, such as the Hadzabe and the Ju/'hoansi (see Chapter 7).

Form	Main Characteristics
Egalitarian	Rough equality between families in access to necessities, possessions, and wealth objects; wide access to and sharing of productive resources; influence and prestige based on age and personal qualities and achievements
Ranked	Limited number of formal social roles or positions (offices, titles) that confer limited authority; access to prestigious titles and offices determined largely by hereditary factors
Stratified	Sharply unequal distribution of material resources and wealth between strata; large inequalities in access to power and social rewards
(a) Caste	Named, endogamous, ranked groups with membership normatively based on birth; occupation and activities constrained by caste membership; interaction between members of different castes governed by social rules (e.g., segregation, pollution)
(b) Class	Vague definition and imprecise membership determined by a combination of birth and achievement; class membership broadly determined by occupation and wealth level, variably affected by inheritance

The distribution of each kind of reward varies among societies. Some societies allow ambitious individuals to acquire wealth, power, and prestige, whereas others make it difficult for anyone to accumulate possessions, gain power over others, or put themselves above their peers socially. It is important to understand that what people think about the distribution of rewards does not necessarily correlate with the actual distribution, especially with wealth, which can be hidden or which takes many forms.

Three Systems

To introduce the ways societies differ in inequality, anthropologists often use an influential classification developed by Morton Fried back in 1967. Fried identified three basic types of societies based on their degree and form of inequality: **egalitarian**, **ranked**, and **stratified**. (The Concept Review provides a quick look at the major differences between the three systems, as well as a summary of the distinction between caste and class.) We need to clarify four points about Fried's classification.

First, the categories do not refer to access to rewards based on gender or age. When we call a society *egalitarian*, for example, we do not mean that women and men receive equal or nearly equal rewards, that elderly people and young people are socially equal, or that unskilled and lazy people are valued just as much as skilled and diligent people. Even in egalitarian

societies, social distinctions exist based on gender, age, and personal qualities. Essentially, *egalitarian* means there are few differences in the rewards received by families or other kinds of kin groups within a society. At the other end of the continuum, in *stratified* societies, there are major differences in rewards between families or kin groups, in addition to other distinctions such as gender, age, and personal qualities.

Second, Fried's three categories are merely points along a continuum of inequality. It is impossible to pigeonhole all human societies into one of these types because most fit somewhere in between the three categories. The terms *egalitarian*, *ranked*, and *stratified* are most useful to distinguish the kinds and range of variation in inequality found among the world's peoples.

Third, this sequence—egalitarian, ranked, stratified—is the temporal order in which the three forms developed. Until about 10,000 years ago, nearly all humans

egalitarian society Form of society in which there is little inequality in access to culturally valued rewards.

ranked society Form of society with a limited number of high-ranking, privileged social positions; groups are ranked relative to one another.

stratified society Form of society with marked and variably heritable differences in access to wealth, power, and prestige; inequality is based mainly on unequal access to productive and valued resources.

lived in egalitarian or ranked societies. Stratification developed in some early chiefdoms and in the great civilizations between 5,000 and 6,000 years ago (see Chapters 7 and 12). By a few centuries ago, stratified societies occupied much of the world, as some peoples and nations conquered and ruled over others.

Fourth, it is important to distinguish two bases for inequality. In ranked and stratified societies, people (some people, at least) may positively value inequality, believing it is necessary for the welfare of all or that it is supernaturally ordained. Alternatively, inequality may exist because it is a regular outcome of how a particular economic and political system works. That is, people (some or most people, at least) may desire or value more equality than actually exists, but their desires and values cannot be realized because the economic or social system continually generates inequality.

Egalitarian Societies

In egalitarian societies, aside from distinctions based on sex and age, minor differences exist among individuals and families in rewards. People who work hard, who have attractive personalities, or who possess valuable skills may be rewarded with respect and prestige from other members of their group. Egalitarian groups have various cultural mechanisms to prevent any individual from becoming too "big." And, even respected people do not have much more in the way of possessions or power than others.

Mobile hunting and gathering peoples—such as the Inuit, Ju/'hoansi, Hadzabe, and BaMbuti—are egalitarian. James Woodburn identified three reasons rewards are comparatively evenly distributed among such foragers:

1. Most obviously, the band or camp must move frequently for effective adaptation (see Chapter 7). Mobility makes it difficult to transport belongings and hence to accumulate possessions or other forms of wealth.

2. The cultural value foragers place on reciprocal sharing (see Chapter 8) prevents individual persons or family groups from becoming wealthier than their band mates. Therefore, even if someone tried to accumulate, he or she would find it difficult to do so because other people demand their share, and failure to adhere to the norms

Like most mobile hunter-gatherers, the Ju/'hoansi are an egalitarian people.

of sharing and to live up to egalitarian values is socially punished by public ridicule or worse.

3. Mobile foraging families are not tied to specific territories but have the right to visit and exploit the resources of many areas, often due to extended family ties (see Chapters 9 and 10). If anyone tries to be the boss or exercise control over behavior, other people have the option to leave and live elsewhere.

In sum, if people move around in their environments a lot, are required to share food and other possessions, and have a range of options about where to live and with whom, then inequality in wealth and power does not have much chance of developing and persisting.

Not all foragers are or were egalitarian, however. As discussed in Chapter 7, the Native Americans of the Northwest Coast lived in ranked societies because, in their rich environment, the three conditions just listed did not exist. Northwest Coast peoples were more sedentary, accumulated wealth for redistribution to validate and acquire rank, and formed kin groups that were associated with particular territories.

Most traditional horticultural peoples also are relatively egalitarian, although some are ranked. In the hundreds of occupied islands of Melanesia, there are tribal peoples (see Chapter 12) who live from tree and root crops, keeping pigs, and fishing if they lived along the coast. In most Melanesian societies, men compete for prestige by organizing large feasts on special occasions—such as weddings and funerals or just to distribute foods and valuables to draw other people into debt. If a man is unusually successful in organizing large feasts, he rises up to become a *big man*—someone whose name is widely known, to whom many men owe goods or favors, and who usually has several wives to help with gardening and pig keeping. Melanesian peoples vary in the degree to which big men have more wealth than other men. In some, there are noticeable differences in possessions, but in others, big men distribute so much of their wealth to others that they live pretty much like everyone else.

Ranked Societies

Any particular Melanesian tribe or even village may have many big men, some "bigger" than others. And the number of big men varies over time, depending on how many men have done well in any decade or generation. This is because "big man" is not an office into which someone is recruited, but an informal status that some men achieve based on their personal ambitions and accomplishments.

In contrast, in ranked societies, there are a limited number of high-ranking social positions, usually titles or some kind of formal offices that grant authority. People who hold the title can issue commands and expect to have them obeyed. The titles also confer high honor on the people who hold them. In most cases, the privilege of holding a title or occupying an office is largely or entirely hereditary within certain families, lineages, or clans. If you are born into a group that does not have the hereditary right to the title or office, normatively (but not always in fact) you cannot succeed to the office regardless of your personal talents.

An excellent example of a ranked society is Tikopia, the small Polynesian island whose kinship system we described in Chapter 10. Tikopia's 1,200 persons were divided into four patriclans, each with its own chief who exercised authority over his clan mates. Each clan in turn was divided into several patrilineages, each with its own head, believed to be the oldest living male descendant of the lineage founder. Alongside this ranking of individuals within a single lineage, the various lineages of a single clan were ranked relative to one another. One lineage of each clan, supposedly the original, senior lineage from which the junior lineages had budded off generations ago, was considered the noble lineage. Members of other lineages of the clan deferred socially to members of the noble lineage, according to Tikopian standards of etiquette. In addition, the noble lineage of each clan selected one of its members as chief of the whole clan. Clan chiefs had authority to punish troublemakers and the duty to perform rituals connected to agriculture and other common concerns.

Chiefs and other members of the noble Tikopia lineages had little more wealth than anyone else, however. The nobility received tribute from other lineages of their clan, but they gave away most of it in the many public activities they organized and financed through redistribution (see Chapter 8). The chief and nobility of each clan could not deny access to land and ocean resources to members of other lineages because each lineage was considered to have inalienable rights to certain pieces of land. High-ranking Tikopians, then, were honored and received tribute from other islanders, but they did not use this tribute to make themselves notably wealthier than lower-ranking people. They could issue commands in certain contexts, but their wealth was not great. It is mainly in this respect that ranked societies contrast with stratified societies.

Stratified Societies

Within a society or nation, a *social stratum* consists of families who have roughly the same access to rewards. Stratified societies have two distinguishing characteristics:

- There are strong inequalities in access to two kinds of rewards: wealth and power. Whether the wealthy and powerful enjoy prestige (or esteem, respect) varies between stratified societies, but there are ways to enhance it, as discussed later. The inequality may last through generations because membership in a stratum is hereditary or because being born into a certain stratum gives individuals better or worse opportunities in life.

- Inequalities are based primarily on unequal access to productive resources such as the land and tools people need to make their living or the education and training needed to succeed. In stratified societies, a minority of people control access to the resources other people need to live at culturally acceptable levels.

Stratified societies vary in their cultural beliefs about the possibilities of social mobility—that is, about movement up and down the social ladder. In some, such as North America, Europe, New Zealand, Australia, Japan, Korea, and other democracies, upward or downward mobility is possible through education, special talents or skills, hard work, good luck, or other circumstances. In contemporary East Asia, educational performance is so important for a child's success that parents who can afford it expend enormous resources in schooling, including cram schools and even prestigious preschools. In other stratified societies, as in traditional India or in Europe before the industrial revolution, one's position is considered fixed, often because of beliefs that existing inequalities are hereditary and/or ordained by supernatural beings.

Social scientists distinguish two kinds of strata: **class** and **caste**. Two general differences between class and caste systems stand out. First, by definition, castes are

class System of stratification in which membership in a stratum can theoretically be altered and intermarriage between strata is allowed.

caste System of stratification in which membership in a stratum is in theory hereditary, strata are endogamous, and contact or relationships among members of different strata are governed by explicit laws, norms, or prohibitions.

endogamous groups: They have cultural norms or laws that require individuals to marry within their caste. As mentioned in Chapter 9, rules that mandate marriage within one's own group have the effect of maintaining the distinctiveness of the group relative to other groups. This is because normatively there is no possibility of upward mobility through intercaste marriage. One's caste membership is theoretically hereditary: One is born into the caste of one's parents, one marries someone in the same caste, and one's children are likewise born into and remain members of one's own caste. In contrast, most class societies allow people to marry someone of a different class; in fact, intermarriage between classes is a common avenue of social mobility.

Second, caste systems have enforced norms or laws regulating social relationships among members of different castes. For example, norms or laws may prohibit direct physical contact between castes or may forbid members of different castes from eating from the same bowl or drinking from the same wells. In some societies, high-caste members believe they will be spiritually polluted if they touch members of other castes. Commonly, they must cleanse themselves after accidental contacts, often with a ritual procedure.

Both of these general differences mean that castes have more permanent membership and more rigid social boundaries than classes. Still, it is not easy to tell whether some particular stratified society has castes or classes. Some societies have elements of both. For instance, some scholars have suggested that black–white relations in the American South were more caste-like than classlike until the mid–twentieth century. There was no possibility of upward mobility into the white caste for blacks because no one could overcome the cultural stigma of dark skin color. Interracial marriage was legally prohibited or culturally taboo, so the two races were virtually endogamous. Explicit laws against certain kinds of contacts and interactions—known as *segregation laws*—forced blacks to live apart from whites, forbade them to enter certain white business establishments and public restrooms, prohibited drinking from the same water fountains, made them send their children to all-black schools, and so forth. Most whites did not believe blacks were polluting in the spiritual sense of the word, but many whites did believe blacks were unclean in another sense and tried to minimize contact with them.

Usually the term *stratification* refers to differences in wealth and power within a single society or nation. There also remain great inequalities between societies and nations, and even between whole continents. Whether future globalization will reduce economic inequalities between nations—and, if so, whether it will be sooner rather than later—is hotly debated. The effect of globalization on inequality *within* nations is also complicated and unclear. (The Global Challenges and Opportunities feature discusses this issue, focusing on the People's Republic of China.)

Many believe inequality is increasing in nations we call developed as a consequence of the growth of those we used to call underdeveloped. In the former, many working-class people are losing high-paying factory jobs—one important reason for Trump's appeal in 2016. The owners of industries who relocate their production factories overseas make higher profits, and their stockholders grow wealthier—an important basis for Sanders's popularity.

Castes in Traditional India

India's traditional caste system is the most famous and best known. It is complex and highly variable from region to region, so we present only a general picture. Traditionally, the people of India recognized five main social categories, four of which are *varna*. The *varna* (meaning "color") are not castes; rather, the *varna* include many different castes. Each *varna* is ranked relative to the others in honor and degree of ritual purity, and each is broadly associated with certain kinds of occupations.

The highest *varna* is the Brahmins, or priests and scholars; next is the *varna* of nobles and warriors, the Kshatriyas; third are the Vaishas, or merchants and artisans; and ranked lowest are the Shudras, or farmers, craftspeople, and certain other laborers. Although the *varna* are associated with certain occupations, not everyone in a given *varna* follows that occupation. A fifth category—outside and ranked below the four *varna*—is the *Dalit* (also called *Untouchables* and *Panchama*) to whom falls work considered polluting to all four *varna*.

The *varna* arose in the second millennium B.P. when the Aryans invaded and conquered what is now northern India, incorporating many of the smaller states that already existed in the region that would become India. The villages in which most Indians formerly lived are divided into much smaller and specific groupings called *jati* (castes, as the term is usually used). For example, in a particular village, the Shudra *varna* might be represented by several *jati* with names such as weaver, potter, and tailor. There are thousands of such castes in India, distributed among the many thousands of villages, with each village containing a variable number of castes.

India's traditional caste hierarchy is integrated with the worldview of Hinduism—the religion still practiced by the majority of Indian people. (Hinduism is incredibly diverse, so here we present only a simplified depiction of it.) In the Hindu worldview, spiritual souls are reborn into different physical bodies at various stages of their existence—this is the doctrine of *reincarnation*. Souls seek an end to the cycle of earthly birth, death, and rebirth, but to achieve this end, each soul must be reborn many times into many bodies, both animal and human. Souls attempt to move from lower forms of life to higher ones: from animals to humans (of various castes) to gods.

The body into which a soul is born depends on how closely that soul adhered to proper standards of behavior in previous lifetimes. For souls placed in human forms in their previous incarnation, standards include avoidance of activities that Hindus believe are polluting. Among the most polluting activities are handling and working with animal carcasses or human corpses, touching excrement and other waste materials, dealing with childbirth, and eating meat. Not only are people who regularly perform these activities polluted themselves, but also any members of a higher caste who come into physical contact with them likewise become polluted and must bathe ritually to cleanse themselves. One's present place in society varies partly with the degree to which one is associated with pure or impure activities.

The caste of a person depends—not perfectly, of course—on actions in previous lives. People are born into a low caste either because their soul has not yet been through enough lifetimes to have reached a higher form or because their misdeeds in a previous lifetime merit reincarnation into a low caste. Thus, in the Hindu worldview it is legitimate that some castes have more honor and power than others.

Each caste (*jati*) is broadly associated with certain occupations. Each village contains a number of castes, most of which are named according to the occupation traditionally performed by their members. Thus, a village might include castes of priests, merchants, blacksmiths, potters, tailors, farmers, weavers, carpenters, washers, barbers, leatherworkers, and "sweepers" (the last refers to those who remove human waste matter from people's houses).

Just as activities are ranked in Hindu beliefs according to their degree of purity and impurity, so occupations and those who perform them are ranked. Working with animal carcasses is defiling, so leatherworking is a defiling occupation, and leatherworkers are so polluting as to be "untouchable." The same applies to

Globalization and Inequality in China

Inequalities at the global level began centuries ago. As early as the 1500s, the products of the two American continents were shipped to Europe. Mesoamerica and the Andes were the homelands of the two great New World civilizations, the Aztec and the Inca. Like the upper classes in Europe, the Aztec and Inca elite surrounded themselves with treasures, many in gold

Chinese entrepreneur Lei Jun speaks at a sub-forum of the World Economic Forum in a 2016 meeting in Tianjin, China. Lei Jun is Chair and CEO of Xiaomi Corporation, a technology company.

and silver. The trade (and plunder) of these precious metals produced huge fortunes for some Europeans and affected balances of military power.

By the 1700s and 1800s, products were pouring out of the conquered regions of the Americas and Asia. In the islands of the Caribbean, northern Brazil, and the American South, enslaved Africans produced the cotton, tobacco, sugar, and cacao that were worn, smoked, eaten, and drunk by western Europeans. In Asia, spices, tea, porcelain (china), hardwoods, and other products produced by peasants and craftsmen were shipped over land or sea to satisfy European appetites and tastes. Britain's colony in India, for example, provided early English textile factories with cotton and other fibers. In the process, India's own highly skilled textile weavers suffered. Although the costs of transporting goods from Asian, African, and American colonies were high, Europe's climate did not allow the production of tropical crops, and the labor costs of both African American slaves and Asian peasants were a fraction of the costs of production.

As these brief examples show, the effects of globalization on inequalities are several centuries old, at least. During the nineteenth and twentieth centuries, the growth of economies in the richer regions of North America, Europe, New Zealand, and Australia dramatically outpaced growth in Africa, Latin America, South Asia, and East Asia (except in Japan). Whether continued globalization in the twenty-first century will increase or decrease the economic gap between poor and rich nations is hotly disputed. (See Chapters 7 and 8 for more on the benefits and costs of globalization.)

A revealing example is China, which has experienced the world's fastest growth since the early 1980s. Although its growth rate slowed in recent years, China's economic growth rate averaged nearly 10 percent until 2010. Reasons include its plentiful labor supply, its central government that seemingly values growth above other national goals, the work ethic of its citizens, and the loosening of restrictions on internal migration and foreign investment. Hundreds of millions of

sweeping: People who remove human wastes from houses or spread excrement over village fields are polluted, and their touch pollutes those of higher castes. Therefore, members of the leatherworking, sweeping, and other castes associated with defiling occupations were traditionally Untouchables.

Untouchables usually live in their own special section of the village, separate from members of higher castes. Because they contaminate temples by their entry, they cannot go inside a temple. Their touch contaminates water, so they must use separate wells. These and other restrictions on their behavior are sometimes extreme. (Such discrimination against people of Untouchable ancestry is now illegal in modern India, although it still occurs in many rural regions.)

Members of high-ranking castes need the services of low-ranking castes. Again, this is because Hinduism defines some essential activities as polluting, so members of castes who would be defiled by these activities need lower castes to perform these services for them. The bullocks needed for farming die, so someone has to remove dead cattle from the village. Brahmin women give birth just as other women do, so the women of some low-ranking caste have to serve as midwives because handling blood and placentas would pollute Brahmin women. Everyone passes bodily wastes, so someone must remove these wastes from the houses of high-caste members, lest these substances pollute their occupants. Accordingly, each caste has its proper role and function in the economic, social, and religious life of the village.

Chinese experienced increases in their living standards by moving from rural villages to work in factories in Shanghai, Guangzhou, Shenzhen, Beijing, and dozens of other cities along the eastern and southern coasts.

Hundreds of thousands of Chinese factory owners, real estate investors, and market entrepreneurs have become fabulously wealthy. However, more hundreds of millions in rural areas have yet to participate significantly in the economic boom. Untold thousands lost their livelihood when local officials did not compensate them when a new factory took over the land they were farming. Hundreds of coal miners have died from mine collapses, and tens of millions of Chinese experience some of the planet's worse air pollution from coal-fired power plants (see Chapter 7). (As you can see, China is a country with lots of large numbers.)

Lately, many migrants (precise numbers are unknown) have returned to their roots in the countryside, setting up businesses or finding employment in emerging interior industries. For many, city life and factory work have not been as rewarding as they had hoped. Most young workers eat at factory dining rooms and live in factory dormitories with numerous roommates sleeping on bunk beds. As the Chinese economy develops, younger workers expect a better life and grow dissatisfied with low wages and poor work conditions that the first generation of factory workers found more acceptable. This has happened repeatedly in the historical spread of industrialism, so China is not unique.

Since the 1980s, China's government has funded education generously. Its colleges and universities turn out more graduates than any other country. In the 2000s, the number of college and university students quadrupled. Well-educated people are not particularly interested in factory work, yet there are not nearly enough professional and service jobs to employ them: In the winter of 2012–2013, the unemployment rate of recent Chinese college graduates was 16 percent. In contrast, only 4 percent of people with an elementary school education were jobless, due to the high demand for factory labor producing for the global market. Like their counterparts in other parts of the world, China's well educated have high expectations that are often frustrated. And the government has plans for 250 million of its citizens to migrate to cities in the next 20 years and has begun constructing their living spaces.

With a land area about equal to that of the United States, China's population is four times larger than that of the United States. Its economy is the world's second largest. It faces serious problems of energy supply and resource depletion. Demonstrations and other forms of social unrest are increasing due to factors like working conditions in factories, widespread corruption, increasing economic inequalities, censorship of information on the Internet and other media, treatment of dissidents, serious air and water pollution, and conflict between the Han majority and several ethnic minorities.

In a nation of nearly 1.4 billion, including 56 groups the government classifies as minorities, Chinese leaders might be correct in believing that effective governing requires measures and policies that citizens of nations with a different past and a vastly contrasting present find abhorrent. Chinese leaders speak of maintaining a harmonious society and keeping China stable. Many scholars of China write about an implicit bargain that the government has made with citizens: The government will keep living standards rising as long as China remains stable. Although many leaders in other developed nations believe this is an undesirable bargain for the Chinese people, most of these nations industrialized over a century ago, and most have had a large middle class for many decades. They might remember things like working conditions, wage rates, racism, and pollution from their own past.

Although the castes are interdependent in that each needs the products and services made by the others, one should not conclude that intercaste relations are harmonious, or that the complementary tasks associated with each caste are entirely mutually beneficial. A great deal of friction and outright conflict exist between individual members of different castes. In fact, local castes as a whole group sometimes organize themselves with a council to pursue their common interests.

Although most castes had names that referred to occupations, in fact, members of a single caste made their living in diverse ways. Most members of lower castes were farmers, regardless of their caste name, and many higher-caste persons engaged in farming as well. Also, there was no simple relationship between caste membership and access to resources or wealth; some Brahmins were poor, some smiths wealthy.

Many people think caste hierarchies and restrictions are no longer important in India. Indeed, given the anonymity of city life, restrictions on behavior clearly are hard to maintain, and many lower-caste urbanites are well-educated, middle-class people. For example, today people with different caste background commonly intermarry. So, caste distinctions have withered (but not died) in urban areas. In parts of the countryside, however, where most people are still farmers, caste distinctions remain, although in weakened form. For decades, the government of India has given preferential treatment in hiring to members of lower castes,

Hinduism regards certain substances and activities as spiritually defiling or polluting. Ritual bathing—here in the Ganges River—removes the pollution.

Bernard P. Wolff/Science Source

and many Indian citizens believe such preferences have gone too far—comparable to debates about affirmative action in the United States.

Class in the United States

An important point to make about classes is that they are seldom organized *as classes.* There are no occasions on which the members of a given class come together for discussion or common action (unlike, say, an extended family or lineage). Indeed, members of a single class do not necessarily believe they have much in common with one another (unlike the members of a labor union). Many people cannot precisely identify the class to which they belong (unlike Indian *jati*). For example, about four-fifths of Americans refer to themselves as "middle class." People cannot say how many classes exist in their nation but use terms like *working class, upper class,* and *super rich.* In fact, there is considerable debate within the social sciences over what the term *class* means, or whether it has anything other than the vaguest meaning.

Class membership might be hard to determine, but no one can deny the differences in wealth, power, and prestige that exist in class societies. The term *class* refers to all the people in a given stratified society who receive comparable levels of rewards. Members of different classes have different access to material resources (income, property, wealth), influential relationships (social networks, political contacts), and "sophisticated" cultural knowledge (formal education, social graces). Unlike caste membership, people are potentially able to move up or down in a class system during their lifetime. Interclass marriage, personal talent, hard work and effort, and good luck can allow upward mobility. More commonly, though, being born into a given class puts some persons so far ahead or behind in life that few people rise or fall very far in the class structure during their lifetime.

In this section, we concentrate on the class structure of the United States. In this country, the kind of work one does (occupation) is often assumed to be the best single overall indication of class membership. ("What kind of work do you do?" or "Where do you work?" is one of the first questions American adults ask of new acquaintances, and the answer gives a lot of information about a person very quickly.) Occupation is generally a good indication of income, and one's income influences so much else: standard of living and overall lifestyle, access of one's children to education, the kinds of people with whom one associates socially, and so on.

One way around the ambiguity of class membership is to define classes on the basis of economic factors, specifically the wealth of individuals and families. Using wealth as the primary basis for assigning class ranking has four major advantages:

1. Wealth can be measured more easily than other indications of class membership, like status or the prestige of one's occupation. However, monetary income alone is not an adequate measure of wealth, as we shall see.

2. Wealth is the best single indicator of the overall benefits individuals and families are receiving from their citizenship in the nation. Money cannot buy love, happiness, intelligence, or many other things, but it can buy you much of what Americans value—including education and consumer goods and, nowadays, more appealing faces and bodies.

3. Extremely high wealth is generally correlated with ownership of productive resources such as industrial factories, financial assets, stocks, and income-producing real estate. Many wealthy people own the nation's large businesses or made their money in finance. Either they built their companies themselves, or their ancestors made fortunes through business activity and passed their ownership along to the current generation. Many of the wealthiest persons gain most of their income from the stock market, which means either they earn large annual dividends or grow rich by buying low and selling high. However, many persons become wealthy by selling their skills on the labor market, in industries like entertainment, media, medicine, law, and sports. That possibility does not exist for most people.

4. Wealth levels broadly determine people's access to political power. Through lobbying efforts, the rich enjoy greater influence on the laws and policies of the nation than their numbers warrant. By providing much of the funding for think tanks and other public advisory groups, the wealthy subsidize the expertise of many economists and other professionals who advise government. People who serve in the government as elected or appointed officials may later work in the private sector, which covets both their expertise and their political connections. Ever since the 2010 Supreme Court verdict in the *Citizen's United* case overturned many restrictions on the contributions of corporations to political campaigns, it has become easier for wealthy persons and groups to provide money to support candidates. The wealthy now have even greater influence on who gets nominated and elected to executive and congressional offices, which is why many liberals want to select future justices who will overturn *Citizen's United*.

For these and other reasons, we can learn most about class inequalities in the United States by focusing on the distribution of wealth.

Income inequality is one measure of the distribution of wealth. Table 13.1 summarizes income inequality for 2014, the latest year for which the U.S. Census Bureau has published information. In the table, American households are divided into fifths (quintiles) based on their 2014 cash income. For example, the poorest one-fifth (20 percent) of households earned 3.1 percent of all income, whereas the richest quintile earned 51.2 percent of the total income earned by all households. The table also shows that the richest 5 percent of American households earned 21.9 percent of the 2014 total family income.

Figure 13.1 portrays these statistics graphically. The X axis shows the amount of income earned. The Y axis shows the number of American households who earned that amount of income in 2014. Notice how many households earn between around $12,000 to $54,000 compared to the few earning over $200,000.

U.S. Census Bureau data over the past 30 years reveal that income inequality has increased markedly.

TABLE 13.1 Distribution of Household Income in the United States, 2014

Quintile	Percentage of Income Earned
Poorest fifth	3.1
Second fifth	8.2
Third fifth	14.3
Fourth fifth	23.2
Richest fifth	51.2
Richest 5 percent	21.9

Source: U.S. Census Bureau (2015).

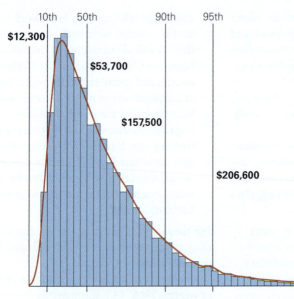

10th   50th   90th   95th

$12,300

$53,700

$157,500

$206,600

Figure 13.1 Distribution of Household Income in the United States, 2014

Source: U.S. Census Bureau (2015).

Between 1960 and 1980, the relative shares of income received by each quintile remained fairly constant. During those 20 years, the bottom three-fifths (the poorest 60 percent) of American households consistently earned about one-third of all cash income. The richest quintile earned a little over 40 percent. However, by 2014, the share of the poorest three-fifths had fallen to 26 percent—a *loss* of about 7 percent. In 2014, the richest one-fifth earned 51 percent of all cash income, a *gain* of around 8 percent from 1980.

To make much the same point, in 1980 the ratio of the income percentage of the most affluent fifth to the poorest fifth was about 10 to 1, whereas in 2014 the ratio was around 16 to 1. Considering the ratio of the richest 5 percent to the poorest 20 percent, income inequality increased even more, from 4 to 1 in 1980 to 7 to 1 in 2014. The relative benefits of economic growth since around 1990 have been distributed unequally, going far more to the affluent than to the poor and even to those who view themselves as middle class.

However, the distribution of income alone does not tell the complete story of inequality in the United States, because figures on annual *income* do not show how much *wealth* is owned by families of different classes. Yearly income figures such as those in Table 13.1 greatly underestimate economic inequality in the United States. People's standard of living is not determined directly by their annual income, nor is their influence on government policies at the local, state, and national levels. By using the distribution of wealth, we see that middle-income families, and even families

generally considered affluent, own little in comparison with the truly wealthy.

Surveys funded by the federal government provide estimates of the net worth (wealth) of American families. *Net worth* includes all family assets (property) owned minus debts. Assets include houses and other real estate, motor vehicles, financial assets like savings and retirement accounts, and stocks and bonds. Debts include mortgages, credit card balances, student loans, and other money owed by an individual or family.

Financial assets vastly increase economic security, for they can be withdrawn from banks or sold on the stock market to increase wealth or keep one's income and property from declining during recessions. Savings and, especially, investments also earn additional future income and wealth, although not without risk.

The Federal Reserve Board (the Fed) is the semi-governmental institution that tries to regulate the economy by affecting interest rates. Every three years, the Fed publishes a *Survey of Consumer Finances* that estimates the wealth held by American families. The most recent survey was conducted in 2013. It reported that the net worth of the richest 3 percent increased from 45 percent in 1989 to 54 percent in 2013. The net worth of the bottom 90 percent fell from 33 percent in 1989 to 25 percent in 2013. Notice the ratios: In 2013 the richest 3 percent had more than twice the percentage wealth of *the bottom 90 percent* of Americans.

The 2013 Federal Reserve survey was not as detailed are some earlier ones, so we can learn more by looking to the 2010 survey. The Economic Policy

Sam Bassett/Getty Images

The difference between the net worth of the very rich and everyone else is much larger than the gap in annual incomes. This couple seems to have what used to be called "jet set" status.

Institute, a private, nonprofit institution, uses Fed surveys and other data to estimate the concentration of wealth in the United States. For 2010, the Economic Policy Institute concluded that the richest 20 percent of families held 89 percent of the wealth, the middle quintile held 2.6 percent, and the poorest quintile had negative net worth (they owed more than they owned). Comparing the 1 percent of rich families to everyone else, the wealthiest 1 percent owned 35.4 percent of the wealth, whereas the bottom 95 percent owned 36.9 percent of the wealth. That is, in 2010 the wealthiest 1 percent had about the same amount of wealth as the bottom 95 percent put together.

Another way to illustrate how wealth inequality has risen over the last few decades is to compare the *wealth ratio* for various years: the ratio of the wealth owned by the very richest Americans to the median wealth. In 1983, the wealthiest 1 percent of Americans owned 131 times the wealth of the median American. By 1998, the wealth ratio grew to 168. In 2010, the ratio was 288.

Maintaining Inequality

One issue in studying stratification is explaining how such large inequalities first developed millennia ago, after tens of thousands of years of humanity living in egalitarian groups. This issue cannot be addressed here, other than noting that inequalities between people usually originated out of a complex combination of intensive agriculture, elite control over scarce resources, large-scale cooperation, and conquest warfare (see Chapter 7). Most archaeologists who study stratification in prehistory agree that significant inequalities (deserving of the term *class*) came into existence with the evolution of civilization

However, knowing the conditions that led to the *origin* of inequalities in the past may not be very relevant to another issue in contemporary societies: How do such high degrees of inequality in stratified societies *persist?* As the United States illustrates, a small percentage of the population typically control most of the wealth and wield a great deal of influence over public affairs. How do they maintain their powers and privileges? Why doesn't inequality produce more conflicts, demonstrations, and other kinds of political action?

In fact, class conflict has surfaced historically in a wide range of stratified societies. Resentment, rebellion, and occasional attempts at revolution occur in stratified societies in all parts of the world (which is not to say that they are universally present). Human lifetimes are so short that most of us live through only a few such events, and most of those events happen far away. In the long term of history, though, a great many powerless and poor people did not simply accept their place in the class hierarchy.

One possible explanation of how stratification persists is that members of the highest stratum (hereafter called the *elite*) use their wealth and power to organize an armed force stronger than that of their opposition. If elites somehow monopolize control over weapons or organize a loyal army, then they can use coercion and threats to maintain their access to rewards and resources. Elites do sometimes use armed force to put down rebellions, and certainly the ever-present threat of coercion and fear of punishment deters resistance to the elite's wealth, prestige, and power.

Yet in most stratified societies, elites only occasionally use force, although the threat is usually present. Use of military or police might is costly to them. Suppose the elite wait for rebellions to occur and then use police or armies to put them down. Even if rebellions fail, suppression by police and armies produces more hatred and resentment and more awareness of the relative wealth and power of the elite. Repression increases fear, just as elites intend, but it also leads to anger and desire for revenge, so it can backfire and provoke a future rebellion.

Notice also that the elite's reliance on brute force and oppression to maintain their wealth and power potentially reduces or eliminates their honor and esteem, one of the three major rewards of stratification, and one that some members of the elite class presumably covet. Furthermore, those who supply the military might—armies, guards, thugs, or police—must be paid or otherwise provided for by the elite. Payment requires resources. Either the elite can take these resources from their own wealth, thus reducing it, or they can increase their exploitation of the majority population, thus breeding still more hatred and resentment toward themselves. Finally, relying entirely on the loyalty of an army is risky because this allegiance may change, as many dictators know or fear. In sum, reliance on threat and armed force alone is both costly and risky.

None of these points deny that armed force is an important way to sustain the powers and privileges of upper-class people. Few elite classes have remained in power for many generations without using force and periodically suppressing rebellions and dissent. Nonetheless, stratification systems that rely entirely or largely on force seem to be short-lived and unstable and in the long term tend to be replaced by those that use other mechanisms. What other mechanisms are available?

Ideologies

We address this question by noting yet another reason coercive force alone is seldom solely responsible for maintaining inequality. A single rebellion can have many causes, but a persistent *pattern* of rebellion is caused mainly by the lower strata's perception that they are exploited or not receiving their fair share of rewards. Seeking out and eliminating rebels does little to change the reasons people rebel. The instigators may be sanctioned or eliminated, but the underlying discontent that causes persistent conflict remains. Imprisoning or killing instigators prevents them from rebelling, but sometimes removing one instigator creates several more instigators, as those who argue that simply wiping out today's terrorist organizations is not sufficient recognize. Sooner or later, there will be new instigators who organize new rebellions and attacks. Furthermore, while armies or police eliminate rebels, innocents are usually killed, injured, or harmed economically. This can alienate those who otherwise would be more passive about their place in the world. For these and other reasons, armed force alone is unlikely to eliminate the perceptions of unfairness, injustice, cultural domination, or other attitudes that cause rebellions and violence.

Elites can maintain their privileges if they can influence the perceptions of the underprivileged about why they are underprivileged. For example, if poor people think it is divine will that they are poor, they are less likely to rebel than if they believe they are poor because of exploitation. Or, if they think the elite use their property and power to benefit everyone in the society, they are less likely to challenge the elite. Or, if they think that a concentration of property and power is inevitable because that's just the way human life is, they will be less likely to resist. Or, if they think that they, too, can acquire property, power, and prestige through their own achievements, they are more likely to put their effort into improving their own position rather than taking the risk of being punished or killed. Finally, if the masses are divided internally—by ethnic identity, by real threats from enemies, by perceived threats from others in their own society, by religious attachments, by regional loyalties, and so forth—then they are less likely to unite in the political arena.

To state the general point, if members of the lower strata adopt beliefs that justify and legitimize the rewards received by the higher stratum, then they are more likely to try to join the system rather than to overthrow it. In such beliefs, the elite have a powerful and relatively cheap tool with which to dampen opposition to their power and privileges. Moreover, these ideas increase the prestige of the elite. If people believe that inequality is the will of the gods, or that the activities of the elite benefit all, or that the elite became elite through intelligence and hard work, then the elite deserve the honor and respect of everyone else. (Not surprisingly, elites easily believe such things about themselves.)

We use the term **ideologies** to refer to those ideas and beliefs that explain inequality as desirable or legitimate. The term *ideology* also has a broader meaning, often referring to any set of ideas held by a group—as in *leftist political ideology* and *feminist ideology*. Here we use the term in the narrow sense, to refer only to ideas that justify the status quo of inequality. Ideologies often are part of a people's worldview (Chapter 2).

In many stratified societies, ideologies are based on religious worldviews. We are familiar with the notion of the *divine right of kings* from feudal Europe—certainly a handy supernatural mandate for kings and aristocracies! Similar notions are common in non-Western stratified societies. For instance, in Bunyoro, a kingdom in East Africa, the health and welfare of the ruler were mystically associated with the fertility and prosperity of the whole kingdom. Anything that threatened his life was believed to be a threat to everyone.

In many ancient civilizations—such as the Inca, the Japanese, and the Egyptian—the ruler himself was believed to be a divine or semidivine being. In pre–twentieth-century China, the emperor had the "mandate of Heaven," meaning that Heaven itself had granted him secular authority over the vast Chinese empire for as long as he ruled it wisely and humanely. In traditional India, as we have seen, Hindu beliefs about reincarnation and pollution were so intertwined with the caste system that they both explained and legitimized its inequalities.

The preceding examples illustrate a few ways religion serves ideological functions. In stratified societies, religion commonly gives the elite a supernatural mandate, provides them with the supernatural means to punish people, and gives them religious duties to perform that are believed to benefit the whole population.

American Secular Ideologies

Do similar kinds of religious ideologies exist in modern industrial societies, some of which are as highly stratified as any preindustrial society?

Some people who are critical of the Judeo-Christian heritage of the West believe this religious tradition supports the accumulation of wealth. In fact, however, many New Testament passages warn Christians about the accumulation of wealth. The best known are the story of the rich man and Lazarus (Luke 16:19–31) and the passages about the rich man who came to Jesus seeking salvation (told in Matthew 19:21–24, Mark 10:21–25, and Luke 18:22–25). Lesser-known scriptures say the poor are blessed and the rich are oppressors (Luke 6:20–24, James 2:2–6, and James 5:1–6). Two passages in Acts (2:44–45 and 4:32–37) seem to instruct Christians to hold their possessions in common, which not only does not support wealth accumulation but also is a rather anticapitalist scripture.

Furthermore, most citizens do not believe that the richest Americans have a divine mandate for their wealth. The wealthiest families do not justify their income and ownership of property and financial assets by invoking religious authority or divine will. They are far more likely to say that they are hard workers or job creators or risk takers. Religion is not generally used to justify the wealth and power of particular individuals and families. At most, some wealthy claim to be blessed, but most take credit for their own success or admit that they are lucky.

Finally, Judeo-Christian teachings historically have been and still are used to support social and political movements that seek to correct inequalities that are believed to be unjust. The nineteenth-century antislavery movement is one example. More recent examples include the civil rights and liberation theology movements. In the political realm, certainly many officeholders attend church and find ways to work their religious faith into their speeches to certain audiences. But few gain politically by claiming they are God's chosen officials. Even suspicion that a politician thinks he or she is carrying out divine will is a political liability (although some citizens will believe it, depending on whether they agree with his or her policies).

In brief, with regard to the issue of who has what and why, most Americans, and Westerners generally,

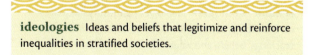

ideologies Ideas and beliefs that legitimize and reinforce inequalities in stratified societies.

AP Photo/Mark J. Terrill

Although American candidates for high political offices usually call attention to their religious faith, those who claim to be divinely chosen rarely succeed. Most voters respond to secular ideologies.

are *secularists:* They explain the unequal distribution of rewards by events here on Earth, not by the will of Heaven.

Ideologies do not have to be based on religion, however. There are only two essential features of ideologies:

1. They justify (legitimize) inequality by affecting people's consciousness, not by threatening or using physical coercion.

2. They are believable to large numbers of people, based on existing cultural knowledge.

In the first condition, *consciousness* refers to cultural attitudes, values, worldviews, and so forth. In the second condition, *believable* means that effective ideologies match people's general ideas about how their society works. Ideologies must make sense in terms of existing cultural knowledge, or they will be ineffective. **Secular ideologies** as well as religious ideologies can have both features.

> **secular ideologies** Ideologies that justify inequality on the basis of societywide benefits rather than religious teachings, beliefs, and values.

Many social scientists argue that secular ideologies take two forms in the modern United States. One is that the whole nation benefits from inequality. Because a few people are very wealthy, many citizens believe that the middle and lower classes are better off than they would be if wealth were distributed more equally. After all, the chance to get rich motivates people to do their best, and we all win when our fellow citizens perform up to their potential. Also, the accumulation and investment of wealth are necessary to create jobs from which lower- and middle-class people benefit. The most familiar example of this notion is the justification for tax cuts for wealthy people (note that a tax cut has the same effect as increasing income). If wealthier people are made even wealthier, the argument (or ideology?) goes, they will invest their extra income in expanding businesses, thus creating jobs that eventually trickle down to the middle and working classes. Giving more income to the rich will grow the economy, thus benefiting everyone, according to this theory (or ideology?) about how the market economy works.

A second secular ideology is that the elite earn their rewards through their own merit and efforts. They are smarter, more ambitious, hardworking, willing to take risks, and so forth. In short, the elite have personal qualities that account for their success. This is, of course, accurate for some members of the elite. However, those who inherited their wealth or were lucky enough to buy the right stock at the right time or to get into (or out of) the right housing market early enough receive the same rewards as those who earned their rewards by using actual skills to perform actual work.

To the extent that they are widely believed, these two ideas fit with Americans' other beliefs about the way people are and how their society works. They are compatible with widespread beliefs about human motivation—people are basically selfish and need strong incentives before they will work hard, take risks, and make the effort to get a good education and have a bright future. Such ideologies also fit with many American values such as individual freedom, progress, the work ethic, and private ownership of property.

Of course, many Americans do not believe these two ideas. (If you do not believe them, then they are not effective ideologies for you.) Others believe these ideas are an accurate portrayal of how the whole nation benefits from economic inequality. (If you fall into this camp, you will think these ideas are objectively true rather than merely ideologies.) Your personal opinion depends on your class, upbringing, ideas about human nature, political views, and so forth.

Can a comparative perspective shed any light on the issue of whether stratification benefits society at large or mainly members of the elite class themselves? To address this question, we look at the major theories of inequality.

Theories of Inequality

Sociologists and anthropologists distinguish two broad theories to analyze stratification. One holds that a high degree of inequality in the distribution of rewards is necessary, morally justified, and beneficial to all members of society. This view is called the **functional theory of inequality**.

A contrary view holds that a high degree of inequality not only is unjust but also robs the whole society of the benefits of much of its potential talent, which lies undeveloped in many of those at the bottom of the socioeconomic ladder. This view is known as the **conflict theory of inequality**. It holds that a high level of inequality offers few benefits to anyone except the elite and, indeed, is harmful to the whole society because of the conflicts it creates and the lack of equal opportunities it entails.

Functionalist Theory

The functionalist theory holds that inequality is necessary for a large and complex society to motivate its most talented and hardworking members to perform the most important roles. Some roles (including jobs) require more skill and training than others. In most cases, the more skill and training required for a job, the fewer the number of people qualified to do the job and the more valuable their abilities are to the whole group. Functionalists argue that high economic rewards are effective ways to recruit the most diligent and qualified individuals into the most socially valuable roles. Unless there are such rewards for those with the talents most of us lack, they will have no incentive to put those talents to work in activities that benefit all of us.

Also, in the functionalist view, inequality is not only socially useful but also morally justified. If society as a whole is to enjoy the fruits of the labor of its small number of well-trained, talented, and hardworking individuals, it is only fair and right that it reward these individuals with material goods, respect, and influence over decision making.

The functionalist analysis of inequality makes sense. People who do the most socially valuable things often get great rewards. However, it is difficult to measure the *social* value of various activities, as the 2007–2008 global financial crisis so clearly shows. From whatever value the financial sector added to the society, we need to subtract the lost value of those who suffered from it. It is reasonable that rewards be proportionate to personal qualities like effort and talent, but the two are not always correlated nor can they be measured.

Two other objections are possible within the framework of the functionalist theory itself. First, there is no reason to believe that the high degree of inequality that *actually exists* in some particular stratified society is necessary to ensure that those with the scarcest talents fill the most valuable roles. In industrialized nations,

functional theory of inequality Theory holding that stratification is a way to reward individuals who contribute the most to society's well-being, making inequality ultimately beneficial to all.

conflict theory of inequality Theory holding that stratification benefits mainly the upper stratum and is the cause of most social unrest and other conflicts in stratified societies, making inequality beneficial to only a few.

for example, how many dollars does it take to motivate a qualified individual to manage a major company? In the United States, chief executive officers (CEOs) of large corporations have enjoyed enormous increases in compensation packages: Between 1978 and 2011, CEO compensation increased 725 percent, whereas the compensation of workers increased 5.7 percent (both figures are adjusted for inflation). In 2016, American CEOs earned 276 times the compensation paid to workers. This is part of a 40-year upward trend from the 1965 earnings ratio (20), the 1978 ratio (30), and the 1995 ratio (123). (Note, though, that the ratio varies enormously over short periods.)

The CEO to worker salary ratio in 2016 was over nine times that in 1978. Were the top executives of American companies responsible for a nine-fold increase in productivity and profits between 1978 and 2011? In 2011, an average worker worked 231 days to earn what a CEO earned in one day. On any given day, is a CEO 231 times more valuable to the company than an ordinary worker? Would companies be managed just as well if their CEOs made only 20 or 50 times what their workers made?

To make the general point, is there a proportional relationship between the compensation (rewards) of elites and their contributions to their groups or to the nation as a whole? Compensation is mostly set by markets, but markets respond to supply and demand, not to the value that some activity or role has for society at large.

For these reasons, one objection to the functionalist theory is that no one knows how much inequality is needed to motivate people. Nor does anyone know how to calculate the benefits that elites actually offer to their group or to society at large. In brief, there is no reason to think that the *high degree* of inequality that actually exists in some stratified society is necessary for the society to benefit from *some degree* of inequality.

Second, functionalists assume the system of stratification effectively places qualified individuals in important roles. It is a large assumption, however, that those who are best able to perform the most important roles are those who are usually recruited for them. In all systems of stratification, there is a powerful element of inheritance of wealth. Even assuming that most members of elite classes of the present day actually earned their rewards, many will pass their resources along to their heirs. Sons and daughters, nieces and nephews, may or may not be talented, hardworking, and meritorious. Even if elite families do not pass their wealth to their children, the latter still have a head start in life from the extra help they get in education,

job prospects, contacts through social networks, and other privileges.

Certainly, children born to poor families can and do succeed, but they must overcome more obstacles than those born to privilege. If every generation were born with nearly equal access to the means to succeed in life, we could be more confident that those who occupy the most important roles are those who are best qualified to fill them. The functionalist theory that those who receive the highest rewards are most deserving would be more plausible if the (metaphorical) playing field in which people compete were leveled.

Suppose there were some way to calculate the amount of inequality that is optimal for a given society. Suppose further that a nation could devise some way of beginning each generation with everyone on an equal footing, with truly equal opportunities to compete. (This could be partly accomplished by steep inheritance taxes, which are mostly opposed by those with wealth and influence.) Then the functionalist theory of inequality might apply. But no stratified society has ever achieved this condition, partly because these questions are unanswerable and partly because the wealthy and powerful would have to consent to such a change, and they have little incentive to do so.

Conflict Theory

The conflict theory agrees with the objections to functionalism just given. But it goes much further. Conflict theorists claim that stratification is based ultimately on control over productive resources, such as land, technology, information, and labor. Once elites gain control over these resources—by whatever means—they get other people to do work that benefits themselves. How this is organized varies among different kinds of economic systems. In ancient preindustrial states and some chiefdoms, the noble class controlled the land and other productive resources and the commoners had to provide tribute and labor to the nobility in return for the privilege of using it. In parts of feudal Europe, serfs were tied to their estate and ordinarily had strong rights over the land they worked, but each year they still had to contribute a certain number of days of work or a certain proportion of their harvest to their lord.

As for the capitalist economic system, Karl Marx—the nineteenth-century founder of what is now called *conflict theory*—argued that capitalist societies include only two fundamental classes. Members of the capitalist class (or *bourgeoisie*) own the factories and tools. Members of the working class (or *proletariat*) have only one thing to sell on the market: their labor. To earn their living, workers must sell their labor to some capitalist. This seems like an equitable arrangement. The capitalists buy the labor they need to operate their factories, mines, and fields to sell goods and make profit. The workers get the jobs they need to support their families by selling their time and skills for a wage set by the market for labor (see Chapter 8).

But, Marx noted, the goods the workers produce must be worth more on the market than the workers themselves receive in wages, or there would be no profit for the capitalists. The difference between the amount capitalists receive for the goods they sell and their costs (including the amount they pay their workers) is *profit.* In Marx's controversial view, profit is based on the exploitation of workers. The belief that workers receive a fair day's wage for a fair day's work is merely an ideology.

Conflict theorists argue that many problems of modern North America are caused (or at least made worse) by increasing inequality, as is the case in much of the world. Much resentment toward "the system"

comes from people's sense that their lives will not get better or are getting worse. Unable to identify the causes of their frustrations, some white conservative groups find scapegoats in African Americans, immigrants, the United Nations, and all those South Asian, South American, and Chinese laborers who work for "peanuts." Unable to make a personally acceptable living in a socially acceptable manner, inner-city youths turn to drug dealing and other kinds of crime. Economic hardship contributes to family breakups. Poorer people need more social programs, funded by taxpayers, who watch stories in the media about people cheating the government and so elect representatives who provide *fewer* services—for the poor, at least. More generally, the sense of national unity and social responsibility is undermined by worsening inequality, according to conflict theorists.

Critics of conflict theory say that conflict theorists are ideologues themselves, though of a different political persuasion. Critics of conflict theory claim that the value-laden term *exploitation* does not adequately characterize relationships between nobles and commoners,

William Taufic/Corbis/Getty Images

Conflict theorists hold that stratification exists and persists because elite classes exploit workers. This woman is boxing up clothing for shipment. Is her employer therefore exploiting her, as Karl Marx claimed?

between lords and serfs, or between capitalists and workers. Of course, if one looks for exploitation in an economic relationship, one can usually find it. Conflict theorists underestimate the valuable services that elite classes perform, such as maintaining social control, organizing the society for the provision of public goods, and accumulating productive resources (capital) put aside to increase future production.

Many conflict theorists assume it is possible to organize a complex society without rewards as unequal as those that exist in real stratified societies. This is an unrealistic view of human nature, according to some critics of the approach. They say this is one reason communism has collapsed almost everywhere. Complex societies are always hierarchically organized, with centralized leadership. Many critics believe the functions of leaders, controllers, and organizers are so valuable to society at large that they deserve the rewards they receive. And who can say what, how much, or what kinds of rewards elites deserve? No one knows, which is why it's best to let markets set reward levels.

Who Benefits?

Contrasting the two theories, we see that functionalism emphasizes the positive aspects of stratification, whereas conflict theory emphasizes the negative side. Functionalists say the class structure benefits society at large, including the less well-off, who would be even less well-off without existing inequalities. Conflict theory points to the costs of stratification not just to those on the bottom of the social ladder but also to society at large. A country or other form of society loses the undeveloped potential of its underprivileged members. Societies also suffer the periodic violent conflicts (rebellions, revolutions) or the ongoing disorder (crimes, labor strikes, political dissent) that result from a high degree of inequality and inherited privilege.

Does anthropology's comparative perspective have anything to say about who benefits from inequality? In premodern stratified societies, elites did indeed perform some vital roles for the whole population, just as functionalists claim. For example, elites organized labor to construct and maintain public works projects, provided relief to regions struck by famine or hardship, promoted long-distance trade, and raised a military force to provide for the defense of the political unit (see Chapter 12). In societies with many thousands or millions of members, some kind of cen-

tral authority may be necessary for such tasks to be coordinated effectively. Cooperation on such a large scale requires leaders to make decisions necessary to organize activities. Provided they make decisions they believe are in the public interest, decision makers deserve rewards.

On the other hand, elites took on some roles that probably developed to maintain their positions at the top of society. Ordinary people regarded the religious functions of elites or of the priests they supported as indispensable to the general welfare, but in fact the rituals did not bring rain, sustain the fertility of land and females, or assuage the anger of the gods. That the elite classes in states and civilizations regulated access to land, irrigation water, and other resources seems socially useful and even necessary. But it was partly because elites themselves controlled so many resources that other people's access to them had to be regulated. Governmental elites provided some law and order, but the elite's power, wealth, and internal political rivalries produced crimes and violent conflicts that otherwise would not have occurred.

From this comparative perspective, we wonder whether some benefits provided by elites in modern nations imply that they deserve the rewards they receive. Perhaps such benefits exist only because of the way the society and its economy is organized. How much of what you pay for a product was spent on advertising it? When you purchase clothing made in Bangladesh, China, or Vietnam, how many of your dollars go to people who actually made the garment compared to those who own the factories in which it was produced and the retailers from whom you bought it?

Who benefits from the inequality in stratified societies? Functionalists are probably correct in assuming that some degree of inequality is needed for motivation. Most people also agree that unequal rewards for unequal efforts and talents is a fair standard. However, we do not know how much inequality is necessary to provide incentives, much less whether some particular stratified society—including whichever one you are a citizen of—has approximately the right amount. We do know that power and privilege are partly or largely inherited, and, therefore, the current members of the upper class are not automatically more talented and diligent than everyone else. Looking at other stratified societies, we see that elites do provide some useful services for the population at large. But we also see that many widespread ideas about their functions are ideologies. Many of the roles regarded as essential are useful because of choices made by previous generations of elites, and present elites use their power to perpetuate them.

Perhaps even the least affluent members of stratified societies would benefit from inequality—if only there were some way to find out what the optimum amount of inequality is for a particular society, if only there were some way to achieve this optimum initially, and if only there were some way to ensure that opportunities to succeed and achieve are equal for children born in varying circumstances. So far, no known human society has ever achieved this utopia.

SUMMARY

1. **Explain the terms *egalitarian, ranked,* and *stratified*.** The terms *egalitarian*, *ranked*, and *stratified* refer to societal differences in inequality in wealth, power, and prestige. How most hunter-gatherers relate to the environment encourages frequent mobility, flexibility, mutual sharing, and modesty, which leads to relative equality in wealth, power, and prestige. In ranked societies such as Tikopia of Polynesia, there are a set number of honored positions (chiefs, titles) to which only a small number of people are eligible to succeed. Stratified societies—found in all ancient civilizations and all modern nations—have marked and enduring inequalities in access to all three kinds of rewards.

2. **Discuss the primary differences between castes and classes.** In caste systems, there is little or no mobility between castes, the castes are legally or normatively endogamous, and higher-caste persons consider those of the lowest castes to be unclean or polluting. Castes are best known from India, where they were integrated into the Hindu doctrines of reincarnation and pollution. Classes exist in all modern countries. In the United States, the best criterion of class membership is wealth. Studies conducted by scholars and by the federal government reveal differences in income and enormous disparities in the distribution of wealth.

3. **Describe how ideologies are important in maintaining inequalities in stratified societies.** Cultural beliefs that inequality is inevitable, divinely ordained, or beneficial to society as a whole are common ideologies that justify and reinforce the power and privilege of elite classes. Among many peoples of the past and present, religious beliefs provide ideologies, as exemplified by most ancient civilizations and states. In modern countries, ideologies tend to be more secular, mainly because effective ideologies must be compatible with people's overall cultural ideas about how their society works. In the United States, secular ideologies include prevalent ideas about the societywide benefits of inequality, about the fairness of unequal rewards for unequal talents and efforts, and about how the well-to-do achieved their wealth.

4. **Evaluate the functional and conflict theories of stratification.** Functionalist and conflict theories offer sharply contrasting ideas about stratification. Functionalists hold that societies offer unequal rewards to those individuals who use their talents to perform the most socially valuable roles. Conflict theorists claim that inequality is based ultimately on control over productive resources. Functionalists are correct that some degree of inequality in rewards is necessary to motivate individuals. However, there is no way of knowing whether a given society has the optimal amount.

14

Religion and Worldview

Paul Chesley/Getty Images

After reading this chapter, you should be able to:

1 **DESCRIBE** how anthropologists define and think about cultural diversity in religion and worldview.

2 **ANALYZE** the strengths and weaknesses of the three main anthropological theories of religion and worldview.

3 **ANALYZE** how witchcraft and sorcery might benefit individuals and groups.

4 **DISCUSS** how anthropologists classify the diversity of human religions and worldviews and analyze the relationships between the four categories and social life.

5 **DESCRIBE** revitalization movements, the conditions under which they are most likely to occur, and what happens to them.

All peoples have some form of religion. Religion is related to worldview (Chapter 2)—conceptions of reality that affect interpretations and perceptions of things and events and, therefore, how individuals act in patterned ways.

Like other dimensions of culture, religion and worldview vary among the world's diverse peoples. In this chapter, we introduce this diversity. We begin with a description of some of the most important aspects of religion from a comparative perspective, using examples. Then we cover some of the main theories social scientists employ to understand religion. Next, we look at some of the major forms of religion that have most interested anthropologists. We conclude by discussing religious movements, which often occur when a people are undergoing rapid change and foreign domination.

Defining Religion

For anthropologists the major difficulty in defining religion is encompassing all the diverse religions of humanity. We cannot define religion simply as belief in a god or even as belief in gods. Some peoples do not have any deities at all, but rather believe in other kinds of spiritual beings and powers that are not gods in the common sense of the word. A nineteenth-century definition that many scholars still use is E. B. Tylor's **animism**, or belief in spiritual beings. Most modern conceptions follow Tylor's lead: All religions include beliefs that some kinds of spiritual or supernatural powers exist. In expanding on Tylor's definition, we also present an overview of religious diversity.

Beliefs About Supernatural Powers

In Chapter 5, we described how nineteenth-century anthropologists proposed that religion had passed through evolutionary stages from simple to complex forms. For Tylor, the three stages of religion were animism, polytheism, and monotheism. Monotheism occurs, he argued, in complex ("advanced," "evolved") societies. But, in fact, elements of animism exist even within religious traditions commonly considered monotheistic. Christianity, for example, has many kinds of spiritual beings such as saints, angels, Satan, and the souls of deceased and living humans.

Spiritual *beings* usually have qualities such as the ability to assume a bodily form, a personality (implying feelings), and a consciousness and will. Usually spiritual beings respond to human actions in some way: If you communicate with them (by chanting, music, prayer, and other ways), they will listen. If your actions displease them, they are likely to react negatively, later if not sooner. Some spiritual beings have human origins or are associated with living or deceased persons such as souls, ancestral ghosts, and important people who did such notable things that they became gods.

animism Belief in spiritual beings.

There are numerous other kinds of beings: spirit helpers, nature spirits, demons, zoomorphic spirits, forest spirits, and so on. The characteristics people attribute to supernatural beings vary enormously: They can be unpredictable or consistent, irrational or reasonable, vengeful or forgiving, amoral or just.

In the religious traditions originating in the ancient Middle East—Judaism, Christianity, and Islam—the supreme being is all-knowing and all-powerful, expects sacrifices or worship, and pays attention to human behavior and morality. The gods that many other peoples believe in have none of these characteristics, however. They can be tricked and manipulated. Often, they are commanded more than worshiped. Some peoples do not believe gods are concerned about the morality of human actions: They do not punish wrongdoing, in either this life or the next. There is no belief that *sin* (violation of a commandment or divine moral precept) even exists.

"Beings" are not the only kind of supernatural powers. The worldview of various peoples includes beliefs in powers that are more like mystical substances or forces than beings. For example, traditionally Polynesians believed in *mana,* a diffuse, incorporeal power that permeated certain people and things. *Mana* lent supernatural potency to objects, which explained unusual qualities such as why some fishing lures worked so well. The gods gave *mana* to certain people, which explained extraordinary success or why chiefs had the right to receive privileges and issue commands. Specific pieces of land were infused with *mana,* which explained why they produced such bountiful harvests.

In contrast to beings such as gods, supernatural *forces* or *substances* like *mana* generally cannot take on a physical appearance and have no will of their own. Rather, they are known mainly by their effects: *Mana* makes a chief successful; pollution sickens a woman or man. In many cultures, beliefs about how powers work are indefinite: One performs a ritual and utters an incantation (spell), and the effect that the rite and spell are intended to cause simply happens. This is generally known as *magic,* discussed later in this chapter.

Myths and Worldviews

Beliefs about supernatural powers are not the only dimension of religion. Religion also includes **myths**—oral or written stories (narratives) about the actions and deeds of supernatural powers and cultural heroes. Sometimes, myths explain how the entire universe was created. They may recount how and why people, animals, plants, and natural features originated. Myths may explain how a people acquired their tools and customs and how they came to live where they do. They often tell why people should or should not act in certain ways and what happened to someone in the past who did something people are forbidden to do. A people's mythology is often their major *teachings*—they learn their group's beliefs about creation, natural phenomena, customs, moral standards, social distinctions, and many other things.

North Americans mostly learn their mythology in formal settings: Myths are taught at church and, to a lesser extent, at home. (Here we need to emphasize that calling the Bible, Quran, Torah, and other religious texts "myths" does not necessarily imply they are mere stories or false accounts of history. In many societies,

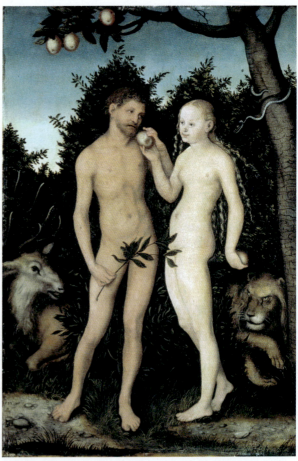

In this depiction of a biblical myth, Eve offers forbidden fruit to Adam. Their original sin explains the origin of evil in the Judeo-Christian worldview.

bpk, Berlin, Staatliche Museen Preussischer Kulturbesitz, Joerg P. Anders, Art Resource NY

~~~
**myths** Stories that recount the deeds of supernatural powers and cultural heroes in the past.
~~~

there are no formal worship services. Elders recount myths informally, sometimes in moments of leisure. Myths are repeated regularly on days set aside for religious performances. They are sung or chanted while one is doing daily tasks.

The fact that myths sometimes are recounted rather casually does not mean that their importance in a people's way of life is negligible. The mythology of a people implies more than stories they tell after dark, recite on appropriate occasions, or use to instruct and perhaps scare children. Mythologies help form a people's worldview—their conceptions of reality and the interpretations of events that happen in society and the natural world. Worldview and myths affect people's beliefs about how they ought to relate to the world and to one another (see Chapter 2), and therefore they affect how people behave in their everyday lives.

Rituals and Symbols

People everywhere believe that gods, ghosts, demons, ancestral spirits, and other supernatural beings take an active interest in worldly affairs, particularly in the lives of human beings. You can ask them for blessings or aid through prayer. Sometimes you can command them to do things for you or for other people. Human behavior can control or influence powers. In the context of religion, the organized performance of behaviors intended to influence spiritual powers is **ritual**. By definition, rituals have certain properties.

Rituals are *stereotyped*: Definite patterns of speech and movement, or definite sequences of events, occur in much the same way in performance after performance. In general, people performing rituals want supernatural powers to do things on their behalf. For example, some central Canadian Inuit believe that their hunts for sea mammals fail because an undersea goddess is angry about the people's misconduct. They persuade the goddess to release the game by performing a ritual in which camp members publicly confess their violations.

Rituals the world over have *symbolic* aspects. These symbolic aspects are so important that some anthropologists define ritual itself as *symbolic behavior*. For example, rituals often occur in *places* that have symbolic significance to the performers. They may be held where some mythological event occurred or where the women who founded a matrilineage were born. Muslims are supposed to make pilgrimages to the holy city of Mecca at least once in their lifetime. Millions of Hindus journey to the city of Varanasi to pray and bathe in Ganga Ma (Mother Ganges). To die and be cremated in Varanasi and have your ashes mix with the river can help you achieve *moksha*, spiritual liberation. Buddhists may go to the site of the Bodhi Tree, where 2,500 years ago Siddhartha's meditation led to his enlightenment and transformation into the Buddha. In Shinto, the ancient indigenous religion of Japan, shrines at which people pray to spirits and to their ancestors are set apart from other spaces by a *torii*, a gate-like structure supported by two pillars.

There are other ritual symbols. Rituals often involve the display, touching, and manipulation of *objects* that symbolize an event (e.g., the cross), a holy person (statues of Jesus and Mary), a relationship (wedding rings, the symbol of holy matrimony), and a variety of other things. Water among many peoples serves as more than just a liquid with practical uses: Bathing in certain rivers or purifying oneself by ritual washing is common among the world's peoples. Buddhist and Hindu temples are filled with statues and relics. The *language* and *behavior* of rituals carry deep symbolic meanings, as in the Christian rituals of worship, hymn singing, prayer, baptism, and communion.

Anthropologists often classify rituals on two bases. The first basis is their *conscious purposes*—the reasons people themselves give for performing rituals. For example, some people believe that divination rituals allow them to acquire information from a supernatural power about some past event, such as illness, or to foretell the future. Familiar examples include tarot cards, crystal balls, and palm reading. There are curing, sorcery, sacrificial, and exorcism rituals. There are rituals to renew the world, to make a man out of a boy and a woman out of a girl, to make people and nature fertile, to bring blessings from deceased ancestors, and to free the soul from a dead person's body.

Many peoples use rituals to control the weather. The Hopi (discussed in Chapter 9) believe the rainfall that replenishes springs and streams and nourishes crops is brought by supernatural beings. These beings, called *kachinas*, live in the peaks of mountains to the west of Hopi villages. They bring life-giving rain to the Hopi cornfields when they come in the form of clouds. In the spring and summer, the Hopi believe, *kachinas* dwell in the villages. During this period, men wearing masks of the *kachinas* perform ritual dances, impersonating and honoring the spirits. The spirit enters the body of the dancer, who thereby becomes the *kachina*. The dances bring rain to the Hopi cornfields.

ritual Organized, stereotyped, symbolic behaviors intended to influence supernatural powers.

In Japan, *torii* symbolically mark the entrance to shrines in which Shinto ritual prayers and offerings to gods and spirits occur. This huge *torii* rests in the bay at Miyajima, near Hiroshima.

The second basis of classifying rituals is their *timing*—on a regular schedule (like weekly worship services or annual religious holidays) or simply whenever some individual or group wants or needs them (like funerals or prayers for a sick person). If rituals are held regularly (seasonally, annually, daily, monthly), they are called *calendrical rituals*. The Hopi, Zuni, and other Pueblo peoples follow a ritual calendar in which certain rituals are performed by certain groups at the same time every year, in the same sequence. The same cycle is repeated the following year.

In contrast, *crisis rituals* are performed whenever some individual or group needs, wants, or asks for them—for purposes of curing, ensuring good hunting or fishing, burying or honoring the dead, or accompanying other events that happen sporadically or unpredictably. The supernatural curing practiced by shamans, described later, is the most widespread type of crisis ritual.

With this brief and broad overview of religion in mind, we consider some of the major theoretical orientations offered to understand or explain religion.

Theories of Religion

Why do all cultures have religious beliefs, myths, and rituals? With regard to beliefs, people cannot confirm the existence of supernatural powers such as ghosts, gods, demons, angels, souls, *mana*, and so forth. Although people who follow a particular religion may believe that traditional accounts of their past reflect historical events, outsiders to the religion are more likely to consider at least parts of them entirely mythical. Indeed, some people who do not share the beliefs of a given culture think such beliefs, which they themselves do not believe, result from ignorance of actual facts or events.

As for rituals, people who are outsiders to a religion and worldview are unlikely to believe that rituals are effective. To nonbelievers, most rituals seem like a waste of time and resources. For example, when a Trobriand Islander plants a yam garden, he does some things that "work" in the way he thinks they do: He clears the land, removes the weeds, and so forth, just as anyone should for success. But a Trobriander also does other things to grow yams and other crops—things that outsiders consider unnecessary and perhaps even wasteful. He hires a magician to perform rites and spells to improve his yam harvest. Outsiders (nonbelievers) to Trobriand beliefs understand what the gardener gets out of the first kind of activity: a yam harvest, if nature cooperates. But what do gardeners gain from magical rites and spells? How did Trobrianders come to believe that magical rites are needed? And why continue to practice them, even when actual experience must often provide evidence that the magic doesn't work?

We can look at this behavior in another way to see a main problem in understanding the rituals of Other cultures. From an outsider's perspective, when the Trobriander plants a crop and weeds his garden, his actions are effective in attaining the goal he has in mind—they work in more or less the way he thinks they do. But when the garden magician performs rites and spells, his actions do not achieve the result he has in mind. The magic does not "really work." How, then, did the Trobrianders get the idea that they do and why keep doing the magic? (Of course, we could simply answer, "Because that is all they know," but there is more to beliefs than just continuing to believe in them.)

Speaking broadly, to those who do not share the particular religion's beliefs, rituals do not have the effects performers intend. The crazy woman is not truly restored to sanity by exorcizing the demon; no spirits really enter the body of the medicine man; there were no genuine witches in Salem, Massachusetts, in 1692. Why, then, do so many people believe in the power of ritual?

Some people who consider themselves sophisticated say that religious beliefs and rituals are rooted in superstition. All anthropologists reject (or should reject) this nonanswer to the question, Why religion? Its ethnocentrism is apparent: Superstition is something that someone else believes in but you do not. Many of our own beliefs seem superstitious to others, and undoubtedly many of the accepted truths of the twenty-first century will be considered superstitions by the twenty-second century. At any rate, even if we think a people's beliefs and practices are superstitious, we still have not explained them. Why does one form of superstition develop in one place and another form in another place?

Perhaps you already know possible answers. If rituals do not have the effects people intend—if weather magic does not affect the real weather, for example—they may have other effects that people find useful or satisfying. If the conscious reasons people give for performing rituals seem inadequate, perhaps their meaning is entirely symbolic: They convey and reinforce deep meanings and values that help people cope with life or that tie people together. As for myths, if they are not accurate historical accounts, perhaps they are symbolic statements that help people make sense of reality and give meaning to real-world things and events. Maybe religious truths are a different kind of truth than scientific truths: They cannot be subjected to tests and experiments to see whether they work the way people think they do, but they work on another level.

Social scientists have proposed many theories for why religion exists. Some theories hold that beliefs, myths, and rituals provide benefits that people want or need but cannot acquire without religion. Broadly, social scientists have proposed three types of theories: intellectual (or cognitive), psychological, and sociological.

Intellectual or Cognitive Approaches

Those who posit the **intellectual approach** (or the **cognitive approach**) assume that humans seek explanations for the world around them. Religious beliefs help satisfy the human desire to understand and explain things and events. Without religion, much of the world would be incomprehensible and inexplicable, which (these scholars argue) would be intolerable to the mind of a conscious, reasoning, problem-solving species like *Homo sapiens*. For example, religion satisfies the human desire for understanding by providing explanations for the movements of the sun, moon, and stars. *Origin myths* explain things like the creation of the sky, land, and water; where animals and plants come from; and where people got their language, tools, rituals, and other customs and beliefs. The essential purpose of religion, in the intellectual view, is to provide people with explanations.

Sir James Frazer was an influential scholar who championed the intellectual approach. His most famous work was *The Golden Bough*, published in 12 volumes

intellectual approach (cognitive approach)
Notion that religious beliefs provide explanations for puzzling things and events.

at around the turn of the twentieth century. One of Frazer's main interests was the development of rational thought. He argued that human thinking progressed through three stages that he called magic, religion, and science. The earliest cultures practiced *magic;* they attempted to control the world by performing rites and spells. Later cultures came to believe in the existence of supernatural beings, who demanded that people worship them or make sacrifices to them, giving birth to *religion.* Finally, people realized that neither magical techniques nor worship of imaginary beings enabled them to explain or control events. With the advent of *science,* the errors of magic and religion were replaced with knowledge of true cause-and-effect relationships. In Frazer's view, magic, religion, and science are alternative worldviews: Each provides people with an intellectual model of the way the world works and a means to manipulate events and people.

The idea of Frazer and others that religious beliefs provide people with explanations for things and events is correct, as far as it goes, but it surely is an incomplete explanation for religion. Religion does satisfy curiosity about the world, but this is not its only function. The people whom Frazer called "savages" possess and use practical knowledge just as "civilized" peoples do—a Trobriander knows that he must care for his yams as well as perform garden magic. Conversely, many scientific people believe in and practice religion—including many persons who make their living practicing the science for which religion supposedly substitutes. Those scientists who go to church apparently find little or no contradiction between their religious beliefs and worship and their scientific knowledge and practice. Religious beliefs do not simply substitute for objective knowledge. People don't "have" religion because they "lack" science. Somehow, the two are complementary.

Although few scholars today hold that religion exists solely or even mainly to provide "prescientific" people with explanations their culture would otherwise lack, the intellectual approach is by no means passé. Clifford Geertz, a leading humanistic theorist (see Chapter 5), argued that religion provides its believers with the assurance that the world is *meaningful*—that events have a place in the grand scheme of things, natural phenomena have understandable causes, suffering and evil happen to good people for some good reason, wrongs will be righted and injustices corrected. Cultural beings (i.e., humans) cannot tolerate events that contradict the basic premises, categories, and worldview of their cultural tradition. Yet such events do occur periodically. Because of religion, people are able to maintain their worldview in spite of events that seem to contradict it. Religion, Geertz believed, reassures believers that the world is orderly rather than chaotic, all within the framework of their existing cultural knowledge.

More recently, Stewart Guthrie also interprets religion in cognitive terms. Guthrie thinks the essence of religion is the belief that natural phenomena have humanlike properties. He points out that people tend to see the world *anthropomorphically:* We tend to attribute human motives, purposes, feelings, senses, and other characteristics to living and nonliving things that are not human. For example, thunder is the voice of the gods, clouds are the spirits of our ancestors, the sun is our life-giving father, Mother Earth is alive, the wind is the breath of a god. Anthropomorphism is natural to human thought, and most of us regularly think or react in this way, as when you think your car hates you, you swear at your computer, or you interact with your pet as if it were a person.

When we see the world as peopled with spirits (as in animism), or think that different gods control various aspects of nature (as in polytheism), or believe that one god created and controls everything (as in monotheism), we are attributing human characteristics to the natural world. In Guthrie's view, this actually is a smart thing to do. If you think there are no spiritual beings making things happen and you are wrong, then the consequences are costly. If the Earth is in fact our mother, but we mistreat her and her children, then she might punish us. But if we think anthropomorphically about the Earth and take steps to worship and protect her, then no harm is done. If there is a war god, and our enemy sacrifices to him but we do not, we may all be killed, so why take the chance? As Guthrie phrases it, in these ways religion is a "good bet."

However, not all rituals resulting from beliefs that humanlike beings control natural processes are harmless. In fact, many rituals are quite costly. They require sacrifices to deities or ancestors, and they consume time and energy that could be used in other ways. In some societies, religious beliefs are costly indeed. In some ancient Mesoamerican civilizations, priests pierced their bodies with thorns to make themselves bleed because they believed the gods demanded blood sacrifices. Humans were also sacrificed. Religion often motivates individuals and groups to do horrific things to others—and sometimes to themselves.

Psychological Approaches

The notion that religion helps people cope with times of trouble, stress, and anxiety is a common one. Sicknesses,

The psychological approach holds that religion provides comfort and reassurance at times of grief, misfortune, anxiety, and fear. This Palestinian woman is grieving at the funeral of loved one.

accidents, misfortunes, injustices, deaths, and other trials and tribulations of life can be better handled emotionally if one believes there is a reason and meaning to them or that one's troubles can be controlled or alleviated by means of ritual. Scholars who make such arguments follow the **psychological approach**.

In anthropology, Bronislaw Malinowski proposed a well-known psychological theory of religion. Malinowski thought that religion (including magic) serves the valuable function of giving people confidence when we are likely to be unsuccessful despite our best efforts. There are always natural phenomena that we cannot control and that constantly threaten to ruin our plans and efforts. Belief in the power of ritual to control these (otherwise uncontrollable) elements instills confidence and removes some of the anxiety that results from the uncertainties of life. Not only do rituals relieve our worries, but they may also help us be more successful in activities by making us more confident of success.

People grow frustrated—and occasionally violent—when they cannot control what happens to them or those they care about. Our lives are filled with uncertainties and unknowable futures. Our families and friends don't always do what we want or what we think is right for them. Accidents happen. Housing prices collapse. Our relatives pass away. Bosses fire us. Crops fail. Professors fail us. We fail ourselves. Religion (and, in this context, especially faith in a power with more knowledge and power than humans have) is there to offer hope and comfort. Often, it helps us cope with frustrated hopes by telling us what we can do to make things better. For example, during a 2007 drought in Georgia, people got together to pray for rain. It did rain later.

Another variant of the psychological theory of religion holds that, as self-conscious beings, we humans are aware of our own mortality. Knowing that we will eventually die causes us great anxiety and leads us to

psychological approach Notion that the emotional or affective satisfactions people gain from religion are primary in interpreting religion.

worry about our own death. Experiencing the serious illness or death of a parent or other relative likewise produces grief and psychological stress for most people. We must have some way of coping emotionally with the grief over the death of our loved ones and with the anxiety caused by the knowledge of our own mortality. Religion helps us cope by denying the finality of death and by leading us to believe in a pleasant afterlife, in which our souls are immortal.

The notion that belief in life after death helps calm our fears and alleviate our anxieties seems reasonable. This theory is tainted by an ethnocentric assumption, however: Although nearly all religions include beliefs about some kind of afterlife, in a great many cultures, that afterlife is far from pleasant. The Dobu people of Melanesia believe that human bodies also have a ghostly form, experienced in the real world as a shadow or a reflection. During life, the ghostly self goes out at night and appears in the dreams of other people. Once the corpse rots after death, the ghosts of people go to a place called the Hill of the Dead, where they have a thin and shadowy existence and mourn for their homeland. How are such beliefs about the afterlife comforting?

Certainly, religion is psychologically useful. For some people some of the time, it relieves anxieties, calms fears, and helps them cope emotionally with life's uncertainties and hardships. That religion often serves such functions seems indisputable. Yet, sometimes religious beliefs actually increase our anxieties, fears, and stress levels. Consider the Kwaio, a people of the Solomon Islands. Kwaio believe that women are polluting to men, so Kwaio wives are expected to take elaborate precautions to avoid polluting their husbands when preparing food for them. If a man dies of an illness, his wife may be blamed, and perhaps killed, for her offense. Whose anxieties and fears are relieved by this belief? Doesn't the belief increase anxieties and fears?

The general point of the Dobu and Kwaio examples is that, from a psychological perspective, religion has two faces. On the one hand, it does—for some people, some of the time, in some respects—help us cope emotionally with times of trouble and hardships. On the other hand, beliefs about supernatural powers and what they do often create fears and anxieties that would not otherwise exist. A pleasant afterlife (Heaven) offers

us comfort and hope. But what *psychological* benefit does the threat of eternal damnation (Hell) offer? This question leads logically to the sociological approach.

Sociological Approaches

"Societies need religion to keep people in line," you may have heard someone say. The idea of this **sociological approach** is that religion helps instill and maintain common values, leads to increased conformity to cultural norms, promotes social cohesion and cooperation, promises eternal rewards for good deeds and threatens eternal damnation for evil acts, and so forth. Those who champion the sociological approach hold that religion exists because of the useful effects it has on human societies—because of its *social functions*. Religion helps societies maintain harmonious social relationships between individuals and groups. It encourages people to respect the rights of others and to perform their proper duties. It is part of the socialization process that instills values in children.

Consider the Ten Commandments, for example, which serve as part of a moral code for Judaism, Islam, and Christianity. Two commandments prescribe how people ought to feel and act toward God and other people, and eight give rules for actions, including the five "thou shalt nots" (see Exodus 20:3–17). Note that five of the divinely ordered prohibitions are against the commission of acts that could result in harm to others, such as killing and stealing.

God gave us commandments that will, if obeyed, lead to good relationships with others and therefore promote earthly social order. More general Judeo-Christian moral guidelines are the Golden Rule ("Do unto others as you would have them do unto you") and love of one's neighbor (Matthew 19:19); both are useful prescriptions for harmonious social life. Confucianism, which originated in China but spread to Korea and Japan, taught a remarkably similar moral lesson: "Do not do to others what you do not want them to do to you."

Religion also enhances the cohesion of society by making people sense their interdependence on one another and on their traditions. Emile Durkheim, a French sociologist of the early twentieth century, was influential in formulating this perspective. Durkheim's view was that the main function of religion in human society is to promote *social solidarity*, meaning that religion has the effect of bringing people together and enhancing their sense of unity, cohesion, and reliance on their society's customs. Groups of people who share

sociological approach Notion that religious beliefs function to maintain the institutions of society as a whole by instilling common values, creating solidarity, controlling behavior, and so forth.

Among the arguments of sociological theories is that religion helps create social bonds and thus increases cohesion in human groups. Shared activities during ritual performances are one way this is achieved, as this ancestral veneration ceremony among the Asmat people of Papua New Guinea illustrates.

the same beliefs and who gather periodically to perform common rituals experience a feeling of oneness and harmony.

The most important social function of religion, Durkheim believed, is to strengthen social solidarity—the feeling that members of the group share common interests and are part of one metaphorical social body. There also are other versions of the sociological approach. One is that religion helps to maintain social order—that is, religion serves as a social control mechanism (see Chapters 12 and 13) by increasing conformity to norms, inculcating shared values in children, reminding people to act responsibly, teaching moral lessons through myths and doctrines, legitimizing the existing social structure, and so forth.

One mechanism by which religion maintains social control is by offering rewards for good behavior and punishments for antisocial behavior. When people have an accident or get sick, they may think they are being punished for some crime or deviant action, for example. This deters the individual from future deviance

and also serves as an example to others, teaching them to act properly in the future. In the afterlife, gods may reward virtue and punish sinful behavior. Such socially useful effects of religion are widespread.

Not all peoples have such beliefs, however. In some worldviews, gods and other kinds of spiritual beings have little interest in the morality or immorality of human actions. There is no concept of sin as behavior that violates a doctrine or divine will, and the fate of a person in this life or in the afterlife is not related to her or his moral character or conduct.

A recent sociological interpretation derives from evolutionary psychology. It assumes that many people are prone to cheat on other members of a group to which they belong if they calculate that it is advantageous to them personally. Cheating means that they only pretend to cooperate with others in the group, but find ways of acquiring the benefits of group membership without paying the costs. Examples of such benefits include security of private property, protection from enemies, earning high wages without working as hard as coworkers, and not paying taxes proportionate to income. Religion helps reduce the frequency of cheating behaviors.

How? Richard Sosis argues that rituals are the key: They lead individuals to make sacrifices that demonstrate commitment to group values and norms. When a person gives up something she or he could otherwise have by undergoing or participating in a ritual, they are signaling to other members of the group that they place its interests above their own. When a group exacts a "price" on its members, only people willing to give up something, or do something costly to themselves, are likely to join and remain. Sosis calls such sacrifices *costly signals*—symbolic acts demonstrating commitment to the group. If you join a church or a cult, there are costs: At the very least, you agree to certain behavioral standards. If the act of joining requires you to pay a price or give up something, your sacrifice signals to others that you are committed to the group's goals and to upholding the group's values. Others trust you more, and you are more likely to cooperate with them because of what you've given up. (Although not religious rituals, think of fraternity initiations and how they help create relations of brotherhood.)

Like the cognitive and psychological approaches, the sociological theory applies sometimes, but not always. At some times, in some places, and in some contexts, religion teaches the difference between right and wrong and thus increases social harmony. Sometimes it strengthens solidarity by bringing people together. It inculcates the belief that good behavior is rewarded, and antisocial behavior is punished eventually, if not immediately. Sometimes it leads people to act in ways that are best for the group, over their personal goals and interests.

But sometimes religion has negative effects, ones that few believe are socially useful. It has contributed to wars and led to persecutions. Although it can help unite the members of one country, or of one faith, it can also promote wars between them and other countries or other faiths. It is a source of disunity as well as unity within many societies, in the past as well as the present. It sometimes contributes to ethnocentrism, racism, intolerance of people who believe differently, gender discrimination, and other socially harmful attitudes and practices. In stratified societies, historically religious beliefs have supported vast social differences in powers and privileges. When used as ideologies, religious beliefs may support all kinds of inequalities and injustices (see Chapter 13). There may be some respects in which such impacts are socially useful, but they are not useful to *everyone*.

Will Religion Disappear?

We have discussed weaknesses as well as insights in all three of the major theoretical approaches. It is unlikely that any of them alone is an adequate general theory of religion. Notice the idea they have in common: Religion is useful to human individuals and to human groups. Perhaps these theories are relevant for the opinion of many atheists that humanity would be better off without religion. With no religions, some atheists think, there would be no faith in mistaken ancient writings or scriptures, less anxiety and fear, no more religious wars or attacks based on other peoples' religions, no possibility of divine will to justify inequalities, and so forth. (Notice the implicit assumption that no nonreligious beliefs and practices would develop to replace these social evils assumed to result from religion.)

In all likelihood those who predict the eventual end of religion are wrong about scientific knowledge replacing religion. A moment's reflection reveals that such opinions derive mainly from only one theory of religion: the intellectual or cognitive. If scientific knowledge becomes more widespread, religion will no longer be necessary to explain the world and events in it. Beliefs that we call religious will wither, myths will be viewed as just old stories, and people will realize that rituals are ineffective.

Such opinions ignore that religion offers things that science does not and cannot provide. A simple example is that medical science explains why people die, but offers no comfort when one of *our* loved ones dies. For that, we need the social support of relatives and friends—funerals are a cultural universal—and many of us find the belief in an afterlife comforting. There are religious services and religious holidays (despite commercialization). Religious teachings and religious rituals provide meaning and purpose to life, which science cannot do as well.

Also, most people today believe both religious teachings and accept scientific findings. This was not always true. The scientific fact that the Earth revolves around the sun was once heresy. Not too long ago, the theory of evolution was condemned as contradicting religious teachings; therefore evolution was ungodly as well as false. When nineteenth-century geologists decided the Earth was much older than scriptures taught, there was much resistance from religious persons. The general point is that religion has been accommodating new scientific ideas and findings for a long time.

There is still resistance to science, of course, and especially to evolution. However, like all other

Commonly, people believe that rituals help individuals acquire something they need or fulfill their wishes. This Peruvian woman is having a ceremony to ensure that she earns enough money to buy a house.

aspects of human life, religious teachings have changed to accommodate technological, cultural, and societal changes. There is no reason to think they will not continue to change. Continual, adjustive change is much more likely to be the future of religion than its disappearance.

Supernatural Explanations of Misfortune

One occurrence that many peoples attribute to the action of spiritual powers is personal misfortune, including death, illness, and events that many Westerners consider accidents. Many beliefs and rituals of various societies are concerned with explaining, preventing, and curing illness and disease, which they believe are caused by something supernatural.

Cross-culturally, two major complexes of beliefs about misfortune are common. First, many peoples believe that sickness or other unfortunate occurrences are caused by the action of spiritual powers. Violations of taboos can lead to sickness. Ancestral spirits of kin groups cause their members to become ill because of conflict or bad feelings within the group. Similar beliefs often apply to accidents that many Westerners attribute to bad luck or carelessness. Drownings, falls, snakebites, prolonged failure to succeed at some activity—such events are culturally interpreted as evidence of unfavorable supernatural intervention. The victim has offended a god or spirit, who brings an "accident" as punishment.

Second, many people think illnesses or other misfortunes are caused by the action of some evil human using special supernatural powers against the afflicted person. The belief that certain people, called *sorcerers* and *witches,* have powers to harm others by mystical means is enormously widespread among humanity. Sometimes, witches and sorcerers are thought to strike randomly and maliciously against people who are innocent of any wrongdoing. More commonly, they direct their evil magic or thoughts toward those against whom they have a grudge. Because they are so puzzling and common among humanity, sorcery and witchcraft are worth considering in more detail.

Sorcery

Sorcery is the performance of rites and spells intended to cause supernatural harm to others; that is, sorcery is a form of evil magic. In some cultures, almost everyone learns to harm their enemies by sorcery techniques. Among such peoples, knowledge of sorcery rites and spells is widespread. In other cultures, sorcery is a more specialized practice; only certain people inherit or acquire the knowledge of how to recite spells and perform the rites correctly.

Most commonly, sorcery relies on two kinds of logical principles or assumptions. Both involve a symbolic identification of something (e.g., an object or action) with something else (e.g., an event or a person).

The *imitative principle* can be stated as "Like produces like." That is, if an object resembles a person and the sorcerer mutilates the object, then the same thing will happen to the person. The so-called voodoo doll is a familiar example. In another kind of imitative magic, the magician or sorcerer mimics the effects she or he wants to produce. For example, sorcerers among the Dobu of Melanesia cast spells by imitating the symptoms of the disease they want their victims to suffer.

The second logical premise underlying magic and sorcery is the *contagious principle,* stated as "Power comes from contact." That is, things once in contact with someone can be used in rites and spells to make things happen to that person. By performing sorcery rites and spells on objects such as hair clippings, bodily excretions, nail parings, umbilical cords, or jewelry and clothing, one can cause harm to one's enemies. In societies in which sorcery rests on the contagious principle, people must dispose of the objects with which they have been in contact, including things like infant umbilical cords, that have come out of or off of their bodies, lest one of their enemies use them for sorcery.

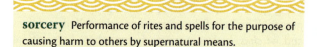

sorcery Performance of rites and spells for the purpose of causing harm to others by supernatural means.

witchcraft Use of psychic powers alone to harm others by supernatural means.

Sorcery practices are related to the social life of a people. For example, who accuses whom of sorcery reflects how individuals and groups relate to one another. In any society, certain kinds of social relationships are especially likely to be beset by conflict. Co-wives of a polygynous man may be jealous over their husband's favors or may compete for an inheritance for their children. People who have married into a kin group or village may be viewed as outsiders who are still loyal to their own natal families. Two men who want the same woman, or two women who want the same man, have reasons to dislike each other. Men who are rivals for a political office have conflicts of interest.

These and other kinds of relationships are sources of tension and conflict within a human group. Which relationships are likely to cause tensions and conflicts depend on the way the society is organized: brothers-in-law are allies in one society, but their interests regularly conflict in another society, for instance. The relationships most likely to be tense are *patterned,* meaning that individuals who have these relationships with one another are most likely to experience conflicts.

Suppose you were brought up among a people who explained illness or accident by sorcery. If you became ill or suffered misfortune, you would not suspect just anyone of causing harm. You would ask, "Who has a motive to perform evil magic against me? Who envies me? Who would profit from my sickness or death? With whom have I recently quarreled?" These people are your prime suspects, and they are the ones you or your family is most likely to accuse.

Members of most cultures reason in much the same way. They believe sorcerers do not strike randomly but harm only their enemies or the people toward whom they feel anger, envy, or ill will. Accusations of sorcery, therefore, usually follow the prevalent lines of social tensions and conflicts: Individuals who have certain kinds of relationships are most likely to suspect and accuse one another, so sorcery accusations usually reflect social tensions and conflicts.

Witchcraft

Witchcraft is another explanation that people in many societies give for personal misfortune. There is no universally applicable distinction between sorcery and witchcraft. Whereas sorcery usually involves the use of rites and spells to commit a foul deed, anthropologists usually define **witchcraft** as the use of psychic power alone to cause harm to others. Sorcerers manipulate objects; witches need only think malevolent thoughts to turn their anger, envy, or hatred into evil deeds. Many cultures believe in the existence of both kinds of malevolent power, so sorcery and witchcraft are often found among the same people. Like sorcery accusations, accusations of witchcraft are likely to be patterned because people most often believe that both witches and sorcerers harm only people they dislike, hate, envy, or with whom they have a conflict.

Cultures vary in the characteristics they attribute to witches and in how witches cause harm. The following examples illustrate the diversity.

- The Navajo of the American Southwest associate witches with the worst imaginable sins. Witches commit incest, bestiality (sex with animals), and necrophilia (sex with corpses); they change themselves into animals; they cannibalize infants; and so on.

- The Nyakyusa of Tanzania hold that witches are motivated mainly by their lust for food; accordingly, they suck dry the udders of people's cattle and devour the internal organs of their human neighbors while they sleep.

- The Azande of South Sudan believe witches possess an inherited substance that leaves their bodies at night and gradually eats away at the flesh and internal organs of their victims. Witches, as well as their victims, are considered unfortunate because the Azande believe a person can be a witch without even knowing it. Witches can do nothing to rid themselves permanently of their power, although they can be forced to stop bewitching some particular individual by overcoming their bad feelings against their victim.

- The Ibibio of Nigeria believe witches operate by removing the spiritual essence (soul) of their enemies and placing it in an animal. This makes the victim sick, and the person dies when the witches slaughter and consume the animal. Sometimes Ibibio witches decide to torture, rather than kill, a person. In that case, they remove the victim's soul and put it in water or hang it over a fireplace or flog it in the evenings. The afflicted person will remain sick until the witches get what they want out of him or her.

- The Lugbara, a people of Uganda, claim that witches—who are always men—walk around at night disguised as rats or other nocturnal animals. Sometimes they defecate blood around the household of their victims, who wake up sick the next morning.

- The Gebusi of Papua New Guinea blame all illnesses on witchcraft. Gebusi attacked and killed so many persons whom they identified as witches that nearly one-third of all deaths among them resulted from revenge against witches.

Someone who does not share these beliefs probably thinks they are logically outrageous. No one's soul leaves his or her body at night to cavort with other witches, for example. It might seem that these beliefs are socially harmful as well, as the Gebusi exemplify. Beliefs about witchcraft, fear of witchcraft, and accusations of witchcraft lead to conflict and aggression among a people. Finally, the punishments that many suspected and "proven" witches receive offend our notions of social justice. As we know from the witch-hunts of European and American history, the truly innocent victims of witchcraft are often the accused witches, who sometimes are cruelly executed for crimes they could not have committed.

Interpretations of Sorcery and Witchcraft

Given the harmful effects and social injustices that frequently result from imagined sorcerers and witches, why do so many of the world's peoples think that some or all of their misfortunes are caused by the supernatural powers of their enemies? Many answers have been offered to such questions. In line with the overall theoretical approaches discussed earlier, the answers fall into two categories: cognitive and social. (For simplicity in the following discussion, we use the term *witchcraft* to refer to both witchcraft and sorcery because the ideas presented have been applied to both kinds of beliefs.)

Cognitive Interpretations

The most influential cognitive interpretation is that witchcraft explains unfortunate events. Most people find the idea of coincidence or accident intellectually unsatisfying when some misfortune happens to them or their loved ones, so they search for other causes. Their logic is something like this: I have enemies who wish me harm, and harm just came to me, so my enemies are responsible.

The best-known example of how people account for misfortune by witchcraft is the Azande of Africa. Azande attribute prolonged serious illnesses and many other personal misfortunes to witchcraft. Ethnographer E. E. Evans-Pritchard (1976, p. 18) describes their beliefs:

> Witchcraft is ubiquitous.... There is no niche or corner of Zande culture into which it does not

twist itself. If blight seizes the groundnut crop it is witchcraft; if the bush is vainly scoured for game it is witchcraft; if women laboriously bail water out of a pool and are rewarded by but a few small fish it is witchcraft; ... if a wife is sulky and unresponsive to her husband it is witchcraft; if a prince is cold and distant with his subject it is witchcraft; if a magical rite fails to achieve its purpose it is witchcraft; if, in fact, any failure or misfortune falls upon any one at any time and in relation to any of the manifold activities of his life it may be due to witchcraft.

This does not mean that Azande are ignorant of cause and effect and therefore attribute every misfortune to some witch who is out to get them. When a man seeks shelter in a granary and its roof falls and injures him, he blames witchcraft. But the Azande know very well that granary roofs collapse because termites eat the wood that supports them. They do not attribute the collapse of granaries in general to witchcraft. It is the collapse of this particular granary at this particular time with this particular person inside that is caused by witchcraft. Don't granaries sometimes fall when no one is sitting inside them? And don't people often relax in granaries without the roof falling? It is the coincidence between the collapse and the presence of a particular person—a coincidence that many other peoples consider bad luck—that Azande explain by witchcraft.

Another cognitive benefit is that witches serve as scapegoats. When things are going poorly, people do not always know why. Witchcraft provides an explanation. It also provides people with a means to do something about the situation: Identify, accuse, and punish the witch responsible. If, as is often the case, things still do not improve, there are always other yet-to-be-identified witches. People can blame many of their troubles on witches—evil enemies conspiring against them—rather than on their personal inadequacies, bad luck, or wider economic or social conditions in their societies. The pattern of blaming particular individuals and groups for one's problems occurs in modern nations as well, although few of their citizens believe in witchcraft.

Social Interpretations

One social interpretation is that witchcraft reinforces the norms and values that help individuals live harmoniously with one another. Every culture has notions of how individuals ideally ought to act toward others. Witches typically are the antithesis of these cultural ideals. They act like animals or actually change themselves into animals. They mate with relatives. They

often put on a false front, pretending to be your friend by day while they eat your liver by night. They have no respect for age or authority. They are in league with the forces of evil (in the Judeo-Christian tradition, witches made compacts with the Devil, agreeing to be his servant in return for worldly pleasures).

All the most despicable personal characteristics of people are wrapped up in the personality of witches, whom everyone is supposed to hate. So, witches symbolize all that is undesirable, wicked, and hateful. Just as one should despise witches, so should one hate all that they stand for. In short, by providing a hated symbol of the abnormal and the antisocial, the witch strengthens cultural conceptions of normatively approved social behavior.

Another interpretation is that witchcraft beliefs serve as a mechanism of social control. This might work in two ways. First, many people believe in the existence of witchcraft but do not know which specific members of their community are witches. This leads individuals to be careful not to make anyone angry; after all, the offended party might be a witch. Second, individuals who fail to conform to local norms of behavior are most likely to be suspected and accused of being witches. People who are always mad at somebody, who carry grudges for prolonged periods, who always seem envious and resentful of the success of others, who have achieved wealth but selfishly refuse to share it in the culturally accepted manner—such violators of these and other normative standards frequently are believed to be the likely perpetrators of witchcraft. Fear of being accused and punished presumably increases adherence to the norms and ideals of behavior.

Probably most readers deny that they believe in sorcery and witchcraft. Those who do believe might have Wicca (or *paganism*) in mind, which obviously is different from the way we have used witchcraft and sorcery to refer to supernatural powers employed for harmful, antisocial purposes. Of course, we could broaden our definitions of sorcery and witchcraft to include Wicca and paganism by removing the antisocial elements. Then Wicca becomes almost the same as *magic*, as anthropologists usually use the term.

Or we could change the definition in another way. We could remove the part of the definition that refers to supernatural powers. Then sorcery and witchcraft would be defined as beliefs that unknown persons harm others using techniques that cannot be demonstrated to be real, that are not observable, or that do not actually exist. In the United States, in the 1950s Senator Joseph McCarthy played on people's fears when he claimed, with no evidence, that the U.S. government and Hollywood had communist infiltrators dedicated to overturning all that Americans hold dear. In the 1980s and 1990s, various supremacists blamed certain political factions and minorities for social and economic problems and what they believed to be the degeneration of their nation's values. Perhaps this is happening again today. Although we might not call them this, will there be more witch-hunts in the twenty-first century?

Varieties of Religious Organization

As we know from earlier chapters, in comparing cultures, anthropologists develop classifications based on differences and similarities. By their very nature, classifications are simplifications of the real world. Those that anthropologists use to describe and understand religious diversity are no exceptions. Classifications must be broad to show contrasts, but that same broadness necessarily ignores most details. As humanistic anthropologists remind us, by categorizing diverse human religions into only few forms or types, we oversimplify and distort.

In previous chapters, we defined categories like nomadic pastoralism, balanced reciprocity, chiefdoms, and ranked societies, and then used particular peoples and cultures as examples of the type or form. In other words, often we described particular cultures to illustrate or exemplify some general category.

We mention this because some humanistically inclined anthropologists (see Chapter 5) are critical of classifications in general. They tend to believe that each culture has so many unique particularities that shoving it into a comparative framework disserves its members and distorts their culture. As we've seen when researching and discussing Other cultures, anthropologists critique cultural constructions about race, kinship, gender, and the like. But anthropologists use constructions ourselves when we make comparisons and contrasts; that is, we have our own constructions that we use to understand Other cultures.

On what basis, then, do comparative anthropologists construct their classifications of Other cultures? Humanistic scholars tend to think the basis is not objective—not based on the reality of actual peoples and cultures, but constructed in the minds of certain (mostly scientifically inclined) anthropologists.

This issue is especially notable for religion and worldview because it so easy to judge the beliefs, myths, and rituals of Others in a negative way. At one extreme, agnostics and atheists may think all things religious are superstitious and that beliefs about ancestral spirits and gods and witches should be eliminated by what they consider education. At the other extreme, in considering the religions of Others, devout believers of certain faiths may view them as the work of Satan leading people astray with pagan rituals, heathenish beliefs, idolatry, and the like.

With such objections in mind, developing contrasts between forms of religion can provide a general picture of religious diversity among humanity. A classification also allows an understanding of the cultural contexts of religious beliefs and practices. To avoid misunderstandings, it is important to be aware that there are many differences between religions and worldviews we place in the same category.

Long ago, Anthony Wallace proposed an influential classification of religions. Wallace originally used the word *cult,* a term that calls to mind exotic and usually short-lived sets of beliefs and practices. To avoid the negative connotations of *cult,* here we use the term *religious organization.* "Organization" emphasizes the social groups and relationships that coordinate activities to control or worship specific supernatural powers for various purposes. It does not mean the entire religion of a people. Rather, a people's total religion includes many different kinds of organizations devoted to different purposes, like curing illness, controlling weather, worshiping gods, hunting animals, divining the future, renewing nature, protecting people from enemies, saving souls, and keeping ancestral spirits happy.

Wallace originally distinguished four types of religious organization:

▌ **Individualistic organization:** Each individual has a personal relationship with one or more supernatural powers, who serve as the person's guardians and protectors. The aid of the powers is solicited when needed for personal goals.

▌ **Shamanistic organization:** Some individuals—shamans—have relationships with supernatural powers that ordinary people lack. They use these

individualistic organization Religious organization based on personal relationships between specific individuals and specific supernatural powers.

shamanistic organization Religious organization in which certain individuals (shamans) have relationships with supernatural powers that ordinary people lack.

CONCEPT REVIEW   Varieties of Religious Organization

Form of Organization	Major Characteristics
Individualistic	Individuals have a special relationship with one or more supernatural powers who serve as personal guardians and protectors. Individuals seek assistance from their guardian spirits when needed.
Shamanistic	Some persons—shamans—have power to contact supernatural beings at times of crisis to help (especially cure) individuals. Shamans may also act on behalf of their band or village to harm enemies.
Communal	Members of a well-defined group gather periodically for collective rituals that generally benefit the group as a whole. Elders often have special roles in rituals.
Ecclesiastical	Societies or their divisions have full-time religious officials—priests—organized into a religious bureaucracy. Priests officiate at calendrical rituals believed to benefit the whole society, usually in large temples dedicated to religious purposes or deities.

powers primarily for socially valuable purposes, to help (especially cure) others in need. They may also act on behalf of their band or village to cause supernatural harm to the group's enemies. Usually shamans organize and direct crisis rituals.

- **Communal organization:** The members of a particular group gather periodically to perform rituals believed to benefit the group as a whole. There are no full-time religious specialists, as is also true of individualistic and shamanistic cults. Usually, leaders who control and direct the rituals are elders or respected members of the group on whose behalf the rituals are performed.

- **Ecclesiastical organization:** Some societies have full-time religious practitioners who form a religious bureaucracy. The actual practice of religion is managed or carried out by formal, specialized officials—priests—who perform mainly calendrical rituals, usually in large temples

communal organization Religious organization in which the members of a group cooperate to perform rituals intended to benefit all.

ecclesiastical organization Religious organization in which full-time priests perform rituals believed to benefit believers or the whole society, usually in large temples dedicated to religious purposes or deities; found mainly in complex societies.

dedicated to religious purposes or deities. This organization is found mainly in complex societies, which supports the priests through taxation or redistributive tribute (see Chapters 8 and 12).

The Concept Review provides a brief overview of these forms of religious organization.

So defined, the religious organizations are not randomly distributed among the world's peoples. Rather, they occur in a rough evolutionary sequence. Most notably, in many foraging bands and horticultural tribes—such as the Inuit, Ju/'hoansi, and Yanomamö—shamanistic rituals are common, whereas ecclesiastical rituals occur mainly in stratified chiefdoms and states. Be aware, though, that the evolutionary matching of kinds of religions with kinds of economic and political organizations is rough and general.

Despite complications, there is a general pattern. The religions of hunter-gatherer bands differ generally and significantly from those of complex chiefdoms and states. Because one of our major points is that religious beliefs, myths, and rituals are embedded in the context of a people's entire cultural system, we also discuss how they relate to economic and political organization.

Individualistic Organizations

The defining characteristic of individualistic religious organizations is that individuals intentionally seek out particular spirits or other supernatural powers to protect and help them. As their name suggests, they emphasize private, even secret, interactions between individual persons and supernatural powers.

The **vision quest** is the best-known example. Vision quests are widespread among Native American peoples but are especially important for Great Plains tribes. To Plains peoples, the world is charged with spiritual energy and power, which exists in inanimate objects, such as rocks or mountains and earth and sky, as well as in living animals and plants. Humans require the aid of supernatural powers and beings in many activities—in hunting, warfare, and times of sickness or other troubles.

Spiritual power most often comes to individuals in visions. Visions play an important role in religious life because through them people achieve the personal contact with the supernatural that is essential for success in many of life's endeavors. Occasionally spiritual powers make contact with individuals for no apparent reason, coming to them as they sleep or even as they are walking or riding alone.

More often, humans—especially young men—seek out these powers through an active search, or quest, whose purpose is to acquire a vision. There are places that supernatural powers are believed to frequent, like certain hills, mountains, or bluffs. A young man goes to such a location alone. There he smokes and fasts, appealing to a power to take pity on him. Among one Native American people, the Crow, sometimes a man will amputate part of a finger or cut his body to arouse pity. The vision commonly appears on the fourth day because four is a sacred number.

The way the power manifests itself varies. Sometimes the man hears the spirit speak to him. Sometimes the spirit comes in the form of a dreamlike story. In other instances, it simply materializes before his eyes, taking the form of a bear, bison, eagle, or some other large animal. Sometimes small animals like rabbits, field mice, and dogs also appear. The power tells the man how it will help him. It might give him the ability to predict the future, locate enemies, find game, become a powerful warrior, or cure illness. It tells him the things he will have to do to keep his power—what songs to sing, how to paint his war shield, how to wear his hair, and so forth. It also tells the man some things he cannot do; for example, if the power comes from an eagle, the man might be prohibited from killing "his brother," the eagle. As long as the man continues to behave in the prescribed manner, the power will be his supernatural protector, or *guardian spirit*. Through the spirit, the man acquires special powers other men do not have.

There is no known culture in which individualistic organizations make up the entire religion. Even among the Native Americans of the Great Plains, among whom the vision quest is unusually well developed, shamanistic and communal organizations also exist.

Shamanistic Organizations

A **shaman** is a person publicly recognized as having a special relationship to supernatural powers, which he or she frequently uses to cure sickness. In many societies (especially among foraging peoples), shamans are the only role that exists in the religious organization; that is, they have abilities not available to ordinary people. Usually, shamans are not full-time specialists. Rather, they assume the role of shaman only when their services are needed, usually in return for a gift or fee. The rest of the time, they live much like everyone else.

People commonly believe shamans possess several qualities. They have access to the power of spiritual beings, which anthropologists usually call *spirit helpers*. The effectiveness of shamans to cure or to cause harm comes from their ability to contact their spirit helpers. Shamans commonly communicate with spirit helpers by achieving an altered state of consciousness, referred to as a *trance*. They reach trance in various ways: through the intake of drugs, ritual chanting, or participation in percussive or rhythmic music. The Tungus, the northeastern Asian people from whom English acquired the word *shaman*, use tambourines and drums to achieve the trance in which they journey to the spirit world to discover the cause of illness.

Peoples who practice shamanism interpret trance as a sign that some spirit, usually one of a shaman's spirit helpers, has physically entered the shaman's body. The spirit takes over (possesses) the shaman's body and speaks to the assembled audience through his or her mouth. When possessed, the shaman becomes a *medium*, or mouthpiece, for the spirits. Shamans may lose control over their actions, and their voices may change quality because a spirit is speaking through them.

---

vision quest Attempt to enlist the aid of supernatural powers by intentionally seeking a dream or vision; characteristic of individualistic religious organizations.

shaman Part-time religious specialist who uses his or her special relationship to supernatural powers for curing members of the shaman's group and harming members of other groups.

Religious healing aids people in societies at all levels of complexity and development. This South Korean woman and her assistants perform a healing ritual. Most South Korean religious healers are women.

Choi Jae-Ku/AFP/Getty Images

People culturally interpret the unusual behavior and strange voice as evidence of genuine possession and as a sign of a shaman's power.

The way a person becomes a shaman varies from people to people, for the details of the role are defined by local cultures. Many scholars argue that shamans are individuals who are unusual in some way: They hear voices, parts of their bodies tremble uncontrollably, they dress or act in strange ways, and so forth. Members of their community interpret their difference as a sign that they have been chosen by a spirit to become a healer. However, just as often shamans are people who act like everyone else when not in the role of shaman. Ju/'hoansi healers use dance and percussive hand clapping to achieve the trance state that makes them powerful and able to diagnose and cure illness. When not in the role of healer, however, they are indistinguishable from other people.

Usually peoples with shamanistic religious organization believe shamans have knowledge and powers

that others lack. Depending on the local culture, shamans acquire knowledge and powers in three major ways. In some cultures, they undergo a period of special training as an apprentice to an experienced shaman, who teaches the novice chants and songs. Among the Navajo of the American Southwest, medicine men are educated for years. They learn the chants, how to arrange ritually powerful objects at the ceremony, and the complex sand paintings necessary to cure people. Among other peoples, shamans must endure difficult deprivations, such as prolonged fasting, the consumption of foods culturally considered disgusting, or years of sexual abstinence. In still other cultures, shamans are individuals who have experienced some unusual event. For example, they may have miraculously recovered from a serious illness or injury, or they claim to have had an unusual dream or vision in which some spirit called them to be its mouthpiece.

In some cultures, shamans, the healing experts, work alone during the actual cures, although many

330 **PART III** The Diversity of Culture

other people may be physically present. Sometimes, though, shamans have helpers in the curing tasks. Among the Navajo, shamans (called "singers") have assistants who fetch objects, help construct the elaborate sand paintings, supply food and drink for all-night cures, and perform other duties. Navajo singers truly need the help of assistants: In olden times, some of the curing ceremonials lasted nine nights.

Some people say that shamanism is the world's oldest profession, by which they mean that among the "simplest" peoples, the shaman is the only person who has special abilities. Perhaps this is true, but shamanism also can be complexly organized. Among the Zuni, who now live on a reservation in western New Mexico, 12 special groups of people (sometimes translated into English as "medicine societies") are recognized as knowledgeable about curing. Different medicine societies know the secret techniques for curing various illnesses. If a Zuni becomes ill with specific symptoms, he or she goes to the appropriate society to be healed. Once healed, the person has learned the secrets of the society and so is usually then initiated into it. Also, South Korea is as modernized as any nation, yet some Koreans still rely on female healers to help solve family and marital problems using rituals called *kut*.

Communal Organizations

Like shamanism, communally organized religions have no full-time specialists who make their living as religious practitioners. They do have leaders—often elderly persons or individuals with a special interest in the results of a ritual—who manipulate symbolic objects or address spiritual beings. Communal rituals are held to intercede with the supernatural on behalf of some group of people, such as a kin group, an age group, a village, or a caste. To illustrate, we consider two widespread kinds of communal rituals organized by descent groups: ancestral rituals and rites of passage.

Ancestral Rituals

Most worldviews hold that people have a spiritual dimension—a *soul*—that lives on after the physical body has perished. Beliefs about the fate of the soul after death vary widely. Some peoples—such as Hindus and Buddhists—believe souls are reincarnated into another person or animal. Others hold that souls pass into a spiritual plane, where they exist eternally with a community of other souls and have no further effect on the living. Still others believe souls become malevolent

after death, turning into ghosts that cause accidents or sickness or terrify the living and so have to be appeased in some way.

Another common belief about the fate of souls after death is that they interact with and affect their living descendants. The many peoples who hold such beliefs perform rituals to induce the spirits of their deceased ancestors to do favors for them or simply to leave them alone. Beliefs and rituals surrounding the interactions between the living and their departed relatives are called **ancestral rituals**, or *ancestor veneration*.

China and other parts of East Asia are famous for ancestor veneration. In the past, and among many families today, patrilineally extended families in China kept tablets and shrines in a prominent place in the house. Printed or engraved on the tablets were the names of the deceased males of the family or lineage, providing a kind of reminder of their existence in the afterlife. Periodically—often even daily—the men of the house and their wives and children gathered and prayed at the shrine. Offerings would be made to ensure the contentment of ancestral spirits in the afterlife, including food, clothing, and ghost money—purchased pieces of paper that were ritually burned so that the ancestors would receive and use them like real money in the afterlife.

The Lugbara of Uganda provide another example. The patrilineage is an important social group to the Lugbara. Lineage elders oversee the interests and harmony of the entire group. They serve as the guardians of the lineage's morality, although they have no power to punish violations physically.

The Lugbara believe the spirit of a deceased person may become an ancestral spirit of her or his lineage. The spirit punishes living descendants who violate Lugbara ideals of behavior toward lineage mates. People who fight with their kinsmen (especially their older relatives), who deceive or steal from their lineage mates, or who fail to carry out their duties toward others are liable to be punished by a spirit. Sometimes this happens because the spirit sees an offense committed and makes the offender ill. More commonly, spirits do not act on their own initiative to make someone sick. Rather, they act on the thoughts of an elder who is indignant because of the actions of some lineage mate. John Middleton (1965, p. 76) describes Lugbara beliefs

> **ancestral rituals** Rituals intended to worship, honor, or beseech the deceased ancestors of a kin group; also called *ancestor veneration*.

about the power of lineage elders to cause illness by invoking ancestral spirits:

> [The elder] sits near his shrines in his compound and thinks about the sinner's behavior. His thoughts are known by the [spirits] and they then send sickness to the offender. He "thinks these words in his heart"; he does not threaten or curse the offender. For a senior man to do this is part of his expected role. It is part of his "work," to "cleanse the lineage home." Indeed, an elder who does not do so when justified would be lacking in sense of duty toward his lineage.

In Lugbara, we see how elders maintain harmony and cooperation in the lineage by invoking the power of deceased members. This is a common feature of ancestral rituals.

Matrilineal peoples have similar ways of recognizing and appeasing ancestors. Consider the Ndembu of Zambia. When an Ndembu woman experiences fertility problems, people often say that she is forgetting her ancestress or doing something disapproved by an ancestress. The cure consists of a lengthy ritual in which many members of the matrilineage make the victim "remember" her relative.

Why do some societies have rituals devoted to spirits of deceased ancestors? Like other "why" questions, this one is controversial. Many anthropologists agree, however, that such beliefs are related to the degree of importance of large, well-defined kin groups in a society. The greater the importance of kin groups such as lineages and clans in making public decisions, regulating access to resources, allocating roles, controlling behavior, and so on, the more likely a society is to develop rituals that control or worship ancestors. This is consistent with sociological interpretations of religion and worldview.

Rites of Passage

Rites of passage of some kind are universal in human cultures (see Chapter 2). Every people celebrate or symbolically mark the stages of life as defined by their culture. Birth and death—the beginning and end of life—are nearly everywhere marked by some kind of ritual process. Most peoples also celebrate transitions between life stages such as puberty, marriage, childbirth, and entry into some new role or position. Rites of passage have long been a major area of field research in anthropology.

Some rites of passage are **initiation rituals**, which incorporate males and/or females into new roles or into new social groups. They are especially well studied, partly because strange and sometimes painful things occur during them. Initiation rituals ceremonially *recognize* or, often, culturally are believed to *cause* bodily changes between childhood and adulthood, often around the time of sexual maturation—which is why they are popularly called *puberty rites.*

Male initiation rituals are common on all continents. However, in some societies in the interior mountains of New Guinea, they often involve psychological trauma and considerable physical pain. Among some New Guinea tribes, the process of making a man out of a boy takes many years. A group of boys nearing puberty goes through the initiation ritual sequence together, as a cohort of age mates. Typically, they are removed from their mothers, and contact with all females is severely restricted. They go to reside with adult men in the communal *men's house* of the village, where they will sleep for most of the rest of their lives and into which they must be "initiated." Usually the rituals occur in several stages, with different events happening to the boys at each stage.

At different stages, the boys are initiated into manhood by undergoing trauma and pain. Commonly adult men berate them for their misdeeds or weakness, make them go without water for long periods, force them to eat unpalatable foods, beat them with switches, place sticks in their noses to induce bleeding, and make cuts in their penises. The various stages frequently take 10 or more years before the boys are "completed" men, ready for marriage and fatherhood, hard physical labor, war, and politicking. Applying Solsis's idea, young men in these societies certainly make substantial sacrifices to signal their commitment to the ideals of manhood in these societies.

Fewer societies make the attainment of adulthood for girls into an initiation ritual. Some say this is because the physical signs of maturity are more obvious in the female body, so it is less essential for them to be socially recognized and proclaimed. Whatever the reason, where they occur, initiation rites for females most often emphasize attainment of physical maturity, instruction in sexual matters and childbearing, and reminders of adult duties as wives and mothers.

rites of passage Rituals celebrating, causing, and/or symbolically marking the stages of life as defined by their culture.

initiation rituals Rites of passage whose purpose is to incorporate males and/or females into new roles or into new social groups.

Mescalero Apache are one Native American people who have ceremonies that recognize and celebrate girls' attainment of puberty. Each year, around the Fourth of July, the people celebrate the attainment of womanhood in a ceremony that lasts four days and four nights. Apache girls in the region who have had their first menses in the last year go to a place where a large tepee is erected. During the ceremony, the girls are regarded as reincarnations of White Painted Woman, a spiritual being who gave many good things to the people. The girls are blessed by singers (specialists who have gone through lengthy training to learn the stories and chants) and by their relatives and friends. Those attending participate in traditional songs and dances dedicated to the four directions and the spirits associated with them.

The Apache ceremony places a lot of emphasis on the girls becoming the Mothers of the Tribe, perhaps because the Apache are a matrilineal people. On the fourth day, singers recount the history of the Apache and the girls are reminded of their ancestry and obligations. The ceremony honors the girls as individuals, reaffirms their commitment to the community and vice versa, urges them to act responsibly, and upholds and re-creates Apache traditions annually. According to ethnographer Claire Farrer (1996, p. 89), "almost invariably, the girls report having been changed, not only into social women but also at a very basic level. They are ready to put aside their childhoods and become full members of their tribe and community." The ceremony thus helps the girls make the social transition to adulthood, with all its rights and responsibilities.

Like ancestor veneration, rites of passage are communal rituals: They require cooperation by the members of a group to achieve socially valuable goals.

Other Communally Organized Rituals

Two kinds of communal religious organizations are widespread and deserve brief description: totemism and seasonal rituals.

Totemism is the belief that human groups have a special mystical relationship with natural objects such as animals, plants, and, sometimes, nonliving things. The object (or objects) with which a group is associated is known as its *totem*. The group most often is a unilineal kin group, such as a clan. The totem frequently serves as the name of the group—for example, the bear clan, the eagle clan, the sun clan.

The nature of the relationship between the members of the group and its totem varies widely. Sometimes the totem is used simply to identify the group and its members, much like our surnames. Often, a mystical

association exists between the group and its totem object. People believe they are like their totem in some respects. Or, the totem may be used as a symbol of differences between clans. In many populations—most notably some of the aboriginal peoples of Australia—the members of a clan believe that their totem produced their ancestors in a mythical period.

Seasonal rituals are usually believed to control natural processes and seasonal rhythms. Eastern Pueblo peoples who have lived along the Rio Grande of New Mexico for hundreds of years organize agricultural, hunting, fertility, and other rituals by season. The same rituals occurred in the same sequence year after year, and the same ceremonial groups are responsible for organizing and staging them. They require large-scale cooperation by an entire community, bringing people together several times a year for a common purpose believed to benefit all. Other Pueblo peoples have seasonal rituals and special ceremonial groups that organize them, although the details vary from people to people.

All these examples show why many kinds of communally organized rituals are also called *rites of solidarity*. The rituals have conscious purposes—respecting ancestors, marking and/or causing transitions from one stage of life to the next, controlling nature. In addition, they provide a ritual means to strengthen and maintain good relationships among the group's members. Also, in most cases, those who lead them are supposed to have good character and to remain pure around the days of the performance, thus upholding values, norms, and other kinds of cultural standards.

Ecclesiastical Organizations

In Chapter 7, we described how occupational specialization accompanied the development of civilization and states. Civilizations and states developed in the Old World cities of ancient Mesopotamia, Egypt, East Asia, and India. They also grew among New World

totemism Form of communal religious organization in which all members of a kin group have mystical relationships with one or more natural objects.

seasonal rituals Form of communal religious organization in which group cooperation is required to ensure the seasonal changes that restore or maintain life.

One hallmark of ecclesiastical religious organization is enormous structures like this Buddhist temple called Daibutsu-den. Originally built in the 700s in Nara, Japan's earliest capital, Daibutsu-den is part of a larger temple complex called Todai-ji.

peoples, such as the ancient Inca, Aztec, and Maya. In these regions, specialization extended into the religious dimension of cultural systems. Rather than organizing rituals on a communal basis—in which a wide range of people controlled and participated in the performance—a formal bureaucracy of religious specialists controlled many public rituals. The religious bureaucracy probably also had a large voice in formulating religious laws, which prescribed certain kinds of punishments for those who violated them.

In this type of religious organization, the specialist is known as a **priest**. It is instructive to contrast priests

priest Kind of religious specialist, usually full-time, who officiates at large-scale, bureaucratically organized rituals that keep the population in proper relationship to deities or cosmic forces.

with shamans. In addition to their more specialized status, priests differ from shamans in several respects.

First, with the exception of people like the Zuni, shamans are not organized as a group, and cooperation between them typically is minimal. Indeed, many peoples believe that enemy shamans engage in supernatural battles with each other, with the stronger shaman winning the battle, resulting in either the recovery or death of the sick person. In contrast, priests are hierarchically organized and are usually subsidized and supported by a formal government, either by the high-ranking chiefs of a large chiefdom or by the state (see Chapter 12). Second, priests undergo a lengthy period of formal training because they must master the complex rituals needed to perform their role. Third, the priests were at or near the top of the social ladder in ancient civilizations, so individual priests lived much better than the population at large. Fourth, shamans typically perform mainly crisis rituals, whenever some person requires their healing or other kinds of services. The rituals at which priests officiate tend to be calendrical—they occur at regular intervals because the powerful gods that the rituals appease demand regular praise or sacrifice.

A final difference is especially revealing. With the development of a *priesthood* comes a strong distinction between priest and layperson. The layperson has little control over the timing of religious performances. The population at large relies on priests to keep it in the proper relationship to supernatural powers. This creates a sense of spiritual dependence on the priests and on the state apparatus that so often sponsors it, a dependence that tends to reinforce and legitimize the high degree of stratification found in states.

These state-sponsored rituals are called *ecclesiastical* (meaning "of or pertaining to the church") because their priests were highly organized and often formed a bureaucratic-like group, and their rituals were usually held in grand buildings that served as temples. The organization of ecclesiastical religions was largely under the control of the government. State officials exacted tribute or taxes to finance the construction of temples, the livelihood of the priests, the sacrifices that often accompanied state rituals, and other expenses needed to support and organize religious activities on a fantastically large scale.

There is little question that ecclesiastical organizations provided rituals, myths, and beliefs that supported the domination of the ruling family or dynasty. (See Chapter 13 for more on ideologies.) The content of the beliefs, myths, and rituals almost invariably expressed the dependence of the entire population on the ruler's well-being and on the periodic performance of rituals. A common belief of official state religions is that the ruler is a god-king: He not only rules by divine mandate but also is himself a god or somehow has divine qualities. This was true of most of the ancient civilizations and of the states that developed in sub-Saharan Africa. The complex chiefdoms of Polynesia and the Americas had comparable ideas.

The ancient complex chiefdoms of Hawaii had marked social distinctions between the noble and commoner classes. The nobility was viewed as endowed with a supernatural power called *mana*, which we discussed earlier in this chapter. *Mana* was partly hereditary, and within a single family the eldest child inherited the most *mana* from his or her parents. The highest-ranking male noble, the paramount chief, was believed to be descended from one of the gods of the islands. This descent gave him the right to rule because he had more *mana* than anyone in the chiefdom. Other nobles (lesser chiefs and their families) were relatives of the paramount chief and thus also were endowed with *mana*. *Mana* gave chiefs the power to curse those who were disloyal or disobedient or who violated some taboo, which further reinforced their authority.

Hawaiians believed the prosperity of a chiefdom and everyone in it depended on the performance of certain religious rituals held in grand temples. Because commoners did not have enough *mana* to enter a temple, only priests and nobles could perform the rituals needed to ensure prosperity. Everyone in the chiefdom thus relied on the social (and religious) elite for their well-being.

In ecclesiastical organizations, many rituals are held to keep the entire polity in a beneficial relationship with supernatural beings. For example, in the state religion of the ancient Aztecs, the gods had to be periodically appeased or they would cause the world to end in a cataclysm. To keep the gods' goodwill, the priesthood periodically performed human sacrifice at temples, offering the heart of the victim (usually a war captive) to the deities. Aztec priests also stuck sharp thorns into their tongues, earlobes, and even genitals as blood offerings to the gods. The ancient Egyptians believed their pharaoh would rule in the afterlife—just as in the present world—so when he died, he took much of his wealth, his wives, and his servants into the next world with him. Japanese believed the emperors of their nation were descended from the sun goddess from about 2,500 years ago. In later Japanese history, the emperors were so set apart from the mundane world that political affairs were handled by the *shogun*, the secular power who ruled in the name of the emperor. The emperor of old China—who was at various times in the history of Chinese civilization the most powerful man on the planet—ruled as long as he had the mandate of Heaven.

Organizing ecclesiastical rituals on a grand scale required enormous resources to construct temples, make offerings at sacrificial altars, support priests, and enforce religious laws. However, such state-sponsored rituals did not necessarily wipe out other kinds of local-level rituals. Commoners usually continued to rely on local shamans to cure them, practiced magic, believed in witches and sorcerers, and worshiped their ancestors. In ancient China, Korea, and Japan, for example, each household and lineage continued to revere its own ancestors through communal rituals and to make offerings to them at family shrines. In Korea, female shamans help families cope with anxieties and stresses even today—even among some Christian families.

In medieval Europe, Catholicism was ecclesiastical. The authority of the Church was tightly interwoven with the exercise of secular power, although conflict often arose between popes and various kings. Only in the past few centuries has the formal alliance between the power of government and the will of the gods been broken for any length of time. We should not assume that even this official separation between church and state will necessarily be permanent. As the recent history of Iran suggests, the intermingling of political and ecclesiastical authorities can be established in the modern world.

Revitalization Movements

So far, we have discussed religion in cultures that are changing slowly. When a people's way of life or physical survival is threatened by contact with powerful outsiders, often they seek the aid and protection of the supernatural. They may form and join a social movement, called a **revitalization movement**.

Revitalization movements are most likely to occur when three conditions coalesce:

1. Rapid change, usually caused by exposure to unfamiliar people, customs, and objects
2. Foreign domination—or widespread fear of foreign domination—which leads to a sense of social, ethnic, or even racial inferiority
3. The perception of relative deprivation, meaning that people sense they lack wealth, power, and esteem relative to those who dominate them

Historically, revitalization movements were especially common during colonialism, in which a foreign power subjugated an indigenous people. (Colonialism did not always lead to revitalization movements, however.)

Revitalization movements usually originate with an individual (a *prophet*) who claims to have had a dream or vision. Sometimes the prophet claims to be a savior (a *messiah*) sent by a spiritual being to save the world from destruction. In the dream or vision, the prophet received a message (a *revelation*) from a god, an ancestor, or another spiritual power.

Revelations typically include two kinds of information given by the spirit or spirits and taught by the prophet. The first is a statement about what is wrong with the present-day world, about why people's lives have changed for the worse. Prophets and followers commonly blame the introduction of corrupting foreign objects and habits—such as tobacco, alcohol, money, new religions, formal schooling, the relaxation of old moral standards—for the troubles of today.

Second, revelations usually include a vision of a new world and a prescription for how to bring it about. In some cases, the message is vague and secular, with the prophet claiming that earthly lives will improve if people do (or stop doing) certain things. However, the message is often *apocalyptic:* The prophet says the present world will end at a certain time, and only those who heed the prophet's message will be saved. The expulsion or death of foreigners is a frequent theme of apocalyptic visions: Foreigners will be drowned in a flood, burned in a fire, swallowed up by an earthquake, or killed by deities or ancestors.

Another common theme is the reversal of existing political and economic dominance relations: Foreigners will work for us, we will have the wealth instead of them, and we will tax them and make laws that they must obey. Nearly always, the prophets' revelations are *syncretic;* that is, they combine elements of traditional myths, beliefs, and rituals with introduced elements.

The following examples from two regions illustrate revitalization movements.

Melanesian Cargo Cults

The area called Melanesia in the southwestern Pacific experienced numerous revitalization movements in the early to mid–twentieth century. Melanesians traditionally placed great cultural value on wealth and its distribution as the means to become a big man or influential leader (see Chapter 13). The value Melanesians placed on wealth led them to be interested in the material possessions of German, English, French, and Australian colonial powers. Because European wealth was brought to the islands by ship or plane, it became known as *cargo,* and the various movements that sprang up with the aim of acquiring it through ritual means are commonly known as **cargo cults**.

To Melanesians, the Europeans they saw were fantastically wealthy, yet the Melanesians seldom saw them do any work to earn their possessions. Europeans who lived in the islands certainly did not know how to construct trucks, produce canned foods, build radios or kerosene lanterns or stoves and so forth. In many traditional Melanesian religions, technology was believed

revitalization movement Religious movement explicitly intended to create a new way of life for a society or group.

cargo cults Melanesian revitalization movements in which prophets claim to know secret rituals that will bring wealth (cargo).

to have been given to people by deities or spirits. It followed logically that European objects came from their god. Furthermore, when the Europeans who lived in Melanesia wanted some new object, they simply made marks on papers and placed them in an envelope or asked for the object by speaking into metal things ("radios"). Some weeks later, the object was delivered in ships or airplanes. Surely, spirits had made the cargo, and the actions of Westerners to persuade their spirits to send cargo were rituals. Melanesians therefore believed that they, too, could acquire this wealth through the correct ritual procedure, which they frequently believed Europeans were selfishly withholding from them.

Numerous prophets sprang up among diverse Melanesian peoples, each with his own vision or dream, each with his own story to explain why the Europeans had cargo and the Melanesians had none, and each claiming to know the secret ritual that would deliver the goods. The prophet often claimed to have received a visit from an ancestor or a native deity, who told him that the whites had been lying to people.

The Garia of the north coast of Papua New Guinea illustrate common themes of cargo cults. Missionaries came to the Garia in the early twentieth century, and the Garia initially adopted Christianity for reasons other than those the missionaries had in mind. They assumed missionaries knew the ritual secrets that were the "road to cargo." In Garia tradition, deities and other spirits had secret names and would give benefits to people who knew them. The missionaries would give cargo to the Garia if only they practiced what the missionaries preached: church attendance, monogamy, worship of the Western God, and cessation of pagan practices such as sorcery and dancing. Based on their belief that the missionary lifestyle and Christian rituals held the secret of cargo, many Garia converted to Christianity early in the twentieth century.

Still the cargo did not arrive. The Garia grew angry as they concluded that missionaries and other Europeans were withholding the true ritual secret of how to get cargo to keep all the wealth for themselves. In the 1930s and 1940s, two Garia prophets arose. They told the people that the missionaries had been lying to them. God and Jesus were both really deities of the Garia, not of whites. Only the Europeans knew the secret names of God and Jesus and asked them for the cargo with secret prayers. All along, Jesus had been trying to deliver the goods to the Garia, but the Jews were holding him captive in Heaven. To free him, the Garia had to perform sacrificial rituals. To show him how poor they were and to make him feel sorry for them,

they had to destroy all their native wealth objects. If they did these things, Jesus would give the cargo to the ancestral spirits of the Garia, who would in turn deliver it to the living.

Native American Movements

Revitalization movements also occurred among Native Americans, whose sufferings at the hands of white traders, settlers, armies, and administrators are well documented. Two movements were especially important, both precipitated by a deterioration of tribal economic, social, and religious life.

Handsome Lake

In the 1600s and 1700s, the Seneca people of New York and Pennsylvania were one of the members of a loose confederation of tribes who agreed to live in peace and come to one another's aid in case of attack by surrounding tribes. The Seneca traditionally were matrilineal horticulturalists. Men hunted, traded for furs, and went on raids against neighboring tribes. Women owned most of the farmland and did most of the planting and harvesting of corn and other crops.

By 1800, the Seneca had lost most of their land to the new state of New York, Euro-American settlers, and land speculators. Whites committed many atrocities against them in the 1780s and 1790s, partly because most Seneca supported the British during the American Revolutionary War. Devastating diseases—such as smallpox and measles, which wiped out millions of Native Americans all over the continent—reduced the tribe to a fraction of its former numbers. Seneca men had been proud warriors and hunters, but these activities became more difficult because of the loss of land and the presence of whites. The American government waged psychological warfare against them, intentionally corrupting their leaders with bribes and liquor and generally attempting to dehumanize and demoralize them.

Seneca men turned to alcohol and drank away most of what little money they could still earn from the fur trade. Neighboring peoples, who once feared the Seneca and other members of the League of the Iroquois, ridiculed them. Witchcraft accusations increased internal conflicts and divisions within their communities. Many women lost their desire for children and took medicines that caused them to abort or become sterile altogether. A way of life—and perhaps an entire people—was dying.

In 1799, a Seneca man named Handsome Lake lay sick. Three angels cured him and gave him a revelation from the Creator. Handsome Lake reported that the Creator was saddened by the life of the people and angry

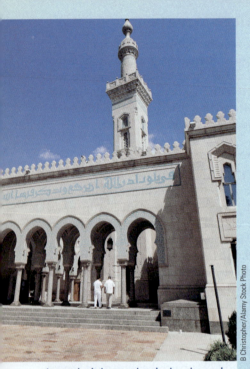

Increasingly international migration and exposure to new religious doctrines bring people of different faiths together, raising challenges of religious accommodation. These men are entering the Islamic Center in Washington, DC.

Most modern nations have *religious pluralism*, meaning that followers of many different religions live inside their boundaries. For centuries, India has been home to Hindus, Muslims, Sikhs, Christians, and Jains. Since 1949, China has been officially atheistic according to its ruling Communist Party, but in fact China has Daoists, Buddhists, Christians, and 20 million Muslims. Muslims are concentrated in China's western provinces, where the Uyghur ethnic group live. Violent clashes between Uyghur and Han sometimes occur, and relations remain uneasy even when there is no overt unrest. Most countries in sub-Saharan Africa are pluralistic, partly because of the way colonial powers established their boundaries and partly because of the spread of Islam and, later, Christianity.

In recent decades, international migration and global contacts have increased religious pluralism. The United Kingdom has hundreds of thousands of Hindus and Muslims, most from its former colonies in South Asia. Turks migrated to Germany and other countries for work and many remained there. European nations like France, the Netherlands, Denmark, and Belgium have large numbers of Muslims who have immigrated from the Middle East.

Most North Americans think of Europe as religiously tolerant (too tolerant, some say), but in recent years several European countries have debated passing regulations and even laws about Muslim dress and mosques. In April 2010, the Belgian parliament prohibited women from wearing clothing that partially or fully covers their faces. Violators could be fined or even jailed up to week. The citizens of Switzerland voted in favor of a law forbidding the construction of more minarets, the tall towers in mosques at which Muslims are called to prayer five times each day. In early 2010, a parliamentary committee in France recommended a ban on Muslim women wearing face veils in hospitals, schools, public transportation, and government offices. In 2012 in France, the public learned that many butchers were following Islamic practices (*halal*) in which butchers kill animals by slitting their throat rather than stunning them to minimize the pain of slaughter. Not surprisingly, much of

because of their drunkenness, witchcraft, and use of abortion medicines. The Seneca must repent such deeds. Handsome Lake had two more visions during the next year. He prophesized an apocalypse in which the world would be destroyed by great drops of fire, consuming those who did not heed his teachings. People could save themselves and delay the apocalypse by publicly confessing their wrongs, giving up sins such as witchcraft and drinking, and performing certain traditional rituals.

The apocalypse did not occur, but Handsome Lake was able to give his teachings a new, more secular twist between 1803 and his death in 1815. He continued to preach temperance because, he said, the Creator had never intended whiskey to be used by Native Americans.

He encouraged peaceful relations with both whites and other native peoples. He urged that the scattered reservations of the Seneca be consolidated, so that the people could live together as one community. Family morality must be impeccable: Sons were to obey their fathers, divorce (commonplace among the matrilineal Seneca in aboriginal times) was no longer to be allowed, and adultery and domestic quarreling were to cease.

Handsome Lake also succeeded in changing the traditional division of labor, in which women cultivated the crops, and men who worked in the garden were considered effeminate. Seneca men took up farming and animal husbandry and even fenced their fields and added new crops to their inventory.

the non-Muslim public was outraged by what they interpreted as cruelty, but butchers claimed it was too expensive to keep up two slaughter methods. In summer 2016, the French government actually outlawed *burkinis*, a swimsuit covering most of the body, which allowed Muslim women to enter waters while preserving Islam's norms of female modesty.

The United States remains predominantly (75 to 80 percent) professed Christian, although there are large differences in doctrines and lifestyles between denominations such as Episcopalians and Southern Baptists. Today students from around the world acquire visas to study in American and Canadian universities. Employers are looking for people who have high-tech professional job skills, for which American workers are either numerically insufficient or overpaid (to use the rationales given by labor or management). Except for the Jewish faith (6 million, or about 2 percent), it is difficult to know the numbers of non-Christian religions represented in the United States. The United States has about 4.7 million Muslims (most of them native-born Americans), 2.7 million Buddhists, 1.1 million Hindus, and 1 million Baha'is. There are also the indigenous religions of Native Americans and beliefs like Wicca.

Given provisions in the Constitution, the United States faces problems of accommodating religious diversity. In 2007, the issue arose in an American university. About 10 percent of the students at the University of Michigan, Dearborn, are Muslim. Muslims should pray five times a day and, as part of their preparation, they should wash their feet. To accommodate the students, the university installed foot-washing stations in some restrooms. Other students objected to what they claimed was special treatment for members of one religious faith. An outside organization, Americans United for Separation of Church and State, got involved because a public university built a facility to accommodate the followers of a particular religious doctrine, which they held to be a violation of the U.S. Constitution. Supporters of the footbaths responded by saying that other students could use the footbaths, such as athletes. They also pointed out that many of the university's holidays and the academic calendar itself accommodates the beliefs of Christians and Jews.

Similar issues have arisen in other universities, including whether cafeterias should be required to prepare special foods (without beef) for Hindus and whether exams should be rescheduled for a particular religious holiday for a religious minority. Some issues have been around for a long time, but their relevance is magnified by religious pluralism. Should Christian prayers be offered at meetings of city councils? Should Christian crèches be displayed on public properties? In the name of equal time, should intelligent design be taught as an alternative to evolution in the classrooms of public schools? (If the answer is yes, then shouldn't public schools also include the origin beliefs of Native Americans such as Navajos and Lakotas, of Hindus, and of numerous other religions?)

Increased religious diversity scares some Americans, including many who do not consider themselves to be religious. Until after 9/11, the religious affiliation of immigrants was not much of an issue in whether their numbers should be controlled. It is worth pointing out, however, that the Catholic faith of Irish and Italian immigrants was an issue when large numbers of those immigrants began to arrive in large numbers. After 9/11 and other events, Americans are more likely to worry about allowing Muslims to enter, legally as well as illegally.

Today, hardly anyone publicly questions the concept of religious freedom as a basic American value, but many feel that this value does not mean that members of all religions should be allowed to immigrate. The appeal of Donald Trump in the 2016 U.S. presidential election was based in part on his explicit anti-immigrant sentiments, especially for people from Muslim countries.

Peyote Religion

Peyote is a cactus that grows in the Rio Grande Valley of Texas and northern Mexico. When eaten, it produces a mild narcotic effect. The ritual use of peyote among northwestern Mexican natives predated European conquest. However, its consumption as the central element in a revitalization movement dates only from the last two decades of the nineteenth century.

In 1875, two southern Plains tribes, the Kiowa and Comanche, lost their land after military defeats. During their confinement to reservations in southwestern Oklahoma, the Lipan Apache introduced them to peyote. By the 1880s, a revitalization movement began after the two tribes began consuming peyote at religious services. Like many movements, peyotism subsequently spread, reaching about 19 Native American groups in Oklahoma by 1899. During the early twentieth century, the church spread rapidly to other native communities throughout the western United States and Canada. The Peyote religion was and is syncretic, adopting many elements of Christian theology and worship along with the consumption of peyote as a sacrament.

The peyote movement had no single prophet or leader. Local churches developed their own versions of services and rituals. One early leader was John Wilson, a Caddo Delaware from western Oklahoma who had learned to ingest peyote from the Comanche. While eating dinner in the early 1890s, Wilson collapsed. Thinking him dead, his family began preparations for the burial. But a Caddoan named Enoch Parker told the family that he had learned in a vision that Wilson was not dead. Indeed, Wilson revived three days later. He reported that a great Water Bird had sucked the breath and sin out of his body, causing his collapse. Jesus brought him back to life after three days, telling him that his sins had been removed and that he was to teach the Native American people to believe in God and to use peyote to communicate with him.

Until his death in 1901, Wilson proselytized the peyote religion among the Osage, Delaware, Quapaw, and other Native American peoples of the area. He preached that they needed to believe in God and Jesus, work hard, act morally, and stop drinking alcohol. They were to abandon their traditional religious practices because the spirits that formerly had aided them could be used for evil as well as good purposes. Wilson attracted a large number of adherents among the Osage, who combined the use of peyote in worship services with the Christian teachings they had learned in mission schools.

Many movements provided meaning and moral direction to Native Americans during a period of rapid and mostly harmful change. The peyote religion continues today on many reservations, especially in the central and western United States. It was legally incorporated as an official church—now known as the Native American Church—in 1918. Those who follow the Peyote Road eat pieces of the cactus during services, treating it as a deeply meaningful sacrament. Many members of the Native American Church say that the Creator intended peyote to be used by them. Periodically, the legislatures of some states have tried to outlaw the use of peyote because the cactus is a legally banned substance defined by the wider society as a dangerous drug. So far, courts have upheld the right of church members to consume peyote as a part of their religious sacraments.

Fate of Revitalization Movements

What ultimately happens to revitalization movements? Many with apocalyptic messages simply disappear when the end of the world does not occur. Other movements have been remarkably tenacious. In Melanesia, certain areas saw the rise and fall of numerous prophets, each claiming to have the cargo secret. People followed again and again because they had no other acceptable explanation for cargo, for why whites had it and they lacked it, or for how they could acquire it. Certainly, their own worldly efforts—working for Europeans in mines and plantations, growing and selling coffee, copra, cocoa, and so forth—did not reward them with the fantastic wealth that whites enjoyed with virtually no effort. Most cargo cults disappeared when the prophecies failed. However, in some regions, cargo cults became political movements or parties. This happened among the Garia, Manus, Tannese, and some Malaitans.

Other movements do not end suddenly, wither away, or transform into a more secular, political movement. They retain their religious character, frequently teaching that contentment is to be found within oneself rather than in worldly material things. After his death in 1815, Handsome Lake's teachings became codified as the Code of Handsome Lake and was influential into modern times. Peyotism also became formally organized. Like many other revitalization movements that give birth to new religions, the adherents of peyotism are thus far largely confined to a single ethnic category: Native Americans.

Other movements grow over the centuries. From humble beginnings, they eventually attract millions of believers. They develop a formal organization, and the religious specialists called priests (including priests, pastors, and the like) replace prophets. The ancient prophets and disciples become the founders of the religion, their lives take on mythical proportions, and their revelations become texts that are considered sacred by believers. Followers become organized into an institutionalized church, which formalizes and codifies the texts so that they become official doctrines and creeds. The teachings and rituals cross national and ethnic boundaries. Beliefs and rituals go from being local to being national to sometimes to being global.

Most of the major religions of the modern world began as revitalization movements, including Judaism, Christianity, Islam, and Buddhism. These religions are sometimes called *world religions* because they have spread outside their original homelands. Today, more and more people are becoming familiar with world religions, not just through books and TV documentaries, but also through firsthand experience. Globalization brings old religions to new places, raising issues of how to accommodate religious pluralism (see the Global Challenges and Opportunities feature).

SUMMARY

1. **Describe how anthropologists define and think about cultural diversity in religion and worldview.** Defining religion is challenging because of the difficulty of encompassing all the diversity of religions found among humanity. Broadly, religion includes three components: beliefs about the nature of supernatural powers, myths about the historical actions of such powers and culture heroes, and symbolic rituals intended to influence them. These components affect a people's worldview and, hence, behavior in the secular world.

2. **Analyze the strengths and weaknesses of the three main anthropological theories of religion and worldview.** Most theories fall into three basic categories. Intellectual or cognitive approaches hold that the most important purpose of religion and worldview is explaining things, events, and actions that are otherwise inexplicable. Psychological theories claim that myths, beliefs, and rituals function to help individuals cope with stresses, fears, uncertainties, grief, and other aspects of their lives. Sociological theorists argue that religion helps hold societies together by imparting common values and norms, punishing and rewarding people according to their behavior, and providing ritualized occasions in which people gather, thus increasing social solidarity. Among one or another people, religion is probably helpful in all these ways. Not only is each theory incomplete, but also for each there are many instances in which religion actually has opposite effects from the theory's principles. It is likely that no single theory can explain religion itself or the great diversity of human religions.

3. **Analyze how witchcraft and sorcery might benefit individuals and groups.** Many peoples believe that supernatural beings or forces cause group or personal misfortune, such as deaths, illnesses, and accidents. The malevolent powers of sorcerers and witches are blamed for misfortune in the worldview of a great many societies. Accusations of sorcery and witchcraft tend to be patterned and to reflect prevalent conflicts and tensions in the organization of society. Although beliefs in sorcery and witchcraft at first glance seem harmful, many anthropologists have argued that they serve useful functions. They might provide emotionally useful explanations for why bad things happen to good people. They also might reinforce right behavior by providing hated symbols of wrong behavior and serve as a social control mechanism.

4. **Discuss how anthropologists classify the diversity of human religions and worldviews and analyze the relationships between the four categories and social life.** Religions and worldviews may be classified according to the ways rituals are organized, although any such classification is necessarily a simplification of the diversity of the world's religions. Four religious organizations are individualistic, shamanistic, communal, and ecclesiastical. In a generalized way, there is an evolutionary sequence to these organizations, as they tend to be associated with different levels of cultural complexity. Ecclesiastical forms are regularly found in complex chiefdoms and states, where they legitimize and rationalize the powers and privileges of ruling families and elite classes.

5. **Describe revitalization movements, the conditions under which they are most likely to occur, and what happens to them.** Revitalization movements originate with prophets who claim to have received a revelation, which usually is syncretic and often apocalyptic. Most often, the movements are indigenous reactions to cope with current oppressive conditions, such as colonial domination. Examples include Melanesian cargo cults, the Handsome Lake movement among the Seneca of New York, and the peyote religion of many North American peoples. Most revitalization movements disappear, but some are transformed and develop into formal churches that evolve into world religions if they eventually attract tens of millions of members.

Art and the Aesthetic

Fazil Aziz/Austrialian Photograph/Getty Images

Handprints or hand stencils on rock faces and in caves are found in Europe, Asia, Australia, and the Americas. Dating from 40,000 b.p. to the present, they are the oldest known and most persistent form of art. Native Australian peoples say that they serve to identify the individual with a particular place and group.

The Pervasiveness of Art

Forms of Artistic Expression
Body Arts
Visual Arts
Performance Arts

Art and Culture
Secular and Religious Art
Art and Gender
Social Functions of Art

After reading this chapter, you should be able to:

1 DISCUSS the disagreement over whether art is or is not a cultural universal.

2 LIST the various forms of body arts.

3 DISCUSS the different forms of visual arts.

4 DISCUSS the different forms of performance arts.

5 EXPLAIN how art is integrated into our religious lives.

6 EXPLAIN how gender, identity, and social status are reflected in art.

Art is one of those elusive terms we all know and use, and think we understand, but it is difficult to define. The difficulty is that art is a multidimensional aspect of human behavior that encompasses, among other things, material objects, song, music, dance, literature, and poetry.

What defines these very different forms of human behavior as "art"? As Clifford Geertz rightly noted, "Art is notoriously hard to talk about. It seems, even when made of words in literary arts, all the more so when made of pigment, sound, stone, or whatever in the nonliterary ones, to exist in the world of its own, beyond the reach of discourse" (1983, p. 94). Also, as anthropologists since Franz Boas have argued, there are no universal standards for art. What is art in one society may not be art in another. Many scholars go even further, agreeing with Toni Fratto that "there is no such thing as art. . . . Art in itself is not a universal human phenomenon but a synthetic Western (cultural) category" (1978, pp. 135–136).

The Western cultural concept of art is of aesthetically beautiful or pleasing objects or actions that exist solely for the sake of themselves. In contrast, non-Western or "primitive" art—if we may call it "art," and we do—is fully incorporated into secular and/ or sacred objects and actions that serve utilitarian or functional purposes. If these distinctions are true, then Western art is not the same as "primitive" art. However, these distinctions are not accurate. First, we commonly define *aesthetics* as referring to something beautiful or pleasing, but it does not have to fit that description. Second, Western art is thought of as having no utilitarian or functional purpose, but it does.

No one would argue that the paintings of Picasso— for example, *Guernica*, which hangs in the Museo Reina Sofia in Madrid, and *Women of Algiers (Version Q),*

which sold at a Christie's auction in New York in 2015— are not art. *Guernica*—Picasso's painting in black, white, and gray of the 1937 bombing of a Basque village during the Spanish civil war—is certainly not beautiful or pleasurable to look at. And it is highly doubtful that the anonymous bidder who paid a record $179 million for *Women of Algiers* did so because he or she was so taken by its "beauty" alone.

We commonly use the word *aesthetic* to mean something beautiful or pleasurable. An alternative meaning of aesthetic is something that evokes an emotion or sensation. Picasso, a Spaniard, painted *Guernica* in Paris during the Spanish civil war. It was not returned to Spain until 1981. The painting evokes such powerful emotions about the war that when first exhibited in Spain, it was protected by bulletproof glass and armed guards for fear that someone would try to destroy it. As for the *Women of Algiers*, we can only speculate why its new owner purchased it.

One could argue that paintings on canvas are certainly nonutilitarian. The only thing we can do with them is hang them on a wall and look at them. To be art, does something have to be nonutilitarian? The difficulty is determining when something stops being utilitarian and becomes art. Richard Anderson uses a Tikopian wooden headrest as an example. Any block of wood, even a log of the proper size, might serve as a headrest. A person might go further by cutting away portions of the block or log to form legs, which Anderson argues still serves the utilitarian purpose of lessening the weight of the block. If, however, the person carves designs on the headrest, this carving becomes its artistic component, and the object becomes art. According to Anderson, it is this artistic component—the design—that transforms the object from the realm of the utilitarian to the realm of art. Thus, is it ornamentation placed on the object—not its functional design—that defines it as art?

In 2014, at a Sotheby's auction in Switzerland, a 1933 Patek Philippe pocket watch was sold for over $24 million. It was original made for Henry Graves, a banker, and has 24 functions in addition to keeping time. Among other things, it has chimes; displays phases of the moon, sunrise, and sunset; offers a "perpetual calendar"; and provides a celestial map of the New York City sky. It is not just any watch: It is the most complicated handmade watch ever made. Why did Henry Graves go to such expense to have a watch produced that has so many functions with, at best, extremely limited utilitarian value? Why was it placed in a gold case and not a silver or even a stainless steel one? Henry Graves wanted something that no one else had—something with meaning to him, a uniquely designed status symbol.

At what point is a piece of wood, stone, metal, or ivory transformed into a work of art? When does noise become music? When do body movements become dance and words become poetry, literature, or song lyrics? **Art** is any product of human behavior that has a cultural meaning not inherent in its visual appearance or sound. But what gives it meaning? Is it the **aesthetic**? The quality that makes objects, actions, or language more beautiful or pleasurable? Is it the aesthetic quality that appeals to our emotions—variously creating feelings of comfort, love, fear, anger, joy, pride, courage, and even hatred?

The power of art as a form of nonverbal communication can be seen in national flags. Although a flag is nothing more than a piece of cloth decorated with different colors and designs that give it meaning, its presence can elicit feelings of comfort and pride among members of its nationality while its destruction by members of another group can elicit feelings of rage. However, is it the aesthetic qualities of a flag that evoke such strong emotions?

Individuals do not emotionally respond to a particular national flag on the basis of how it looks; they respond to what it symbolizes. The cultural meaning of a particular artistic object or action is unrelated to its aesthetic qualities. It is not the aesthetic attributes of

art Any product of human behavior that has a cultural meaning not inherent in its visual appearance or sound.

aesthetic Quality that makes objects, actions, or language more beautiful or pleasurable.

Guernica that evoke emotions among Spaniards; it is the cultural historical event that it recalls and symbolizes that gives it meaning. Had Picasso entitled it *Human and Animal Body Parts in Black, Gray, and White,* the emotion evoked by the painting would have been very different; people would probably be wondering why it was in an art museum. It is not the aesthetic attributes of *Women of Algiers* that resulted in its record auction price. Had an unknown artist offered the bidder an identical painting at a street fair for $10 or so, he or she would not have purchased it. It is the fact that Pablo Picasso, a well-recognized famous artist, painted the picture that gives the painting its cultural meaning and value. Similarly, the buyer of the Patek Philippe watch was not buying a watch, but rather a unique watch. It is its uniqueness that gives the watch its cultural meaning and value.

Art is something we can see, we can hear, we can make, we can participate in, and we can emotionally experience. It may be permanent as in a design painted or carved on a piece of wood, or it may be transitory as in the performance of a dance or song. One can argue, and we will, that individuals are constantly modifying their material possessions and behaviors to enhance their aesthetic appeal to them personally. However, most of these creations of our imagination have meaning only to us; they are idiosyncratic and not cultural. They are not yet art. Only when modifications to particular objects or behaviors have a cultural meaning—one that is recognized by at least some other members of the society—does it become art; it isour most important form of nonverbal communication.

As we will discuss, in human society art serves to identify us as individuals—as well as our gender, our relative age, our social groups and status, our economic status, and our political and/or ethnic allegiances—while also being a means of communication with the supernatural. In our daily lives we are all Sherlock Holmes—analyzing, usually unconsciously, the people and objects around us for the visual and behavioral clues to tell us who they are and what they are doing or have done.

The reason why some scholars see a difference between Western art and so-called primitive art is ethnocentrism: Westerners do not respond emotionally to "primitive" art. One can only imagine what a nineteenth-century Plains Indian or an Australian Aborigine would have thought of a Picasso painting.

Because of its complexity and pervasiveness in human behavior, we cannot discuss art in the manner that we discuss other aspects of culture, such as social organization, legal systems, and religion. Thus, in this chapter we examine only certain aspects of art:

the pervasiveness of art in our lives, forms of artistic expression, and the cultural meaning of art.

The Pervasiveness of Art

As anthropologists have long noted, Native American peoples had no word for art in their languages. Similarly, other traditional peoples in other parts of the world lack words for art. The reason for this is that art is integrated into virtually every aspect of their lives and is so pervasive that they do not think of it as something separate and distinct. The idea of "art for art's sake" is a recent Western cultural phenomenon that in some ways both distracts and diminishes the reality of human creative expressions.

If we define art broadly, then it permeates virtually every aspect of our lives. All of us search for and attempt to create that which is aesthetically pleasing; thus, we are all artists. Creative artistic expressions are found in even the most mundane and commonplace acts of the daily lives of all peoples. Consider, for example, two behaviors that most of us think of as mundane rather than artistic: dressing for the day and residing in a particular place.

We begin the day by ornamenting our bodies. From among our clothes, we make choices about what to wear based on colors and styles appropriate for the day's events. We make choices on how to wear our hair and even the color of our hair. We may paint our faces and further adorn our bodies with jewelry of varying kinds, worn on our fingers and arms, around our necks, in our ears, noses, and—in recent years—other parts of our bodies. Some of us have our bodies permanently decorated with tattoos. By these everyday acts, we are artists, attempting to enhance the aesthetic qualities of our persons by making ourselves a work of art. We are also creating a visual public image of ourselves—telling others who we are or who we would like to be. In this regard, some individuals are more adept communicators than others.

Consider your home. In finding or building a place to live, we do not just look for something that will meet our budgets and physical needs; aesthetic appeal also plays an important role. We may alter our homes by changing walls, adding rooms, remodeling the bathroom or the kitchen, and repainting things in different colors inside and outside. We decorate the inside with furniture, rugs, paintings, posters, mirrors, and a host of knickknacks and smaller things. If we have a yard, we may remove or add trees, shrubs, flowerbeds, and fences. Even temporary apartment and college dormitory dwellers try to make a place their own. Although some of these additions and changes may be of utilitarian value or need, most serve to enhance the aesthetic appeal of the place where we live while also telling others who we are.

Even in our daily lives, then, we attempt to immerse ourselves in the aesthetic. The search for the aesthetic is reflected in the appearance of our persons and our homes, as well as in our places of worship, recreation, and work. Much of our day is filled with music, song, dance, drama, comedy, literature, and sports, which we listen to, participate in, and sometimes create. Art is a cultural universal. But beyond this, the artistic impulse is seen in the everyday lives of individual human beings.

Forms of Artistic Expression

Although art permeates all aspects of human activity—from clothing and furniture to music and theater—space constraints do not permit us to discuss all these diverse forms of artistic expression. For this reason, we limit our discussion to certain categories: body arts, visual arts, and performance arts. The Concept Review outlines these three categories of art.

CONCEPT REVIEW	Forms of Artistic Expression
Body Arts	Art created by physically changing the body, including but not limited to physical alterations, painting, tattooing, and scarification
Visual Arts	Art made from tangible objects that are part of the material culture of a people, including but not limited to basketry, pottery, textiles, clothing, jewelry, tools, furniture, painting, masks, and sculpture
Performance Arts	Art meant to be heard, seen, or personally performed, including music, song, dance, and theater

Body Arts

People around the world are highly creative in altering their physical appearance. Almost anything that can be done to the human body is probably being done or has been done in the past. **Body arts**, or the temporary or permanent enhancements of the human body, are found in all societies. For convenience, we focus on the body arts of physical alterations, body painting, and tattooing and scarification.

Physical Alterations

In most societies, people attempt to physically alter their bodies. Head and body hair is treated in many different ways. In Western societies, hair is styled and often artificially colored. Some people shave their head, their beard, and even their legs and armpits. Others let their beard and mustache grow and style them in various ways. In some societies these actions may be a matter of fashion or personal taste; in other societies, such actions may have deeper cultural meanings.

In parts of Africa, a woman's status—for example, whether she is unmarried or married, or is a mother or a widow—is indicated by her hairstyle. Among the Hopis, adolescent girls of marriageable age wear their hair in a large whorl on each side of the head, creating the so-called butterfly hairstyle. After marriage, they wear their hair long and parted in the middle. Children among the Omaha had their hair cut in patterns indicating their clan membership.

Wearing beards is not always a matter of personal taste and fashion. In many societies—such as Hasidic Jews, Mennonites, Amish, some Muslim sects, and Sikhs—wearing a beard is an act of religious belief. In the ancient world, social status was frequently associated with beards. In Egypt, only the nobility were allowed to wear beards. Not only did noblemen wear beards, but women of the nobility frequently wore artificial beards as well to indicate their social rank. In contrast, in ancient Greece, only the nobility were allowed to be clean-shaven; men of commoner status had to let their beards grow.

Hair alterations are usually reversible because hair will grow back. Other parts of the body are altered permanently. Cranial deformation or head shaping has been and is still widely practiced among some peoples of the world. The skull of a baby is soft, and, if the baby's head is bound, the shape of the skull can be permanently changed, flattening the back and the forehead or lengthening the head. In parts of France, cranial deformation was virtually universal until the eighteenth century. A baby's face was tightly wrapped in linen, resulting in a flattened skull and ears. In the Netherlands, babies once wore tight-fitting caps that depressed the front portion of the skull. The elite classes of the ancient Andean civilizations elongated the skull, as did the ancient Egyptians. Some peoples of Central Africa bound the heads of female babies to create elongated skulls that came to a point in the back.

Some peoples permanently altered other parts of the body as well. In China, the feet of girls of high-status families were bound at the age of 5 or 6 to keep them small. Not only were small feet considered attractive, but also foot binding was a visible indication that the family was sufficiently wealthy that its women did not have to engage in physical labor.

Among the Karen Padaung of Myanmar (formerly Burma), starting at about age 5, girls have brass rings placed around their necks. As they grow older, more rings are added so that by the time they reach adulthood, their shoulders have been pressed down, making their necks appear longer.

The most widespread form of physical alterations is **body piercing** of some part of the body for the attachment of ornaments. Ear piercing is probably the most common and widespread. One or more small holes are pierced in one or both ears for the attachment of metal ornaments or feathers. However, some groups—such as the Maya, Aztecs, and many other Native American societies—cut open and stretch their earlobes so they could insert decorated clay, wood, stone, or metal ear spools, some 2 or more inches in diameter.

In parts of Africa and among many Native American peoples, holes were cut in the lower or the upper lip or both and were expanded so that large lip plugs, up to 3 inches in diameter, could be inserted. Sometimes, only women wore these discs, other times only men, and in some cases both. Among the Inuit (Eskimo) and Aleut, both men and women wore one or two *labrets* (ornaments) in their lower lips. Only high-status women among the Northwest Coast societies wore labrets in their lips. Among groups such as the Suya and Kayapo of the Amazon Basin, only men wore discs, in their lower lip. In Africa, only women wore discs, and usually only in the lower lip. Some groups, however, like the Sara in Chad, wore discs in both their upper and lower lips, while the Malonde women of East Africa wore them only in their upper lip.

> **body arts** The temporary or permanent enhancements of the human body.
>
> **body piercing** Decoration of the body by piercing holes in parts of the body for the attachment of ornaments.

Nose piercing takes two forms: nostril piercing and nasal septum piercing. With nostril piercing, one or more holes are made in the nostril. In South Asia and the Middle East, many women wear a gold ring or jewel in their right nostril. In other parts of the world, men and women place feathers or other decorative items in their nostril piercing. More extreme are nasal septum piercings found in Native America, Africa, and Oceania. In some cases, people insert nose rings in gold or brass through the opening; others insert bone, tusk, or shell ornaments or feathers.

Today, the widest range of body piercings is found in North America and Europe. Not only do many individuals have ear, nose, and lip piercings; some have piercings in their tongues, eyebrows, nose bridges, breasts, and pubic areas as well.

Body Painting

Body painting is a less drastic and temporary way of changing an individual's appearance and thus status. Some peoples paint only their faces, while others paint almost their entire bodies. In some cases, body painting has religious significance and meaning; in other cases, it is purely secular, designed to enhance the person's physical appearance.

Many peoples in Papua New Guinea cover their faces and limbs with white clay when a relative or important person dies, as a sign of mourning and respect for the deceased. The aboriginal peoples of Australia traditionally painted their bodies with red and yellow ochre, white clay, charcoal, and other pigments. During rituals, individuals were painted with elaborate designs covering most of the body. The colors and designs were standardized and had symbolic meaning. Ritual specialists who knew these designs did the painting for religious ceremonies. Outside of ritual contexts, for many Australian peoples, body painting was a secular and daily activity, performed by family members on one another. Individuals were free to use whatever colors and designs pleased them, so long as they were not ritual designs.

Among the most famous body painters are the Nuba of the Sudan. Nuba body painting serves to note the individual's age, kin group, and ritual status as well as enhancing appearance by emphasizing physical strength and health. Starting at about age 5, girls paint their bodies completely in either red or yellow ochre. They continue painting until the beginning of their first pregnancy.

Although some men just paint their bodies in black, others paint their bodies in elaborate designs using a range of contrasting colors. While all men paint their bodies, young men between the ages of about 14 and 25

mediacolor's/Alamy

The Nuba men of Sudan are widely known for their elaborated body painting.

are the most active painters. Unless they are involved in some seasonal agricultural task, they paint a new design on their body every day or two. This painting frequently requires an hour or two of work. To prepare their bodies, they shave off all their body hair, including the eyebrows and pubic hair, since virtually all parts of their bodies maybe be painted. Some designs are nonrepresentational bars and bands; others are representational, usually of animals. New designs may also be incorporated. In their body painting, Nuba men attempt to achieve both balance and symmetry.

Tattooing and Scarification

Tattooing and the related practice of **scarification** are widespread. Tattoo designs—achieved by etching and placing a colored pigment under the skin—have been

body painting Decoration of the body by painting designs.

tattooing Decoration of the body with designs by cutting and placing colored pigments under the skin.

scarification Decoration of the body by scarring the skin to produce designs on the body.

practiced by diverse peoples. When the skin is too dark to easily see tattoo designs, people may use scarification, which is the deliberate scarring of the skin to produce designs on the body.

Tattooing has a long history as an art form. It was practiced by the ancient Egyptians as well as by the ancient Scythians, Thracians, and Romans in Europe. The ancient Bretons, at the time of the Roman conquest, were reported to have had their bodies elaborately tattooed with the images of animals. In the fourth century C.E., when Christianity became the official religion of the Roman empire, tattooing was forbidden on religious grounds—it was an affront to God. Tattooing virtually disappeared among European peoples until the eighteenth century, when it was discovered in the Pacific and Asia by sailors and reintroduced to Europe as a purely secular art.

Robert Brain noted an important difference between body painting and tattooing and scarification: Paint is removable, whereas tattooing and scarification are indelible and permanent. As a result, tattooing and scarification are usually associated with societies in which there are permanent differences in social status. Peoples also differed in terms of complexity of designs and parts of the body tattooed. Among some people, tattooing was limited to a few lines on the face, chest, or arms. For others, complex designs covered most of the body from the face to the legs. In some cases, every adult had some tattoos; in other societies, only certain individuals had tattoos. The significance and meaning of tattoos varied, but most had socioreligious meaning. The more fully tattooed an individual was, the higher the social status.

The adornment of the body with tattoos is most elaborate in the scattered islands of Polynesia. In fact, the word *tattoo* itself is Polynesian. The word, like the practice of tattooing sailors, came into use as a result of the voyages of Western explorers and whalers in the seventeenth and later centuries. Tongans, Samoans, Marquesans, Tahitians, the Maori of New Zealand, and most other Polynesian peoples practiced tattooing, which in all these places was connected to social distinctions such as class or rank, sex, religious roles, and specialization. Polynesian peoples are all historically related, so it is not surprising that marking the body with tattoos is found on almost all islands, albeit to different degrees and with somewhat different styles.

Many Maori had large areas of their bodies covered with tattoos, which could be on the torso, thighs, buttocks, calves, and, most notably, the face. Skilled tattoo artists used several instruments to incise the curvilinear patterns characteristic of most Maori tattoos. One was a small chisel made of bone, which was etched into the skin with a hammer. Apparently, no anesthetic was used to relieve the pain; and, in fact, tolerating the pain of the procedure may have been part of its cultural significance. To make pigment, the Maori burned several kinds of wood for their ashes. After making the cuts, the artist rubbed the pigment into the wounds to leave permanent markings. The most skilled tattoo artists were rewarded with high prestige and chiefly patronage, and their craft was in such high demand that they traveled widely over New Zealand's two huge islands.

Both Maori men and women wore tattoos, although men's bodies were more thoroughly covered. For both sexes, tattoos were considered not merely as body ornamentation or as an expression of personal identity: Having tattoos brought certain privileges. Men who did not undergo tattooing could not build canoe houses, carve wood, make weapons, or weave nets. Women who did not have tattoos could not help in the gardens with sweet potatoes, the Maori staple vegetable crop.

Maori facial tattoos, called *moko*, have special importance. Women were tattooed on the lips and chin, often near the time of their marriage. Men's facial tattoos were designed by splitting the face into four fields—left versus right of the nose and upper versus lower at roughly eye level. *Moko* were basically symmetrical on the vertical axis, with curvilinear designs on the forehead and eyebrows, cheeks, and mouth regions. In many cases, virtually the man's entire face was tattooed. Not just any *moko* design could be worn by just any man; designs were related to factors such as hereditary status, place of birth, and achievement in battle. Thus, there were social restrictions placed on the wearing of facial tattoos, suggesting that they were important symbols of group identity and personal achievement. North Americans might see echoes of their own styles of clothing, jewelry, hairstyle, and other personal ornamentations in Maori and other Polynesian tattoos.

On other Polynesian islands, tattooing was similar to the Maori in broad pattern but varied in detail. In Samoa, for instance, a group of boys was tattooed together on the hips and thighs in their early teens, accompanied by much ceremony. The primary recipient of the tattoo was the son of a high-ranking chief, and other boys participated to share his pain and, therefore, publicly show their respect and loyalty. Supposedly, Samoan women disdained men as sexual partners if they did not have tattoos. Traditionally, Samoan girls received tattoos only on the backs of their knees, which they were not supposed to reveal to others. It is interesting that in Samoa, greater and more elaborate male tattoos were connected to different sexually based biological functions. There was a saying (Milner, 1969, p. 20): "The man grows up and is tattooed. The woman grows up and she gives birth." According to one interpretation, voluntary tattooing gives pain to men just as childbirth causes pain to women. Perhaps the male experience of pain by tattooing is connected to Samoan women's contempt for men without tattoos.

In all of Polynesia, it was the people of the Marquesas whose bodies were most covered by tattoos. The highest-ranking chiefs had tattoos even on the soles of their feet. Alfred Gell argues that this relatively thorough tattooing in the Marquesas wrapped the body in images in order to protect it from spiritual dangers.

Decorating the body by cutting and creating scars, or scarification, is less common than tattooing among the world's peoples. Like tattooing, scarification is practiced for numerous reasons. Depending on the culture, both men and women may be scarred. Sometimes the scarred design is on the face; in other cases, the chest, breast, back, and even the legs and arms may be elaborately covered with such designs. Sometimes scarification forms part of the puberty rite or some other initiation rite. Among the Nuer of South Sudan, a series of horizontal cuts is made on the foreheads of men who have completed male initiation rituals. These cuts symbolically mark and communicate a young man's maturity and courage. After the cuts scarify, the scars become permanent symbols of Nuer manhood.

Visual Arts

Visual arts are produced from tangible objects, so they are part of the **material culture** of a people. They may be religious or secular in meaning and use. Usually, they are permanent in that they are meant to last for a long time, but sometimes they are created for a one-time use only and then destroyed. Visual arts encompass a wide range of basketry, ceramics, textiles, clothing, jewelry, tools, paintings, masks, and sculpture, to name only a few examples. Metal, wood, stone, leather, feathers, shell, and paper made of fibers, pigments, and other materials are used in their creation. The two main factors that transform a material item into a visual art are form and ornamentation.

Form

The physical form or shape of an object is a reflection of its utilitarian function, the materials available, the technical knowledge and skill of the person producing it, and the general lifestyle of the society. Nomadic or seminomadic foraging and pastoral peoples often produce items that are lightweight and easily transportable. One might think the visual arts of these peoples are less refined than those of more settled peoples. But Inuit peoples of the Arctic precisely carved small art objects out of soft soapstone and decorated many of their portable tools with figures of animals. In addition, the nomadic peoples of the American plains elaborately painted their shields and hides and heavily decorated their clothing and moccasins with paint, quills, and beadwork, thus allowing people to carry their art along with them. Native Americans of the western United States, especially the Southwest, used pigment to paint or hard stones to etch images of animals, celestial objects, people, mythological beings, and other things on rocks. The prehistoric peoples who created these images might have moved according to the season, but their art was stationary and long lasting. Today, we know these images as pictographs and petroglyphs, also called *rock art*.

Although rock may seem like a difficult object to use as a canvas, the world's peoples have used other unusual materials as well, including sand (as we shall see later). Of course, the availability of wood, stone, clay, hides, and other natural materials does influence what people can create and how. The kinds of tools the artist uses to paint, etch, or sculpt are also important influences on the final artwork. Metal tools have advantages over stone tools in giving artistic form to a raw material. Peoples also differ in their technical knowledge of how to work stone or wood and how to model clay or metals.

Within these natural and technical limitations, the form of an object is the result of the interplay of utilitarian function and aesthetic style. The function/style debate has long interested archaeologists. Prehistoric stone tools display a bewildering variety of forms. In North American archaeology, extensive typologies have been created to classify projectile point types, which differ in size, relative length and width, and shape (straight, concave, convex, or even serrated). Some are unnotched; others are notched on the bases or sides. Many of these differences are undoubtedly related to function, but others seem to be purely stylistic.

visual arts Arts produced in a tangible form, including basketry, pottery, textiles, paintings, drawings, sculptures, masks, carvings, and the like.

material culture Artifacts and other physical, visible manifestations of culture, including art, architectural features, tools, consumer goods, clothing, and writing.

These men in Morocco are producing traditional pottery.

Great variability is also present in the vessel shapes and decorations of another archaeological favorite—pottery. Pottery vessels vary tremendously from one group to another, as well as within the same group of people over time.

Ornamentation

Ornamentation is design added to the physical form of an object. Humans are highly creative in developing ways of adding ornamentation to material items. Ornamental designs may be woven or carved into an object. They may be painted, incised, molded, or sewn onto an object. Or a combination of these techniques may be used to decorate an object.

In basketry and textiles, designs are commonly woven onto the item during its construction. For baskets, different colors of plant fibers, either natural or artificially dyed, are used for the designs. The same is true in the weaving of textiles, for which different-colored yarns are used. Not all textile designs are created using fibers of contrasting colors. By using a variety of techniques, weavers may create different designs within a fabric using only a single color.

Carving refers to creating a design by removing parts of the original form. Wood, stone, clay, ivory, shell, and bone may have carved designs. An object may be carved in three dimensions so that the form itself becomes the design, as in a piece of sculpture. Or the form of the object will remain the same, with only shallow relief carving of a design on the surface.

Painting is certainly one of the easiest and most versatile methods of ornamenting an object. It is possibly the oldest method of ornamentation; European cave paintings are at least 20,000 years old. All one needs to paint is a range of colors. To make colored pigments, a variety of different materials may be mixed with water, oil, or fat, such as charcoal, plant materials, and natural mineral pigments. Paintings can be applied to wood, stone, clay, textiles, paper, or leather. Paintings can be applied to flat surfaces (such as cave walls), exposed rocks or cliff walls, wooden furniture, or canvas. They may be made on round or irregular surfaces, such as pottery, masks, and sculpture.

Incising consists of decorating an object by scratching lines into the surface. Like painting, incising appears to be one of the earliest ways of adding designs to an item. Incising is most commonly used on ivory, bone, and shell. In these cases, the scratched lines are frequently accentuated by adding some type of colored pigment, usually black or a dark color, so one can more readily see the design itself. Incised designs are also occasionally used for decorating clay pots and leather.

Designs on ceramics and metal are commonly modeled by raising certain areas above the surface. There are two ways in which this form of ornamentation can be accomplished. One is by making additions to the object after the surface area is finished. In pottery, for example, artists form designs by placing little balls or coils of clay on the surface after the body of the pot has been formed. A similar technique is sometimes used in adding designs to metal items, as when metal wires shaped into designs are welded to the surface. More commonly, though, molds are created with designs carved into the surface area. Clay can be forced into these molds, or metal poured into them. After the object is removed from the mold, the design areas stand out as raised areas on the object's surface.

Sewing is often used to add ornamentation to cloth or leather. Glass, bone, or shell beads may be sewn onto an item, forming designs, as on moccasins or clothing. Designs may be created by sewing with various colored threads of hair, plant fiber, quills, or metal, or by sewing different colors of fabrics together, as in a patchwork quilt.

Although meaningful cross-cultural studies of visual arts are difficult, comparative studies have been made of stylistic elements found in ornamental designs. Working with the idea that art reflects the creator's view of society, John Fischer studied the use of stylistic elements in 28 different societies around the world. He divided the societies based on the extent of their social equality and inequality (see Chapter 13), thinking that the artistic expressions of egalitarian (primarily foraging) societies would differ from those of socially stratified (primarily intensive agricultural) societies. He examined the stylistic elements in terms of their relative complexity, use of space, symmetry, and boundedness. Fischer found that in egalitarian societies, designs tended to repeat similar, symmetrical elements, with large areas of empty space without enclosures. In more stratified societies, ornamentation was characterized by asymmetrical designs that integrated unlike elements and included more fully filled enclosed areas. Fischer interpreted these differences as symbolically reflecting the differing social realities of egalitarian and stratified peoples. Egalitarian peoples tend to live in small, scattered isolated groups, whereas in stratified societies, people live in crowded communities.

This discussion has only touched upon some of the ways in which peoples add ornamentation to objects. When it comes to ornamenting objects, humans are highly creative. When most people think of artistic creativity, they think of the artist as creating a novel object (e.g., a unique drawing or sculpture) using some medium (e.g., paper or wood). Looking in broad cross-cultural perspective, we see that humanity as a whole has also been enormously creative not only in its styles but also in its techniques of ornamentation and in some of the surprising materials used.

Art of the Northwest Coast: An Example of Style

In the visual arts, the artist creates some two-dimensional image, such as a painting or drawing, or three-dimensional form, such as a sculpture or mask. Cultures vary in many ways in their visual arts: the themes or subjects portrayed, the purposes of the artwork, the relationship between the artist and the public, and so forth.

Stylistic conventions are an important variation. In visual arts, stylistic symbolism may be especially significant because artists in many cultures are not especially concerned with realistic portrayals of people or nature but use conventional representations understood by themselves and the public. But, even when the intention is a realistic portrayal, symbolic representation may be necessary. In a painting or drawing, for example, three-dimensional reality is portrayed on a two-dimensional surface, and the stylistic conventions of different cultures may handle this problem of representation in various ways.

The art of some of the Native Americans of the Northwest Coast, from southern Alaska to Oregon, is one example of stylistic variation in imagery and two-dimensional representation. Although they were hunters, gatherers, and fishers—rather than cultivators—Northwest Coast peoples were largely sedentary villagers, which was made possible by the abundance and reliability of coastal and riverine food resources, especially fish (see Chapter 7). Their social and political organization included large descent groups, chiefly roles, and hierarchical ranking (see Chapter 13). Sponsoring the creation of art objects, displaying them, and/or using them in ceremonies were the ways groups and high-ranking people proclaimed their wealth and social position.

Northwest Coast art is famous for its sheer quantity, quality, and style. Many major Canadian and American museums contain substantial collections of masks, wooden sculptures, incised silver jewelry,

Along the Northwest Coast, houses were elaborately decorated with designs that were symbolic of the family and its heritage. This Tlingit house is in Ketchikan, Alaska.

Chlaus Lotscher/Getty Images

exaggerated dorsal fin. Using such conventional design elements, Northwest Coast artists carved animals onto boxes, masks used in a multitude of ceremonies, huge cedar tree trunks representing a group's or individual's ancestry (commonly mislabeled "totem poles"), and other three-dimensional objects.

Painters are familiar with the problem of representing the world on flat surfaces. In the Western and many other artistic traditions, three dimensions are represented on two-dimensional surfaces (canvas or paper) by techniques such as relative sizes of images, perspective, and coloration, all intended to create the visual illusion of depth. Northwest Coast artists painted on many two-dimensional surfaces, including the flat sides of boxes and communal house fronts. They also wove representations of animals into blankets and incised lines into bracelets and other metal jewelry. Most often, their work on flat surfaces tried to retain many of the design elements characteristic of each animal, so that each animal representation would be readily identifiable. A common technique was to split the animal down the middle and paint profiles on each half of the surface. The result was a representation that distorted the actual shape of the body and its characteristic parts, but retained the elements that conventionally identified the animal.

Yet another stylistic characteristic of Northwest Coast art is an apparent intolerance of empty spaces. The subject's body, limbs, and even hands and feet were generally filled in by design elements. Most commonly, curvilinear patterns, stylized eyes, or faces were painted or carved inside body parts. Thus, one frequently observes a face on an animal's torso or an eye pattern on a leg joint.

Performance Arts

Performance arts encompass music, song, and dance, which use voice, instruments, and movement to delight the senses and communicate. (Theater/drama is also a performance art, but we do not cover it here.) Music, song, and dance are closely interrelated. Dancing is usually to the accompaniment of music, especially rhythms created partly by drumming, clapping, or other kinds of percussion. Singing is often accompanied by instrumental music. Traditional religious ceremonies and pageants commonly integrate music, song, and dance.

An interesting aspect of performance arts is that not only do we watch or listen to such formal performances, but we also frequently perform them ourselves, in many cases for pure pleasure. We play our own pianos or guitars, we sing in the shower or as we drive, and we take part in social dances.

carved boxes, finely woven blankets, and sometimes larger objects such as so-called totem poles and painted house fronts. Animals, humans, and spirits are the most common subjects of the art of these peoples, although many creations represent animal-human-spirit at the same time. Because of the unique style used to represent these subjects, most Northwest Coast art is easily recognizable.

Animals such as beavers, ravens, hawks, frogs, bears, and killer whales were common subjects of the art, but their depiction was not intended to be realistic. Artists created animals by combining design elements representing what was culturally considered their most distinctive body parts. For example, beavers are shown with two large incisors, a scaly (often hatched) tail, a rounded nose, and forepaws (often holding a stick). Hawks are portrayed by emphasizing their distinctive beak, which is turned backward and often touches the face. Frogs are suggested by wide and toothless mouths. Bears usually are identified by paws with claws and a large and heavily toothed mouth. Images of killer whales have a large toothed mouth, a blowhole, and an

performance arts Forms of art such as music, percussion, song, dance, and theater/drama that involve sound and/or stylized body movements.

Some anthropologists have questioned the dual dimension of these art forms. Speaking only of dance, Adrienne Kaeppler has asked, "Is participation in rock and roll in any way comparable to watching ballet? Indeed, should 'dances of participation' and 'dances of presentation' be classified as the same phenomenon either in our own or other cultures, let alone cross-culturally?" (1978). She further questions whether dance performances for the gods should be categorized with social dancing, because their purposes are so different.

Similar questions may be asked of music and song, which so often are part of religious rituals. For example, Osage rituals integrated music, song, dance, and theatrical performances to communicate ideas that could not be expressed by words alone. Over a hundred years ago, Francis LaFlesche argued that these rituals were not merely prayers for supernatural assistance but were educational as well. They were a manner of recording and transmitting the collective knowledge of the society, communicating social messages to the assembled participants. Thus, even within a society, the purposes of performance arts may differ significantly, depending on whether they are religious or secular in nature.

People raised in the Judeo-Christian religious tradition are quite familiar with the many functions of music in religious services. The lyrics of familiar hymns sung to praise God are an integral part of worship rituals. Music also helps to create the mood and sense of reverence for the service and is capable of altering the emotional state of the participants. The shared experience of singing in unison may help draw the congregation together, enhancing what many Christian denominations call their fellowship. In these and other ways, music is important in making the congregation receptive to the messages delivered by the sermon and prayers.

Music and other forms of performance arts are essential to the religious experience for diverse peoples in all parts of the world. The Voudon (Voodoo) religion of the Caribbean heavily incorporates performance arts into religious ceremonies. Followers of Voudon consider themselves people who "serve the spirits" (*loa*). Many *loa* originated and now live in West Africa, where the ancestors of modern Afro-Caribbean peoples were

Michele Alfieri/Shutterstock.com

Masks, such as these worn by the Dogon people in Mali, are a widespread form of visual art. The masks are integral to the performance art of this dance.

enslaved during the era of the slave trade beginning in about 1500. Voudon temples are elaborately decorated with sacred objects, paintings, and symbolic representations of various *loa*, which show the devotion of the worshipers and make the temple attractive to the spirits. Through drumming, music, and energetic dancing, Voudon worshipers induce the *loa* to leave their spiritual homes and take over the bodies of those who worship them. When the *loa* possess their human servants, the latter speak with the voices of the *loa*, wear the *loa*'s favorite clothing, eat their foods, drink their beverages, and generally assume their identity. Visiting petitioners with problems can ask questions of the worshiper/*loa*, who may answer with directions about what course of action to take. Voudon drumming, music, and dancing are so totally integrated into temple rituals that the religion is unimaginable without it.

Among many peoples, music, dance, and other forms of performance arts are essential elements of curing ceremonials. !Kung shamans use percussion, song, and dance to induce the trance state they believe is necessary for curing sick people. The power to heal, !Kung believe, comes from a substance called *nlum*, which, when heated up by dancing and trance, allows shamans to draw sickness out of people. As the women produce a definite rhythm by clapping and singing, the curers circle the fire in short, synchronous dance steps. The experience of music and dance causes the *nlum* inside their bodies to boil up into their heads, inducing trance. In this spiritually powerful state, shamans heal by placing hands on the sick, shrieking at the same time to drive out the affliction.

Music is essential to the healing process among many other African peoples. The Tumbuka-speaking peoples of northern Malawi combine singing, drumming, and dancing in all-night curing sessions. Some kinds of illness are caused by a category of spirits called *vimbuza*. *Vimbuza* are the powerful spiritual energy of foreign peoples and wild animals (especially lions). *Vimbuza* cause various kinds of illness and even death when they possess someone. Tumbuka believe that health requires a balance between the body's cold and hot forces (similar to the "humours" of old Europe). When *vimbuza* enter the body, they create an imbalance between hot and cold forces, leading to the buildup of heat that is culturally interpreted as sickness.

Tumbuka diviner-healers (curers) both diagnose illnesses and direct elaborate healing ceremonies that include drumming, music, and dance. The most essential part of the curing ritual is a shared musical experience in the context of a group gathering, with every individual present expected to contribute to the music making. Even patients themselves participate in the total experience by singing, clapping, and dancing. As the sick person dances to the accompanying rhythm of drums and music, the heat inside the person's body increases. This leads the possessing spirit to expend excess energy and cool off. By thus restoring the balance between hot and cold, the individual is cured, at least temporarily. Steven Friedson, who worked among the Tumbuka, briefly summarizes the importance of music and performance to healing among just a few African cultures:

> Africans approach healing through music and dance. Azande "witch doctors" eat special divinatory medicines, activated by drumming, singing, and dancing. In northern Nigeria among the Hausa, the sounds of the *garaya* (two-stringed plucked lute) and *buta* (gourd rattle) call the divine horsemen of the sacred city of Jangare to descend into the heads of *boorii* adepts, thus healing the people they have made sick. Similarly, the various *orisha* and *voudon* spirits of the Guinea Coast, called by their drum motto, mount their horses (possess their devotees). The resultant spirit-possession dance, though religious in nature, is in the first instance often a therapy for those afflicted by the same spirits. Spirit affliction is healed through music and dance in Ethiopia and Sudan, wherever *zar* cults occur. . . . Central, southern, and parts of Equatorial Africa have examples of the *ng'oma* type of healing complex, whose name . . . points to the centrality of music in curative rites.

(Friedson, 1998, pp. 273–274)

In the early 1980s, the authors of this book first heard about a medical practice that involves integrating music into the treatment of both biomedical and psychological disorders. At the time, we thought the field—now called *music therapy*—was a new mode of treatment and a new occupation. As the preceding examples illustrate, many other cultures have long recognized the connection between music and healing and have integrated the performance arts into their treatments.

Like other forms of aesthetic expression, comparative studies of performance arts are difficult and few. Alan Lomax's comparative studies of dance and song rank with the most ambitious. Lomax and his collaborators analyzed film footage of peoples from around the world, comparing their body movements in everyday activities with their dance movements. They found that dance movements were formalized repetitions of the movements found in daily life. Lomax further argued that the form of the dance was correlated with the relative complexity of the society.

In his comparative study of songs, Lomax found that differences in song styles were also correlated with societal complexity. The songs of less complex peoples, such as egalitarian foragers, included more vocables (sounds, not words). Words were not enunciated as clearly in their songs, and there was more repetition of vocables and words. The songs of the most complex peoples included fewer vocables, less repetition, and more words, which were more clearly enunciated.

Although Lomax's conclusions concerning the correlation between dance and song and relative cultural complexity have been questioned, there are some interesting parallels between his findings and those of Fischer on stylistic elements in ornamental designs.

Art and Culture

Many anthropologists are interested in art as nonverbal communication. As we have already seen with the examples of body, visual, and performance arts, art is embedded in a cultural context. Three of many features of this context are religion, gender, and identity.

Secular and Religious Art

In our discussions of the various forms of art, we mentioned that certain artistic products are sacred and others are not. There are both sacred and secular designs, forms, dances, songs, music, and literature. This division between secular and sacred cuts across many types of art and across most cultures.

In contemporary industrial society, the greatest artistic energies are expended in the creation of secular art, although such art may at times include religious themes. If, for example, you examine the works of the greatest Western painters, architects, and composers of the last century, you will find that most of their work is secular. This was not always true. The great art of earlier periods was for the most part concerned with religion, partly because religious and political authorities often sponsored artists and their creations. For example, the pyramids and great temples of ancient Egypt were related to conceptions of the afterlife and other dimensions of the supernatural world. While visiting pyramids and great statues of the pharaohs, one must remember that the pharaohs were gods on Earth.

In classical Greece, the cradle of Western culture's artistic traditions, religion was a central focus for most of the greatest artistic accomplishments. The Parthenon in Athens was the temple of Athena. Most of the greatest Greek public statuary depicted gods such as Poseidon, Zeus, Apollo, and Aphrodite. Much Greek drama had strong religious overtones and was associated with the god Dionysus. In Rome, secular art became more prominent. The great buildings were usually palaces and theaters, while public monuments honoring the triumphs of living or recently deceased heroes filled Roman cities. In the Middle Ages, religion regained preeminence. The great buildings of the medieval and Renaissance periods were cathedrals, while the greatest artists of the time labored to fill these buildings with frescoes, mosaics, paintings, statuary, and other artistic works as well as music, song, and pageantry dedicated to the worship of God.

The 1700s saw an emphasis on reason and science, the industrial revolution, the rise of capitalism, and the beginnings of modern political democracy. Ever since, Western art has become increasingly secular. The largest buildings in our cities are no longer dedicated to religion, but to government, commerce, or athletics. Contemporary painters choose secular subjects—from realistic landscapes and buildings to abstract designs and cans of Campbell's soup. The most illustrious composers and performers today seldom produce or perform religious music; instead they focus on secular and, at times, even irreligious themes. For those of us who grew up in a society dominated by secular art, it is important to remember that for most peoples and for most of human history, religion and religious art have been preeminent. The most elaborate artistic achievements of a great many peoples are associated with religious ceremonies: visual arts, music, dances, ornamentations, architecture, and their associated mythologies.

We have already discussed examples of the integration of performance arts like music and dance into African healing practices. The Navajo of the American Southwest are another people who involve art—both visual and verbal—in their curing rituals. In Navajo belief, the most common cause of illness is the loss of harmony with the environment, often because of the person's violation of a taboo or another transgression. When illness strikes and a diagnosis is made, a Navajo "singer" (curer or shaman) is called on to organize a complex curing ceremony.

In curing ceremonies (and there were traditionally dozens of such ceremonies), the singer addresses and calls on the Holy People, who are spiritual beings believed by Navajo to have the power to restore sick people to harmony and beauty. Ceremonies usually occur in a *hogan* (house) at night, and in theory the procedures must be executed perfectly for the cure to work.

For the ceremony, the singer creates images of the Holy People out of colored sand, called sand paintings. Navajo sand paintings are visual representations of the Holy People that are created, used in a single ceremony, and then destroyed. Most sand paintings are stylized scenes of events involving Holy People that occurred in the mythological past. Each sand painting is part of a ceremony that also includes other sacred objects (such as rattles and prayer sticks) and lengthy songs or chants recited by the singer. The songs/chants that are recited over the sand painting and the patient may last for hours. Most songs/chants tell of the myths depicted in the specific sand painting.

In their years of learning to become singers, Navajo singers must memorize the lengthy songs and chants they recite over sick people to restore their harmony with the world. Singers also learn to make sand paintings that represent specific mythical scenes and events. To make the images, a singer—usually with the help of family members and/or apprentices—collects, grinds, and mixes sand and other materials of various colors, including white, red, yellow, black, and blue, with charcoal, corn pollen, and other plant materials. Pictures are created by carefully dribbling fine grains of sand through the fingers onto the prepared floor of the hogan.

There are literally hundreds of sand paintings. Most ceremonies involve a combination of many sand paintings used in association with particular chants. Because some are quite large and enormously detailed, they often take hours to create. But all must be exact representations of the ideal model of the mythical scene or event depicted. The images are stylized drawings of the Holy People, many of whom are depicted with weapons and armor. Most scenes represented in the sand paintings are from particular myths familiar to the patient and audience.

Sand paintings are made for the express purpose of inducing the Holy People to come to the hogan where the ceremony is held. The Holy People are attracted by their images in the sand painting, and, once consecrated with pollen, the sand images and the Holy People become one and the same and thus holy. This process of transforming the sand figures into actual spiritual beings is termed *transubstantiation* and is a commonly occurring feature of religious art. The very same idea is found in the Eucharist of the Roman Catholic Church, with the conversion of wine and bread into the "blood and body of Christ." During the Navajo ceremony, the patient is seated on the sand painting itself, which is now imbued with the presence of the Holy People. The singer completes the transfer of power to the patient when he rubs the patient's body with the sand of the images of the Holy People. After each phase of the ceremony is finished, the sand painting is destroyed, and the sand is carefully removed from the hogan.

Navajo sand paintings certainly are works of art. Some non-Navajos who have seen them think it is a shame to destroy such beautiful images that the singers and their helpers have worked so hard to create. But in the context of Navajo beliefs, sand paintings are made for specific curing ceremonials held for particular patients. That is their purpose—not expressing the singer's creativity, making an artistic statement, celebrating Navajo culture, or publicly displaying the singer's talents. For Navajo, fulfilling that purpose requires that the paintings not be permanent.

Navajo sand paintings and the singing of curers are clearly religious, but the division between their secular and religious purposes is not always obvious, particular to nonmembers of the society. If you travel in the Southwest, you will see Navajo "sand paintings" for sale. Many of these have depictions of the Holy People. However, they have not been consecrated with pollen. They are nothing but sand glued on a board. Perhaps not surprisingly, some traditional Navajo object to this use.

Somewhat different are the so-called *kachina* dolls of the neighboring Hopi. *Kachinas* are the supernatural spirits of the Hopi, and the *kachina* ceremonies or dances are among their most important religious activities. When a man puts on a sacred *kachina* mask, that spirit becomes embodied in him. During certain of these ceremonies, the *kachinas* (the men wearing the masks) will give the girls figures carved out of cottonwood and painted in the image of *kachinas*. Although called "dolls," they are neither toys nor sacred items. They are mnemonic devices to help the children learn about, and recognize, the 500 or so different *kachina* spirits. As secular objects, *kachina* "dolls" are sold to visitors. (See the Global Challenges and Opportunities feature for more about marketing the art of traditional cultures.)

Religious symbolism is often used to decorate clothing and other secular objects, but it does not necessarily make them sacred or imbue them with power. Religious symbolism can limit artistic expression, and the use of certain types of motifs or themes may be religiously forbidden. The Quran prohibits the use of human images, which are viewed as idolatry. Thus, many Islamic peoples extended this ban to include any pictorial representation of humans or animals. As a result, much of the art of Islamic peoples is devoid of naturalistic representations, focusing instead on elaborate geometric or curvilinear designs. Another example of religious influence on secular art can be seen among the Shakers; they emphasized singing and dancing as important parts of their religious services but prohibited the use of musical instruments.

Art and Gender

Gender differences are often reflected in body, visual, and performance arts. Colors and designs are sometimes considered male or female, most familiarly reflected in clothing and body decoration. Gender also influences who creates and performs certain types of visual and performance arts. The BaMbuti Pygmies of the African rain forest have a ritual performance involving dance and music they call *molimo*. They view the forest as their parent and, like any parent, the forest looks after its children—themselves. Therefore, when misfortune strikes, it must be because the forest is asleep. To wake up the forest, at night the women and children retire to their huts while the men make *molimo* music outside. Women are not supposed to know that the *molimo* is just a long, flutelike instrument stored in a local stream, but instead believe it to be some kind of forest animal. (In fact, women seem to know all about the *molimo*.)

As discussed in Chapter 11, men and women are usually involved in the production of different types of material items, and usually the individuals involved in production decorate the items as well. In many cases, the aesthetic qualities of the items are an integral part of the production process itself, as with the shape of a pottery vessel or metal tool, or the design in a blanket or a basket. In other instances, however, decorative arts are separate and distinct from the production of the basic item, and decorative artists may be defined by gender.

Among the Plains Indians, beadwork and quillwork were produced by women. The only men who produced beadwork and quillwork were *berdaches*, men who dressed and acted as women (see Chapter 11). Although both women and men painted hides, there were distinct differences in subject matter. Women painted only geometric designs. The hide containers called *parfleches* used for the storage of food and clothing were made by women and were painted only in geometric designs. Representational designs of people, horses, and other animals and supernatural beings were painted only by men. Tepees and buffalo robes, though made by women, were painted by either men or women, depending on whether the design was to be geometric (by women) or representational (by men).

Some visual art objects are made for specific rituals or ceremonies. Initiation rites are usually held for only one sex (see Chapter 14). The art produced for them, therefore, is sometimes "sex specific." In many cultures of the highlands of Papua New Guinea, long bamboo flutes are played at male initiation ceremonies. Women are not supposed to know about the existence of the flutes. Many initiation ceremonies also include carved and painted masks, supposedly kept secret from women and uninitiated boys.

Performance arts are often carried out during religious ceremonies. Men have historically played the dominant role in most religions. Not surprisingly, in most societies, men dominate the performance arts associated with religion. For example, even though many of the Hopi *kachinas* (spirits) are female, in *kachina* dances all dancers—even those impersonating female spirits—are male. In ancient Greek drama, the roles of women were played by men. In western Europe, women were not allowed to participate in certain performance arts long after they had become secularized. The role of Juliet, in the original productions of Shakespeare's play, was performed by a young boy because women could not be actors in Shakespeare's time. It was not until the late seventeenth century that women could perform in the English theater.

Social Functions of Art

Does art exist solely to satisfy the human desire for the aesthetic? Perhaps, but if so, why have humans expended such incredible energy in its creation? Perhaps art also has a critical role in human social life and cultural existence. Through the use of art, people can express their identities as members of particular groups, while at the same time demonstrating their individuality. Through the production, consumption, and use of art, we can express our personal individuality, our group identities (including ethnic affiliation), and even our social status.

Individuality

Many of us attempt to express our individuality by creating or displaying art, as shown by the widespread appeal of handmade goods produced by skilled craftspeople. Since the advent of the industrial revolution, the attraction of handmade over machine-made goods has been their individuality. This individuality derives not solely from the differing technical skill of the makers; it is also the result of the artists' conscious attempt to make every item unique by varying colors and designs. Thus, if one looks at Oriental rugs; Native American jewelry, pottery, and baskets; Maya textiles from Guatemala; or wood carvings from New Guinea,

Globalization and, more recently, the global economy are influencing all forms of artistic expression—body arts, visual arts, and performance arts. Increasingly, traditional art forms are being commoditized and marketed in competition with other art forms. Because this is a highly complex topic, this discussion is limited to something manageable: how integration into the market economy is affecting the traditional visual arts.

As we discussed at the beginning of this chapter, members of more developed societies commonly, though incorrectly, believe that for an object to be considered art, it can have no function other than being a decorative, aesthetically pleasing object—a painting, a sculpture, a vase, and so forth. Thus, art is sharply distinguished from that which has a utilitarian use. In contrast, in traditional societies, there are no "decorative objects": Virtually every material object has some utilitarian function, secular or religious. Thus, by necessity, artistic expression has to be incorporated into utilitarian objects—the form of and ornamentation on clothing, pottery, basketry, household items, sacred objects, tools, and weapons. However, people differ on which types of utilitarian objects are most suitable for this artistic expression.

Because religion is by nature highly conservative and less subject to change, we are going to focus on secular art. The traditional secular arts of the native peoples of the United State are an ideal example for two reasons. First, over a century ago, these peoples became integrated into an industrialized market economy. Thus, these societies have already experienced the changes that other traditional peoples in the world are only now confronting. Second, anthropologists and other scholars have studied the arts of Native American people to a greater extent than any comparable population in the world. Yet there is such complexity in the changes in Native American art that we are limiting this discussion to the changes in only two of these artistic traditions: Plains beadwork and Pueblo pottery.

Until the last decades of the nineteenth century, most Native Americans produced their own clothing and domestic goods. These items were produced by hand and usually were intended only for other family members; trade in these items was limited. The category of utilitarian goods in which their artistic traditions found their greatest expression varied regionally. Among the nomadic groups on the Great Plains, it was usually in leather goods: clothing, footwear, cradleboards, and storage and personal bags. Initially, these items were decorated with painted designs or designs made of sewn and dyed porcupine quills. Later, after they acquired European glass trade beads, beadwork became the primary means of decorating these items.

Every Plains society developed its own preferences in designs and colors. Although some were more talented and creative than others, virtually every woman, and a few men, produced beadwork. Although beaded clothing and footwear were worn daily, particularly fine items were reserved to be worn only for special occasions.

Among the Pueblo peoples of the Southwest, their greatest secular artistic expressions were found in their pottery. Settled, farming peoples, these tribes regarded pottery as extremely important in their daily lives, and they made a wide variety of different utilitarian pots: mixing bowls, serving bowls, storage jars, water ollas, water canteens, and many others. These pots were usually decorated with painted designs. Like the peoples of the Plains, every Pueblo developed its own distinctive style of pottery, and every potter attempted to develop her own. Rarely were two pots identical in their painted designs. This same basic characteristic of secular art finding its greatest expressions in only certain aspects of the utilitarian material culture is generally true for traditional, pre-industrial peoples throughout the world.

The industrial revolution, which we discussed in Chapter 4, dramatically reduced the production of individually crafted handmade domestic items in the United States and western Europe. Mills and factories mass-produced cloth, clothing, pots, pans, dishes, tools, furniture, and similar utilitarian goods. In many cases, these items were finer and more durable that handcrafted items; but in all cases, they were far less labor intensive and thus less costly.

Very quickly, manufactured goods replaced traditional handmade goods among the peoples of western Europe and the dominant society in the Americas. While the middle and lower classes could purchase mass-produced manufactured utilitarian goods from the local stores or the Sears-Roebuck catalog, the wealthier wanted something finer, something unique, something handmade. This resulted in the so-called Arts and Crafts movement, which emerged in the United States and western Europe during the late nineteenth century, producing handcrafted furniture, pottery, metalwork, and other domestic

Every summer since 1922, the Indian Market has been held in Santa Fe, New Mexico. More than any other event, this market has helped elevate the status of Pueblo pottery from curio to art form.

Robert Alexander/Getty Images

goods for the home. In other words, finely crafted, unique, handmade domestic objects, although still utilitarian, were being transformed—if not into art then at least into something different, more desirable, and certainly more expensive.

During this same period, the Native American peoples of the Plains and Pueblos saw their economies greatly altered as they became integrated into the local U.S. market economy. Machine-made mass-produced clothing and ceramic and metal pots, pans, dishes, and other household items started quickly replacing handmade pottery among the Pueblos and beaded clothing among the Plains peoples in their daily lives. Their utilitarian value greatly diminished, these items were now produced in far lower quantities— in some cases precipitously. Initially, it appeared that beadwork and pottery production among some of these societies might actually vanish, along with the art traditions associated with them. However, they were saved in part by commoditizing their art for a newly emerging market in souvenirs or curios.

The last decades of the nineteenth century witnessed the convergence of Western tourism and an increasing nostalgia for the American past. These factors, together with the prevalent belief in the "vanishing Indian," made Indian items an ideal souvenir for travelers or those who wanted mementos of the vanishing past. In this new market, Native Americans items were not being sold for utilitarian use or for their aesthetic appeal, but rather as something strange, exotic, or nostalgic. Pueblo pottery was ideally suited for this new market because pottery could be readily displayed as decorative objects on shelves or tables.

Plains beadwork was more problematic in that it could not be easily displayed; moreover, with few exceptions, tourists did not wish to dress "like an Indian." A tourist might buy a pair of beaded moccasins and wear them a few times before putting them away, but other beaded items had little appeal. A beaded cradleboard or beaded dress might have exotic appeal, but few people wanted to hang one on their wall. Plains peoples did develop a few specialty items for the non-Indian trade, such as beaded watch pockets, gauntlets, women's purses, and valises for men. However, the market for such items was small relative to the Plains population. Another factor that affected an item's marketability as a souvenir or curio was that it had to be relatively inexpensive.

Thus, the market economy had different effects on these two artistic traditions. Plains beadwork became more limited as the members of these societies made a distinction between their "daily clothes," which were mass-produced machine goods, and their beaded "Indian clothes," which were now only worn on special occasions. Production of other beaded items, such as storage bags and cradleboards, also declined or disappeared. As a result, fewer and fewer women became active beadworkers, and beadworking became a specialized occupation within the native communities, with a few individuals making and selling items to other members of the native community. Thus, the primary market for beaded items remained other natives.

In contrast, although less pottery was being used within the Pueblos, the demand for Pueblo pottery by nonnatives was dramatically increasing and changing the Pueblo pottery tradition. Pueblo potters began producing new inexpensive items for tourists. Pots became smaller, and wide variety of new forms appeared, such as pitchers, teapots, candlesticks, ashtrays, animal and human figures, cups, plates, and handled baskets. By the 1920s, a few potters, such as Maria Martinez, were beginning to be recognized for their outstanding work and began signing their names to their pottery. However, these individuals were the exception. The primary market until well after World War II was still for inexpensive curio or souvenir pots made by anonymous potters.

In the 1960s and 1970s, Native American traditional arts were redefined by the dominant society as "ethnic art," and their prices escalated; "Indian curio stores" became "Indian art galleries." The making of Indian art became so lucrative that non-Indians started producing "Indian art." In 1990, Congress passed the Indian Arts and Crafts Act, stating that only objects made by an enrolled member of a federally recognized tribe could be sold as "Indian made."

The rising value of Indian art had minimal effect on Plains beadwork, as the market remained primarily other Indians for their personal use. In contrast, Pueblo pottery has been dramatically affected. Not only could an individual earn a good living, but also a well-known potter could become relatively prosperous. Now marketed to nonnatives as art, all pieces are now signed by the potter. In attempts to gain ever-higher prices for work, in an increasingly competitive market potters have created innovative forms and decorating techniques to readily distinguish their work from that of others.

In summary, Plains beadwork and Pueblo pottery represent the two extremes of the effects of the market economy on the traditional secular art of Native American peoples. Today, most beadwork and most pottery are no longer produced by family members for family members, but by artisans for sale to others. However, these two markets are very different. Beadwork has remained an artistic tradition associated with utilitarian goods that are marketed to other members of the native community. Its daily utilitarian function has disappeared, replaced by its social function of maintaining the identity of the group. Pueblo pottery is now produced primarily as objects of decorative art for sale to nonnatives. Its daily utilitarian function has almost disappeared, superseded by its economic role as an important source of cash income. Although some pottery still strongly reflects the Pueblo artistic tradition, increasingly the pottery produced by Pueblo artisans reflects the aesthetic tastes of nonnative buyers. As a result, unlike beadwork, much of it has lost its ethnic identity; it is just "art."

The traditional visual arts of the Plains and Pueblo peoples have survived because they have become commoditized. Plains beadworkers have found a highly specialized local market: other members of their community. Pueblo potters have established a national/global market for their pottery as either art or ethnic art. As other traditional peoples throughout the world are increasingly integrated into the global market economy, their art traditions will confront similar challenges.

rarely does one find two identical items. If they are identical, it is probably because they were produced for the commercial market.

Similarly, our clothing and houses express our individuality. Even though we usually conform to the norms of our society in clothing styles, most of us abhor uniforms, and thus we enhance our clothes in some manner to make them uniquely ours. People also attempt to express their individuality in their homes. Although all Maori dwellings were carved and painted, different designs and images were used. Today in suburban North America, builders of subdivisions usually vary the houses by using a range of floor plans, building materials, and colors. Many residents of older neighborhoods, though, still think the new subdivisions lack character, style, and individuality.

Social Identity

As well as displaying our individuality, art is a means of expressing social identity: publicly displaying what kind of person you are or with which group of people you identify. In the 1960s and early 1970s, many young people wore long hair, beads, and baggy clothes decorated with peace signs and upside-down flags. Some traveled the country in old Volkswagen minibuses or school buses that were painted in strange colors and designs. The minute you saw them, you knew they were hippies. Clothing styles, hairstyles, and other art forms are commonly used to indicate social group identity— from the black leather jackets painted with club emblems of motorcycle gangs to the shepherd crook spears and red sashes of the Cheyenne Dog Soldier society.

Art is also commonly used to express social membership through ethnic affiliation. In Chapter 16, we discuss ethnic boundary markers in more detail, but here it is important to note that art often expresses ethnic identity. Clothing styles and decoration are important visual markers of ethnic identity. Plaid kilts are markers of Scots as much as beaded clothing and feather headdresses are of Native Americans. A woman in Guatemala wearing a *huipil* is a Maya. If you see a man wearing a cowboy hat and boots in Europe, you can guess that he is probably an American tourist.

Ethnicity is expressed in more than clothing. The full range of artistic forms—body, visual, and performance arts—is employed to display one's ethnic identity. Thus, we speak of ethnic art, ethnic dance, ethnic music, ethnic songs, ethnic literature, and ethnic foods. Despite our use of the word *ethnic* in such contexts, ultimately, of course, all art is ethnic art because it is associated with a specific ethnic group and everyone is a part of some ethnic group. For various reasons, people value and pay premium prices for the art produced by ethnic groups other than their own.

From an anthropological perspective, much of the multicultural movement in contemporary North America—and particularly in colleges and universities— is really about understanding and appreciating "ethnic" forms of artistic expression. When Euro-Americans talk about "other cultures," often they are referring to African, Hispanic, Asian, and other non–Euro-Americans. When they "celebrate diversity," often they are celebrating differences in literature and other forms of verbal art, interpreting graffiti as a legitimate art form, listening to African or Mexican music, eating South Asian or Vietnamese foods, and so forth. Overall, the multicultural movement has had a positive influence on intercultural tolerance and understanding. In fact, multiculturalism is part of what anthropologists have been trying to get across to their students for nearly a century. But perhaps appreciating multicultural diversity should mean far more than celebrating diversity in forms of artistic expression.

Social Status

Finally, relative social status within societies is reflected in the use of art. As discussed earlier, body arts are frequently an indicator of social status. Other art forms also indicate status. In many ranked and stratified societies, the right to use certain art forms may be tied to the property of families or status groups. Only certain individuals have the right to wear or use particular colors or designs, sing particular songs, dance particular dances, and even tell particular stories. This control over the use or performance of particular artistic expression is a symbolic indicator of individual social position within the society.

Similarly, in contemporary Western society, we use art to demonstrate our relative status. We display our status in our homes, automobiles, furnishings, and clothing, communicating to the world, "Look what we can afford to buy." We also demonstrate our status in what we hang on our walls, read, listen to, and watch. In our consumption of visual and performance arts, the evaluation, of course, is more subjective and difficult to measure. But for many people, opera, ballet, and classical music have higher status than comedy, square dancing, and country or rap music. Classical literature has higher status than romance novels, science fiction, and comic books.

1. **Discuss the disagreement over whether art is or is not a cultural universal.** All cultures have artistic objects, designs, songs, dances, and other ways of expressing their appreciation of the aesthetic. The aesthetic impulse is universal, although cultures vary in their ways of expressing it and in the social functions and cultural meanings they attach to it. However, people raised in the Western tradition are inclined to think of art as something set apart from everyday life—as when we use the phrase "fine arts"—yet we all express ourselves aesthetically in many ways, including how we dress and decorate our homes.

2. **List the various forms of body arts.** People around the world change their body's appearance by means such as physical alterations, application of body paints, tattooing, and scarification. These decorations of the body are used for a variety of purposes, including beautification, expression of individual or group identity, display of privilege or social position, and symbolic indication of social maturity.

3. **Discuss the different forms of visual arts.** In the visual arts, humankind as a whole has shown enormous creativity in form, style, design, technique, material, and many other features. Ornamentation of tools, clothing, basketry, houses, and practically all other material objects is a universal practice.

4. **Discuss the different forms of performance arts.** Performance arts include the use of sound and movement for both aesthetic and communicative purposes. In preindustrial cultures, performances of music (including song and percussion), dance, and theater often involve audience participation, as they often do in the everyday lives of people everywhere. Often, performance art is tightly integrated into a people's spiritual and religious life.

5. **Explain how art is integrated into our religious lives.** Many forms of art may have begun as sacred in that they were connected to the appeal to or worship of spiritual beings. Certainly, the religious elements of artistic expression are important not only in the history of Western art but also in the artistic traditions of people the world over. In their complex curing ceremonies, Navajo singers used both visual arts (sand paintings) and performance arts (chants/songs) in appealing to the Holy People. Distinguishing between sacred and secular art seems like a simple thing, but objects with religious significance are often used for practical purposes.

6. **Explain how gender, identity, and social status are reflected in art.** Art is connected to other social and cultural elements such as gender, identity, and status. In many societies, certain arts and art forms are associated with women and others with men. Ethnic identity is commonly expressed in art and serves as an ethnic boundary marker. Finally, within societies, relative social status is frequently expressed in the consumption of art.

16 Ethnicity and Ethnic Conflict

AHMAD AL-RUBAYE/Getty Images

The multi-sided ethnic/sectarian conflicts in Syria and Iraq demonstrate the political instability inherent in "artificial countries." Created by the French and the British out of portions of the Ottoman Empire at the end of World War I, they lack any internal socio-political cohesion.

Ethnic Groups
   Situational Nature of Ethnic Identity
   Attributes of Ethnic Groups
   Fluidity of Ethnic Groups
   Types of Ethnic Groups

Civilizations

The Problem of Stateless Nationalities
   Conflict in Northern Ireland and in Israel and Palestine

Conflict Between Ethnic Nationalities and Political Boundaries

Responses to Ethnic Conflict
   Homogenization
   Segregation
   Accommodation
   Results

Consequences of Globalization

After reading this chapter, you should be able to:

1 **DEFINE** ethnic group.

2 **EXPLAIN** what we mean when we say ethnic identity is situational.

3 **EXPLAIN** the attributes of ethnic groups.

4 **DESCRIBE** the different levels of ethnic identity.

5 **EXPLAIN** why ethnic conflict is so prevalent in the world today and describe an artificial country.

6 **EXPLAIN** ethnic homogenization.

7 **ELABORATE** on the meanings of ethnic segregation and ethnic accommodation.

With the collapse of the Soviet Union and the end of the Cold War in the 1990s, many people thought we had entered a new, safer, and more peaceful era. But instead of peace, we are now faced with growing conflicts that are becoming ever-more violent and destructive. In the past decade or so, several million people have fallen victim to wars, while tens of millions more have joined the ranks of refugees. Central governments exist in name only in parts of Africa and Asia. Large regions of some of these countries are under the control of rebel armies or outlaw groups. Concerns increase about nuclear proliferation and biological warfare. Concerns are also rising about terrorist groups and their expanding capabilities for destruction. It is not just that conflict is a problem—it is a *growing* problem. Most, but not all, of these conflicts are essentially ethnic conflicts.

Globalization has changed the nature of ethnic conflict. In the not-too-distant past, ethnic conflicts were limited to particular geographic regions or countries. With vastly improved transportation and communications systems, however, together with increasing international migrations of peoples and the emergence of ethnically mixed urban populations, conflicts are no longer geographically localized. Ethnic groups increasingly have the potential to strike their enemy anywhere in the world.

Associated with this increased capability, the tactics of ethnic guerrilla warfare also changed—from targeting primarily opposing armies and paramilitary groups to the targeting of civilian populations. The first evidence of this change came in 1972, when the Irish Republican Army began bombings in London. The following year, the Black September Organization, a Palestinian militant group, killed 11 Israeli athletes competing in the Olympic Games in Munich, Germany. Since the 1970s, many other groups have become involved in such attacks. In 1985, Sikh separatists allegedly bombed an Air India flight between Montreal and London. In 1995, Basque separatists began attacking targets throughout Spain. In 2002 and again in 2010, Chechen rebels attacked civilian targets in Moscow, almost 1,000 miles from Chechnya.

Even more frightening, globalization has also resulted in the emergence of a higher and more ominous level of ethnic identity and conflict between *civilizations*. In Samuel Huntington's terminology, a **civilization** consists of a large number of otherwise linguistically and socially distinct ethnic groups who share a common, usually religious, cultural tradition that unites them in opposition to members of ethnic groups from other civilizations (discussed further below).

By the beginning of the twenty-first century, a pan-Islamic identity had begun to emerge. The 1979 occupation of Afghanistan by the Soviet Union led to the emergence of the *mujahedeen*—a group of loosely affiliated Afghan Islamic ethnic groups and Islamic

civilization In Huntington's terms, a grouping of nationalities on the basis of a shared or common cultural historical tradition; in most cases, this shared cultural tradition takes the form of religion.

volunteers from throughout the world. In the late 1980s, Al Qaeda, a separate group of Arabic-speaking Sunni Muslims, emerged. After the withdrawal of Soviet troops in 1989, Al Qaeda, operating from Afghanistan, expanded its war against the West—carrying out terrorist attacks on New York City and Washington (2001), Madrid (2004), and London (2005).

The U.S.-led invasions of Afghanistan and Iraq, with the military support of other primarily Western countries, served to validate Al Qaeda's assertions in the minds of many Islamic peoples. The failure of the United States to reestablish a functioning central government in Iraq after the 2003 invasion resulted in a multisided civil war involving varying factions of Sunnis, Shiites, and Kurds. Al Qaeda found support among a faction of Sunni Arabs.

Al Qaeda in Iraq eventually splintered, and by 2013 the Islamic State of Iraq and Levant—ISIL—had emerged. In 2014, ISIL (or ISIS) demanded the alliance of all devout Muslims in the world, declaring a global jihad. By late 2015, having established control of much of Iraq and Syria, ISIS had a network of affiliated groups stretching from the Philippines and Malaysia; west to Algeria, Mali, and Nigeria; and south to Yemen and Somalia. With secret operatives in Europe, they staged attacks in Paris (2015), Brussels (2016), and Turkey (2016). ISIS and its affiliates have globalized the conflict—not just targeting Christians and Jews, but Hindus and Buddhists as well as Shiites and other Islamic groups whom they consider non-Muslims—in their attempt to establish a global Islamic caliphate.

Ethnic Groups

Over the past few decades, the terms *ethnic* and *ethnicity* have become part of our everyday vocabulary, as have the terms *ethnic food, ethnic vote, ethnic conflict, ethnic clothes, ethnic neighborhood,* and *ethnic studies.* In the 1960s, anthropologists began studying ethnicity as a distinct social phenomenon, and since that time literature on ethnicity has proliferated. Part of the increased scholarly interest in ethnic groups came as a result of Nathan Glazer and Daniel Moynihan's study of ethnic groups in New York City. They found that

[I]n the third generation, the descendants of the immigrants confronted each other, and knew they

were both Americans, in the same dress, with the same language, using the same artifacts, troubled by the same thing, but they voted differently, had different ideas about education and sex, and were still, in many essential ways, as different from one another as their grandfathers had been.

(Glazer & Moynihan, 1963, p. 13)

Thus, while a population may develop a new ethnic identity, in this case American, they will retain many of their earlier cultural believes and practices.

What is an ethnic group? First, it is necessary to realize that all peoples, not just minority populations, have an ethnic group identity. In essence, an **ethnic group** is a named social category of people based on perceptions of shared social experience or ancestry. Members of the ethnic group see themselves as sharing cultural traditions and history that distinguish them from other groups.

Ethnic group identity has a strong psychological or emotional component that divides the people of the world into opposing categories of "us" and "them." In contrast to social stratification (discussed in Chapter 13), which divides and unifies people along a series of horizontal axes on the basis of socioeconomic factors, ethnic identities divide and unify people along a series of vertical axes. Thus, ethnic groups, at least theoretically, cut across socioeconomic class differences, drawing members from all strata of the population.

Before discussing the significance of ethnic differences and conflicts in the modern world, we need to examine the varying dimensions of ethnic group identity, including (1) the situational nature of ethnic identity, (2) the attributes of ethnic groups, (3) the fluidity of ethnic group identity, and (4) the types of ethnic groups.

Situational Nature of Ethnic Identity

One of the more complicated aspects of ethnicity is that an individual's ethnic group identity is seldom absolute. A person may assume a number of different ethnic identities, depending on the social situation. For example, in the United States, an individual may simultaneously be an American, a Euro-American, an Italian American, and a Sicilian American. The particular ethnic identity chosen varies with the social context. When in Europe or among Europeans, the person would assume the identity of American, in contrast to German, French, or Italian. In the United States, the same individual might assume the identity of Euro-American, as opposed to African American or Native

---

ethnic group Named social group based on perceptions of shared ancestry, cultural traditions, and common history that culturally distinguish that group from other groups.

American. Among Euro-Americans, the person might take the ethnic identity of Italian American, as opposed to Irish American or Polish American. When among Italian Americans, the individual might be identified as Sicilian American, as opposed to an Italian American whose family came from Rome, Naples, or some other region of Italy.

The situational nature of ethnic identity demonstrates what some have called the **hierarchical nesting** of identity. A particular ethnic group forms part of a larger collection of ethnic groups of like social magnitude. In turn, these ethnic groups may collectively form still another higher level of ethnic identity, which may be nested in yet another higher level. Thus, ethnic identity does not simply divide the world into categories of "us" and "them" but into varying, hierarchically ranked categories of "us" and "them."

Attributes of Ethnic Groups

Two main attributes help to define and identify an ethnic group: an origin myth and ethnic boundary markers.

Origin Myth

Each ethnic group is the product of a unique set of social and historical events. The common or shared historical experiences that serve to unite and distinguish the group from other groups and give it a distinct social identity constitute the group's **origin myth**. By *myth*, we do not mean to imply that the historical events did not really happen or that the group is not what it claims to be. We mean only that these particular experiences serve as the ideological charter for the group's common identity and provide the members with a sense of being different from other people. Origin myths play an integral part in creating and maintaining ethnic group identity: They define and describe the origin and collective cultural historical experiences of the group.

Not all historical events are equally important; origin myths make selective references. Wars and conflicts are frequently emphasized because they clearly distinguish "us" from "them."

The origin myth imbues the group's members with feelings of distinctiveness and, often, superiority in relation to other groups. What makes an origin myth so powerful is that mythic themes and concepts are embedded in virtually every aspect of the people's popular culture: stories (written and oral), songs, dances, games, music, theater, film, and art. So pervasive are these mythic images in everyday life that members of the group learn them passively rather than consciously. Thus, all members of the group are well versed in the

basic tenets of the group myth, and in the minds of most, these ideas become an unquestioned truth.

In larger, more sophisticated groups, the origin myth also takes the form of a written, purportedly objective history formally taught in schools. American history as taught in elementary school and high school is not merely the objective, political history of a particular nation-state; it is also the story of the American people. Thus, it serves as the officially sanctioned origin myth of the American ethnic group. Similarly, English, French, Japanese, and Russian history as taught in their schools is the authorized origin myth of those groups.

When you realize that history as taught in schools is, in fact, the collective origin myth of the group, you realize the significance of including or excluding a particular subgroup of the population. Using American history as an example, we can see how historical events play a critical role in the emergence and definition of a distinctively American ethnic identity. Among these events are the landing of the *Mayflower*, the American Revolution, the Civil War, the westward expansion, and the world wars. Certain historical groups, such as cowboys and cavalry, are used as embodiments of American ideals and identity. Americans are the descendants of the various peoples who collectively participated in these and other group-defining events.

Thus, it is not surprising that every American subgroup is sensitive to its portrayal in these events. To African Americans, it is important that American history acknowledges that the first man to die in the American Revolution was an African American and that African Americans fought as soldiers in the Revolutionary War and Civil War, that a high percentage of cowboys were African Americans, and that African American cavalrymen played an important part in winning the West. Similarly, public acknowledgment and recognition that their groups were active participants in some, if not all, of the major defining events of American history are equally important for American populations. Although Christopher Columbus never actually saw what is today the United States, we celebrate Columbus Day, in recognition of the contributions of Italian Americans. We have monuments and

---

hierarchical nesting Occurs when an ethnic group is part of a larger collection of ethnic groups, which together constitute a higher level of ethnic identity.

origin myth Collective history of an ethnic group that defines which subgroups are part of it and its relationship to other ethnic groups.

parks recognizing the contribution of General Tadeusz Kosciuszko, the Polish volunteer who fought in the American Revolution, which serves to honor not only him but also Polish Americans. The public honoring of the Japanese American volunteers who fought in World War II is to recognize not just their individual patriotism but the patriotism of the Japanese American community in general. It is inclusion in the collective origin myth that legitimizes a people's status as members of the group.

Ethnic Boundary Markers

Every ethnic group has a way of determining or expressing membership. An overt factor used to demonstrate or denote group membership is called an **ethnic boundary marker**. Ethnic boundary markers are important not only to identify group members to one another but also to demonstrate identity to and distinctiveness from nonmembers. Because these markers distinguish members from all other groups, a single boundary marker is seldom sufficient. A marker that might distinguish one ethnic group from a second group may not distinguish it from a third group. Thus, combinations of markers have to be used. Differences in language, religion, physical appearance, or particular cultural traits may serve as ethnic boundary markers.

As we discussed in Chapter 3, speech style and language are symbols of personal identity: We send covert messages about the kind of person we are by how we speak. Language, therefore, frequently serves as an ethnic boundary marker. A person's native language is the primary indicator of ethnic group identity in many areas of the world. In the southwestern United States, Hopi and Navajo members are readily distinguished by their language alone.

However, just because two populations share a common language does not mean they share a common identity, any more than the fact that two populations speak different languages means they have two distinct identities. For example, the Serbs, Croats, and Bosniaks of what was Yugoslavia speak dialects of Serbo-Croatian. They are, however, distinct and historically antagonistic ethnic groups. Conversely, a person may be Irish and speak either Gaelic or English as a native language. At one time the German government granted automatic citizenship to ethnic German

refugees from eastern Europe, but a difficulty in assimilating these refugees was that many spoke only Polish or Russian. Thus, one does not have to speak German to be an ethnic German.

While the spoken language may not clearly distinguish two groups, the *orthography,* or written forms of the language, may. Serbo-Croatian is written using three different alphabets. The Serbs use Cyrillic, the Croatians use Roman, and the Bosniaks use Arabic characters. Yiddish spoken by the Ashkenazi Jews is basically a dialect of German. However, German is written in Roman script, while Yiddish uses the Hebrew alphabet. Urdu and Hindi are the same language, but Urdu is written in Perso-Arabic script, while Hindi is written using Nagari script.

Like language, religion may serve as an ethnic boundary marker. The major world religions—such as Christianity, Islam, and Buddhism—encompass numerous distinct groups, so that religious affiliation does not always indicate ethnic affiliation. But, in many cases, religion and ethnic group more or less correspond. The Jews may be categorized as either a religious or an ethnic group. Similarly, the Sikhs in India constitute both a religious and an ethnic group.

In still other situations, religious differences may be the most important marker of ethnic identity. As we mentioned earlier, the Serbs, Croats, and Bosniaks speak the same language; the most important distinction between these three groups is that the Serbs are Eastern Orthodox, the Croats are Catholic, and the Bosniaks are Muslim. Conversely, the Chinese ethnic identity transcends religious differences. A person is still Chinese, or Han, whether he or she is a Christian, Taoist, Buddhist, or Marxist atheist. However, Chinese Muslims, called Hui, are one of the officially recognized 56 ethnic groups of China.

Physical characteristics, or phenotypes, can sometimes indicate ethnic identity. It is impossible to identify Germans, Dutch, Danes, and other northern European ethnic groups by their physical characteristics. A similar situation is found in those regions of the world in which populations have been in long association with one another. Thus, physical characteristics do not distinguish a Zulu from a Swazi, a Chinese from a Korean, or a Choctaw from a Chickasaw.

However, with the massive movements of people, particularly over the past few hundred years, physical characteristics have increasingly emerged as a marker of ethnic identity. Members of the three major ethnic groups in Malaysia—Malays, East Indians, and Chinese—are readily distinguishable by their physical appearance. The significance or lack of significance

ethnic boundary marker Any overt characteristic that can be used to indicate ethnic group membership.

of physical characteristics in ethnic identity may also vary with the level of ethnic identity we are considering. The American identity includes virtually the full range of human physical types. However, at a lower level of identity—Euro-American, African American, and Native American—physical characteristics do serve as one marker of ethnic identity. Yet within these groups, physical characteristics alone cannot be the only marker. Some Native Americans physically look like Euro-Americans or African Americans, while some African Americans might be identified as Euro-Americans or Native Americans on the basis of their physical appearance alone.

A wide variety of cultural traits, clothing, house types, personal adornment, food, technology, economic activities, or general lifestyle may also serve as ethnic boundary markers. Over the past 100 years, a rapid homogenization of world material culture, food habits, and technology has erased many of the more overt cultural markers. Today, you do not have to be Mexican to enjoy tacos, Italian to eat pizza, or Japanese to have sushi. Similarly, you can dine on hamburgers, the all-American food, in Japan, Oman, Russia, Mexico, and most other countries. Cultural traits remain, however, the most important, diverse, and complex category of ethnic boundary markers. For the sake of brevity, we limit our discussion to one trait—clothing (see also Chapter 15).

Clothing styles have historically been the most overt single indicator of ethnic identity. Not that long ago, almost every ethnic group had its own unique style of dress. Even today, a Scottish American who wants to publicly indicate his ethnic identity can wear a kilt, and a German American may wear his lederhosen. Similarly, on certain occasions, Native Americans wear "Indian clothes" decorated with beadwork. These are not everyday garments and are worn only in social situations in which people want to emphasize their ethnic identity.

In many regions of the world, however, people still wear "ethnic" clothes every day. In highland Guatemala, clothing, particularly women's clothing, readily identifies the ethnic affiliation of the wearer. Guatemalan clothing styles actually indicate two levels of ethnic identity. If a woman wears a *huipil*, a loose-fitting blouse that slips over the head, she is a Native American. The style, colors, and designs on the *huipil* further identify where a particular woman is from: Nahuala, Chichicastenango, Solola, or one of the other hundred or so Native American communities in highland Guatemala. Ladinas, women who are not Native American, dress in Western-style clothes.

Garrick Bailey

The dress of this woman not only identifies her as a Maya Indian but also indicates that she is from the town of Santa Maria Nebaj in Guatemala.

Fluidity of Ethnic Groups

Ethnic groups are not stable groupings. Ethnic groups vanish, individuals and even communities change ethnic identities, and new ethnic groups come into existence.

During the past 500 years, numerous ethnic groups have vanished. Massachusetts, Erie, and Susquehannock were not originally place names but the names of now vanished Native American ethnic groups. Still other ethnic groups in Asia, Africa, Oceania, Europe, and the Americas have vanished as well.

Extinction of an ethnic group seldom means biological extinction, though. In most cases, the members of one group are absorbed into the population of a larger group. The Tasmanians of Australia are typical of what happened to many smaller ethnic groups. Numbering at most 5,000 when the British began colonizing the island of Tasmania in 1802, the population was so ravaged by wars and massacres that only a handful survived by 1850; the Tasmanians as a viable ethnic group had ceased to exist. In 1869, the last full-blooded Tasmanian man died, and in 1888, the last full-blooded Tasmanian woman died. Even today, however, mixed-blood descendants of the Tasmanians can be found among the Australian population.

Both individuals and communities can move between ethnic groups. During the sixteenth and seventeenth centuries, French Protestants, called Huguenots, fled persecution in France and settled in large numbers in England and the English colonies in North America. These people quickly became absorbed into the English population. Over the past 200 years, Americans have absorbed numerous immigrant populations.

Ethnogenesis is the emergence of a new ethnic group. Ethnogenesis usually occurs in one of two ways: (1) A portion of an existing ethnic group splits away and forms a new ethnic group, or (2) members of two or more existing ethnic groups fuse to form a new ethnic group.

Probably the most common cause of ethnogenesis is the division of an existing ethnic group. At one time, the Osage, Kansa, Omaha, Ponca, and Quapaw Indians of the central United States were a single ethnic group. The origin myths of these peoples tell how at different times portions broke away, until there were five distinct groups. In the 1700s, small groups of Muskogee/Creek Indians began moving south into Florida, where they eventually developed a distinct identity as the Seminole. Similarly, as Bantu-speaking peoples spread throughout Central and southern Africa, they became separated, and new ethnic groups formed. As the Spanish empire in the Americas disintegrated during the early 1800s, new regional ethnic identities (such as Mexican, Guatemalan, Peruvian, and Chilean) began to emerge among the Spanish-speaking peoples in that region. In 1652, the Dutch began settling near the Cape of Good Hope in southern Africa. These people eventually developed their own distinctive dialect of Dutch, called Afrikaans, and their own ethnic identity: Boers.

In other cases, members of two or more ethnic groups fuse, and a new ethnic identity emerges. In Chapter 4 we discussed the Saramaka and the Garifuna; there are countless more. In England, the Angles, the Saxons, and the Jutes merged and became known as the English. Furthermore, the original Euro-American

ethnic group was not the result of a split among the English people but rather a fusion of English, Dutch, German, Scots, Irish, French Huguenots, Scots-Irish, and other European settlers residing on the coast of North America. Most African American groups in the Americas are the result of the fusion of numerous distinct African groups. Intermarriage between French traders and Native Americans in Canada resulted in the emergence of the Métis—a socially and culturally distinct population. Similarly, in South Africa, the Cape Coloureds, a people of mixed Dutch and Khoikhoi ancestry, are socially and politically distinct from both whites and Africans.

Types of Ethnic Groups

From our discussion and examples so far, it should be apparent that the term *ethnic group* covers a range of social groupings. In general, ethnic groups fall into two main categories: national and subnational.

A **nationality** is an ethnic group that claims exclusive rights to a discrete geographic region, which is its **homeland**. Implicit in this concept is the assumption of an inherent right to political autonomy and self-determination. In contrast, a **subnationality** lacks the concept of a distinct and separate homeland and the associated rights to separate political sovereignty and self-determination. A subnational group sees itself as a dependent and politically subordinate subset of a nationality.

Although it is easy to define the difference between ethnic nationalities and subnationalities, it may be far more difficult to classify particular groups. The ethnic groups in the United States demonstrate some of the classification challenges. With some ethnic groups, there is no doubt: Italian Americans, German Americans, Polish Americans, Scottish Americans, and Irish Americans are all subnational groups. At another level of identity, the same is true for African Americans. None of these groups has a concept of a distinct and separate geographic homeland within the United States. Hence, they are subnational groups that, together with many other groups, collectively constitute the American ethnic nationality.

For other ethnic groups within the United States, their status is not as clear. What is the status of Native American groups such as the Navajo, the Hopi, the Cheyenne, and the Cherokee? These groups have historic homelands within the United States. They also have histories quite distinct from those of other Americans. In recent years, they have been asserting increased political autonomy and self-determination within their

ethnogenesis Creation of a new ethnic group.

nationality Ethnic group that claims a right to a discrete homeland and to political autonomy and self-determination.

homeland Geographic region over which a particular ethnic group feels it has exclusive rights.

subnationality Dependent subgroup within a larger nationality that lacks the concept of a separate homeland and makes no claim to any inherent right to political autonomy and self-determination.

reservations or what were their reservations. Although there is disagreement, many Native American individuals and groups still consider themselves distinct nationalities. For example, many Iroquois in the United States and Canada still see themselves as members of a distinct and sovereign nation, even issuing their own passports. The U.S. government recognizes most American Indian groups as distinct groups with collective legal and political rights. No other ethnic groups in the United States have officially recognized governments and limited rights of self-determination.

There are also some differences of opinion concerning the ethnic status of Spanish-speaking people in the southwestern United States. Until the mid–nineteenth century, Texas, New Mexico, Arizona, and California were part of Mexico, when the United States acquired this region through military conquest. Most of the native Spanish-speaking people in this region think of themselves as Mexican American or Spanish American or Hispanic—a subnational group. There is, however, a group who sees themselves as Mexicans living in a land that is rightfully part of Mexico, in a region they call Atzlán.

The distinction between nationality and subnational ethnic group is important because of their different political implications. As we shall see, the demands of subnational groups for equal rights and treatment have long been a source of conflict in countries such as the United States. However, these groups compete within the existing political framework. In contrast, the demands of nationalities for independence and sovereignty create major political problems.

Civilizations

There are higher levels of identity than ethnic nationalities. (The Concept Review outlines a hierarchy of ethnic identity.) There are identities that create aggregates of ethnic groups for joint action. Just like with ethnic groups, these identities divide the world into larger groupings of "us" and "them." Frequently these identities are based on speaking a common language, which is the result of a partially shared history. Not surprisingly, when in conflict with other peoples, the Americans, Canadians, English, Australians, New Zealanders, and other English-speaking peoples are usually supportive of one another. The reason is not just that these groups share a common language but that they also share common cultural values, norms, and worldview as well. Thus, they understand each other better that they understand other people. The same is true of Spanish-speaking peoples in Latin America, Arabic-speaking peoples in North Africa and the Middle East, and Turkic-speaking peoples in the Middle East and Central Asia, to note only a few examples.

There is, however, still a higher level that Samuel Huntington, one of America's foremost political scientists, noted in his widely read book, *The Clash of Civilizations and the Remaking of World Order*. As mentioned at the beginning of the chapter, Huntington sees the world coalescing into seven or eight *civilizations*, which he identifies as Western (Protestant-Catholic), Slavic-Orthodox (Christians), Confucian, Japanese, Islamic, Hindu, Latin American, and possibly African. Huntington argues that increasing contact between peoples is not serving to lessen cultural differences, but rather to make people more acutely aware of those cultural factors that divide them. People are increasingly identifying with others of like cultural heritage. The result is a political realignment based on cultural heritage, or "civilizations."

To Huntington, religious traditions indicate fundamental cultural differences between peoples, and religion forms the cultural core of what he calls civilizations. Huntington does not see the coalescence of civilizations as replacing existing ethnic identities or ending internal conflicts. He does, however, see these various civilizations increasingly competing with one

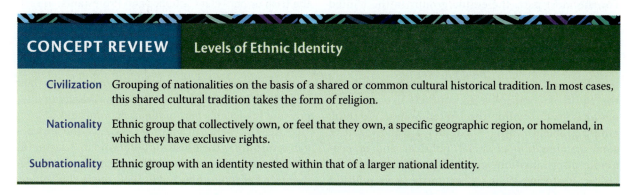

CONCEPT REVIEW   Levels of Ethnic Identity

Civilization	Grouping of nationalities on the basis of a shared or common cultural historical tradition. In most cases, this shared cultural tradition takes the form of religion.
Nationality	Ethnic group that collectively own, or feel that they own, a specific geographic region, or homeland, in which they have exclusive rights.
Subnationality	Ethnic group with an identity nested within that of a larger national identity.

another and the boundaries separating these civilizations becoming the "fault lines" along which future conflicts will occur. Ethnic and ideological wars will be superseded by wars between civilizations; the most imminent of these clashes is between Western and Islamic civilizations, which we discussed at the start of this chapter.

Most anthropologists see problems with Huntington's concept. One of the main problems is with his definition of the "seven or eight" civilizations. Should Japanese be considered a separate civilization, or is it a part of a larger East Asian civilization? Should Western and Slavic-Orthodox be two separate civilizations or one Christian civilization? Should Latin American be separate from Western? On the other hand, he seems to be correct in his assertion that increased contact is resulting in a heightened awareness of cultural similarities and differences between peoples. All other things being equal, ethnic groups have a tendency to identify with groups most like themselves. For lack of a better term, we can apply the word *civilization* to the larger aggregates of ethnic nationalities. However, it is not clear how many such civilizations exist and which ethnic nationalities belong to these aggregates.

The Problem of Stateless Nationalities

It is difficult for most Americans to understand the causes and bitterness of ethnic conflict in other parts of the world. We think of *nationality* and *nation* as one and the same. An American is any person who is a citizen of the United States. Most of us think of ourselves primarily as Americans and only secondarily as Irish, Italian, or Japanese Americans.

This mindset about the meaning and significance of ethnicity is due mainly to our history as a nation of immigrants; with the exception of Native Americans, most immigrants renounced their claims to their national homelands when they came to the New World. For the most part, the ethnic groups in the United States are subnationalities, not nationalities. Thus, from our common perception, a Russian is a person from Russia, a Nigerian is a citizen from Nigeria, and so forth. Equating country of origin with ethnic nationality, we view ethnic conflicts in other regions of the world as comparable to conflicts between subnational groups within the United States. We think ethnic problems within a country are the result of some combination of social, political, and/or economic discrimination—resolvable and reparable by political reforms—and we minimize their political

significance. However, armed ethnic conflicts are not between subnational groups but between distinct nationalities. Let's take a closer look at two particularly contentious trouble spots: the conflicts in Northern Ireland and those between Israel and Palestine.

Conflict in Northern Ireland and in Israel and Palestine

In 1922, after several centuries of British colonial domination and periodic rebellions by the native Irish, the Irish Free State (now the Republic of Ireland) was established. Not all of Ireland was given independence, however. In the seventeenth century, to control the Irish, the British evicted Irish farmers from the northernmost portion of the island and colonized the region with Scottish Presbyterians, who became known as the Ulster Scots, or Scots-Irish in the United States.

The Ulster Scots did not identify themselves as Irish and had no desire to become part of an independent Ireland. Recognizing the wishes of the Ulster Scots, at independence in 1922, the British partitioned the island. The northern six counties became Northern Ireland and remained part of the United Kingdom. Many Irish did not and do not accept the legality of this partitioning of Ireland. To them, Northern Ireland is part of the Irish homeland and thus should be part of the Republic of Ireland. In 1968, the Irish Republican Army (IRA), a secretive guerrilla army that is illegal in the Republic of Ireland, began waging a guerrilla war with the objective of reuniting Northern Ireland with the Republic of Ireland. Bombings, ambushes, and assassinations claimed more than 2,200 lives before the IRA announced in 2005 that it would end its military operations. Several splinter groups have still not agreed, and sporadic bombings and shootings still occur.

The news media frequently report the problems in Northern Ireland as conflict between the British and the Irish or between Catholics and Protestants; in reality, it is neither. The root of the problem is the clashing claims of two rival and hostile ethnic groups: the Irish and the Ulster Scots. The Ulster Scots, or Scots-Irish, have emerged over the past 400 years as a distinct nationality who claim the northern part of Ireland as their homeland. In contrast, the Irish see the area as an integral and inalienable part of the Irish homeland.

After an absence of almost 2,000 years, the Jews began returning to their historic homeland in Palestine in 1882. During the early twentieth century, Jewish settlements in Palestine grew, and in 1948, the Jewish settlers proclaimed the state of Israel. In the war that followed, the Arab League (Jordan, Egypt, Syria, and Iraq) was defeated, and the Israelis gained control over most of the area west of the Jordan River and the Sinai. Periodic fighting continued, however. The 1967 Six Day War resulted in the Israeli occupation of the Palestinian areas of the West Bank and the Gaza Strip, but it did not bring an end to the fighting. For the past 75 years, conflict between Israelis and Palestinians has been constant, varying only in the intensity and the nature of the violence. The problem is similar to the problem in Northern Ireland: two nationalities—Israelis and Palestinians—claiming the same geographic region as their legitimate homeland.

Although some progress has been made recently toward peaceful settlements of the conflicts in Northern Ireland and between Israelis and Palestinians, such agreements are tenuous. These situations remain volatile. In Israel and Northern Ireland, it is impossible to resolve the conflict to the total satisfaction of both nationalities.

Conflict Between Ethnic Nationalities and Political Boundaries

These conflicts in Northern Ireland and Israel/Palestine vividly illustrate the strength of nationalist sentiments. In both cases, we see groups of educated, rational human beings willing to sacrifice their lives and economic well-being in unending conflicts for what they consider their nationality's legitimate political rights. Such conflicts are more common in the modern world than most of us realize. The world is divided into about 200 countries, but there are 3,000 to 5,000 distinct ethnic nationalities. As a result, the populations of most countries encompass many distinct nationalities. China officially recognizes 56 distinct nationalities. Some estimates are as high as 300 ethnic nationalities in Indonesia. Ethiopia has at least 70 nationalities. Only a handful of countries are peopled by members of a single nationality and are thus ethnically homogeneous.

The ethnic nationality problem is further complicated because current political boundaries frequently divide members of a nationality and their historic homelands. For example, Hungarians are found not only in Hungary but also in the adjacent portions of Romania and Serbia. Somalis live not only in Somalia but also in the neighboring regions of Ethiopia and Kenya. The world is filled with ethnic groups who do not fully recognize the legitimacy of "their" central government and who aspire or may potentially aspire to political sovereignty or unification with another country.

For the most part, nationality problems were not created by the nationalities themselves. As we discussed in Chapter 4, the current political boundaries for most of the world are legacies of European colonialism and expansion, drawn by Europeans for their own interests with little regard for the interests of any indigenous peoples or the boundaries of the ethnic groups affected. As a result, most European colonial possessions were a polyglot of ethnic groups, many of whom had long histories of hostilities toward one another. Sometimes the land and people of an ethnic group were divided between two or more European colonies. To make matters worse, colonial powers frequently moved people from one colony to another to supply labor. For example, the British settled Indian laborers in Burma (Myanmar), Malaya (Malaysia), Fiji, Ceylon (Sri Lanka), Kenya, Uganda, South Africa, Trinidad, and British Guiana (Guyana).

The end of the colonial period did not end the ethnic conflicts in the world. As European powers granted independence to their colonies, they made little attempt to redefine political boundaries. In most cases, these newly independent countries had the same boundaries and ethnic composition as the former colonies. Because these political divisions were imposed from the outside by European military power, some scholars have termed such a former colony an **artificial country**, a country with no historic political cohesion. For many ethnic groups, independence only meant that their European colonial rulers were replaced by a new set of rulers who in many cases belonged to ethnic groups with whom they were historical hostile.

One rare effort by a colonial power to redefine the political boundaries of a colony to avoid internal conflicts occurred with the partitioning of India by the British in 1947. British India consisted of several hundred distinct ethnic groups as well as two major religious divisions. India did not exist—and had never existed—as a unified country before British domination. As independence approached in the 1940s, hostilities between rival Muslim and Hindu factions became so intense that British officials decided that a unified, independent India was impossible.

They determined that India had to be divided into two countries: India (predominantly Hindu) and Pakistan (predominantly Muslim). The problem was the lack of clear geographic boundaries separating

artificial country Multinationality country created by external powers; usually applied to a former colony.

Although one might assume this picture is of somewhere in South Asia, this Hindu temple is in Middlesex County, New Jersey.

Today over 215 million people, or 3 percent of the world population, live in a country other than the one in which they were born—a much higher percentage than at any other time in human history. The global economy has changed the patterns of migration. Between 1500 and World War II, most migration was from Europe and Africa to the Americas. While the Americas, particularly the United States, are still a major destination for migrants, most of the migrants to the United States are now from Asia and Latin America.

transnational Member of an ethnic community living outside his or her country of origin.

For the first time, Europe has become a major destination for migrants from Asia and Africa. Within Asia, the Persian Gulf states have become a destination for migrants from South and Southeast Asia.

Not only has the magnitude and direction of human migration changed and increased, but the nature of the new overseas ethnic communities formed by these migrants has changed as well. We have seen the increasing development of what some are calling **transnational** ethnic communities. However, it is important to note than not all immigrants form transnational communities, and such communities have existed throughout history. It is the number and importance of these communities that have increased significantly in recent decades.

Transnational ethnic communities are communities of a particular ethnic group that are geographically scattered. Some members of the group remain within the home country; others live in ethnic enclaves in other countries and frequently on other continents.

Unlike earlier immigrant groups to the Americas and even most immigrants today, members of these ethnic enclaves maintain their social boundaries, their languages, and their religious and cultural traditions. They are not attempting to assimilate into the new neighboring populations. They do not subordinate their ethnic or their political identities to that of the dominant ethnic group among whom they live or to their country of residence. They have a tendency to either directly or indirectly be involved in the politics of their homeland. Economically, they are only partially integrated into the economy where they live, frequently sending money to relatives who remain at "home" and owning homes and even businesses in their home country. This feeling of primary identity with their ancestral homeland and ethnic group persists even among their descendants who were born overseas. Why is this

phenomenon more prevalent today than in the past?

First, it is natural for an individual to be proud of his or her ethnic group. It is also natural for individuals to feel more social cohesion with other individuals whose cultural behaviors and practices they understand and with whom they share basic beliefs. It is an unusual individual who totally rejects his or her native ethnic community and joins another. Thus, not surprisingly, immigrant ethnic groups tend to settle together and form enclaves.

Contemporary immigrant groups fall into two major categories: economic immigrants and political refugees. Political refugees are not voluntary immigrants. They have relocated from their home country for only one reason—they had to. Few political refugees move to another country with the idea that they are going to remain there permanently; their intention is to eventually return. Thus, they create transnational communities. However, only a small portion of immigrants are political refugees. The vast majority are economic immigrants.

Americans have a tendency to misjudge the motives of economic immigrants. In our folk mythology, we commonly see these people as coming to America in search of "a new life" and not just economic opportunity. This myth is only partially correct. Many of the European immigrants during the late nineteenth and early twentieth centuries did reject their homeland. Many would not even have their children learn their ancestral language. They wanted them to be "Americans." However, the myth is based on those immigrants who stayed. Although there are no official records, it appears that perhaps one-third of the European immigrants returned to Europe; during the Great Depression of the 1930s, more immigrants returned to Europe than came from Europe. A high percentage of economic immigrants have always come for economic opportunity, with the ultimate objective of eventually returning to their homeland.

There are political as well as social and cultural reasons that transnational communities have proliferated during the last 50 or so years. It is important to remember that Canada and the United States are the most predisposed of developed countries to attempt to socially and politically integrate immigrants. Although most European countries have naturalization programs for immigrants, they are more stringent, and in most cases, the children of noncitizens born within their borders are not given automatic citizenship. For the millions of residents from South and Southeast Asia living in the Persian Gulf states, there is no choice—they are never going to be socially or politically integrated into the local Arab population. They are guest and foreign workers and will always remain such. It is expected that they will eventually return home.

The main barrier to the integration of recent immigrants to the United States and Canada is the degree of social and culture difference. In the century prior to World War II, the greatest immigration to these countries was from Europe. These immigrants were overwhelmingly Christians and Jews, just like the dominant populations of their home countries. In addition, although unlike the dominant population, most were from eastern and southern Europe, and they still shared the same basic Western cultural beliefs and values. In contrast, many of the more recent immigrants to Europe and the United States and Canada are from very different cultural traditions and religions. Many are Muslim, Buddhist, and Hindu. Religion and culture tend to more sharply socially segregate and distinguish them from the members of the dominant society, making assimilation more difficult.

Finally, earlier immigrants had difficulty maintaining social and economic contact with their family and friends in their homelands. The postal service and the trans-Atlantic or trans-Pacific telephone services were slow and expensive—even if family members or friends back home had access to phone service. Travel home by boat was slow and expensive (if they could afford it). Thus, once in the Americas, contact with their native communities was limited, and over time it eroded.

Recent advances in communications and transportation technology have changed this scenario dramatically. Today—thanks to e-mail, Facebook, Twitter, Skype, iPhones, and cell phones—communication with distant family and friends is quick and inexpensive. Money transfers can be made electronically, while legal documents can be faxed or scanned. In addition, thanks to the Internet, one can be well informed about news and events at home, and air travel is quick and relatively inexpensive if one wants to visit home.

There has been still another important change in the immigrant population. Before World War II, most immigrants were poor unskilled or semiskilled laborers or farmers. Today, a growing portion of this population consists of highly educated and technologically skilled individuals: MDs, PhDs, teachers, engineers, accountants, health professionals, and even business and financial managers and executives.

What is happening is that ethnic groups are being geographically dispersed. Most will remain in the home community, while others will live in scattered enclaves in different countries throughout the world. Thanks to modern information technology, they can remain in constant social contact—not only with family and friends in their home community, but with family and friends in other scattered enclaves as well. Individuals can readily travel between these communities for business, weddings, funerals, and other events. Among many of these groups, marriages are arranged with individuals back home or in other enclaves. Money also readily flows between members in these dispersed communities for economic support and business investments.

Despite being geographically separated, the members of the ethnic group thus maintain their collective social and economic cohesiveness and solidarity. Unlike past immigrations, ethnic identity is not being changed or eroded. Many ethnic nationalities are becoming globalized. This globalization has many consequences. Nonresident members of these groups are an important source of the capital and technical expertise needed for the economic development of the home community, which is usually less developed. At the same time, nonresident members of some stateless ethnic groups are frequently the source of money and material support for secessionist movements in their homelands.

Involvement of nonresident immigrants in the politics of their homeland is not new or unexpected. In the early twentieth century, for example, Irish immigrants and their children in the United States were an important source of money, guns, and volunteers for the Irish Republican Army in their revolt against British rule; and the first president of the new Republic of Ireland was Éamon de Valera, who was born in New York City.

these groups; in many regions, the populations were mixed Hindu and Muslim. An East Pakistan and a West Pakistan were carved out on either side, separated by 1,000 miles of what was to be India. However, the princely state of Kashmir was not partitioned because while the vast majority of the population was Muslim, wealthy Hindu owned most of the land, and the ruler was a Sikh. Thus, the future status of Kashmir was left undetermined.

After the official announcement of the boundaries, massive migrations began as millions of Muslims and Hindus found themselves on the wrong sides of the borders. (See the Global Challenges and Opportunities feature for more about transnational ethnic communities.) Extremists on both sides stimulated these migrations, by massacring Muslims living in what was to become India and Hindus in what was to become Pakistan. Some estimate that as many as 1 million people were killed in these riots. The granting of actual independence to the two countries in 1947 made the situation worse because of the Kashmir question. The new Indian army quickly occupied Kashmir, and the first India-Pakistan war broke out. This war formally ended in 1949, with most of Kashmir occupied by India. However, the Kashmir issue is far from settled as a militant Muslim activist movement still exists, and Pakistani and Indian troops still occasionally exchange gunfire.

The creation of two separate states out of British India addressed—but did not solve—only one of the region's ethnic/religious problems. The day before independence, the Naga people in India's easternmost Assam province declared an independent Nagaland. In 1963, the Indian government, in an attempt to pacify the Naga secessionists, created the new state of Nagaland with limited autonomy. However, periodic armed clashes still occurred between Naga nationalists and Indian authorities.

More recently, a Sikh separatist movement emerged, demanding an independent Khalistan in Punjab. The violent tactics of the Sikh nationalists resulted in the Indian army attacking the holiest Sikh religious shrine, the Golden Temple in Amritsar, in 1984. Later that year, two Sikhs assassinated Indira Gandhi, the prime minister of India, causing more violence between Sikhs and Hindus. In 1985, Sikh militants bombed an Air India flight en route between Montreal and London.

A militant Sikh separatist movement continues today although most of its active members live in communities outside India. In addition, there are active separatist movements among the Bodo, Gurkha, Tripuri, and Tamil. In addition to these problems with India's religious and ethnic minorities, Hindu extremists are becoming increasingly hostile to non-Hindu minorities.

Pakistan has also experienced internal ethnic difficulties. Historically, both parts of Pakistan were, and are, Muslim, but there were major ethnic differences between the two. East Pakistanis were predominantly Bengali; West Pakistan was more heterogeneous ethnically but dominated by the Punjabi. Although West Pakistan had a smaller population, the capital was located there after independence, and the Punjabi gained dominance in the government and the military. In West Pakistan, the Balochi, who sought an independent Balochistan soon after independence, started a separatist movement. However, the first major conflict emerged with the Bengalis in East Pakistan. Although the Bengalis were economically exploited and discriminated against, it was not until the government attempted to impose the Urdu language in the schools of East Pakistan that the situation came to a head. In 1971, the East Pakistanis revolted and, after a short but bloody war aided by India, succeeded in establishing the state of Bangladesh.

The independence of Bangladesh did not totally solve its ethnic problems for its Bengali majority. The tribal peoples of the Chittagong Hill Tracts now have a militant separatist movement. Nor did the separation of Bangladesh end the ethnic problems of present-day Pakistan. The government and the military are still controlled by Punjabi, who constitute about 45 percent of the population. There are active nationalism movements among both the Balochi and the Sindhi peoples.

However, the greatest potential internal ethnic threat in Pakistan is with the Pushtun, who constitute over 15 percent of the population concentrated along the border with Afghanistan. Since the mid–eighteenth century, the Pushtun have politically dominated Afghanistan, which is a de facto Pushtun state. The present border was created by the British in 1893 and inherited by Pakistan in 1947. The border politically divides the Pushtun peoples, about one-third of whom live in Afghanistan and two-thirds in Pakistan. Neither the Pushtun nor the government of Afghanistan fully acknowledges this border. The Pushtun are a tribal people known for their military prowess, and neither the British nor the Pakistani governments have ever attempted to bring them under their direct political control. Nor has Pakistan, like the British before them, attempted to fully control the border. Following the British pattern, the Pushtun tribal areas in Pakistan along the border are designated as either Federally Administered Tribal Areas or

Provincially Administered Tribal Areas. These areas are and have been politically autonomous.

During the period of Soviet military occupation of Afghanistan from 1979 to 1989, many Afghan Pushtuns took refuge among the Pushtuns in Pakistan. From bases in these areas, Pushtun leaders organized and equipped the Pushtun *mujahedeen* militias to fight the Soviets. In the civil wars that followed the Soviet withdrawal, the Taliban, an ethnically Pushtun religious political movement, gained control of most of Afghanistan and gave sanctuary to Al Qaeda, a pan-Islamic group who had supported them in their war with the Soviets.

On September 11, 2001, Al Qaeda staged their attack on the World Trade Center and the Pentagon. In response, the United States attacked Afghanistan. Defeated, the Taliban and Al Qaeda took refuge in the Pushtun tribal areas of Pakistan. It is from these bases in the tribal areas that the Taliban are now staging their attacks on NATO and government forces in Afghanistan. As long as the Taliban are able to operate with impunity from their bases in Pakistan, the conflict in Afghanistan can continue indefinitely. Under pressure from the United States, the Pakistani army has staged limited attacks on Taliban bases, and the Taliban have responded with terrorist attacks in Pakistan. The vast majority of Pushtun tribal groups appear either neutral or anti-Taliban. The fear is that if the Pakistani army invades the tribal areas, it would result in the Taliban becoming a Pushtun nationalist movement, which would greatly increase the scope and complexity of the present conflict.

British India was by far the largest and most ethnically complex of the former European colonial possessions. Similar secessionist movements have taken place and are still occurring throughout the old colonial world—the Muslim ethnic groups on Mindanao in the Philippines, the Acehnese and Papuan peoples in Indonesia, the Karen and Kachin peoples in Myanmar (Burma), the Bakongo peoples in the Cabinda portion of Angola, the Tuareg in Mali and Niger, and the Lozi in Namibia, to name only some.

Two major secessionist movements have been crushed in bloody wars: the Tamils in Sri Lanka and the Igbo in Nigeria. In addition to the Bengalis in Bangladesh, two separatist movements have been successful in gaining independence: South Sudan and Eritrea. In other places, such as Rwanda and Burundi, conflict between rival ethnic groups has resulted in massive genocide. Certainly, it is facile to lay all the blame on colonialism for these and other conflicts in the postcolonial era. But it is undeniable that violence between ethnic nationalities, each believing its political and territorial claims are legitimate, is one of colonialism's most unfortunate and long-lasting legacies.

Not all ethnic conflicts are confined to the old colonial world, however. For example, the Kurds (who live in the mountainous regions of Turkey, Iraq, Iran, and Syria) have had an active separatist movement since the 1960s. At different times, they have fought the Turks, the Iraqis, the Iranians, and, more recently, ISIS. Another example is between China and Tibet. In 1950, China invaded and occupied Tibet, a region that the Chinese consider part of China. A Tibetan revolt in 1959 was crushed, but Tibetans still seek political autonomy under the Dalai Lama, their spiritual leader.

Recently, some of the most violent ethnic conflicts have been in Europe and the former Soviet Union. In the early 1990s, Yugoslavia disintegrated as the republics of Slovenia, Croatia, Bosnia, and Macedonia proclaimed their independence. Yugoslavia was reduced to only two of the former six republics: Serbia and Montenegro. Hundreds of thousands of ethnic Serbs found themselves living in Croatia and Bosnia. Supported by the Serb-controlled Yugoslavian army, Serb nationalists in Croatia and Bosnia rebelled, took control of regions in both republics, and demanded unification with Serbia. With more than 100,000 dead and more than 1 million homeless, the war in Bosnia has been the bloodiest and most destructive war in Europe since World War II. In 1995, the Bosniaks, Croats, and Serbs reached an agreement. Fighting stopped, and NATO troops occupied zones between the warring factions.

Ethnic conflict spread to the Kosovo province of Serbia in 1998, when the Albanian majority in the province organized the Albanian Liberation Army and called for an independent Kosovo. Attempts by the Serbs to crush the rebellion resulted in armed intervention by NATO forces in 1999 and the military occupation of the province. In 2000, ethnic conflict spread to Macedonia as Albanian nationalists rebelled against Macedonian control of their regions of the country. NATO peacekeepers are today in Macedonia. The question remains whether long-term workable political solutions can be found for the ethnic problems in Bosnia, Kosovo, and Macedonia.

This is only a sampling of armed nationalist conflicts. Nationalist movements are difficult to defuse. In most cases, the recognized national governments lack the military resources to fully defeat them. Even when a government has overwhelming resources, such as the British in Northern Ireland, guerrilla wars are difficult to win decisively. As a result, few separatist movements have been extinguished. In some cases, the central governments have either disintegrated or lost control over most of the country. In other cases, the central governments have adopted policies of geographic containment and lessening of direct conflict.

A graphic example of this containment approach is in Western Sahara, formerly Spanish Sahara. In the early 1970s, Spain committed itself to a policy of independence and self-determination for its colony. However, in 1976, before independence was achieved, Morocco occupied the northern portion of the region, claiming it was historically part of Morocco. In 1979, Morocco occupied the southern portion of the region. The Spanish did not resist the Moroccan occupation. But the local Sahrawi population rejected Moroccan domination, formed the Polisario Front, and started a guerrilla war. Unable to defeat the guerrillas but unwilling to withdraw, the Moroccan government partitioned the region with a 2,500-kilometer-long sand "wall" equipped with electronic devices to detect movements; the purpose of the wall was to separate the portion Morocco controlled from the area it did not control. In 1989, the Moroccan government agreed to a referendum sponsored by the United Nations, but as of today, the future of Western Sahara has yet to be resolved.

Almost yearly the number of unresolved ethnic conflicts increases, and the number of peoples and regions affected widens. There are about 150 ongoing armed conflicts in the world today, and the majority of these may be classified as nationalist movements. Central governments as a whole have been unsuccessful in achieving complete military victories over separatist groups, but nationalist separatist groups themselves seldom have been successful in achieving political victories.

Bangladesh was recognized by the United Nations only because it was a *fait accompli,* backed by the overwhelming military support of India. In contrast, the United Nations was extremely slow to extend recognition to Slovenia and Croatia. Only when it appeared that Yugoslavia might militarily intervene did the United Nations act, and then only in hopes of preventing a war. The recent problems of chaos and starvation in Somalia have been limited to the southern portion of the country. When the central government of Somalia disintegrated in 1991, the leaders in the north declared their independence and established their state of Somaliland. Although Somaliland is politically stable, it has yet to be granted recognition by any country. The United Nations and the Organization of African Unity (OAU) have taken the position that northern and southern Somalia will "remain" united, and they act as if no government exists in the north.

One may well ask why separatist movements are seldom extended official recognition. In Chapter 1, Article 1, of the Charter of the United Nations, the right of a people to self-determination is recognized. The United Nations, however, also recognizes the sovereignty and territorial integrity of existing states. Thus, recognition of a secessionist group would be considered intervention in the affairs of a sovereign member state.

Other governments have also pledged not to recognize separatist states. In 1964, the OAU adopted the policy that "the borders of African States on the day of independence constitute a tangible reality," and thus it firmly opposes any changes in the political boundaries of Africa. The real, unstated reason is that almost every country in the world has one or more minority nationalities that either have or potentially may develop an independence movement. Therefore, existing countries make both formal and informal agreements to maintain the political status quo.

However, in Sudan an exception was made. In the 1980s conflict arose between the Arabic Islam peoples of northern Sudan and the non-Muslim Nilotic peoples of the south. After a bloody war, the new country of South Sudan was established and recognized by both the UN and the OAU in 2011.

Responses to Ethnic Conflict

How do countries respond to internal ethnic conflicts? The most obvious solution is to divide the country, giving the members of each dissatisfied nationality their own land and independence and allowing them to establish their own country or merge with another country. Peaceful solutions to ethnic questions are rare, however. Most governments would rather fight a long, destructive, and inclusive war than officially recognize the independence of a rebellious nationality. Governments take this stance partly because they fear setting a precedent. As a result, most ethnic conflicts have been resolved—and future solutions will probably have to be sought—within the existing political structure.

Historically, such internal responses to ethnic issues have taken three forms: (1) ethnic homogenization of the population through the elimination of rival ethnic groups, (2) segregation of ethnic groups, and (3) political accommodation of ethnic groups.

Genocide is a frequent consequence of ethnic conflict. Here, forensic experts uncover the bodies of Bosniaks murdered by Serbs after the capture of Srebrenica in 1995.

Homogenization

Ethnic homogenization is the process by which one ethnic group attempts to eliminate rival ethnic groups within a particular region or country. Historically, ethnic homogenization has taken one of two main forms: ethnic cleansing or assimilation. The term *ethnic cleansing* entered our vocabulary in reference to the warfare in the republics of what was formerly Yugoslavia. **Ethnic cleansing** is the physical elimination of an unwanted ethnic group or groups from particular geographic areas. It involves genocide and/or relocation.

Genocide is the deliberate and systematic attempt to physically destroy the members of the rival population. The objective may be the total destruction of the group, the reduction of their numbers, or a stimulus for the surviving members of the group to migrate. The process is the same: the indiscriminate slaughter of men, women, and children of the targeted ethnic group.

Today, when we think of genocide, we think of the recent events in Sudan, Bosnia, or Rwanda or the killing of millions of Jews and Gypsies by the Germans during World War II, but genocide has been a recurrent event in human history. Only the magnitude of the killing has varied. In the late 1970s and early 1980s, the Guatemalan army massacred thousands of Native Americans. The Turks instituted a policy of systematic killing of Armenians during the early years of the last century. During the colonial period, the English, Dutch,

ethnic homogenization Elimination of ethnic difference within a region or country, historically involving ethnic cleaning or assimilation.

ethnic cleansing Physical elimination or removal of an unwanted ethnic group or groups from a country or a particular geographic region; usually involves genocide and/or relocation of the population.

genocide Deliberate and systematic attempt to eliminate the members of an ethnic category or cultural tradition by killing the members of the group.

French, Spanish, Portuguese, Belgians, and Germans were periodically guilty of genocide. Incidents of genocide are found even in American history, beginning with the slaughter of the Pequots in Connecticut in 1637 and ending with the massacre of more than 150 Sioux at Wounded Knee, South Dakota, in 1890. Genocide has been and still is a far too common response to ethnic conflict and rivalry.

Relocation is the forced resettlement of an unwanted ethnic group in a new geographic location. The forced relocation of the target population may be either in conjunction with genocide, as in the Darfur region of Sudan, or separate from it. Sometimes the unwanted group is forced outside the boundaries of the country, becoming what today we term **refugees**. In other cases, an ethnic group is forcibly moved to a new area within the boundaries of the existing state, where it is assumed the group will pose less of a problem.

At the outbreak of World War II, the Soviet Union was home to several million ethnic Germans who had settled in Russia during the eighteenth century. In 1924, a separate German autonomous republic within Russia was established along the Volga River for the so-called Volga Germans. When Germany attacked the Soviet Union in 1941, Stalin, fearing that the ethnic Germans might join the invaders, ordered them moved from Russia and Ukraine to Kazakhstan, Siberia, and other remote areas.

After World War II, the boundaries of much of eastern Europe were redrawn. That portion of Germany located east of the Oder River was given to Poland, and 7 million German residents were forcibly evicted. At the same time, Czechoslovakia evicted almost 3 million resident Germans from their homes. After independence, many East African countries expelled many East Indians who had settled there during the colonial period.

In American history, Native Americans were regularly relocated as the frontier moved west. The largest and best known of these relocations occurred in the 1830s, when the Five Civilized Tribes were forced to move (along the so-called Trail of Tears) from their homes in the southeastern states to what is today Oklahoma. Most indigenous tribes of the United States experienced similar resettlement programs. In Bosnia and Croatia, the main objective of all the combatants had been the relocation of the other ethnic populations. The killings, rapes, and destruction were the tactics used to encourage them to abandon their homes.

Assimilation is the social absorption of one ethnic group by another dominant one. Assimilation may be total, in which the ethnic identity of one group is lost, or partial, in which one ethnic group assumes a subordinate identity. Assimilation may be either forced or passive.

In **forced assimilation**, the government adopts policies designed to deliberately and systematically destroy or change the ethnic identity of a particular group. The ultimate objective is the absorption of the group into the dominant ethnic group. A key target of a forced assimilation policy is the elimination of ethnic boundary markers: language, religion, modes of dress, and any cultural institution that readily distinguishes the population. If these boundary markers are destroyed, the group loses much of its social cohesiveness. For example, until recently, the Bulgarian government pursued a policy designed to assimilate its Turkish population. Turks were not free to practice their Islamic religion, and they were forced to speak Bulgarian in public and adopt Bulgarian names.

One of the best examples of forced assimilation was the Indian policy of the United States in the latter part of the nineteenth and early twentieth centuries. Federal policy attacked Native American ethnic identity from several directions. Reservation lands, which were owned communally, were broken up, and the land was allotted (deeded) to individual members of the tribe in order to destroy community or village life. Many ceremonies such as the Sun Dance and the Peyote religion were made illegal. Traditional or hereditary tribal leaders were not recognized, and tribal governments were either dissolved or reorganized along an American political model. People who worked for the government were commonly forced to cut their hair and wear "citizen's" (Western-style) clothes. Native American children were taken from their families and placed in boarding schools, where they were forbidden to speak their native language, had their hair cut, were made to dress in citizen's clothes, were taught Euro-American technical skills, and were indoctrinated with Euro-American Christian

relocation Forced removal of the members of a particular ethnic group from one geographic region to another.

refugees Individuals and families who temporarily take up residence in another region or country to escape famine, warfare, or some other life-threatening event.

assimilation Social absorption of the members of one ethnic group into another, with the consequent abandonment of the former group's identity.

forced assimilation Social absorption of one ethnic group by another ethnic group through the use of force.

values and attitudes. As the head of the Carlisle Indian School said, "You have to destroy the Indian to save the man." Canada and Australia established similar policies for the assimilation of aboriginal peoples.

Assimilation need not be the result of a conscious official policy to solve an "ethnic problem" by incorporating the population into the cultural mainstream. Another form, called **passive assimilation**, occurs without any formal planning or political coercion. Unless strong social barriers prevent assimilation, social and economic forces frequently result in more dominant ethnic groups absorbing members of less powerful groups with whom they are in contact. The dominant ethnic group does not necessarily have to be the largest, but it must be the most socially prestigious and economically powerful group.

Many of the governments in Latin America have historically followed a laissez-faire policy toward Native American groups. Guatemala has not had a policy of forced assimilation. In Guatemala, the primary differences between Ladinos and Native Americans are not biological but social and cultural, and people who are identified as Native Americans are (informally) socially and economically discriminated against. As a result, more ambitious and educated Native Americans frequently have abandoned their native languages, dress, and lifestyles (ethnic boundary markers) and reidentified themselves as Ladinos. During the past 100 years, the Native American population in Guatemala has decreased from about 75 percent of the total population to less than 50 percent; passive assimilation is the primary cause of this decline.

History shows that there are other ways of managing ethnic differences. People do not have to resort to ethnic homogenization; segregation and accommodation are other responses, as we explore below.

Segregation

The political, social, and economic **segregation** of different ethnic groups has a long history in human society. In these situations, the dominant ethnic group does not attempt to eliminate the group, but rather places legal restrictions on the actions of the members of the group. In most cases, they have no political rights. They may not be permitted to own land, or they may own land in only certain restricted areas. Marriage between them and members of the dominant group may be prohibited. They may also be restricted to certain economic occupations. Not only is there no attempt to assimilate them into the dominant ethnic groups, but also legal restrictions maintain their ethnic identities.

There are two major reasons such ethnic relationships develop: (1) The dependent ethnic group performs a needed economic role, or (2) the dependent ethnic group is so powerless that it presents no threat, economic or political, to the dominant society. The Jews and Gypsies in Europe are examples of groups that survived as segregated ethnic groups. Jews were merchants and craftspeople at a time when most Christian Europeans were farmers. Thus, the dominant society was economically dependent on them. Gypsies, on the other hand, were a small, powerless group that presented no threat to the dominant society.

African Americans performed critical agricultural labor in the American South. After the Civil War and the end of slavery, the southern states passed so-called Jim Crow laws, which placed political, social, and economic restraints on African Americans. These new laws kept African Americans from threatening the continued political and economic dominance of Euro-Americans, while allowing Euro-American farmers and landowners the continued use of their labor. In contrast, government officials segregated Native Americans from the general population by placing them on reservations where their actions could be controlled. It was not until 1924 that U.S. citizenship was extended to all Native Americans, and not until 1948 that Native Americans living on reservations were allowed to vote in state and local elections in Arizona and New Mexico.

Accommodation

An alternative to ethnic homogenization or segregation is some form of political **accommodation** that formally recognizes and supports the ethnic and cultural differences of the population. Along with being formally recognized and supported, ethnic groups are given some degree of localized autonomy.

Accommodation takes many forms. One form is to adopt a strategy of officially recognized ethnic pluralism.

passive assimilation Voluntary social absorption of one ethnic group by another ethnic group.

segregation Enforced separation of ethnic groups, in which the dominant ethnic group places legal restrictions on the actions of the members of the other group.

accommodation Creation of social and political systems that provide for and support ethnic group differences together with local autonomy.

For instance, Canada has two main nationalities: Anglo-Canadians (English speaking) and French Canadians (French speaking). Both English and French are formally acknowledged as official languages. Although Quebec is the only province in which French Canadians are the majority, French speakers are found throughout other provinces. Within Quebec, French is the official language.

Belgium also has two major national groups: the Flemish (Dutch speakers) and the Walloons (French speakers). Both Flemish and Walloon are the official languages of Belgium, although internal political divisions are officially either Flemish or Walloon. The capital, Brussels, is officially bilingual. The former Czechoslovakia was also officially bilingual—Czech and Slovak.

However, many countries are home to more than two main nationalities, none of which are dominant. Yugoslavia had eight major nationalities: Serbs, Croats, Bosniaks, Slovenes, Montenegrins, Macedonians, Hungarians, and Albanians. The largest of these groups, the Serbs, constituted only about one-third of the population. Recognizing the long history of hostility and conflict between these groups, after World War II, Marshal Josip Broz Tito, the head of their liberation army and prime minister, adopted an ambitious scheme to give each group its own region of political control and autonomy. Separate republics were established for the Serbs, Croats, Slovenians, Montenegrins, and Macedonians. Although no separate republic was created for the Bosniaks (Muslims), they were the largest group in the ethnically mixed republic of Bosnia. The Albanians and Hungarians were given autonomous provinces within the republic of Serbia. Yugoslavia was organized as a confederacy, with a relatively limited central government and with a great deal of local autonomy given to each of the republics.

However, in most countries, one nationality constitutes the majority of the population and politically and economically dominates the smaller nationalities within its borders. For various reasons, some countries have created a limited number of regional enclaves and given these minorities some degree of political autonomy within these enclaves.

In the 1920s, the Soviet Union created a large number of internal "autonomous" ethnic political units called *republics, okrugs,* and *oblasts.* The degree of internal autonomy varied by category. Republics had the most autonomy and could have their own official language. With the collapse of the Soviet Union, many of the republics became independent countries; however, many of the smaller ones were incorporated into modern Russia. China also has "autonomous" ethnic areas; the five largest—Tibet, Guangxi, Ningxia, Inner Mongolia, and Xinjiang—are "autonomous regions." In addition, there are more than 100 smaller "autonomous prefectures" with some ethnic groups occupying several geographically scattered prefectures.

As we have discussed, along its border with Afghanistan, Pakistan has what it terms tribal areas for the Pushtun. In these tribal areas, their traditional institutions govern the Pushtun with virtually no interference from the central government.

Further examples include the United Kingdom, which in 1998 and 1999 allowed for the creation of regional parliaments for Scotland, Wales, and Northern Ireland. With a predominantly Inuit population, Denmark made Greenland an autonomous region in 1979. In 2009, Greenland adopted Kalaalligut (an Inuit language) as its official language. Canada established Nunavut, a separate territory, for the Inuit in 1999. In addition to French and English, Inuktiut and Inuinnagtun, two Inuit languages, are the official languages of the territory. The Philippines established an autonomous region in 1989 for the Muslims on Mindanao. Indonesia established Aceh as an autonomous area in 1999. Panama has a number of autonomous areas for Native American groups. In 1952, the United States granted "commonwealth" status to Puerto Rico and in the 1970s, following a policy of self-determination, began extending increased autonomy to the over 350 federally recognized native tribes. These are just some of the autonomous ethnic areas of the world. However, it is important to note that the degree of autonomy differs greatly from one to another.

Results

Having looked at the various means by which people have responded to ethnic differences, we can now examine the results. (Please see the Concept Review box for an outline of the responses to ethnic differences.)

What are the results of ethnic cleansing? No American can deny that ethnic cleansing does not work. In most regions of the United States, one need only look about them. How many Native American faces do you see? Yet America was once entirely Native American. American Indian peoples were massacred and the defeated survivors driven steadily westward to lands considered less desirable. Today, most Native Americans live in the western states.

Setting aside the moral issues, ethnic cleansing is seldom a permanent solution. Except for very small groups, rarely has one ethnic nationality been successful in

Ethnic Homogenization	The elimination of ethnic difference within a region or country, historically involving ethnic cleansing, genocide, or relocation.
(a) Ethnic Cleansing	Elimination or removal of an unwanted ethnic group from a country or a particular geographic region; usually involves genocide and/or relocation of the population.
(b) Genocide	Deliberate and systematic attempt to eliminate the members of an ethnic category or cultural tradition by killing the members of the group.
(c) Relocation	Forced resettlement of an unwanted ethnic group in a new geographic location—sometimes outside the boundaries of a region or country and sometimes to a restricted area within the existing state.
Assimilation	Social absorption of one ethnic group by another dominant one; may be forced or passive.
(a) Forced Assimilation	Dominant group's process of systematically destroying or changing the social identity of an ethnic group by eliminating their ethnic boundary markers.
(b) Passive Assimilation	Dominant group's process of absorbing the social identity of an ethnic group through conscious or unconscious social and economic discrimination and "voluntary" elimination of ethnic boundary markers.
Segregation	Type of assimilation in which an ethnic group is politically, socially, and economically separated, limiting the group's contact with other ethnic groups.
Accommodation	Type of assimilation in which a balanced political relationship between two or more ethnic groups is created, with each allowed to maintain its own social identity and cultural traditions with some degree of local autonomy.

destroying another. Even though it may be greatly reduced in number, the targeted group usually survives. The history of genocidal attacks by the other group becomes an integral part of the origin myth of the victimized group and thus serves to strengthen—not weaken—its identity. Genocide also creates hatred and distrust between groups that can persist for centuries after the actual event and make future political cooperation difficult, if not impossible.

Relocation also produces mixed results. As in the case of genocide, the forced removal of a people becomes part of their origin myth and strengthens their cohesion and identity. Among the Cherokee of both North Carolina and Oklahoma, the Indian removal of the 1830s has become a defining element of their ethnic identity. Removal of a people from their homeland in no way negates their claims to the lands they lost. Four hundred years after the Irish were evicted from Northern Ireland, the Irish Republican Army is fighting to reclaim this portion of the lost Irish homeland. The Jews were expelled from Jerusalem in the first century C.E. and dispersed over

Europe, North Africa, and the Middle East. Yet, in the past century, the Jews have returned to Israel to reclaim their homeland. The collective memory of a nationality is long. Old wrongs are seldom forgotten, and lost homelands are never truly relinquished.

Assimilation—whether passive or forced—is not always effective, either. There is no question that throughout history, smaller groups have been absorbed by larger groups, but assimilation is usually a slow and uncertain process. As we discussed, over the past 100 years in Guatemala, Native Americans have slowly declined as a percentage of the total population. We might therefore assume that passive assimilation has proved effective in this case. However, considering absolute rather than relative population, we find that the Native American population actually increased from 1 million to about 4 million during the same period. The main problem with passive assimilation, then, is that population growth often creates new members at least as fast as members become assimilated.

Another problem is that people are not willing give up their ethnic identity; if they did, forced assimilation would not be necessary. The forced assimilation policies in the United States were unsuccessful in regard to Native Americans. Loss of language, material culture, and other cultural institutions that functioned as ethnic boundary markers did not destroy ethnic identity or group cohesiveness because new cultural institutions and ethnic boundary markers emerged to replace the old. From a population of only about 250,000 in 1890, the Native American population of the United States has risen to more than 2 million today, and their major political demands are for greater tribal self-determination.

So genocide, relocation, and forced or passive assimilation may be effective to a greater or lesser degree, but none of these practices, under most circumstances, truly resolves ethnic problems. More often, they postpone the formulation of workable policies and are even counterproductive—they worsen rather than alleviate conflicts. Besides these "pragmatic" considerations, genocide and forced assimilation are so morally abhorrent that few modern governments would publicly admit to pursuing such policies. Relocation, likewise, poses ethical dilemmas; most groups are moved against their will, and some other nationality must be relocated to make room for the migrants. In the modern world, there is nowhere to relocate to without violating some other group's territorial rights. Finally, as we have seen, passive assimilation is usually slow and its result uncertain.

Political accommodation and local autonomy is the only practical and morally acceptable solution. But how well does it work, and what are the problems in maintaining a multinational state? First, we will look at the countries that have adopted the strategy of recognized ethnic pluralism.

In January 1993, by mutual agreement, Czechoslovakia peacefully split into the Czech Republic (now Czechia) and Slovakia. Simlarly, in Canada in the 1960s, a separatist movement emerged among the French Canadians in Quebec; in the 1976 elections, the Parti Québécois, the separatist party, won control of the government of Quebec. Although in a 1980 referendum in Quebec voters rejected separation from Canada, the issue was not resolved; in 1995, a second referendum was held on Quebec separation and failed by less than 1 percent. There are still many people in Quebec who support separation from Canada. At some time in the future, there may be a third referendum. Belgium has an active Flemish nationalist movement.

In every case, many, if not the majority, of the members of the smaller of the two national ethnic groups want independence. This is not because their individual rights or liberties are threatened; rather, they feel their collective ethnic identity is being eroded or diminished. As for Yugoslavia, after Tito's death in 1980, the presidency of Yugoslavia revolved among the presidents of six republics. In 1991, Slovenia declared its independence. As discussed earlier in this chapter, many of the other republics quickly followed suit, and a series of extremely bloody multisided wars frequently broke out, resulting in the disintegration of Yugoslavia.

The creation of politically autonomous regions for ethnic minorities within countries with a numerically dominant ethnic nationality has also had mixed results. Russia and China have both had problems with secessionist movements within some of their autonomous regions. In 1994–1995 and again in 1999–2000, secessionists in the autonomous Chechen Republic were involved in extremely bloody and destructive rebellions. Even today, Chechen separatists stage terrorist attacks in Russia itself.

There are active secessions movements among the Tibetans and Uyghurs in the autonomous regions of Tibet and Xinjiang in China. Indonesia and the Philippines created autonomous areas as a response to succession movements; however, succession movements among the Aceh in Indonesia and the Muslim groups in the southern Philippines continue. The United States created the special political status for Puerto Rico in response to an increasingly militant independence movement. There was even an attempt to assassinate President Harry Truman in 1950. This strategy was successful only in that the Puerto Rican separatists today are attempting to achieve independence through political means.

The creation within the United Kingdom of separate parliaments for Scotland and Wales has not been sufficient for many Scot and Welsh nationalists—they want total independence within the European Union. In 2014 a referendum on Scottish independence was defeated. However, the U.K.'s recent vote to leave the European Union has caused some Scottish leaders to call for a new referendum. Spain is home to a number of linguistically and culturally distinct groups. In 1978 the government divided the country into 17 communities, each with its own parliament and local autonomy in an attempt to accommodate these differences. In 2015 the Catalonian nationalist parties gained a large majority of the seats in the parliament of Catalonia and began planning for independence from Spain.

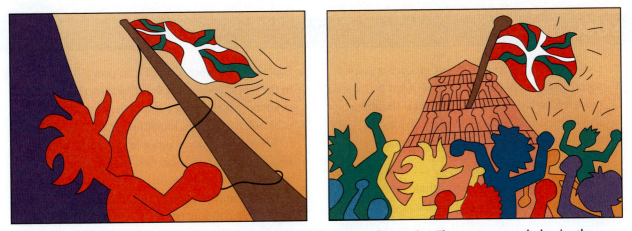

Nationalist organizations use various means to communicate their message of separation. These cartoon panels showing the Basque flag are from a booklet distributed by Basque separatists in northern Spain.

There are two problems with addressing nationality differences through the creation of autonomous regions. One is how much autonomy does the particular ethnic group actually have? In most cases, the group has only limited internal control over its population and resources. The second is that autonomy is not the same as sovereignty, and many groups aspire for total independence.

Finally, it is important to note that countries that are home to multiple ethnic nationalities are inherently unstable unless one ethnic group's dominance over the others is so great as to be indisputable. Otherwise, there has to be an excepted and stable social, political, and economic balance between the resident ethnic nationalities. The two factors that most seriously threaten the political stability of such countries are differential rates of population growth and relative differences in economic development. If the population of one group grows more rapidly than that of another, it threatens the existing social and political balance of the country. Differences in economic growth may result in changes in the relative economic well-being of the different nationalities and the feeling of exploitation by some.

Consequences of Globalization

There is no simple solution to ethnic conflict, and globalization is resulting in conflicting trends. The evolving **global economy** requires ever-closer cooperation between countries. At the same time the massive migration of peoples is resulting in larger countries becoming increasingly ethnically diverse.

One would think that these factors would lessen ethnic conflict. However, that does not appear to be the case. As noted, Glazer and Moynihan found that while ethnic groups may lose many of their superficial differences, basic cultural differences persist despite several generations of intensive contact. Similarly, as noted, Huntington argues that increasing contact between peoples does not serve to lessen cultural differences but rather makes people more aware of these differences. Are they correct?

At the same time, the global economy is resulting in a dramatic increase in the degree of economic inequality in the world. The widening inequality is not just between individuals, economic groups, and countries, but between geographic regions and ethnic groups as well. Also, as we discussed in Chapter 12, in many places in the world, the national government has diminished economic importance in the lives of the people. As a result, there fewer compelling economic reasons for large ethnic minorities to remain politically tied to their existing national government. There is little doubt that Scotland and Catalonia can become independent countries with few, if any, significant economic consequences.

Will we see a continuing political fragmentation of existing national government into independent countries, autonomous regions, and/or special legal statuses to empower particular ethnic groups? If so, what will be the consequences?

global economy Integrated global market in which goods and services are bought and sold globally with prices determined by supply and demand.

SUMMARY

1. **Define ethnic group.** An ethnic group is a named social grouping of people based on what is perceived as shared ancestry, cultural traditions, and history. Ethnic group identity divides the world into categories of "us" and "them."

2. **Explain what we mean when we say ethnic identity is situational.** An individual's ethnic group identity is seldom absolute but changes with the social context. An individual may assume various hierarchically ranked identities. This characteristic is called the hierarchical nesting quality of identity.

3. **Explain the attributes of ethnic groups.** The two main attributes of an ethnic group are origin myths and ethnic boundary markers. The origin myth or history describes the common or shared historical experiences that define the social boundaries of the group. Ethnic boundary markers are those overt characteristics that make its members identifiable. Ethnic boundary markers may include language, religion, physical characteristics, and other cultural traits such as clothing, house types, personal adornment, food, and so on.

4. **Describe the different levels of ethnic identity.** There are three categories of ethnic identity: nationality, subnationality, and civilization. An ethnic nationality is an ethnic group that shares a feeling of homeland and the inherent right to political sovereignty. A subnational group is an identity nested in a larger national identity. A subnationality claims neither a separate homeland nor rights to political sovereignty. Recently, some scholars have argued that another important level of ethnic identity is emerging: civilization. A civilization is a grouping of a number of distinct nationalities on the basis of a shared or common cultural historical tradition, generally religion.

5. **Explain why ethnic conflict is so prevalent in the world today, and describe an artificial country.** Much of the conflict in the world today is between ethnic nationalities. There are 3,000 to 5,000 ethnic nationalities in the world but only about 200 separate countries. Most countries are artificial countries, whose boundaries and thus ethnic composition were a product of European imperialism. Ethnic conflict is the result of stateless nationalities wanting to establish their own independent countries.

6. **Explain ethnic homogenization.** Frequently, more powerful groups have attempted to resolve ethnic differences by the elimination rival ethnic groups. In some cases, the men, women, and children of the rival group are killed—this is known as genocide. In other cases, the members of the rival ethnic group are physically removed from a geographic area—this is known as relocation. Finally, in still other cases, the dominant group attempts to assimilate the other group or groups by eliminating their ethnic boundary markers in hopes of destroying their identity.

7. **Elaborate on the meanings of ethnic segregation and ethnic accommodation.** If the dominant group does not wish to destroy a rival group, it may adopt either policies of segregation or accommodation. Segregation consists of legally limiting the rights and movements of the members of the group. Accommodation consists of formally recognizing and supporting the cultural differences that define the group and in many cases designating a particular geographic region in which members of the group have some degree of collective group autonomy.

17

World Problems and the Practice of Anthropology

Despite decades of protest by Native American leaders, international indigenous rights organizations, and the adoption of the UN's Declaration on the Rights of Indigenous Peoples in 2007, Belo Monte Dam on the Xingu River in Brazil is scheduled for completion in 2019.

Applied Anthropology

Health and Health Care
Medical Anthropology
Scientific Medicine and Traditional Healing

Population Growth
Anthropological Perspectives on Population Growth
Costs and Benefits of Children in LDCs

World Hunger
Scarcity or Inequality?
Is Technology Transfer the Answer?
Agricultural Alternatives

Anthropologists as Advocates
Indigenous Peoples Today
Vanishing Knowledge
Medicines We Have Learned
Adaptive Wisdom
Cultural Alternatives

1 **DEFINE** applied anthropology and discuss its importance today in understanding the cultures of other peoples.

2 **DEFINE** medical anthropology.

3 **COMPARE** the differences between Western or scientific medicine and most traditional systems of healing.

4 **IDENTIFY** the unfavorable consequences of rapid population growth.

5 **EXPLAIN** why the population growth rates are high in the poorer regions of the world.

6 **DESCRIBE** the two explanations for world hunger.

7 **IDENTIFY** some of the possible solutions for hunger.

8 **DISCUSS** how globalization is changing the lives of indigenous peoples and destroying the cultural traditions of these peoples.

9 **ANALYZE** the potential importance of the cultural knowledge of indigenous peoples.

Increasing numbers of anthropologists today are using their training to help solve human problems. In the private sector, for example, anthropologists work in a variety of roles—from training international businesspeople to become culturally sensitive when dealing with people from other countries, to observing how humans interact with machines. Governmental agencies and international organizations employ anthropological expertise to address problems connected to development, health, education, social services, and ethnic relations. In the first part of this chapter, we show some of the specific contributions anthropologists have made to understanding the problems of population growth and hunger. In the second part, we discuss the anthropologist as advocate.

Applied Anthropology

As we mentioned at the beginning of this book, *applied anthropology* is most simply defined as the application of anthropological perspectives, theory, empirical knowledge of cultures, and methods to help assess and solve human problems. The subfield has grown dramatically since the early 1970s, partly because the number of people earning PhDs in anthropology has outstripped the number of academic jobs available and partly because larger numbers of anthropologists want to use their expertise to help people and organizations.

What special talents or insights do applied anthropologists bring to problem solving? What unique contributions can anthropologists make to programs and agencies? The simple answer is that anthropologies do not think like other people. In studying and explaining the issues, applied anthropologists combine the holistic and relativistic perspectives, which we discussed in Chapter 2. We think you will see that this combined perspective makes a major difference in more fully understanding some of the cultural issues involved in health, population growth, and world hunger. Finally, we will discuss the role of anthropologists as advocates for smaller indigenous peoples of the world.

Quite often, applied anthropologists work in lesser-developed countries (LDCs), which are often collectively known as the Third World. Terms such as *developed, less developed, First World*, and *Third World* convey a certain prejudice resulting from a Western view (e.g., Third World to whom?). Because they are familiar terms, however, we continue to use them as shorthand descriptions of major world regions.

Health and Health Care
Medical Anthropology

The study of health and health care falls under the heading of medical anthropology, the largest and most rapidly growing specialty in applied anthropology.

Although most medical anthropologists are cultural anthropologists, sometimes physical anthropologists, linguists, and even archaeologists are involved in the study of health issues. Here, however, we address medical anthropology as an aspect of cultural anthropology.

First, it is important to note that health is a critical issue in every society, and every culture has a manner of dealing with disease and illness. Second, it is important to note that cultural behaviors, and changes in these behaviors, can have health-related consequences for a community.

Cultural anthropologists study a wide range of health and health-related topics. Here, we discuss only two broad overlapping categories: (1) the study of what can be called traditional or folk medicine and (2) programs by which Western or scientific medical practices can be made compatible with traditional medical beliefs and practices.

Scientific Medicine and Traditional Healing

Traditional medical beliefs and practices differ greatly not only from scientific medicine or Western medicine but from one another as well. Thus, there is tremendous

cultural diversity in health and health care. Without understanding these differences, it is impossible to adequately address the health concerns of a particular community. These differences fall into interrelated areas: the causes of particular illnesses and the treatment of these illnesses.

In his cross-cultural study of illness, G. P. Murdock found that explanations of illness fell into one of two categories: natural causation and supernatural causation. Natural causation "accounts for the impairment of health as a physiological consequence of some experience of the victim in a manner that would appear reasonable to modern medical science" (1980, p. 9), such as infection, stress, organic deterioration, or an accident. Supernatural causation accounts for the health impairment as the consequence of something "supernatural," such as fate, contagion, sorcery, soul loss, spirit aggression, and so forth. Western or scientific medicine explains all illness as the result of natural causes. Non-Western or traditional medicine most frequently uses some combination of natural and supernatural causes to explain illnesses. How a society explains the causes of illness in turn affects the curing practices used by their medical practitioners.

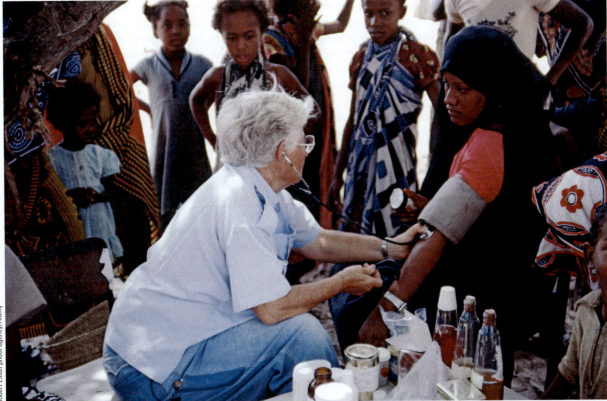

Robert Estall photo agency/Alamy

Western medical professionals, such as this doctor working in Kenya, frequently confront cultural barriers in treating traditional peoples. One role of medical anthropologists is to study traditional health beliefs and practices to improve the delivery of health services for traditional peoples.

Scientific medicine views illness as solely a physical problem—the result of natural causes—thus its treatment focuses on the physical elimination, alteration, or containment of the illness to either correct, cure, or give some degree of physical relief to the patient. To achieve these objectives, scientific medicine relies heavily on the use of surgical techniques and/or various drugs. In contrast, traditional medicine usually takes what is sometimes called a holistic approach to treatment: treating the mental, physical, and spiritual aspects of the illness. Thus, treatment usually involves, in part, religious healing rituals.

Numbering over 300,000, the Navajo are not only the largest native group in the United States but also the most studied of any tribal group in the world. The Navajo make a distinction between what might be considered commonplace and what might be considered serious illnesses. Commonplace illnesses are treated by bonesetters and herbalists. Serious illnesses result "from the disturbance of the normal order, harmony, or balance among the elements of the universe" (Wyman, 1983, p. 536). To cure an individual with a serious illness, this order, harmony, or balance has to be restored.

Because the cause is supernatural, both the diagnosis and the cure take the form of religious rituals. Health and healing are a central focus of Navajo life, as virtually all Navajo religious ceremonies are healing rituals with a patient. Making a distinction between symptoms and causes, the individual first sees a diagnostician, usually a "hand trembler"—an individual with an inherent ability to determine the cause of the illness. By passing his hand over the body of the individual, he determines the cause and which ritual the individual needs to restore harmony or balance. A highly trained specialist called a "singer" performs the actual ritual. Because the learning of a ritual or "sing" usually requires several years of study as an apprentice to an established singer, each singer is a specialist in only a limited number of rituals of the several dozen possible rituals used. Varying in length from an hour to nine days, the rituals involve songs, memorized prescribed prayers, sand paintings, the taking of various herbs, ritual bathing with yucca, and/or offerings of corn pollen.

There are two important limitations on traditional Navajo healing. First, these rituals can only be performed within a specific geographic region, the traditional Navajo area defined by their four sacred mountains. Second, they require a trained singer who knows the needed ritual.

The number of singers has declined relative to the total population during the twentieth century. Some of the rituals have become extinct or known only by very few individuals. As a result of these and other factors, the Navajo have added two new religious healing traditions: the Native American Church and Pentecostal Christianity.

A pan-Indian religion, the Native American Church (NAC), involving the use of the peyote cactus, first became popular among the Navajo in the 1930s (see discussion in Chapter 13). Health and the curing of illness are the primary reasons for meetings among the Navajo. Held from sundown to sunrise and presided over by a "roadman," NAC meetings involve spontaneous prayers and the ingestion of peyote to restore the health. Because only limited ritual knowledge is required to conduct a meeting, it is far easier to become a roadman than a traditional singer. Also, because they last only one night, peyote meetings are far less time-consuming and costly for the patient and the patient's family than most traditional Navajo healing rituals. Another advantage of the NAC is that its meetings are not geographically restricted to the land between the four sacred mountains and so can be observed by Navajo living well removed from the reservation.

Euro-American Christian missionaries began working among the Navajo in the nineteenth century, operating many of the early clinics, hospitals, and schools on the reservations. These missionaries were openly hostile to traditional Navajo religious practices. As a result, relatively few Navajo actually converted to Christianity.

This started to change in the 1950s when traveling Protestant evangelical ministers began holding tent revivals on reservations that emphasized spiritual healing. Because of the lack of a formal organizational structure, any individual so motivated could become a minister and establish his or her own church. As a result, independent Pentecostal churches with Navajo ministers quickly appeared and spread throughout the reservations. Although some prayer and healing meetings are held for individuals in homes, most are held in churches or large tent camp meetings. These larger meetings usually involve sermons and Bible readings, hymn singing, the giving of testimony, and prayers for healing. For individuals, healing may involve laying on of the hands, the use of oils, Bible readings, and healing prayers by the entire congregation. Pentecostal meetings, like NAC meetings, are not restricted by geography. However, they also have an advantage over NAC in that an ill individual does not have to schedule a special meeting but may attend any of the regularly scheduled Pentecostal meetings or revivals.

There is and has been antagonism between many of the traditional religious leaders and the leaders of the Native American Church and the Pentecostal churches.

However, for the most part, individual Navajos appear to move among the three groups, depending on the particular circumstances.

The traditional Navajo do not see any conflict between their ideas and religious practices and scientific medicine as provided by the Indian Health Service and/or the Navajo tribe. As noted, they make a distinction between the symptoms and the cure. Thus, when Western medical care can provide effective treatment, as in the case of surgical procedures or medicines such as antibiotics, they have no difficulty in accepting this care. Western medicine is seen as only addressing the symptoms.

Perhaps not surprisingly, Western-trained physicians are at times equated with traditional herbalists and bonesetters, not with singers. The causes of illness are supernatural, and the actual cure thus requires a religious healing ceremony to restore harmony and balance. The main problem has not been the Navajo rejection of scientific medicine but rather the reverse— the Western-trained health professionals and their hostility and rejection of traditional Navajo healing practices. Some physicians would even reject patients who had undergone a traditional healing ritual.

In what may have been the earliest example of applied medical anthropology, in 1944, Alexander and Dorothea Leighton wrote *The Navajo Door.* This

> introduction to the health beliefs and practices of the Navajos [was] written . . . for Indian Bureau employees providing medical care. The message in part was that Navajo ceremonials, while not adequate therapy for appendicitis or tuberculosis, did have great psychotherapeutic and social value; traditional healers were to be respected as potentially valuable allies.
>
> (cited in Kunitz, 1983, p. 149)

In his 1983 study of the changes in morbidity patterns among the Navajo, Stephen Kunitz found that while death rates from infectious diseases—particularly tuberculosis— had declined dramatically, death rates from alcohol-related accidents, alcoholic cirrhosis, homicide, and suicide, particularly among young adults in their 20s and 30s, had considerably increased. Since that study, drug abuse could also be added to these health problems.

Kunitz argues that the added social conflict within families and communities, which are the underlying causes of these health issues, are in large part the result of stress brought on by mounting poverty on the reservation. Poverty is a health issue that cannot be addressed by scientific medicine. However, one can also argue that while the three healing traditions now utilized by the Navajo cannot alleviate poverty on the

reservation, by stressing the spiritual harmony and balance within the family and the community, they can ease some of the social problems and conflict that result from health problems.

Population Growth

One of the consequences of globalization has been the phenomenal increase in world population. In the last 50 years, world population has more than doubled, jumping from 2.5 billion to more than 7 billion. Most of this growth is occurring in the poorer countries of the world, which creates a wide range of problems. Whereas the standard of living in the developed countries of North America, Europe, and Japan is increasing, the standard of living for most of the rest of the world's people is declining, and differences in population growth rates are the primary reason. In addition, overpopulation in Latin America, Africa, and parts of Asia is resulting in increasing ethnic and social conflict, environmental degradation, and massive migrations of people from the underdeveloped to the more developed countries of the world. Why are the poorest peoples of the world continuing to have large families, while the wealthier peoples are having fewer and fewer children? What is the reason for this inverse correlation?

Anthropological Perspectives on Population Growth

Anthropological insight on this issue is twofold. First, anthropologists study human behavior holistically, in terms of the total system in which people live their everyday lives. For the issue of population growth, anthropologists study reproductive behavior, including the choices couples make about how many children to have. By understanding the overall context of behavior, anthropologists can understand how the birthrates of a region result from local conditions—especially economic conditions faced by many rural poor. The second prong of anthropological insight involves their detailed fieldwork in local communities to uncover the major causes of high birthrates in Third World settings.

There is an apparent paradox about the comparatively high birthrates of many underdeveloped countries. An average North American family is able to afford more children than an average Nigerian family. Canadians and Americans have more money to house, feed, clothe, educate, and otherwise provide for their children. Yet they usually have only two or three children, whereas the Nigerian family averages six or seven. And this is the most puzzling thing about high fertility: It continues despite its adverse consequences for those very nations that experience it and whose citizens cause it—the LDCs.

Why do people in these countries continue to have so many children? Are Asian, Africans, and Latin Americans too ignorant to realize they cannot afford to support so many children? Do they not see the strain that all these children put on their nations' educational, health, and agricultural systems? Does the refusal of couples in these countries to practice birth control even when condoms and pills are available represent a perfect example of their backwardness and ignorance?

Not at all.

Costs and Benefits of Children in LDCs

Too often, when we learn that rural people in parts of the Third World average six, seven, or more children per couple, we think this is economically irrational. They must be having large families for other noneconomic reasons. Probably children are highly valued in their traditional culture. Or maybe men have higher prestige if they have lots of children. Perhaps they are not educated enough to recognize the effects of having such large families. Or it could be that they don't know how to prevent pregnancy.

Part of our error comes from our failure to grasp the conditions of their lives that lead them to bear more children than we do. Just because children are an economic liability in a highly mobile, industrialized, urbanized, market economy, this does not mean they are a liability everywhere. Many demographers argue that rural people in LDCs have high fertility not simply because of cultural preferences but because children are economically useful. Village-level ethnographic studies suggest that children do indeed offer a variety of material benefits to their parents in LDCs.

One such study was done in the Punjab region of northern India by anthropologist Mahmood Mamdani. He researched a family planning project that aimed to reduce the birthrate in seven villages. Mamdani found that in the village of Manupur, people accepted the birth control pills and condoms offered by the staff of the program, but most refused to use them. The reaction of the project's administrators was like that of many outsiders when local people do not behave in ways they seemingly ought to behave: They blamed the ignorance and conservatism of the villagers. To the staff, the benefits of having fewer children seemed obvious. The amount of land available to most people was barely adequate, so by reducing family size, people could stop the fragmentation of land that was contributing to their poverty.

However, the village's parents interpreted their economic circumstances differently. They believed that children—especially sons—were economically beneficial, not harmful. Villagers of all castes and all economic levels reported that children were helpful to a household in many ways. They helped with everyday tasks such as washing, gathering animal dung to use as fertilizer, weeding fields, collecting firewood, and caring for livestock. Even young children supplemented family income by doing small jobs for neighbors. When they grew up, sons were the major source of support for their elderly parents because one or more of them usually continued to live with their parents and farm the land or work in other occupations. Adult sons often went to cities, where part of the money they earned from their jobs was sent back to help their parents and siblings.

In short, Mamdani argued, the residents of Manupur recognized that the benefits of children exceeded their costs to the parents. Outsiders did not recognize this fact because they did not fully grasp the economic circumstances under which people were actually living.

Like people everywhere, however, the people of this region of India proved capable of altering their behavior as their circumstances changed. In 1982, 10 years after Mamdani's study, Moni Nag and Neeraj Kak restudied the village of Manupur. They found that couples had changed their attitudes about desirable family size: About half of all couples were now using contraception or had accepted sterilization after they had two sons. The reason was that changing economic conditions in the region had made children less valuable to families. Parents did not need as much children's labor as before. The introduction of new crops and farming methods had almost eliminated grazing land in the region, so boys were no longer useful for tending cattle. Increasing reliance on purchased chemical fertilizers reduced the value of children's labor in collecting cattle dung to spread on fields. Chemical weed killers reduced the amount of handwork necessary for weeding. A new crop, rice, did not require as much work as the old staples.

The increased value of formal education also led people to have fewer children. Because more outside skilled jobs were available, parents became more interested in providing a secondary education that would increase their children's ability to acquire high-paying jobs. Opportunities for women increased, and secondary school enrollment rates for girls more than doubled between 1970 and 1982. Sending more children to secondary school raised the costs of childrearing. Parents had to pay for clothing and textbooks for their children who attended school, which was a significant expense for poorer families. Accordingly, they wanted and had fewer children.

Finally, most couples believed that having lots of sons was not as necessary as it had been 10 years earlier. People still desired sons for old-age support, but many believed sons were not as dependable as they used to be. Many sons no longer brought their wives with them to live on the family land, but instead left the village to live on their own. One elderly man who was interviewed reported that

> Children are of no use any more in old age of parents. They also do not do any work while going to school. My son in the military does not keep any connection with me. My son living with me has two sons and one daughter. I have advised him to get a vasectomy.

> (Nag & Kak, 1984, p. 666)

All these and other changes increased the economic costs and decreased the benefits of having large families, and couples reacted to these changes by having fewer children. In this region of northern India, then, ideas and attitudes about desirable family sizes were not fixed by tradition but changed as people adapted their family sizes to changing circumstances.

Researchers in other parts of the world also report that children offer many economic benefits to their parents, explaining why high fertility persists in most LDCs. On the densely populated Indonesian island of Java, rural parents do not have to wait for their children to grow up to acquire the benefits of their labor. Children ages 6 to 8 spend three to four hours daily tending livestock, gathering firewood, and caring for their younger siblings. By the time they are 14, girls work almost nine hours a day in child care, food preparation, household chores, handicrafts, and other activities.

Most of the labor of children does not contribute directly to their family's cash income or food supply, so it is easy to see how outsiders might conclude that children are unproductive. However, children accomplish many household maintenance tasks that require little experience and skill, which frees the labor of adult family members for activities that do bring in money or food. Ethnographer Benjamin White suggests that large families are more successful economically than small families in Java. Ethnographers working in rural Nepal, Bangladesh, Samoa, and the Philippines have reported similar findings. Unlike suburban and urban North Americans, farming families in LDCs use much of the time of even young children productively. As children grow older, they are used to diversify the economic activities of a household, earning cash themselves or performing subsistence work that frees their parents for wage labor.

In many countries, the grown children of rural people migrate to a city in their own country or to a developed country. They acquire jobs—which are well paid relative to what they could earn in their own villages—and send much of the cash back to their families. Such remittances contribute half or more of the family income in Western Samoa, Tonga, and some other small nations of the Pacific—both because migrants feel a continuing sense of obligation to their parents and siblings back home and because many of them hope to return to their islands someday. Remittances are also a major source of family income (and, as a byproduct, of national income) in countries like Nigeria, Ghana, Pakistan, India, Mexico, Central America, and parts of the Middle East.

In most parts of the world, children are also the major source of economic support in their parents' old age because rural villagers lack pension plans and Social Security. As Stanley Freed and Ruth Freed have pointed out, in many parts of India parents prefer to bear two or three sons to ensure themselves of having one adult son to live with them, in case one son dies or moves elsewhere.

Such factors mean that children are perceived (in most cases, correctly) as both more valuable and less costly than most citizens of the developed world perceive them. We should not assume that couples in LDCs are too ignorant to understand the costs of having many children or to appreciate the benefits of small families. Nor should we think they are prisoners of their "traditional cultural values," which have not changed fast enough to keep up with changing conditions. Instead, we should assume that they make reproductive decisions just as we do. Then we can begin to understand the economic and other conditions of their lives that often lead them to want more children than affluent couples in urbanized, industrialized countries want. We can also see why birthrates are falling in so many LDCs today. It is not simply the increased family planning education and the recent availability of contraceptive devices. Lowered fertility is also a response to the increased urbanization of most nations, to the growth in wage employment over subsistence farming, to the rising emphasis on education for girls as well as boys, and to other factors that have changed the circumstances of family lives.

As we have seen, rising human numbers contribute to the resource shortages faced by LDCs today. One of the resources in shortest supply is one of the things people cannot do without: food. Most North Americans see malnutrition and overpopulation as two sides of the same coin. In the popular view, the "fact" that there are "too many people" in the world is the major reason there is "too little food to go around." And the solution to world hunger is more food—that is, increased production by the application of modern agricultural technologies. In the next section, we try to convince you that neither the problem (too many people) nor the solution (more production through better technology) is this simple.

World Hunger

Hunger is endemic in much of the world today. The United Nations estimated that from 2014 to 2015, almost 800 million people went to bed hungry every night and that over 29,000 people die of hunger or hunger-related causes every day. Hunger afflicts poor people in parts of South Sudan, Mozambique, Ethiopia, Chad, Bolivia, Peru, Bangladesh, Pakistan, and India. Even in countries considered moderately developed or rapidly developing, there are regions of extreme poverty and hunger, as in Indonesia, Egypt, Brazil, and Mexico.

Women and children constitute the vast majority of the malnourished. Children are especially at risk; if malnutrition does not kill them, it frequently causes lifelong mental and physical disabilities. In this section, we discuss the conditions that contribute to hunger in the Third World. Our focus is on chronic malnutrition or undernutrition on a worldwide scale, not on a short-term famine in particular countries or regions. (The reason we focus on *chronic* hunger is that the immediate causes of famine are more likely to be political upheavals and conflicts that disrupt food production or distribution rather than economic or demographic forces.) First, we discuss two alternative explanations for hunger. Then we describe attempts to increase the food supply by modern technological methods, showing why such attempts are so often unsuccessful

scarcity explanation of hunger Theory that, due to overpopulation, there are not enough land, water, and other resources to feed all the people of a country or region an adequate diet, given current technology.

inequality explanation of hunger Theory that hunger is not caused by absolute scarcity but by the unequal distribution of resources and how these resources are used.

and counterproductive. Throughout, we suggest anthropological insights into the problem.

Scarcity or Inequality?

What causes hunger? In any given region, people are hungry for a variety of reasons. On a worldwide basis, however, two explanations for hunger are most commonly offered. The first, which we call the **scarcity explanation of hunger**, is that the major cause of widespread hunger in LDCs is *overpopulation*: Populations have grown so large that available land and technology cannot produce enough food to feed them. The second, which we call the **inequality explanation of hunger**, holds that the *unequal distribution of resources* is largely responsible for chronic hunger on a worldwide basis: So many people are hungry today because they lack access to the resources (especially land) needed to produce food.

The scarcity explanation holds that not enough food-producing resources exist to provide the poor with adequate nutrition. In countries like India, Bangladesh, El Salvador, Kenya, and Ethiopia, populations have grown so large in the last century or two that there is not enough land to feed everyone. This argument maintains that food-producing resources like land, water, fertilizer, and technology are absolutely scarce—that is, there are not enough resources for the size of the population. In brief, the scarcity explanation holds that hunger is caused by too many people.

Although not our focus here, the scarcity explanation accounts for starvation by saying that chronic hunger turns into outright famine when some sort of disaster strikes. With so many people chronically undernourished, anything that disrupts food production (e.g., droughts, floods, plant diseases, insect infestations, or political disturbances) will reduce food supplies enough to turn hungry people into starving people.

The inequality explanation arose, in part, as a reaction to the excesses of the scarcity explanation, which (some believe) blames the victims of hunger by saying that their own (reproductive) behavior causes their hunger. The inequality explanation holds that resources are not absolutely scarce. In fact, there is enough productive capacity in the land of practically every nation to feed its people an adequate diet, if only this productive capacity were used to meet the needs of the poor. Instead, too many productive resources are used to increase the profits of wealthy landowners and to fulfill the wants of the more affluent citizens of the world.

The inequality explanation says that poor people are hungry because of the way both the international economy and their own national economies allocate productive resources. The international (global) economy allocates resources on the basis of ability to pay, not on need. For example, if affluent North American consumers want coffee and sugar, wealthy and politically powerful landowners in Central America will devote their land to coffee and sugar plantations for export, because this is how they can make the most money. If North Americans want tomatoes and other vegetables during the winter, large landowners in northwestern Mexico will produce them, rather than the beans and corn that are major staples for Mexican peasants. The national economies of countries with hungry people work in a similar way. Urban elites have the money to buy luxuries, and urban middle- and working-class families pressure governments to keep food prices low. As a result, too much land is used to produce crops sold to city dwellers at prices made so low by government policy that the rural poor cannot feed themselves. In brief, according to the inequality explanation, hunger is caused mainly by the use of and unequal access to resources.

Which explanation is correct? As is often the case, the two are not mutually exclusive. Both are correct to a certain degree, depending on time and place. The scarcity explanation is correct when, all else being equal, the amount of land available per person has been and continues to be reduced by population growth. Moreover, as the population grows, land of increasingly poorer quality has to be cultivated, reducing its productivity. And as families grow poorer, they have less money to acquire new land or to buy fertilizer or other products that will increase the productivity of their land. These arguments are the kind we encounter regularly in the popular news media. It is hard to see how such conclusions can be wrong.

But these conclusions tell only part of the story. The explanation for hunger is more complex than "too many people" combined with "low farm productivity." Hunger is created by human institutions as much as by population increase and unproductive technologies and farming methods. For example, at a growth rate of 3 percent a year, a population will double in less than 25 years. Does this mean that in 25 years everybody will have only half the amount of food? Of course not. Land that formerly was underused will be brought into fuller production, more labor-intensive methods of cultivation can produce higher yields per acre, people can change their diets and eat less meat, and so on. People will adjust their cultivation methods, work patterns, eating habits, and other behaviors to the new conditions rather than tolerate being hungry.

Or, rather, people will adjust if they have access to the resources they need to do so. And this is a large part of the problem in many LDCs: It is not just that there are too few resources, but that too few people own or control the resources available. In their books *Food First* and *World Hunger: Twelve Myths*, Frances Moore Lappé and Joseph Collins question what they call "the myth of scarcity." They claim that every nation could provide an adequate diet for its citizens if its productive resources were more equitably distributed.

We do not attempt to present a complete discussion of the evidence to show that inequality is as important as scarcity in explaining hunger around the world. There are several excellent contemporary studies by anthropologists of the relationships among population, resource distribution, and hunger. Here, we discuss a well-known historical example, the Irish potato famine of 1845–1850, because it personally affected the ancestors of so many North Americans and because it illustrates the changes that are occurring in agricultural production in the world today.

In the early nineteenth century, Ireland was an agriculturally diverse country in which large landowners controlled most of the land. Politically and economically, the island was controlled by England. Starting in the last decades of the eighteenth century, large landowners had begun increasingly allotting their land to the production of cash crops for export to England, where the industrial revolution was transforming the economy. English mills needed Irish wool and flax in their production of textiles, and England needed Irish wheat, meat, butter, and other food products to help feed the increasing numbers of factory workers.

Ireland's export of wool, in particular, had resulted in a significant reduction of land available for farming, as many wealthy landowners evicted their tenant farmers to turn their land into sheep pastures. Still other large landowners focused on raising wheat, flax, and other exportable grains. Only a small portion of the population of Ireland worked on the large estates or in the towns or cities. The vast majority of the population survived as small subsistence farmers. Their landholdings, either owned or rented, were so small—usually less than 5 acres—that they had to plant a crop that yielded the most in terms of subsistence value. Thus, they planted potatoes, which, in a normal year, would yield sufficient food to feed their family, with a small surplus they could sell. The sale of a few potatoes and some irregular wage work produced the only cash income most families had. Malnutrition was common in rural Ireland during the early nineteenth century.

In 1845, the potato blight struck, destroying between a third and half of the potato crop. The severity of the blight varied from one part of the country to another. However, in almost every region, small farmers quickly found themselves short of food, with little if any cash, little in the way of property to sell, and little chance of finding wage work. Many families were quickly reduced to starvation. As the blight continued in 1846 and 1847, conditions became increasingly difficult. Several million starving people began wandering the countryside in a desperate search for food or jobs or anything to keep them alive. Many simply abandoned their farms, while others were evicted for nonpayment of rent. Tens of thousands gathered in the port cities, where, ironically, a few found work loading ships with wool, flax, wheat, meat, butter, and other agricultural products for shipment to England.

Starvation in Ireland was not the result of a lack of agricultural resources; rather, it was the result of the people of Ireland not having the money to purchase the food that was grown and exported. One estimate found that, during the famine, Ireland was exporting to England food sufficient to support 18 million people. In 1845, the population of Ireland had been about 8.5 million. When the famine ended in 1850, only about 6.5 million remained. An estimated 1 million people had died of starvation or related causes, while another 1 million had emigrated to North America, England, or Australia.

The economic relationship between agricultural Ireland and industrialized England that existed during the early nineteenth century is seen on a global scale today. Poorer, primarily agricultural countries are increasingly allocating their resources to the production of exports to wealthier, more developed countries, while at the same time their populations are growing rapidly.

There is no denying that population growth contributes to hunger and poverty. But we should not conclude that "too many people" is *the* problem, or that the scarcity explanation is sufficient. Population growth always occurs within a political and economic context, and this context greatly influences the degree to which poor people can adjust to it. In a similar vein, it is fascinating that many economists recognize that famines do not result mainly from an absolute scarcity of food, but rather from the inability of some groups— usually the poorest groups—to gain access to food. There is also increasing recognition that development ought to be measured by more than income and ought to mean more than material affluence.

The combination of population growth and increasing land concentration is doubly devastating. Even if

Increasingly, lesser-developed countries allocate food-producing resources for the production of cash crops for exportation.

the poor manage to hang on to their land, they will become poorer if their numbers grow. If their increased poverty makes it necessary for them to borrow from the wealthy, to sell part of their land to raise cash, or to work for low wages to make ends meet, they are likely to grow poorer still. This double crunch is precisely the experience of the rural poor in many LDCs.

Is Technology Transfer the Answer?

One commonly proposed solution for world hunger is to apply modern scientific know-how and technology to areas in which agriculture is still technologically underdeveloped. This solution seems simple: Thanks to agricultural machinery, plant breeding, modern fertilizers, pest control methods, advances in irrigation technology, genetic engineering, and so on, the developed countries have solved the nutrition problem for most of their people. We have developed science and technology and applied it to agriculture. Lesser-developed countries need only adopt our know-how and technology to solve their hunger problems. In this view, the main thing hungry countries need is a transfer of our food-production technology.

There are many problems with the **technology-transfer solution**. We can touch on only a few. First, many of the methods developed for application in temperate climates fail miserably when transported to the tropics, where most hungry people live. This is largely because of the profound differences between tropical and temperate soils and climates.

Second, many experts doubt that so-called high-tech solutions to food problems are appropriate to economic conditions in LDCs. Labor is much more available than capital in these nations, so to substitute technology (machinery, herbicides, artificial fertilizers, and so forth) for labor is to waste a plentiful factor of production in favor of a scarce one. Besides, those who need to increase production the most—the poorest farmers—are those who can least afford new technology. And borrowing money for new investments involves risks because many small farmers who borrow from rich landowners lose their land if they default.

Third, new technologies often come as a package deal. For instance, new crop varieties usually require large amounts of water, pesticides, and fertilizers to do well. Small farmers must adopt the whole expensive package for success. The expense—combined with the logistics of long-term supply of each element of the package in countries with uncertain transportation and political regimes—makes many farmers wary of innovations. Further, many new high-yielding varieties of crops are hybrids, which means that farmers cannot select next year's seeds from this year's harvest. Rather, they must purchase their seeds every year from large companies, many of which operate internationally. Is it a good idea to make the world's farmers dependent on a few suppliers of genetic material for their crops?

Fourth, agricultural experts from the developed world often report that peasant farmers resist change. Sometimes, peasants cling tenaciously to their traditional crops, varieties, and methods of cultivation even when genuine improvements are made available to them. This famed cultural conservatism of peasants seems downright irrational to many technical experts.

But some anthropologists who have conducted village-level fieldwork offer an alternative interpretation of peasant resistance to change. Living in intimate contact with local people, fieldworkers are sometimes able to perceive problems the way peasants do. Subsistence farmers who are barely feeding their families cannot afford to drop below the minimum level of food production it takes to survive. Traditional crops and varieties give some yield even when uncontrollable environmental forces are unfavorable because over the generations they have adapted to local fluctuations of climate, disease, and pests. The new varieties might not fare as well. Because the consequences of crop failure are more severe for poor subsistence farmers than for well-off commercial farmers, the poor farmers minimize their risks by using tried-and-true crop varieties and methods. Thus, peasant cultural conservatism may be a sound strategy, given the conditions of peasant lives.

Finally, the technology that some believe is wise to transfer to other parts of the world may not be as effective or as efficient as anticipated. Modern mechanized agriculture requires a large amount of energy to produce its high yields. Studies done in the 1970s suggest that on modern commercial farms in the United States, on average about 1 calorie of energy is required to produce about 2 calories of food. The "energy subsidy" to agriculture goes into producing and running tractors, harvesters, irrigation facilities, chemical fertilizers, herbicides, pesticides, and other inputs. The payoff for this energy subsidy is enormously high yields, in terms of both yields per acre and yields per farmworker. In traditional agricultural systems, however, for every 1 calorie of energy expended in agricultural production, 15–50 calories of food energy are returned (the amount depends, of course, on local conditions, cultivation methods, crop type, and a multitude of other factors). The main reason traditional agriculture is so much more energy efficient is that human labor energy, supplemented by the muscle energy of draft animals, is the major energy input.

Many questions follow from this difference in energy subsidy. Is there enough energy for modern mechanized agricultural methods to be widely adopted around the world? If there is, can the rural poor of the Third World afford them? What will happen if the rural poor have to compete on a local level with the well-off farmers who can afford to purchase and maintain the new technologies? What will be the local and global

technology-transfer solution Theory that developing nations can best solve their hunger problems by adopting the technology and production methods of modern mechanized agriculture.

environmental consequences of agricultural mechanization on such a large scale? The worldwide price of oil was high in 2012, but what will happen to the price if tens or hundreds of millions of additional farmers mechanize their operations? Can such methods be used indefinitely—are they ecologically sustainable?

We raise such questions not because the answers are obvious. Some experts—mainly economists—believe that the new problems new technologies create will be solved by even newer technologies. Others say it is too risky to count on a future of uncertain technological salvation, and the consequences of being wrong are too severe to do so. Some believe that whatever future scarcities of energy or other resources occur will stimulate the search for alternative sources, so that the free market will save us. Others claim that we are near the limits of our planet's ability to produce affordable food and other products.

To point out that technology transfers are not economically or ecologically feasible for many regions is not to say that modern food-producing methods are always harmful or should not even be considered as solutions for world hunger. It merely points out that mechanized technologies have problems of their own and that experts do not have all the answers. Are there other solutions that avoid or minimize some of the problems with transfers of technology? Some agricultural scientists, anthropologists, and other scholars are researching alternative methods of boosting food production—methods that are productive and sustainable yet avoid some of the high energy requirements and the problems associated with mechanized agriculture.

Agricultural Alternatives

Since the early 1980s, increasing numbers of agricultural scientists have been taking another look at traditional farming practices—that is, methods of cultivating the soil that have been used for decades or centuries by the people living in a particular region. In the past, technical experts in agricultural development often scorned traditional farming methods, which they viewed as inefficient and overly labor intensive. But today, there is increasing awareness of the benefits of traditional methods.

This awareness stems partly from the failure of many agricultural development programs for the Third World. It also stems from the environmental movement that began in developed countries in the 1970s, which called attention to the negative environmental impacts of mechanized agriculture. In addition to the high energy requirements of mechanized agriculture

previously discussed, some farming practices commonly used in developed countries cause environmental problems. Such problems include water pollution from fertilizer runoff, poisoning of farmworkers and wildlife from agricultural chemicals, soil erosion from failure to rotate crops, and increasing resistance of insects because of exclusive reliance on pesticides.

In addition to negative environmental impacts, technologies such as machinery, pesticides, herbicides, and fungicides are too expensive for many traditional farmers. Sometimes they are inappropriate or uneconomical to use on the small plots that are characteristic of farms in many parts of the world. They may be unfamiliar to local people, who understandably are reluctant to abandon proven cultivation methods for alternatives they perceive to be riskier.

Considerations such as these led some agricultural scientists to consider whether there are *viable* alternatives to mechanized agricultural technologies and practices. Some experts believe there are. The main goals of such alternatives are minimization of negative environmental impacts, affordability to small farmers, reliance on technologies and locally available resources, adaptation to local environmental conditions, and long-term sustainability.

Over the centuries, traditional farming systems have evolved that meet many of these goals. Increasingly, agricultural scientists and development agencies look at traditional agriculture not as a system that should be replaced but as a set of farming techniques they can learn from. Much research on this topic is ongoing; here, we present brief descriptions of only two traditional methods: intercropping and resource management.

Intercropping

One method used by traditional farmers in many parts of the world (in the tropics, especially) is *intercropping*, also known as *multiple cropping* or *polyculture*. In contrast to monoculture, intercropping involves the intermingling of numerous crops in a single plot or field. It has been practiced for centuries by shifting cultivators, whose plots usually contain dozens of crops and varieties.

Although intercropped fields look untidy, this method offers several benefits, stemming from the diversity of crops growing together in a relatively small space. Many plant diseases and pests attack only one or a few crops, so if there are several different crops, yields may still be good despite an outbreak. In regions where water supply is a problem and rainfall is erratic, some crops suffer during droughts, but others will still produce a harvest. The varying growth patterns and root structures of diverse crops have useful ecological benefits: Erosion is reduced because more of the soil is covered, and sun-loving weeds are suppressed by the shade of the crops themselves.

Traditional farmers in some parts of the world have learned over the centuries that many crops grow better when planted together. Leguminous crops—such as beans, peas, and peanuts—take nitrogen (a necessary plant nutrient) from the air and store it in their roots. Intercropping legumes with crops that need lots of nitrogen can increase yields. This is done in Mexico and Central America, where traditional farmers have long intercropped corn, beans, and squash. The stout corn plants provide support for the bean vines to climb, and the ground-hugging squash plants keep the soil covered. African farmers intercrop sorghum with peanuts and millet with cowpea with similar benefits.

Traditional Resource Management Practices

In many parts of the world, traditional farmers actively take steps to control the plant species growing in areas that, to outsiders, look wild or abandoned. They are, in other words, managing their resources so they can continue to use them indefinitely. Two brief examples illustrate these management practices.

The Kayapo of the Xingu River basin of Brazil farm in the forest by shifting cultivation. According to anthropologist Darrell Posey, who has worked among the Kayapo for years, the Kayapo manage the forest carefully. One of their traditional practices is the creation of "islands" of forest in deforested areas. They move composted soil made from termite and ant nests and vegetation into open areas and transplant crops and other useful plants. The created and managed environment provides plant foods, medicines, and building materials and attracts some of the animals hunted by the Kayapo.

The Lacandon Maya of the state of Chiapas in southern Mexico practice slash-and-burn agriculture. Although the staple crop is corn, they plant many other crops in the cleared fields, including several tree species that yield fruit. Lacandon farmers clear and plant new plots frequently, but they do not simply abandon a plot once its main crops are harvested. Rather, they return to it for many years to harvest the long-lived fruit trees and other species they planted. Even while the natural forest is regrowing, the Lacandon continue to use the land. They manage their fallowing fields and thus integrate their exploitation of the land with the natural process of forest regeneration.

We have presented some of the reasons many scientists and others concerned with agricultural development are reconsidering traditional agriculture. It is all too easy to romanticize traditional farmers, to think that they really have had the answers all along, and that only recently have so-called experts been forced to pay attention. This view, too, is simplistic. In all likelihood, solutions to the food crisis will require a mixture of traditional and modern technologies. It is, however, encouraging that the knowledge and methods embedded in traditional agricultural adaptations are taken seriously by the World Bank and other institutions in a position to make critical decisions.

Anthropologists as Advocates

Anthropologists do not merely define problems. From the earliest origins of the discipline, anthropologists as individuals have been politically active, using the information and insights gained from their research to voice their concerns about a wide range of public policy issues. Franz Boas (see Chapter 5) took an active role in attacking racist stereotypes during the first decades of the twentieth century and publicly opposed U.S. immigration laws based on racist ideas. Margaret Mead (see Chapter 5) was certainly the best-known advocate for women's rights in the United States during the mid–twentieth century. As individuals, anthropologists have been and still are activists concerned with a wide range of particular and global issues. However, no single issue has concerned anthropologists as a group more than the rights of indigenous peoples.

This should not be surprising. Much of anthropological research has focused on the study of these peoples, and field research is a highly personal experience. As a result, anthropologists as a group more clearly understand the problems of these peoples than other outsiders, and collectively we know them and value them not just as individuals but also as friends.

In the late nineteenth century, American anthropologists were engaged in advocating the rights of American Indian peoples. As members of the Lake Mohonk Conference, the Association on American Indian Affairs, and other Indian rights organizations, they lobbied Congress for changes in the laws concerning American Indian tribes. However, their involvement was as individuals.

The emergence of applied anthropology in the 1940s saw anthropologists becoming increasingly concerned with the contemporary problems facing indigenous peoples. In the 1950s, Sol Tax called for anthropologists to not just research these problems but to become active advocates for native peoples—engaged in what he called **action anthropology**. In 1961 Tax found funding for and coordinated the American Indian Chicago Conference. During this weeklong conference, 467 Native American people from 90 different communities drafted the "Declaration of Indian Purpose." This conference and the Boulder Workshop for Indian college students that followed led to the creation of the National Indian Youth Council—the first national American Indian activist organization.

In 1972, David Mayberry-Lewis, a Harvard anthropologist, and his wife Pia cofounded Cultural Survival, the largest U.S.-based organization advocating the rights of indigenous peoples. The director of Survival International, the major London-based indigenous rights organization, is British anthropologist Stephen Corry. Throughout the twentieth century and today, anthropologists continue to fight for the rights of indigenous peoples. Thus, it is fitting that we end this book by advocating the rights of indigenous peoples to preserve their cultural systems.

Indigenous Peoples Today

Anthropologists frequently use the term *indigenous peoples*—a label that is somewhat ambiguous in that it refers to any native people. Anthropologists also use the equally ambiguous terms *tribal peoples* and *Fourth World peoples* as synonyms for *indigenous peoples*. Not surprisingly, there are disagreements about which particular societies should or should not be considered "indigenous," "tribal," or "Fourth World."

Complicating the issue are the different number estimates. The Human Rights Council of the United Nations estimates that there are 370 million "indigenous peoples" in the modern world, whereas Survival International estimates that there are about 150 million "tribal peoples" living in about 60 countries. Although here we use the term *indigenous peoples*, we use it as a synonym for *tribal* or *Fourth World peoples*. **Indigenous peoples** refers to those foraging, horticultural, and/or pastoral societies that have yet to be economically or politically integrated into the market economy and governmental system of the countries or regions in which they live.

As such, indigenous peoples survive as ethnic enclaves within larger nation-states. The governments, controlled by the dominant ethnic group or groups of these countries, usually claim ultimate authority over the land, resources, and lives of the indigenous peoples who live within their officially recognized national borders. For indigenous peoples, the colonial world still exists. Among them are indigenous peoples of the Americas; aboriginal peoples of Australia and other islands of the Pacific; the Sami (formerly known as the Lapps) of northern Europe; and hundreds, if not several thousand, smaller ethnic groups in Asia and Africa.

These small, culturally distinct societies have survived up to the present day in the remote jungles, swamps, mountains, deserts, tundra, and other "undeveloped" regions of the world for only one reason: They did not have anything their larger and far more powerful neighbors wanted.

The global economy is rapidly changing indigenous peoples' relationship with the outside world. The growth of industrialization together with a global population explosion is creating ever-increasing demands for food, timber, minerals, energy, and water. The lands presently occupied by these indigenous peoples constitute the last "undeveloped" or "underdeveloped" lands in the world; the lands of the indigenous peoples are the last frontier. The world's remaining jungles and woodlands are rapidly being cleared for timber and/or for new farms and ranches. Vast river valleys are being damned and flooded for hydroelectric power. No region is too remote or isolated to be safe from development if rich deposits of oil, natural gas, iron, copper, nickel, bauxite (aluminum ore), gold, diamonds, or other valuable minerals are discovered.

The rights of indigenous peoples became an issue at the time of Columbus's landing in the Americas. Questions of whether the native peoples of the Americas—or, for that matter, any non-Christian indigenous people—had any inherent rights to their land, resources, or political sovereignty were debated in Spain. Although legal particulars differed from one colonial power to another as well as over time, a basic consensus was reached early in the colonial period: Indigenous peoples did have some rights based on prior occupancy. However, more "civilized" peoples could unilaterally claim dominion over them and make use of any land and resources that were either not utilized or were "underutilized." "Civilized" peoples had both a right and an

---

action anthropology Public support for and facilitation of indigenous communities and organizations in their attempts to protect their human rights.

indigenous peoples Those foraging, horticultural, and/or pastoral societies that have yet to be economically or politically integrated into the market economy and governmental system of the countries or regions in which they live.

obligation to uplift indigenous peoples and to act in their best interest. "Civilized" peoples also had the right to travel and trade wherever they wanted free of interference from indigenous peoples. Finally, if an indigenous people resisted, then the "civilized" peoples had the right to use military force against them. Racist, ethnocentrist, and social Darwinist ideas about the inevitability and desirability of progress provided the moral justification for the treatment of indigenous peoples.

Such attitudes and policies affected the governing of most indigenous peoples in European colonies. With the collapse of these colonial empires, the leaders of the new independent countries adopted the same basic attitudes and policies toward the resources of the indigenous minority communities. Here, we discuss three groups in three different regions of the world to show some of the ways in which globalization is destroying the lives of indigenous peoples.

The San

Within the southern African nation of Botswana lies the Central Kalahari Game Reserve (CKGR); larger in land area than Switzerland, it is the second largest game reserve in all Africa. The CKGR was established in 1961, partly to provide the indigenous hunter-gatherers of the region—the San—with adequate resources for their subsistence needs and partly to protect its abundant wildlife.

In the 1960s and 1970s, local groups of San used the territory as they always had for subsistence foraging: hunting and gathering of food plants. In the 1980s, European environmentalists began pressuring Botswana officials to remove the people from the CKGR and declared the area solely a game reserve, with no hunting allowed. By the 1990s, the San were encouraged to move outside the reserve by various methods, including failure to repair a needed well, intimidation by selective enforcement of game laws, and (allegedly) severe physical punishments of accused poachers.

By 2002, the government had resettled nearly all of the resident San—about 1,000 individuals—into two settlements outside the boundaries of the reserve; there—having no jobs, no wild plant foods to gather, and no animals to hunt—they live primarily off of government-issued rations. This action was taken partly in the name of conservation. However, the government also argued that it was for the good of the San, so "that they may be provided with modern facilities, schools, clinics, etc. and to integrate them into modern society." According to Robert Hitchcock (1999, p. 54) the San "expressed that the reason they were being removed was so that well-to-do private citizens could set up lucrative safari camps in the reserve." In 2002, the San filed a legal case in the High Court of Botswana. In 2006, the court finally ruled that their eviction was unlawful and unconstitutional, that they had a right to live on the reserve, and that the government had to issue them hunting permits. Justice Phumaphi of the Botswana High Court stated that forbidding the San to hunt was "tantamount to condemning [them] to death."

Despite the court ruling, the government still attempted to keep the San from returning to the reserve by capping their only water well and by at first refusing to issue hunting permits for San hunters and arresting hunters. Later they began allowing a few to hunt on the reserve. Meanwhile, a new deluxe tourist lodge, complete with a swimming pool, was established. However, the San were not allowed take water from the lodge swimming pool or any of the water wells on the reserve, which are for animals. In responding to criticism, the Bushman welfare minister stated, "To those who think for some reason that opening lodges for tourists in the Kalahari while we are banning the Bushmen from accessing their water borehole [well] is immoral, I say, 'would you prefer your tourists sweaty?'" He added, "They should have realized by now, it will be much better for them to go back to the relocation camps, where there is no shortage of home-brew and other alcoholic beverages to quench their thirst, rather than persisting in living on their 'ancestral land' in the Kalahari."

Arguing that their right to hunt was irrelevant, if they did not have access to water, the San took their case to court and asked for the water well to be opened. In February 2011, Botswana's Court of Appeals ruled in favor of the San, stating that their treatment was "degrading." The San now have the right to open one or more water wells; however, they have to do this at their own expense. Nevertheless, government officials have in most cases ignored the rulings of the court. As one relocated San stated, "We thought the government would help us. . . . But I think the government is killing us."

Although the Botswanan government had always stated that the reason for removing the San from the reserve was to protect wildlife, it had been rumored that the government was secretly leasing diamond mining rights to parts of the reserve. In 2014, Gem Diamonds opened a mine in the CKGR at the cost of almost $5 billion. In 2015, the Gem Diamond mine—together with the Botswanan Tourist Board, a local bank, and a luxury hotel and casino—began sponsoring an annual Kalahari Challenge: a three-day, 237-kilometer bicycle race in the reserve. What the Botswanan government has done is stolen the land while attempting to destroy the culture of a small, powerless group of people whose ancestors had lived in the Kalahari Desert for tens of thousands of years—all for the benefit of a foreign-owned mining company and the pleasure of wealthy foreign eco-tourists and bicycling enthusiasts.

Dongria Kondh

Numbering only about 8,000, the Dongria Kondh are a small indigenous people in India. Living in the jungle-covered Niyamgiri Hills in Odisha (Orissa) state, the Dongria Kondh support themselves by growing small crops of millet, peas, and beans and by collecting fruits, plants, and palm oil in the jungle, some of which they sell in the towns at the foot of the hills. As one young tribal member stated, "We get everything from the jungle like the fruits we take to the market. This is . . . our source of life."

Speaking their own distinct language, Kui, they are neither Hindu nor Muslim. They have their own native religion: The mountains are their temples—the homes of their gods and the places they pray and make sacrifices. The region is so remote that their villages lack schools, electricity, television, and telephones. Only a few have had any formal education.

Their isolation is rapidly ending, however. Vedanta Resources, a London-based but Indian-controlled multinational corporation, has constructed a $1 billion aluminum refinery at the base of the Niyamgiri Hills. The government of Odisha, one of the poorest states in India, agreed to allow Vedanta to strip-mine the Niyamgiri Hills for bauxite ore, from which aluminum is made. This open-pit mine will necessitate not only the clearing of much of the jungle, but the destruction of most of the hills as well. For the Dongria Kondh, the strip mining will destroy not just their economy and religion, but their whole way of life. Local environmentalists attempted to legally stop the development in court, arguing that the mining violates the Indian Forest Conservation Act. In July 2009, activists in London demonstrated at the annual meeting of Vedanta.

In October 2009, after a nine-month investigation, the British government found, among other things, that Vedanta "did not respect the rights of the Dongria Kondh" and "did not consider the impact of the construction of the mine on . . . [their] rights." The government further stated "a change in the company's behaviour is essential." Although legally a British company, Vedanta ignored the government's rulings, saying that because its majority owners were Indian nationals, it was really an Indian company. Despite national and international outcry,

The physical and cultural survival of the Yanomamö and other Amazonian peoples is threatened by opening up their traditional lands to mining, logging, ranching, and other extractive industries.

Vedanta still proceeded with the project, while the issue remained unresolved in the Indian court system.

In December 2012, the Dongria Kondh, together with thousands of other indigenous peoples, demonstrated to voice their opposition to the mine before India's Supreme Court announced its final decision. Finally, in April 2013, the Supreme Court ruled, stating,

> If the project, affects their [tribal] religious rights, especially their right to worship their deity known as Niyam Raja, in the hill tops of the Niyamgiri range of hills, that right has to be preserved and protected. We find that this aspect of the matter has not been placed before the Gram Sabha [local self-governments] for their active consideration.

The court then requested that the Gram Sabha of the two local districts inform the united environmental ministry of their decision within three months.

In 2013, a referendum was held in the Gram Sabha representing the Dongria Kondh. In a unanimous vote, the mine was rejected, and Vedanta announced that it would not seek to mine the hill until it had the consent of the community. In 2015, the state of Odisha resumed consultations with the tribe over the mine, arguing that the 2013 referendum was flawed. Thus, the future of the hill has not been resolved: There is too much money involved, and Vedanta has already invested $1 billion.

Kayapo

Brazil began planning for a massive development of hydroelectric dams in the Amazon Basin in the mid-1970s; however, it was not until the late 1980s, with funding from the World Bank, that preparation began in earnest.

The plan called for a major hydroelectric dam to be built on the lower Xingu River. With a relatively small reservoir covering only about 150 square miles of jungle, this dam would be capable of producing 11,000 megawatts of electricity, making it potentially one of the world's three largest producers. However, for three to five months during the dry season, the lower Xingu dam would be able to produce little if any electricity. Thus, the construction of the lower Xingu dam would necessitate the construction of five other dams on the upper Xingu. Although these new dams would not produce as much electricity as the dam on the lower Xingu, controlled water releases into the river from the larger upstream reservoirs would allow the main dam to generate the maximum amount of electricity throughout the year. The largest of these upstream reservoirs would flood over 2,500 square miles of forest, while the reservoirs of the other four would cover several thousand additional square miles. The result would be a massive flooding of the valley of the Xingu and its tributaries, affecting the lands of 37 different native tribes numbering 25,000 people and resulting in the relocation of many of them.

Realizing that these reservoirs would flood their lands and those of their neighbors, leaders of the Kayapo contacted other indigenous leaders to protest. In early 1988, two Kayapo leaders traveled to Washington with anthropologist Darrell Posey to speak against the project to officials of the World Bank and U.S. congressional officials. In February 1989, a large multitribal meeting, the Altamira Gathering, was held to show their opposition. With worldwide news coverage and support from international organizations, the World Bank deferred action on the loan funding the dam project.

In July 2005, without any consultations with the indigenous groups, the Brazilian National Congress approved the construction of what is now called the Belo Monte Dam on the lower Xingu River. There are two likely reasons the Brazilian government changed its position: (1) A Chinese-Brazilian company is planning to build the world's largest aluminum refinery in the region, and (2) the financial support from China means Brazil no longer needs a loan from the World Bank.

Despite renewed protest by the Kayapo and other tribes and legal delays in local courts, in April 2010, the Brazilian government awarded the contract for the construction of the Belo Monte Dam pending approval from the Brazilian Institute of Environment and Renewable Natural Resources. The institute gave full approval in June 2011.

In May 2013, 22,000 construction workers were on site, starting to build the dam, when 200 native people from 8 indigenous groups occupied part of the construction site. The government responded by saying that they would not negotiate with native peoples, and they did not. As the dam neared completion in early 2016, a court order delayed the testing of its turbines and fined its owner Norte Energia and the government $200,000 for failing to provide for the indigenous groups affected by the dam's construction. With the $18 billion Belo Monte Dam scheduled for completion in 2019, the struggle has now shifted to attempting stop the construction of the upstream dams.

Before Americans become too judgmental about the actions of other governments, we have to remember our own not-too-distant past. The following details some of these troubling actions.

In 1882, the federal government acknowledged that 518 acres of farmland in Cataract Canyon belonged to the Havasupai. However, all of their land outside the canyon belonged to the federal government. In 1919, Grand Canyon National Park was created on the lands surrounding Cataract Canyon. At different times, park officials have attempted to stop the Havasupai people's seasonal hunting and gathering activities in the park as well as to relocate them to another more distant reservation. In the 1930s, the Havasupai camp near the park visitor center was burned by rangers who claimed that it was an eyesore and that the Havasupai had no right to be there. It was not until 1975 that the Havasupai Reservation was official expanded to include the land outside their small canyon.

In the mid-1940s, the Mandan, Hidatsa, and Arikara peoples of the Fort Berthold Reservation in North Dakota were as they had always been: farmers cultivating the rich farmlands along the Missouri River. In 1947, the U.S. government forced the sale of over 150,000 acres of their best land and built the Garrison Dam, flooding the richest portion of the reservation.

Fishing for salmon at Celilo Falls on the Columbia River was the main economic activity of the Wishram and Wasco Native American peoples. In 1952, construction began on the Dalles Dam, which flooded the falls and destroyed the fishing economy.

In 1960, the U.S. government built the Kinzua Dam at the border of Pennsylvania and New York on the Allegheny River. The dam flooded 10,000 acres of the Alleghany Reservation in New York, forcing the relocation of 600 Seneca Indians.

The rich coal deposits of Black Mesa in northern Arizona had been known since the nineteenth century. In the 1960s, Peabody Coal wanted to develop these coal deposits to supply nearby coal-powered electrical generators. However, the title to the land was in dispute. Although the mine area was fully occupied, as it had been for 150 years or more, by scattered Navajo pastoral families, the Hopi, whose farming villages were located about 25 miles to the southwest, also had a claim. Although a 50-50 split in the mineral royalties was readily negotiated, the problem of surface ownership remained. In 1963, federal courts decided the Hopi and Navajo had an equal land title, and the U.S. Congress ordered the land divided in 1974. In 1977, the courts drew the boundary, giving much of the surface in the mine area to the Hopi and ordering between 10,000 and 13,000 Navajos to relocate. Deborah Lacerenza (1988, n.p.) summarizes what happened: "The idea that this relocation was caused by a land dispute between the Navajo and Hopi is a distortion . . . a diversion created by business interest in order to gain access to the land and its energy resources."

Do indigenous peoples have the right to control the use of their own lands? Do indigenous peoples have the right to live the way they wish, to determine their own futures? What is the difference between the San and the Germans, the Dongria Kondh and the Japanese, the Kayapo and the Russians? All six groups have their own distinct histories, homelands, languages, cultural traditions, and political institutions. The only difference is that unlike the Germans, Japanese, and Russians, the indigenous groups are too small and powerless to effectively resist.

In 1982, the United Nations created the Working Group on Indigenous Populations (WGIP) with the purpose of developing standards for the protection of indigenous peoples. In the decades that followed, the WGIP and then other United Nations bodies worked with indigenous leaders as well as representatives of national governments to draft a declaration concerning the rights of indigenous peoples. On September 13, 2007, the United Nations General Assembly adopted the Declaration on the Rights of Indigenous Peoples. Here we quote only a few of the more important points relative to indigenous rights directly related to their political status and landholdings.

Several articles address the political rights of indigenous peoples: "Indigenous peoples have the right of self-determination [and] by virtue of that right . . . freely determine their political status" (Article 3); "the right to autonomy or self-government in matters relating to their internal and local affairs" (Article 4); and "the right to promote, develop and maintain their institutional structures and . . . in the cases where they exist, juridical systems or customs, in accordance with international human rights standards" (Article 34).

Other articles address the issues of land, resources, and economic development: "Indigenous peoples have the right to the lands, territories and resources which they have traditionally owned, occupied or otherwise used or acquired" (Article 26); "the right to be secure in the enjoyment of their own means of subsistence and development, and to freely engage in all their traditional and other economic activities" (Article 20); "the right to determine and develop priorities and strategies for the development or use of their lands or territories and other resources" (Article 32); and "the right to the conservation and protection of the environment and the productive capacity of their lands or territories and resources" (Article 28).

Finally, the declaration states that "indigenous peoples shall not be forcibly removed from their lands or territories" (Article 10), and it gives peoples "the right to . . . restitution or . . . fair and equitable compensation, for lands, territories and resources which they have traditionally owned or otherwise occupied or used, and which have been confiscated, taken, occupied, used or damaged without their free, prior and informed consent" (Article 28).

The United Nations General Assembly adopted the declaration with 143 countries voting in favor, 11 countries abstaining, and 4 countries—the United States, Canada, Australia, and New Zealand—voting against. Later these four countries adopted it.

Although Botswana, India, and Brazil voted in favor of the declaration, the actions of these governments since 2007 in regard to the San, the Dongria Kondh, and the Kayapo are clearly violations of the declaration.

The declaration is a nonbinding resolution, meaning it is not international law. It is merely a statement as to what *should* be, not what *shall* be. Tourism is an important source of revenue in Botswana, Odisha is one of the poorest states in India and needs the jobs that the refinery and mine will create, and Brazil badly needs electricity for its rapidly expanding economy.

Not only did Peru support the declaration, but also Peruvian representatives played an important role in drafting the declaration. However, in February 2009, the Peruvian government signed oil leases for portions of the Amazon Basin occupied by native groups. In protest, members of several indigenous groups, armed with bows and arrows, blocked the main road, while others with canoes blockaded a major river. The response? The Peruvian navy destroyed the river blockade, and the police, using helicopters and assault rifles, attacked the roadblock, leaving at least 30 dead. In defending these attacks, President Alan García told the Peruvian people, "The lands of the Amazon belong to you, to you sons, to all the nation, to all Peruvians not just to a small group lives there." What García was saying is that the economic needs of the 28 million people of Peru were more important than the rights of the 300,000 or so indigenous peoples of the Amazon.

The vast majority of world leaders may agree in principle with the ideas set forth in the declaration. Unfortunately, the vast majority of leaders of underdeveloped and developing countries also agree with President García. The recognition of the rights of their indigenous peoples is a luxury they do not feel their countries can afford.

Vanishing Knowledge

Anthropologists are especially concerned with the rights of indigenous peoples for several reasons. First, because of our interest in cultural diversity, we are more aware than most people of what has happened to non-Western cultures in the past several centuries. Second, we identify with indigenous peoples partly because so many of us have worked among them. Third, our professional training gives us a relativistic outlook on the many ways of being human, so we can appreciate other peoples' customs and beliefs as viable alternatives to our own. Finally, the fieldwork experience often affects our attitudes about our own societies—deep immersion in other cultural traditions leaves some of us not so sure about our commitment to our own.

Whether an anthropologist or not, one can appreciate the rights of any group of people to have their lives, property, and resources secure from domination by powerful outsiders. The most important factors in considering the rights of indigenous peoples to be left alone are ethical ones. Don't people everywhere have the right to live their lives free from the unwanted interference of those more powerful and wealthy than themselves? Does any government, regardless of its problems, have the right to dispossess people from land they have lived on and used for centuries, if not longer?

Ethical concerns for the human rights of indigenous peoples, combined with a respect for their cultural traditions, are the primary reasons for granting their rights to survive as living communities. But if the ethical arguments alone are not compelling, other arguments are based on more practical concerns. For example, the long-term welfare of all humanity may be jeopardized by the loss of cultural diversity on our planet. Think about the cultural heritage of humanity as a whole. Consider *all* the knowledge accumulated by *all* humanity over hundreds of generations. Imagine, in other words, human culture—here defined as the sum of all knowledge stored in the cultural traditions of all humans alive today.

Some of the knowledge in present-day human culture has been widely disseminated in the past few centuries by means of written language. We may call it *global knowledge* (but do not mean to imply that it is true or universally known). Although some global knowledge will be lost or replaced, much of the knowledge stored in writing (or, more recently, on computer discs or "the cloud") will be preserved and added to over the coming decades and centuries. Other knowledge in human culture is *local knowledge*—it is stored only in the heads of members of particular cultures, many of which are endangered. Most local knowledge will disappear if those cultural traditions disappear—even if the people themselves survive.

How much of this local knowledge is knowledge that may in the future prove useful to all humanity? No one knows. But no one can doubt that the rest of the world has much to learn from indigenous cultures. In fact, much of what had been only the local knowledge of some indigenous culture has been incorporated into global knowledge, as a consequence of contact with the West and other colonizing peoples. We conclude this book with a small sample of some of the medical and adaptive wisdom of indigenous peoples, whose local knowledge has already contributed so much to the world.

Medicines We Have Learned

"The Medicine Man Will See You Now," proclaimed a headline in a 1993 edition of *Business Week*. The accompanying article described a California pharmaceutical company that sends ethnobotanists and other scientists into rain forests to learn from indigenous shamans. Companies as well as scholars are beginning to understand that the traditional remedies long used by preindustrial peoples often have genuine medical value. In fact, many of the important drugs in use today were derived from indigenous knowledge. Here, we provide only a few examples of the medicines originally discovered by indigenous peoples that now have worldwide significance. An enjoyable source of more examples is the 1993 book *Tales of a Shaman's Apprentice*, by Mark Plotkin.

Malaria remains a debilitating, although usually not fatal, sickness in tropical and subtropical regions. Its main treatment is quinine, a component of the bark of the cinchona tree. Europeans in the seventeenth century learned of the value of quinine from Peruvian Indians.

The Madagascar periwinkle has long been used in folk medicine to treat diabetes. Researchers first became interested in the plant as a substitute for oral insulin, but it seems to have little value for this purpose. During their investigation, however, scientists discovered that extracts from periwinkle yielded dramatic successes in treating childhood leukemia, Hodgkin's disease, and some other cancers. Drugs based on the plant—notably vincristine and vinblastine—remain the major treatments for these otherwise fatal diseases.

Muscle relaxants are important drugs to surgeons. A popular one is curare, made from the chondodendron vine. Taken in large amounts, curare can paralyze the respiratory organs and lead to death. This property was recognized by South American Indians, who used it as arrow poison for hunting birds, monkeys, and other game and from whom medical science learned of the drug's value.

B. & C. Alexander/Science Source

Indigenous peoples, such as these Indonesian medicine men, commonly have an extensive and potentially important knowledge of the curative powers of plants. How much medical knowledge of healers in indigenous cultures will be lost?

The ancient Greeks and several North American Indian tribes used the bark of willows for relief from pain and fever. In the nineteenth century, scientists succeeded in artificially synthesizing this compound that today we call "aspirin."

There is no way of knowing how many plants used by surviving indigenous peoples could prove medically effective. The potential is great. According to pharmacologist Norman Farnsworth, about one-fourth of all prescribed drugs in the United States contain active ingredients extracted from higher plants. The world contains more than 250,000 species of higher plants. Although as many as 40,000 of these plants may have medical or nutritional value, only about 1,100 of these have been well studied. Botanists and medical researchers are coming to realize what indigenous peoples already have discovered, through centuries of trial and error: Certain plants are effective remedies for diseases. The value of indigenous peoples' medical wisdom to all of humanity is potentially great.

Adaptive Wisdom

Many preindustrial peoples have lived in and exploited their natural environments for centuries. Earlier in this chapter, we discussed the problems of technology in attempting to overcome hunger and some of the important traditional agricultural alternatives used by indigenous peoples such as the Kayapo and the

Lacandon Maya. They have learned to control insect pests and diseases that attack the plants on which they depend, and to do so without using expensive and often dangerous artificial chemicals. They have often learned how to make nature work for them while minimizing the deterioration of their environments. They have, in short, incorporated much adaptive wisdom into their cultural traditions. Following are possible benefits that all humanity might gain by preserving the ecological knowledge of indigenous peoples.

Preservation of Crop Varieties

In all cultivation systems, natural selection operates in the farmers' fields. Like wild plants, crops are subject to drought, disease, insects, and other natural elements, which select for the survival of the individual plants best adapted to withstand these hazards. In addition, crops are subject to human selection. For example, crop varieties most susceptible to drought or local diseases are harvested in smaller quantities than drought- and disease-resistant varieties. Perhaps without knowing it, the cultivator replants mainly those varieties best adapted to survive the onslaughts of drought and local diseases.

This tuning of plant varieties to the local environment, with all its hazards and fluctuations, goes on automatically so long as the crops harvested from the fields are replanted in the same area. Thanks to the unintentional and intentional selection by hundreds of generations of indigenous cultivators around the world, each species of crop (e.g., beans, potatoes, wheat) evolved a large number of *land races,* or distinct varieties adapted to local conditions.

Over the course of human history, several thousand species of plants have been used for food, but less than a hundred of these were ever domesticated. Of all the plants that have been domesticated, today only a handful provides significant amounts of food for the world's people. In fact, only four crops—wheat, rice, maize, and potato—provide almost half of the world's total consumption of food.

Since around 1950, plant geneticists and agricultural scientists have developed new varieties of wheat, corn, rice, and potatoes capable of giving higher yields if they receive proper amounts of water and fertilizers. These new strains were developed by crossing and recrossing native land races collected from all over the world. The aim was to achieve a "green revolution" that would end world hunger by increasing production. Many new varieties are hybrids, which means that farmers must receive a new supply of seeds yearly from governmental or private sources.

Ironically, having been bred from the genetic material present in their diverse ancestors, the new strains now threaten to drive their ancestors to extinction. As farmers in Asia, Africa, and the Americas plant the seeds of artificially bred varieties, the traditional varieties—the land races that are the product of generations of natural and human selection—fall into disuse, and many have disappeared.

Why should we care? Increasingly, agricultural experts are realizing the dangers of dependence on a few varieties. If crops that are nearly identical genetically are planted in the same area year after year, a new variety of pest or disease will eventually evolve to attack them. The famous Irish potato famine of the 1840s, which we discussed earlier, was directly related to the genetic uniformity of the potato because all the potatoes in Ireland were apparently descended from only a few plants. The United States has also suffered serious economic losses: The corn blight of 1970 destroyed about 15 percent of the American crop. Losses would have been less severe had most American farmers not planted a single variety of corn.

Many plant breeders are alarmed at the prospect of losing much of the genetic diversity of domesticated plants. Today, they are searching remote regions for surviving land races that contain genes that one day might prove valuable. (The seeds are stored in seed banks for future study.) The searchers have been successful, although no one knows how much of the genetic diversity of crops such as wheat and corn has already disappeared.

The knowledge of indigenous peoples is an important resource in the effort to preserve land races. In many parts of the world—the Andes, Central America, Amazonia, the Middle East, and elsewhere—cultivators still grow ancient varieties of crops. They know where these varieties yield best, how to plant and care for them, how to prepare them for eating, and so on. In the Andes, for instance, over 3,000 potato varieties survive among the indigenous peoples. Many have specific ecological requirements, and some are even unique to a single valley. Research is now under way to determine how well specific land races will grow in other areas to help solve food supply problems elsewhere. It is important to preserve the genetic information encoded in these varieties for future generations.

Indigenous peoples who still retain the hard-won knowledge of their ancestors and who still use the often-maligned "traditional crop varieties" are important informational resources in the effort to save the genetic diversity of crops on which humanity depends.

"Undiscovered" Useful Species

In addition to their familiarity with local crop varieties that have potential worldwide significance, many indigenous peoples cultivate or use crop species that are currently unimportant to the rest of the world. One example is amaranth, a grain native to the Americas that was of great importance to the Indians in prehistoric times. The great Mesoamerican civilizations made extensive use of the plant in their religious rituals. This led the Spanish conquerors, in their anxiety to root out heathenism, to burn fields of amaranth and prohibit its consumption. Otherwise, it—like maize, potatoes, beans, squash, and other American crops—might have diffused to other continents. Amaranth remains an important food to some indigenous peoples of highland Latin America, who retain knowledge of its properties and requirements. Its unusually high protein content is just starting to make it an attractive grain to some modern consumers in other parts of North America and might someday make it valuable throughout the rest of the world.

Other plants used by native peoples have the potential to become important elsewhere. Quinoa, now grown mainly in Peruvian valleys, has twice the protein content of corn and has long been recognized as a domesticate with great potential. The tepary bean, now grown mainly by the O'odham of the American Southwest, can survive and yield well during extreme droughts, which might make it cultivatable in other arid regions of the world. Another legume, the winged bean, has long been cultivated by the native peoples of Papua New Guinea, and it has helped nourish people in 50 other tropical countries.

Besides food, indigenous peoples have discovered many other uses for the plants found in their habitats. Scientific researchers today are attesting to the validity of much native knowledge about the use of plants as sources of fuel, oils, medicines, and other beneficial substances, including poisons. Forest peoples of Southeast Asia use the toxic roots of a local woody climbing plant as a fish poison. The root is so powerful that a mixture of 1 part root to 300,000 parts water will kill fish. From the indigenous tribes, scientists learned of the toxicity of these roots, which allowed them to isolate the rotenoid now used as an insecticide spray for plants and as dips and dusting powders for livestock.

Scientists no doubt will rediscover many other useful plants that today they know nothing about—if the tropical forests in which most endangered plant species are found last long enough. Their task will be easier if the original discoverers—indigenous peoples—are around to teach them what their ancestors learned.

Cultural Alternatives

There is another kind of practical lesson we might learn from surviving indigenous peoples. Industrialized humans have developed technologies that discover, extract, and transform natural resources on a scale undreamed of a century ago. To North Americans and many other citizens of the developed world, "progress" is almost synonymous with "having more things." Yet whether our economies can continue to produce ever-increasing supplies of goods is questionable. Many of us are frightened by the thought that economic growth might not continue. The fear that we will be forced to accept a stagnation or even a decline in our levels of material consumption no doubt contributes to the interest today's undergraduates have in careers they believe are most likely to earn high incomes for themselves and their future families.

On the other hand, some individuals and groups in the affluent, developed world have questioned the value of what most of their fellow citizens call "economic progress." They think the environmental and familial costs of the unceasing drive to accumulate and to succeed in a highly competitive environment are not worth the benefits. Some of them believe material affluence cannot bring happiness because it is gained at the high cost of the emotional gratifications that spring from community relationships, from supportive family and friendship ties, and from adherence to what some call spiritual values (see the Global Challenges and Opportunities feature).

Most readers of this book are the beneficiaries of economic progress. At the same time, we should be careful not to become the victims of the mentality of progress—of that unceasing desire to earn more, to have more, to succeed more. If the industrial bubble does not burst in our lifetime, then most of us who live in the developed world will spend our lives in a continuous effort to increase our consumption of goods. We will do so despite the fact that our efforts will never be sufficient to get us all we want because no one can consume goods as fast as companies can turn them out and advertisers can create new desires for them. We will do so despite the fact that many of our marriages and families will be torn apart by the effort, and many of us will suffer psychologically and physically from stress-related disorders. Sadly, most of us pursue our dollars and goods unthinkingly because we remain ignorant of any alternative way of living.

The world's remaining indigenous peoples provide us with such alternatives. They do not and did not live in a primitive paradise. Subjugation of neighboring

What is the purpose of the global economy? Judging by the frenzied behavior of many, if not most, of the peoples of the world, it appears to be to satisfy an insatiable demand for material goods and narcissistic pleasures. Is wealth only measured in material goods? Does the country or people with the most toys win? It certainly appears that way.

When we think of development, we almost invariably think only in terms of economic development. To us, the economic development of a country, a state, or a region is easily measured; it is a matter of dollars and cents. We need only to look at the gross national product (GNP) or the per capita incomes. If we compare countries in terms of their growth of GNP, then we can determine which are the most economically successful—the winners. However, are the gross production figures the only—or even the best—measure of development? Are per-capita incomes the best measure of the standard of living of the society?

Nobel Prize–winning economist Amartya Sen argues that growth in the GNP alone is not a particularly good indicator of development. As a child in India, he lived through the great famine of 1943, during which 3 million people died. Perhaps not surprisingly, one of his interests as an economist is famine. He has discovered that famines were not solely or even primarily the result of food shortages. Instead, famines are frequently the result of market forces that increase the cost of food while depressing incomes to the point that families can no longer purchase adequate food. Just as famines are not necessarily the result of food shortages, the growth in the GNP of a country does not in itself result in increased prosperity. The GNP might be growing with little economic benefit to many, if not most, of the people.

Sen also questions how we measure standards of living. Is it merely a question of relative income? The Indian state of Kerala is an excellent example that per-capita income figures alone are not always the best measure of quality of life. Covering only 24,000 square miles along the southwest coast of India, Kerala is home to 33 million people. Depending primarily on agriculture, Kerala is a poor state, even by Indian standards. In terms of gross domestic product (GDP), Kerala averages only about $1,000 per capita, $200 less than India as a whole, and only 1/26 that of the United States. By such economic measures alone, residents of Kerala would appear to have a very poor standard of living. If we look at Kerala in terms of health, education, and other social issues, however, we see a far different picture.

In terms of health, the people of Kerala are better off than most other peoples in India and in countries with much higher incomes. Their infant mortality rate is among the lowest in the developing world. Their life expectancy is 72 years—11 years longer than the average for India, and only 4 years shorter than the United States.

Even more impressive are their achievements in education. Well-maintained schools are scattered throughout the state, and education is virtually universal. As a result, 90 percent of the people are literate—an achievement that places Kerala on the same level as the far more prosperous peoples of Spain and Singapore.

Social discrimination is less of a problem than in other parts of India and most of the world. Protests against the caste system began in Kerala in the middle of the nineteenth century, and in no other part of India has this system been so expunged from social consciousness. Although there are sizable Muslim and Christian minorities in the state, there have not been the religious conflicts that have beset most of India.

However, possibly the major factor that distinguishes Kerala from other parts of India and most parts of the world is its relative equality in income and opportunity. In the 1960s, the state government abolished landlordism and redistributed the land to 1.5 million tenant families. Kerala also has a relatively high minimum wage. This wage has discouraged industrial development, and, as a result, Kerala has an unemployment rate of 25 percent. Because most families have land on which they can garden, however, they are shielded from destitution.

Sen is not arguing that Kerala is a utopian paradise. What he is arguing is that the relative health, education, and social harmony of a community are far better measures of a people's development than material wealth. The relative quality of life of a people cannot be measured by wealth alone, and the people of Kerala have made their choice.

The Thrissur Pooram Elephant Festival in Kerala, India, celebrates the end of the harvest.

Frans Lanting Studio/Alamy

peoples, exploitation by the wealthy and powerful, degradation of women, warfare, and other ideas and practices many of us find abhorrent existed among some preindustrial peoples, just as they do today. Yet, we also find other cultural conditions that some of us long to recover: closer family ties, greater self-sufficiency, smaller communities, more personal and enduring social relationships, and more humane, more moral values.

No anthropologist can tell you whether life is better or worse in preindustrial communities; indeed, we cannot agree on the meaning of *better*. We do know that humanity is diverse. We know that this diversity means that human beings—ourselves included—have many alternative ways of living meaningful and satisfying lives. In the end, it is these cultural alternatives provided by indigenous peoples that might have the greatest value to humankind.

Perhaps a people themselves are the only ones qualified to judge the quality of their lives, to decide what it will take to lend meaning and dignity to their existence. We hope we have convinced you that there are many ways of being human, and we hope you have learned to appreciate some of the alternative ways of living experienced by various human populations. We hope you will agree that some of these alternatives are worth preserving, both in their own right and for the long-term well-being of all humanity.

SUMMARY

1. **Define applied anthropology and discuss its importance today in understanding the cultures of other peoples.** Anthropological expertise is useful for solving human problems because the way anthropologists look at people and cultures (our worldview) differs somewhat from the views of other professionals. Applied anthropologists have conducted research relevant to both global and local-level problems.

2. **Define medical anthropology.** Medical anthropology is the study of all aspects of health and health care for the purpose of improving the health of the people of the world.

3. **Compare the differences between Western or scientific medicine and most traditional systems of healing.** Explanation of illness usually falls into two broad categories: natural causation, which accounts for illness as a physiological consequence of some experience of the individual; and supernatural causation, which accounts for illness as the consequence of some supernatural experience. Western or scientific medicine sees and treats illness as the result of natural causes, whereas many traditional medical practices are based on the belief that illness is at least in part the result of supernatural causes.

4. **Identify the unfavorable consequences of rapid population growth.** Population growth has many unfavorable consequences. It contributes to serious environmental problems, low economic productivity, urban sprawl and shantytowns, political conflicts, and even war. This is the main paradox of population growth: The high fertility of a country's citizens is mainly responsible for the growth, yet their high fertility contributes to many of their nation's problems.

5. **Explain why the population growth rates are high in the poorer regions of the world.** High fertility in LDCs is likewise a consequence of the overall economic and social environment that constrains reproductive behavior. Ethnographic studies suggest that children are a net economic asset rather than a liability in the rural areas of the Third World. Children are productive family members at a young age. They seek jobs with local people to supplement the family income. When older, they go to cities or to foreign countries and send money back home. They provide old-age security for their parents. Under such conditions, high fertility and large families are beneficial.

6. **Describe the two explanations for world hunger.** Population growth is often believed to be the major cause of world hunger. This is the

scarcity explanation of hunger, which holds that overpopulation leads to chronic malnutrition and periodic massive starvation. The alternative is the inequality explanation. It holds that land and other food-producing resources are in fact sufficient to provide an adequate diet for the whole world. Hunger is caused by the way local and world economies allocate resources. These two explanations of hunger are compatible: Population growth contributes to hunger by increasing the scarcity of food production resources, yet prevalent inequalities in access to productive resources aggravate the scarcity and prevent people from adjusting to it.

7. **Identify some of the possible solutions for hunger.** Technology transfer is a viable solution to hunger in LDCs, according to many. But there are numerous problems with this solution. Temperate agricultural methods often do not work well in tropical climates and soils. New technologies sometimes harm rather than help the poorest families. Peasants often do not adopt new technologies and crop varieties because they perceive them as not worth the costs or because they cannot afford to assume the risks of failure. Mechanized agriculture requires so much energy to produce food that it may not be affordable to Third World farmers and may not be sustainable in the long run. Agricultural scientists, anthropologists, and others have been researching alternative farming methods long used by traditional peoples of the world. Traditional methods such as intercropping and resource management hold promise for increasing food production sustainably. It is likely that a combination of solutions will be necessary to alleviate problems of hunger and poverty.

8. **Discuss how globalization is changing the lives of indigenous peoples and destroying the cultural traditions of these peoples.** Smaller indigenous foraging, farming, and herding peoples have existed until the present day in isolated and remote regions of the world. They have survived primarily because they had nothing their more powerful neighbors wanted. Globalization and the global

economy are today threatening the continued existence of these peoples. The forests and jungles that many depend on are being cut for timber and/ or farmland and ranchland. Mining and energy development is destroying their land and polluting their water. The construction of hydroelectric dams is flooding their valleys. The national governments that claim dominion over them are ignoring their rights in the name of development.

9. **Analyze the potential importance of the cultural knowledge of indigenous peoples.** Ethical considerations alone are a sufficient reason these peoples should be allowed to remain in their communities, on their traditional lands, living in the ways of their ancestors, if that is their choice. Pragmatic considerations are also important because these people still retain a vast body of knowledge—knowledge that is of great potential value to all humanity. Science has already adapted several important medicines and treatments from indigenous peoples. Many other plants with medical value will probably be discovered, if the tropical forests and the cultural knowledge of their indigenous inhabitants last long enough. Adaptive wisdom is to be found in the traditions of indigenous peoples. Land races of important crops still survive and might contain genetic materials from which useful foods might someday be bred. Crops that today are used primarily by indigenous peoples—such as amaranth, quinoa, tepary bean, and the winged bean—might eventually have worldwide significance. Nonfood plants are also important as insecticides, oils, fibers, and other products. Indigenous people also provide us with alternative cultural models, showing us that material living standards do not necessarily relate to life satisfaction. The diversity of the human species shows that we can live meaningful and wholly satisfying lives without the technologies and huge quantities of consumer goods we consider necessary to our economic welfare. The remaining preindustrial cultures allow us to see that there is more than one narrow road to personal fulfillment, cultural health, and national dignity and prestige.

Glossary

accommodation Creation of social and political systems that provide for and support ethnic group differences together with local autonomy.

action anthropology Public support for and facilitation by anthropologists of indigenous communities and organizations in their attempts to protect their human rights.

aesthetic A quality that makes objects, actions, or language more beautiful or pleasurable.

agriculture Purposeful planting, cultivation, care, and harvest of domesticated food plants (crops); also called **cultivation**.

ambilineal descent Form of descent in which relationships may be traced through both females and males; also called **cognatic descent**.

ambilocal residence Residence form in which couples choose whether to live with the wife's or the husband's family.

ancestral rituals Rituals intended to worship, honor, or beseech the deceased ancestors of a kin group; also called *ancestor veneration*.

animism Belief in spiritual beings.

anthropological linguistics Subfield that focuses on the interrelationships between language and other aspects of a people's culture.

anthropology Academic discipline that studies all of humanity from a broad biological and cultural perspective.

applied anthropology Subfield applying anthropological perspectives, theory, empirical knowledge of cultures, and methods to help assess and solve real-world problems; practitioners are often employed by a governmental agency or private organization.

archaeology Investigation of past cultures through excavation of material remains.

art Any product of human behavior that has a cultural meaning not inherent in its visual appearance or sound.

artificial country Multinationality country created by external powers; usually applied to a former colony.

assimilation Social absorption of the members of one ethnic group into another, with the consequent abandonment of the former group's identity.

authority Recognized right of an individual to command another to act in a particular way; legitimate power.

balanced reciprocity Exchange of products or services considered to have roughly equal value; social purposes usually motivate the exchange.

band Small foraging group with flexible composition that migrates seasonally.

big man Political leader who does not occupy a formal office and whose leadership is based on influence, not authority.

bilateral kinship Form of kinship in which individuals trace their kinship relationships equally through both parents.

bilocal residence Residence form in which couples move between the households of both sets of parents.

biological determinism Idea that biologically (genetically) inherited differences between populations are important influences on the cultural differences between them.

biological anthropology Major subfield of anthropology that studies the biological dimensions of humans and other primates; also called **physical anthropology**.

body arts The temporary or permanent enhancements of the human body.

body painting Decoration of the body by painting designs.

body piercing Decoration of the body by piercing holes in parts of the body for the attachment of ornaments.

borrowing The spread or diffusion of cultural knowledge from members of one society to those of another society.

bound morpheme Morpheme attached to a free morpheme to alter its meaning.

brideservice Custom in which a man spends a period of time working for the family of his wife.

bridewealth Custom in which a prospective groom and his relatives are required to transfer goods to the relatives of the bride to create or validate the marriage.

capitalism Market economy; emphasizes capital accumulation through profitmaking as the key to economic growth and maximum material welfare.

cargo cults Melanesian revitalization movements in which prophets claim to know secret rituals that will bring wealth (cargo).

caste System of stratification in which membership in a stratum is in theory hereditary, strata are endogamous, and contact or relationships among members of different strata are governed by explicit laws, norms, or prohibitions.

chiefdom Centralized political system with authority vested in formal, usually hereditary, offices or titles.

civilization First meaning: A level of cultural complexity characterized by intensive agriculture, cities, monumental architecture, writing systems, metallurgy, and craft specialization (Chapter 7). Second meaning: In Huntington's terms, groupings of nationalities on the basis of shared or common cultural historical traditions; in most cases, this shared cultural tradition takes the form of religion (Chapter 16).

clan Named unilineal descent group, some of whose members are unable to trace how they are related but who still believe themselves to be related and who periodically associate or cooperate.

class System of stratification in which membership in a stratum can theoretically be altered and intermarriage between strata is allowed.

classification of reality The ways in which the members of a culture divide up the natural and social world into categories, usually linguistically encoded; also known as **cultural construction of reality**.

cognatic descent Form of descent in which relationships may be traced through both females and males; also called **ambilineal descent**.

cognitive approach Notion that religious beliefs provide explanations for puzzling things and events; also called **intellectual approach**.

Columbian Exchange Exchange of people, diseases, domesticated animals and plants, and other cultural knowledge between the peoples of the Old World and the New World.

communal organization Religious organization in which the members of a group cooperate to perform rituals intended to benefit all.

comparative methods Methods that test hypotheses by systematically comparing elements from many cultures.

comparative perspective Insistence by anthropologists that valid hypotheses and theories about humanity be tested with information from a wide range of cultures.

composite band Autonomous (independent) political unit consisting of several extended families that live together for most or all of the year.

configurationalism Theoretical idea that each culture historically develops its own unique thematic patterns around which beliefs, values, and behaviors are oriented.

conflict theory of inequality Theory holding that stratification benefits mainly the upper stratum and is the cause of most social unrest and other conflicts in stratified societies, making inequality beneficial to only a few.

consultant Member of a society who provides information to a fieldworker, often through formal interviews or surveys; also called informant.

controlled comparisons Methodology for testing a hypothesis using historic changes in societies.

court legal system System in which authority for settling disputes and punishing crimes is formally vested in a single individual or group.

court of mediation Court system in which judges attempt to reach compromise solutions, based on the cultural norms and values of the parties involved, that will restore the social cohesion of the community.

court of regulation Court system that uses codified laws, with formally prescribed rights, duties, and sanctions.

cross-cultural comparison Methodology for testing a hypothesis using a sample of societies drawn from around the world.

cultivation Purposeful planting, cultivation, care, and harvest of domesticated food plants (crops); also called **agriculture**.

cultural anthropology Subfield that studies the way of life of contemporary and historically recent human societies and cultures; also called **social anthropology** and **sociocultural anthropology**.

cultural construction of gender Idea that the characteristics a people attribute to males and females are culturally, not biologically, determined; also called the **social construction of gender**.

cultural construction of kinship Idea that the kinship relationships a given people recognize do not perfectly reflect biological relationships; revealed in the kinship terminology.

cultural construction of reality The ways in which the members of a culture divide up the natural and social world into categories, usually linguistically encoded; also known as **classification of reality**.

cultural determinism Notion that the beliefs and behaviors of individuals are programmed by their culture.

cultural identity Cultural tradition a group of people recognizes as its own; the shared customs and beliefs that define how a group sees itself as distinctive.

cultural integration Interrelationships among the various components (elements, subsystems) of a cultural system.

cultural knowledge Information, skills, attitudes, conceptions, beliefs, values, and other mental components of culture that people socially learn during enculturation.

cultural materialism Scientific theoretical orientation claiming that the main influences on cultural differences and similarities are technology, environment, and how people produce and distribute resources; also called **materialism**.

cultural relativism Notion that one should not judge the behavior of other peoples using the standards of one's own culture.

cultural universals Elements of culture that exist in all known human groups or societies.

culture The shared, socially learned knowledge and patterns of behavior characteristic of some group of people.

culture shock The feeling of uncertainty and anxiety an individual experiences when placed in a strange cultural setting.

descent group Group whose members believe themselves to be descended from a common ancestor.

diachronic Describing changes in a culture over time.

dialect Variation in a single language based on factors such as region, subculture, ethnic identity, and socioeconomic class.

discovery New cultural knowledge independently discovered by members of the society through observation, experimentation, or chance.

domestication The purposeful planting, cultivation, and harvest of selected plants and the taming and breeding of certain species of animals in order to increase their usefulness to humans.

dowry Custom in which the family of a woman transfers property or wealth to her and/or to her husband and his family upon her marriage.

ecclesiastical organization Religious organization in which full-time priests perform rituals believed to benefit believers or the whole society, usually in large temples dedicated to religious purposes or deities; found mainly in complex societies.

egalitarian society Form of society in which there is little inequality in access to culturally valued rewards.

enculturation Transmission (by means of social learning) of cultural knowledge to the next generation; also called **socialization**.

endogamous rules Marriage rules requiring individuals to marry some member of their own social group or category.

ethnic boundary marker Any overt characteristic that can be used to indicate ethnic group membership.

ethnic cleansing Physical elimination or removal of an unwanted ethnic group or groups from a country or a particular geographic region; usually involves genocide and/or relocation of the population.

ethnic group Named social group based on perceptions of shared ancestry, cultural traditions, and common history that culturally distinguish that group from other groups.

ethnic homogenization Elimination of ethnic difference within a region or country, historically involving ethnic cleaning or assimilation.

ethnocentrism Attitude or opinion that the morals, values, and customs of one's own culture are superior to those of other peoples.

ethnogenesis Creation of a new ethnic group.

ethnographic fieldwork Collection of information from living people about their way of life; see also **fieldwork**.

ethnography Written description of the way of life of some human population.

ethnohistoric research Study of a people's culture using written accounts and other records.

ethnohistory Study of past cultures using written accounts and other documents.

ethnology Study of human cultures from a comparative perspective.

evolutionary psychology Scientific approach emphasizing that humans are subject to similar evolutionary forces as other animals; associated with the hypothesis that human behavior patterns enhance genetic fitness; also called **sociobiology**.

exogamous rules Marriage rules prohibiting individuals from marrying a member of their own social group or category.

extended family Nuclear families related through culturally variable kinship ties.

feud Method of dispute settlement in self-help legal systems involving multiple but balanced killings between members of two or more kin groups.

fictive kinship Condition in which people who are not biologically related behave as if they are relatives.

fieldwork Ethnographic research that involves observing and interviewing members of a community in order to document and describe their way of life; see also **ethnographic fieldwork**.

foraging Harvest of wild (undomesticated) plants and animals; also called **hunting and gathering**.

forced assimilation Social absorption of one ethnic group by another ethnic group through the use of force.

forensic anthropology Specialization within physical anthropology that analyzes and identifies human remains.

form of descent Principle through which a people trace their descent from previous generations.

free morpheme Morpheme that can be used alone.

functional theory of inequality Theory holding that stratification is a way to reward individuals who contribute the most to society's well-being, making inequality ultimately beneficial to all.

functionalism Theoretical orientation that analyzes cultural elements in terms of their useful effects to individuals or to the persistence of the whole society.

gender crossing Custom by which a person of one sex is allowed to adopt the roles and behavior of the opposite sex, with little or no stigma or punishment.

gendered division of labor Kinds of productive activities and tasks assigned to women versus men in a culture; also called **sexual division of labor**.

gender roles Rights and duties individuals have because of their perceived identities as males, females, or another gender category; also called **sex roles**.

gender stratification Degree to which men and women are unequal in dimensions such as status, power, or influence; access to valued resources; eligibility for social positions; and ability to make decisions about their own lives.

generalized reciprocity Giving of products or services without expectation of a return of equal value at any definite future time.

genocide Deliberate and systematic attempt to eliminate the members of an ethnic category or cultural tradition by killing the members of the group.

global economy Integrated global market in which goods and services are bought and sold globally with prices determined by supply and demand.

global trade The economic exchange of goods and products between the different peoples of the world via established trade networks.

globalization The flow of cultural knowledge, directly or indirectly, among the different peoples of the world.

globalization of production Process of corporations that are headquartered in one country relocating their production facilities to other countries to reduce production costs and remain globally competitive.

grammar Knowledge shared by those who speak and understand a language, including sounds, rules for combining sounds into sequences, meanings of these sequences, and constructing sentences by combining words according to precise rules.

group marriage Several women and several men are married to one another simultaneously.

herding Tending, breeding, and harvesting the products of livestock, which are taken to seasonally available pasturelands and water; also called **pastoralism**.

hierarchical nesting Occurs when an ethnic group is part of a larger collection of ethnic groups, which together constitute a higher level of ethnic identity.

historic archaeology Field that investigates the past of literate peoples through excavation of sites and analysis of artifacts and other material remains.

historical particularism Theoretical orientation emphasizing that each culture is the unique product of all the influences to which it has been subjected in its past, making cross-cultural generalizations questionable; also called *historicism*.

holistic perspective Assumption that any aspect of a culture is integrated with other aspects, so that no dimension of culture can be understood in isolation.

homeland Geographic region over which a particular ethnic group feels it has exclusive rights.

horticulture Methods of cultivation using hand tools powered by human muscles and in which land use is extensive.

household Dwelling or compound inhabited by biological relatives or fictive kin who cooperate and share some resources; in some contexts, a kin group of one or more nuclear families who live in the same physical space.

human variation Physical differences among human populations; an interest of physical anthropologists.

humanistic approach Orientation that mistrusts attempts to explain cultural differences and similarities and cultural changes in favor of achieving an empathetic understanding of particular cultures.

hunting and gathering Harvest of wild (undomesticated) plants and animals; also called **foraging**.

ideologies Ideas and beliefs that legitimize and reinforce inequalities in stratified societies.

incest taboos Prohibitions against sexual intercourse between certain kinds of relatives.

incipient court Court system in which judicial authorities meet, frequently informally, in private to discuss issues and determine solutions to be imposed. Evidence is not formally collected, and the parties involved in these cases are not formally consulted.

indigenous peoples Those foraging, horticultural, and/or pastoral societies that have yet to be economically or politically integrated into the market economy and governmental system

of the countries or regions in which they live.

individualistic organization Religious organization based on personal relationships between specific individuals and specific supernatural powers.

industrialism Development of technology to harness the energy of fossil fuels to increase productivity, profits, and the availability of consumer commodities.

industrial revolution Historical period in the eighteenth and nineteenth centuries during which predominantly agrarian societies became industrialized and urban through the harnessing of energy in fossil fuels.

inequality Degree to which individuals, groups, and categories differ in their access to culturally valued rewards.

inequality explanation of hunger Theory that hunger is not caused by absolute scarcity but by the unequal distribution of resources and how these resources are used.

influence Ability to convince people they should act as suggested.

informant Member of a society who provides information to a fieldworker, often through formal interviews or surveys; also called **consultant**.

initiation rituals Rites of passage whose purpose is to incorporate males and/or females into new roles or into new social groups.

innovation Creation of a new cultural trait by combining two or more existing traits.

intellectual approach Notion that religious beliefs provide explanations for puzzling things and events; also called the **cognitive approach**.

intensive agriculture Systems of cultivation in which plots are planted annually or semiannually; usually involves irrigation, natural fertilizers, and (in the Old World) plows powered by animals.

interpretive anthropology Contemporary approach that analyzes cultural elements by explicating their meanings to people and understanding them in their local context; generally emphasizes cultural diversity and the unique qualities of particular cultures.

interviewing Collecting cultural data by systematic questioning; may be

structured (using questionnaires) or unstructured (open-ended).

key consultant Member of a society who is especially knowledgeable about some subject and who supplies information to a fieldworker; also called *key informant*.

kin group Group of people who culturally view themselves as relatives, cooperate in certain activities, and share a sense of identity as kinfolk.

kin terms Labels that individuals use to refer to their relatives of various kinds.

kindred All the bilateral relatives recognized by an individual.

kinship terminology Logically consistent system by which people classify their relatives into labeled categories or kinds of relatives.

laissez-faire Belief that economic freedom results in the best results for society as a whole; mistrust in government interference with free markets; also called **neoliberalism**.

language Shared knowledge used by speakers to send and hearers to understand messages.

law Type of social control characterized by the presence of authority, intention of universal application, obligation, and sanction.

levirate Custom whereby a widow marries a male relative (usually a brother) of her deceased husband.

lineage Unilineal descent group larger than an extended family whose members can actually trace how they are related.

linguistic relativity hypothesis Idea that language significantly shapes the perceptions and worldview of its speakers; also called **Sapir-Whorf hypothesis**.

market Exchange by means of buying and selling, using money.

market economy Economy organized by market principles: prices determined by supply and demand; individuals and families rely on the market for livelihood; free-market allocation of resources, products, and services; self-regulation and decentralization of decision making.

market globalization Process through which the world's national economies become integrated into a single global exchange system organized by market principles.

marriage alliances Relationships created between families or kin groups by virtue of intermarriage between them.

material culture Artifacts and other physical, visible manifestations of culture, including art, architectural features, tools, consumer goods, clothing, and writing.

materialism Scientific theoretical orientation claiming that the main influences on cultural differences and similarities are technology, environment, and how people produce and distribute resources; also called **cultural materialism**.

matrifocal family Family group consisting of a mother and her children, with a man only loosely attached or not present at all.

matrilineal descent Form of descent in which individuals trace their primary kinship relationships through their mothers.

matrilocal residence Residence form in which couples live with or near the wife's parents.

medical anthropology Specialization that researches the connections between cultural beliefs and habits and the spread and treatment of diseases and illnesses.

money Objects that serve as exchange media in a wide range of transactions of goods, services (including labor), or both.

monogamy Each individual is allowed to have only one spouse at a time.

morpheme Combination of phonemes that communicates a standardized meaning.

morphology Study of the units of meaning in language.

multiple gender identities Definitions of sexual identities beyond the female and male duality, including third and fourth genders such as man-woman or woman-man.

myths Stories that recount the deeds of supernatural powers and cultural heroes in the past.

nationality Ethnic group that claims a right to a discrete homeland and to political autonomy and self-determination.

negative reciprocity Reciprocal exchange motivated largely by the desire to obtain products or services.

neoevolutionism New evolutionism, or the mid–twentieth-century rebirth of evolutionary approaches to studying and explaining culture.

neoliberalism Belief that economic freedom results in the best results for society as a whole; mistrust in government interference with free markets; also called **laissez-faire**.

neolocal residence Residence form in which a couple establishes a separate household apart from both the husband's and the wife's parents.

New World The landmasses of North and South America.

nomadism Seasonal mobility, often involving migration to high-altitude areas during the hottest and driest parts of the year.

nonunilineal descent Form of descent in which individuals do not regularly associate with either matrilineal or patrilineal relatives, but make choices about whom to live with, whose land to use, and so forth.

norms Shared ideals and/or expectations about how certain people ought to act in given situations.

nuclear family Family consisting of a married couple and their unmarried children.

Old World The landmasses of Europe, Asia, and Africa.

origin myth Collective history of an ethnic group that defines which subgroups are part of it and its relationship to other ethnic groups.

paleoanthropology Specialization within biological anthropology that investigates the biological evolution of the human species.

participant observation Main technique used in conducting ethnographic fieldwork, involving living among a people and participating in their daily activities.

passive assimilation Voluntary social absorption of one ethnic group by another ethnic group.

pastoralism Tending, breeding, and harvesting the products of livestock, which are taken to seasonally available pasturelands and water; also called herding.

patrilineal descent Form of descent in which individuals trace their most important kinship relationships through their fathers.

patrilocal residence Residence form in which couples live with or near the husband's parents.

patterns of behavior Within a single culture, the behavior most people perform when they are in certain culturally defined situations.

peasants Rural people who live by a combination of subsistence agriculture and market sale, integrated into a larger society politically and economically.

performance arts Forms of art such as music, percussion, song, dance, and theater/drama that involve sound and/or stylized body movements.

phoneme Smallest unit of sound that speakers recognize as distinctive from other sounds; when one phoneme is substituted for another in a morpheme, the meaning of the morpheme alters.

phonology Study of the sound system of language.

physical anthropology Major subfield of anthropology that studies the biological dimensions of humans and other primates; also called **biological anthropology**.

polyandry One woman is allowed to have multiple husbands at one time.

polygamy Multiple spouses.

polygyny One man is allowed to have multiple wives at one time.

postmarital residence pattern Household in which the majority of newly married couples establish their own residence.

postmodernism Philosophical viewpoint emphasizing the relativity of all knowledge, including science; focus is on how the knowledge of a particular time and place is constructed, especially on how power relations affect the creation and spread of ideas and beliefs.

prehistoric archaeology Field that uses excavations and analysis of material remains to investigate cultures that existed before the development of writing.

priest Kind of religious specialist, often full-time, who officiates at large-scale, bureaucratically organized rituals that keep the population in proper relationship to deities or cosmic forces.

primatology Part of biological anthropology that studies primates, including monkeys and apes.

psychological approach Notion that the emotional or affective satisfactions people gain from religion are primary in interpreting religion.

ranked society Form of society with a limited number of high-ranking privileged social positions; groups are ranked relative to one another.

rapport Working relationship between the researcher and the members of the community he or she is studying.

reasonable-person model Model used in legal reasoning that basically asks how a reasonable individual should have acted under these circumstances.

recall ethnography Technique for reconstructing a cultural system at a slightly earlier period by interviewing older individuals who lived during that period.

reciprocity Exchange of products or objects between two or more individuals or groups.

redistribution Collection of products or money from an organized group or society, followed by a reallocation to the group by a central authority.

refugees Individuals and families who temporarily take up residence in another region or country to escape famine, warfare, or some other life-threatening event.

relocation Forced removal of the members of a particular ethnic group from one geographic region to another.

resident population The people who live or lived in a particular region of the world at a specific time; may or may not refer to an indigenous people.

revitalization movement Religious movement explicitly intended to create a new way of life for a society or a group.

rites of passage Rituals celebrating, causing, and/or symbolically marking the stages of life as defined by their culture.

ritual Organized, stereotyped, symbolic behaviors intended to influence supernatural powers.

role Rights and duties that individuals receive because of their perceived personal identity or membership in a social group.

Sapir-Whorf hypothesis Idea that language significantly shapes the perceptions and worldview of its speakers; also called **linguistic relativity hypothesis**.

scarcity explanation of hunger Theory that, due to overpopulation, there are not enough land, water, and other resources to feed all the people of a country or region an adequate diet, given current technology.

scarification Scarring of the skin to produce designs on the body.

scientific approach Approach suggesting that human cultural differences and similarities can be explained in the much the same ways as biologists explain life and its evolution.

seasonal rituals Form of communal religious organization in which group cooperation is required to ensure the seasonal changes that restore or maintain life.

secular ideologies Ideologies that justify inequality on the basis of societywide benefits rather than religious teachings, beliefs, and values.

segregation Enforced separation of ethnic groups, in which the dominant ethnic group places legal restrictions on the actions of the members of the other group.

self-help legal system Informal legal system in societies without a centralized political system in which authorities who settle disputes are defined by the circumstances of the case; also called *ad hoc system*.

semantic domain Class of things or properties perceived as alike in some fundamental respect; hierarchically organized.

sex roles Rights and duties individuals have because of their perceived identities as males, females, or another gender category; also called **gender roles**.

sexual dimorphism Physical differences based on genetic differences between females and males.

sexual division of labor Kinds of productive activities and tasks assigned to women versus men in a culture; also called **gendered division of labor**.

shaman Part-time religious specialist who uses his or her special relationship to supernatural powers for curing members of the shaman's group and harming members of other groups.

shamanistic organization Religious organization in which certain individuals (shamans) have relationships with supernatural powers that ordinary people lack.

simple band Autonomous or independent political unit, often consisting of little more than an extended family, with informal leadership vested in one of the older family members.

social anthropology Subfield that studies the way of life of contemporary and historically recent human societies and cultures; also called **cultural anthropology** and **sociocultural anthropology**.

social construction of gender Idea that the characteristics a people attribute to males and females are culturally, not biologically, determined; also called the **cultural construction of gender**.

social control Mechanism by which behavior is constrained and directed into acceptable channels, thus maintaining conformity.

social Darwinism View that the degree of success in achieving social rewards is determined by the inherent (inborn) characteristics of individuals and groups.

social distance Degree to which cultural norms specify that two individuals or groups should be helpful to, intimate with, or emotionally attached to one another.

socialism Economy in which government makes decisions about product prices, wages and employment, what is produced, and accumulation of income and wealth.

socialization Transmission (by means of social learning) of cultural knowledge to the next generation; also called **enculturation**.

social welfare capitalism Capitalist economy in which a legitimate function of government is protection of workers and society from the harmful impacts of free markets; involves extensive regulations of business and worker protections.

sociobiology Scientific approach emphasizing that humans are subject to similar evolutionary forces as other animals; associated with the hypothesis that human behavior patterns enhance genetic fitness; also called **evolutionary psychology**.

sociocultural anthropology Subfield that studies the way of life of contemporary and historically recent human societies and cultures; also called **cultural anthropology** and **social anthropology**.

society A socially distinct group of people who share a common identity, language, and culture.

sociolinguistics Specialty within cultural anthropology that studies how language is related to culture and the social uses of speech.

sociological approach Notion that religious beliefs function to maintain the institutions of society as a whole by instilling common values, creating solidarity, controlling behavior, and so forth.

sodality Formal institution that cuts across communities and serves to unite geographically scattered groups; may be based on kin groups (clans or lineages) or on groups that are not based on kin (age grades or warrior societies).

sorcery Performance of rites and spells for the purpose of causing harm to others by supernatural means.

sororate Custom whereby a widower marries a female relative of his deceased wife.

state Centralized, multilevel political unit characterized by the presence of a bureaucracy that acts on behalf of the ruling elite.

stereotyping Having preconceived mental images of a group that bias the way one perceives group members and interprets their behavior.

stratified society Form of society with marked and variably heritable differences in access to wealth, power, and prestige; inequality is based mainly on unequal access to productive and valued resources.

subculture Cultural differences characteristic of members of various ethnic groups, regions, religions, and so forth within a single society or country.

subnationality Dependent subgroup within a larger nationality that lacks the concept of a separate homeland and makes no claim to any inherent right to political autonomy and self-determination.

surplus Amount of food or other goods a worker produces in excess of the amount consumed by the individual or the individual's dependents.

synchronic Describing a culture at one period in time.

symbols Objects, behaviors, and other phenomena whose culturally defined meanings have no necessary relationship to their inherent physical qualities; symbols are arbitrary and conventional.

tattooing Decorating of the body with designs by cutting and placing colored pigments under the skin.

technology-transfer solution Theory that developing nations can best solve their hunger problems by adopting the technology and production methods of modern mechanized agriculture.

tone language Language in which changing voice pitch within a word alters the entire meaning of the word.

totemism Form of communal religious organization in which all members of a kin group have mystical relationships with one or more natural objects.

transhumance Pastoral pattern involving migration to different elevations to respond to seasonal differences in the availability of pasturelands.

transnational Member of an ethnic community living outside his or her country of origin.

tribe Autonomous political unit encompassing a number of distinct, geographically dispersed communities held together by sodalities.

tribute Rendering of products (usually including food) to an authority such as a chief.

unilineal descent Descent through one line, including patrilineal and matrilineal descent.

unilineal descent group Group of relatives formed by tracing kinship relationships through only one sex, either female or male, but not both.

unilineal evolutionism Nineteenth-century theory holding that all human ways of life pass through a similar sequence of stages in their development.

unilineally extended family Group of nuclear families formed by tracing kinship relationships through only one sex.

values Shared ideas or standards about the worth of goals and lifestyles.

vision quest Attempt to enlist the aid of supernatural powers by intentionally seeking a dream or vision; characteristic of individualistic religious organizations.

visual arts Arts produced in a tangible form, including basketry, pottery, textiles, paintings, drawings, sculptures, masks, carvings, and the like.

witchcraft Use of psychic powers alone to harm others by supernatural means.

worldview The way in which people interpret reality and events, including how they see themselves relating to the world around them.

Notes

Chapter 1—The Study of Humanity

Subfields of Anthropology

A short article summarizing the capacities of humans versus chimpanzees is Balter (2008). The description of the Denisovan and Neandertal impact on Melanesians is summarized from Vernot et al. (2016). Recent data on "Hobbits" is from Culotta (2016) and van den Berghe et al. (2016). Jaubert et al. (2016) describe the circular structure made by Neandertals in a French cave. Material on cannibalism in Jamestown is from Joseph Stromberg, "Starving Settlers in Jamestown Colony Resorted to Cannibalism," in *Smithsonian* magazine: http://www.smithsonianmag.com/history/starving-settlers-in-jamestown-colony-resorted-to-cannibalism-46000815/?no-ist (retrieved September 13, 2016).

Cultural Anthropology Today

The examples of fieldworkers studying North America are drawn from Lane (2009), Johnson (2007), Luhrmann (2012), and Nagle (2013).

Anthropological Perspectives on Cultures

The account of the incident among the Jarawa is drawn from a *New York Times* article by Ellen Barry and Hari Kumar, "Baby Killing Tests India's Protection of an Aboriginal Culture," March 13, 2016, p. A1.

Chapter 2—Culture

Tylor's definition of culture is from Tylor (1871, p. 1).

Defining Culture

The material on the Yanomamö and Semai is drawn from Chagnon (1983) and Dentan (1968), respectively. Most general concepts (e.g., ethnic identity, subculture) are from our general knowledge of the literature. Information about mass killings under the subheading "Socially Learned" was summarized from a wide variety of news sources.

Cultural Knowledge

Edward Hall's two early books (1959 and 1966) were among the first to systematically discuss the importance of nonverbal communication in everyday social interaction. Victor Turner (1967) applied the concepts of multivocality and condensation to ritual symbols. The example of symbolic behavior from Micronesia is from Jim Peoples's own research. Information on Navajo witchcraft comes from Kluckhohn (1944). Reichel-Dolmatoff (1971) describes shamanism among the Tukano. Information on Hanunoo ethnobotanical classification is from Conklin (1957). Discussion of the cultural construction of race was put together by ourselves but is familiar to most anthropologists and in accord with the AAA statement on race: http://www.americananthro.org /ConnectWithAAA/Content.aspx?ItemNumber=2583.

The Origins of Culture

On the early bone flutes in Germany, see Conrad, Malina, and Munzel (2009); on the first known beads in Morocco, see Bouzouggar et al. (2007); on the use of silcrete and fire to harden stone used for microliths, see Kyle Brown et al. (2012a and 2012b). The use of abalone shells to process ochre is reported by Hensilwood et al. (2002; 2011). All interpretations and speculations about the origins of culture are ours.

Biology and Cultural Differences

The phrase "wired for culture" is from Pagel (2012). The example of lactose intolerance is well known, but Arjamaa and Vuorisalo (2010) place it in the context of coevolution. Murdock (1949) was the first to provide a systematic list of cultural universals, but more thorough coverage is provided in Donald Brown (1991).

Chapter 3—Culture and Language

The Power of Language

Information on the five distinguishing features of human language is from Hockett's (1960) seminal discussion. Ideas about their applications and extensions are our own.

How Language Works

The examples of Thai aspiration and Nupe tones are taken from Fromkin and Rodman's (1988) textbook. The author's (J.P.) own knowledge is the basis for the discussion of the Kosraen language. Information on Native American words incorporated into English is taken from Nestor (2003) and Weatherford (1991). An authoritative website with words compiled by Mark Rosenfelder is http://www.zompist.com /indianwd.html (retrieved September 13, 2016).

Global Challenges and Opportunities

Data for Global Challenges and Opportunities are taken from SIL International's website Ethnologue.com and Walsh (2005).

Communication and Social Behavior

Hall (1959 and 1966) originated many ideas about proxemics. We thank Kathryn Meyer and Gary deCoker for help with the example of Japanese honorifics. Chagnon (1983) discusses the Yanomamö name taboo.

Language and Culture

The Aztec 52-year calendar cycle is described by Berdan (2005) and Michael Smith (2012). A concise description of the Sapir-Whorf hypothesis is in Donald Brown (1991). We consulted reviews by Leavitt (2006), Lucy (1997), and Penelope Brown (2006). Levinson (2003) describes the Guugu Yimithirr. Deutscher (2010) is a readable book covering the effects of language on perceptions and worldviews.

CHAPTER 4—CULTURAL DIVERSITY AND GLOBALIZATION

Cultural Change and Diversity

This section has been adapted from George Foster (1962), Steward (1955 and 1977), Leslie White (1959), Service (1962 and 1971), and Sahlins and Service (1960).

The World Before Globalization

The main sources relied on for this section were Fagan (2002) and Wenke (1990). The overview of globalization was derived from Stavrianos (1998), Wolf (1982), and Diamond (1999). Additional information for the period from the fifteenth through the eighteenth centuries was taken from Braudel (1979a and 1979b) and Frank (1998). The discussion of the Columbian Exchange is from Crosby (1972). Additional data on the Americas are drawn from Stannard (1992), Kehoe (1992), Thornton (1987), and Wolf (1969); and on Africa from Davidson (1969), Oliver and Fage (1962), Mintz (1986), and Miracle (1966 and 1967).

The Global Economy

For general information on the global economy, we have drawn from several studies: Giddens (2000), Hines (2000), Hutton and Giddens (2000), Klein (1999), Robbins (1999), and general reading. The portion on the development of free trade is in large part from the website of the World Trade Organization (www.wto.org). Information on shipping is from the International Chamber of Shipping website (http://www.ics-shipping.org/shipping-facts/shipping-facts). The information on information technology is from general reading. The basic inspiration for the portion on the ways in which the global economy directly and indirectly is affecting global culture is from Berger (1997). However, we have defined different categories in some cases and elaborated on others.

For the portion on the globalization of knowledge, we have relied on general reading as well as upon Haynes (2014), Marklein (2013), and the Cross-Border Educational Research Team (www.globalhighered.org). See also two New York Times articles: (1) by Lisa Foderaro called "More Foreign-Born Scholars Lead U.S. Universities," March 10, 2011 and (2) by Katie Zezima called, "A Guide to Branch Campuses," April 17, 2011.

Information on Internet usage is from the Internet World Stats website (http://www.internetworldstats.com).

For data on wealth distribution, see the Credit Suisse Global Wealth Report 2013 (http://publication.creditsuisse.com) and the World Council of Churches (2000). For data on immigration issues, we drew heavily from the *Migration News* (http://migration.ucdavis.edu/). Additional current data on economic, social, migration, and other issues are taken from news reports in the *Washington Post, Christian Science Monitor,* the BBC News website (http://www.bbc.com/news), and television and radio news reports. Other portions were inspired by Robbins (1999) and Mahbubani (2012), supplemented by general readings.

Global Challenges and Opportunities

The portion on the Gurifuna or Black Caribs is from Marshall (1973) and Sweeney (2007). Information on the Saramaka is from Price and Price (1980), Price (2012), and Orellana (2008).

CHAPTER 5—THE DEVELOPMENT OF ANTHROPOLOGICAL THOUGHT

The Emergence of Anthropology

Unilineal evolutionary theory is best known from the works of Tylor (1865, 1871) and Morgan (1877). The times and places of the founding of the first anthropology programs in the United States are from Black (1991).

Anthropological Thought in the Early Twentieth Century

The best single source of writings on Boas is a collection of his articles (1966). Configurationalism is best known from Benedict (1934). The critique of historical particularist assumptions is taken from Harris (1968). Malinowski's ideas about the functions of institutions, behaviors, and beliefs were first presented in a 1944 book, reprinted as Malinowski (1960). Good sources on structural-functionalism are Radcliffe-Brown (1922 and 1965) and Nadel (1951).

Global Challenges and Opportunities

Kuwayama (2004) provides part of the material used in the Global Challenges and Opportunities feature.

The Rebirth of Evolutionism in the Mid–Twentieth Century

See Leslie White (1949 and 1959). Steward's most influential articles appear in two volumes (1955 and 1977).

Anthropological Thought Today

The general discussion of controversies over the scientific and humanistic approaches is based on our own knowledge and interpretations.

Scientific Approaches

Dawkins (1976) and E. O. Wilson (1975, 1978) were instrumental works that popularized sociobiology. Books by Marvin Harris (1977, 1979, 1985, 1999) were influential in the development of modern materialist thought. Harris's work and Mark Cohen (1977) emphasized the importance of population pressure. Sanderson (1999 and 2007) provides nice summaries of current evolutionary theory and defends it from both old and new critics.

Humanistic Approaches

On interpretive anthropology, good sources are early works by Geertz (1973 and 1980).

Either, Or, or Both?

Discussion of controversies over the 2010 long-range plan of the AAA is drawn from two articles in the online *New York Times* by Nicholas Wade: "Anthropology as a Science? Statement Deepens a Rift" (December 10, 2010) and "Anthropology Group Tries to Soothe Tempers After Dropping the Word 'Science'" (December 13, 2010). On its website, the AAA responds in "AAA Responds to Public Controversy over Science in Anthropology."

CHAPTER 6—METHODS OF INVESTIGATION

Ethnographic Methods

The discussion of ethnographic field methods is based on the authors' field experiences and numerous informal discussions with colleagues about the problems and issues they encountered during their field research. The discussions of particular field research problems with the Navajo are from Sasaki (1960, p. viii) and Kluckhohn (1944, p. 7). The discussion of suicide in the Trobriand Islands is derived from Malinowski (1926). The problems of collecting genealogies among the Yanomamö are recounted by Chagnon (1983). The discussion of how to evaluate a particular historical account was influenced by Naroll (1962). See also Hickerson (1970) on the ethnohistoric method and Fogelson (1989) for a discussion of interpretation of historical events. The data on Captain Cook is from Sahlins (1981 and 1995) and Obeyesekere (1992).

Comparative Methods

For information on cross-cultural research, see Ember and Ember, "Basic Guide to Cross-Cultural Research" and the Human Relations Area Files (see http://hraf.yale.edu/). The cross-cultural test of the sorcery and social control hypothesis is from Whiting (1950). The basic discussion of controlled comparisons is drawn from Eggan (1954). Data on matrilineal and patrilineal societies are from Allen (1984) and Bailey (1989).

Global Challenges and Opportunities

The historical discussion was from general reading. The quote and statements of Leslie White on Zia are from White (1962). The discussion of the Native American Protection and Repatriation Act as well as the discussion of international repatriation is from the National NAGPRA website (www.nps.gov/nagpra), while the discussion of the UN Declaration on the Rights of Indigenous Peoples is from the UN website (http://www.un.org/esa/socdev/unpfii/documents/DRIPS_en.pdf). The information on the Pitjantjatjara cases is from Michael Brown (2003, pp. 33–34). The discussion on the San is from the WIMSA website (http://www.osisa.org/education/regional/working-group-indigenous-minorities-southern-africa-wimsa) and Stephenson (2003). The Protocols for Native American Archival Materials can be found at the website (www2.nau.edu/libnap-p/protocols.html); the Hopi protocols are available at ww8.nau.edu/hcpo-p/ResProto.pdf.

See the website of the American Anthropological Association for its Code of Ethics (http://ethics.aaanet.org/category/statement/).

CHAPTER 7—CULTURE AND NATURE: INTERACTING WITH THE ENVIRONMENT

Hunting and Gathering

Dobyns (1983) provided most of the information on the distribution of foragers in North America used in Figure 7.1. Denevan (1992) and Krech (1999) discuss the use of fire to provide habitat for game animals among prehistoric Native Americans. Information on specific foragers is taken from the following sources: BaMbuti (Turnbull, 1962), Hadza (Woodburn, 1968), Netsilik (Balikci, 1970), Western Shoshone (Steward, 1938 and 1955), Ju/'hoansi (Lee, 1969, 1979, 2003), Northwest Coast (Ferguson, 1984), and Cheyenne (Hoebel, 1978). Information on the current conditions among the Hadzabe from is drawn from two articles in the *Survival International* website: (1) "Hadzabe Celebrate Land Victory," November 6, 2007, http://www.survivalinternational.org/news/2579 (retrieved June 28, 2016); (2) "Tanzania: Hadza Tribe Celebrates First Land Titles," November 11, 2011, http://www.survivalinternational.org/news/7859 (retrieved June 28, 2016). Comparative information on foraging working hours is from Kelly (2006).

Domestication

Bowles (2011) uses archaeological, ethnographic, and historic evidence to conclude that early farming was not more productive than foraging. Bocquet-Appel (2011) uses prehistoric burial evidence to claim that mortality generally increased and fertility increased after agriculture. Diamond (1999) summarizes dates and places of plant and animal domestication and provides reasons for both developments. Sources consulted on the origins of plant domestication are Barton et al. (2009), Crawford (2009), Denham et al. (2003), Dillehay et al. (2007), D. Fuller et al. (2009), Pickersgill (2007), Pope et al. (2001), T. D. Price (2009), and Zeder (2008). Historian Alfred Crosby (1972 and 1986) pioneered the study of the extraordinary impacts of the transfer of crops and livestock between the Old World and New World. Mann (2011) updates and extends Crosby's work on the Columbian Exchange, which includes pathogens.

Horticulture

Mark Cohen (1989) provides an overview of evidence about the health of prehistoric foragers. Sources used to draw the North American portion of the map on the distribution of horticulture are Dobyns (1983) and Doolittle (1992). Material on shifting cultivation is from Conklin (1957) and Ruddle (1974). See Bradfield (1971) on dry land gardening among the Pueblo (mainly the Hopi).

Intensive Agriculture

Differences between extensive and intensive agriculture are described in Boserup (1965) and Grigg (1974). Material on intensive agriculture in the New World is drawn from our general knowledge and from Donkin (1979). On peasant revolts, see Eric Wolf (1969). Johnson and Earle (1987) analyze the relationship between intensification and cultural evolution. Gregory Clark (2007) argues that the overall quality of human life did not improve until after the industrial revolution.

Pastoralism

Porter (1965) discusses the subsistence risk reduction benefit of pastoralism. Schneider (1981) shows the negative relationship between the distribution of the tsetse fly and cattle pastoralism in Africa. A short source on the Karimojong is Dyson-Hudson and Dyson-Hudson (1969).

Industrialism

Most material in this section is drawn from our general knowledge of the industrial revolution and its consequences. Strauss, Rupp, and Love (2013) provided the inspiration and data on power and energy slaves. The ratio of farmers to the U.S. population is drawn from "The Voice of Agriculture," http://www.fb.org/newsroom/fastfacts/, an online source sponsored by the American Farm Bureau.

Globalization and the Environment

Economy (2004 and 2007) provided much background for the information on China. The Chinese government's efforts to reduce dependence on coal is from our general knowledge. Specific information in the text is from an article by Michael Forsythe, "China Curbs Plans for More Coal-Fired Power Plants," April 25, 2016, *New York Times*, p. B1. Recent information about China's environmental damage is drawn from two *New York Times* articles by Edward Wong: "Cost of Environmental Damage in China Growing Rapidly amid Industrialization," March 30, 2013, p. A4 and "On Scale of 0 to 500, Beijing's Air Quality Tops 'Crazy Bad' at 755," January 13, 2013, p. A16.

Global Challenges and Opportunities

Factual information for the discussion in the Global Challenges and Opportunities feature was taken from several sources. Three *New York Times* articles available online provided the information on the G-8 meeting in July 2009: (1) Peter Baker, "Poorer Nations Reject a Target on Emission Cuts," July 8, 2009; (2) Betinna Wassener, "Where Iron Is Bigger Than Oil or Gold," July 10, 2009; and (3) Keith Bradsher, "U.S. Officials Press China on Climate," July 15, 2009. On the Copenhagen meetings in December 2009, we consulted John Bowder, "5 Nations Forge Pact on Climate; Goals Go Unmet," December 19, 2010, *New York Times*; and John Bowder, "Countries Submit Emissions Goals," February 2, 2010, *New York Times*. Four entries from Johansen (2009) were helpful in summarizing the impacts of global warming: (1) "Agriculture and Warming" (pp. 10–16); (2) "Bangladesh, Sea Level Rise in" (pp. 83–84); (3) "China and Global Warming" (pp. 144–149); and (4) "Gulf of Mexico: Prospective Climate Changes" (pp. 319–321).

CHAPTER 8— EXCHANGE IN ECONOMIC SYSTEMS

Information sources in the chapter opening vignette on Bank Americard is from the history given by the Bank of America (http://about.bankofamerica.com/en-us/our-story/birth-of-modern-credit-card.html#fbid=Yhy1dIxiW7d) and from the National Public Radio podcast "99% Invisible" of January 19, 2016 (http://99percentinvisible.org/episode/the-fresno-drop/).

Economic Systems

Sahlins (1965) first distinguished the three forms of exchange.

Reciprocity

Lee (1979, 2003) describes Ju/'hoansi sharing and *hxaro*. Kelly (2006) generalizes some of Lee's points to other foragers. Malinowski (1922) describes Trobriand *wasi*. The Maring discussion is from Rappaport (1968) and Peoples (1982).

Redistribution

Alkire (1977), Sahlins (1958), Oliver (1989), and Peoples (1985) describe tribute in Micronesia and Polynesia.

Market Exchange

Neale (1976) remains a good general source on money, although many features in the text are our own ideas. Schneider (1981) describes some African monies. Pospíšil (1978) discusses the multiple uses of money among the Kapauku. Distinctions between market exchange and market economies are from our own general knowledge, as is that between the two forms and ideas of capitalism that we call *neoliberalism* and *social welfare capitalism*. Ho (2009) conducted the ethnographic interviews with Wall Street investment bankers, but she is not responsible for our interpretations and conclusion.

Globalization and Markets

General information in this section is from our own knowledge and opinions. Foley (2013) is a brief source on American uses of corn. Information on U.S. corn prices is from a University of Illinois's farmdoc website, http://www.farmdoc.illinois.edu/manage/uspricehistory/USPrice.asp (retrieved July 5, 2016). USDA (2016) estimates the net energy balance of ethanol for 2015. Levitt (2011) provides information on the impact of ethanol production and speculation on Mexican corn tortilla prices.

Information on corn also came from two news sources: (1) James C. McKinley, "Cost of Corn Soars, Forcing Mexico to Set Price Limits," *New York Times,* January 19, 2007 (online, retrieved June 13, 2012) and (2) Manuel Foig-Franzia, "A Culinary and Cultural Staple in Crisis," *Washington Post,* January 26, 2007 (online, retrieved June 13, 2012).

Information on the collapse of the Bangladesh clothing factory is from a variety of news sources. The *New York Times* reported specific facts in three articles: (1) Julfikar Ali Manik and Jim Yardley, "Building Collapse in Bangladesh Leaves Scores Dead," April 24, 2013 (online, retrieved May 27, 2013); (2) Steven Greenhouse, "Retailers Are Pressed on Safety at Factories," May 11, 2013 (online, retrieved May 27, 2013); (3) Jim Yardley, "Report on Deadly Factory Collapse in Bangladesh Finds Widespread Blame," May 23, 2013 (online, retrieved May 27, 2013). Jason Burke's article in the British newspaper *The Guardian* updated the causes of the Rana Plaza building collapse: www.theguardian.com/world/2015/apr/22/garment-workers-in-bangladesh-still-suffering-two-years-after-factory-collapse (retrieved July 5, 2016).

Global Challenges and Opportunities

For the Global Challenges and Opportunities feature, Michael Brown (2003) discusses issues of ownership of native cultures. Information on the 2009 West Sedona sweat lodge tragedy is from an article by John Dougherty, "Death at Sweat Lodge Brings Soul Searching," *New York Times,* October 11, 2009.

CHAPTER 9—MARRIAGES AND FAMILIES

For the opening vignette, we consulted the Pew website, http://www.pewresearch.org/fact-tank/2014/12/22/less-than-half-of-u-s-kids-today-live-in-a-traditional-family/.

Some Definitions

2010 U.S. Census Bureau data are from the website *Households and Families 2010,* available at https://www.census.gov/prod/cen2010/briefs/c2010br-14.pdf (retrieved September 16, 2016).

Incest Taboos

Tylor (1888) first proposed the "marry out or die out" theory. "Familiarity breeds disinterest" was originally the idea of Westermarck (1926). On Taiwan, see Arthur Wolf (1970). On Israeli kibbutz, see Shepher (1971). On Lebanese cousin marriages, see McCabe (1983).

Marriage

Information on the Musuo is from Hua (2001). The material on Nayar marriage is from Gough (1959). Hart, Pilling, and Goodale (1988) describe Tiwi marriage and other aspects of Tiwi culture. Jane Goodale (1971) provides information about Tiwi wives.

Variations in Marriage Beliefs and Practices

Goldstein (1987) and LeVine (1988) describe Tibetan polyandry and its advantages to husbands and the wife. Chagnon (1983) discusses the importance of marriage alliances among the Yanomamö. The challenges of Tierney (2000) do not alter Chagnon's conclusions about marriage alliances. Kuper (1963) describes Swazi bridewealth. See Lee (1979, pp. 240–242) on Ju/'hoansi brideservice. See Goody and Tambiah (1973) and Harrell and Dickey (1985) on dowry. Material on Indian dowry deaths is from our general knowledge and an article by Rahul Bedi in *The Telegraph,* "Indian Dowry Deaths on the Rise," February 27, 2012.

Global Challenges and Opportunities

Specific information in the Global Challenges and Opportunities feature is drawn from the following sources: Bernstein (1983); CIA *The World Factbook* (https://www.cia.gov/library/publications/resources/the-world-factbook/index.html, retrieved September 19, 2016); James Brooke, "Japan Farms: An Old Man's Game," *New York Times,* November 7, 2003; Kunio (1988); Joji Sakurai, "Japan Looks to Foreign Brides to Save Its Villages," *Delaware Gazette,* May 19, 1997, p. 12; Zielenziger (2007); and Jenike (2003).

Same-Sex Marriage and the Culture Wars

A regularly updated source of factual information is the website of the National Conference of State Legislatures, last updated in June 2015, http://www.ncsl.org/research/human-services/same-sex-marriage-laws.aspx (retrieved September 10, 2016). Other specific information in this section is from the following news sources: Nate Silver, "How Opinion on Same-Sex Marriage Is Changing, and What It Means," *New York Times,* March 26,

2013 (online, retrieved June 6, 2013); David Von Drehle, "How Gay Marriage Won," *Time,* April 8, 2013, pp. 16–24; Adam Liptak, "Supreme Court Bolsters Gay Marriage with Two Major Rulings," *New York Times,* June 26, 2013 (online, retrieved June 27, 2013); Jeremy W. Peters, "Effects of Ruling on Same-Sex Marriage Start Rippling Out Through Government," *New York Times,* July 9, 2013 (online, retrieved July 11, 2013); Frank Newport, "Religion Big Factor for Americans Against Same-Sex Marriage." Gallup Politics, December 5, 2012 (http://www.gallup.com/poll/159089/religion%20major-factor-americans-opposed-sex-marriage.aspx).

Postmarital Residence Patterns

We use the frequencies of different residence patterns reported in Pasternak (1976, p. 44). Ember and Ember (1971 and 1972) and Pasternak (1976) have discussed the influences on residence patterns.

Family and Household Forms

Murdock (1949) first suggested how forms of postmarital residence produce various forms of the family and household. Pasternak, Ember, and Ember (1976) suggest an economic hypothesis for why extended families exist.

CHAPTER 10—KINSHIP AND DESCENT

Unilineal Descent

Information on the frequencies of patrilineal and matrilineal descent are from Aberle (1961) and Divale and Harris (1976). Firth (1936 and 1965) describes the functions of Tikopian lineages and clans. See Eggan (1950) on Hopi matrilineal descent.

Global Challenges and Opportunities

Information in the Global Challenges and Opportunities feature is from our general knowledge and from *China Daily* (November 5, 2003), Fong (2004), Jackson and Howe (2006), and Yan (2006).

Nonunilineal Descent

Cognatic descent in Polynesia is discussed in Firth (1968), Howard and Kirkpatrick (1989), and Douglas Oliver (1989). The Samoan 'aiga is described in Melvin Ember (1959), Holmes and Holmes (1992), and Douglas Oliver (1989).

Influences on Kinship Systems

We consulted Aberle (1961); Alexander (1974); Divale (1974); Divale and Harris (1976); Carol Ember (1974); Ember and Ember (1971); Ember, Ember, and Pasternak (1974); and Holden and Mace (2003).

Cultural Construction of Kinship

The diagrams portraying the terminological systems are from our own knowledge. Aberle (1961) and Pasternak (1976) provide statistical data on the general but imperfect correlation between forms of descent and terminological systems.

CHAPTER 11—GENDER IN COMPARATIVE PERSPECTIVE

Cultural Construction of Gender

The Hua material is from Meigs (1988 and 1990). Quantitative data on occupational distributions for 2014 are from the

United States Bureau of Labor Statistics (2015). The same BLS table also reports the changing percentages of women who earn more income than their husbands.

Multiple Gender Identities

The primary sources of generalized information on Native American peoples are Roscoe (2000) and Nanda (2000). Information on the Zuni is from Roscoe (1991). Hoebel (1978) discusses Two Spirits among Cheyenne. Epple (1998) interprets *nadleehi* among Navajo. Nanda (1999) provides factual material on *hijra*. Our attention was called to the rise in unisex names by an article in the *New York Times* by Alex Williams, "Is Hayden a Boy or Girl? Both. 'Post-Gender' Baby Names Are on the Rise," August 18, 2016 (online, retrieved August 19, 2016). See also nameberry.com/blog/post-gender-baby-names for a list of names the authors of the site consider unisex.

The Gendered Division of Labor

Table 11.1 was constructed from data in Murdock and Provost (1973). On female hunting among BaMbuti and Agta, see Turnbull (1962) and Estioko-Griffin (1986), respectively. On the possibility that strenuous exercise inhibits ovulation, see Graham (1985). The influence of female child-care responsibilities on the division of labor was first made forcibly by Judith Brown (1970a). The discussion of why female contributions to subsistence tend to decline with intensification draws on information in Carol Ember (1983); Martin and Voorhies (1975); Boserup (1970); Burton and White (1984); and White, Burton, and Dow (1981). The Kofyar material is from Stone, Stone, and Netting (1995). Holden and Mace (1999) conducted the comparative study suggesting that small variations in sexual dimorphism depend on female contributions to subsistence.

Gender Stratification

The general discussion is drawn from previous editions, which included material from di Leonardo (1991), Leacock (1978), Rosaldo and Lamphere (1974), and Sacks (1982). The information about Andalusia is from Gilmore (1980, 1990). The suggestion that women's status improves with age in many cultures is from Judith Brown (1988). Sanday (2002) challenges the common definition of matriarchy. Information on the Iroquois is from Albers (1989), Stockard (2002), and Judith Brown (1970b). Lepowsky (1993) describes gender egalitarianism among the Vanatinai. On BaMbuti and Aka, see Turnbull (1962) and Hewlett (1992). The idea that women's control over key resources frequently leads to high overall status is discussed in Sanday (1973 and 1981). Friedl (1975 and 1978) was one of the first to argue that women's status in hunting and gathering cultures is positively related to the importance of women's ability to control the distribution of the products they produce. Yoruba material is from Barnes (1990).

Data on the employment of wives in the United States in 2013 are reported in Bureau of Labor Statistics (2015). Schlegel (1972) discusses why matrilineality and matrilocality tend to give women high status, all else equal. Information on Chinese wives is from Margery Wolf (1972) and our general knowledge.

Global Challenges and Opportunities

Information in the Global Challenges and Opportunities feature is from Adrian (2003), CIA (2010), and Vogel (1991).

CHAPTER 12—THE ORGANIZATION OF POLITICAL LIFE

Forms of Political Organization

The definitions and ideas concerning political structure were influenced by Steward (1955), Service (1962), Cohen and Service (1978), Krader (1968), and Fried (1967). Ethnographic examples were taken from the following sources: Comanche from Hoebel (1940) and Wallace and Hoebel (1952); Tahiti from Goldman (1970); and Inca from D'Altroy (1987), LaLone and LaLone (1987), LeVine (1987), and Metraux (1969).

Social Control and Law

For the basic definition of law as well as many of the concepts about legal systems, we relied on Hoebel (1954), Pospíšil (1958), Fallers (1969), Newman (1983), and Gluckman (1972 and 1973). Ethnographic examples were taken from the following sources: Comanche from Hoebel (1940), Cheyenne from Llewellyn and Hoebel (1941), Nuer from Evans-Pritchard (1940), Jívaro from Harner (1973), and Barotse from Gluckman (1972 and 1973).

Global Challenges and Opportunities

The information on the Panama Papers was taken from general news accounts. In addition, BBC World Service produced "Panama Papers" (July 4, 2016) in which they discussed the operations of shell companies in the British Virgin Islands. Information on the size of the problem of offshore banking was from Zucman (2015) as well as a special BBC report (www.bbc.com/news/business-18944097/ (retrieved April 8, 2016). In 2015, Citizens for Tax Justice (CTJ) produced "Offshore Shell Games 2015" in which they name major U.S. corporations involved: http://ctj.org/ctjreports/2015/10/ (retrieved April 9, 2016).

Data on the World Trade Organization and disputes are from their website (www.wto.org). There are varying estimates as to the job losses in the United States due to outsourcing. For the best discussion, see Atkinson, Stewart, Andes, and Ezell (2012).

The use of shell companies by Apple Inc. and particularly their use of the "double Irish" strategy have attracted a great deal of attention. See also the *New York Times* article by Charles Duhigg and David Kocieniewski called "How Apple Sidesteps Billions in Taxes," April 29, 2012; the *Daily Mail* article called "How Apple (Legally) Avoided Paying Billions in Taxes Last Year—Despite Record Profits" by Daniel Bates, April 30, 2012; and the Apple website (www.Apple.com). For data on Walmart see their website (corporate.walmart.com /our-story/our-history) and Chan (2011).

The general information on economic size of multinational corporations is based on news reports over the past few years and the websites of the United Nations (www.un.org), the World Bank (www.worldbank.org), the International Monetary Fund (www.imf.org), the World Trade Organization (www.wto.org), and *Fortune* magazine's "Global 500" report (http://fortune.com/global500/2014/).

The discussion of free trade and WTO is based in large part on Chomsky (2000), "The MAI Shell Game: The World Trade Organization (WTO)" from the Public Citizen Global Trade Watch website (www.tradewatch.org); "The WTO in

Brief" from the World Trade Organization website (www.wto.org); and "Is Globalization Shifting Power from Nation States to Undemocratic Organizations?" from the Globalisation Guide website (www.globalisationguide.org).

CHAPTER 13—SOCIAL INEQUALITY AND STRATIFICATION

Equalities and Inequalities: Three Systems

Fried (1967) first introduced the classification of societies into egalitarian, ranked, and stratified. Woodburn (1982) discusses reasons for egalitarianism among foragers. Information on Tikopia is from Firth (1936). Berreman (1959) long ago noted the similarity of race relations in the American South to caste systems.

Global Challenges and Opportunities

For the Global Challenges and Opportunities feature, we used our general knowledge and information from the following sources: Chang (2009); *New York Times* article by David Barboza and Hiroko Tabuchi, "Power Grows for Striking Chinese Workers," June 9, 2010, p. B1; and also *New York Times* article by Edward Wong, "As China Aids Labor, Unrest Is Still Rising," June 21, 2010, p. A1.

Castes in Traditional India

The traditional Indian caste system and its relationship to Hinduism are discussed in Dumont (1980), Hiebert (1971), Mandelbaum (1970), and Tyler (1973).

Classes in Industrial Societies: The United States

Data on the 2014 distribution of U.S. income is drawn from the U.S. Census Bureau (2015). Table 2 supplied quintile percentages for Table 13.1. Table A.2 provides the distribution of income by quintile from 1967 to 2010 used in the body of the text. Quantitative information on the distribution of wealth in the United States for 2010 is from Economic Policy Institute (2012). The 2016 CEO-to-worker income ratio is from the Economic Policy Institute's website: http://www.epi.org/publication/ceos-make-276-times-more-than-typical-workers/ (retrieved August 2, 2016).

Maintaining Inequality

This narrative came from our general knowledge and opinions.

Theories of Inequality

Davis and Moore (1945) originated the functionalist theory. Conflict theory goes back to Marx (1967, original 1867). Dahrendorf (1959) was important in formulating conflict theory in sociology. Lenski (1966) remains an excellent source, comparing and evaluating the functionalist and conflict theories.

CHAPTER 14—RELIGION AND WORLDVIEW

Defining Religion

Tylor (1871) defined religion as animism. Shore (1989) summarizes Polynesian *mana*. The Hopi information is from Frigout (1979) and our general knowledge.

Theories of Religion

The Trobriand magic example is from Malinowski (1954). Frazer's intellectual theory is from Frazer (1963). Geertz (1965) argued that religion provides meaning. The anthropomorphic theory is Guthrie's (1993). Malinowski (1954) argued that magic and religion alleviate anxieties during times of stress and uncertainty. Dobu beliefs about the fate of the dead are discussed in Fortune (1932, pp. 179–188). Kwaio pollution is described in Keesing (1982). The theory that ritual behavior creates social solidarity goes back to Durkheim (1915). Sosis (2004) and Sosis and Alcorta (2003) championed the costly signal theory of religion, which arguably is a form of the sociological theory.

Supernatural Explanations of Misfortune

The distinction between imitative and contagious magic is Frazer's (1963). Fortune (1932) describes Dobu sorcery. The witchcraft examples are from Kluckhohn (1944, Navajo); Monica Wilson (1951, Nyakyusa); Evans-Pritchard (1976, Zande); Offiong (1983, Ibibio); Middleton (1965, Lugbara), and Knauft (1985). Kluckhohn (1944) hypothesizes that Navajo witchcraft beliefs reduce overt, socially disruptive hostilities.

Varieties of Religious Organization

Wallace (1966) formulated and named the kinds of cult organizations. The vision quest material is from Lowie (1954 and 1956) and our general knowledge. Middleton (1965) describes the Lugbara ancestral cult. Victor Turner (1967) describes women's fertility rituals among the Ndembu. Farrer (1996) is a readable ethnography of Mescalero Apache girls' puberty rituals.

Revitalization Movements

A general description of cargo cults is in Worsley (1968). Lawrence (1964) describes several Garia movements. On Handsome Lake's movement among the Seneca, see Wallace (1969). Stewart (1980) and Edward Anderson (1996) describe peyotism among Native Americans.

Global Challenges and Opportunities

Specific information for the Global Challenges and Opportunities feature came from the following sources: "In France, Politicians Make Halal Meat a Campaign Issue," National Public Radio broadcast, March 16, 2012; *World Almanac and Book of Facts 2007* (pp. 711–712); Tamar Lewin article, "Muslims' Footbaths Set Off Debate," *Columbus Dispatch*, August 12, 2007, p. G2; and "Belgium: Toward a Ban on Veils," *Time*, May 17, 2010, p. 13.

CHAPTER 15—ART AND THE AESTHETIC

Many of the ideas for this chapter came from Geertz (1983), Hunter and Whitten (1975), Richard Anderson (1989), and Fratto (1978). Information on *Guernica* was from general sources, while information on *The Women of Algiers* is from BBC News, May 12, 2015. The auction of the Patek Philippe watch is from Simons (2014) and Mulier and Pulvirent (2014). Other sources of general information used in this chapter were Lipman and Winchester (1974), Hobson (1987), and Harvey (1937). Specific information on art in particular cultures is drawn from Colton (1959, Hopi); Connelly (1979, Hopi); Hoebel (1978, Cheyenne); and Hail (1980, Plains Indians).

Forms of Artistic Expression

The general discussion of body arts is based primarily on Brain (1979). Nuba body paint is from Faris (1972) and from a conversation with Faris. Information on Polynesian tattooing is from Gell (1993), Hage et al. (1995), and Simmons (1983). A 1998 research paper by undergraduate Maureen McCardel of Ohio Wesleyan University also was helpful on Polynesian tattooing.

Close (1989) provides a good summary of the archaeological debate over style versus function. Material on the Northwest Coast art is from our general knowledge, with specific points drawn from Richard Anderson (1989), Boas (1955), Furst and Furst (1982), and Holm (1965 and 1972). The comparative information on style in visual arts is from Fischer (1961).

We drew from the studies of Kaeppler (1978) and Lomax (1962 and 1968). Good sources on *Voudon* are Metraux (1972) and Wade Davis's (1985) controversial book. We drew information on !Kung healing from Lee (2003) and Shostak (1983) and on Tumbuka healing from Friedson (1998). A source of case studies on various performances and healing is Laderman and Roseman (1996). An informative and heavily illustrated source for students on Native American dance is Heth (1993). For a discussion of the individual in art, see Warner (1986).

Art and Culture

Information on the use of sand paintings and song/chants in Navajo curing ceremonials is taken from Sandner (1991), Reichard (1950 and 1977), and Parezo (1991). BaMbuti *molimo* is described in Turnbull (1962).

Global Challenges and Opportunities

This feature is based on general reading together with Tanner (1975) and Hail (1980).

Chapter 16—Ethnicity and Ethnic Conflict

There is a vast body of literature in anthropology and sociology on ethnicity and related issues. Because the entire chapter draws on the sources given here, we have not divided these notes into sections. Our ideas on the nature and significance of ethnicity have been most strongly influenced by the studies of Barth (1958 and 1969), Vincent (1974), Khlief (1979), Glazer and Moynihan (1963 and 1975), Bennett (1975), Himes (1974), DeVos and Romanucci-Ross (1975), Ronald Cohen (1978), Tax (1967), Nietschmann (1988), Horowitz (1985), Huntington (2011), and Jackson and Hudman (1990a and 1990b). For discussions of international legal and political issues, see Alfredsson (1989) and Swepton (1989).

For additional data on particular ethnic groups and historical events, we have drawn on a number of sources: *CIA World Factbook* (2013–2014), Canfield (1986), Ember and Ember (2001), Gerner (1994), Hajda and Beissinger (1990), Foster (1980), Bodley (1999), Eric Wolf (1982), Stavrianos (1998), Davidson (1969), Carmack (1988), Kehoe (1992), McAlister (1973), Handler (1988), Richard Price (1979), and the Library of Congress online Country Studies (http://countrystudies.us), as well as general news accounts and discussions with colleagues and students from Angola, Saudi Arabia, Oman, Bangladesh, Indonesia, Pakistan, and Malaysia. See also two articles by Selig Harrison: *New York Times* article, "The Pashtun Time Bomb," August 1, 2007, and *Washington Post* article, "Pakistan's Ethnic Fault Line," May 11, 2009. Most of the information on current ethnic conflicts, such as ISIS, is taken from current news reports, the website of the BBC (http://www.bbc.com/news /world) being the primary source.

Ideas and information on migration and transnational groups are from general reading, and Al-Ali and Koser (2001), Tsakiri (2005), Hirsch (2012), and the websites of the Ministry of Overseas Indian Affairs (http://www.mea .gov.in/overseas-indian-affairs.htm) and the Immigration Policy Institute (http://www.migrationpolicy.org/programs /migration-information-source). See also *New York Times* article by Kirk Semple called, "Many U.S. Immigrants' Children Seek American Dream Abroad," April 15, 2012.

Chapter 17—World Problems and the Practice of Anthropology

Applied Anthropology

The ideas about the unique contributions of anthropology to problem solving are our own.

Health

The discussion of western and traditional medicine is based on Murdock (1980). The data on Navajo healing and health are from Wyman (1983), Kunitz (1983), Csordas (2000), and Lewton (2000).

Population Growth

The economic interpretation of high birthrates in the Punjabi villages was presented by Mamdani (1973). The 1982 study of the same area is reported in Nag and Kak (1984). Data on large Javanese and Nepalese families appear in Benjamin White (1973) and Nag, White, and Peet (1978). Nardi (1981 and 1983), Shankman (1976), and Small (1997) discuss the importance of remittances in Samoa and Tonga. Freed and Freed (1985) discuss why Indian couples think they need more than one son.

World Hunger

The inequality explanation of hunger is stated and defended in lay terms in Lappé and Collins (1977 and 1986). Data on the Irish famine are from O'Grada (1989), Kinealy (1995), and Woodham-Smith (1991). The discussion of the effects of the green revolution on Javanese peasants is from Franke (1974). Allen Johnson (1971) discusses risk minimization among peasants. The quantitative data on the energetic efficiency of various food systems are compiled from information given in Pimentel et al. (1973 and 1975) and Pimentel and Pimentel (1979).

The potential value of traditional farming methods for the modern world is described in Altieri (1987) and Wilken (1987). The advantages of intercropping and other traditional methods are covered in Innis (1980), Gliessman and Grantham (1990), and Paul Harrison (1987). Traditional resource management is covered by Alcorn (1981) and Posey (1983, 1984, 1985). Nations and Nigh (1980) discuss the potential of Lacandon Maya shifting cultivation.

Anthropologists as Advocates

The anthropologist as advocate is best discussed by Peterson (1974). The early roles of anthropologists in American Indian rights issues are discussed in Mark (1987). For Boas and the issue of racism, see Stocking (1974); and for Mead, see Mark (1999). For information on Sol Tax and the American Indian Chicago Conference, see Hauptman and Campisi (1988).

For the best general discussion of the evolution of European attitudes to indigenous peoples, see Berkhofer (1978). Germany's policies toward the Herero are discussed in Bodley (1999). Shelton Davis (1977) discusses the impact on indigenous tribes of Brazil's efforts to develop the Amazon Basin. The best summary of the San issue until 2015 is "Twenty Years After Bushmen First Petition UN, Abuse Continues" (www.survivalinternational.org/news/11189). For additional information on San relocation, see Hitchcock (1999); Hitchcock, Biesele, and Lee (2003); and the websites of BBC News (http://www.bbc.com/news/world/africa) and Survival International (http://www.survivalinternational.org/tribes/bushmen). The quote about government policy is from the Botswana Tourism Board (http://www.botswanatourism.co.bw/), and the quote of the Bushman Welfare Minister is from Survival International (www.survivalinternational.org/news/5705).

The Dongria Kondh materials are from the websites of Survival International (http://www.survivalinternational.org/tribes/dongria), BBC World News (http://news.bbc.co.uk/2/hi/south_asia/7486252.stm), and *The Guardian* article by Maseeh Rahman, "India Blocks Vedanta Mine on Dongria-Kondh Tribe's Sacred Hill," August 24, 2010. The quote of the Indian Supreme Court is from NDTV (http://www.downtoearth.org.in/coverage/dongrias-decide-41620). The Kayapo and Belo Monte Dam materials are from Terrence Turner (1989), Ava Goodale (2003), Fearnside (2006), BBC News (http://news.bbc.co.uk/2/mobile/americas/8633786.stm), the *Huffington Post* (http://www.huffingtonpost.com/bianca-jagger/the-belo-monte-dam-an-env_b_1614057.html), Amazon Watch (http://amazonwatch.org/work/belo-monte-dam), and *The Guardian* article by Jonathan Watts, "Belo Monte Dam Operations Delayed by Brazil Court Ruling on Indigenous People," January 15, 2016. See also the Piaracu Declaration (https://www.internationalrivers.org/sites/default/files/attached-files/piaracudeclaration_en.pdf).

The information concerning the U.S. treatment of Native American societies is from general reading. The quote on Black Mesa is from Lacerenza (1988). On the conflict between the Peruvian government and the tribes of the Amazon, see BBC News (http://www.bbc.com/news/10399962). The statement of President Garcia is from the website of Tribe (http://indiancountrytodaymedianetwork.com/2009/06/01/fight-against-president-garcia-laws-intensify-84134).

The *Business Week* issue referred to is from March 1, 1993. The examples of medicines learned about from indigenous peoples are taken from Lewis and Elvin-Lewis (1977). Farnsworth (1984) argues that many more plants will be discovered to have medical uses. A good discussion of the insights of "traditional medicine" is in Fabrega (1975). The discussion of the erosion of the genetic diversity of major food crops is from our general knowledge and Harlan (1975). The material on amaranth is from Sokolov (1986). Information on the Declaration on the Rights of Indigenous Peoples was taken from the United Nations website (http://www.un.org) and from the BBC News website (http://news.bbc.co.uk).

Global Challenges and Opportunities

Ideas in this feature are taken from Sen (1984 and 1987) and Kapur (1998).

Bibliography

Aberle, David F. 1961. "Matrilineal Descent in Cross-Cultural Perspective." In *Matrilineal Kinship,* edited by David M. Schneider and Kathleen Gough, pp. 655–727. Berkeley: University of California Press.

Adams, Richard N. 1982. *Paradoxical Harvest.* Cambridge: Cambridge University Press.

———. 1988. "Energy and the Regulation of Nation States." *Cultural Dynamics* 1:46–61.

Adler, Daniel S. 2009. "The Earliest Musical Tradition." *Nature* 460: 695–696.

Adrian, Bonnie. 2003. *Framing the Bride: Globalizing Beauty and Romance in Taiwan's Bridal Industry.* Berkeley: University of California Press.

Al-Ali, Nadje, and Kalid Koser. 2001. *New Approaches to Migration? Transnational Communities and the Transformation of Home.* Oxford: Routledge.

Albers, Patricia C. 1989. "From Illusion to Illumination: Anthropological Studies of American Indian Women." In *Gender and Anthropology: Critical Reviews for Research and Teaching,* edited by Sandra Morgen, pp. 132–170. Washington, D.C.: American Anthropological Association.

Alcorn, Janice. 1981. "Huastec Non-Crop Resource Management." *Human Ecology* 9:395–417.

Alexander, Richard. 1974. "The Evolution of Social Behavior." *Annual Review of Ecology and Systematics* 5:325–383.

Alfredsson, Gudmundur. 1989. "The United Nations and the Rights of Indigenous Peoples." *Current Anthropology* 30:255–259.

Alkire, William H. 1977. *An Introduction to the Peoples and Cultures of Micronesia,* 2nd ed. Menlo Park, Calif.: Cummings.

Allen, Michael. 1984. "Elders, Chiefs, and Big Men: Authority Legitimation and Political Evolution in Melanesia." *American Ethnologist* 11:20–41.

Altieri, Miguel A. 1987. *Agroecology: The Scientific Basis of Alternative Agriculture.* Boulder, Colo.: Westview.

Anderson, Edward F. 1996. *Peyote: The Divine Cactus,* 2nd ed. Tucson: University of Arizona Press.

Anderson, Richard L. 1989. *Art in Small-Scale Societies,* 2nd ed. Englewood Cliffs, N.J.: Prentice Hall.

Arjamaa, Olli, and Timo Vuorisalo. 2010. "Gene-Culture Coevolution and Human Diet." *American Scientist* 98:140–147.

Atkinson, Robert D., Luke A. Stewart, Scott M. Andes, and Stephen J. Ezell. 2012. *Worse Than the Great Depression: What Experts Are Missing About American Manufacturing Decline.* Washington D.C.: The Information Technology & Innovation Foundation Report.

Aveni, Anthony. 1995. *Empires of Time.* New York: Kodansha America.

Bailey, Garrick. 1989. "Descent and Social Survival of Native Horticultural Societies of the Eastern United States." Paper presented at the American Anthropological Association meetings, Washington, D.C.

Balikci, Asen. 1970. *The Netsilik Eskimo.* Garden City, N.Y.: Natural History Press.

Balter, Michael. 2008. "Why We're Different: Probing the Gap Between Apes and Humans." *Science* 319:404–405.

Barnes, Sandra T. 1990. "Women, Property, and Power." In *Beyond the Second Sex,* edited by Peggy Reeves Sanday and Ruth Gallagher Goodenough, pp. 253–280. Philadelphia: University of Pennsylvania Press.

Barth, Fredrik. 1958. "Ecological Relationships of Ethnic Groups in Swat, North Pakistan." *American Anthropologist* 60:1079–1089.

———. 1969. *Ethnic Groups and Boundaries.* Boston: Little, Brown and Company.

Barton, Loukas, et al. 2009. "Agricultural Origins and the Isotopic Identity of Domestication in Northern China." *Proceedings of the National Academy of Sciences* 106 (14):5523–5528.

Benedict, Ruth. 1934. *Patterns of Culture.* Boston: Houghton Mifflin.

Bennett, John (Ed.). 1975. "The New Ethnicity: Perspectives from Ethnology." *1973 Proceedings of the American Ethnological Society.* St. Paul, Minn.: West.

Berdan, Frances. 2004. *Aztecs of Central Mexico: An Imperial Society,* 2nd edition. Belmont, CA: Cengage Learning.

Berger, Peter. 1997. "Four Faces of Global Culture." *National Interest* 49:419–427.

Berkhofer, Jr., Robert F. 1978. *The White Man's Indian: Images of the American Indian from Columbus to the Present.* New York: Knopf.

Bernstein, Gail. 1983. *Haruko's World: A Japanese Farm Woman and Her Community.* Stanford, Calif.: Stanford University Press.

Berreman, Gerald D. 1959. "Caste in India and the United States." *American Journal of Sociology* 66:120–127.

Black, Nancy Johnson. 1991. "What Is Anthropology?" In *Introduction to*

Library Research in Anthropology, edited by John Weeks, pp. 1–5. Boulder, Colo.: Westview.

Boas, Franz. 1955. *Primitive Art.* New York: Dover.

———. 1966. *Race, Language and Culture.* New York: Free Press (original 1940).

Bocquet-Appel, Jean-Pierre. 2011. "When the World's Population Took Off." *Science* 333:560–561.

Bodley, John H. 1968. *Justice and Judgement Among the Tiv.* London: Oxford University Press.

———. 1999. *Victims of Progress,* 4th ed. Palo Alto, Calif.: Mayfield.

Boserup, Ester. 1965. *The Conditions of Agricultural Growth.* Chicago: Aldine.

———. 1970. *Women's Role in Economic Development.* New York: St. Martin's.

Bouzouggar, Abdeljalil, et al. 2007. "82,000-Year-Old Shell Beads from North Africa and Implications for the Origins of Modern Human Behavior." *Proceedings of the National Academy of Sciences* 104:9964–9969.

Bower, Bruce. 2010. "Evolution's Bad Girl." *Science News (January* 16):22–25.

Bowles, Samuel. 2011. "Cultivation of Cereals by the First Farmers Was Not More Productive Than Foraging." *Proceedings of the National Academy of Sciences* 108 (12):4760–4765.

Bradfield, Maitland. 1971. "The Changing Pattern of Hopi Agriculture." Royal Anthropological Institute of Great Britain and Ireland Occasional Paper, no. 30. London: Royal Anthropological Institute.

Brain, Robert. 1979. *The Decorated Body.* New York: Harper & Row.

Braudel, Fernand. 1979a. *The Structures of Everyday Life. Civilization & Capitalism 15th–18th Century,* vol. 1. New York: Harper & Row.

———. 1979b. *The Wheels of Commerce. Civilization & Capitalism 15th–18th Century,* vol. 2. New York: Harper & Row.

Brown, Donald E. 1991. *Human Universals.* New York: McGraw-Hill.

Brown, Judith K. 1970a. "Economic Organization and the Position of Women Among the Iroquois." *Ethnohistory* 17:131–167.

———. 1970b. "A Note on the Division of Labor by Sex." *American Anthropologist* 72:1073–1078.

———. 1988. "Cross-Cultural Perspectives on Middle-Aged Women." In *Cultural Constructions of "Woman,"* edited by Pauline Kolenda, pp. 73–100. Salem, Wisc.: Sheffield.

Brown, Kyle S., et al. 2012a. "An Early and Enduring Advanced Technology Originating 71,000 Years Ago in South Africa." *Nature* 491:590–593.

———. 2012b. "Fire as an Engineering Tool of Early Modern Humans." *Science* 325:859–862.

Brown, Michael F. 2003. *Who Owns Native Culture?* Cambridge, Mass.: Harvard University Press.

Brown, Penelope. 2006. "Cognitive Anthropology." In *Language, Culture, and Society,* edited by Christine Jourdan and Kevin Tuite, pp. 96–114. New York: Cambridge University Press.

Bureau of Labor Statistics. 2015. *Women in the Labor Force: A Databook.* Report 1059. http://www.bls.gov/opub /reports/womens-databook/archive /women-in-the-labor-force-a-databook -2015.pdf (retrieved July 31, 2016)

Burton, Michael L., and Douglas R. White. 1984. "Sexual Division of Labor in Agriculture." *American Anthropologist* 86:568–583.

Canfield, Robert L. 1986. "Ethnic, Regional, and Sectarian Alignments in Afghanistan." In *The State, Religion, and Ethnic Politics: Afghanistan, Iran, and Pakistan,* edited by Ali Banuazizi and M. Weiner, pp. 75–103. Syracuse, N.Y.: Syracuse University Press.

Carmack, Robert (Ed.). 1988. *Harvest of Violence.* Norman: University of Oklahoma Press.

Central Intelligence Agency. 2013–2014. *The World Factbook.* https://www.cia .gov/library/publications/the-world -factbook/index.html (October 11, 2016)

Chagnon, Napoleon A. 1983. *Yanomamö: The Fierce People,* 3rd ed. New York: Holt, Rinehart & Winston.

Chan, Anita (Ed.). 2011. *Walmart in China.* Ithaca, N.Y.: Cornell University Press.

Chang, Leslie T. 2009. *Factory Girls: From Village to City in Changing China.* New York: Spiegel & Grau.

Chen, Keith. 2013. "The Effect on Language on Economic Behavior: Evidence from Savings Rates, Health Behaviors, and Retirement Assets." *American Economic Review* 103 (2):690–731.

Chomsky, Noam. 2000. "Control of Our Lives." Lecture presented February 26, 2000, Albuquerque, New Mexico.

Clark, Gregory. 2007. *A Farewell to Alms: A Brief Economic History of the World.* Princeton, N.J.: Princeton University Press.

Close, Angela E. 1989. "Identifying Style in Stone Artifacts: A Case Study from the Nile Valley." In "Alternative Approaches to Lithic Analysis," edited by Donald Henry and George Odell. *Archaeological Papers of the American Anthropological Association* 1:3–26.

Cohen, Mark Nathan. 1977. *The Food Crisis in Prehistory.* New Haven, Conn.: Yale University Press.

———. 1989. *Health and the Rise of Civilization.* New Haven, Conn.: Yale University Press.

Cohen, Ronald. 1978. "Ethnicity: Problem and Focus in Anthropology." *Annual Review of Anthropology* 7.

Cohen, Ronald, and Elman Service. 1978. *Origins of the State: The Anthropology of Political Evolution.* Philadelphia: Institute for the Study of Human Issues.

Colton, Harold S. 1959. *Hopi Kachina Dolls.* Albuquerque: University of New Mexico Press.

Commission for the Creation of Yanomami Park (CCPY). 1989a. "Brazilian Government Reduces Yanomami Territory by 70 Percent." *Cultural Survival Quarterly* 13:47.

———. 1989b. "The Threatened Yanomami." *Cultural Survival Quarterly* 13:45–46.

Committee for Human Rights, American Anthropological Association. 2001. "The Yanomami of Brazil: Human Rights Update." http:// s3.amazonaws.com/rdcms-aaa/files /production/public/FileDownloads /pdfs/cmtes/cfhr/upload/The

-Yanomami-of-Brazil-rptyano10.pdf (retrieved October 11, 2016)

Conklin, Harold. 1957. "Hanunoo Agriculture." FAO Forestry Development Paper, no. 12. Rome: Food and Agriculture Organization of the United Nations.

Connelly, John C. 1979. "Hopi Social Organization." In *Handbook of North American Indians*, vol. 9, *Southwest*, edited by Alfonso Ortiz, pp. 539–553. Washington, D.C.: Smithsonian Institution.

Conrad, Nicholas J., Maria Malina, and Susanne C. Munzel. 2009. "New Flutes Document the Earliest Musical Tradition in Southwestern Germany." *Nature* 460: 737–740.

Crawford, Gary W. 2009. "Agricultural Origins in North China Pushed Back to the Pleistocene-Holocene Boundary." *Proceedings of the National Academy of Sciences* 106 (18):7271–7272.

Crosby, Alfred W. 1972. *The Columbian Exchange*. Westport, Conn.: Greenwood.

———. 1986. *Ecological Imperialism: Biological and Cultural Consequences of 1492*. Westport, Conn.: Praeger.

Csordas, Thomas J. 2000. "The Navajo Healing Project" *Medical Anthropology Quarterly* 14 (4):463–475.

Culotta, Elizabeth. 2016. "Likely Hobbit Ancestors Lived 600,000 Years Earlier." *Science* 352:1260–1261.

Dahrendorf, Ralf. 1959. *Class and Class Conflict in Industrial Society*. Berkeley: University of California Press.

D'Altroy, Terence N. 1987. "Transitions in Power: Centralization of Wanka Political Organization Under Inka Rule." *Ethnohistory* 34:78–102.

D'Errico, Francesco, et al. 2005. "*Nassarius kraussianus* Shell Beads from Blombos Cave: Evidence for Symbolic Behaviour in the Middle Stone Age." *Journal of Human Evolution* 48:3–24.

———. 2012. "Early Evidence of San Material Culture Represented by Organic Artifacts from Border Cave, South Africa." *Proceedings of the National Academy of Sciences* 109 (33):131214–131219.

Davidson, Basil. 1961. *The African Slave Trade: Precolonial History 1450–1850*. Boston: Atlantic-Little Brown.

———. 1969. *Africa in History*. New York: Macmillan.

Davis, Kingsley, and Wilbert E. Moore. 1945. "Some Principles of Stratification." *American Sociological Review* 10: 242–249.

Davis, Shelton H. 1977. *Victims of the Miracle*. Cambridge: Cambridge University Press.

Davis, Wade. 1985. *The Serpent and the Rainbow*. New York: Warner Books.

Dawkins, Richard. 1976. *The Selfish Gene*. Oxford: Oxford University Press.

Denevan, William M. 1992. "The Pristine Myth: The Landscape of the Americas in 1492." *Annals of the Association of American Geographers* 82:369–385.

Denham, T. P., et al. 2003. "Origins of Agriculture at Kuk Swamp in the Highlands of New Guinea." *Science* 301:189–193.

Dentan, Robert Knox. 1968. *The Semai: A Nonviolent People of Malaya*. New York: Holt, Rinehart & Winston.

Deutscher, Guy. 2010. *Through the Looking Glass: Why the World Looks Different in Other Languages*. New York: Metropolitan Books.

DeVos, George, and Lola Romanusci-Ross (Eds.). 1975. *Ethnic Identity: Cultural Continuities and Change*. Palo Alto, Calif.: Mayfield.

di Leonardo, Micaela (Ed.). 1991. *Gender at the Crossroads of Knowledge*. Berkeley: University of California Press.

Diamond, Jared. 1999. *Guns, Germs, and Steel*. New York: Norton.

Dillehay, Tom, Jack Rossen, Thomas Andrus, and David Williams. 2007. "Preceramic Adoption of Squash, Peanut, and Cotton in Northern Peru." *Science* 316:1890–1893.

Divale, William T. 1974. "Migration, External Warfare, and Matrilocal Residence." *Behavior Science Research* 9:75–133.

Divale, William T., and Marvin Harris. 1976. "Population, Warfare, and the Male Supremacist Complex." *American Anthropologist* 78:521–538.

Dobyns, Henry F. 1976. *Native American Historical Demography: A Critical Bibliography*. Bloomington: Indiana University Press.

———. 1983. *Their Numbers Become Thinned*. Knoxville: University of Tennessee Press.

Donkin, Robin. 1979. *Agricultural Terracing in the Aboriginal New World*. Tucson: University of Arizona Press.

Doolittle, William E. 1992. "Agriculture in North America on the Eve of Contact: A Reassessment." *Annals of the Association of American Geographers* 82:386–401.

Dozier, Edward P. 1970. *The Pueblo Indians of North America*. Prospect Heights, Ill.: Waveland Press (reissued 1983).

Dumont, Louis. 1980. *Homo Hierarchicus: The Caste System and Its Implications*. Chicago: University of Chicago Press.

Durkheim, Émile. 1915. *The Elementary Forms of the Religious Life*. London: Allen and Unwin.

Dyson-Hudson, Rada, and Neville Dyson-Hudson. 1969. "Subsistence Herding in Uganda." *Scientific American* 220:76–89.

Economic Policy Institute. 2012. *The State of Working America*, 12th ed. Ithaca, N.Y.: Cornell University Press.

Economy, Elizabeth C. 2004. *River Runs Black: The Environmental Challenge to China's Future*. Ithaca, N.Y.: Cornell University Press.

———. 2007. "The Great Leap Backward?" *Foreign Affairs* (September/October).

Eggan, Fred. 1950. *Social Organization of the Western Pueblos*. Chicago: University of Chicago Press.

———. 1954. "Social Anthropology and the Method of Controlled Comparison." *American Anthropologist* 56:743–761.

Ember, Carol. 1974. "An Evaluation of Alternative Theories of Matrilocal Versus Patrilocal Residence." *Behavior Science Research* 9:135–149.

———. 1983. "The Relative Decline in Women's Contribution to Agriculture with Intensification." *American Anthropologist* 85:285–304.

Ember, Carol R., and Melvin Ember. (n.d.). "Basic Guide to Cross-Cultural Research." HRAF website. http://hraf .yale.edu/cross-cultural-research/basic -guide-to-cross-cultural-research/

Ember, Melvin. 1959. "The Nonunilinear Descent Groups of Samoa." *American Anthropologist* 61:573–577.

Ember, Melvin, and Carol R. Ember. 1971. "The Conditions Favoring Matrilocal Versus Patrilocal Residence." *American Anthropologist* 73:571–594.

———. 1972. "The Conditions Favoring Multilocal Residence." *Southwestern Journal of Anthropology* 28:382–400.

Ember, Melvin, and Carol R. Ember (Eds.). 2001. *Countries and Their Cultures,* 4 vols. New York: Macmillan Reference USA.

Ember, Melvin, Carol R. Ember, and Burton Pasternak. 1974. "On the Development of Unilineal Descent." *Journal of Anthropological Research* 30:69–94.

Epple, Carolyn. 1998. "Coming to Terms with Navajo Nadleehi: A Critique of Berdache, 'Gay,' 'Alternate Gender,' and 'Two Spirit.'" *American Ethnologist* 25:267–290.

Estioko-Griffin, Agnes. 1986. "Daughters of the Forest." *Natural History* 95:36–43.

Ethnologue, Languages of the World. 2016. *World Languages.* www .ethnologue.com/world (retrieved September 15, 2016)

Evans-Pritchard, E. E. 1940. *The Nuer.* Oxford: Clarendon.

———. 1976. *Witchcraft, Oracles, and Magic Among the Azande,* abridged ed. Oxford: Clarendon Press.

Ewers, John. 1955. "The Horse in Blackfoot Indian Culture." Bureau of American Ethnology, Bulletin 159. Washington, D.C.: U.S. Government Printing Office.

Fabrega, H., Jr. 1975. "The Need for an Ethnomedical Science." *Science* 189:969–975.

Fagan, Brian. 2002. *Archaeology: A Brief Introduction,* 8th ed. Englewood, Cliffs, N.J.: Prentice Hall.

Fallers, Lloyd A. 1969. *Law Without Precedent.* Chicago: University of Chicago Press.

Faris, James. 1972. *Nuba Personal Art.* Toronto: University of Toronto.

Farnsworth, Norman R. 1984. "How Can the Well Be Dry When It Is Filled with Water?" *Economic Botany* 38:4–13.

Farrer, Claire F. 1996. *Thunder Rides a Black Horse.* 2nd ed. Prospect Heights, Ill.: Waveland Press.

Fearnside, Phillip M. 2006. "Dams in the Amazon: Belo Monte and Brazil's Hydroelectric Development of the Xingu River Basin." *Environmental Management* 20 (10):1–13.

Ferguson, R. Brian. 1984. "A Reexamination of the Causes of Northwest Coast Warfare." In *Warfare, Culture, and Environment,* edited by R. Brian Ferguson, pp. 267–328. Orlando, Fla.: Academic Press.

Fine, Gary Allan. 2007. *Authors of the Storm: Meteorologists and the Culture of Prediction.* Chicago: University of Chicago Press.

Firth, Raymond. 1936. *We, the Tikopia.* Boston: Beacon.

———. 1965. *Primitive Polynesian Economy.* New York: Norton.

———. 1968. "A Note on Descent Groups in Polynesia." In *Kinship and Social Organization,* edited by Paul Bohannan and John Middleton, pp. 213–223. Garden City, N.Y.: Natural History Press.

Fischer, John. 1961. "Art Styles as Cultural Cognitive Maps." *American Anthropologist* 63:80–84.

Fogelson, Raymond D. 1989. "The Ethno-history of Events and Nonevents." *Ethnohistory* 36:133–147.

Foley, Jonathan. 2013. "It's Time to Rethink America's Corn System." *Scientific American.* www .scientificamerican.com/article /time-to-rethink-corn/ (retrieved July 5, 2016).

Fong, Vanessa. 2004. *Only Hope: Coming of Age Under China's One-Child Policy.* Stanford, Calif.: Stanford University Press.

Fortune, Reo. 1932. *Sorcerers of Dobu.* New York: Dutton.

Foster, Charles R. (Ed.). 1980. *Nations Without a State: Ethnic Minorities of Western Europe.* New York: Praeger.

Foster, George. 1962. *Traditional Cultures and the Impact of Technological Change.* New York: Harper & Row.

Frank, Andre Gunder. 1998. *ReOrient: Global Economy in the Asian Age.* Berkeley: University of California Press.

Franke, Richard W. 1974. "Miracle Seeds and Shattered Dreams in Java." *Natural History* 83:10–18, 84–88.

Fratto, Toni Flores. 1978. "Undefining Art: Irrelevant Categorization in the Anthropology of Aesthetics." *Dialectical Anthropology* 3 (2):129–138.

Frazer, Sir James George. 1963. *The Golden Bough,* abridged ed. Toronto: Macmillan (original 1911–1915).

Freed, Stanley A., and Ruth S. Freed. 1985. "One Son Is No Sons." *Natural History* 94:10–15.

Freeman, Derek. 1983. *Margaret Mead and Samoa.* Cambridge, Mass.: Harvard University Press.

Fried, Morton. 1967. *The Evolution of Political Society.* New York: Random House.

Friedl, Ernestine. 1975. *Women and Men: An Anthropologist's View.* New York: Holt, Rinehart & Winston.

———. 1978. "Society and Sex Roles." In *Anthropology 98/99,* edited by Elvio Angeloni, pp. 122–126. Guilford, Conn.: Dushkin.

Friedson, Steven. 1998. "Tumbuka Healing." In *The Garland Encyclopedia of World Music,* vol. 1, edited by Ruth M. Stone, pp. 271–284. New York: Garland.

Frigout, Arlette. 1979. "Hopi Ceremonial Organization." In *Handbook of North American Indians,* vol. 9, *Southwest,* edited by Alfonso Ortiz, pp. 564–576. Washington, D.C.: Smithsonian Institution.

Fromkin, Victoria, and Robert Rodman. 1988. *An Introduction to Language,*

4th ed. New York: Holt, Rinehart & Winston.

Fuller, D., et al. 2009. "The Domestication Process and Domestication Rate in Rice: Spikelet Bases from the Lower Yangtze." *Science* 323: 1607–1610.

Furst, Peter T., and Jill L. Furst. 1982. *North American Indian Art.* New York: Rizzoli International.

Geertz, Clifford. 1965. "Religion as a Cultural System." In *Anthropological Approaches to the Study of Religion,* edited by Michael Banton, pp. 1–46. Association of Social Anthropologists Monographs, no. 3. London: Tavistock.

———. 1973. *The Interpretation of Cultures.* New York: Basic Books.

———. 1980. *Negara.* Princeton, N.J.: Princeton University Press.

———. 1983. *Local Knowledge: Further Essays on Interpretive Anthropology.* New York: Basic Books.

Gell, Alfred. 1993. *Wrapping in Images.* Oxford: Clarendon Press.

Gerner, Deborah J. 1994. *One Land, Two Peoples: The Conflict over Palestine.* Boulder, Colo.: Westview.

Giddens, Anthony. 2000. *Runaway World: How Globalization Is Reshaping Our Lives.* New York: Routledge.

Gilmore, David D. 1980. *The People of the Plain.* New York: Columbia University Press.

———. 1990. *Manhood in the Making.* New Haven, Conn.: Yale University Press.

Gladwell, Malcolm. 2001. "The Mosquito Killer." *New Yorker* (July 2):42–51.

Glazer, Nathan, and Daniel P. Moynihan. 1963. *Beyond the Melting Pot.* Cambridge, Mass.: Harvard University Press.

Glazer, Nathan, and Daniel P. Moynihan (Eds.). 1975. *Ethnicity: Theory and Experience.* Cambridge, Mass.: Harvard University Press.

Gliessman, Stephen, and Robert Grantham. 1990. "Agroecology: Reshaping Agricultural Development." In *Lessons of the Rain Forest,* edited by Suzanne Head and Robert Heinzman, pp. 196–207. San Francisco: Sierra Club Books.

Gluckman, Max. 1972. *The Ideas in Barotse Jurisprudence.* Manchester: Manchester University Press.

———. 1973. *The Judicial Process Among the Barotse.* Manchester: Manchester University Press.

Goldman, Irving. 1970. *Ancient Polynesian Society.* Chicago: University of Chicago Press.

Goldstein, Melvyn C. 1987 "When Brothers Share a Wife." *Natural History* 96 (3):38–49.

Goodale, Ava Y. 2003. "The Kayapo Indians' Struggle in Brazil." www .action-bioscience.org/environment /goodale.html (retrieved October 11, 2016)

Goodale, Jane C. 1971. *Tiwi Wives.* Seattle: University of Washington Press.

Goodenough, Ward H. 1961. "Comment on Cultural Evolution." *Daedalus* 90:521–528.

Goody, Jack, and S. J. Tambiah. 1973. *Bridewealth and Dowry.* Cambridge: Cambridge University Press.

Gough, E. Kathleen. 1959. "The Nayars and the Definition of Marriage." *Journal of the Royal Anthropological Institute* 89:23–24.

Graham, Susan Brandt. 1985. "Running and Menstrual Dysfunction: Recent Medical Discoveries Provide New Insights into the Human Division of Labor by Sex." *American Anthropologist* 87:878–882.

Grigg, David. 1974. *The Agricultural Systems of the World.* Cambridge: Cambridge University Press.

Guthrie, Stewart. 1993. *Faces in the Clouds: A New Theory of Religion.* Oxford: Oxford University Press.

Hage, Per, Frank Harary, and Bojka Milicic. 1995. "Tattooing, Gender and Social Stratification in Micro-Polynesia." *Journal of the Royal Anthropological Institute (N.S.)* 2:335–350.

Hail, Barbara. 1980. *Hau, Kola: The Plains Indian Collection of the Haffenreffer Museum.* Providence, R.I.: Haffenreffer Museum of Anthropology, Brown University.

Hajda, Lubomyr, and Mark Beissinger (Eds.). 1990. *The Nationalities Factor in Soviet Politics and Society.* Boulder, Colo.: Westview.

Hall, Edward T. 1959. *The Silent Language.* Greenwich, Conn.: Fawcett.

———. 1966. *The Hidden Dimension.* Garden City, N.Y.: Doubleday.

Handler, Richard. 1988. *Nationalism and the Politics of Culture in Quebec.* Madison: University of Wisconsin Press.

Harding, Susan Friend. 2000. *The Book of Jerry Falwell: Fundamentalist Language and Politics.* Princeton, N.J.: Princeton University Press.

Harkin, Michael E., and David Rich Lewis. 2007. *Native Americans and the Environment.* Lincoln: University of Nebraska Press.

Harlan, Jack R. 1975. "Our Vanishing Genetic Resources." *Science* 188:618–621.

Harner, Michael J. 1973. *The Jívaro.* Garden City, N.Y.: Doubleday-Anchor.

Harrell, Stevan, and Sara A. Dickey. 1985. "Dowry Systems in Complex Societies." *Ethnology* 24:105–120.

Harris, Marvin. 1968. *The Rise of Anthropological Theory.* New York: Crowell.

———. 1977. *Cannibals and Kings.* New York: Random House.

———. 1979. *Cultural Materialism.* New York: Vintage Books.

———. 1985. *Good to Eat.* New York: Simon & Schuster.

———. 1999. *Theories of Culture in Postmodern Times.* Walnut Creek, Calif.: Altamira Press.

Harrison, Paul. 1987. *The Greening of Africa.* New York: Penguin.

Hart, C. W. M., Arnold R. Pilling, and Jane C. Goodale. 1988. *The Tiwi of North Australia.* Belmont, Calif.: Wadsworth.

Harvey, Paul. 1937. *The Oxford Companion to Classical Literature.* Oxford: Clarendon Press.

Hauptman, Lawrence, and Jack Campisi. 1988. "The Voice of Eastern Indians: The American Indian Chicago Conference of 1961 and the Movement for Federal Recognition." *Proceedings of the American Philosophical Society* 132 (4):316–329.

Haynes, Devon. 2014. "Number of International Students Continues to Climb." *U.S. News*. www.usnews.com/education/best-colleges/articles/2014/11/17/ (retrieved February 29, 2016)

Henshilwood, Christopher S., et al. 2002. "Emergence of Modern Human Behavior: Middle Stone Age Engravings from South Africa." *Science* 295: 1278–1280.

———. 2011. "A 100,000-Year-Old Ochre-Processing Workshop at Blombos Cave, South Africa." *Science* 334:219–222.

Hepner, George F., and Jesse O. McKee. 1992. *World Regional Geography: A Global Approach*. St. Paul, Minn.: West.

Heth, Charlotte (Ed.). 1993. *Native American Dance*. Washington, D.C.: Smithsonian Institution.

Hewlett, Barry S. 1992. *Intimate Fathers*. Ann Arbor: University of Michigan Press.

Hickerson, Harold. 1970. *The Chippewa and Their Neighbors: A Study in Ethnohistory*. New York: Holt, Rinehart & Winston.

Hiebert, P. G. 1971. *Konduru: Structure and Integration in a Hindu Village*. Minneapolis: University of Minnesota Press.

Himes, Joseph S. 1974. *Racial and Ethnic Relations*. Dubuque, Ia.: Brown.

Hines, Colin. 2000. *Localization: A Global Manifesto*. London: Earthscan Publications.

Hirsch, Michelle. 2012, May 14. "U.S. Educated Immigrants Return to Their Homelands." *Fiscal Times*. http://www.thefiscaltimes.com/Articles/2012/05/14/US-Educated-Immigrants-Return-to-Their-Homelands (retrieved October 11, 2016)

Hitchcock, Robert K. 1999. "Resource Rights and Resettlement Among the San of Botswana." *Cultural Survival Quarterly* 22 (4):51–55.

Hitchcock, Robert K., Megan Biesele, and Richard B. Lee. 2003. "The San of Southern Africa: A Status Report, 2003." http://s3.amazonaws.com/rdcms-aaa/files/production/public/FileDownloads/pdfs/cmtes/cfhr/upload/The-San-of-Southern-Africa-A-Status-Report-2003.pdf (retrieved October 11, 2016)

Ho, Karen. 2009. *Liquidated: An Ethnography of Wall Street*. Durham, N.C.: Duke University Press.

Hobson, Christine. 1987. *The World of the Pharaohs*. New York: Thames and Hudson.

Hockett, Charles F. 1960. "The Origin of Speech." *Scientific American* 203:88–96.

Hoebel, E. Adamson. 1940. *The Political Organization and Law-Ways of the Comanche Indians*. American Anthropological Association, Memoir 54. Menasha, Wisc.: American Anthropological Association.

———. 1954. *The Law of Primitive Man*. Cambridge, Mass.: Harvard University Press.

———. 1978. *The Cheyennes*, 2nd ed. New York: Holt, Rinehart & Winston.

Holden, Clare Janake, and Ruth Mace. 1999. "Sexual Dimorphism in Stature and Women's Work: A Phylogenetic Cross-Cultural Analysis." *American Journal of Physical Anthropology* 111:27–45.

———. 2003. "Spread of Cattle Led to the Loss of Matrilineal Descent in Africa: A Coevolutionary Analysis." *Proceedings of the Royal Society of London B*: 270:2425–2433.

Holm, Bill. 1965. *Northwest Coast Indian Art: An Analysis of Form*. Seattle: University of Washington Press.

———. 1972. *Crooked Beak of Heaven*. Seattle: University of Washington Press.

Holmes, Lowell D., and Ellen Rhoads Holmes. 1992. *Samoan Village Then and Now*, 2nd ed. Fort Worth, Tex.: Harcourt Brace Jovanovich.

Horowitz, Donald L. 1985. *Ethnic Groups in Conflict*. Berkeley: University of California Press.

Howard, Alan, and John Kirkpatrick. 1989. "Social Organization." In *Developments in Polynesian Ethnology*, edited by Alan Howard and Robert Borofsky, pp. 47–94. Honolulu: University of Hawaii Press.

Hua, Cai. 2001. *A Society Without Fathers or Husbands: The Na of China* (translated by Asti Hustvedt). New York: Zone Books.

Hunter, David E., and Phillip Whitten (Eds.). 1975. *Encyclopedia of Anthropology*. New York: Harper & Row.

Huntington, Samuel P. 2011. *The Clash of Civilizations and the Remaking of World Order*. New York: Simon & Schuster.

Hutton, Will, and Anthony Giddens (Eds.). 2000. *Global Capitalism*. New York: New Press.

Innis, Donald Q. 1980. "The Future of Traditional Agriculture." *Focus* 30:1–8.

Izady, Mehrdad R. 1992. *The Kurds*. Washington, D.C.: Taylor & Francis.

Jackson, Richard, and Neil Howe. 2006. "The Greying of the Middle Kingdom: The Demographics and Economics of Retirement Policy in China." *European Papers on the New Welfare*, paper no. 4. http://eng.newwelfare.org/2006/02/12/the-greying-of-the-middle-kingdom-the-demographics-and-economics-of-retirement-policy-in-china/#.V_0Yd5MrJkU (retrieved October 11, 2016)

Jackson, Richard, and Lloyd E. Hudman. 1990a. *Cultural Geography: The Global Discipline*. St. Paul, Minn.: West.

———. 1990b. *Cultural Geography: People, Places and Environment*. St. Paul, Minn.: West.

Jaubert, Jacques, et al. 2016. "Early Neandertal Constructions Deep in Bruniquel Cave in Southwestern France." *Nature*. doi:10.1038/nature18291

Jenike, Brenda Robb. 2003. "Parental Care and Shifting Family Obligations in Urban Japan." In *Demographic Change and the Family in Japan's Aging Society*, edited by John W. Traphagan and John Knight, pp. 177–201. Albany: State University of New York Press.

Johansen, Bruce E. 2009. *The Encyclopedia of Global Warming Science and Technology*. Santa Barbara: ABC-CLIO.

Johnson, Allen W. 1971. "Security and Risk-Taking Among Poor Peasants: A Brazilian Case." In *Studies in Economic Anthropology*, edited by George Dalton, pp. 143–150. American Anthropological Association Special Publication, no. 7.

Washington, D.C.: American Anthropological Association.

Johnson, Allen W., and Timothy Earle. 1987. *The Evolution of Human Societies.* Stanford, Calif.: Stanford University Press.

Johnson, Ericka. 2007. *Dreaming of a Mail Order Husband: Russian-American Internet Romance.* Durham, N.C.: Duke University Press.

Julien, Catherine J. 1988. "How Inca Decimal Administration Worked." *Ethnohistory* 35:257–279.

Jurmain, Robert, Lynn Kilgore, Wenda Trevathan, and Russell L. Ciochon. 2008. *Introduction to Physical Anthropology,* 11th ed. Belmont, Calif.: Wadsworth.

Kaeppler, Adrienne L. 1978. "Dance in Anthropological Perspective." *Annual Review of Anthropology* 7:31–49.

Kalb, Laurie Beth. 1994. *Crafting Devotions: Tradition in Contemporary New Mexico Santos.* Albuquerque: University of New Mexico Press.

Kapur, Akash. 1998. "The Indian State of Kerala Has Everything Against It—Except Success." *Atlantic Monthly* (September):40–45.

Keesing, Roger M. 1982. *Kwaio Religion.* New York: Columbia University Press.

Kehoe, Alice B. 1992. *North American Indians: A Comprehensive Account,* 2nd ed. Englewood Cliffs, N.J.: Prentice Hall.

Kelly, Robert L. 2006. *The Foraging Spectrum: Diversity in Hunter-Gatherer Lifeways.* Clinton Corners, NY: Eliot Werner Publications.

Khlief, Bud B. 1979. "Language as Identity: Toward an Ethnography of Welsh Nationalism." *Ethnicity* 6 (4):346–357.

Kinealy, Christine. 1995. *This Great Calamity: The Irish Famine 1845–52.* Boulder, Colo.: Roberts Rinehart.

Klein, Naomi. 1999. *No Logo.* New York: Picador.

Kluckhohn, Clyde. 1944. *Navajo Witchcraft.* Boston: Beacon.

Knauft, B. M. 1985. *Good Company and Violence: Sorcery and Social Action in a Lowland New Guinea Society.* Berkeley: University of California Press.

Krader, Lawrence. 1968. *Formation of the State.* Englewood Cliffs, N.J.: Prentice Hall.

Kraybill, Donald B. 1989. *The Riddle of Amish Culture.* Baltimore, Md.: Johns Hopkins University Press.

Krech, Shepard. 1999. *The Ecological Indian: Myth and History.* New York: Norton.

Kunio, Sato. 1988. "Wives for Farmers: A Critical Import." *Japan Quarterly* (July–September):253–259.

Kunitz, Stephen J. 1983. *Disease Change and the Role of Medicine.* Berkeley: University of California Press.

Kuper, Hilda. 1963. *The Swazi: A South African Kingdom.* New York: Holt, Rinehart & Winston.

Kuwayama, Takami. 2004. *Native Anthropology.* Melbourne: Trans Pacific Press.

Lacerenza, Deborah. 1988. "An Historical Overview of the Navajo Relocation." *Cultural Survival Quarterly* 12 (3). https://www.culturalsurvival.org /publications/cultural-survival-quarterly /united-states/historical-overview -navajo-relocation (retrieved October 11, 2016)

Laderman, Carol, and Marina Roseman (Eds.). 1996. *The Performance of Healing.* New York: Routledge.

LaFlesche, Francis. 1905. *Who Was the Medicine Man?* Hampton, Va.: Hampton Institute Press.

———. 1925. "The Osage Tribe: Rite of Vigil." In *39th Annual Report of the Bureau of American Ethnology (1917–18),* pp. 523–833. Washington, D.C.: U.S. Government Printing Office.

———. 1928. "The Osage Tribe: Two Versions of the Child-Naming Rite." In *43rd Annual Report of the Bureau of American Ethnology (1925–1926),* pp. 23–164. Washington, D.C.: U.S. Government Printing Office.

LaLone, Mary B., and Darrell E. LaLone. 1987. "The Inka State in the Southern Highlands: State Administrative and Production Enclaves." *Ethnohistory* 34:47–62.

Lane, Carrie. 2009. "Man Enough to Let My Wife Support Me: How Changing Models of Career and Gender Are Reshaping the Experience of Unemployment." *American Ethnologist* 36:681–692.

Lappé, Frances Moore, and Joseph Collins. 1977. *Food First.* New York: Ballantine Books.

———. 1986. *World Hunger: Twelve Myths.* New York: Grove Press.

Lawrence, Peter. 1964. *Road Belong Cargo.* Manchester: Manchester University Press.

Leacock, Eleanor. 1978. "Women's Status in Egalitarian Society: Implications for Social Evolution." *Current Anthropology* 19:247–275.

Leacock, Eleanor, and Nancy Lurie (Eds.). 1971. *North American Indians in Historical Perspective.* New York: Random House.

Leavitt, John. 2006. "Linguistic Relativities." In *Language, Culture, and Society,* edited by Christine Jourdan and Kevin Tuite, pp. 47–61. New York: Cambridge University Press.

Lee, Richard B. 1969. "!Kung Bushman Subsistence: An Input-Output Analysis." In *Environment and Social Behavior,* edited by Andrew P. Vayda, pp. 47–79. Garden City, N.Y.: Natural History Press.

———. 1979. *The !Kung San.* Cambridge: Cambridge University Press.

———. 2003. *The Dobe Ju/'hoansi,* 3rd ed. Belmont, Calif.: Wadsworth.

Lenski, Gerhard E. 1966. *Power and Privilege.* New York: McGraw-Hill.

Lepowsky, Maria. 1993. *Fruit of the Motherland: Gender in an Egalitarian Society.* New York: Columbia University Press.

LeVine, Terry Yarov. 1987. "Inka Labor Service at the Regional Level: The Functional Reality." *Ethnohistory* 34:14–46.

Levinson, Stephen. 2003. *Space in Language and Cognition: Explorations in Cognitive Diversity.* Cambridge: Cambridge University Press.

Levitt, Tom. 2011, September 13. "Mexico's Poor Suffer as Food Speculation Fuels Tortilla Crisis." *The Ecologist.* http://www.theecologist.org /trial_investigations/1051194/mexicos _poor_suffer_as_food_speculation _fuels_tortilla_crisis.html (retrieved October 11, 2016)

Lewis, Walter H., and Memory P. F. Elvin-Lewis. 1977. *Medical Botany.* New York: Wiley.

Lewton, Elizabeth L. 2000. "Identity and Healing in Three Navajo Religious Traditions: Sa'ah Naaghai Bik'eh Hozho." *Medical Anthropology Quarterly* 14 (4):476–497.

Lieberman, Philip. 2007. "The Evolution of Human Speech." *Current Anthropology* 48:39–53.

Lipman, Jean, and Alice Winchester. 1974. *The Flowering of American Folk Art.* New York: Viking.

Llewellyn, Karl, and E. Adamson Hoebel. 1941. *The Cheyenne Way.* Norman: University of Oklahoma Press.

Lomax, Alan. 1962. "Song Structure and Social Structure." *Ethnology* 1:425–451.

———. 1968. "Folk Song Style and Culture." American Association for the Advancement of Science Publication, no. 88. Washington, D.C.: American Association for Advancement of Science.

Love, Thomas. 2008. "Anthropology and the Fossil Fuel Era." *Anthropology Today* 24 (2):3–4.

Lowie, Robert H. 1954 Indians of the Plains. Garden City, N.Y.: American Museum of Natural History.

———. 1956. *The Crow Indians.* New York: Holt, Rinehart & Winston (original 1935).

Lucy, John A. 1997. "Linguistic Relativity." *Annual Review of Anthropology* 26:291–312.

Luhrmann, T. M. 2012. *When God Talks Back: Understanding the American Evangelical Relationship with God.* New York: Vintage Books.

Mahbubani, Kishore. 2012, February 7. "Western Capitalism Has Much to Learn from Asia." *Financial Times.* http://www.mahbubani.net/articles%20by%20dean/Western%20capitalism%20has%20much%20to%20learn%20from%20Asia.pdf (October 11, 2016)

Malinowski, Bronislaw. 1922. *Argonauts of the Western Pacific.* New York: Dutton.

———. 1926. *Crime and Custom in Savage Society.* London: Routledge & Kegan Paul.

———. 1954. *Magic, Science and Religion.* Garden City, N.Y.: Doubleday.

———. 1960. *A Scientific Theory of Culture and Other Essays.* New York: Oxford University Press (original 1944).

Mamdani, Mahmood. 1973. *The Myth of Population Control: Family, Caste, and Class in an Indian Village.* New York: Monthly Review Press.

Mandelbaum, David G. 1970. *Society in India.* 2 vols. Berkeley: University of California Press.

Mann, Charles. 2011. *1493: Uncovering the New World Columbus Created.* New York: Knopf.

Mark, Joan. 1987. *A Stranger in Her Native Land: Alice Fletcher and the American Indians.* Lincoln: University of Nebraska Press.

———. 1999. *Margaret Mead: Coming of Age in America.* New York: Oxford University Press.

Marklein, Mary Beth. 2013, November 14. "Colleges Go Abroad with Branch Campuses." *USA Today.*

Marlowe, F. W. 2010. *The Hadza: Hunter-Gatherers of Tanzania.* Berkeley: University of California Press.

Marshall, Bernard. 1973. "The Black Caribs: Native Resistance to British Penetration into the Windward Side of St. Vincent 1763–1773." *Caribbean Quarterly* 19 (4):4–19.

Marshall, Mac. 1979. *Weekend Warriors.* Palo Alto, Calif.: Mayfield.

Martin, M. Kay, and Barbara Voorhies. 1975. *Female of the Species.* New York: Columbia University Press.

Marx, Karl. 1967. *Capital,* vol. 1. New York: International Publishers (original 1867).

Mayo, Katherine. 1927. *Mother India.* New York: Harcourt, Brace.

McAlister, John T. (Ed.). 1973. *Southeast Asia: The Politics of National Integration.* New York: Random House.

McCabe, Justin. 1983. "FBD Marriage: Further Support for the Westermarck Hypothesis of the Incest Taboo." *American Anthropologist* 85:50–69.

McDonald, Kim. 1995. "Unearthing Sins of the Past." *Chronicle of Higher Education* (October 6):A12, A20.

Mead, Margaret. 1928. *Coming of Age in Samoa.* New York: Morrow.

Meigs, Anna S. 1988. *Food, Sex, and Pollution: A New Guinea Religion.* New Brunswick, N.J.: Rutgers University Press.

———. 1990. "Multiple Gender Ideologies and Statuses." In *Beyond the Second Sex,* edited by Peggy Reeves Sanday and Ruth M. Gallagher Goodenough, pp. 99–112. Philadelphia: University of Pennsylvania Press.

Metraux, Alfred. 1969. *The History of the Incas.* New York: Pantheon Books.

———. 1972. *Voodoo in Haiti.* New York: Schocken Books.

Middleton, John. 1965. *The Lugbara of Uganda.* New York: Holt, Rinehart & Winston.

Milner, G. B. 1969. "Siamese Twins, Bird, and the Double Helix." *Man* 4:5–23.

Mintz, Sidney W. 1986. *Sweetness and Power: The Place of Sugar in Modern History.* New York: Penguin Books.

Miracle, Marvin P. 1966. *Maize in Tropical Africa.* Madison: University of Wisconsin Press.

———. 1967. *Agriculture in the Congo Basin.* Madison: University of Wisconsin Press.

Morgan, Lewis Henry. 1877. *Ancient Society.* New York: World.

Mountford, Charles P. 1976. *Nomads of the Australian Desert.* Melbourne: Rigby.

Mukherjee, Siddhartha. 2016. *The Gene: An Intimate History.* New York: Scribner.

Mulier, Thomas, and Stephen Pulvirent. 2014. "Patek Philippe Watch Sets Auction Record Price in Geneva." *Bloomberg.* http://www.bloomberg.com/news/articles/2014-11-12/patek-philippe-watch-sets-auction-record-price-in-geneva (retrieved July 26, 2016)

Mulroy, Kevin. 2004. "Seminole Maroons." In *Handbook of North American Indians,* vol. 14, *Southeast,* edited by Raymond D. Fogelson, pp. 465–477. Washington, D.C.: Smithsonian Institution.

Murdock, George Peter. 1949. *Social Structure.* New York: Free Press.

———. 1980. *Theories of Illness.* Pittsburgh: University of Pittsburgh Press.

Murdock, George P., and Caterina Provost. 1973. "Factors in the Division of Labor by Sex: A Cross-Cultural Analysis." *Ethnology* 12:203–225.

Nadel, S. F. 1951. *The Foundations of Social Anthropology.* London: Cohen & West.

Nag, Moni, and Neeraj Kak. 1984. "Demographic Transition in a Punjab Village." *Population and Development Review* 10:661–678.

Nag, Moni, Benjamin N. F. White, and R. Creighton Peet. 1978. "An Anthropological Approach to the Study of the Economic Value of Children in Java and Nepal." *Current Anthropology* 19:293–306.

Nagle, Robin. 2013. *Picking Up: On the Streets and Behind the Trucks with the Sanitation Workers of New York City.* New York: Farrar, Straus and Giroux.

Nanda, Serena. 1999. *Neither Man nor Woman: The Hijras of India.* Belmont, Calif.: Wadsworth.

———. 2000. *Gender Diversity: Cross-Cultural Variations.* Prospect Heights, Ill.: Waveland Press.

Nardi, Bonnie. 1981. "Modes of Explanation in Anthropological Population Theory." *American Anthropologist* 83:28–56.

———. 1983. "Goals in Reproductive Decision Making." *American Ethnologist* 10:697–714.

Naroll, Raoul. 1962. *Data Quality Control—A New Research Technique.* New York: Free Press.

Nations, James, and Robert Nigh. 1980. "The Evolutionary Potential of Lacandon Maya Sustained-Yield Tropical Forest Agriculture." *Journal of Anthropological Research* 36:1–30.

Neale, Walter C. 1976. *Monies in Societies.* San Francisco: Chandler and Sharp.

Nestor, Sandy. 2003. *Indian Placenames in America: Volume 1: Cities, Towns and Villages.* London: McFarland.

Newman, Katherine S. 1983. *Law and Economic Organization: A Comparative Study of Pre-Industrial Societies.* Cambridge: Cambridge University Press.

Nietschmann, Bernard. 1988. "Third World War: The Global Conflict over the Rights of Indigenous Nations." *Utne Reader* (November/December):84–91.

Oboler, Regina Smith. 1985. *Women, Power, and Economic Change.* Stanford, CA: Stanford University Press.

Obeyesekere, Gananath. 1992. *The Apotheosis of Captain Cook: European Mythmaking in the Pacific.* Princeton, N.J.: Princeton University Press.

Offiong, Daniel. 1983. "Witchcraft Among the Ibibio of Nigeria." *African Studies Review* 26:107–124.

O'Grada, Cormac. 1989. *Ireland Before and After the Famine: Explorations in Economic History 1800–1925.* Manchester: University of Manchester Press.

Oliver, Douglas L. 1989. *Oceania: The Native Cultures of Australia and the Pacific Islands.* Honolulu: University of Hawaii Press.

Oliver, Roland, and J. D. Fage. 1962. *A Short History of Africa.* Baltimore: Penguin.

Orellana, Marcos A. 2008. "*Saramaka v Suriname.*" *American Journal of International Law* 102 (4):841–847.

Ortiz, Alfonso. 1969. *The Tewa World.* Chicago: University of Chicago Press.

Pagel, Mark. 2012. *Wired for Culture: Origins of the Human Social Mind.* New York: Norton.

Parezo, Nancy J. 1991. *Navajo Sandpainting: From Religious Act to Commercial Art.* Albuquerque: University of New Mexico Press.

Pasternak, Burton. 1976. *Introduction to Kinship and Social Organization.* Englewood Cliffs, N.J.: Prentice Hall.

Pasternak, Burton, Carol R. Ember, and Melvin Ember. 1976. "On the Conditions Favoring Extended Family Households." *Journal of Anthropological Research* 32:109–123.

Peoples, James G. 1982. "Individual or Group Advantage? A Reinterpretation of the Maring Ritual Cycle." *Current Anthropology* 23:291–309.

———. 1985. *Island in Trust.* Boulder, Colo.: Westview.

———. 2007. "Materialist Particularity in Nuclear Micronesia." In *Studying Societies and Cultures: Marvin Harris's Cultural Materialism and Its Legacy,* pp. 104–127. Boulder, Colo.: Paradigm.

Petersen, Glenn. 2009. "Kanengamah and Pohnpei's Politics of Concealment". *American Anthropologist* 95 (2): 334–352.

Peterson, John. 1974. "The Anthropologist as Advocate." *Human Organization* 33:311–318.

Pickersgill, Barbara. 2007. "Domestication of Plants in the Americas: Insights from Mendelian and Molecular Genetics." *Annals of Botany* 1–16.

Pimentel, David, et al. 1973. "Food Production and the Energy Crisis." *Science* 182:443–449.

———. 1975. "Energy and Land Constraints in Food Protein Production." *Science* 190:754–761.

Pimentel, David, and Marcia Pimentel. 1979. *Food, Energy and Society.* New York: Wiley.

Plotkin, Mark J. 1993. *Tales of a Shaman's Apprentice.* New York: Viking.

Pope, Kevin O., et al. 2001. "Origin and Environmental Setting of Ancient Agriculture in the Lowlands of Mesoamerica." *Science* 292:1370–1373.

Porter, Philip W. 1965. "Environmental Potentials and Economic Opportunities—A Background for Cultural Adaptation." *American Anthropologist* 67:409–420.

Posey, Darrell. 1983. "Indigenous Ecological Knowledge and Development of the Amazon." In *The Dilemma of Amazonian Development,* edited by Emilio Moran, pp. 225–257. Boulder, Colo.: Westview.

———. 1984. "A Preliminary Report on Diversified Management of Tropical Forest by the Kayapo Indians of the Brazilian Amazon." *Advances in Economic Botany* 1:112–126.

———. 1985. "Indigenous Management of Tropical Forest Ecosystems: The Case of the Kayapó Indians of the Brazilian Amazon." *Agroforestry Systems* 3: 139–158.

Pospíšil, Leopold. 1958. *Kapauku Papuans and Their Law.* Yale University Publications in Anthropology, no. 54. New Haven, Conn.: Yale University Press.

———. 1978. *The Kapauku Papuans of West New Guinea,* 2nd ed. New York: Holt, Rinehart & Winston.

Price, Richard (Ed.). 1979. *Maroon Societies: Rebel Slave Communities in the Americas.* Baltimore, Md.: Johns Hopkins University Press.

———. 2012, July 30. "*Saramaka People v Suriname*: A Human Rights Victory and Its Messy Aftermath." *Cultural Survival Quarterly.* https://www.culturalsurvival.org/news/saramaka-people-v-suriname-human-rights-victory-and-its-messy-aftermath (retrieved October 11, 2016)

Price, Sally, and Richard Price. 1980. *Afro-American Arts of the Suriname Rainforest.* Berkeley: University of California Press.

Price, T. Douglas. 2009. "Ancient Farming in Eastern North America." *Proceedings of the National Academy of Sciences* 106 (16):6427–6428.

Radcliffe-Brown, A. R. 1922. *The Andaman Islanders.* Cambridge: Cambridge University Press.

———. 1965. *Structure and Function in Primitive Societies.* New York: Free Press.

Rappaport, Roy. 1968. *Pigs for the Ancestors.* New Haven, Conn.: Yale University Press.

Reichard, Gladys A. 1950. *Navaho Religion.* Princeton, N.J.: Princeton University Press.

———. 1977. *Navajo Medicine Man Sandpaintings.* New York: Dover.

Reichel-Dolmatoff, Gerardo. 1971. *Amazonian Cosmos.* Chicago: University of Chicago Press.

Ridley, Matt. 2010. *The Rational Optimist: How Prosperity Evolves.* New York: HarperCollins.

Robbins, Richard H. 1999. *Global Problems and the Culture of Capitalism.* Boston: Allyn & Bacon.

Rosaldo, Michelle Z., and Louise Lamphere (Eds.). 1974. *Women, Culture, and Society.* Stanford, Calif.: Stanford University Press.

Roscoe, Will. 1991. *The Zuni Man-Woman.* Albuquerque: University of New Mexico Press.

———. 2000. *Changing Ones: Third and Fourth Genders in Native North America.* New York: St. Martin's.

Rostow, W. W. 1978. *The World Economy: History and Prospect.* Austin: University of Texas Press.

Ruddle, Kenneth. 1974. *The Yukpa Autosubsistence System: A Study of Shifting Cultivation and Ancillary Activities in Colombia and Venezuela.* Berkeley: University of California Press.

Sabadish, Natalie, and Lawrence Mishel. 2013, June 26. "CEO Pay in 2012 Was Extraordinarily High Relative to Typical Workers and Other High Earners." *Economic Policy Institute.* http://www.epi.org/publication/ceo-pay-2012-extraordinarily-high/ (retrieved October 11, 2016)

Sacks, Karen. 1982. *Sisters and Wives.* Urbana: University of Illinois Press.

Sahlins, Marshall. 1958. *Social Stratification in Polynesia.* Seattle: University of Washington Press.

———. 1965. "On the Sociology of Primitive Exchange." In *The Relevance of Models for Social Anthropology,* edited by Michael Banton, pp. 139–236. London: Tavistock.

———. 1972. *Stone Age Economics.* New York: Aldine.

———. 1981. *Historical Metaphors and Mythical Realities: Structure in the Early History of the Sandwich Island Kingdom.* Ann Arbor: University of Michigan Press.

———. 1995. *How "Natives" Think: About Captain Cook, for Example.* Chicago: University of Chicago Press.

Sahlins, Marshall, and Elman Service (Eds.). 1960. *Evolution and Culture.* Ann Arbor: University of Michigan.

Sanday, Peggy R. 1973. "Toward a Theory of the Status of Women." *American Anthropologist* 75:1682–1700.

———. 1981. *Female Power and Male Dominance.* Cambridge: Cambridge University Press.

———. 2002. *Women at the Center: Life in a Modern Matriarchy.* Ithaca, N.Y.: Cornell University Press.

Sanderson, Stephen K. 1999. *Social Transformations,* expanded ed. New York: Rowman & Littlefield.

———. 2007. *Evolutionism and Its Critics.* Boulder, Colo.: Paradigm.

Sandner, Donald. 1991. *Navajo Symbols of Healing.* Rochester, Vt.: Healing Arts Press.

Sapir, Edward. 1964. "The Status of Linguistics as a Science." In *Edward Sapir,* edited by David G. Mandelbaum, pp. 65–77. Berkeley: University of California Press (original 1929)

Sasaki, Tom. 1960. *Fruitland, New Mexico: A Navaho Community in Transition.* Ithaca, N.Y.: Cornell University Press.

Schlegel, Alice. 1972. *Male Dominance and Female Autonomy.* New Haven, Conn.: HRAF Press.

Schneider, Harold K. 1981. *The Africans.* Englewood Cliffs, N.J.: Prentice Hall.

Sen, Amartya. 1984. *Resources, Values and Development.* Cambridge, Mass.: Harvard University Press.

———. 1987. *The Standard of Living.* Cambridge: Cambridge University Press.

Service, Elman. 1962. *Primitive Social Organization: An Evolutionary Perspective.* New York: Random House.

———. 1971. *Cultural Evolutionism: Theory in Practice.* New York: Holt, Rinehart and Winston.

Shankman, Paul. 1976. *Migration and Underdevelopment: The Case of Western Samoa.* Boulder, Colo.: Westview.

Shapouri, Hosein, James A. Duffield, and Michael Wang. 2002. *The Energy Balance of Corn Ethanol: An Update.* U.S. Department of Agriculture. Agricultural Economics Report No. 813.

Sheper-Hughes, Nancy. 1992. *Death Without Weeping: The Violence of Everyday Life in Brazil.* Berkeley: University of California Press.

Shepher, Joseph. 1971. "Mate Selection Among Second Generation Kibbutz Adolescents and Adults: Incest Avoidance and Negative Imprinting." *Archives of Sexual Behavior* 1:293–307.

Shore, Bradd. 1989. "Mana and Tapu." In *Developments in Polynesian Ethnology,* edited by Alan Howard and Robert Borofsky, pp. 137–173. Honolulu: University of Hawaii Press.

Shostak, Marjorie. 1983. *Nisa: The Life and Words of a !Kung Woman.* New York: Vintage.

Simmons, Dave. 1983. "Moko." In *Art and Artists of Oceania*, pp. 226–243. Palmerston North, New Zealand: Dunmore Press.

Simons, Jake Wallis. 2014, November 12. "World's Most Complicated Patek Philippe Gold Watch Sells for Record $24.4 Million." http://www.cnn.com/2014/11/12/business/24-million-gold-watch-sothebys-record-patek-philippe/ (retrieved July 26, 2016)

Small, Cathy. 1997. *Voyages*. Ithaca, N.Y., and London: Cornell University Press.

Smith, Michael, 2012. *The Aztecs*, 3rd ed. West Sussex, U.K.: Wiley-Blackwell.

Sokolov, Raymond. 1986. "The Good Seed." *Natural History* 95:102–105.

Sosis, Richard. 2004. "The Adaptive Value of Religious Ritual." *American Scientist* 92 (2):166–172.

Sosis, Richard, and Candace Alcorta. 2003. "Signaling, Solidarity, and the Sacred: The Evolution of Religious Behavior." *Evolutionary Anthropology* 12:264–274.

Stannard, David E. 1992. *American Holocaust: The Conquest of the New World*. New York: Oxford University Press.

Stavrianos, Leften S. 1998. *The World Since 1500: A Global History*, 8th ed. Englewood Cliffs, N.J.: Prentice Hall.

Stephenson, David. 2003. "San Reach Landmark IPR Benefit-Sharing Accord for Diet Pill." *Cultural Survival Quarterly* 27 (3). https://www.culturalsurvival.org/publications/cultural-survival-quarterly/san-reach-landmark-ipr-benefit-sharing-accord-diet-pill (retrieved October 11, 2016)

Steward, Julian H. 1938. *Basin-Plateau Sociopolitical Groups*. Bureau of American Ethnology Bulletin 120. Washington, D.C.: U.S. Government Printing Office.

———. 1955. *Theory of Culture Change*. Urbana: University of Illinois Press.

———. 1977. *Evolution and Ecology: Essays on Social Transformation*, edited by Jane C. Steward and Robert F. Murphy. Urbana: University of Illinois Press.

Stewart, Omer C. 1980. "The Native American Church." In *Anthropology on the Great Plains*, edited by W. Raymond Wood and Margot Liberty, pp. 188–196. Lincoln: University of Nebraska Press.

Stockard, Janice E. 2002. *Marriage in Culture*. Fort Worth, Tex.: Harcourt.

Stocking, Jr., George W. 1974. *The Shaping of American Anthropology, 1883–1911*. New York: Basic Books.

Stone, Arthur A., Joseph E. Schwartz, Joan E. Broderick, and Angus Deaton. 2010. "A Snapshot of the Age Distribution of Psychological Well-Being in the United States". *Proceedings of the National Academy of Sciences* 107 (22):9985–9990.

Stone, M. Priscilla, Glenn Davis Stone, and Robert M. Netting. 1995. "The Sexual Division of Labor in Kofyar Agriculture." *American Ethnologist* 22:165–186.

Strauss, Sarah, Stephanie Rupp, and Thomas Love (Eds.). 2013. *Cultures of Energy*. Walnut Creek, CA: Left Coast Press.

Stromberg, Joseph. 2013, April 30. "Starving Settlers in Jamestown Colony Resorted to Cannibalism." *Smithsonian Magazine*. http://www.smithsonianmag.com/history/starving-settlers-in-jamestown-colony-resorted-to-cannibalism-46000815/?no-ist (Retrieved September 13, 2016)

Sturm, Cirse, and Kristy J. Feldhousen-Giles. 2008. "The Freedmen." In *Handbook of North American Indians*, edited by William Sturtevant, vol. 2, *Indians in Contemporary Society*, pp. 275–284. Washington, D.C.: Smithsonian Institution.

Survival International. 2007, November 6. "Hadzabe Celebrate Land Victory." http://www.survivalinternational.org/news/2579 (retrieved June 28, 2016)

———. 2011, November 11. "Tanzania: Hadza Tribe Celebrates First Land Titles." http://www.survivalinternational.org/news/7859 (retrieved June 28, 2016)

Swanson, Guy. 1960. *The Birth of the Gods*. Ann Arbor: University of Michigan Press.

Sweeney, James L. 2007. "Caribs, Maroons, Jacobins, Brigands, and Sugar Barons: The Last Stand of the Black Caribs on St. Vincent." *The African Diaspora Archaeological Network*. March newsletter.

Swepton, Lee. 1989. "Indigenous and Tribal Peoples and International Law: Recent Developments." *Current Anthropology* 30:259–264.

Talheim, T., et al. 2014. "Large-Scale Psychological Differences Within China Explained by Rice Versus Wheat Agriculture." *Science* 344:603–608.

Tanner, Clara Lee. 1975. *Southwest Indian Craft Arts*. Tucson: University of Arizona Press.

Tax, Sol (Ed.). 1967 *Acculturation in the Americas*. New York: Cooper Square.

Thornton, Russell. 1987. *American Indian Holocaust and Survival: A Population History Since 1492*. Norman: University of Oklahoma Press.

Tierney, Patrick. 2000. *Darkness in El Dorado*. New York: Norton.

Tsakiri, Elisa. 2005. "Transnational Communities and Identity." *Refugee Survey Quarterly* 24 (4):102–104.

Turnbull, Colin M. 1962. *The Forest People*. New York: Simon & Schuster.

Turner, Terence. 1989. "Kayapo Plan Meeting to Discuss Dams." *Cultural Survival Quarterly* 13:20–22.

Turner, Victor. 1967. *The Forest of Symbols*. Ithaca, N.Y.: Cornell University Press.

Tyler, Stephen A. 1973. *India: An Anthropological Perspective*. Pacific Palisades, Calif.: Goodyear.

Tylor, Edward B. 1865. *Researches into the Early History of Mankind and the Development of Civilization*. London: J. Murray.

———. 1871. *Primitive Culture*. London: J. Murray.

———. 1888. "On a Method of Investigating the Development of Institutions, Applied to Laws of Marriage and Descent. *Journal of the Royal Anthropological Institute* 18:245–272.

United Nations. 2007. "Declaration on the Rights of Indigenous Peoples." www.un.org/esa/socdev/unpfii/documents/DRIPS_en.pdf

United States Census Bureau. 2015. *Income and Poverty in the United States,*

2014. Current Population Reports. http://www.census.gov/content/dam/Census/library/publications/2015/demo/p60-252.pdf (retrieved August 3, 2016)

United States Department of Agriculture. 2016. *2015 Energy Balance for the Corn-Ethanol Industry.* http://www.usda.gov/oce/reports/energy/2015EnergyBalanceCornEthanol.pdf (retrieved July 5, 2016)

Valeri, Valerio. 1985. *Kingship and Sacrifice: Ritual and Society in Ancient Hawaii.* Chicago: University of Chicago Press.

van den Bergh, G., et al. 2016. "*Homo floresiensis*-like Fossils from the Early Middle Pleistocene of Flores." *Nature.* doi:10.1038/nature17999

Vernot, Benjamin, et al. 2016, March 17. "Excavating Neandertal and Denisovan DNA from the Genomes of Melanesian Individuals." *Science.* http://science.sciencemag.org/content/early/2016/03/16/science (retrieved October 11, 2016)

Vincent, Joan. 1974. "The Structuring of Ethnicity." *Human Organization* 33:375–379.

Vogel, Ezra F. 1991. *The Four Little Dragons: The Spread of Industrialization in East Asia.* Cambridge, Mass.: Harvard University Press.

Wallace, Anthony F. C. 1966. *Religion: An Anthropological View.* New York: Random House.

———. 1969. *The Death and Rebirth of the Seneca.* New York: Vintage Books.

Wallace, Ernest, and E. Adamson Hoebel. 1952. *The Comanches: Lords of the South Plains.* Norman: University of Oklahoma Press.

Walsh, Michael. 2005. "Will Indigenous Languages Survive?" *Annual Review of Anthropology* 34:293–315.

Warner, John Anson. 1986. "The Individual in Native American Art: A Sociological View." In *The Arts of the North American Indian: Native Traditions in Evolution,* edited by Edwin L. Wade, pp. 171–202. New York: Hudson Hills Press.

Wax, Emily. 2007. "An Ancient Indian Craft Left in Tatters." *Washington Post National Weekly Edition (*June 11–17), p. 21.

Weatherford, Jack. 1991. *Native Roots: How the Indians Enriched America.* New York: Fawcett Columbine.

Wenke, Robert. 1990. *Patterns in Prehistory: Humankind's First Three Million Years,* 3rd ed. New York: Oxford University Press.

Wesley, Daniel. 2016, April 3. "Double Irish Deception: How Google—Apple—Facebook Avoid Paying Taxes." *CREDITLOAN.* https://visualeconomics.creditloan.com/double-irish-deception-how-google-apple-facebook-avoid-paying-taxes/ (retrieved April 3, 2016)

Westermarck, Edward. 1926 *A Short History of Marriage.* New York: MacMillan.

White, Benjamin N. F. 1973. "Demand for Labor and Population Growth in Colonial Java." *Human Ecology* 1:217–236.

White, Douglas R., Michael L. Burton, and Malcolm M. Dow. 1981. "Sexual Division of Labor in African Agriculture: A Network Autocorrelation Analysis." *American Anthropologist* 83:824–849.

White, Leslie. 1949. *The Science of Culture.* New York: Grove Press.

———. 1959. *The Evolution of Culture.* New York: McGraw-Hill.

———. 1962. *The Pueblo of Sia New Mexico.* Smithsonian Institution Bureau of American Ethnology, Bulletin 184. Washington D.C.: U.S. Government Printing Office.

Whiting, Beatrice. 1950. *Paiute Sorcery.* Viking Fund Publications in Anthropology 15. New York: Viking.

Wilken, Gene C. 1987. *Good Farmers: Traditional Resource Management in Mexico and Central America.* Berkeley: University of California Press.

Wilson, E. O. 1975. *Sociobiology: The New Synthesis.* Cambridge, Mass.: Harvard University Press.

———. 1978. *On Human Nature.* Cambridge, Mass.: Harvard University Press.

Wilson, Monica. 1951. *Good Company.* Oxford: Oxford University Press.

Wolf, Arthur. 1970. "Childhood Association and Sexual Attraction: A Further Test of the Westermarck Hypothesis." *American Anthropologist* 72:503–515.

Wolf, Eric. 1969. *Peasant Wars of the Twentieth Century.* New York: Harper & Row.

———. 1982. *Europe and the People Without History.* Berkeley: University of California Press.

Wolf, Margery. 1972. *Women and the Family in Rural Taiwan.* Stanford, Calif.: Stanford University Press.

Woodburn, James. 1968. "An Introduction to Hadza Ecology." In *Man the Hunter,* edited by Richard B. Lee and Irven DeVore, pp. 49–55. Chicago: Aldine.

———. 1982. "Egalitarian Societies." *Man* 17:431–451.

Woodham-Smith, Cecil. 1991. *The Great Hunger; Ireland 1845–1849.* London: Penguin Books.

World Bank. 1999. *World Development Report 1998/9.* New York: Oxford.

World Council of Churches. 2000. "There Are Alternatives to Globalization." Dossier prepared by the Justice, Peace and Creation team.

Wormsley, William E. 1993. *The White Man Will Eat You!* Fort Worth, Tex.: Harcourt Brace Jovanovich.

Worsley, Peter. 1968. *The Trumpet Shall Sound.* New York: Schocken Books.

Wyman, Leland C. 1983. "Navajo Ceremonial System." In *Handbook of North American Indians,* vol. 10, *Southwest,* edited by Alfonso Ortiz, pp. 536–557. Washington, D.C.: Smithsonian Institution.

Yan, Yunxiang. 2006. "Girl Power: Young Women and the Waning of Patriarchy in Rural North China." *Ethnology* 45 (2):105–123.

Zeder, Melinda. 2008. "Domestication and Early Agriculture in the Mediterranean Basin: Origins, Diffusion, and Impact." *Proceedings of the National Academy of Sciences* 105 (33):11597–11604.

Zielenziger, Michael. 2007. *Shutting Out the Sun.* New York: Vintage Books.

Zucman, Gabriel. 2015. *The Hidden Wealth of Nations: The Scourge of Tax Havens.* Chicago: University of Chicago Press.

People and Cultures Index

pastoralists, 78–79
Pentecostal Christianity, 388
sand paintings, 356
singers, 331, 388
spiritual powers, 248
third-gender persons, 246
transvestism, 247–248
tribal products, 184
Western medicine, 389
witchcraft, 34, 121, 325
Naxi, 196
Nayar marriage, 198
Ndembu, 32, 332
Ndyuka, 83
Netsilik, 141
New Guinea. *See* Papua New Guinea
Northwest Coast peoples
 art, 351–352
 hunting and gathering, 143
 labrets, 346
 ranked society, 295
Nuba, 347
Nuer, 196, 284–285, 349
Numic peoples, 105
Nyakyusa, 325

O
Ojibwa, 143
Omaha people
 hairstyle, 346
 kinship terminology, 236, 237–238
 origin myth, 368
 transvestism, 247
Omani Arabs, 71, 76
Osage, 247, 340, 353, 368
Oto, 247

P
Papua New Guinea
 body painting, 347
 contact with Europeans, 85
 male initiation rituals, 357
 puberty rites, 332
Papuan people, 375
Pawnee, 247
Pequots, 378
Pitjantjatjara people, 123
Plains peoples
 beadwork, 358, 359
 bison, 141

vision quest, 329
women and art, 357
Pohnpei, 292
Polynesia/Polynesian culture
 god-king, 335
 mana, 314
 map, 73
 ranked society, 295
 respect language, 58
 scattered volcanic island
  groups, 74
 tattooing, 348
 tribute payments, 174
Ponca, 247, 368
Powhaten, 7
Pueblo peoples
 cultivation, 149
 pottery, 359
 ritual calendar, 316
 seasonal rituals, 333
Pushtun peoples, 374–375, 380
Pygmies of Central America, 35

Q
Quapaw, 340, 368
Quebecois, 67

S
Sami people, 155, 398
Samoan people
 'aiga, 230–231
 chief, 275
 family size, 391
 tattooing, 348
San people, 70, 123, 399–400
Sara, 346
Saramak (Saramacca), 83–84
Semei, 29
Seminoles, 83, 368
Seneca people, 337–338, 402
Shoshone
 foraging, 138
 nonunilineal descent, 231
 property rights, 141
 resource allocation, 140
Sindhi people, 374
South Korea/Korean culture
 female shamans, 335
 honorifics, 58–59
 kut, 331

religious leaders, 330
sibling terminology, 233
touching (females holding
 hands), 33
Sumerians, 49
Suya, 346
Swazi marriage, 208

T
Tahitians, 174, 230, 275–276, 348
Taiwanese weddings, 264–265
Tannese, 340
Tibetans, 4
Tikopia, 226–227, 295
Timucua, 83
Tiwi marriage, 198–199
Toltec, 152
Tongans, 348
Trobriand Islanders
 balanced reciprocity *(wasi)*, 171
 cultural norms, 120
 Malinowski, Bronislaw, 102
 yam garden, 317
Tuareg, 375
Tukano people, 34
Tumbuka, 354
Turkana, 155

U
United Kingdom. *See* Great Britain/
 British culture
United States/American culture
 anti-slavery movement, 305
 arts and crafts movement, 358–359
 census form, 34
 CEO compensation, 308
 Christianity, 339
 citizenship examinations, 42
 civil rights movement, 210
 class, 300–303
 contract archaeology, 7
 corn blight (1970), 405
 court of regulation, 289
 cultural enclaves, 27
 equal opportunity, 31
 ethanol, 182
 greenhouse gas emissions, 163
 health care, 174–175
 household income, 301–302
 households, 191

Subject Index

Boas, Franz, 17, 97–98, 343, 397
Body arts, 346–349
Body painting, 347
Body piercing, 346–347
Borrowing, 68
Botany Bay, 80
Botswana, 399, 403
Bound morpheme, 52
Bourgeoisie, 309
Brain, Robert, 348
Breadwinning, 250–251
Brexit vote, 382
BRIC countries, 161, 163
Brideservice, 208
Bridewealth, 207–208
British East India Company, 80
British functionalism, 100–101
British Virgin Islands, 278
Bronze Age, 93
Brown, Judith, 255
Brussels terrorist attacks (March, 2016), 28
Buddhism, 315, 334
Bureaucrat, 277
Burkinis, 339
Bush, George W., 209
Business cycles, 179
Buta, 354

C

Cai Hua, 196
Calendrical rituals, 316
Cannibalism, 7
Cannon Mills, 186
Capitalism
    business cycles, 179
    defined, 178
    market principles, 178
    neoliberalism, 180
    philosophical basis, 180
    productivity, 181
    profit, 178
    social welfare, 180
    socialism, contrasted, 178–179
"Cardinal directions," 63
Careers in anthropology, 10
Cargo, 336
Cargo cults, 336–337, 340
Caribs, 82
Carving, 350

Caste, 293, 296
Catalonian nationalist parties, 382
Cataract Canyon, 402
Catholicism, 335–336
Cattle domestication, 42
Cattle herding. *See* Pastoralism
Cave paintings, 350
Census form, 34
Central Kalahari Game Reserve (CKGR), 399
Central Mosque (London), 24
CEO compensation, 308
Cereal crops, 257
Chagnon, Napoleon, 125
Changing Ones (Roscoe), 246
Cheating, 321
Chechen rebels, 363, 382
Chen, Keith, 64
Cheney, Dick, 211
Chief executive officer (CEO) compensation, 308
Chiefdom, 275–276
Child care, 255
Childhood familiarity hypothesis, 193
Chimpanzees, 3–4, 17, 38
China-Tibetan conflict, 375
Chinampas, 151
Chittagong Hill Tracts, 374
Christian God, 130
Christianity, 313, 339
Circumcision, 16
Cisgender (cis), 250
Citizen's United case, 301
Citizenship examinations, 42
Civil rights movement, 210
Civilization, 95, 152–153, 363, 369–370
Clan, 225–226
Clan brother/sister, 225
Clan house/clan mother, 228
Clark, Gregory, 153
Clash of Civilizations and the Remaking of World Order, The (Huntington), 369
Class, 296
Class conflict, 304
Classical Greece, 355. *See also* Ancient civilizations
Classical literature, 360

Classification of reality, 33
Clean Air Act, 279
Climate change, 146, 162–163
Clinton, Bill, 209
Clothing styles, 367
Code of Ethics (AAA), 124
Code of Hammurabi, 288
Code of Handsome Lake, 340
Code talkers, 121
Coevolution, 42
Cognatic descent, 230–231
Cognatic descent group, 230
Cognitive approach, 317–318
"Collection of Ethnography," 128
Collins, Joseph, 393
Columbian Exchange, 74, 75
Columbus, Christopher, 74, 365
Columbus Day, 365
Coming of Age in Soma (Mead), 17, 98
Communal organizations, 328, 331–333
Communication
    language. *See* Language and speech
    miscommunication when people from different parts of world interact, 17
    nonverbal. *See* Nonverbal communication
Communist Revolution (1949), 209, 222
Comparative methods, 128–132
Comparative perspective, 13–14
Composite band, 272–273
Compound words, 52, 53
Concept review
    cultural knowledge, 30
    descent and kinship, 231
    ethnic conflict, 381
    ethnic identity, 369
    female/male differences and division of labor, 253
    forms of artistic expression, 345
    forms of exchange in economic systems, 169
    kinship groups, 191
    language, 49
    legal systems, 283
    methods of investigation, 132
    political organizations, 271

evolution, 93–94
fieldwork tradition, 101–104
functionalism, 100–101
Herodotus, 92
historical particularism, 97–100
Malinowski, Bronislaw, 102
Morgan's stages of "savagery,"
  "barbarism" and "civilization,"
  94–95
neoevolutionism, 104
Polo, Marco, 92
"science of culture," 96, 104
Steward, Julian, 104–105
unilineal evolutionism, 94–96
White, Leslie, 104
Diachronic, 118
Diachronic ethnohistoric research,
  126–128
Dialects, 50
Diamond, Jared, 146
Diner's Club card, 167
Dionysian culture theme, 100
Discovery, 68
Displacement, 48–49
Divine right of kings, 305
DNA, 4
Do-no-harm principle, 124
Dog Soldier society, 360
DOMA (Defense of Marriage Act),
  209, 210
Domestic corporation, 278
Domestication of plants and animals,
  69, 143–147
  advantages/disadvantages, 146–
    147
  defined, 143
  New World crops, 144
  New World livestock, 144–145
  Old World crops, 144
  Old World livestock, 144
  reasons for development of agri-
    culture, 146
Double Irish, 279
Dowry, 208–209
Dreaming of a Mail-Order Husband:
  Russian American Internet
  Romance (Johnson), 10
Dry land gardening, 148–149
Durkheim, Emile, 320, 321
Dutch Guiana, 84
Duties, 29

Dwarfism, 5
Dying languages, 57

E

Ear piercing, 346
Early European expansion, 74–79
  Africa, 75
  Americas, 74–75
  Asia, 75–76
  Columbian Exchange, 74
  conversion of native peoples to
    Christianity, 77, 78
  Manila galleons, 76
  New World crops, 76
  Portuguese expansion, 75–76
  slave-for-gun trade, 76
  slavery, 75
  Spanish conquistadores, 74–75, 77
  world-changing events, 74
East African cattle complex, 155
Ecclesiastical organization, 328,
  333–336
Ecological anthropology, 105
Ecological tourism, 185
Economic freedom, 180
Economic immigrants, 372
Economic Policy Institute, 303
Economic progress, 406, 408
Economics, 167
Educational anthropology, 9
Egalitarian society, 293, 294–295, 351
Eggan, Fred, 130
Ego, 214
Ego focused kindred, 230
Electricity, 158
Elites, 298, 304, 310
Emasculation, 249
Enculturation, 25, 47
Endangered languages, 57
Endogamous rules, 199–200
Endogamy, 199
Energy and society, 158
Energy slaves, 158
Energy subsidy, 395
English language, 57
Enlightenment period, 94, 112
Environmental issues. *See* Human-
  environment interactions
Equal opportunity, 31
Eritrea, 375
Eskimo kinship terminology, 234–235

Esoteric (secret) knowledge, 292
Essentializing other peoples, 260
Estioko-Griffin, Agnes, 253
Ethanol, 182, 183
Ethiopia, 371
Ethnic boundary markers, 366–367
Ethnic cleansing, 377
Ethnic group, 364
Ethnic homogenization, 377
Ethnic stereotyping, 120–121
Ethnically diverse, 88
Ethnicity and ethnic conflict, 362–
  384
  accommodation, 379–380
  artificial country, 371
  assimilation, 378–379
  civilizations, 369–370
  clothing styles, 367
  concept review, 369, 381
  ethnic boundary markers, 366–367
  ethnogenesis, 368
  fluidity of ethnic groups, 367–368
  genocide, 377–378
  geographic containment, 376
  globalization, 383
  homogenization, 377–379
  Israeli-Palestinian conflict, 370–
    371
  language, 366
  Northern Ireland conflict, 370
  origin myth, 365–366
  physical characteristics, 366–367
  political boundaries/secessionist
    movements, 371–376
  race/ethnicity, contrasted, 36
  religion, 366
  relocation, 378
  responses to ethnic conflict,
    376–383
  segregation, 379
  situational nature of ethnic iden-
    tity, 364–365
  social identity, 36
  stateless nationalities, 370–376
  terrorism, 363
  transnational communities,
    372–373
  types of ethnic groups, 368–369
Ethnocentric bias, 128
Ethnocentrism, 14, 127
Ethnogenesis, 368

farming the land. *See* Domestication of plants and animals

foraging. *See* Hunting and gathering

globalization, 161–164

herding. *See* Pastoralism

horticulture, 69, 147–149

industrialism. *See* Industrialism

intensive agriculture. *See* Intensive agriculture

overview/summary, 156–157

who should pay to reduce global warming, 162–163

Human migration, 88

Human Relations Area Files (HRAF), 128

Human tragedies, 186–187

Human variation, 4

Humanistic approach, 108–114

  criticism of scientific approach, 110

  defined, 109

  human-environment interactions, 136

  interpretive anthropology, 111

  language, 109

  overview (concept review), 113

  postmodernism, 111

  scientific approach, compared, 113

  uniqueness of humanity, 109

  weaknesses of materialist orientation, 109, 110

Hunger. *See* World hunger

Huno, 281

Hunting, 252–253

Hunting and gathering, 69, 137–143

  bands, 139–140

  concept review, 157

  defined, 136

  division of labor, 138

  generalized reciprocity, 170

  key features, 141

  map, 137

  nonunilineal descent, 231

  property rights, 140, 141

  quality of life, 142

  reciprocal sharing, 140

  resource allocation, 140–141

  seasonal mobility, 138

  seasonal congregation and dispersal, 138–139

what happened to hunters/gatherers?, 141–143

Huntington, Samuel, 363, 369, 383

Husband-father, 266

Hutton, James, 93

Hxaro, 171

Hydraulic fracturing (fracking), 182

Hydroelectricity, 158

I

Ideas, 22

Ideologies, 304–305, 306

Igbo, 375

Imitative principle, 324

Immigrants, 11, 26

Inbreeding avoidance hypothesis, 193

Incest taboos, 192–195

  childhood familiarity hypothesis, 193

  family disruption hypothesis, 192–193

  inbreeding avoidance hypothesis, 193

  Lebanon, 194

  "marry out or die out," 192

  Taiwan, 194

Incipient court, 286–287

Incising, 350–351

Income inequality, 301–302

India-Pakistan War, 374

Indian art, 359

Indian Arts and Crafts Act, 359

Indian clothes, 367

Indian Market (Santa Fe, New Mexico), 358

Indian Removal Act (1830), 83

Indian schools, 248

Individualistic organization, 327, 328–329

Individuality, 357, 360

Indonesia, 371

Induna, 288

Indus River Valley, 152

Industrial market economies, 168

Industrial revolution, 79–81, 94, 158, 358

Industrialism, 157–161

  defined, 136

  energy and society, 158

  food production and distribution, 158–159

fossil fuels, 158

globalization of production, 159–160

rural-urban migration, 158

transportation, 159

Inequality, 292. *See also* Social inequality and stratification

Inequality explanation of hunger, 392, 393

Influence, 272

Informant, 125

Initiation rituals, 332

Inmarriage, 199

Innovation, 68

"Innovator," 26

Intellectual approach, 317–318

Intensification, 108

Intensive agriculture, 70–71, 150–153

  ancient times, 153

  cereal crops, 257

  chinampas, 151

  civilization, 152–153

  concept review, 157

  cultivation tasks, 257

  cultural consequences, 151–153

  defined, 150

  high productivity, 151

  large-scale political and economic organization, 151–152

  map, 150

  peasants, 153

  stepped terraces, 151

  surplus produce, 151

  survival of, into 21st century, 153

  tax, 151

  wet rice regions, 150, 151

Intercropping, 396–397

International academic conferences, 87

International migration, 24

International regulations, 182

Internationally competitive, 182

Internet and information revolution, 86–87

Interpretive anthropology, 111

Interracial couples, 200

Interviewing, 119–120

Intimate distance, 55

Inuinnagtun, 380

Inuktiut, 380

productivity, 48
Romance languages, 53
Sapir-Whorf hypothesis, 62, 63
semantic domains, 61
sentences, 48
sociolinguistics, 55
sound systems, 51
spatial directions, 63
terms of address, 58
tone language, 51
verb-tense modifiers, 64
vocal tract, 46–47
words and meanings, 51–53
worldview, 62
Lappé, Frances Moore, 393
Law, 282–283
Lazarus, 305
Leakey, Richard, 5
Lebanon, 194
Lee, Richard, 140, 142
Legal sanctions, 282
Legal systems
concept review, 283
court of mediation, 287–288
court of regulation, 288–289
court systems, 286–289
incipient court, 286–287
self-help system, 283–286
Legal tender, 175
"Legalese," 61
Leguminous crops, 397
Leighton, Alexander and Dorothea, 389
Leopard-skin chief, 284–285
Lepowsky, Maria, 261, 262
Lesser-developed countries (LDCs)
children, 390–392
family size, 390–391
hunger. See World hunger
population growth, 389–392
Levirate, 206–207
LGBTQIA persons
anti-gay (religious beliefs) legislation, 31
changes in attitude, 250
North Carolina anti-trans people legislation, 31
same-sex marriage, 209–211
same-sex relationships, 248
Lhamana, 247

"Like produces like" (imitative principle), 324
Likombwa, 288
Lineage, 225
Lingua franca, 57
Linguistic communities, 56
Linguistic extinction, 56
Linguistic relativity hypothesis, 62, 63
Linguistics, 8
Lip piercing, 346
Liquidated: An Ethnography of Wall Street (Ho), 181
Little emperors, 223
Loa, 354
Local knowledge, 403
Lomax, Alan, 354, 355
Long-haul trucking industry, 159
Lono, 127
Love, Thomas, 158
Low touch culture, 55
Lowie, Robert, 98
Lunda, 76
Lyell, Charles, 93
Lying, 40

M
Macaques, 38
Machu Picchu, 277
Madagascar periwinkle, 404
Maize, 182–183
Male circumcision, 16
Malinowski, Bronislaw, 100, 102, 120, 318
Mamdani, Mahmood, 390
"Man Enough to Let My Wife Support Me: How Changing Models of Career and Gender Are Reshaping the Experience of Unemployment" (Lane), 10
Man-woman, 246, 248
Mana, 314, 335
Manahune, 276
Mandarin language, 57
Manila galleons, 76
Manupur, 390
Mao Zedong, 222
Maps
ancient civilizations, 152
horticulture, 148

hunting and gathering, 137
intensive agriculture, 150
Old World, 73
pastoralism, 154
Maquiladoras, 183
Marital exchanges, 207–209
Market
concept review, 169
defined, 168
exchange, 177
market economies and capitalism, 177–181
money, 175–176
productivity, 181–182
Market economy, 178
Market exchange, 175, 177
Market globalization, 183
Market norms, 177
Marriage alliances, 206–207
Marriage and families, 189–216. *See also* Kinship and descent
brideservice, 208
bridewealth, 207–208
definitions, 190–192
dowry, 208–209
enculturation practices, 40
extended households, 214–215
functions of marriage, 197
household forms, 214–215
how many spouses?, 200–201
incest taboos, 192–195
interracial couples, 200
Japanese customs, 202–203
kinship diagram, 213–214
levirate/sororate, 206–207
marital exchanges, 207–209
marriage, defined, 195–196
marriage alliances, 206–207
marriage rules, 199–200
matrifocal households, 214
Nayar marriage, 198
polyandry, 205–206
polygyny, 201–205
postmarital residence patterns, 211–213
same-sex marriage, 209–211
Tiwi marriage, 198–199
wedding ceremony, 206
Marriage rules, 199–200
"Marry out or die out," 192

Neandertals, 4, 5
Negative reciprocity, 172–173
Neoevolutionism, 104
Neoliberalism, 180, 182
Neolocal residence, 212
Nestlé, 26
Net worth, 302
New African peoples of the
    Americas, 82–84
New World, 71
New World crops, 76, 144
New World livestock, 144–145
New York Stock Exchange, 179
Ng'oma type of healing complex,
    354
Nile Valley, 152
9/11 terrorist attacks, 28
Nineteenth Amendment, 262
Nixtamalización, 183
Niyamgiri Hills, 400
Nlum, 354
"No Fat Valley," 125
Nokia, 26
Nomadism, 154, 156
Nomads of the Australian Desert
    (Mountford), 123
Nonfood plants, 406, 409
Nonunilineal descent, 229–231
Nonverbal communication, 32–33
    distance, 55
    facial expressions, 54
    proxemics, 55
    symbolic behaviors, 55
    touching, 55
Norms, 30–31, 40, 59
Norte Energia, 401
North American Church (NAC), 340,
    388
North American Free Trade
    Agreement (NAFTA), 86, 164
North Carolina anti-trans people
    legislation, 31
Northern Ireland conflict, 370
Nose piercing, 347
Nostril piercing, 347
Nu, 243, 244
Nuclear family, 190
Nuclear family incest, 192. *See also*
    Incest taboos
Nuclear power sources, 158

Nunavut, 380
Nupe language, 51

O
Oba, 122
Obama, Barack, 34
Obamacare, 175
Obeyesekere, Gananath, 127
Oblasts, 380
Oboler, Regina Smith, 196
Obsidian, 173
Occupational culture, 24
Oceania, 80–81
    chiefdoms, 275
    cultural isolation, 73
    nasal septum piercing, 347
Odisha, 400–401, 403
Off-shore college campuses, 87
Offshoring, 279, 280
Oklahoma City bombing, 28
Okrugs, 380
Old World, 71, 72
Old World crops, 144
Old World diseases, 75
Old World livestock, 144
On the Origin of Species (Darwin), 93
One-child policy, 223
Only Hope (Fong), 223
O'odham, 406
Open-ended questions, 119
Opium War, 80
Organization of African Unity
    (OAU), 164, 376
Organization of American States, 164
Organization of political life, 269–290
    bands, 271–273
    chiefdoms, 275–276
    concept review, 271
    Inca empire, 277, 281
    law, 282–283
    legal systems. *See* Legal systems
    politicization of the laws, 289
    social control, 282
    states, 276–277
    tribes, 273–275
Origin myth, 365–366
Original myths, 317
Orisha, 354
Orlando, Florida, nightclub mass
    shooting, 28

Ornamentation, 350–351
Orthography, 366
Osh-Tisch, 248
Ostracize, 282
"Other" cultures, 92
Outline of Cultural Materials,
    128
Outmarriage, 199
Overview. *See* Concept review
Oyo, 76

P
Pacific Island nations, 163
Paganism, 326
Pagel, Mark, 38
Painting, 350
Painting/carving representations of
    nature, 37
Pakistan, 371, 374, 380
Paleoanthropology, 4–5, 94
Pan troglodytes, 17. *See also*
    Chimpanzees
Panama Papers, 278
Panasonic, 26
Panchama, 297
Parallel cousins, 223
Parasaito, 203
Parfleches, 357
Paris Accord, 162
Parker, Enoch, 340
Parthenon, 72, 355
Parti Québécois, 382
Participant observation, 102, 120
Passive assimilation, 379
Pastoralism, 70, 153–156
    advantages, 155–156
    concept review, 157
    defined, 136
    edible food and drink, 155
    map, 154
    mobility, 155
    nomadism, 154, 156
    patrilineal descent, 231–232
    regions unsuitable or marginal for
        farming, 155
    subsistence risk reduction, 155
    transhumance, 154
    tribal products, 185
Patek Philippe pocket watch (1933),
    344

Self-sacrificial acts of devotion, 107
Selfish behavior, 177
Semantic domain, 61
Semicolonial regions, 80
Seminole War (1835-42), 83
Sen, Amartya, 407
Separatist movements, 371–376
Sepoy Mutiny, 80
September 11 terrorist attacks, 28
Serbo-Croatian, 366
Serial monogamy, 206
Seven Years War, 82
Sewing, 351
Sexual dimorphism, 242
Sexual division of labor, 250.
     See also Gendered division
     of labor
Sexual Life of Savages, The
     (Malinowski), 102
Shakers, 357
Shaman, 329
Shamanistic organization, 327–328,
     329–331
Shareholder value, 181
Sharing, 139–140
Shechem, 207
Shell companies, 278
Shifting cultivation, 148
Shinto, 315
Shiva, 248, 249
Shoat, 156
Shogun, 335
Shotgun questioning, 119
Sibling terminology, 233
Sikh separatist movement, 374
Sikhs, 366
Silk Road, 71, 155
Simple band, 272
Singers, 331, 355, 356, 388
Singing (songs), 352, 355
Sioux Two Spirits, 247
Six Day War, 371
Skin color, 4
Skype, 86
Slash and burn, 148
Slave-for-gun trade, 76
Slave wars, 75, 90
Slavery, 75
Smith, Adam, 178
Social anthropology, 7

Social construction of gender,
     242–244
Social control, 282
Social Darwinism, 41
Social distance, 55, 173
Social fathers, 242
Social identity, 241, 360
Social inequality and stratification,
     291–311
   American secular ideologies,
     305–307
   caste, 296
   CEO compensation, 308
   China, 298–299
   class, 296
   class conflict, 304
   concept review, 293
   conflict theory, 308–310
   egalitarian societies, 294–295
   elites, 304, 310
   functionalist theory, 307–308, 310
   ideologies, 304–305
   income inequality, 301–302
   India (caste system), 297–300
   maintaining inequality, 303–307
   ranked societies, 295
   rewards, 292
   stratified societies, 296–297
   United States (class), 300–303
   wealth inequality, 302–303
   who benefits?, 310–311
Social justice, 179
Social norms, 177
Social reality, 34–36
Social solidarity, 320, 321
Social status, 360
Social stratum, 296
Social welfare capitalism, 180
Socialism, 178, 179
Socialization, 25
Socialized medicine, 181
Society, 67
Sociobiology, 106–107
Sociocultural anthropology, 7
Sociolinguistics, 55
Sociological approach, 320–322
Sodality, 273–274
Sodomy laws, 250
Soetoro, Ann Dunham, 34
Somalia, 376

Somaliland, 376
Songhai empire, 76
Sorcery, 128–129, 324. *See also*
     Witchcraft
Sororate, 206–207
Sosis, Richard, 322, 332
Sound systems, 51
Sources of cultural change, 68
South Sudan, 376
Soviet Union, 380
Spanglish, 11
Spanish-American War, 81
Spanish conquistadores, 74–75, 77
Spanish language, 57
Spanish Sahara, 376
Spatial directions, 63
Speech, 22. *See also* Language and
     speech
Spirit helpers, 329
Spirit-possession dance, 354
Spiritual beings, 313
Spiritual powers, 248
Srebrenica massacre, 377
Stalin, Joseph, 378
Standard American English
     (SAE), 50
State, 152, 276–277
Stateless nationalities, 370–376
Status, 292, 360
Status of women, 258. *See also*
     Gender stratification
Stepped terraces, 151
Stereotyping, 120–121
Stevenson, Matilda Coxe, 247
Steward, Julian, 104–105
Stone Age, 93
Stone money, 176
Stonewall riots, 250
Stratification. *See* Gender stratifica-
     tion; Social inequality and strat-
     ification
Stratified society, 293, 296–297, 351
Strength, 254–255
Structured interview, 119
Subculture, 24–25
Subfields of anthropology, 2–8
   anthropological linguistics, 8
   archaeology, 6–7
   biological/physical anthropology,
     3–6

concept review, 3
cultural anthropology, 7–8
Subnationality, 368
Subsidiary companies, 279
Subsidized health insurance/medicine, 175
Sudan, 376
Suez Canal, 80
Suicide bombers, 107
Summary/overview. *See* Concept review
Sun Dance, 274
Supermarkets, 159
Supernatural causation of illness, 387
Supernatural explanations of misfortune, 323–327
Supernatural powers, 226, 228, 313–314
Supernatural sanctions, 282
Superstition, 317
Supreme being, 314
Suriname, 82, 84
Surnames, 237
Surplus, 151
Survey of Consumer Finances, 302
Survival International, 398
Sweat lodge ceremony, 185
Sweet Medicine chief, 274
Symbolic glyphs, 72
Symbols
arbitrary/conventional, 32
cultural knowledge, 32–33
defined, 32
multivocality/condensation, 32
Synchronic, 118
Synchronic ethnographic fieldwork, 118–126
Syncretic revelations, 336

T
Taboo, 59
Tabu, 276
Tai chi, 185
Taiwan, 194
Tales of a Shaman's Apprentice (Plotkin), 404
Tamils, 375
Tariffs, 85
Tasmania, 73
Tasmanians, 367

Tattooing, 347–349
Tax, 151, 174
Tax, Sol, 397–398
Tax avoidance schemes, 279
Tax evasion, 278
Tax haven, 278
Tax-haven subsidiaries, 279
Technological determinism, 104
Technology-transfer solution, 394–396
Ten Commandments, 320
Tense modifiers, 64
Tepary bean, 406
Ter, 285
Terms of address, 58
Terrorist attacks, 27–28, 363–364
Textile designs, 350
"the Hobbit," 5
Third-gender persons, 246
Third World nations, 13, 386. *See also* Lesser-developed countries (LDCs)
Thrissur Pooram Elephant Festival, 407
Tito, Josip Broz, 380
Tiwi Wives (Goodale), 199
Tlingit house, 352
Todai-ji, 334
Tone language, 51
Tonga Islands, 81
Toolmaking, 37
Torii, 315, 316
Totem, 333
Totemism, 333
Touching, 55
Trade agreements, 85–86, 164
Trade partnership, 171
Traditional cultural behaviors, 88
Traditional healing, 387–389
Traditional resource management practices, 397
Trail of Tears, 378
Trance, 329
Transfer payments, 174
Transhumance, 154
Transnational ethnic communities, 372–373
Transportation, 159
Transubstantiation, 356
Transvestism, 247–248

Tribal peoples, 398. *See also* Indigenous peoples
Tribal products, 184–185
Tribal war chief, 274
Tribe, 273–275
Tribute, 173–174
Triple A, 9. *See also* American Anthropological Association (AAA)
Trucking industry, 159
Truman, Harry, 382
Trump, Donald, 60, 292, 297, 339
Turner, Victor, 32
Tuvalu, 163
Two Spirits, 245–248
Tylor, E. B., 21, 95, 96, 106, 192, 313
Tzeltal language, 63

U
Ugandan chimpanzees, 3
Ulster Scots, 370
Underdeveloped nations, 13
understandingrace.org, 36
Unilineal descent, 220–228
clan, 225–226
defined, 220
descent groups, 224–228
genealogical depth, 224
Hopi (matrilineal society), 227–228
lineage, 225
matrilineal descent, 220, 222, 224
matrilineal descent group, 224
patrilineal descent, 220, 221
patrilineal descent group, 224
supernatural powers, 226, 228
Tikopia (patrilineal society), 226–227
unilineally extended family, 225
Unilineal evolutionism, 94–96, 105, 128
Unilineally extended family, 225
United Nations Development Programme, 9
United Nations Universal Declaration of Human Rights, 16
Universal Declaration of Human Rights, 16
Unselfish behavior, 106
Unstructured interview, 119